The Late Medieval Age of Crisis and Renewal, 1300–1500

A Biographical Dictionary

Edited by
CLAYTON J. DREES

The Great Cultural Eras of the Western World
Ronald H. Fritze, Series Adviser

GREENWOOD PRESS
Westport, Connecticut • London

Library of Congress Cataloging-in-Publication Data

The late medieval age of crisis and renewal, 1300–1500 : a biographical dictionary /
edited by Clayton J. Drees.
     p. cm.—(The great cultural eras of the Western world)
    Includes bibliographical references and index.
    ISBN 0–313–30588–9 (alk. paper)
    1. Civilization, Medieval—Dictionaries. 2. Europe—History—476–1492—Biography—
Dictionaries. 3. Europe—History—1492–1517—Biography—Dictionaries. 4. Europe—
Social conditions—To 1492—Dictionaries. I. Drees, Clayton J. II. Series.
CB353.L38 2001
940.1—dc21   00–022335

British Library Cataloguing in Publication Data is available.

Library of Congress Catalog Card Number: 00–022335
ISBN: 0–313–30588–9

First published in 2001

Greenwood Press, 88 Post Road West, Westport, CT 06881
An imprint of Greenwood Publishing Group, Inc.
www.greenwood.com

Printed in the United States of America

The paper used in this book complies with the
Permanent Paper Standard issued by the National
Information Standards Organization (Z39.48–1984).

10 9 8 7 6 5 4 3 2 1

Contents

Introduction

This volume features biographical vignettes of important figures who lived in Europe during the fourteenth and fifteenth centuries. As such, it encompasses a period that witnessed a great deal of both crisis and renewal. As Europe emerged from the late Middle Ages, social, demographic, and economic calamities—some of them devastating in their scope and consequences—changed the way Europeans viewed their universe and their place in it. Old notions of community, spirituality, prosperity, and creativity were swept away in the successive crises of war, religious contention, and plague that seemed to dominate the fourteenth-century experience. Yet these disruptive changes allowed a fresh breeze of cultural renewal to blow over Europe to build upon, and in some ways to replace, the exhausted intellectual energies of the passing medieval age. Germinating at the very climax of crisis in the fourteenth century, this seed of renewal sprouted first in Italy and then, over time, spread through the Continent and was carried forth to the world in the vessels and minds of bold explorers. Thus in apparent disaster was born cultural refreshment. In loss Europeans discovered opportunity, and in crisis they found renewal, a rebirth of interest in ancient wisdom and human achievement that we have come to call the Renaissance.

The medieval world that was visited by crisis in the fourteenth century had evolved only very slowly from the time of the collapse of the Roman Empire in the fifth century A.D. Late medieval Europe was still an overwhelmingly agrarian society, based upon the feudal relationship between protective landlord and serving or rent-paying peasant, and was still defined by the agricultural season cycle and by a "great chain of being" social order that assigned each individual his or her position in a collective Christian universe. Some medieval men and women, however, also lived in towns by the fourteenth century. There master craftsmen plied their trades as members of powerful guilds, while others traveled to regional fairs and even across Europe to more distant markets to sell goods for profit as merchants. One unifying element in this social and economic milieu was the Roman church, to which the vast majority of western Europeans belonged and in whose teachings they unequivocally believed. The church, directed from Rome by the pope through regional bishops and local parish priests, provided Christians with a rich ceremonial culture, a strict moral code, and the means (sacraments, pilgrimages, and good works) by which they might attain everlasting life in heaven after death. The influence of the church in the daily lives of late medieval believers was all-pervasive and extended not only to the organization of time (liturgical calendar) and the economy (landownership), but also to the intellectual enterprises of the age. Great universities had appeared all over western Europe during the twelfth and thirteenth centuries. These institutions were largely staffed by Franciscan and Dominican professors who, though they spent some time teaching the seven liberal arts to their students, otherwise considered and debated the truths of universals and theology through the Scholastic reconciliation of faith and reason achieved by the thirteenth-century thinker Thomas Aquinas.

The church also played an active role in the ordering and management of kingdoms. By the fourteenth century rulers of emerging feudal states such as France, England, Scotland, the Holy Roman Empire, Castile, Aragon, Burgundy and others sought to fulfill their God-given "priestly" duty to protect Christian society from the threats of religious heresy and Muslim encroachment. Such rulers often employed educated prelates as royal advisors, in this way allowing some of Christendom's most able and ambitious intellects to rise to positions of great power in the service of both the Crown and the church. Late medieval Europe was, therefore, a largely agrarian, commercially and intellectually active, Christian and hierarchical world that had remained relatively insulated and had changed only very gradually during the preceding millennium. Yet, unknown to these people who lived out their lives in the cyclical certainty of an invariable Christian universe, cataclysmic changes were at hand.

Unexpected as crisis may have been, when it came, it struck with vehemence at the very heart of the European experience. One of the most difficult ordeals of the late medieval age began innocently enough in 1305 when the newly elected French pope, *Clement V, decided to remain in southern France rather than return to the traditional seat of papal authority in Rome. (In this volume, an asterisk indicates a cross-reference to another entry.) This was not unusual at a time when pontiffs were often away from the Eternal City for long periods of time, but Pope Clement's decision soon became a precedent as successive popes at first remained and then established their permanent residence in the Provençal town of Avignon. So began what critics called the Babylonian Captivity of the papacy, a seventy-three-year span during which the bishops of Rome, and with them directive power over the entire church, remained absent from the See of St. Peter. This crisis of papal residence and dominion violently shook the foundations of Christendom as educated and simple believers alike questioned pontifical authority and the very truth of church doctrines themselves. Then between 1376 and 1378, when Pope Gregory XI finally did restore the papacy to Rome, a group of French cardinals elected their own pope in Avignon, and so began the great Papal Schism. This proved to be a second and far more serious crisis for the church as two and sometimes three rival popes excommunicated one another in attempts to attract papal tax revenues and the support of European monarchs. The schism took several church councils and nearly forty years to heal, but doubts sown among the Christian faithful during this divisive time never really faded and were exacerbated later in the fifteenth century when a series of particularly corrupt popes in Rome further alienated an already-wary populace.

Another crisis of the late Middle Ages primarily involved France, and to a lesser extent England, when these two kingdoms clashed in the so-called Hundred Years' War. Actually a series of battles and skirmishes during the period 1337–1453, this struggle sorely tested the French people since most of the fighting occurred on their soil. It was also a particularly destructive war in that both armies were largely composed of mercenary troops who plundered freely and lived off the land rather than carry their own supplies. The war also saw the first use in Europe of firearms, which, although they were primitive and often more dangerous to the gunners than to the target, nevertheless opened the door to the use of more sophisticated and accurate guns as the conflict dragged on. The Hundred Years' War was in some respects the first "modern" war in its ravaging effects on civilians and the countryside, in the sheer size of the war effort on the part of the combatants, and in the more "national" character of a conflict that loomed larger than the dynastic and feudal clashes of old.

Easily the most catastrophic event of the fourteenth century, and perhaps in the entire history of Europe, was the epidemic known as the Black Death, which initially swept through the Continent between 1347 and 1351 and returned intermittently during the next few centuries. We now know that the Black Death was a combination of bubonic plague, carried by fleas that jumped from rats to human hosts, and pneumonia, which struck Europeans already weakened by a shortage of food due to overpopulation and a series of poor harvests. After flea-infested rats arrived in Italy late in 1347 aboard trading vessels from the Levant, the lethal disease spread quickly until, in a few years' time, it had claimed the lives of some 40 percent of Europe's total population. Very few regions were spared, and no social class or religious order escaped its deadly hand. Europeans were stunned and confused by the onslaught of the plague. Many thought that the disease was airborne and so quarantined themselves or sought to cover their mouths and noses; others believed that God was punishing Christians for their sins in anticipation of the dreaded Apocalypse. Whatever their opinions, the Black Death certainly caused many believers to doubt a church that God had apparently forsaken, and although men and women would continue through succeeding centuries to follow Christianity, it is evident that the unflinching devotion of the Middle Ages was tempered by skepticism and indifference in the wake of this great demographic disaster. Economically, the Black Death most profoundly decreased the supply of labor both on feudal manors and in the towns. Landlords thus relaxed demands on their remaining peasants to keep them from running off, and sometimes converted arable lands to pasture to reduce their dependence on peasant workers. Meanwhile, towns were hardest hit by the plague, mainly because townsfolk lived in close quarters and filthy conditions; many towns were simply abandoned by craftsmen and merchants who no longer had buyers for their goods. The Black Death shocked and terrified as it killed off millions of people, but it also solved—for those who survived it—a number of serious economic and social problems such as overpopulation and scarcity of foodstuffs. In the religious disquiet it caused, the plague also helped release Christians from their preoccupation with the formal and ritualistic practice of their faith. In effect, it freed them to begin to think for themselves, to discover previously forgotten or forbidden worlds, and to renew their search for knowledge in directions left unexplored for a millennium and more.

The crises of divided church, war, and plague did much violence to late medieval society, it is true, but these traumas also cleared the social and cultural air, so to speak, in turn allowing those who survived to rebuild their world with new vigor and creativity. Italy, an urbanized land that had suffered much from the Black Death, was one of the first regions of Europe to recover. Indeed, parts of Italy were already beginning the process of intellectual and political *renovatio* even before the arrival of the awful disease in the middle of the fourteenth century. Northern Italians had freed themselves from the authority of the Holy Roman Emperor as early as the twelfth century and had established a patchwork of independent city-states across the Po valley and down through Tuscany and the Romagna. Many of these states created communal forms of government— actually, oligarchies of prominent citizens—that styled themselves "republics" and rotated important offices and assembly seats among members of the most influential families in town. Eventually some of the communal governments proved unable to control the various family factions competing for power in the city-states and so gave way first to invited *podestà* judges from other cities and then to *signoria* governments run by a single individual or family. Thus by the middle of the fifteenth century Milan was under the control first of the Visconti and then the Sforza dukes, Florence was ruled by the Medici, and various smaller towns such as Ferrara, Mantua, and Urbino were governed by the Este, Gonzaga, and Montefeltro families, respectively. These city-states interacted with one another commercially and diplomatically, and it was in this early microcosm of the modern United Nations that the art of diplomatic correspondence, negotiation, and representation was born. These cities also fought small wars, but since condottieri (mercenaries) were usually hired for this purpose, the wars were seldom destructive and few soldiers were killed—mercenaries always hoped to survive to fight another day. Above all, the northern Italian city-states enjoyed great commercial prosperity as their textile and banking houses served the needs of all Europe, and their merchants became wealthy middlemen in the luxury import/export business between the Levant and northern Europe. The Milanese, Florentines, and Venetians were doing so well by the turn of the fifteenth century, in fact, that many successful entrepreneurs in these cities began to turn their attention and their considerable fortunes to the support of learned and artistic pursuits. It was this patronage, or the ability to pay the expenses of artists and writers so that they might be free to create, that in many significant ways fueled the cultural renewal of the Renaissance.

The dominant intellectual trend of the great European renewal was humanism, a reawakening of interest in the art, literature, history, and philosophy of the ancient Greeks and Romans. Such studies were called humanistic because they celebrated the achievements of human beings, an attitude that diverged from the medieval emphasis on the divine and was perhaps a result of religious insecurity following the Black Death. Humanistic scholarship also required a mastery of the ancient Greek and Latin languages so that original ideas could be read and digested in their original form without distortion from imperfect translations. Humanism first took root in Italy, naturally enough, because Italians were surrounded by, and drew inspiration from, the architectural monuments of their great Roman past. Soon the governments of fourteenth-century Italian city-states were fashioning themselves after the ancient republic of Rome. Newly aware of a forgotten corpus of ancient wisdom that crusading contact with the Islamic world had revealed, Italian scholars gradually rediscovered the ideas of pre-Christian thinkers whose works had languished in neglected corners of monastic libraries for centuries.

*Francesco Petrarch was among the first to appreciate the moral and political lessons offered by the ancients, and he undertook a quest—or sent forth his students in his later years—to bring their "lost" works to light once more. Petrarch was followed by other scholars such as *Leonardo Bruni and *Leon Battista Alberti, both of whom believed that a humanistic education was best employed in the service of the city-state. Indeed, Alberti preached that accumulation of wealth and ambition for political power were laudable aspects of the human condition because only with these tools could men serve their states most effectively. It was also Alberti who promoted himself as the archetypical Renaissance man, an individual with humanistic learning who commanded several languages, who was a great soldier and athlete, and who was witty and urbane enough in polite company to attract the all-important patronage of great civic leaders. As the focus of scholarly activity in quattrocento (1400s) Italy, humanism broke with the old Christian values of poverty, humility, and contemplative simplicity and instead substituted an image of *virtù*, or cleverness, courage, boldness, style, and classical learning, as the new ideal. In humanism Italians found release from conformity to the collective Christian chain of being, they found freedom to develop their own human talents as individuals, and they found an opportunity to renew themselves and their culture in the previously ignored or prohibited ideas of ancient teachers.

If humanism provided the initial spark of European intellectual renewal, then other forms of human creativity soon found expression in its wake. The fourteenth century, devastated by crisis as it may have been, was also an age of great achievement in the literary arts. This was the time in Italy of *Dante and *Giovanni Boccaccio, two Florentines who consciously chose to write in their native Tuscan vernacular, and who thus diverged from the medieval focus on works of theology, penned in Latin and intended for a narrow clerical audience. These innovators brought entertaining poetry and tales to lay readers and listeners through the vernacular and, at the same time, so popularized their Tuscan dialect that it became the basis of modern written Italian. England also enjoyed a heady literary moment around the turn of the fifteenth century when *Geoffrey Chaucer, *William Langland, and others produced masterworks in varying dialects of what was then "Middle" English. Popular literature in vernacular languages such as these, coupled with the development of the movable-type printing press in Germany in the mid-fifteenth century, did much to encourage literacy across Europe. Laypersons now possessed not only the desire to learn to read works that interested them, but also the financial means to buy cheaper and more plentiful printed books.

The plastic arts, too, experienced a creative resurgence under the brushes and chisels of men newly freed from the artistic conventions of old. Inspired by the realism they observed in Greco-Roman statues and mosaics all around them, Italian artists became "humanists" themselves as they experimented with perspective and shadow to achieve depth in their work, just as the ancients had once done. The symbolic, static, two-dimensional creations of the Middle Ages now gave way to vibrant, colorful, and, above all, realistic portrayals of human figures in their urban and natural settings. As with literature, this artistic revival did not occur exclusively in Italy but spread beyond the Alps to the urbanized regions of Flanders and the Rhine valley in Germany, and to France and Spain in the west. Although religious themes remained popular in Renaissance art, bold painters and sculptors also flirted with secular and even pagan subjects from the mythology and history of the Greeks and Romans. They were encouraged in this by wealthy patrons who were so captivated by the humanistic lessons of the ancients that they were willing to support the creative genius that brought these lessons to life on plaster, stone, and canvas in their chapels and villas. Indeed, the church itself was often the most willing and generous patron of both sacred and secular art. Popes such as *Nicholas V and *Pius II, former humanist scholars who had as younger men produced classical translations and even bawdy poetry, now commissioned writers, painters, and sculptors to help transform Rome into an unrivaled center of learning and beauty. Yet as many churchmen shared in the exuberance of the Renaissance spirit, some also neglected their clerical duties to live more completely in the secular world.

The fifteenth century was not a healthy time for the institutional Roman church. Crises such as the Black Death, the Avignon "captivity" and the great Papal Schism had caused large numbers of the faithful to doubt their confused and seemingly inept clergy. Many believers now turned their attention from saving their immortal souls to building their financial and political fortunes in this world, and, to a certain extent, some churchmen could not resist the temptation to follow their lead. If the middle of the fifteenth century produced worldly popes more devoted to humanism and art than to their pastoral cares, then the end of the century gave Christendom a series of popes far less worthy of the title "vicar of Christ" than their predecessors. *Innocent VIII is thought to have sired as many as sixteen illegitimate children, while *Alexander VI was a grand manipulator of Italian geopolitics through the agency of his notorious offspring Cesare and Lucrezia Borgia. With degenerate pontifical leadership such as this, it is small wonder that some Christians fell away from formal church obedience and either embraced the "heretical" teachings of reformers or else wandered off to seek a more personal, intense, and satisfying spirituality on their own. Born in the absurdity of the Papal Schism, heresiarchs *John Wyclif of England and *Jan Hus of Bohemia denounced church corruption while attracting followers with messages of apostolic simplicity and scriptural authority. The movements they generated were subsequently attacked by a threatened church and its secular allies, but not before these reformers were able to show Europeans an alternate and often more appealing religious path. Other alienated believers fled the ritualized Roman church to establish small spiritual communities of their own or undertook ascetic and contemplative exercises that sometimes led to mystical experiences of the divine. This new piety was known as the *devotio moderna*; it was not heretical in that the church never officially condemned its practices or adherents, but like heresy, it offered sustenance to the spiritually starved. Mystics such as *Walter Hilton and *Juliana of Norwich in England, and adherents of the Brethren of the Common Life such as *Gerhard Groote and *Thomas à Kempis in the Rhine valley, discovered by themselves a more individual and profound religious truth than anything the institutional church could offer. It was a blend of these forces—the corruption and worldliness of Rome and the spiritual innovations of reformers—that would spark the Protestant and Tridentine renewal of Christianity during the sixteenth century.

The final phase of cultural renewal in the early modern period occurred when the creative genius of Italy began to spread to northern and western Europe at the end of the fifteenth century. Scholars from Germany, England, France, and Spain traveled to Italy to study classical art and imbibe the lessons of humanism, and they returned to their homelands with this "new learning" to share with their countrymen. Northerners, however, used their newfound humanistic skills not only to grasp the wisdom of ancient pagan thinkers, but to translate more accurately and to clarify their understanding of ancient Christian sources as well. Although many of the great Christian humanists of the early modern age belong to the sixteenth century, and thus to the next volume in this series, important early practitioners included England's *John Colet, Germany's *Regiomontanus, and Spain's *Francisco Jiménez de Cisneros. These and other scholars helped inaugurate a period of theological, literary, and artistic brilliance in northern and western Europe that was fueled, as the Italian renewal had once been, by the political stability of emerging centralized states and by the prosperity of contact with a rich new world.

By the late fifteenth century the tiny city-states of Italy were dwarfed economically and militarily by the much larger kingdoms of France, Spain, England, and the Holy Roman Empire. A French invasion in 1494 overwhelmed the independent and contentious little world of Italy, clearly demonstrating that the center of power had now shifted to the North Sea and the Atlantic seaboard. This was partly due to the ability of these larger kingdoms to command enormous tax revenues and armies, but it was also partly due to a new source of wealth that was beginning to trickle in from places previously unknown or inaccessible to Europeans. Thanks to significant advances in navigational technology learned from crusading and commercial contacts with the Muslim world, European explorers ventured forth first along the coast of Africa and then out into the open Atlantic. They went in search of a route to the East Indies, where the luxury goods Italians had once purchased from Muslim middlemen in the Levant could be acquired, it was hoped, at cut-rate prices from the original suppliers themselves. What these intrepid explorers encountered, however, was an entirely new and unimagined world that, within a decade of its "discovery," they were scrambling to exploit and settle for profit. By the turn of the sixteenth century Europeans had indeed undertaken the renewal of their old world from within, but they had also achieved its complete redefinition from without by sailing forth to find their place in a new global universe.

The following figures were men and women who made important contributions to European culture in the fourteenth and fifteenth centuries, the "age of crisis and renewal" that is the theme of this volume. They are included here because they were great thinkers, saints, artists, patrons, rebels, poets, scientists, theologians, historians, and linguists. Others have deliberately been omitted because their accomplishments were primarily political or military and so do not properly belong in this volume. It can be said that any era exceeds the sum total of the lives and achievements of those individuals who shaped it, set its tone, and helped create its singular character in history, and the late medieval and early modern period is no exception. Though every era is necessarily the result of that which preceded it, and is in turn the foundation of that which is to come, the arbitrary division of time that we call the Renaissance still holds unique lessons for those who would appreciate the richness of the human experience.

The Late Medieval Age
of
Crisis and Renewal,
1300–1500

A

Abravanel, Isaac ben-Judah (1437–1508), was born in Lisbon to an important Jewish family known for its learning and especially for its public service to the royal families of Spain and Portugal. Although Isaac's grandfather was forced to convert to Christianity in the Spanish riots of 1391, he fled to Lisbon by 1397 and there reembraced Judaism. Both Isaac and his father served the royal family of Portugal, his father working for the infante Ferdinand, while Isaac acted as the treasurer for King *Alfonso V, "the African," However, Alfonso's successor, *João II, accused Isaac of plotting against him in 1481, forcing the family to flee to Spain. There Abravanel became a scholar, writing biblical commentaries while serving as an important financier and diplomat for *Ferdinand and *Isabel and becoming very wealthy himself. Nevertheless, in the family's third exile, the Abravanels were thrown out of Spain along with all other Jews in 1492. Although, as he later put it, Abravanel had pleaded until his throat was sore with King Ferdinand not to evict the Jews, who would give all they possessed for their country, all such arguments failed. The Abravanels found refuge in Naples, where Isaac worked as court treasurer for King *Ferrante I and later for Ferrante's son Alfonso II, while also composing a commentary on the Book of Kings. The French invasion of Naples in 1494 forced Abravanel, along with the Neapolitan royal family, to flee to Messina, returning in 1496. Abravanel's son Samuel and daughter-in-law Bienvenida later led the Neapolitan Jewish community until it suffered yet another expulsion in 1541. Abravanel's final move was to Venice in 1503, where he wrote most of his major works and served as a diplomat, negotiating an important treaty with Portugal. He died in Venice in 1508.

Abravanel was an important scholar whose works reflected his wide-ranging education, both secular (including classical literature) and religious (Jewish and Christian theology). He has been called the last of the great medieval Spanish Jewish philosophers and the first of the Renaissance humanists, for his work encompassed both perspectives. He contributed original insights into biblical commentary and acted as an inspired commentator for and mediator of Maimonides' thought. Abravanel's work met that of Maimonides especially on the three subjects of the creation of the world, the prophecies, and the principles of Judaism. Arguing against *Levi Gersonides, Abravanel claimed that the creation of the world *ex nihilo* was the only religiously acceptable explanation. His commentary on *The Guide to the Perplexed* is considered his masterpiece.

Abravanel was also an important thinker in the fields of politics and history, where his perspective is considered to have been more Renaissance than medieval. Given his and his family's history of service to the kings of Spain, Portugal, and Naples, his attitude toward government is particularly interesting. Abravanel preferred the governments of such Italian city-states as Venice, Florence, and Genoa to absolute monarchies, though he did argue that where kings exist, they must be obeyed. He interpreted the Torah and the biblical tradition of chosen judges as a pattern for government, arguing that the history of Israel demonstrated that the collective will of many people represented by a judge was better than the absolute will of one man. The Messiah, he said will be a judge and a prophet, not a king. These writings were influential in the sixteenth- and seventeenth-century Jewish messianic movements. His other writings included commentaries on the Torah and the prophets and on the Passover Haggadah; three messianic works called *Migdal Yeshu'ot* (Tower of salvation); two works on the creation of the world, *Shamayim hadashim* and *Mifalot Elohim*; works concerning Jewish dogma; and a short work on *The Form of Elements*. His biblical commentary influenced Christian biblical commentators in the seventeenth and eighteenth centuries. At least two other works on philosophy and divine justice have been lost.

Bibliography: Solomon Gaon, *The Influence of the Catholic Theologian Alfonso Tostado on the Pentateuch Commentary of Isaac Abravanel*, 1993; Ben-Zion Netanyahu, *Don Isaac Abravanel*, 1982.

Deborah S. Ellis

Afonso V, "the African," King of Portugal. *See* Alfonso V, "the African," King of Portugal.

D'Agnolo, Donato. *See* Bramante, Donato d'Agnolo Lazzari.

Agricola, Alexander (c. 1446–1506), was an early Renaissance musician of the Franco-Flemish school. He was one of the leading polyphonic composers of his generation, succeeding Johannes Ockeghem, and sang at the courts of *Charles VIII of France, Galeazzo Maria Sforza, and Philip the Fair of Burgundy, the future *Philip I of Spain.

Alexander Agricola was born in Ghent, probably around 1446. He was the son of Heinric Ackerman and Lijsbette Naps; his brother, Jan, appears to have been active as a singer-composer at a church in 's Hertogenbosch during the last two decades of the fifteenth century. Following a practice common in humanistic circles, Alexander Latinized his paternal name. Little is known of his early formative years. Married to a Florentine in 1470, he gained employment at the court chapel of Galeazzo Maria Sforza in Milan and remained there from approximately 1471 to 1474. By 1476 he had returned north, acquiring a position as chanter at the Cathedral of Cambrai. His whereabouts during the period 1477–91 remain a matter of speculation. However, in the summer of 1491, when he embarked on a new trip to Italy, he held an appointment as a chapel singer for Charles VIII of France. For the next few years he was seen visiting the courts at Mantua, Florence, and Naples. *Ferrante I of Naples tried, without success, to retain him as a singer at a generous annual salary of 300 ducats. By 6 August 1500 Agricola was a chaplain and singer for Philip the Fair, duke of Burgundy. In his employment at the Brussels court chapel, he had ample opportunity to interact with Pierre de La Rue, whose musical style was similar to his own. Agricola accompanied the duke on trips to Spain in 1501–3 and 1505–6. He is reported to have been sixty years old when he died near Valladolid in mid-August 1506.

Agricola's music gained wide diffusion in contemporary manuscript and print. In addition to eight complete masses, various credos, hymns, motets, magnificats, and lamentations, his extant work includes a significant corpus of secular music, popular songs in French, Italian, Latin, and Dutch. His six-part version of *Fortuna desperata*, an Italian *canzona*, shows him at the height of contrapuntal intricacy. The Venetian printer Ottaviano Petrucci included a sample of Agricola's music in *Harmonice musices odhecaton* (1501), the first printed volume of polyphonic music produced with movable type, and subsequently published five of the musician's masses in *Missae Alexandri Agricolae* (1504). Like Ockeghem, Agricola frequently used a borrowed cantus firmus melody as a structural device to organize his compositions. His mass *In myne Zyn* was unique inasmuch as he patterned it after one of his own secular chansons. His music, generally elaborate, rhythmically complex, often florid, maintained an unbroken melodic flow by avoiding simultaneous cadencing in all voices.

Bibliography: Rob C. Wegman, "Agricola, Bordon, and Obrecht at Ghent: Discoveries and Revisions," *Revue Belge de Musicologie* 51 (1997): 23–62.

Jan Pendergrass

Agricola, Rudolf (1444–85), a northern humanist who was praised by Erasmus as "another Virgil" for his eloquence in Latin, authored a handbook on rhetorical dialectics. Rudolf Agricola (Latin for Roelof Huysman) was born in Baflo near Groningen in the Netherlands, where his father, Hendrik Vries, was parish priest. On the day Rudolf was born, Hendrik was made abbot of the influential Benedictine monastery at nearby Selwerd, thus allowing him to boast of "becoming a father twice on the same day." Agricola received his early education at St. Martin's School at Groningen, where he showed himself a precocious student. In 1456, at the age of twelve, he matriculated at the University of Erfurt, receiving his bachelor's degree two years later. He continued his study in Cologne and Louvain, where he received his master of arts degree in 1465. His interest in classical authors probably prompted him, like many other northern humanists, to travel to Italy in 1468. In Pavia he initially studied law, but soon abandoned this to pursue his interest in the liberal arts. To refine his knowledge of Greek, he transferred to the University of Ferrara in 1474, where a strong liberal arts curriculum had been established under the patronage of the Este dukes. His fame as a speaker was such that he was asked to deliver the annual inaugural speech at the university in 1476. Agricola, who was not only versed in the liberal arts but was also an accomplished musician, supported himself by playing the organ at the court of Duke *Ercole 1 d'Este.

While Agricola was in Ferrara, he started his main work, *De inventione dialectica*, which he completed during a stay at Dillingen in 1479 on his journey back to the Netherlands. The book offered a practical course in argumentation and became widespread as a handbook of rhetorical dialectics at major universities, replacing texts such as Quintillan's *Institutio oratoria*, Cicero's *De inventione*, and the pseudo-Ciceronian *Rhetorica ad Herennium*. Echoing Cicero's dictum that every speech is to "teach, move, and delight," Agricola's *De inventione dialectica* provided an original rhetorical layout that treated topics, analyzed the form and function of dialectics, and finally offered practical guidelines for the art of argumentation, persuasion, and composition.

On his return to the Netherlands in 1480, Agricola was offered the position of town secretary in the city of Groningen. During his stay in Groningen he was a frequent visitor at the nearby Cistercian Abbey of Aduard, which in his time was "more an academy than a monastery," as one of his contemporaries put it. With a circle of prominent humanists such as Wessel Gansfort, *Alexander Hegius, Rudolf von Langen, Antoon Vrije, and Wilhelmus Frederici regularly visiting, the abbey grew into a prominent center of humanist learning. Although Agricola frequently complained about his position at Groningen, he declined several other job offers, one as a secretary and educator at the court of Emperor *Maximilian I, another as principal of the city school in Antwerp. He feared that these positions would restrict him academically. As a consolation for not accepting the position in Antwerp, he later wrote a letter, *De formando studio*, to Antwerp's school principal, Jacques Barbireau. The letter has frequently been considered a program for humanist education. Agricola considered two questions: first, the student's choice of study (philosophy was the worthiest field), and second, the key to success in study. The latter lay in the student's ability to understand and memorize, as well as in the creative application of the material.

In 1484 Agricola moved to Heidelberg at the invitation of his friend Johann von Dalberg to become professor at the university there. One of his main intentions, to learn Hebrew, was never fulfilled, however. Illness cut his professorship at Heidelberg short. On the way back from a trip to Rome to congratulate Pope *Innocent VIII on his election, he fell ill and died of fever on 27 October 1485.

Agricola's corpus is small; his fame with his contemporaries rested more on his inspiring personality than on the abundance of his writings. Apart from the works already mentioned, occasional orations, translations of Greek classics, and several letters have survived. Among the addressees of his letters were his old study friend from Pavia, Johann von Dalberg, the brothers Johann and Dietrich von Plieningen (both Agricola's students), and *Johann Reuchlin. Dietrich von Plieningen wrote an interesting and detailed biography of Agricola between 1494 and 1499. Agricola's Latin poetry consisted mainly of poems for special occasions, as well as a religious poem, *Anna mater*, composed shortly before his move to Heidelberg in 1484. Agricola's influence on later humanists, such as Desiderius Erasmus (who met Agricola in Deventer at the age of twelve) and Philip Melanchthon, was considerable.

Bibliography: Fokke Akkerman and Arjo Vanderjagt, eds., *Rodolphus Agricola Phrisius*, Brill's Studies in Intellectual History 6, 1988; Eckhard Bernstein, *German Humanism*, 1983; Lewis W. Spitz, *The Religious Renaissance of the German Humanists*, 1963.

Frans A. van Liere

Ailly, Pierre d' (1351–1420). Arguably the single most important player in ending the Great Schism, Pierre d'Ailly was one of the key proponents of the conciliarist solution that resulted in the election of Pope Martin V in 1417. An able administrator, d'Ailly completed his career as a cardinal of the church; he was a learned and prolific scholar whose thought shows the influence of the humanistic and nominalist tendencies of the College of Navarre. D'Ailly produced treatises on ecclesiology and ecclesiastical reform, logic, astrology, and geography and argued the case for the Immaculate Conception before Pope Clement VII.

Pierre d'Ailly was born on 14 March 1351 in Compiègne, a short distance from Paris, in a home adjoining the walls of the local Franciscan house. His family was a prosperous burgher clan that still owned property in its native Picardy. Around 1364 d'Ailly was sent to Paris to study at the progressive and prestigious College of Navarre. He began lecturing in the arts in 1368, was chosen procurator of the French kingdom in 1372, and received his degree in theology in 1381, four years younger than was usual. The Great Schism had begun in 1378 with the election of *Urban VI and subsequently of Clement VII. At the time, d'Ailly remained silent, but by 1381 he wrote a short treatise in the form of an ironic fictional letter from hell, the *Epistola Diaboli Leviathan*, arguing in favor of a general council. He made the close acquaintance in these years of his pupil and protégé *Jean Gerson, as well as two close advisors to King Charles V: the bishop, later cardinal, Jean de La Grange, and the crusader knight Philippe de Mézières.

In 1384 d'Ailly was appointed rector of the College of Navarre at the University of Paris and found himself embroiled in complicated political disputes between the university, the pope, and King *Charles VI and his regent uncles. In 1387 d'Ailly made a name for himself by persuading Clement VII to affirm the Immaculate Conception of the Virgin Mary. Shortly thereafter, late in 1389, he was appointed chaplain to the king and, a few months later, chancellor of the university, as both pope and king maneuvered for favorable relations with each other and the university.

In 1394 d'Ailly and Gilles des Champs made a recommendation on ending the schism based on a general referendum of the university. Composed in its final form by Nicholas of Clamanges, the document outlines three ways to end the schism: the *via cessionis*, in which both popes resigned, allowing a new election; the *via compromissi*, in which both popes submitted to the judgment of a third party; and the *via concilii*, the calling of a general council. Most, including d'Ailly himself, hoped that both popes would resign. Indeed, d'Ailly was persuaded of the good will of Clement's successor, *Benedict XIII, and inclined away from the *via concilii*, believing that Benedict would be willing to abdicate. In 1395 Benedict appointed d'Ailly to his first bishopric, in Le Puy, and two years later moved him to Cambrai. This last appointment was a testament to Benedict's faith in d'Ailly's courage and political skill, as it required him to confront a hostile duke of Burgundy, *Philip the Bold, in a diocese split between adherents to Urban and to Benedict. It also cost d'Ailly support in Paris among those who saw him as a papal partisan and believed him susceptible to what amounted to bribery because he backed away from calls for a council to end the schism. While d'Ailly was in Cambrai, and partly in response to a letter from Jean de Montreuil in praise of the *Roman de la Rose*, in 1401 he composed *Le jardin amoureux de l'âme dévote*, in which he rewrote the Roman missal as a religious allegory along the lines of the mystical interpretation of the Song of Songs.

Back in Paris in 1402, d'Ailly wrote his *Tractatus de materia concilli generalis*, in which he agreed to a general council, but as a council of the Avignon church and only with the reinstatement of obedience to Benedict XIII, from whom it had been withdrawn by France in 1398. In 1403 obedience was indeed restored to Benedict, but this seemed to quiet d'Ailly, who declined the opportunity to admonish the pope. With the assassination of the duke of Orléans in 1407, Paris became a hostile place for supporters of the pope, among whom d'Ailly was counted, so again he retreated to Cambrai. During this time he wrote a life for his Celestine friends of the founder of their order, Pope Celestine V, who had abdicated his throne in 1294.

D'Ailly attended the conciliarist Council of Pisa (1409) with high hopes, but the resultant election of Alexander V only complicated matters further, as both Gregory XII and Benedict XIII further dug in their heels. Following the disappointing conclusion of the council, d'Ailly again undertook a short period of rest. Among the works produced during this time was his *Imago mundi* (1410), a compendium of ancient and earlier medieval sources on geography and astrology that was later read and annotated by *Christopher Columbus.

In 1411 d'Ailly was appointed cardinal by John XXIII, and in 1413, papal legate in Germany, which posts he held at the time of the Council of Constance (1414–18). D'Ailly exerted considerable influence during the council, participating prominently in most of its defining moments, including the condemnations of John XXIII and *Jan Hus. In 1416 he presented to the council his *Tractatus de reformatione ecclesiae.* At the end, d'Ailly played a pivotal role in resolving a dispute between the English and French, resulting in the election of Martin V on 11 November 1417, which ended the schism. After the council, d'Ailly was appointed papal legate to Avignon and died there on 9 August 1420, at the age of sixty-nine.

Bibliography: Alan E. Bernstein, *Pierre d'Ailly and the Blanchard Affair: University and Chancellor of Paris at the Beginning of the Great Schism*, 1978; Francis Oakley, *The Political Thought of Pierre d'Ailly: The Voluntarist Tradition*, 1964; Laura Ackerman Smoller, *History, Prophecy, and the Stars: The Christian Astrology of Pierre d'Ailly, 1350–1420*, 1994.

Jeffrey Fisher

Albarno, Montréal d' (d. 1354), known to the Italians as Fra Moriale, was a French mercenary and leader of the condottieri Great Company in Italy in the early 1350s. A former Knight of St. John, this Provençal soldier was elected leader of the Great Company of condottieri after the resignation of Duke Werner of Urslingen in 1351. When Montréal joined the Great Company, it was fighting for the Hungarians against the city-state of Naples. After the defeat of the Neapolitans and Werner's resignation, the Great Company remained in Italy under Montréal's direction. From 1353 to 1354 this company of 7,000 men-at-arms and 2,000 crossbowmen, with approximately 20,000 camp followers, operated in central Italy. A skilled leader, Montréal was able to use his force to extort protection money from a number of Tuscan and Umbrian cities, including Florence, Pisa, Siena, and Rimini.

In 1354, before beginning a campaign against the archbishop of Milan on behalf of Padua, Ferrara, and Mantua, he left the company in Lombardy under the command of Conrad of Landau while he made a brief trip to Rome. Montréal's object for this trip was to collect money owed to him by the papacy for past service. On his arrival in Rome, however, he was seized at the command of the demagogue *Cola di Rienzo. Rienzo, attempting to regain his former political power in Rome, tried and executed Montréal as a brigand and murderer. Rienzo himself died several weeks later at the hands of a Roman mob. Conrad of Landau assumed the leadership of the Great Company, which in the years to come became closely associated with another band of condottieri led by the German Bongarten.

Bibliography: Michael Mallett, *Mercenaries and Their Masters: Warfare in Renaissance Italy*, 1974; Geoffrey Trease, *The Condottieri: Soldiers of Fortune*, 1971.

Angela B. Fulk

Alberti, Leon Battista (1404–72), famous as an athlete, musician, mathematician, poet, writer, artist and architect, was the most representative figure of the early Italian Renaissance. Alberti personified the cultural shift from the medieval world of revealed truth based on religion into a world of humanistic values based on inquiry and the resurgence of classical modes of art and thought, particularly of ancient Rome. Alberti's emblem, the winged eye, symbolized the union of supreme insight with supreme power.

Born out of wedlock, Alberti was cheated out of his inheritance at age sixteen when his father died, yet he still managed to become a student in Padua under the famous teacher Barsizza. A precocious student, he wrote a Latin comedy, *Philodoxeos* (c. 1426), which he passed off as an ancient work, finally acknowledging it as his own many years later. He went to Florence around 1428, where he met the most advanced artists of his time, including *Filippo Brunelleschi, *Donatello, *Lorenzo Ghiberti, Luca Della Robia, and *Masaccio. Continuing his work in Bologna, he studied law and became an apostolic abbreviator at the court of Pope *Eugenius IV in 1432, following the Curia to Florence and Bologna a year later. He returned to Rome in 1443, where he remained for the rest of his life.

Alberti is mainly known for his writings, which span the breadth of knowledge of the humanist mind. While he was working for the Curia, he wrote *Descriptio urbis Romae*, a description of the monuments of Rome; consistent with the spirit of his times, he insisted that Rome was culturally continuous, but with periods of rise and decline. Around 1433 he wrote *Della famiglia*, a work dedicated to domestic and civil life, in which he revealed his darker side and anticipated Niccolò Machiavelli in some of his observations on the human condition. In 1435–36 he wrote *Della pittura*, dedicated to his artist friends in Florence, which contained the first description of perspective construction as well as the "four elements of color" of red, blue, green, and gray. That he did not distinguish between light and pigment probably accounts for his including gray as a color, since he did correctly identify the primaries, as well as white and black, in various light intensities. Around the same time he wrote the first Italian grammar. Writing in the Italian vernacular himself, he encouraged others to do so as well. He also wrote on sculpture, philosophy, and mathematics. Finally, he wrote his treatise on architecture, *De re aedificatoria*. This was the first work on architecture to appear since the *De architectura* of the Roman Vitruvius in 27 B.C. He began it around 1452 and worked on it for the rest of his life. It was published posthumously in 1485 by his brother Bernardo. In it, he stated his views on proportion and elucidated the orders of architecture. He argued that beauty was not just in the subjective eye of the beholder but was rather a matter of correct proportions in which all parts relate to each other. He became authoritative in these matters for generations to come. His bay-arch-bay prescription for facades became very popular and had a great deal to do with the development of the modern proscenium theatre via the works of Gian Battista Aleotti (1546–1636). In book 8, chapter 7, in a discussion of classical theatres, Alberti explained the first scientific view of the phenomenon of acoustics.

Alberti designed a number of memorable buildings that were considered models of the classical style. He designed Sigismondo Malatesta's "temple" (*Il Tempio Malatestiano*) at Rimini, a monument to both Christianity and paganism, as well as Sigismondo himself, all rolled into one. In the Church of S. Andrea at Mantua he combined the Roman temple front, the triumphal arch, a dome, and the *thermae* (Roman baths) in his design. He also used the basic rhythm of bay-arch-bay for both the facade and the internal elevations. He remodeled the facade of Santa Maria Novella in Florence (1456–70) and gave it the classical columns, pediment, and scroll buttresses that are considered by some to be the beginning of the mannerist style, though this is usually attributed to Michelangelo for his design of the Laurentian Library. At Ferrara he designed the campanile for the Gothic cathedral, San Giorgio. He formulated the "five orders" that became common in Renaissance architecture and introduced them in his most important work, the Rucellai Palace in Florence (1446–51). Based on the Colosseum in Rome, it was the first Renaissance building in which a system of classical pilasters articulated a trilevel facade. Alberti regarded architecture as a civic activity and may be considered the first advocate of city planning.

Bibliography: Joan Gadol, *Leon Battista Alberti: Universal Man of the Early Renaissance*, 1969; H. W. Janson, *History of Art*, 3rd ed., 1986; Giorgio Vasari, *Lives of the Most Eminent Painters, Sculptors, and Architects*, 1568/1976.

C. Thomas Ault

Alexander VI, Pope (b. 1431, r. 1492–1503).

Rodrigo de Borja y Doms was corrupt, worldly, treacherous, and ambitious. His excesses and practices as pope were a contributing factor to the Protestant Reformation.

Rodrigo was born into the Spanish branch of the powerful Borgia family. His uncle, Alfonso, bishop of Valencia, supervised his education under Gaspare da Verona and endowed the teenager with ecclesiastical benefices. Rodrigo studied canon law at the University of Bologna. In 1456 his uncle, Pope Calixtus III, appointed the libidinous Rodrigo a cardinal. Calixtus sent Rodrigo to be papal legate in the March of Ancona. Impressed with Rodrigo's diplomatic skills, Calixtus next appointed him commander in the papal army, president of the Sacra Rota (the ecclesiastical high court), and vice chancellor of the Roman church.

In this last office Rodrigo amassed immense personal wealth, patronized the arts, and lived as a Renaissance prince. In 1460 Pope *Pius II reprimanded Rodrigo on several occasions for overly licentious behavior. Rodrigo did not temper his decadent behavior in light of these remonstrances, but learned instead to exercise a discretion so complete that the mother, or mothers, of his first three children—Pedro Luis in 1462 and Isabella and Girolama between 1467 and 1471—are unknown. He provided livings for his children, mainly in his native Spain. In 1473 Rodrigo began a ten-year affair with Vanozza dei Catanei. He had four children by Vanozza: Cesare in 1475, Juan in 1477, Lucrezia in 1480, and Jofre in 1481. Rodrigo removed his children from their mother's house to legitimize them, and thus began his lavish devotion to the offspring whose chaotic lives would trouble his pontificate. At *Innocent VIII's death in 1492 Rodrigo was elected Pope Alexander VI in a tumultuous conclave of the Sacred College, whose ranks he had joined by means of simony and bribery.

As a pope, Alexander at first looked promising. He renewed the war against the Ottoman Turks; he strengthened law enforcement in Rome; he ran an austere household; he clarified the organization of the papal courts; he set aside time for petitioners; and he promised, initially, to avoid nepotism and to keep his children at a distance. He also received the blessing of the Roman populace. Alexander quickly became the first pope not only to favor relatives, but also to honor his own children, and, perhaps most important, to flaunt a mistress, Giulia Farnese, openly. Within a month Alexander granted Cesare the See of Valencia, made his nephew, Juan Borgia Lanzol, a cardinal, and created two other Borgias captains of the Palatine Guard. In 1493, eighteen-year-old Cesare became a cardinal. Determined to unite the kingdoms of Italy under his own leadership, Alexander used his children as diplomatic and political pawns and so betrothed Lucrezia, at the age of thirteen, to Giovanni Sforza of Pesaro in northern Italy.

By 1494 Alexander's children had become a constant cause of worry. Juan was gambling heavily, spent his nights in brothels, was known to molest honest citizens and kill dogs and cats for sport, and had yet to consummate his marriage to the cousin of King *Ferdinand of Spain—a political connection of extreme importance to Alexander's design. Alexander's position was challenged by King *Charles VIII of France, who laid claim to the Kingdom of Naples and easily moved his army through Italy, capturing Rome by the end of the year. When he threatened the pope with deposition, Alexander turned to the Turkish sovereign, Bayezid II, for assistance. In a meeting with Charles, Alexander received the customary obeisance from the French monarch, but he continued to reject Charles's Italian claims. As Charles moved on to Naples, Alexander fled to Perugia with his daughter Lucrezia and formed alliances with Milan, Venice, and the holy Roman emperor, who demanded the withdrawal of the French from Italy. Alexander returned to Rome, congratulating himself on the victory over France.

In 1497 Giovanni Sforza fell out of favor with Alexander, who desired a more advantageous political match for Lucrezia. Sforza fled Rome, asking Lucrezia to follow. Amid rumors of incest between Alexander and Sforza's seventeen-year-old wife, and afraid that Alexander would take away his small fiefdom, Sforza acquiesced, and the marriage was annulled by papal decree on the grounds of impotence. In June Alexander's favorite son Juan was murdered, it was rumored at the hand of Cesare. Alexander was devastated. During this upheaval Alexander's moral turpitude and treachery were strongly condemned by *Girolamo Savonarola, a Dominican friar and the pope's most vocal critic. Savonarola had usurped political control of Florence in 1494 and led a group of detractors who denounced the irreligious practices of Alexander. Savonarola had supported Charles VIII's march into Italy, hoping for political reform in Italy. In 1498 he was condemned as a heretic and hanged by papal decree.

The loss of his son marked a change in Alexander's papacy. He announced a clerical reform program that clarified liturgical duties, conduct, and morals. Still, Alexander did not follow his own example. In 1498 Alexander selected a new husband/political alliance for Lucrezia, Alfonso II of Naples, a political marriage that turned into a love match. Shortly afterward, Cesare resigned his cardinalate and married Charlotte d'Albret to create an alliance with the French king Louis XII. His marriage to a French princess meant that Lucrezia's marriage had to end because their alliances were in conflict. Alfonso fled for his safety. The couple was reunited, and within a month Lucrezia gave birth to a boy, Rodrigo. It is believed that Alexander and/or Cesare later had Alfonso attacked on the steps of St. Peter's in 1500. Though Alfonso survived, he was subsequently strangled during his recuperation. With Alfonso dead, the alliance with France could go forward, advancing Alexander's political ambitions. Via siege and assassination, Cesare brought northern Italy under Borgia control, conquering the duchies of Romagna, Umbria, and Emilia. In Rome, Alexander shattered the power of the Orsini and Colonna families and concluded an alliance with Spain. Lucrezia eventually married as her third husband Alfonso I d'Este, duke of Ferrara.

In 1500, the Holy Year of Jubilee, Cesare was invested as papal vicar of the Romagna and then confirmed as captain general of the church. Cesare continued his tyrannical reign, supported by his father. In the summer of 1503 both Alexander and Cesare became ill, and rumors suggesting poison circulated widely. In August, ill with a malarial fever, Alexander made his confession and received Communion in the presence of five cardinals. Pope Alexander VI died around the hour of vespers. His funeral and burial were inglorious. The coffin was too small for Alexander's bloated body, which had to be punched into it. Neither a priest nor anyone else would attend the body.

Alexander's religious convictions cannot be questioned, but scandal and injustice accompanied each activity in his infamous career. Even within Renaissance standards of behavior for princes of the church, his ruthless pursuit of political influence and ceaseless aggrandizement of his family were excessive. Alexander VI holds a notoriously high position on the list of the so-called bad popes.

Bibliography: Ivan Cloulas, *The Borgias*, 1989; Marion Johnson, *The Borgias*, 1981; Michael Mallett, *The Borgias: The Rise and Fall of a Renaissance Dynasty*, 1969.

Kristopher Bell

Alfonso V, "the African," King of Portugal (b. 1432, r. 1438–81),

commonly spelled Afonso, nicknamed "African," was born in 1432, the son of Duarte (in English, Edward) and nephew of Prince *Henry the Navigator. His uncle Pedro acted as regent during the boy's minority. Nicknamed "African" because of his victories in Morocco, Alfonso neglected the crucial task of geographical discovery that his uncle Henry had encouraged. Irresponsible distribution of Crown funds and property, as well as a disastrous attempt to claim the throne of Castile, also contributed to making Alfonso's reign unfortunate for his country.

On 9 September 1438 Alfonso's father, King Duarte, died of plague. Six-year-old Alfonso was crowned his successor, but a struggle immediately ensued over who would control the kingdom until he came of age. Duarte had specified that Alfonso's mother, Queen Leonor, should be in sole charge of the government after his death, but her claim to the regency was disputed on the grounds that she was a woman and a foreigner (Aragonese). The other two candidates put forward for the regency at this time were Duarte's brother Pedro and Pedro's illegitimate half brother Afonso, count of Barcelos. Both attempted to connect themselves with the young king through marriage; Pedro offered his daughter Isabel as Alfonso's bride, and Barcelos his granddaughter. Prince Henry proposed a compromise solution that would divide the responsibilities of government between Leonor and Pedro, and when this proposal was spurned by the Barcelos party, he went further, this time suggesting a six-part division of government. Each of the three feuding parties would have control of one or more governing offices, with the remaining business conducted by a council. This compromise was also rejected, however, and the quarrel continued until Leonor was officially deposed as regent by the Portuguese Cortes and Pedro was installed in 1440. Leonor subsequently traveled to Castile, where she attempted to win support for her cause, and where she died in 1445.

In 1446 Alfonso reached his legal majority at age fourteen. He agreed to marry his cousin Isabel and requested that Pedro continue to govern the kingdom. Alfonso, however, proved indecisive and distrustful of Pedro. Barcelos, now duke of Bragaña, seized the chance to drive a wedge between the king and his uncle. After the marriage of Alfonso and Isabel in 1447, Bragaña persuaded Alfonso to end the regency, and Pedro retired to his estates. With Pedro absent from court, the Bragaña faction slandered him with the charge that he had poisoned Leonor and Duarte and had planned the death of Alfonso in order to seize the throne. Alfonso forbade all nobles to visit Pedro and demanded that Pedro surrender his arms. Pedro refused, displaying his contempt for the teenaged king. Despite Prince Henry's attempts to make peace, civil war broke out between the parties, and on 20 May 1449 Pedro was killed by a stray arrow in battle at Alfarrobeira.

The Bragaña family continued to wield great influence throughout Alfonso's reign. He rewarded them with lands and titles, including the newly created title of marquis. The only apparent limit to their influence was their inability to persuade the king to divorce Pedro's daughter. In 1455 Isabel gave birth to an heir to the throne, the future *João II. During that same year Alfonso allied himself to Castile by marrying his sister Juana to King *Enrique IV. Constantinople had fallen to the Turks in 1453, and Alfonso responded to a renewed papal call to crusade by capturing Alcacer-Seguir in Morocco in 1458. This outpost proved costly and difficult to retain. He gave some measure of support to Prince Henry's expeditions of discovery, but neglected this enterprise altogether after Henry's death in 1460. In 1461 Alfonso's extravagant spending prompted the Cortes to extract a promise from him not to give away his resources "with so much freedom and so unnecessarily." He failed to keep this promise.

Alfonso's greatest moment of success came in August 1471 when he conquered Tangier. After this victory he became known as "Alfonso the African." In 1474, with the death of Enrique IV of Castile, Alfonso's thoughts turned to uniting that kingdom with his own. A widower by this time, he married Enrique's daughter (and his own niece), *Juana la Beltraneja, and claimed the kingdom of Castile. He was opposed by Enrique's half sister *Isabel and her husband, *Ferdinand of Aragon. The succession of Castile was left in doubt because Juana was commonly believed to be illegitimate, and Enrique had vacillated several times before his death between the two women in naming his heir. In need of support, Alfonso sailed to France, where *Louis XI offered to approach the pope in order to legitimize Alfonso's marriage to Juana. In Alfonso's absence, his son João ruled in Portugal. The promised French aid never materialized, and as the discouraged Alfonso prepared to return to Portugal, he made the abrupt decision to renounce the monarchy and become a monk. After dispatching a set of letters that announced this decision, he disappeared. He was presently found and persuaded to return to the throne, where the remaining years of his reign were undistinguished. His marriage with Juana was dissolved, and she chose to enter a convent. By 1481 Alfonso had again decided to abdicate the throne, but he died before this plan could be effected on 28 August 1481. He was succeeded by his son, João II.

Bibliography: H. V. Livermore, *A New History of Portugal*, 1966; Malyn Newitt, ed., *The First Portuguese Colonial Empire*, 1986.

Angela B. Fulk

Alfonso V, "the Magnanimous," King of Aragon, Naples, and Sicily
(b. 1396, r. 1412–58), was the true founder of Iberian rule in Italy, a leading

example of chivalrous conduct and courtly display, and a patron of artists and writers, including *Lorenzo Valla, who wrote on the Donation of Constantine at Alfonso's behest. Alfonso was a modern king striving to build a modern regime, but was faced with a backward and highly divided Iberian society. Repeatedly thwarted by conflicting local interests, Alfonso had no real choice but to move his power base to the Italian holdings of his house, which he expanded greatly. In so doing, he laid down a foundation upon which his successors, including the Habsburgs, were able to build.

Alfonso V was born, probably on 18 December 1396, somewhere in Castile. His father was Fernando of Antequera (1379–1416), scion of the well-connected Trastámara line then dominating Spain. His mother was Leonor de Albuquerque (d. 1436), an equally well connected Castilian heiress. Through his marriage, Fernando became one of the richest and most powerful men in Spain, and his Aragonese descent placed him in contention for the Crown of Aragon in 1412 when the old direct line died out. Alfonso became Fernando's heir in 1412 and was actively involved in his father's affairs until Fernando's death in 1416, when the young Alfonso became king himself, a position he was to hold for some forty-two years in one of the longest and most successful reigns of the age.

Alfonso's life may be divided into four major periods: (1) his childhood and youth, including his years as heir apparent (1396–1416), (2) his first, largely abortive foray into Italy as king (1416–23), (3) a forced return to Spain to deal with Castilian politics and his own family's threatened position (1424–32), and (4) a renewed period of Italian intervention (1432–58) during which Alfonso was finally able to seize the Kingdom of Naples (1442). It subsequently became his headquarters and the new power base from which he intervened actively in Italian affairs, above all against archrival Genoa and its allies.

During Alfonso's lifetime the kingdom of Aragon was highly fragmented and was dominated by powerful noble families that continually used their hereditary power and privileges to thwart royal interests. The other major components of the kingdom, Catalonia and Valencia, the latter a conquest march, also had their strongly entrenched local factions, including, in the case of Catalonia, the powerful urban community of Barcelona with its overseas interests. When he became king in 1416 Alfonso had, as a consequence, little direct control and few regular sources of income and was disadvantaged as a Castilian outsider. For his income, he was highly dependent upon the dispensations of the various Cortes, which usually only granted subsidies in exchange for concessions of additional rights and privileges, further weakening already-limited royal power. To enhance his position, Alfonso looked to Catalonia, its overseas interests, and the overseas components of his kingdom, which included the Balearic Islands, Sardinia, and Sicily. To these domains Alfonso sought, unsuccessfully, to add Corsica, controlled by his lifelong enemy Genoa, but he quickly became embroiled instead in the affairs of Naples, where he briefly became, heir of the fickle Jovanna II, regent of the kingdom, until she changed her mind.

Frustrated in Italy and faced with civil war in Castile, Alfonso was forced to return to Spain in 1424, where he remained for almost a decade, but he never lost his Italian ambitions. Ultimately tiring of endless Castilian intrigues, Alfonso returned to Italy and fought a long and bitter series of wars against Jovanna II and her French supporter, *René, duke of Anjou. He finally triumphed in 1442, taking Naples again after being expelled ignominiously in 1423. Once in control of Naples, despite a number of setbacks, one of which left him a captive in Milan, Alfonso made himself into one of the dominant influences in Italy, in large part based upon his more regular and more abundant Italian revenues. He died still planning war against Genoa.

Alfonso was married to Maria of Castile (1401–58), who, although she lived apart from her husband for most of her life and was apparently unloved by him, remained loyal and proved a highly capable regent in Aragon during the decades of the king's absence. The couple had no children, but Alfonso did have several illegitimate children, including *Ferrante, whom Alfonso made his heir in Naples. His brother Juan II took over Aragon and the other Aragonese domains.

Bibliography: Jerry H. Bentley, *Politics and Culture in Renaissance Naples*, 1987; T. N. Bisson, *The Medieval Crown of Aragon: A Short History*, 1986; Alan Ryder, *Alfonso the Magnanimous, King of Aragon, Naples, and Sicily, 1396–1458*, 1990.

Paul D. Buell

Alfonso Fernández de Madrigal. *See* Tostado, Alfonso.

Alfonso Fernández de Palencia. *See* Palencia, Alfonso Fernández de.

Alighieri, Dante. *See* Dante Alighieri.

Álvaro de Luna. *See* Luna, Álvaro de.

Amboise, Georges d' (1460–1510), cardinal, was a descendant of the Norman lords of Amboise. D'Amboise rose to great prominence during Louis XII's reign, although he never held a formal ministerial office.

At age nineteen d'Amboise was created bishop of Montauban, and by age twenty-three he had joined the Orléanist party. In 1482 he became archbishop of Narbonne, and in 1493 he acquired the eminent French archdiocese of Rouen. Shortly after Louis's accession to the throne in 1498, Pope *Alexander VI granted d'Amboise a cardinal's hat, and by 1502 his growing influence increased when he was made legate *a latere* (a papal ambassador).

D'Amboise quickly became involved in many facets of Louis's government. He was a member of the Conseil des Affaires and was very active in foreign affairs. He was Louis's governor of Milan for four years, with full royal authority. On 6 April 1500 he officially entered the city and accepted its surrender in exchange for a royal pardon. At d'Amboise's request, Louis sent the cardinal's nephew, Charles de Chaumont d'Amboise, to be the commander of the French army in Milan.

Cardinal d'Amboise was Louis's primary diplomat. He became close to Niccolò Machiavelli, negotiated with rebellious Swiss troops, and was always sent first into conquered regions. He also handled the delicate negotiations between Archduke Philip of Austria (future *Phillip I of Spain) and Louis regarding the proposed marriage of their children, Louise and Charles. Afterwards, he traveled on to meet with Charles's grandfather, Holy Roman Emperor *Maximilian I, and gained his approval for the match on 13 October 1501. In 1505 it was d'Amboise who was sent to receive Milan's investitures from the emperor and to swear homage for the duchy. It was also the cardinal who met privately with Margaret of Austria, Charles of Habsburg's regent, at the Conference of Cambrai.

The cardinal was an active reformer of both secular and religious institutions. He was the impetus behind Louis's 1498 edict that limited the privileges of the University of Paris, its faculty, and its students. Despite a huge outcry, the royal will was asserted, and the university backed down. D'Amboise was more active in church reform. In March 1502 he issued a decree designed to curb prodigious abuses in religious houses. He declared that monasteries must submit to formal visitations by a panel of bishops. The Dominicans, who were the first to "fail" the visitation, refused to reform, and so d'Amboise used force to remove them from their houses and from Paris. This process was repeated with the Benedictines and the Franciscans. Before his death in 1510, the cardinal was also working toward reform in the Carmelite orders. Despite these valiant efforts, the reform was not entirely successful since the measures taken were too scattered to have a large impact.

Cardinal d'Amboise had his faults, but apparently pluralism and sexual misconduct were not counted among them by contemporaries. He was politically astute, and his shrewd maneuvers helped a rather ineffectual king become a solid one. He could also be generous. Records show that the cardinal donated goodly sums to the poor coffers, offered unsecured loans to his neighbors, and rebuilt the cathedral at Rouen from his own resources.

Absenteeism was one of the sins that could be laid at d'Amboise's feet, and avarice was another. Grandiosity was perhaps his biggest fault. He enjoyed ceremonies such as Queen Anne's coronation on 18 December 1504, where he was as much a focus as was the new consort. D'Amboise enthusiastically embraced Italian Renaissance architecture and poured vast sums into rebuilding his château, Gaillon, which was not completed until a year after his death. The cardinal also enjoyed politicking and was not above underhanded maneuvering to defeat his enemies. For example, when Marshal Pierre de Rohan, sieur de Gié, was arrested on charges of treason in 1504, d'Amboise threw himself wholeheartedly into the cause against his former ally. When Gié retired in disgrace, the cardinal became the sole administrator of the realm. D'Amboise's major ambition was to become pope, an office that he openly coveted, and that

.orenzo Ghiberti. Ghiberti designed the frame and provided the painter with
example of monumental sculpture. Particularly distinctive was the height-
d plasticity of the figures and the careful use of drapery to indicate mass,
ile the animated predella compositions also betrayed Fra Angelico's interest
Ghiberti's relief sculpture. Despite its monumental quality, the work is not
rowly representational. The imitation of visible reality increasingly became
nical to Fra Angelico's definition of a work's spiritual import, since the
estic figures served primarily a dogmatic function. The Linaiuoli Tabernacle
v the painter to the attention of two powerful rival families, the Medici and
Strozzi, and resulted in important commissions, including the Strozzi *Dep-
ion* (early to mid-1430s; Florence, Museo di S. Marco) and the extensive
ram of decoration for the Dominican Convent of S. Marco funded by *Code Medici.

1436 the Sylvestrine Monastery of S. Marco in Florence was ceded to the
inican community at Fiesole. The dilapidated buildings were renovated at
xpense of the Medici family, and Fra Angelico was entrusted with a dec-
e program that included a huge altarpiece for the church and more than
frescoes for the convent. The San Marco program included the work of
ants (their number and identity are not known), but many of the compo-
s are certainly autograph. Work began around 1440 and continued inter-
tly for at least a decade. The S. Marco work reinforced an earlier departure
m and iconography—seen initially in the frescoes at S. Domenico at
e (c. 1435)—since it moved away from the three-dimensional accuracy of
pieces in favor of an austerity designed to stimulate meditation and the
er's religious imagination. The altarpiece (c. 1440–41), a *Virgin and Child
ned*, combined Dominican and Medicean interests; saints important to the
figured alongside images and motifs that sprang from the conventions
ninican iconography. Sparse decoration and minimal incident characterize
coes designed for the convent dormitories and bear witness to the artist's
o fuse image and beholder in a transcendent meditational moment. The
s that decorate the more public ground floor, however, never forgetful of
ntemplative function, make more of a concession to narrative. The *An-
ion* fresco contrasts eloquently with the painting at Cortona. A cell-like
replaces the elaborate architecture of the earlier work; the figures are
nd motionless; and nothing distracts the eye from the mystical union.
ugh the work at S. Marco was not yet complete, toward the end of 1445
elico moved to Rome. There he undertook a series of commissions in
Vatican palace and St. Peter's for Pope *Eugenius IV, but the only
work is the cycle of the lives of Sts. Stephen and Lawrence executed
ubsequent pope, *Nicholas V, and found in his private chapel. The
narrative and rich detail of these scenes distinguish them sharply from
rco frescoes and make traditional assessments of stylistic development
Also executed during his Roman sojourn were the frescoes at Orvieto
commission never completed. In 1450 Fra Angelico returned to Fiesole

Louis did everything possible to gain for him. His early de:
these hopes.

By 1508 the cardinal was incapacitated by gout, yet
control of government. Knowing that his death was i
penned his will in 1509. On 25 May 1510 the cardinal suc
Upon hearing of his death, King Louis wept bitterly. If the
as to who really ruled France, the chaos that ensued afte
case.

Bibliography: Frederic J. Baumgartner, *Louis XII*, 1994.

Andrés de Escobar. *See* Escobar, Andrés de.

Andrew of Wyntoun. *See* Wyntoun, Andrew of.

Angelico, Fra (c. 1395/1400–1455), originally
Italian painter and Dominican friar. Equally at home
uscript illumination and with the bold modeling of
cles, Fra Angelico put the sturdy realism of his Ren
the service of an entirely nonrational, devotional an

Fra Angelico's origins are obscure, and document
Guido di Piero at the end of the fourteenth century
moved at an unknown date to Florence and traine
minator. Sometime between 1417 and 1425 he en
at the Observant (reformed) Convent of S. Dome
name Fra Giovanni. By 1417 he had received his f
of 1425 refer to him as the author of an altarpiec
was in charge of a large and prestigious workshop
was his most important pupil. Early pieces displa
*Masaccio, and Gentile da Fabriano include a
1500) depicting the *Virgin and Child Enthrone
Barnabas, Dominic, and Peter Martyr* (Fiesole,
1428) executed for the Dominican nuns of Flo
*and Child with SS. Dominic, John the Baptist,
nas* (now in Florence's Museo di S. Marco), a
S. Domenico in Cortona. The Cortona *Annur
tuous piece in the artist's oeuvre, demonstrate
temporary spatial innovations and marked
windowlike perspective of the S. Marco altar

The commission by the Florentine Arte de'
Tabernacle (executed c. 1433–36) signaled
largest single panel of the Virgin and Child
triptych was the result of the collaboration

to take up the post of prior at S. Domenico for the customary two years. Thereafter documentation is scarce, but later work included the altarpiece for S. Bonaventura at Bosco ai Frati (c. 1450–52, now in Florence, Museo di S. Marco). In March 1452 Fra Angelico declined a commission for fresco decoration in Prato and likely returned to Rome. He died there in February 1455 and is buried at S. Maria sopra Minerva. He was beatified in 1984, confirming a saintly status accorded him in biographies since the sixteenth century.

Bibliography: Georges Didi-Huberman, *Fra Angelico: Dissemblance and Figuration*, 1995; William Hood, *Fra Angelico at San Marco*, 1993.

Nicola McDonald

Anjou, René, Duke of. *See* René, Duke of Anjou.

Anne Valois, Duchesse de Bourbon. *See* Valois, Anne, Duchesse de Bourbon.

Antoine de La Sale. *See* La Sale, Antoine de.

Antonio de Nebrija. *See* Nebrija, Antonio de.

Arc, Joan of. *See* Joan of Arc.

Arévalo, Rodrigo Sánchez de. *See* Sánchez de Arévalo, Rodrigo.

Artevelde, Jacob van (c. 1290–1345), was the charismatic dictator of Ghent. Van Artevelde played an important role in the early conflicts of the Hundred Years' War. Often depicted as a democratic reformer, he was an unusual figure for his time, a rich merchant who became virtual ruler of Flanders for seven years.

Jacob van Artevelde burst upon the Flemish scene in 1337 when Ghent, one of the most prosperous of northern European cities, exploded in rebellion against the count of Flanders, Louis of Nevers. Flanders was poised on a precipice between the ambitions of the French king Philip VI, who sought more complete control over it, and its need for cordial relations with England, which supplied wool for its cloth industries. Louis of Nevers, since his marriage in 1320 to the daughter of Philip V of France, had remained close to his French suzerains. By 1337, however, such close relations with France were doing the Flemish cloth industry no good; because of his own hostilities with France, *Edward III of England had closed off the wool supply to Flanders in retaliation. Ghent, Bruges, and Ypres, the three biggest industrial cities of Flanders, reacted in open revolt.

Van Artevelde was a brewer, a broker of food products, and, by the time of the Ghent rebellion, one of the richest men in the city. In December 1337 an emergency government of five captains, one of whom was van Artevelde, was established to stabilize the city. Louis of Nevers fled Flanders for France. Thus began the rule over Flanders of a man who had held no previous public office. Van Artevelde did possess, however, the attributes of a demagogue: charisma, persuasive oratorical skills, and the support of the common people. Van Artevelde soon made his mark by directing Flanders into an alliance with the English king, Edward III.

In December 1339 van Artevelde became a hero to his subjects by negotiating with Edward III a very favorable treaty for Flanders. The Flemings were to have unlimited access to English wool and a subsidy of 140,000 livres for military equipment. The English promised to restore the former Flemish castellanies of Lille, Douai, and Orchies, which *Philip IV, "the Fair," of France had annexed to the royal domain. If the French attacked, the English swore to devote an English fleet and troops to the defense of Flanders. In return, van Artevelde guaranteed military aid to the English in their conflicts against France and recognized Edward III as the rightful king of England and France. This agreement brought Flanders into the early battles of the Hundred Years' War.

Van Artevelde ruled Flanders with an iron hand, even holding under house arrest the rightful count, Louis of Nevers, when Philip VI sent him back to Ghent. In fact, van Artevelde was little more than an autocratic dictator. *Jean Froissart wrote that everywhere he went, van Artevelde was attended by sixty to eighty armed men and that he put to death any who opposed him. He put down any revolt against his authority and packed official positions in Ghent with his friends, relatives, and allies. Despite his ruthlessness, however, van Artevelde retained massive popular support for a time. He also enjoyed the personal friendship of Edward III.

By 1345, however, van Artevelde's power in Flanders was declining. He and his troops had not acquitted themselves well during the siege of Tournai in the summer of 1340, and he was no longer on good terms with many of the guilds that had supported his rise to power in the first place. He openly displayed his wealth and success, displeasing the common people. His subjects began to become suspicious of van Artevelde's ambitions and his close relationship with Edward III. Rumors abounded that van Artevelde intended to supplant the rightful count of Flanders with Edward III's eldest son, *Edward, the future Black Prince. Finally, his heavy-handed methods of ruling the Flemish cities were simply no longer successful. On 17 July 1345, at his home in Ghent, van Artevelde was surprised by a mob of unruly men led by a rival who chased him outdoors and beat him to death. For a time, Edward III was upset by the murder of Jacob van Artevelde, a man whom he believed was the key to the Anglo-Flemish alliance. He provided financial support and protection to van Artevelde's family, who went to live in England for some years.

Historians have represented Jacob van Artevelde in paradoxical terms. To some, he was a champion of the common people who fought for the continuing economic prosperity of Flemish cloth industries. To others, he was a ruthless autocrat, too corrupted by his own excessive ambitions to be an effective ruler.

In any case, his importance to England's cause in the early years of the Hundred Years' War is undeniable.

Bibliography: David Nicholas, *The van Arteveldes of Ghent: The Varieties of Vendetta and the Hero in History*, 1988; Hans van Werveke, *Jacques van Artevelde*, 1942.

Dana L. Sample

Artois, Robert of. *See* Robert of Artois.

Aureoli, Peter (1280?–1322), nicknamed "doctor facundus," was a Franciscan Scholastic philosopher and theologian. He authored commentaries on the *Sentences* of Peter Lombard, several Scholastic treatises, *quaestiones* and sermons, most notably on the Immaculate Conception and evangelical poverty, and exegetical works. Although his philosophy was influenced by Augustine, Aristotle, and Averroës, Aureoli was too much of an independent thinker to fit into any medieval "school." His philosophy formed an important chain between the philosophical realism of John Duns Scotus and the nominalism of *William of Ockham. Aureoli was probably born near Gourdon in Aquitaine in southwestern France. In the first decade of the fourteenth century he studied in Paris, probably with Duns Scotus. From 1312 to 1314 he lectured at the seminaries of the Franciscans, first in Bologna and later in Toulouse.

Aureoli's earliest work, *De usu paupere* (1311), dealt with the controversy in the Franciscan order between Conventual and Spiritual factions. While he remained faithful to his Franciscan vow of strict poverty and criticized the lax attitudes of some of the Conventual Franciscans, Aureoli opposed the ascetic rigorism of the more radical Spiritual Franciscans and their allies, the Fraticelli. Evangelical poverty was mandatory, but he felt that the moderate use of goods not owned personally was certainly allowed to Franciscans, Aureoli asserted that the pope was the ultimate authority in this matter, and his stance was not too different from *Clement V's bull *Exivi de paradiso* (1312), which sought to settle the matter of the extent of evangelical poverty. Here and in his treatise *De conceptione*, Aureoli showed himself a defender of papal infallibility while at the same time arguing for a stricter separation of temporal and spiritual powers.

Aureoli's *De conceptione beatae Mariae virginis* deserves mention as one of the earliest arguments in favor of the Immaculate Conception of the Virgin Mary. It was composed as a sermon for clerics in 1314; in a later treatise, the *Repercussorium*, he defended the same views against an attack by an unnamed Dominican friar.

In 1316 Aureoli started to lecture on the *Sentences* of Peter Lombard in Paris at the request of the general chapter of the Franciscans in Naples. In 1318 he obtained his master's degree in theology. His commentary on the *Sentences* probably originated during his lectureship in Bologna and Toulouse and was revised in Paris before 1319. It survived in two redactions, one as reported by his students and another as an abbreviated commentary in his own hand, on the first book of the *Sentences* only. These commentaries can be considered Aureoli's main work, containing his most important contribution to philosophy on the topic of epistemology. For Aureoli, to know an object was not, as Thomas Aquinas and Duns Scotus had defined it, the intellectual reception of an intelligible form or a reproduction in one's mind of a really existing extramental idea. Instead, he defined perception as an active effect of the intellect that created in the mind an "apparent being." Aureoli cited the examples of several optical illusions to show that the mind's "apparent being" did not always correspond to the extramental reality. For someone traveling on a ship, for instance, the trees on the shore seemed to move. He thus showed that the sensitive and intellectual powers of the mind had an active and formative role in cognition. Only in true vision did extramental reality and "apparent being" coincide. Aureoli's skeptical epistemological stance vis-à-vis cognition is sometimes called conceptualism, as opposed to realism. By defining cognition mainly in psychological terms, he eventually opened the way to Ockham's nominalist theories of cognition, even though he consistently opposed a more nominalist interpretation of his own theories.

Aureoli's exegetical work, the *Compendium on the Literal Sense of Scripture* (1319), included a commentary on the Apocalypse that mingled a historicizing approach with a more traditional moral exegesis. In 1320 Aureoli was elected provincial minister of Aquitaine, and shortly thereafter, in 1321, he was appointed archbishop of Aix. He died in Avignon in 1322.

Bibliography: Etienne Gilson, *History of Christian Philosophy in the Middle Ages*, 1955; Katherine H. Tachau, *Vision and Certitude in the Age of Ockham: Optics, Epistemology, and the Foundations of Semantics, 1250–1345*, 1988.

Frans A. van Liere

Avignon, Juan de (fl. c. 1418),

was a Spanish physician and author. Very little biographical information is extant about Juan de Avignon, who was a practicing physician in Seville around 1418. It is known that he moved from Avignon to Seville because he was in service to the archbishop of Seville, Don Pedro Barroso. It is assumed that he remained in the city the rest of his life, where he published his *Sevillana medicina* for the purpose not only of instructing his son but also of recording what he had seen as a practicing physician in Seville.

The *Sevillana medicina* was compiled by Juan de Avignon in 1418 or 1419 and was published in 1545 by another doctor, the *licenciado* Monardes. This work was an extensive treatise, not only on general medical matters but also on the specific circumstances pertaining to living in the city of Seville. Juan de Avignon wrote of topics ranging from good and bad "air" to problems of infertility. He not only gave diagnoses of symptoms and treatments for disease, but also recommended healthful habits (particularly the importance of iron in the diet) and corrected errors both noted and experienced. One of the *Sevillana Medicina*'s most historically valuable aspects was its catalog of ailments predominant in Seville during this particular period.

The *Sevillana medicina* was one of the earliest works of medical topography written in Europe; it was the third of this genre, the first being Benjamin Ben-Jone Tudelensis's work on Zaragoza, completed in 1273. Juan de Avignon's contribution was a true corpus of doctrine for medical science, integrating what today would be considered holistic medicine. Many of his observations and recommendations have been confirmed in modern medical practice, and he excelled in employing scientific rigor in the creation of his treatise.

Bibliography: Nancy G. Siraisi, *Medieval and Early Renaissance Medicine*, 1990.

Rowena Hernández Múzquiz

Ayala, Pero López de. *See* López de Ayala, Pero.

B

Baconthorpe, John (c. 1290–c. 1350?), was an English Carmelite friar and the major theological writer of his order in the fourteenth century. His influence reached its peak during the 1600s when his writings were recommended as manuals of theology for the order.

John Baconthorpe (or Bachon, as he was known on the Continent) was born around 1290 in the village of Baconthorpe in Norfolk, England, and joined the Carmelites probably in nearby Burnham Norton. (Older authorities give Blakeney, but that house was founded some years later.) He was sent to study first at Oxford around 1312 and then in Paris, where he was taught by the Carmelite theologian Gul Terreni. Baconthorpe gave his student lectures on the Bible and the *Sentences* of Peter Lombard between 1316 and 1318, and he received his bachelor's in theology by 27 July 1321, when he is recorded as a witness at the revocation of his errors by Jean de Pouilly. He incepted as a doctor probably in 1322 and took his place as regent master in the Carmelite *studium* (seminary). Book 1 of his commentary on the *Sentences* of Peter Lombard was completed on 23 April 1325, and he delivered his *Quodlibeta* 1 and 2 (responses to theological problems) during this period.

He returned to Cambridge by the end of 1326 or early 1327. On the resignation of the English provincial Richard Blyton, Baconthorpe was elected in his place. On 20 January 1327 he was probably one of the two Carmelites present at the abdication of King Edward II. In 1330, though, he was accused of complicity in the earl of Kent's plot and, as a result, was banished. He returned to Paris and resumed his teaching. During this period he delivered his *Quodlibeta* 3 and was probably one of the three Carmelite theologians summoned to Avignon to defend Pope *John XXII against attacks on papal supremacy.

In 1333 Baconthorpe resigned as English provincial, probably due to his absence abroad. When he returned is unknown, but he was lecturing in Oxford by 1344, as he referred to a discussion that year with *Thomas Bradwardine on foreknowledge and predestination. He died in London sometime between 1349 and 1352.

Baconthorpe's intellectual ability was extraordinary, and as an early writer commented, he was "a man small in his person but great in learning and knowledge." Known as the "Doctor resolutus," he wrote extensively, and over one hundred titles have been attributed to him, most of which, however, are now lost. His major work, his commentary on the *Sentences*, and the three *Quodlibeta* were frequently reprinted (most recently in 1969). In his theology, he was better as a critic than a synthesist: he analyzed the opinions of others in great detail, pointing out where they were wrong, then sought a solution that contained and explained the other viewpoints. His *postill* (commentary) on St. Matthew's Gospel illustrated well his originality of approach as compared with his contemporaries. In it, he rejected any moralizing on pagan tables, the use of classical literature, sophistry, and elaborate divisions of a subject into themes, aiming instead to model himself on Jesus' use of the parables with their simple, direct conclusions. Baconthorpe was not averse to using the writings of pagan philosophers to support his theology and was also accused of adopting ideas from the Arab philosopher Averroës. However, he was too original a thinker to simply accept opinions from others, although it is clear that he drew inspiration from non-Christian sources. In regard to the church, he was a traditionalist, a staunch defender of the papacy against its critics, but he expressed his views with originality and conviction. Although Baconthorpe's four small works on the Carmelite order repeat many of the historical legends about its foundation, they are noted for their spirituality and Marian devotion.

Bibliography: James P. Etzweiler, "John Baconthorpe: 'Prince of Averroists'?" *Franciscan Studies* 36 (1976): 148–76; Beryl Smalley, "John Baconthorpe's Postill on St. Matthew," in *Studies in Medieval Thought and Learning*, 1981.

Richard Copsey

Bardi, Contessina (c. 1400–1473), also called Lotta, was the wife of the famous political leader and cultural patron of Florence, *Cosimo de Medici (1389–1464). In his life of Cosimo, *Vespasiano da Bisticci, a bookseller and biographer of many famous Florentines of his day, only refers to Contessina as the butt of her husband's rather acerbic wit. Historians, too, have generally not taken Contessina seriously, viewing her as solely concerned with domestic and familial matters, ignorant of and uninvolved in affairs outside that arena.

Contessina's exact date of birth is unknown; it has been variously given as 1391, 1392, or around 1400. The latter date is the most likely, given that she married Cosimo about 1414 and would have been considered then too old to marry, by Florentine standards, if she had been born in the early 1390s. Her two children were called *Piero ("the Gouty," 1414–69) and Giovanni (1421–63).

Contessina came from a noble feudal family. Her father was Alessandro di

Sozzo Bardi, count of Vernio, and her mother, named Cammilla, was the daughter of Raniero di Galdo Pannochieschi, count of Elci. The marriage to Contessina linked Cosimo de Medici to several powerful noble families in Tuscany, and the Medici later relied upon the Bardi for military support. The Bardi, who had been excluded from Florentine politics because of their status as magnates, were readmitted to the Florentine political class in 1434 upon Cosimo de Medici's assumption of de facto power.

Contessina's surviving correspondence of some thirty or so letters written (or dictated) between 1428 and 1473 were all, with one exception, addressed to members of her marital and natal families. These letters reveal a woman whose life was family centered, and who was concerned for her husband's and sons' health (all three of them suffered from gout), the provision of household goods and foodstuffs, and the successful management of various family estates in the city and the country. This devotion to household and family was what contemporaries would have expected of an upper-class woman whose primary responsibility was, after all, that of childbearer and domestic manager. This was reflected also in the Florentine political system, which was modeled on that of the classical republics. Consequently, the consorts of Florence's chief citizens, and, indeed, women generally, had no formal role in the regime.

However, this did not mean that Contessina could not exercise considerable influence within the Medici family. Part of her responsibility as Cosimo's wife was to play host to important dignitaries. In 1459, for example, she hosted the visiting duke of Milan, Galeazzo Maria Sforza, at the Medici palace. Contessina was also willing to advise her son Giovanni on political matters if she felt it appropriate to do so. After being widowed in 1464, Contessina was sometimes asked by relatives and others to intercede on their behalf with *Lorenzo, her grandson, with whom she enjoyed a close relationship.

Contessina died sometime between 26 September and 25 October 1473. Her death is known to have occurred within that time period because Contessina's daughter-in-law, *Lucrezia Tornabuoni de Medici, had reported that she was well on 25 September of that year and Luigi Pulci, a vernacular poet and Medicean client, told Lucrezia in a letter of 26 October of his deep sadness at Contessina's passing, including his regret at not being able to see her one more time. Contessina's death was also acknowledged by the abbess of the Convent of San Matteo in Pisa in a letter to Lucrezia Tornabuoni a fortnight later. Contessina's position of influence within the Medici family was well understood by her contemporaries.

Bibliography: Y. Maguire, *The Women of the Medici*, 1927; Janet Ross, *Lives of the Early Medici as Told in Their Correspondence*, 1910.

Natalie Tomas

Beauchamp, Richard (d. 1481). An ecclesiastic who benefited from the patronage of *Henry VI and *Edward IV, Richard Beauchamp was best known as the bishop of Salisbury Diocese in England, a position that he held from 1450 until his death in 1481. Supported by royal patronage, Beauchamp defended his episcopal overlordship over the citizens of Salisbury. His other principal achievement was his role in the building of St. George's Chapel at Windsor Castle, one of the primary examples of perpendicular architecture in England.

Beauchamp was born to Sir William Beauchamp, a prominent politician who served periodically as speaker for the House of Commons in Parliament. His mother was Elizabeth, the daughter of Sir John Roche and Sir William's second wife. Although little is known about Beauchamp's early life, he probably studied at Exeter College, Oxford, where he obtained a doctorate in canon law by 1442. Beauchamp worked as a canon lawyer, and his service as a royal chaplain and a Chancery clerk resulted in his being named the bishop of Hereford in 1448, until which time he had been serving as the archdeacon of Suffolk. During his brief eighteen-month tenure as Hereford's prelate, Beauchamp distinguished himself as the first bishop to visit Hereford Cathedral officially.

Beauchamp's brief tenure as bishop of Hereford ended in 1450 when a papal bull translated him to Salisbury. This diocese was still recovering from Jack Cade's rebellion, during which Beauchamp's predecessor Bishop Aiscough had been killed by a mob. Beauchamp's primary challenge was fighting the efforts of Salisbury's citizens to undercut his episcopal authority over the borough. By 1465 Beauchamp was confronted directly by the city council, which seized a plot of land that Beauchamp had granted to William Swayne, another burgess of Salisbury. Beauchamp proved to be a crafty and astute administrator who called on his ties to the royal exchequer to put additional pressure on the mayor and commonalty of Salisbury in 1466. Although the citizens were acquitted in 1473, they had been weakened by their legal expenses and loss of rents, factors that led to the end of their dispute with Beauchamp in 1474. From this time until the beginning of the Reformation, episcopal overlordship in Salisbury was accepted by the fathers of the city.

Although his dispute with the citizens of Salisbury was his most noted accomplishment as its bishop, Beauchamp's other activities during his episcopate reflect his commitment to improving spiritual life within his see. Early in his episcopate, Beauchamp joined the movement in Salisbury to secure the canonization of Osmund, who had founded Old Sarum in the eleventh century. His efforts contributed to Osmund's canonization in 1456, after a sixty-year campaign. Beauchamp was also active in rewriting the statutes of St. Nicholas's Hospital, reflecting its relatively new status as an almshouse. He met the threat of Lollardy by forming a commission to discover and try heretics in 1475. In the same year Beauchamp devoted considerable time to exploring the reasons for the low numbers of vicars in the diocese. In these acts and in his dispute with the citizens of Salisbury, Beauchamp consistently used his abilities as an administrator and a leader to strengthen the role of the bishop of Salisbury and to improve the quality of religious life within his diocese.

Beauchamp also served as a diplomat, first as an emissary between the Lancastrians and the Yorkists, and later as an envoy to France. Beauchamp's royal ties led to his being named the first chancellor of the Order of the Garter in 1475. His ties to the Order of the Garter may have begun decades before that, as some evidence suggests that he was a chaplain to the order as early as 1457. His chancellorship of the order probably helped Beauchamp secure the deanship of Windsor, which he was granted in addition to his bishopric in 1478. Beauchamp was also given the opportunity to use his skills as an architect when he served as master and surveyor of St. George's Chapel, Windsor, begun under the patronage of Edward IV in 1475. The chapel's paneling and vaults with flattened four-centered arches (ribbing rising from four connected arches) are important examples of the perpendicular architecture of late medieval England.

Bibliography: Andrew D. Brown, *Popular Piety in Late Medieval England: The Diocese of Salisbury, 1250–1550*, 1995; R. B. Pugh and Elizabeth Criltall, eds., The Victoria History of the Counties of England, vols. 3 and 6, 1956 and 1962.

Kristine Lynn Rabberman

Beaufort, Henry (1374–1447), cardinal and bishop of Winchester, was a younger son of *John of Gaunt by his mistress Catherine Swynford. Half brother to *Henry IV and therefore uncle to Henry V and *Henry VI, Beaufort combined his blood ties with his enormous wealth and considerable ability to thrust himself into the center of Lancastrian and European politics. Employing his wealth for political purposes, Beaufort influenced and even shaped English policies during the first half of Henry VI's reign, defending the Lancastrian regal claims to France and thereby prolonging the Hundred Years' War.

After spending much of his youth in Aachen reading civil and canon law, Beaufort began his rise to prominence when he was appointed to several prebendaries in the 1390s that provided the young man with an income to support his theological studies at Oxford. After succeeding to the chancellorship of the university, Beaufort was promoted to the See of Lincoln in 1398. Although the bishop played no role in his half brother's successful revolt against *Richard II in 1399, Henry IV's need for loyal and capable servants led him to induce Beaufort to enter the political world, where the bishop remained for the rest of his life. In 1402 Beaufort left Oxford to play an active role in that year's Parliament and help secure a large clerical subsidy. In 1403 Beaufort became lord chancellor, in which position he worked closely with his brothers on Anglo-French relations, the Hanseatic conflicts, and Owen Glyndwr's rebellion in Wales. In the midst of the Welsh crisis, Beaufort handled the Parliament of 1404 deftly, and in November 1404 he was translated to the bishopric of Winchester, the wealthiest see in England, thereby increasing his influence within the church. After 1405 the bishop retired from the chancellorship but remained on the king's council and continued to manage royal policy in Parliament. For the remainder of the reign, the bishop became the focus of a political faction attached to the Prince of Wales that directed its efforts against the earl of Arundel's party.

Following Henry V's accession in 1413, Beaufort returned to the chancellorship for a time and served his nephew in matters of diplomacy and finance, probably functioning as treasurer as well. Involved in the negotiations that ultimately led to war against France, Beaufort defended Henry V's claim to the French throne in a masterful speech before Parliament immediately following the Battle of Agincourt, invoking divine authority to fill royal coffers. Falling from grace in 1417, Beaufort involved himself in the Council of Constance in an attempt to end the Great Schism. Although it appears that Beaufort was briefly considered for the papacy, an idea attractive to the English, the new pope Martin V appointed Beaufort as cardinal legate, thereby exempting him from Canterbury's jurisdiction while simultaneously, in violation of English tradition, allowing Beaufort to retain the bishopric of Winchester *in commendam* (in title and receipt of revenues though not in residence). This state of affairs annoyed and alarmed the king, who feared a renewal of papal interference in the church in England. When Beaufort was threatened in 1418 with *praemunire*, the series of fourteenth-century statutes limiting papal jurisdiction in England, his relationship with his nephew ebbed dramatically.

The accession of the infant Henry VI in 1422 transformed the state of affairs in England. Beaufort, who had intended to focus his energies as an Anglo-papal intermediary, resumed instead his position on the royal council as lord chancellor. Beaufort employed his wealth and political connections to cement his position, thereby threatening the influence of the child king's uncle *Humphrey, duke of Gloucester. Beaufort and his brother John, duke of Bedford, worked in concert to continue Henry V's policy of Lancastrian expansionism in France, but the English alliance with Burgundy was threatened when Gloucester, acting on his own, invaded the Low Countries; his failure divided the council, antagonized Burgundy, and amplified his personal rivalry with the cardinal. Despite Bedford's support, Beaufort surrendered the chancellorship in 1426 in exchange for a formal, if temporary, reconciliation with Gloucester. The loss of office did not considerably enfeeble the cardinal's influence, for his position as the king's primary creditor allotted to him a stranglehold on import taxes and, therefore, a powerful sway over state policy.

Beaufort, disillusioned, retired from English affairs in 1426 to pursue his ecclesiastical duties. Wearing the mantle of cardinal legate in central Europe, Beaufort led the papal crusade against the Hussites. Though his army met with disastrous defeat at Mies, Beaufort returned to his native island to raise another army with papal support and ecclesiastical financing. Yet domestic matters intervened in 1429 when England fell on the defensive in northern France, obliging the cardinal to turn his attentions once more to the Anglo-French war. Offering his crusading army to bolster the English efforts, Beaufort subsequently gave his political and financial support to a relief expedition led by the newly crowned, if still youthful and inexperienced, Henry VI. Yet Beaufort quarrelled with Bedford over political control in France, opening himself to a renewed personal attack by Gloucester in 1431. Though Beaufort persevered with parliamentary support, the atmosphere hampered efforts to fund adequately more French campaigns, resulting in further English losses. By 1433 Beaufort and Bedford had renewed their commitment to the French war, again with the duke in the field and the bishop raising money and conducting diplomacy, but Burgundy's desertion from the war in 1435 and Bedford's almost simultaneous death devastated both England's military position and Beaufort's protection against Gloucester. Despite an English rally in the following year, financed with Beaufort money, the English remained unable to reinforce their military position without the Burgundian alliance.

Following the disasters of 1436, Beaufort pinned his hopes on a peace with Burgundy, reestablishing trade with the Low Countries in 1439, but the aged cardinal failed to secure peace with France. As Beaufort's political influence waned, he began to withdraw from politics. Yet, as if to highlight the Crown's dependence on the cardinal's money, Beaufort returned to the council in 1442 to support yet another grand campaign on the Continent, but the anticlimactic failures of that year foreshadowed his permanent retirement from politics. It was only at the end of his life that the immensely gifted and wealthy cardinal found time briefly to pursue educational, artistic, and pastoral work. It is emblematic of the cleric, ensnared by the political exigencies of his troubled age, that his great riches failed to provide gifts to posterity equivalent to those of his immediate predecessor, *William of Wykeham, or successor, William Waynfleet, in Winchester.

In his life, Henry Cardinal Beaufort employed his many skills and fortunes in the services of his king. His influence on the council, his consistently good relations with the House of Commons, and his political leverage as a major royal creditor enabled him to influence and even direct royal policy in the critical years of Henry VI's minority. This cardinal, the first bishop of the royal blood since the twelfth century, remained resolved to continue Henry VI's imperial policies, a determination that ultimately met disaster due to the inherent fragility of the Lancastrian military and political position.

Bibliography: Ralph A. Griffiths, *The Reign of King Henry VI: The Exercise of Royal Authority, 1422–1461*, 1981; G. L. Harriss, *Cardinal Beaufort: A Study of Lancastrian Ascendancy and Decline*, 1988; K. B. McFarlane, *England in the Fifteenth Century: Collected Essays*, 1981.

James C. Owens

Beaufort, Margaret (1441–1509). As one of fifteenth-century England's two royal mothers, Lady Margaret Beaufort was an enigma in English history. Married four times, she was also the mother and grandmother of two kings of England, *Henry VII and Henry VIII. She represented the quickly changing fortunes that so defined the medieval world. The image she projected, both publicly and privately, was in essence a duality, the shrewd and politically active side balanced by piety and education.

Lady Margaret's roots were hardly the most exalted, for the Beaufort line was the result of a liaison between *John of Gaunt, duke of Lancaster, and his mistress, Catherine Swynford. Margaret's father, John, duke of Somerset, descended from this line, which received its name from the castle in France where the first of the Beaufort line were born. The Beaufort family was legitimized in 1391, and although Margaret herself was the product of a lawful union, she was never to know her father. The duke of Somerset committed suicide after a failed expedition during the Hundred Years' War, almost one year after the birth of his daughter Margaret on 31 May 1441. When Margaret was three years old, she was given to her father's friend, William de la Pole, earl of Suffolk, as his ward. Since Margaret was already heiress to a sizable fortune, her wardship and eventual marriage were of great interest to all. Margaret was considered a more-than-suitable match, and de la Pole attempted to marry his only son, John, to Margaret, thus transferring her wardship to him. Since marriage was much more a means of profit than an expression of love, the fact that Margaret was married at the age of six is hardly unusual. Her marriage contract, however, contained a clause allowing her to dissolve the marriage when she wished, and in 1453 she took advantage of this clause. Her wardship was then divided evenly in 1453 between the sons of Owen Tudor and Katherine of France, Edmund and Jasper. She married Edmund Tudor at the age of twelve, and a year later she was widowed and pregnant with Edmund's child. The future Henry VII was born on 28 January 1457. His mother Margaret was not yet fifteen, and as a result of her youth, the birth was a difficult one, resulting in her inability ever to conceive again.

The quest began anew to find a husband for Margaret. Although she was only fifteen, Margaret's shrewd instincts were evident. Her chief concern was the welfare of her child, and then her own safety. Therefore, on 6 April 1457 Margaret married Sir Henry Stafford, her second cousin. Their marriage occurred in the midst of some of the worst of the Wars of the Roses, and Stafford staunchly supported the Lancastrian line. However, the Yorkist victory in the key Battle of Towton caused the separation of Margaret and her son, and the wardship of young Henry Tudor, lord of Richmond, was transferred to the Yorkist Lord William Herbert, an ally of the Yorkist king *Edward IV. Uncertainty increased, however, with the death of Lord Herbert, a situation that Margaret used to her advantage in 1469 to demonstrate her loyalty to the Crown. Thus she essentially switched sides in order to protect her son. When *Henry VI was restored to the throne in 1470, the Lancastrian restoration gave Margaret the opportunity to secure the interests of her son. However, the king's death in 1471 left Margaret Beaufort, nearly the last of the Beaufort line, to defend the Lancastrian cause, and so she entrusted the guardianship of young Henry Tudor to her ex–brother-in-law, Jasper Tudor. Not long after this occurrence, Sir Henry

Stafford, Margaret's husband, died in battle, but Margaret's widowhood was brief, and by June 1472 she had remarried again, this time to Lord Thomas Stanley. This marriage was a carefully arranged match from which Margaret stood to benefit. Marriage to someone of Stanley's stature and to someone who had the trust of King Edward IV was hardly undesirable. Margaret's new position within the Yorkist party allowed her to negotiate the return of her son from exile and in 1482 to secure his return in good faith to the court. In the 1482 document arranging his return, Margaret was the key negotiator between the king and her husband, a feat uncommon for the medieval woman.

The unexpected occurred in April 1483 with the death of Edward IV. After the usurpation of the throne by *Richard III, Margaret's life took a difficult turn, and she pursued a dangerous course of action. Realizing the amount of opposition to the Yorkist usurper, she abandoned her allegiance to Richard III in order to rescue the two sons of Edward IV imprisoned in the Tower of London. The attempt to storm the tower in 1483, however, failed, and so a new strategy to promote Henry Tudor as the next king was devised. Margaret's role in the conspiracy of 1483 was not only the result of love for her son but the culmination of her political career, a sign of her fortitude in the midst of political turmoil.

The coronation of Henry VII on 30 October 1485 was a triumph for Lady Margaret and reunited mother and son to govern England. Margaret's role as the king's mother was just as important as that of Henry's queen, Elizabeth of York, if not more so. Margaret used her trusted officials to keep watch over the kingdom as well as the organization of the government.

Not only did Margaret seem to have her way in public life, she was truly regal in private life as well. In early 1499 she took a vow of chastity while her husband was still alive, an unusual undertaking in the medieval era. This was most likely not a calculated slight against Stanley, but rather a political action. Henry VII perhaps may have wanted to accord more political responsibility to his mother without the influence of his stepfather. Under the influence of her spiritual advisor, John Fisher, Margaret established an endowment for the construction of St. John's College in Cambridge. While this reflects her interest in education, it also was a testament to the spirituality of the fifteenth-century queen.

Lady Margaret Beaufort was by no means a docile woman; she owned her own land, she had taken a vow of chastity, and she had even translated many works, including *The Imitation of Christ* by *Thomas à Kempis. Her life was notable also for its longevity; she outlived her son, who died on 21 April 1509, and survived to see the coronation of her grandson, Henry VIII, on 22 April 1509. Lady Margaret followed her son in death on 29 June 1509, and at her death she left a signed charter for the establishment of St. John's College. More important, she left behind the legacy of a woman who cultivated cultural and political contacts in the interest of the welfare of her son.

Bibliography: Michael K. Jones and Malcolm G. Underwood, *The King's Mother: Lady Margaret Beaufort Countess of Richmond and Derby*, 1992; John Carmi Parsons, ed., *Medieval Queenship*, 1993; E.M.G. Routh, *Lady Margaret: A Memoir*, 1924.

Jennifer L. Harrison

Beaujeau, Pierre de, Duc de Bourbon (1438–1503), also known as Pierre de Bourbon, sire de Beaujeau, was the fourth son of Charles, duke of Bourbon, by his marriage with Agnes, daughter of the duke of Burgundy. He was the protégé and favorite of his aunt, the duchess of Orléans, in whose household he was raised. Brought up in an atmosphere of antipathy to the throne, Beaujeau was sympathetic to the ambitions of the House of Orléans, but when the king offered him in 1465 the hand of his eldest daughter, Beaujeau changed his alliance, marrying in 1473 the twelve-year old *Anne Valois (1461–1522), the eldest child of *Louis XI. Repaying his benefactor with loyal and capable service, Beaujeau became the lieutenant governor of the kingdom. When Louis XI was on his deathbed, he asked Beaujeau to watch over the young dauphin and help shape the destiny of France.

At this point in Beaujeau's biography, scholars diverge in opinion regarding the true nature of Anne of Beaujeau's influence. The popular tradition assigns to Anne rather than to her husband the responsibility for the government during *Charles VIII's minority, whereas nineteenth-century academic tradition asserts that authority was wielded by Beaujeau himself. Contemporary scholars follow the popular tradition, citing both the sympathetic letters of Jaligny, the Beaujeau secretary, and the unsympathetic letters of the dukes of Orléans and Brittany. The grievance in these letters was not that Beaujeau had too much influence, but that Anne had monopolized power. She was called "Madame" by her contemporaries, and it is evident that diplomatic agents addressed their letters to her, not Beaujeau.

Beaujeau was a trusted servant of the Crown and always presided over the council, and it appeared that it was he who guided the government. But Anne had a quality of mind that was austere, powerful, and awe-inspiring, giving her a limitless capacity for personal rule. Beaujeau himself was intelligent but unimaginative, with strong common sense, the gentle type of man who can execute a policy but not initiate it, who can obey but not command. If he presided over the council, it was because Anne was prudent enough to disguise her power.

The regency of the Beaujeaus ended when Charles VIII turned twenty-one in 1491 and took over in December the reins of the country for himself. Pierre de Beaujeau inherited upon his father's death in 1488 estates that made him one of the wealthiest princes in Europe, while he and Anne were also preoccupied at that time with the birth of their daughter Suzanne (1491–1521). With the dawn of the rule of Charles VIII, the tale of Pierre de Beaujeau disappeared quietly from the political stage as the inheritance of the Bourbon duchy passed to Charles, constable of Bourbon, Suzanne's husband, in 1503.

Bibliography: Pierre Pradel, *Anne de France, 1461–1522*, 1986.

Dominique Tieman

Beauneveu, André (1337–1403). Known as a painter and sculptor (only his sculpture remains), André Beauneveu is recognized today for his humanist approach to creating lifelike and realistic funeral effigies and religious statues in the late medieval court of Charles V of France. Beauneveu was from Valenciennes near Hainaut, and his artistic talent was recognized as early as 1359, as he is mentioned in a group of receipts from Yolande de Bar. He was called "Master André" in his work on the chapel of the Castle of Nieppe by the same Yolande de Bar, and by 1363 he was working as a painter on the Hôtel de Ville in Valenciennes. In 1364 he came into the service of Charles V. The aging king, impressed with his talent, commanded him to sculpt the royal funeral effigy as well as those of his grandparents, Philip VI and Jeanne of Burgundy, and of his father, Jean the Good. The three male effigies are found today in the Cathedral of St. Dennis, but the female was destroyed in 1793. The payments for these statues continued until June 1366, but the effigy of Charles V, being so superior to the other three, suggests that Beauneveu abandoned his work on the retrospective effigies and focused on that of the reigning king, since it proved to be the only statue of Charles V executed in his lifetime.

Beauneyeu's royal service ended and between 1366 and 1372 the artist visited England with his friend Jean Froissart, clerk of the chamber of Queen Philippa of Hainaut. Scholars suggest that Beauneveu worked with Jean of Liège on the tomb of Queen Philippa, and he was the author of the only statue of the young countess of Lancaster (d. 1369). When he returned to France, he worked unceasingly until his death in 1403. The sculptures attributed to him include the tomb of Louis of Mâle, count of Flanders, in the Cathedral of Notre Dame of Courtrai and possibly a statue of the Virgin Mary for the belfry of Ypres. He was also artistic advisor for the Cathedral of Cambrai.

Unfortunately, the effigy of Charles V is the only sculpture that scholars are absolutely certain was executed by Beauneveu. The problem of attribution to Beauneveu is complicated by the fact that he worked for Charles V at the same time as the artist Jean of Liège, and for the *Jean Valois, duc de Berry at the same time as Jean of Cambrai. The same sculptures, according to scholars, can be attributed equally to one of these three artists. Nevertheless, two great ensembles are indisputedly attributed to Beauneveu. One features the six statues of *Beau Pilier* done between 1376 and 1380 in the Cathedral of Amiens representing Charles V, his two sons, and three of his councilors, Cardinal Jean de La Grange, Bureau de La Rivière, and the admiral Jean de Vienne. The other ensemble includes the statues of the Great Room in the Palace of Poitiers commissioned between 1389 and 1395 by the duke of Berry and Queen Isabeau of Bavaria, regents of *Charles VI, in honor of the marriage between the duke and Jeanne of Boulogne. André Beauneveu's legacy is that of a hard-working artist who balanced shifting patronage with exploration of the new orientations of humanism toward individuality and realism in art.

Bibliography: Stephen K. Scher, "The Sculpture of Andre Beauneveu," Ph.D. diss., Yale University, 1966.

Dominique Tieman

Bellini, Gentile (c. 1429–1507), was a Venetian painter especially known for portraits and paintings of public events. He was also one of the early proponents of the medium of oil paint and the support of canvas.

Along with Vittore Carpaccio, Giovanni Mansueti, and others, Gentile practiced the so-called eyewitness style of fifteenth-century Venetian narrative painting. This style was characterized by meticulous attention to detail, a focus on all parts of the image, and the inclusion of portraits and other mundane particulars within a painting whose subject was often in the background, to one side, or otherwise slightly obscured. In contrast to Florentine style, in which the subject is the most prominent aspect, in Venetian style every detail received the same amount of attention and focus in order to make the depiction seem more real. Some have said of this style that the concern for detail detracted from the focus on the whole and led to misinterpretation. Giorgio Vasari, educated in the Florentine style, occasionally identified a subject as an episode in the foreground when the true subject was elsewhere.

Born into the most distinguished painting family in Venice, the son of Jacopo Bellini, older brother of *Giovanni Bellini, and brother-in-law of *Andrea Mantegna, Gentile trained in his father's workshop. His first recorded collaboration with his father was in 1460, an altarpiece for the Gattamelata Chapel in Sant Antonio in Padua; in 1465 he signed and dated his first known independent work, a portrait of Venetian patriarch Lorenzo Giustiniani.

In 1466 Gentile made his reputation by finishing the *Passion* cycle that Jacopo had begun for the Scuola Grande di San Marco in Venice (destroyed in 1485). Gentile's success with the *Passion* cycle led to a commission in 1474 to redecorate the Sala del Maggior Consiglio in the Palazzo Ducale. He was assigned to paint portraits of each doge and twenty-two paintings showing legendary events from the life of Doge Alexander III.

In 1479 Gentile was sent on a mission for the Signoria to the court of Mehmed II in Constantinople. He brought along a book of his father's drawings as a gift. He painted a view of Venice and portraits of Mehmed and members of his court. During his stay, Mehmed presented him with a gold chain. Gentile probably returned to Venice in 1481 and resumed work on the Sala del Maggior Consiglio, on which Giovanni and others had continued to work in Gentile's absence. Gentile worked at the palace until no later than 1495; the paintings were destroyed by fire in 1577.

Gentile's next major commission was the *True Cross* cycle for the Scuola

Grande di San Giovanni Evangelista. He supervised artists including Lazzaro Bastiani, Carpaccio, Benedetto Diana, and Mansueti. Of the eight paintings in the cycle, Gentile did three: *The Procession in the Piazza San Marco* (1496), *The Miracle at the Bridge of San Lorenzo* (1500), and *The Healing of Pietro de' Ludovici* (1501).

Gentile's last major commission came in 1504. The Scuola Grande di San Marco again hired him, this time to decorate its Albergo. Before his death in 1507 he had begun a large painting, *Saint Mark Preaching in Alexandria*, which Giovanni finished, and had submitted a sketch for *The Martyrdom of Saint Mark*. *Saint Mark Preaching* shows suggestions of Mamluk architecture and costumes that indicate that Gentile may have gone to Jerusalem while he was in the eastern Mediterranean. He included his own self-portrait, wearing the chain from Mehmed II in the painting.

Although today Giovanni is considered the more talented Bellini brother, in their day Gentile had a more prominent position. A true assessment of his development and importance is difficult because so much of his work has been destroyed. His style suited the aesthetic tastes of his time, although his manner was quickly eclipsed by the more focused, expressive style of Venetian artists of the following generation.

Bibliography: Patricia Brown, *Venetian Narrative Painting in the Age of Carpaccio*, 1988; Peter Humfrey, "The Bellinesque Life of St. Mark Cycle for the Scuola Grande di San Marco in Venice in Its Original Arrangement," *Zeitschrift für Kunstgeschichte* 48 (1985): 225–42.

Susanne Breckenridge

Bellini, Giovanni (c. 1431/36–1516), son of Jacopo Bellini, was a Venetian painter. Giovanni Bellini was born into one of the major dynasties of painters in quattrocento Venice. Receptive throughout his life to many artistic and technical influences (although he is recorded as having left Venice only once), he extensively modernized Venetian painting and propelled it toward the great achievements of the following century.

Bellini started to paint in the late 1440s and by 1459 was already head of a workshop that expanded alongside the master's increasing dominance of Venetian art. Under the influence of his father's workshop, he specialized early in small and medium-size devotional panels for private ownership. In his larger series of Virgin and Child portrayals, he explored ever further the moving relationship between the mother and the son. He enriched the hieratic majesty of Byzantine icons by using an infinite variety of compositional devices and by reflecting and amplifying the pathos of the figures in a wide range of backgrounds and landscapes. Other similar images for private devotion included half-length representations of the Suffering Christ and various Pietà groups, of which the one in the Brera in Milan (1460s) is the most accomplished. Around 1460 some of Bellini's works showed the influence of *Andrea Mantegna, his brother-in-law, who introduced him to classical and Tuscan art. They nonetheless reveal distinctive personal elements; thus in the *Agony in the Garden* (early 1460s), based on a composition by Mantegna, light and landscape participate fully in the drama, and the minerality of Mantegna's figures and landscape seems animated. From the early 1470s his innovative choice of the oil medium (imported to Venice through Flemish works and by Antonello of Messina) instead of tempera allowed Bellini to distinguish himself more radically and to create atmospheres defined by softer tonal transitions and outlines.

Bellini pursued his research on light and space in large altarpieces. The *Polyptych of St. *Vincent Ferrer* (c. 1464–68), probably his first major public commission, the *Coronation of the Virgin* (c. 1473), the *Frari Triptych* (1488), and the *S. Zaccaria Altarpiece* (1505), for example, were landmarks in the progressive coordination of elements. The old system of polyptychs merely juxtaposed the frame, figures, throne, and background (architecture or landscape), but Bellini increasingly united these elements through the vibration of light within a strict spatial organization. The *S. Giobbe Altarpiece* (c. 1480) exemplified Bellini's attempt to define volume subtly by using a light that combined deep shadows with the pervading reflections of a golden mosaic to link the pictorial space with that of the spectator in the church.

Bellini, first associated with his brother *Gentile, then alone after Gentile's death in 1507, undertook or completed several narrative paintings and, after 1479, worked regularly for the doge's palace, where he was commissioned to paint scenes of Venetian history. He was much admired by his contemporaries for this historical cycle, which was destroyed in 1577. Bellini excelled also in portraits of ruling patricians (whether in votive pictures, history cycles, or, increasingly toward the end of the fifteenth century, independent portraits). The portrait of *Doge Leonardo Loredan* (c. 1501) is revelatory of his analytical precision, influenced by the Flemish masters, and of his insistence on the sitter's social status.

In the early cinquecento, despite his leading position in Venice, Bellini still endeavored to adapt to the innovations of his own pupils, Giorgioni and Titian, thus continuing the quest for colors and lights that he had initiated himself and that was to be the distinctive feature of the sixteenth-century Venetian school. In these late years he painted a small number of profane subjects, including the *Feast of the Gods* for Alfonso d'Este (1514) and the seminude *Woman at Her Toilet* (1516), destined to be an influential model.

Throughout his career Giovanni Bellini assimilated an incomparable variety of influences and durably transformed almost all genres of painting (altarpieces, Passion scenes, landscapes, and portraits). He is a major landmark in the history of oil painting. Through him Venice, discarding the outdated practices of Gothic painting, became the privileged alternative to Florence, initiating an artistic rivalry that was to be fully developed in the sixteenth century.

Bibliography: Rona Goffen, *Giovanni Bellini*, 1989; Norbert Huse and Wolfgang Wolters, *The Art of Renaissance Venice*, 1990.

E. Helene Tronc

Beltrán de la Cueva (d. 1492). A favorite in the courts of King *Enrique IV of Castile and Queen *Isabel of Spain, Beltrán de la Cueva played a lesser ministerial role in the turbulent and mercurial court politics of early modern Spain. Beltrán was born a caballero in early-fifteenth-century Spain. As the son of a town councilman, he was well equipped to enter the world of high court politics when King Enrique IV of Castile made him a grandee (noble) in 1456. An elaborate dresser and skilled in the niceties of court life, Beltrán de la Cueva quickly became a favorite at the Castilian court.

Within two years Beltrán became Enrique's *mayordomo* (chief steward), which gave him the opportunity to influence royal decisions and which troubled others at court vying for power and the king's favor. When Beltrán began to escort Queen Juana to various court functions in addition to his political and ministerial duties, rumors flew that he was the queen's illicit lover. To make matters worse for royal reputations, many people believed that the king was impotent, despite having several mistresses, and was thus unable to sire an heir.

When the queen gave birth to the princess *Juana in 1462, Beltrán, instead of the king, was rumored to be the true father. Consequently, Juana (1462–1530) was branded illegitimate and was burdened with the scurrilous nickname "la Beltraneja," meaning "of Beltran." Twelve years later the aspersions cast on Juana's legitimacy forced her to renounce her rightful claim to the Castilian throne in favor of her aunt, Isabel I of Castile.

Unflustered by the scandal that linked his wife and minister, Enrique IV raised Beltrán to aristocratic standing during Juana's baptismal ceremonies by naming him the count of Ledesma. This newly conferred honor and Beltrán's status as the king's favorite disgruntled many at the faction-laden court, who were themselves covetous of the king's favor.

In 1462 Beltrán married Mencia de Mendoza, the daughter of the second marquis of Santillana. This alliance further solidified his diplomatic standing and political power at the Castilian court. In 1464 Enrique awarded Beltrán the mastership of the Order of Santiago, which comprised the greatest landed estates in all of Castile, outside of the Crown's own holdings. More important, this land was considered part of the birthright of Isabel's brother Alfonso, and not the king's possession to bestow upon his favorite. This award raised tremendous resentment throughout Castile and helped spark the civil war against King Enrique in 1464.

At the death of Enrique IV in 1474, the fortunes of Beltrán and Castile shifted with the disputed accession of Isabel I to the vacant throne. Crowned along with her husband *Ferdinand, the new queen swiftly cemented her position as the legitimate heir to the Castilian throne. While Enrique's daughter Juana found support among several important Castilian families, Isabel gained even stronger champions throughout Old and New Castile, Andalusia, and even Portugal. At this time Beltrán abruptly redirected his loyalties to the new queen and abandoned the cause of Juana, Isabel's long-standing rival and his presumed daughter. By the time the civil war ended with the Treaty of Alcacoras in 1479, Isabel was the acknowledged ruler of Castile and the queen of Spain.

Beltrán immediately sought to curry favor with the increasingly powerful new queen. Seizing on the Catholic monarch's intense religious zeal, Beltran helped lead a small army in Córdoba as part of Isabel's larger campaign to reconquer Spain and oust the Moors from the peninsula. He remained in favor throughout Ferdinand and Isabel's reign until he died in 1492.

Bibliography: Nancy Rubin, *Isabella of Castile: The First Renaissance Queen*, 1991.

Susanna Calkins

Beltraneja, Juana la. *See* Juana of Castile.

Benedict XII, Pope (b. 1284, r. 1334–42), formerly Jacques Fournier, the second pope to rule from Avignon. Benedict XII was dedicated to the reform of both the papacy and the church, but his tendency to seek political compromise at times gave his pontificate an appearance of indecisiveness.

Born in Saverdun to a wealthy bourgeois family, Jacques Fournier entered the Cistercian order at a young age. He studied theology in Paris and became abbot of Fontfroide in 1311. In 1317 he became bishop, first of Pamiers and later of Mirepoix. As bishop of the latter see, he set up an Inquisition tribunal to fight heresy and proceeded against the Waldensians and Cathars in his diocese with great zeal, showing himself an excellent interrogator and scrupulous judge. The voluminous proceedings of these Inquisition trials form the source of Emmanuel Le Roy Ladurie's famous book *Montaillou*. In 1327 Fournier became cardinal; both his inquisitorial and theological abilities were much valued by Pope *John XXII, who asked his opinion on several matters, such as the heresy of the Fraticelli and the Beatific Vision controversy.

After the death of John XXII in 1334, the assembled cardinals elected Benedict XII after a conclave of only seven days. His first papal bull, *Benedictus Deus* (1336), sought to end the dispute about the Beatific Vision, a matter left unsettled by his predecessor. Also known as the "white cardinal" because he kept wearing his Cistercian habit even after he received his cardinal's hat, Benedict remained a stern ascetic after his papal election, dedicated to ending nepotism, corruption, and malpractice among the clergy. He reduced the papal bureaucracy, widened the distribution of benefices, and tried to ensure that livings were given only to clergy of good repute. He greatly reduced the number of clergy residing in Avignon. The beneficial effect of most of these measures was, however, undone by the extravagance of his spendthrift successor, *Clement VI.

Benedict's most important reform involved the large religious orders, which often made him unpopular among their more indulgent members. Under his direction the Cistercians (1335), Benedictines (1336), Regular Canons (1336), and Franciscans (1337) all received new constitutions. Only the Dominicans successfully resisted his plans for reform and centralization. His reform of the Franciscans also dashed the hopes of the more radical Spiritual groups in that order to reach a reconciliation with the Holy See.

Despite a conciliatory policy, the conflict with the German emperor *Louis of Bavaria, a legacy of Benedict's stubborn predecessor John XXII, was never resolved. Benedict's pacific efforts were obstructed by King Philip VI of France and Robert of Anjou, king of Naples, who had no wish to see peace between Louis and the Holy See. The negotiations ended in 1337 when Louis entered an alliance with King *Edward III of England, who was eager to find anti-French allies. It was mainly the German clergy, suffering most from the interdict that John XXII had imposed upon the empire in 1324, who urged Louis to resume the negotiations in 1338. But the conflict would not be resolved until Louis was deposed in 1346 and the German electors chose Charles IV of Bohemia in his place.

Benedict XII was the first Avignon pope to give up all hope of returning to an anarchy-ridden Italy. He began the building of a palace at Avignon as a permanent papal residence. Benedict died on 25 April 1342.

Bibliography: Emmanuel Le Roy Ladurie, *Montaillou*, 1978; Guillaume Mollat, *The Popes at Avignon, 1305–1378*, 1963; Yves Renouard, *The Avignon Papacy, 1305–1403*, 1970.

Frans A. van Liere

Benedict XIII, Anti-pope (b. 1342, r. 1394–1423),

formerly Pedro de Luna, was an antipope during the Great Schism (1378–1417). A pugnacious pontiff, he outlived five rival popes and never relented his position nor his conviction that he was the rightful pope.

Pedro Martini de Luna was born in 1342 in the castle of Illueca, Aragon, in Spain. Some authors assign 1328 as the date of his birth, but M. Seidlmayer offered documentary evidence in 1933 that he was born in 1342 and not 1328. The date of his death at Peñíscola is also unsure, and authors waver between November 1422 and May 1423. The latter date is most often cited.

The counts of Luna were powerful Aragonese magnates. Pedro was born the youngest son of his family; his interest in law and government brought him to Montpellier, in southwestern France, to study canon and civil law. At this renowned medieval university he received his doctoral degree, and he later chaired in canon law at the same institution. His training explains in part his behavior during the schism. Ever a legal mind, abstract, technical, and argumentative, he considered his position as strong as that of his predecessor. If nobody debated the legality of Clement VII's position, why should they have debated his?

On 30 December 1375 Pope Gregory XI, still in Avignon, elevated Pedro to the cardinalate as cardinal deacon of Santa Maria in Cosmedin. Leaving Montpellier, after a short sojourn in Avignon, he followed Gregory XI to Rome in 1377. At the death of that pontiff in 1378, Pedro participated in the tumultuous conclave that elected the Italian archbishop of Bari, Bartolomeo Prignano, as *Urban VI on 8 April. In June 1378 he followed several non-Italian cardinals to Agnani, using as an excuse the Roman heat, and then to Fondi, where, on 20 September 1378, he was one of the cardinals who elected the antipope Robert of Geneva, Clement VII.

Unable to defend his position in Italy, Clement retreated back to Avignon, where he used Pedro's connections to assert his rights. Pedro was sent as legate to Castile, Aragon, Navarre, and Portugal in order to bring these kingdoms to Clement's obedience. In 1393 he was sent to France, Brabant, Flanders, Scotland, England, and Ireland. While resting from his travels, he resided mainly in Paris, in close proximity to the university and aware of its conciliar schemes to heal the schism.

When Clement VII died, Pedro was back in Avignon, and on 28 September 1394 he was elected pope as Benedict XIII. As one of two popes, he always agreed in theory with the idea of abdicating, but rather than submit to secular pressures, he chose "discussion" with his rivals. He received many embassies between 1395 and 1396, including one headed by King *Charles VI of France's brother and uncles, but Benedict never gave up his position. Frustrated, the French clergy finally voted to renounce their obedience in May 1398. That resolution was announced in Avignon in early September 1398, and so some thirty of Benedict's cardinals left the city for Villeneuve, on French territory. Fearing for his life, Benedict retreated to the papal palace and was there besieged by French troops. Their efforts to storm the place failed, and so the siege lasted until May 1399. Benedict eventually obtained the protection of Louis d'Orléans (Charles VI's brother) and was virtually kept prisoner in his palace until his escape on 12 March 1403. Negotiations, which had been ongoing, accelerated with his escape, and France finally restored its obedience in May.

Benedict went on negotiating with the Roman popes and proposed various meeting places in Italy and France at which to discuss a solution to the schism. He absorbed his most severe blow in 1407 when his main protector, Louis d'Orléans, was assassinated. Benedict lost his French revenues quickly after that, when France decided on neutrality in the crisis in 1408.

Benedict opened his own council in Perpignan in November 1408 to discuss a solution to the schism, but in 1409 cardinals of both obediences decided to convene independently in Pisa; they deposed him and his Roman rivals and elected Alexander V. Benedict nevertheless kept Scotland, Aragon, Castile, and Sicily on his side, and from 1408 until 1415 he resided in Perpignan. Once again, visitors pleaded with him to abdicate, but to no avail. After 1415 he retired to his own castle at Peñíscola, near Valencia, Spain, a place he called his "Noah's Ark." The Council of Constance deposed him again on 27 July 1417, but he died considering himself the rightful pope. Pedro was an avid reader and built a substantial library in Avignon and Peñíscola. He was interested in ceremony and liturgy and wrote two treatises on canon law, *De concilio generali* and *De novo schismate*.

Bibliography: Alec Glasfurd, *The Antipope Peter de Luna, 1342–1423: A Study in Obstinacy*, 1965; Francis McGurk, ed., *Calendar of Papal Letters to Scotland of Benedict XIII of Avignon, 1394–1419*, Scottish History Society 4th series, vol. 13, 1976; M. Seidlmayer, *Geschichte Italiens*, 1934/1962.

Joelle Rollo-Koster

Bernardino of Siena (1380–1444) was a Franciscan Observant and one of the most successful popular preachers of the fifteenth century. After his death, he became both a canonized saint and a subject of religious art. His monogram for the name of Jesus, YHS surrounded by the rays of the sun, also became a common artistic motif.

Bernardino was born in Massa Marittima in 1380, the son of a Sienese father and a local mother. Orphaned at an early age, he was raised by relatives and educated in Siena. After studying canon law, Bernardino became a Franciscan (1402) affiliated with the Observant branch of the order, which wished to follow a more rigorous interpretation of the rule. He was ordained a priest in 1404 and undertook the role of a traveling preacher. He also helped bring about internal peace in Crema (1421), and the Observants made him their vicar general for Umbria and Tuscany. Bernardino's preaching emphasized the name of Jesus, and his YHS monogram became famous. It also was a focus of hostile comment, much of it deriving from rival orders of friars. In 1424 charges of heresy and idolatry were made, and Martin V called the friar to Rome in 1426 to reply to them. Bernardino triumphed over his foes, and he soon was preaching to attentive audiences in the Eternal City. More accusations followed, but *Eugenius IV issued a bull dismissing all charges of heresy against him.

Bernardino did not devote all of his time to preaching. He served as the vicar general of the Observants for Italy in 1438–39. He found Pope Eugenius a continuous supporter, but the duke of Milan had to help him resist a summons to appear before the Council of Basel on renewed heresy charges. Bernardino found another friend in *Sigismund of Luxembourg, whose imperial coronation he attended. The friar also took part in the Council of Florence and made further efforts to promote peace and reform within the cities of Italy. These efforts brought him three offers of bishoprics, all of which he refused even though the three mitres representing them later became part of his iconography.

By 1440 Bernardino was aging, and *John Capistrano was appointed to aid in his work as vicar general. Even so, he desired to relinquish the office. No infirmity could keep him from preaching, and he made final visits to several Italian cities in 1443–44. In 1444 Bernardino undertook his last preaching tour, going to Aquila, where he died and was buried. Bernardino of Siena was canonized by *Nicholas V in 1450.

Bernardino's sermons survive in two forms, fully documented Latin texts, which could serve as models for other preachers, and transcriptions of his vernacular sermons. The reports reveal eloquence and pungent turns of phrase, such as the friar's uncomplimentary descriptions of elaborate hairdos. The friar also could address his individual hearers directly, for example, by telling women in the audience to go home and fetch their husbands. Conversion of life was preached, as was devotion to the Holy Name. He attacked abuses like vanity of dress, simony, and usury and rooted out pagan practices, for example, by making the Fonte Tecta near Arezzo into a Christian shrine. Bernardino preached with such sincerity that he overcame charges of heresy and won over auditors as sophisticated as the jurist Prosdocimo de' Conti. He left the Franciscan Observants securely established; and other influential preachers, among them Capistrano, followed in his footsteps.

Bibliography: Thomas M. Izbicki, "Pyres of Vanities: Mendicant Preaching on the Vanity of Women and Its Lay Audience," in *De Ore Domini: Preacher and Word in the Middle Ages*, ed. Thomas Amos, Eugene Green, and Beverly Kienzle, 1989; Iris Origo, *The World of San Bernardino*, 1962.

Thomas M. Izbicki

Berry, Jean Valois, Duke of. *See* Valois, Jean, Duc de Berry.

Bertrand, Pierre, (1280–1349), cardinal, also known as Peter of Saint-Clement. In his capacity as a canonist and bureaucrat, Pierre Cardinal Bertrand served both the house of Valois and the Avignonese papacy during the turbulent years of the early fourteenth century. Pierre Bertrand (also Petrus Bertrandus or Petrus S. Clementis) was born in Annonay, near Vienne, in 1280 to a physician named Mathieu Bertrand and his wife Agnès Empérière. Pierre studied law at Avignon and theology at Montpellier, becoming a doctor each field in 1301. He taught as a professor at Avignon, Montpellier, Orléans, and Paris in quick succession. At the 1314 Parlement of Paris, he pled the case of Louis of Nevers against *Robert of Artois, earning the attention of the French royal house. In 1315 he was named *clerc du regent* to the Parlement; three years later he was promoted to the Council of State under Philip V as a *clerc-poursuivant*. In 1320 he became the chancellor of Queen Jeanne of Burgundy, who later made him the executor of her estate.

Bertrand's ecclesiastical career took off along with his political ambitions. He was promoted from canon to dean at Notre-Dame du Puy in 1314, was named a canon at Bayeux in 1316, and acted as archdeacon of Billom while he was a canon of Paris in 1319. In January 1320 he was named bishop of Nevers and attended an Avignon council under that title, where he spoke against the heresy of the Beguines and Beghards. He avoided consecration at Nevers in an attempt to retain other offices, but was consecrated bishop of Autun later that year. As bishop of Autun, he attended the Council of Vincennes called by Philip VI, where he defended the church's rights together with Archbishop Pierre Roger of Sens (later *Clement VI).

In 1330, after his participation in the Council of Vincennes, Bertrand was named archbishop of Bourges; the following year he was raised to the rank of cardinal of Saint-Clement by Pope *John XXII at the request of Philip VI. He continued to serve the French Crown, helping to marry off the king's sisters and attempting to negotiate a peace between *Louis of Bavaria and Frederick of Austria. Under John XXII, *Benedict XII, and Clement VI, Bertrand represented the papacy as well. He acted as legate for the abortive crusade of 1332 and was sent to the Papal States in 1338 to handle problems related to the Spiritual Franciscan movement. He was also a papal legate while helping negotiate the Treaty of Flanders between Philip VI of France and *Edward III of England. His last years were spent at the Priory of Montault, near Avignon, where he died on 24 June 1349.

The positions Bertrand held at Vincennes were detailed in his *Libellus super jurisdictione ecclesiastica et temporali*, in which he maintained the separation of clerical and secular jurisdictions and defended the right of prelates to name justices and notaries within their jurisdictions. According to Bertrand, ecclesiastical courts should have the right to try personal cases from "mixed causes," for example, cases in which clerics were attacked by laypeople, as well as purely clerical incidents. The church could also rule on material possessions, even in entirely secular cases. However, he agreed that certain clerical abuses had to stop, including threats of excommunication to royal officials. Although he was largely concerned with maintaining the status quo, he was willing to advocate certain reforming measures on the part of both church and state. The "appeal from abuse" in canon law is thought to date from the theses he advanced at Vincennes.

Copies of Bertrand's legal works and letters were left to the Parisian college of Autun, which he founded. These were stolen by a lawyer in 1575, but manuscripts remain in the Vatican and the Bibliothèque Nationale in Paris. Aside from the *Libellus super jurisdictione*, he added to a treatise by *Durand of Saint-Pourçain entitled *De origine potestatum et jurisdictionum* and penned several commentaries on different collections of decretals and papal acts.

Bertrand made significant contributions to canon law and hence to modern formulations of civil jurisdiction. His shifting allegiances, his rise from a relatively middle-class background, and his role in the ongoing conflicts between the papacy, the French Crown, and the spectre of popular heresy make him emblematic of the age in which he lived.

Bibliography: Stephan Kuttner, *Studies in the History of Medieval Canon Law*, 1990; Dorothy M. Owen, *The Medieval Canon Law: Teaching, Literature, and Transmission*, 1990.

Wendy Love Anderson

Bertrand du Guesclin. *See* Guesclin, Bertrand du.

Bessarion, John (1399?–1472), was a Byzantine humanist, scholar, church-man, philosopher, and manuscript collector. He was born at Trebizond to a family of modest means, but was educated by Manuel Chrysococcus in Con-stantinople along with fellow student George Scholarius. Bessarion became a monk in 1423 and a deacon in 1426 and was ordained in 1431. He then traveled to Mistra and studied with George Gemistos Plethon. After settling a dispute between the Byzantine emperor and his brother, Bessarion established himself in Constantinople as the abbot of the Monastery of St. Basil. His career contin-ued to flourish, and he was named archbishop of Nicaea in 1437. He never assumed his seat and instead accompanied John VIII Palaeologus and the Byz-antine delegation to the Council of Ferrara-Florence in 1438. Bessarion served as one of the primary spokesmen for the Greek side and was a staunch advocate of the union of the Eastern and Western churches. He accepted the Roman position on the *filioque* controversy and was a major force in the eventual sign-ing of the decree of union in 1439.

Bessarion converted to Catholicism, and Pope *Eugenius IV, impressed with the Greek scholar and churchman, made him a cardinal in 1439. From then on Bessarion lived in Italy, moving to Rome in 1443, undertaking scholarly activity, and keeping busy as a papal legate. He was the governor of Bologna from 1450 to 1455 and was himself a candidate for the papacy in 1455 and 1471. After the fall of Constantinople to the Turks in 1453, he traveled to Naples, Germany, Venice, and France trying to raise support for a crusade, but to no avail. His home in Rome was a center of philosophy and learning, especially for refugee Greek scholars and princes fleeing from the capture of Constantinople. He was elected the expatriate Latin patriarch of Constantinople in 1463 and died in Ravenna, Italy, on 18 November 1472.

Bessarion's early writings included letters, panegyrics, orations, and various other documents for the imperial court. Like Plethon, Bessarion was a Platonist (with Neoplatonic leanings), but he saw the value of Aristotelian thought and sought to reconcile the two philosophical systems. Bessarion translated Aris-totle's *Metaphysics* and composed the Platonic treatises *De natura et arte* and the well-known *In calumniatorem Platonis*, which was a defense of Plato against the attack of George Trapezountios in *Comparationes Aristotelis et Platonis*. With the patronage of the popes *Nicholas V, Paul II, and *Pius II, Bessarion translated patristic Greek literature into Latin and presided over an important Greek revival in Italy. He also assembled a large collection of between 800 and 900 manuscripts (approximately 600 in Greek); he presented the collection to the Venetian senate in 1468, and it became the center of the Biblioteca Marciana. His associates included *Nicholas of Cusa, *Marsiglio Ficino, and a wide range of important fifteenth-century scholars and philosophers. Bessarion combined Byzantine scholastic training with a mastery of Latin humanism; *Lorenzo Valla called him "inter Graecos latinissimus, inter Latinos graecissimus" ("among the

Greeks the greatest Latinist, among the Latinists, the greatest Greek"). Bessarion and his Greek academy were an important influence on the Italian Renaissance.

Bibliography: Deno John Geanakoplos, *Greek Scholars in Venice: Studies in the Dissemination of Greek Learning from Byzantium to Western Europe*, 1962; N. G. Wilson, *From Byzantium to Italy: Greek Studies in the Italian Renaissance*, 1992.

Andrew Scheil

Biel, Gabriel (c. 1410–95), a German philosopher and theologian known as "Doctor profundissimus," is significant for being among the last of the pre-Reformation Scholastic thinkers and for the influence of his Ockhamist thought on Martin Luther. Biel was born at Speyer, was ordained in his youth, and received his arts education at Heidelberg (1432–38), where he taught until 1443. He then studied theology at Erfurt and Cologne, reading Albertus Magnus, Thomas Aquinas, and John Duns Scotus, the principal thinkers of the *via antiqua*, as well as *William of Ockham, the herald of the *via moderna*. Biel became a popular cathedral preacher at Mainz (1457–65) and in 1468 joined the Brethren of the Common Life, serving as provost at various houses in the Upper Rhine and in Baden-Württemberg until 1484. He was appointed regent master of theology at the University of Tübingen and in 1491 retired to the nearby house of the Brethren, where he died.

While Biel was at Mainz, he produced the strongly papalist *Defensorium obedientiae apostolicae* (1462), defending the interdict *Pius II had imposed on Mainz in response to Diether von Isenburg's rebellious archiepiscopate. While he was living with the Brethren, Biel wrote *De communi vita clericorum*, a clear and loving explanation of the order's principles explicating both the nonmonastic nature of the communities and their foundations in the *devotio moderna*, the new spirituality of the fourteenth and fifteenth centuries. While Biel embraced the communalism of the Brethren, he did not advocate the earlier Franciscan repudiation of the institution of private property ownership per se; his *Tractatus de potestate et utilitate monetarum* exemplified the complexity and sensitivity of late Scholastic thought on the doctrine of just price, the nature of currency, and the evils of usury. Biel's *Sacri canonis missae expositio* became a classic treatment of eucharistic theology, influential into the early sixteenth century.

Biel's philosophical and theological reputation rests on his *Collectorium*, his elucidation and continuation of Ockham's commentary on the *Sentences* of Peter Lombard, which Biel wrote while teaching theology at Tübingen. The *Collectorium* was conceived to be the classic statement of *via moderna*, influencing Philip Melanchthon and Martin Luther, as well as Tridentine Catholic theologians. Biel's position can best be described as that of an Ockhamist seeking common ground with Thomism and Scotism, countering the still-common belief that the *moderni* represented skepticism and a rejection of the synthesis of philosophical and theological concerns.

While his approach was nominalistic, drawing on Ockham, Marsilius von Inghen, and *Pierre d'Ailly, Biel's attention in the *Collectorium* is less upon logical and ontological problems than it is on the metaphysics of the covenants binding God and man. Consequently, analysis of problems associated with defining divine power, justification and grace, and predestination characterized his thought. Biel has been assessed variously as a Pelagian (an advocate of the heresy that salvation is possible without grace) by Luther and as an occasionalist (believing that God is the sole cause of all created action) by later Catholic thinkers.

Biel, following Ockham, relied on the widely used Scholastic distinction between absolute and ordained divine power, holding that God could accept a sinner without grace or reject one in a state of grace in his absolute power, if God so willed. Thus the truly meritorious aspect of good human acts did not lie in the acts themselves, but in God's predestined acceptance of them. But God had bound himself to reward good actions with grace, which meant that God's ordained power recognized human acts as good in themselves and rewarded them accordingly. So people who did their best using their natural powers were assured of reward according to God's ordained system. Earlier critics of the *moderni*, including Archbishop *Thomas Bradwardine, accused them of obviating the need for grace by making human actions good enough to merit salvation.

Biel believed that Ockhamism could avoid accusations of Pelagianism by emphasizing the *moderni*'s denial of the Scotistic and Thomistic divisibility of God's person and divine attributes. Absence of difference of any kind between God's willing and knowing entailed absence of an order of decisions in the divine mind. The result was that God's ordained power was not preceded by absolute power, and human action's meriting grace by ordained power was commensurate with predestination by absolute power. Martin Luther, having studied Biel's nominalistic theology, would coldly dismiss Biel's defense of Ockhamism as effectively Pelagian.

Bibliography: John Farthing, *Thomas Aquinas and Gabriel Biel*, 1988; Heiko Oberman, *The Harvest of Medieval Theology*, 1963.

Stephen E. Lahey

Binchois, Gilles (c. 1400–1460), also known as de Bins or de Binche, was a Franco-Flemish composer of sacred and secular polyphonic music active at the Burgundian court chapel from approximately 1427 to 1452. His chansons were among the most fashionable of his day, furnishing material for popular *basses danses*, for mass cycles by Johannes Ockeghem and Johannes Bedyngham, and for various musical settings by Johannes Ghiselin, *Alexander Agricola, and others. Among the many literary texts he set to music were famous poems by *Christine de Pizan (*Deuil angoisseux*), Charles d'Orléans (*Mon cuer chante*), and *Alain Chartier (*Triste plaisir*).

Gilles Binchois was born, most likely in Hainaut province, around 1400. His father Jean de Binche is believed to have been a councilor to William IV of Hainaut. Gilles's earliest known employment was as an organist at Sainte-Waudru in Mons from 1419 to 1423. In 1424, with the English present in northern France, he came into contact with William de la Pole, earl of Suffolk, and composed at his request a now-lost rondeau, "Ainsi que à la foiz my souvient." Soon afterward, presumably by 1427, he found employment as a singer and composer at the court chapel of Philip the Good of Burgundy and remained there for the next twenty-five years. In 1452 he retired to Soignies, in the diocese of Cambrai, where he had recently been appointed provost at the collegiate church of Saint-Vincent. Although he was not an ordained priest, he held prebends at Bruges, Mons, Cassel, and Soignies that, combined with payments he continued to receive from the Burgundian court, provided him a comfortable annual income of more than 1,000 livres.

Although he apparently wrote no complete mass cycles, his production of sacred music was considerable and varied, including twenty-eight paired and single mass movements, six magnificats, and sundry devotional and ceremonial pieces. The four-voice motet *Nove cantum melodie*, written to commemorate the baptism of Prince Antoine of Burgundy on 18 January 1431, stands out as his only isorhythmic composition. Its quadruplum text curiously recorded the names of eighteen of the singers present at the ceremony. The text of another piece, his three-voice motet *Domitor Hectoris*, offered an interesting exercise in allegorical exegesis by linking the Greek myth of Achilles and Telephus to Old and New Testament doctrine. Striking examples of fauxbourdon, an improvised form of polyphonic chanting embraced by his contemporaries Guillaume Dufay and John Dunstable, appeared in the settings for psalms *In exitu Israel* and *Inter natos mulierum*, in the hymn *Te Deum laudamus*, and in several magnificats.

Considered the epitome of Burgundian style, Binchois's fifty-five to sixty extant chansons represent perhaps only a fraction of the secular music he actually produced. Most surviving pieces are three-voice settings for rondeaux or ballades and rely on triple time. Octave-leap cadences are a common trait. His song texts almost invariably embrace the themes of courtly love, be it the joyful thought of serving one's mistress in "Joyeux penser," the persistent fear of rejection in "De plus en plus" and "Se j'eusse," or the despair of impossible love in "Seule esgarée." "Triste plaisir" and "Ah! Doloureux," typical of his art, are laced with a nostalgic sense of melancholy. At times, one must wonder that Ockeghem, in a musical eulogy, should have named him "père de joyeuseté" (the father of joyfulness). Binchois died at Soignies on 20 September 1460.

Bibliography: Dennis Slavin, "Some Distinctive Features of Songs by Binchois: Cadential Voice Leading and the Articulation of Form," *Journal of Musicology* 10 (1992): 342–61.

Jan Pendergrass

Bisticci, Vespasiano da. *See* Vespasiano da Bisticci.

Boccaccio, Giovanni (1313–75). Though readers in the fifteenth century remembered him as a writer of erudite Latin, Giovanni Boccaccio has been best known since for his works in Italian, especially his *Decameron*. The latter is a collection of one hundred tales told on ten consecutive days by ten different narrators (seven women and three men) hiding in the countryside while the bubonic plague rages in Florence. Still others knew him as the writer of Italian romances. *Geoffrey Chaucer, for instance, may never have seen the *Decameron*, but he based his *Troilus and Criseyde* on Boccaccio's *Filostrato*, his "Franklin's Tale" on Boccaccio's *Filocolo* (an early, rambling romance based on the legend of Florio and Biancifiore), and "The Knight's Tale" on the *Teseida* (a romance with epic trappings). Boccaccio also wrote a number of other poems and fictions, including *La caccia di Diana, Comedia delle ninfe fiorentine* (the *Ameto*), *Amorosa visione*, his short novel *Elegia di madonna Fiametta, Il ninfale fiesolano, Il corbaccio*, and Latin eclogues.

Giovanni Boccaccio was born in Tuscany, the illegitimate son of the merchant Boccaccino di Chellino, who legally adopted him soon after birth. Boccaccio then lived with his father and, after 1319, Chellino's new bride, Margherita dei Mardoli. Boccaccino intended his son to be a merchant and provided him with a good teacher (Giovanni di Domenico Mazzuoli da Strada); Boccaccio was then taught commercial activities and money matters by his father, his uncle, and other associates. In 1327, when Giovanni was fourteen, his father was sent to Naples by the Bardi Company (a large Florentine banking company), and he took his son with him. Boccaccio did not return to Florence until he was twenty-eight years old.

Most of Boccaccio's years in Naples were not, however, spent on commerce. While the father wanted his son to continue the business, the latter took a decided distaste to it, and by the time he was eighteen, Boccaccio had convinced his father to let him leave. There was a condition, however; Boccaccio had to study canon law. So for at least six years, Boccaccio was a student at the Studio in Naples. Fortunately, the study of law required Latin, and this allowed Boccaccio to perfect his knowledge of the language while studying Latin poetry, particularly after his father left for Paris in 1332. He began to visit the royal library and was befriended by the court librarian, Paolo da Perugia, who introduced him to the classics.

At the same time, Boccaccio became a regular visitor at the Angevin court, perhaps introduced by his ambitious friend Niccolò Acciaiuoli (later the seneschal of Catherine de Valois Courtenay, King Robert's sister-in-law). Boccaccio's *Caccia di Diana, Filocolo, Filostrato,* and *Teseida* all date from his days in aristocratic circles at court. When Boccaccio finally left Naples in 1341, he went unwillingly, forced by the rupture of relations between Florence and the Angevins and the retreat of the Florentine banking companies that soon followed (Boccaccino lost his connection with the Bardi and was likely in financial difficulties). Probably the father tried again to interest him in mercantile activities; certainly Boccaccio wrote unhappy letters of complaint about having to live in his father's house in Florence.

The years that followed, however, were enormously productive ones for Boccaccio, who in the next four or five years wrote *Ameto, Amorosa visione, Fiam-
metta*, and *Il Ninfale fiesolano*. Boccaccio was by now a well-known man of
letters. He also became something of a diplomat, for the government of Florence
increasingly entrusted him with missions to other cities and states. In 1345–46,
for instance, he was sent to Ravenna, and in 1347–48 he was in Forlì at the
court of Francesco Ordelaffi. When the bubonic plague took half the population
of Florence in 1348, Boccaccino and his second wife (Bice de Bostichi) were
among its victims; this made Boccaccio the head of his family, with a stepbrother in his charge. In 1350 he was "ambaxiator" to Romagna. Later that year
the city of Florence sent Boccaccio to Ravenna to give ten gold florins to
*Dante's daughter, Sister Beatrice, belatedly compensating the great poet of
Florence who died in exile. Soon after Boccaccio's return, *Francesco Petrarch
passed through Florence and became Boccaccio's guest; the assemblage of poets
and scholars gathered there established a "school" of friends of Petrarch in
Florence, and this led to a number of visits and letters between the two writers.
More official positions followed in the months to come. Boccaccio was, first,
bursar of the Chamber of the Commune and then bursar and delegate of the
Signoria. From late 1351 to early 1352 he was "ambaxiator solemnis" to *Louis
of Bavaria. Two months later Boccaccio arrived in Padua with official letters
for Petrarch, offering him a chair at the Studio, which had reopened in 1349
(Petrarch declined the offer). Yet sometime in these active years, between 1349
and 1353, Boccaccio probably wrote the *Decameron*.

In the years following the *Decameron*, Boccaccio continued to travel for both
Florentine and private reasons. In April 1353, for instance, he was in Romagna,
perhaps on another diplomatic mission; in July he was in Forli, and he spent
the rest of the summer in Ravenna. Violante, the young daughter whose death
he mourned in an eclogue and two affectionate letters, may have been born there
a few years earlier; she died in 1355 while Boccaccio was vainly trying to visit
Acciaiuoli in Naples. In all, Boccaccio had at least five illegitimate children.
His diplomatic journeys, meanwhile, became steadily more important, and in
1354 he was given an important embassy to Pope *Innocent VI at Avignon.

It was 1357 before Boccaccio returned seriously to his scholarship, writing
and rewriting *De montibus silvis, fontibus, lacubus, fluminibus, stagnus seu palu-
dibus, et de nominibus maris, Del claris mulieribus, Genealogia deorum gen-
tilium*, and *De casibus virorum illustrium*. These were the works that first placed
Boccaccio in libraries all over Europe. In 1359 Boccaccio set off for Milan to
visit Petrarch and devoted the following winter to promoting new translations
of Homer. The next year Innocent VI granted a dispensation to Boccaccio for
his illegitimacy. Perhaps he received a church dignity. At any rate, in the face
of new political turmoil in Florence, Boccaccio retired to Certaldo, emerging
briefly in 1365 and 1367 when he took on two diplomatic missions to the court
of Urban V. Only in 1368, after visiting Petrarch again, did Boccaccio decide
to copy and revise his *Decameron*. Petrarch enthusiastically shared the copy

with friends, and the Decameron was soon read throughout Europe. By 1371 Boccaccio had retired to his estate at Certaldo where he continued to edit and add to several of his previous works. He also traveled, and gave public readings from Dante's Divine Comedy, until his death in December 1375.

Bibliography: Giovanni Boccaccio, *The Decameron*, 1993; Vittore Branca, *Boccaccio: The Man and His Workds*, 1976; Judith Powers Serafini-Sauli, *Giovanni Boccaccio*, 1982.

Kathyrn Jacobs

Bondol, Jean de (c. 1330–85?),

whose name is also spelled Boudolf, was a painter of Bruges who was also active in Paris from 1368 to 1381. He worked in the court of Charles V and was, before 1374, *pictor regis* (the king's painter). Bondol was trained in the Flemish style of naturalistic rendering of detail and figure, which he combined with the more elegant court style of Paris, as did many Flemish artists who worked in France. In 1374 he was granted an annual salary of two hundred livres "on this condition that he shall be held to serve in all works of painting that the King shall command without other wages, either for himself or for his servant." Bondol's extant work includes illuminated manuscripts for Charles V and the *Angers Apocalypse*, which he executed with Nicholas Bataille. In 1371 he painted the portrait of Charles V in the *Bible historiée* (The Hague, Rijksmuseum Meermanno-Westreenianum, MS. 10 B 23, fol. 2). The monarch is shown accepting the Bible from the donor, Jean de Vaudetar. Rather than presenting the king in his finery, Bondol painted him in the costume of a master of the University of Paris. Here the artist incorporated the naturalism of the body, volumetric beneath its gown, with its portrait head, and the flat, conservative decoration of the background. The figures were placed within a "diaphragm arch" that served to set the composition apart from the viewer, rather like a stage setting, while the artist used one-point perspective. This amalgamation of ideas reflects the Franco-Flemish work typical of the Parisian court style. In the *Bible of Jean de Sy* (Paris, Bibliothèque Nationale, MS. fr. 15397, c. 1380), Bondol employed the same combination of stylistic features as in the *Bible historiée*.

Certainly the largest of Bondol's surviving works is the *Angers Apocalypse*, which is a tapestry measuring 16 by 470 feet. The project was a 1377 commission from Charles V's brother, Duke Louis of Anjou, for which he "borrowed" Bondol from the Parisian court. The Flemish painter was responsible for the plan and execution of the cartoons for the tapestry. It seems that he used an illustrated Apocalypse in the king's collection as a model for the Apocalypse scenes. There are seven panels containing more than ninety scenes, based upon the prototype. Although the style of Bataille's tapestry contains more of the linearism of the International Gothic, popular throughout Europe, many of the figures show the style of Bondol, with swelling curves and volumes beneath their clothing. The *Apocalypse* was designed to decorate the walls of the duke of Anjou's bedroom, a constant reminder of the eschaton (the Day of Judgment) and the reign of Antichrist. The model selected by Bondol was of the type that combined Scripture with depictions of St. John, author of the Revelation or Apocalypse, who served to introduce the various scenes and to act as a means to lead the eye of the viewer through the prophecies.

Bibliography: E. Panofsky, *Early Netherlandish Painting*, 1971.

Marian Hollinger

Bondone, Giotto di. *See* Giotto di Bondone.

Boner, Ulrich (c. 1290–1349), was the author of the first complete German translation and edition of Aesop's fables. The author of a collection of Aesopian fables identifies himself as "Bonerius" in the preface and the epilogue to his work, entitled *Edelstein* (The gem): "He who brought this out of the Latin into German . . . is called Bonerius." Very little else is known about the author, who seems to be identical with the Dominican friar Ulrich Boner mentioned several times in local deeds between 1324 and 1350. He dedicated his work to one John of Ringgenberg (1291–1350). This dedication supplies a terminus ante quem for his work and has been used to place Boner in the political and geographical sphere of Berne, Switzerland, an assumption that is supported by the dialect of his writing.

The *Edelstein* represents the first complete edition of Aesop's fables in the Middle High German language. The formal model of Boner's text was the Middle High German exemplum in rhymed couplets (*Reimpaarspruch*), a form characteristic of other exempla collections such as the Stricker's. Boner used two medieval Latin fable collections as his sources: the *Anonymus neveleti* for the first part, and Avianus's collection for the second. Boner himself supplemented these texts with moralizing short narratives, which are also found in popular exempla collections such as the *Alphabetum narrationum*. Characteristic of Boner's use of his sources is his arrangement of pairs of fables under a common topical heading; the criteria for their selection, however, vary widely. Genuine additions by Boner himself are the four introductory fables and the concluding fable in the epilogue. The latter informed his readers about the collection's objective, to present God's creation as a mirror in order to formulate rules for the proper behavior of humankind. A further addition consisted of Boner's own interpretations of the exempla: often a string of sentencelike summaries that repeated the fable's moralization.

Boner's perception of nature went beyond that of a pure mirror function, and his interpretation was clearly ethical when in his prologue he defined true wisdom as the knowledge that "all creatures teach us . . . to love God." Notwithstanding his own words, however, Boner preserved the inherent moral indifference of the genre and played on the fable's own logic of justifying human behavior solely according to its usefulness. Thus a virtuous life should be embraced since it is the only guarantee of success, whereas its opposite inevitably leads to failure. In cases where individual fables obviously contradicted this observation, he circumvented this problem by referring to the temporality of all earthly success. Another characteristic of the fable that Boner preserved was the genre's inherent social and political conservatism. He sanctioned the politically shrewd behavior of those who accepted and adapted themselves to the existing conditions without questioning them: "Poor people should heed that they are not to seek the companionship of those who are far more wealthy than they are." The popularity of Boner's work was relatively short-lived and waned after 1476 when another German collection of fables, Steinhoewel's *Esop*, began to replace the *Edelstein*.

Bibliography: Klaus Grubmüller, *Meister Esopus: Untersuchungen zu Geschichte und Funktion der Fabel im Mittelalter*, Münchener Texte und Untersuchungen zur deutschen Literatur des Mittelalters, vol. 56, 1977: 297–374.

Martin Blum

Bosch, Hieronymus (c. 1450–1516),

was born Jeroen van Aken and became a noted Netherlandish artist. The most idiosyncratic and outlandish of fifteenth-century northern European painters, Bosch is remembered primarily as the inventor of extraordinary, enigmatic images. Distinguished by the free fusion of disparate elements, animate and inanimate, the peculiarities of his oeuvre have given rise to lively debates among modern scholars.

Jeroen van Aken was born around 1450 in 's Hertogenbosch, northern Brabant, to a family of painters. It is assumed that he received his early training from his father, Antonius, and his paternal uncles. He undoubtedly went on to head a workshop, but there is no extant reference to it or to any of Bosch's assistants. There is no evidence for journeys away from 's Hertogenbosch, and despite illustrious commissions, his artistic career seems to have been confined to the distinctive milieu of his provincial birthplace, a center of religious culture, with its peculiarly bourgeois fusion of secular and sacred—shaped by the *devotio moderna*, preoccupied with things eschatological, and driven by fear. The influence of 's Hertogenbosch on Bosch cannot be overestimated. Bosch was first documented in 1474, was first mentioned as a painter in 1480–81, and was first identified by his place of origin in 1504. In 1481 he married Aleyt Goyarts van den Meervenne (d. 1522–23), the daughter of a prosperous local patrician. Tax records placed Bosch in the wealthiest 10 percent of 's Hertogenbosch's citizens. A member of the town's social elite, he was a member (ordinary 1486–87, sworn 1488) of 's Hertogenbosch's wealthy confraternity, the Brotherhood of Our Lady. The confraternity afforded him useful social contacts and provided him with his first commissions. Bosch died in 1516, apparently childless.

There is no satisfactory classification, chronological or stylistic, of Bosch's paintings. None are dated, many survive only as fragments, others are unsigned, and some are known only from copies. The division of Bosch's work according to subject matter, religious and moral, is less fraught with contradiction, but even this forces distinctions that at times run counter to his work's inherent ambiguity. Rough chronological estimates date his maturity to the decade following 1500, and his major work (including most of the monumental triptychs) is commonly assigned to this period. Early (1470–85) and middle (1485–1500) periods are sometimes also identified.

The nature of Bosch's eschatological vision, his decidedly pessimistic interpretation of doomsday, is neatly captured in the Vienna *Last Judgment*. The subdued grisaille of the outer wings gives way, when the triptych is open, to a riotous scene of apocalyptic torment. The left panel depicts Adam and Eve's expulsion from Eden, surmounted by the Fall of the Rebel Angels. In the center, a myriad of brightly colored creatures litter the foreground as the scene recedes into dense blackness, relieved only by the glow of smoldering fires. The left panel represents a hell that is indistinguishable from earth. A small, light-encircled Christ sits in judgment at the top of the central panel and is distinguished by his distance from the painting's activity and by the small number of his elect.

The only serious alternative Bosch envisaged to a life of almost certain damnation was furnished by the example of the hermit saints. Paintings of Sts. Jerome, Anthony, and Giles (depicted both alone and together) figure prominently among the artist's extant works; the hermit saint's unique invulnerability is most fully elaborated in Lisbon's *Temptation of St. Anthony* triptych. Anthony's temptations and the chaotic disport of innumerable devils fill the canvas, but the viewer's eye is directed to the picture's center, where a tranquil St. Anthony raises his hand in benediction. The painter's bizarre amalgamation of the human, animal, and inanimate, an audacious reinvention of manuscript marginalia, here displays a complexity of form that is unusual even for Bosch.

The most enigmatic of Bosch's paintings, and probably his most famous, is the *Garden of Earthly Delights* (Madrid, Prado). A luxuriant earth, peopled with a panoply of naked cavorters, is framed by panels of Eden (left) and hell (right). The ambiguity of the central panel, paradisiacal or diabolical, is almost certainly intended, reminding the viewer of the fundamental nature of sexuality, but also of its inherently pernicious quality. The erotic symbolism of the scene becomes clear when the iconography (much of it decrypted by Dirk Bax) is read as a visual translation of popular puns and metaphors. Other religious paintings by Bosch included various incidents from the Old Testament (most no longer extant) as well as scenes from the life of Christ, predominantly his childhood and Passion.

Popular culture (proverbs, popular ballads and songs, familiar sayings), reinterpreted in the interest of a bourgeois ethical scheme, lies behind the majority of Bosch's secular moralizing works. The equation of vice with folly, and its attribution to the lower classes and social deviants, provided Bosch with the material for a wide range of works, including *Stone Operation* (Madrid, Prado), *Ship of Fools* (Paris, Louvre), *Haywain* (Madrid, Prado), and *Death of the Miser* (Washington, D.C., National Gallery). Although these works found their way, by the late sixteenth century, into the collections of the Spanish aristocracy (avid admirers of "El Bosco"), they seem to have catered originally to an upper-middle-class urban clientele familiar with their "folk" language. Indeed, many of Bosch's later admirers enjoyed his work largely for the idiosyncrasy of his diabolical creations, which by then were emptied of their moral significance. Bosch stands apart from the mainstream of Netherlandish painting, and his animated formulations were executed with little concern for the naturalistic problems of his contemporaries. He inspired a thriving industry of imitators, and his most lasting impact was on the work of Pieter Bruegel the Elder.

Bibliography: Dirk Bax, *Hieronymus Bosch: His Picture-Writing Deciphered*, 1979; W. S. Gibson, *Hieronymus Bosch*, 1973.

Nicola McDonald

Botticelli, Sandro (1444–1510), was born Alessandro di Mariano Filipepi. A leading painter of the Florentine school, misunderstood for centuries until he was rediscovered by the Pre-Raphaelites, Botticelli is now considered one of the great humanist painters of allegorical representations of sacred and mythical themes. He enjoyed the patronage of the Medici rulers of Florence. Important works include *Primavera* (Uffizi, Florence), *Birth of Venus* (Uffizi, Florence), *Madonna of the Pomegranate* (Uffizi, Florence), and *Mystic Nativity* (National Gallery, London).

Alessandro di Mariano Filipepi was born in 1444 to a tanner, Mariano Filipepi. He came to be known as Botticelli through his older brother, "Il Botticelli" (little wine barrel), a broker of some wealth, who contributed to Sandro's education. Apprenticed under *Filippo Lippi, influenced by *Andrea del Verrocchio, Botticelli was an independent master by 1470. In 1472 he joined the Compagnia di S. Luca, whose records show that he took Filippino Lippi as an apprentice. At this time the Medici became his patrons. For the joust of 28 January 1475 he painted the banner for *Giuliano de Medici. Botticelli painted a fresco of the hanged Pazzi conspirators (1478) over the Porta della Dogana in Via de' Gondi to mark Giuliano's murder; it was destroyed when the Florentine Republic was reestablished and the Medici were expelled from Florence in 1494. Botticelli painted the well-known portrait of Giuliano de Medici (National Gallery of Art, Washington, D.C.) sometime later.

In the early 1480s Botticelli had close contact with *Domenico Ghirlandaio and *Pietro Perugino. In 1480 he painted in situ the fresco *St. Augustine's Vision of the Death of St. Jerome* in the Ognissanti at the same time Ghirlandaio executed *St. Jerome in His Study*. In 1481 he joined Perugino, Cosimo Rosselli, and Ghirlandaio to decorate the Sistine Chapel. Botticelli painted the *Story of Moses*, the *Punishment of Korah*, and the *Temptation of Christ*, as well as a number of papal portraits. These frescoes show that he had not yet fully mastered placing several stages of narrative in one grand composition that, achieved in the earlier *Primavera* (1478), is one of his great artistic achievements. By the autumn of 1482 Botticelli, Ghirlandaio, and Perugino were all commissioned to fresco the Sala dell'Orologio (Sala dei Gigli) of the Palazza della Signoria in Florence.

Between 1478 and 1490 Botticelli painted his great mythologies. Heavily influenced by the humanism of his patron, *Lorenzo de Medici, Botticelli produced poetic allegorical works such as *Primavera* and the *Birth of Venus* (1484). The importance of *Primavera* is universally acknowledged. Its conception was based upon contemporary Neoplatonic vernacular poetry, most probably *Angelo Poliziano's *Stanze* (itself heavily influenced by Lorenzo de Medici), in which Venus was the allegory of love. Botticelli achieved a synthesis of the antique and the new by generalizing classical mythological imagery while detailing it with decorations of contemporary vernacular fashion. For instance, the ancient gods were costumed in contemporary masquerade such as that worn by Florentines attending the civic festivals sponsored by Lorenzo. Botticelli mastered the synthesis of *antico* and *nuovo*, poetry and painting, and philosophy and politics with *Birth of Venus*. The subject was the same as that of *Primavera*, the advent of Venus in spring, but emboldened by Venus in full classical naked form as Venus *pudica* (shamed), significant as the first reappearance of the nude Venus since antiquity.

Venus reappeared in Botticelli's religious works such as the *Madonna of the Pomegranate* (1487), demonstrating the attempt to reconcile classical naturalism with Christian spirituality. The slight melancholy first felt in the *Birth of Venus* was fully evident in this later work. By the beginning of the 1490s Botticelli underwent a discernible crisis of style in his search for a retrospective form of religious expression. He had been deeply influenced by the Dominican *Girolamo Savonarola, who preached against representing female saints in contemporary garb, considering such portrayals improper and lascivious. Botticelli's *Mystic Nativity* (1501) reflected an increasingly apocalyptic world view. The imagery was adapted from the eschatology of Joachim of Fiore. The inscription alluded to the Second Coming of Christ in fulfillment of Revelation, as demonstrated by the political instability attendant upon Lorenzo de Medici's death. Heavily imbued with Savonarola's religious fanaticism, the *Mystic Nativity* equally reflected the synthesis of theology and poetry attempted by the Laurentians, a group of humanists formerly supported by Lorenzo who had subsequently followed Savonarola.

Whether it was because of religious fundamentalism, artistic retrospection, his eclipse by Michelangelo, *Leonardo da Vinci, and Raphael, or the reestablishment of the Florentine Republic, the *Mystic Nativity* was Botticelli's last important commission. In 1504 he joined the judges of the competition between Leonardo and Michelangelo for the Sala dei Cinquecento, Palazzo della Signoria, and belonged to the group deciding the placement of Michelangelo's *David*, the symbol of Florentine liberty. Botticelli died on 17 May 1510 in Florence.

Bibliography: H. P. Horne, *Alessandro Filipepi, Commonly Called Sandro Botticelli, Painter of Florence*, 1986; R. Lightbown, *Sandro Botticelli: Life and Work*, 1989; L. Venturi, *Botticelli*, 1961.

Patricia Cossard

Bourbon, Anne Valois, Duchesse de. *See* Valois, Anne, Duchesse de Bourbon.

Bourchier, Thomas (1411–86), cardinal and archbishop of Canterbury. Thomas Bourchier (also spelled Bourgchier), the great-grandson of *Edward III, had the longest service (twenty-two years) of any archbishop of Canterbury up to the twentieth century and also achieved the cardinalate. In addition, he played a key role as both peacemaker and partisan during the conflict that later historians dubbed the "Wars of the Roses."

The third son of William Bourchier, comte d'Eu, and Anne Plantagenet, second daughter of Thomas of Woodstock, duke of Gloucester and youngest son of Edward III, Thomas Bourchier had three elder brothers, including Humphrey Stafford, duke of Buckingham. The young Thomas Bourchier attended Oxford, resident at the then-thriving Neville's Inn. In 1424, at age thirteen, he received the prebend of Colwick in Lichfield, and by 1433 he had two more prebends, one at West Thurrock in Hastings and another in Lincoln, as well as the deanship of St. Martin-le-Grand in London. That year, though only twenty-two and not yet of canonical age, he received the nomination to the See of Worcester. This nomination had more to do with his family connections and the jockeying for power in the realm between the Beaufort/Bedford and Gloucester factions. In Bourchier's case, the support of *Henry Cardinal Beaufort, the duke of Bedford, and Archbishop Kemp proved decisive. However, Pope *Eugenius IV instead named Thomas Brouns, dean of Salisbury. Though this led to an immediate strain in Anglo-papal relations at a crucial moment in the war with France, the pope undoubtedly questioned the wisdom of appointing one so young to a bishopric, minor and in the west of England though it might be. Fortunately for all concerned, the See of Rochester had in the meantime become vacant, and the translation of Brouns to Rochester and the appointment of Bourchier to Worcester managed to save both the honor and the positions of all concerned. Accordingly, Bourchier entered upon his duties as bishop of Worcester on 15 April 1435.

Rather unfortunately for all concerned, the see at Ely immediately fell vacant. *Humphrey, Duke of Gloucester, sought to secure the translation of Bishop Thomas Rudbourne of St. David's to Ely, but his foes in the Beaufort/Bedford affinity in riposte championed Bourchier; indeed, John, Lord Tiptoft, bullied the chapter at Ely into electing Bourchier as its next bishop. Pope Eugenius IV at first agreed, hoping to avoid the factionalism involved with Bourchier's appointment to Worcester. Unfortunately for him and nearly everyone involved, however, the king's council as a whole nominated a third man, Cardinal Louis de Luxembourg, the archbishop of Rouen and the Lancastrian chancellor of France. The dispute over Ely bitterly dragged on for the next two years, further damaging Anglo-papal relations. In the end, Gloucester dropped his support of Rudbourne, Luxembourg received Ely *in commendam* for life (having the revenues but not the title), and Bourchier received the title but no pallium and no revenues until Luxembourg's death. When this occurred in 1443, Bourchier took office and had the temporalities restored to him on 27 February 1444. In the meantime, he served as chancellor of Oxford University from 1434 to 1437.

Bourchier first played the role of peacemaker between *Henry VI and the duke of York during the crisis of 1452. Along with Bishop William Waynflete of Winchester, the earls of Salisbury and Warwick, and Lords Sudeley and Beauchamp, Bourchier mediated an agreement between the two by which the king initiated an inquiry into the conduct of the duke of Somerset in losing the Hundred Years' War, with the latter (York's archenemy) committed to the Tower for the duration of the inquest. Despite York's subsequent humiliation and arrest upon the king's decision to go back upon his word, York bore Bourchier no ill will. Indeed, in 1454, after the death of the archbishop of Canterbury, Richard of York, acting as protector of the realm during the first of Henry VI's many mental incapacities, nominated Bourchier as the next archbishop, and thus Bourchier attained the pinnacle of the English church on 24 January 1455, at the age of forty-four. Despite his family connections, Bourchier's diplomatic skills (as evidenced many times over in the years from 1452 to 1454) had proved the chief recommendation for this promotion.

Still, by no means could York always count upon Bourchier's support. Thus at the end of 1454 Bourchier played a key role in ending York's protectorship and restoring personal rule to the momentarily lucid Henry VI; but Bourchier did play a pivotal role in forging yet another agreement between York and Henry. Perhaps as a reward, Bourchier accepted his appointment as chancellor of England on 7 March 1455. Though mediation efforts continued, Bourchier's efforts came to naught and ended in the first Battle of St. Albans on 22 May 1455. York's triumph, which included the capture of the again "confused" Henry VI, enabled him to proclaim a second protectorate. At the succeeding July Parliament, York and his supporters received a full pardon and immunity for any and all actions committed to that time. Bourchier's elder brother Henry, Viscount Bourchier, also received the treasurership of England.

However, by the succeeding February the king had once more recovered, and York again resigned his protectorship, thanks in no small part to the efforts of Bourchier, still loyal to a king in control of his mental facilities. Increasingly, however, with the king a shadow of his former self, the government fell into the hands of Queen Margaret of Anjou, with whom both York and Bourchier had increasing problems. In August 1456 the queen moved the court to Coventry, then England's third-largest city and a royalist stronghold. At a great council held that October, both Bourchiers lost their offices to men loyal to the queen, and the government remained resident in the West Midlands for the next five years. As Queen Margaret increasingly sought to exert royal power and bring the realm under her control, the country plunged further into disorder, tumult, and near civil war, driving York, Bourchier, and others further into opposition.

These machinations eventually led to the Battle of Ludlow on 12 October 1459 and the subsequent attainder of York and his affinity. However, the failure to capture any of the leading Yorkists or their bases in Ireland and Calais led to disaster the next year. At the end of June 1460 the earls of Salisbury and Warwick, along with York's eldest son, *Edward (IV), earl of March, crossed the Channel from their base in Calais and entered London on 2 July. The next day, at St. Paul's, in front of the Convocation of Canterbury, the three earls publicly enunciated their grievances and swore on the cross of St. Thomas Becket that they harbored no designs against the king himself, only against his "evil counselors." Bourchier, on behalf of the convocation, agreed to see the king to mediate a settlement, but these efforts broke down when the Yorkists and royalists fought the Battle of Northampton on 11 July. The Yorkist victory there led to the capture of the king (and the death of Bourchier's half brother, the duke of Buckingham, who fought on the royalist side), and the political climate remained tense.

Nevertheless, Bourchier continued to seek reconciliation. Again he brokered a settlement at a parliament convened later that year whereby Henry VI retained the title of king for life, while York became his heir as well as protector of the realm. Bourchier's agreement might have held but for the queen's continued hostility and Richard of York's death in a minor skirmish at Wakefield. Bourchier's attempts at reconciliation finally evaporated after the queen's victory at the second Battle of St. Albans, when she had many Yorkists summarily executed. However, upon the seizure of London by York's eldest son and heir, Edward of March, Bourchier publicly proclaimed his support for the Yorkist cause on 28 June of that year when he crowned March as King Edward IV. The Battle of Towton later that year confirmed Edward's position, and by 26 May 1465 Bourchier had also crowned Elizabeth Woodville as the new queen of England. For reward, Edward IV asked the pope to make Bourchier a cardinal, and in 1467 the pope agreed. However, due to political machinations on the part of Queen Margaret, then in France, and the brief restoration of Henry VI in 1471, Bourchier did not receive his cardinal's hat until 31 May 1473.

In the meantime, Bourchier proved his loyalty yet again. In 1471, after Edward IV had fled the country and Henry VI had been restored to power, Bourchier not only raised troops for Edward but also succeeded in mediating a reconcilliation between the king and the duke of Clarence. All these efforts proved of critical importance in Edward's final victory at Tewkesbury later that year.

Though Edward IV never appointed him to a major office in the government, Bourchier continued active in the king's council, officiating at all state functions, serving on local commissions, managing the Convocation of Canterbury in Edward's interest, and lending the Crown large sums of money. Additionally, Edward gave him effective control of the realm during his 1475 French campaign, and Bourchier subsequently served as a diplomat during negotiations that led to the 1475 Treaty of Picquigny.

In 1483, upon the death of Edward IV, Bourchier entered the final stage of his involvement in political affairs. First, he headed the deputation from the council to Edward's widowed queen and persuaded her to deliver up her second son (Richard, duke of York) for safekeeping to his uncle, *Richard (III), duke of Gloucester. Within three weeks Bourchier officiated at the coronation of Gloucester as King Richard III. We do not know, except by surmise, his feelings toward Richard III after the disappearance of the princes in the Tower, or the state of his support for either Richard or Henry Tudor. We do know that Bourchier formally crowned the latter as King *Henry VII in 1485 and married the king to the Yorkist heiress Elizabeth of York the following year. These actions may, however, have resulted more from his position as cardinal primate of England than from any personal stake in the outcome, or they may simply reflect the state of affairs brought about by Richard's death at Bosworth and Henry Tudor's emergence as the only effective claimant to the throne.

Though Bourchier Oxford educated and once chancellor of the university, he never had a reputation for personal erudition. Instead, he cultivated a reputation as a magnificent host, as well as a patron of learning and the arts. Throughout his long tenure as archbishop of Canterbury he variously entertained or supported Edward IV, the patriarch of Antioch, and various men of learning and the arts. Bourchier died at the age of seventy-five, at Knowle, on 30 March 1486. He was buried in Canterbury Cathedral, and one can still visit his tomb there.

Bibliography: Ralph A. Griffiths, *The Reign of King Henry VI: The Exercise of Royal Authority, 1422–1461*, 1981; Charles Ross, *Edward IV*, 1974.

Jerome S. Arkenburg

Bouts, Dirc (Dieric, Dirk, Thierry) (c. 1415–75), was a native of Haarlem. It is thought that he may have studied painting with Albert van Ouwater. Bouts went to Louvain, Flanders, in 1457 and in 1468 became the city's official painter. Documents indicate that he was married twice and had at least two sons, Aelbrecht and Dirc the Younger. Contracts survive for the painter that provide a glimpse into the world of fifteenth-century Flemish painters. Many of the characteristic features of Bouts's painting reflect trends and styles of his immediate predecessors and colleagues, among whom were *Jan van Eyck, *Rogier van der Weyden, and Petrus Christus.

Although the majority of Bouts's subjects were religious, there are also surviving portraits and other secular commissions. His work contained stylistic kinships with Flemish naturalism and with the more linear qualities of the International Gothic. Bouts merged the particularized naturalism of Flemish tradition with the more internalized, spiritual qualities for which van der Weyden was so highly regarded. The earliest extant work, the *Infancy Altarpiece* (c. 1445), contained in its four panels of *The Annunciation to the Virgin, The Visitation, The Nativity*, and *The Adoration of the Magi* marked influences from both Christus and van der Weyden. His altarpiece of *The Deposition* (c. 1450–55) also bore references to van der Weyden's style, but Bouts was never merely an imitator of his fellow painters. Although his figures were tall and slender, they were not weightless, as in the International Gothic manner. They possess volume and character and seem to inhabit a sort of intermediary stage between the reality of the worldly plane and a subliminal spiritual realm. Bouts's figures did not have the effusive emphasis of psychological drama of the most popular of van der Weyden's panels, nor did they have the elegance of Jan van Eyck's richly garbed and bejeweled actors. They functioned, rather, as intermediaries between the everyday world of the fifteenth-century viewer and the spiritual realm.

Bouts's major work, and one of two projects for which there is documentation, was the *Altarpiece of the Last Supper* (c. 1464–67). The contract for this triptych has survived, allowing scholars to understand how such a commission was executed. This work illustrates the artist's ability to blend the secular and the religious, influenced by other Flemish painters, but made distinctly his own. He united the Old and New Testament types under the tutelage of theological supervisors (as the contract stated), but placed these types into a context that characteristically blended this world and the next.

Two of four panels depicting the *Justice of Emperor Otto III*, which was a commission for the city hall of Louvain, today survive as examples of Bouts's secular subject matter. Some portraits have also been attributed to his workshop.

Bibliography: E. Panofsky, *Early Netherlandish Painting*, 1971.

Marian Hollinger

Bracciolini, Gian Francesco Poggio (1380–1459),

was also known as Poggius Florentinus. An exemplar of Italian Renaissance humanism, Bracciolini is best known both for his discovery of important works by ancient authors and for his own dialogues and epistles. His life was characterized by the unending search for ancient manuscripts, accompanied by the conviction that these texts could serve as models not only of writing but also of a moral society.

Poggio Bracciolini was born on 11 February 1380 in Terranuova in the upper Valdarno region to Guccio Bracciolini, a pharmacist, and Iacoba Frutti, the daughter of a local notary. Although his earliest education was in Arezzo, Bracciolini's humanistic formation began in earnest in Florence, where he went around 1400 for notarial training. Bracciolini supported his studies by working as a scribe, an activity that earned him the admiration of prominent humanists in Florence. Within this circle, Bracciolini acquired his expertise in Latin, as well as his passion for the recovery of ancient Latin manuscripts.

Encouraged by his friend *Leonardo Bruni, Bracciolini left Florence for Rome in 1403. There he served first as secretary for Cardinal Landolfo Maramaldo, bishop of Bari, and later as apostolic scriptor in the papal Curia under Boniface IX. During this tumultuous period Bracciolini served both the legitimate pope Alexander V and the Pisan pope John XXIII. The latter appointed him to the coveted position of apostolic secretary. In 1414 Bracciolini attended the Council of Constance, which deposed John XXIII and dissolved the Pisan Curia on 29 May 1415. He remained in Constance devoting himself to manuscript research, an activity he had already begun in Italy. During his forays into the library of Saint Gallen, conducted independently and with Cencio de' Rustici and Bartolomeo da Montepulciano, Bracciolini discovered a complete copy of Quintilian's *Institution oratoria*, Vegetius's *Epitoma rei militaris*, and many other previously unknown texts.

In the spring of 1417 Bracciolini uncovered the *De rerum natura* of Lucretius, the *Astronomica* of Manilius, and the *Punica* of Silius Italicus, as well as many other writings in libraries in Fulda, Germany. During the summer of the same year Bracciolini discovered several Ciceronian orations in Langres, France, and Cologne, as well as Statius's *Silvae*, the *Vita Aristotelis*, another copy of Quintilian's *Institution oratoria*, and other codices. Bracciolini diligently copied the texts he found, a boon for later generations because many of the originals were later lost.

Although Bracciolini had gained considerable fame as a researcher by this point, he was initially unsuccessful in securing the promised position of apostolic secretary. Instead, under Martin V, elected at Constance on 11 November 1417, he served as scriptor. In 1418 Bracciolini went to England at the invitation of Cardinal *Henry Beaufort of Winchester, where he spent several unhappy years, temporarily shifting his focus from humanistic to religious works.

In 1423 Bracciolini returned to Rome, where he finally was appointed apostolic secretary to Pope Martin V. He also participated fairly actively in the political events of the time, without ceasing his research on both manuscripts and archaeological objects. After Martin V's death, Bracciolini followed his successor, *Eugenius IV (1431–47) throughout Italy, renewing old friendships, especially in his hometown of Florence. In 1436, the same year Bracciolini wrote a dialogue on the advantages and disadvantages of marriage (*An seni sit uxor ducenda*), he married eighteen-year-old Vaggia de' Buondelmonti of Florence. He and Vaggia had six children, and Bracciolini acquired a house in the Tuscan countryside, which served as his most permanent home for the rest of his life. Bracciolini wrote most of his more important works during this period. His dialogues included *De avaritia* (1428–29), *De nobilitate* (1440), *De infelicitate principum* (1440), *De varietate fortunae* (1448), *Contra hypocritas* (1447–48), and *De miseria humanae condicionis* (1455). His *Facetiae*, a collection of obscene stories, was published in fragments between 1438 and 1452 and remained quite popular throughout the Renaissance. Bracciolini is also known for his letters, which he edited and gathered together in several collections, as well as invectives and funeral elegies.

In 1447 Tommaso Parentucelli, a friend of Bracciolini's, was elected Pope *Nicholas V. Despite the favor he found in Rome, Bracciolini longed to return to Florence, which he finally did in 1453. There he assumed the post of *cancelliere* (chancellor) of the Florentine Republic. He began his last work, the *Historiae Florentini populi*, during this period. In 1458 Bracciolini retired to his country home, where he died on 30 October 1459, leaving the *Historiae Florentini populi* unfinished. He is buried in the Church of Santa Croce in Florence.

Bracciolini is significant for his Latin manuscript discoveries as well as his understanding of the cultural significance of these works. His own writing is notable for its descriptive narrative and was intended to serve as a moral looking glass.

Bibliography: Phyllis Walter Goodhart Gordon, ed., *Two Renaissance Book Hunters: The Letters of Poggius Bracciolini to Nicolaus de Niccolis*, 1974; D. Marsh, *The Quattrocento Dialogue*, 1980.

Anne M. Schuchman

Bradwardine, Thomas (1290?–1349), known as "Doctor profundus," distinguished himself in several areas of early-fourteenth-century intellectual and political life. He wrote on theology, mathematics, logic, and physics and also served as confessor to *Edward III, accompanying him on his French military operations during the Hundred Years' War.

As with many fourteenth-century figures, little is known of Bradwardine's early life. He was born sometime between 1290 and 1300 somewhere in Sussex. In 1323 Bradwardine was a fellow of Merton College, Oxford, and he became associated with a group interested in physics, including William Heytesbury, *Richard Swineshead, and John Dumbleton. The Merton school differentiated dynamics (the causes and forces of motion) from the new study of kinematics (the observable effects of motion).

From 1325 to 1327 Bradwardine served as proctor of Merton College and in 1333 became canon of Lincoln. Shortly thereafter, he accepted the patronage of Richard de Bury, bishop of Durham, and entered his household in 1335. The bishop advanced Bradwardine's career, helping him to the chancellorship of St. Paul's in London in 1337. In 1339 Bradwardine served as chaplain and confessor to King Edward III.

It is convenient to consider his theological works separately from his writings in physics and mathematics, although these areas of thought were obviously closely related in Bradwardine's work. Bradwardine's *De causa Dei contra Pelagium et de virtute causarum* appeared in 1344 and was directed polemically against a group of thinkers (probably *William of Ockham and his followers) whom Bradwardine called "modern Pelagians." These "modern Pelagians" emphasized free will in human action, whereas Bradwardine stressed in *De causa Dei* that God is both first mover and primary cause; therefore no human action is possible without God's prior willing or foreknowledge. God did not act as a spectator of future events but actively willed these events. This work may have influenced the views on predestination of *John Wyclif. *De causa Dei* appeared in a 1618 edition edited by Henry Savile, indicating continued interest in Bradwardine's theology into the seventeenth century. Bradwardine's *De futuris contingentibus* also discussed problems of God's foreknowledge and future action. Bradwardine influenced thinking on grace, free will, and predestination outside the universities, and he was mentioned by *Geoffrey Chaucer in "The Nun's Priest's Tale" as an authority (along with Augustine and Boethius) on necessity and free will. Another important political and religious work of Bradwardine was his *Sermo epinicius*, delivered before Edward III in 1346 in honor of the English victory at Crécy.

In the realm of natural philosophy and mathematics, Bradwardine wrote *Geometria speculativa* and *Arithmetica speculativa*. His most lasting scientific contribution, *Tractatus de proportionibus velocitatum in motibus* (Treatise on the proportions of velocities in movements) of 1328, examined the unsatisfactory Aristotelian law of motion. Motion in the Aristotelian theory occurs when a particular force overcomes the resistance of the medium. Bradwardine demonstrated that Aristotle's formulation could not hold for all possible cases, and so he proposed his own mathematical law of motion in its place.

The primary significance of *De proportionibus* and its theory of motion is that it used sophisticated mathematics (anticipating logarithms) to express a law of physics, aiding in the development of mathematical physics that was crowned by the later achievements of Galilean and Newtonian mechanics. Bradwardine clearly demonstrated the power of mathematical expression as a tool for investigating nature. The Merton school with which Bradwardine was associated also developed the "mean-speed theorem," which states that given a fixed interval of time, an accelerated body moves the same distance as if it were traveling with a uniform speed equivalent to the average or mean speed during its acceleration.

Bradwardine reached the pinnacle of his career in 1349 when he was consecrated archbishop of Canterbury by Pope *Clement VI, the highest ecclesiastical appointment in England. He was unable to enjoy this office, however, succumbing to the Black Death one month after his appointment.

Bibliography: H. Lamar Crosby, ed., *Thomas of Bradwardine: His Tractatus de Proportionibus: Its Significance for the Development of Mathematical Physics*, 1961; Gordon Leff, *Bradwardine and the Pelagians*, 1957.

Alan S. Weber

Bramante, Donato d'Agnolo Lazzari (1444–1514), generally known as Bramante, was the outstanding architect of the High Renaissance. Born near Urbino, where he is said to have had his early training as an artist in the *Duke Federigo Montefeltro of Urbino's palace, he began as a painter and painted the *Philosophers* (1447) at the Palazzo del Podestà, possibly under the influence of Melozzo da Forlì. He also painted the *Men at Arms* and *Christ at the Column* (1480–85), both now in the Brerai in Milan. He began to work as an architect in Milan, where he quickly established his reputation. His cloisters at the Monastery of S. Ambrogio show his concern for architecture based on Roman forms, as do his constructions of the arm he added to S. Maria delle Grazie (1492–97) and the small choir at S. Maria presso S. Satiro. In the latter he used his knowledge of perspective to create an illusion of depth in the choir, which was actually only a few feet long. Bramante left Milan in 1499 due to the French invasion and went to Rome to become the leading architect of his day. Like *Filippo Brunelleschi and *Leonardo da Vinci before him, he was attracted to the classical symmetry of the centrally planned church. He represented this ideal of a building in which each part is related to its neighbor and identical forms are repeated on a radial plan. His tiny chapel, S. Pietro in Montorio (1500–1502), called "Il Tempietto," in a Vatican courtyard is the foremost example of Bramante's ideals. It has acquired a reputation disproportionate to its size and is generally regarded as the most perfect monument of the High Renaissance. Built on the alleged site of St. Peter's crucifixion, it is based on a Roman round temple with a Tuscan peristyle on astylobate surmounted by a drum and dome within a balustrade. He did many works in Rome, including the cloister at Sta. Maria della Pace, the huge amphitheatre of the Belvedere in the Vatican, and the original plan for St. Peter's. From 1503 onwards, Bramante was engaged primarily on the latter two tasks. Pope Julius II made the bold decision to tear down the old St. Peter's, then 1,200 years old and in bad repair, and build a new edifice for the mother church of Christianity. Bramante was commissioned to create the design and produced a completely symmetrical plan on the Greek-cross model, laid out like Brunelleschi's Pazzi Chapel in Florence. A central dome was surrounded by symmetrical, subsidiary spaces. The first stone was laid in 1506, but little had been achieved when Bramante died in 1514, and the four large piers he designed to support the massive dome he envisioned proved inadequate. This concept had to be rebuilt by Michelangelo, who succeeded him as designer of St. Peter's and modified the plan, making it less angular and giving it an entrance facade and a less angular exterior. Carlo Maderno lengthened Michelangelo's facade into a nave, severely compromising the dome and converting the plan to a Latin cross, but Bramante's radiating plan around a dome was retained and is still seen at St. Peter's today.

Bibliography: George L. Hersey, *High Renaissance Art in St. Peter's and the Vatican*, 1993; H. W. Janson, *History of Art*, 3rd ed., 1986; Giorgio Vasari, *Lives of the Most Eminent Painters, Sculptors and Architects*, 1568/1976.

C. Thomas Ault

Brant, Sebastian (1457–1521). Often identified as one of the earliest German Christian humanists, Brant was a university teacher and a jurist who specialized in Roman civil and canon law. Brant, a conservative Catholic, was an active scholar who worked as an editor and translator of classical authors (especially Virgil), legal commentaries, and grammar texts. He was also a poet in his own right who wrote both in the vernacular and in Latin. In addition, Brant frequently served as a counselor to Emperor *Maximilian. Brant was a contemporary and acquaintance of the artist Albrecht Dürer and the poet-humanist Desiderius Erasmus. Hans Holbein the Elder and Albrecht Dürer both produced portraits of Brant.

Brant's best-known work, both to his contemporaries and to later generations, was *Das Narrenschiff* (The ship of fools). Written in Early New High German and composed in rhyming couplets of iambic dimeter, *Das Narrenschiff* is a long poem divided into 112 chapters. Each chapter ranges from 33 to over 200 lines and describes a different kind of fool. The chapters were usually accompanied by a corresponding woodcut in the original edition (published in 1494) and in early editions published before the sixteenth century. Brant embraced the technology of printing as a promising new way to disseminate didactic and satirical works. He hoped that classical didactic and satirical works or writings (such as *Das Narrenschiff*) modeled on classical styles would stimulate intellectual rigor and thus inspire renewed spiritual devotion in those who indulged in the worldly excesses and spiritual laxity of his day.

Sebastian Brant was born in Strassburg in 1457, the oldest of three boys born to Diebold and Barbara Brant. Diebold Brant, an innkeeper, died suddenly when Sebastian was ten years old. Barbara Brant kept the family together and managed to provide tutors for Brant. He matriculated at the University of Basel in 1475, where he was licensed to teach and practice law in 1484. Shortly thereafter he married Elisabeth Burg. They settled in Basel until 1501, when Brant began his productive career. He was a popular teacher and prolific scholar. After obtaining his advanced degree, Brant edited several works, including Augustine's *City of God* and a Vulgate Bible. He produced commentaries on canon and civil law and wrote his first law text during this period, *Expositiones sive declarationes*, which gained wide circulation. Brant acted as a legal advisor in local matters as well, and in 1499 he edited the decretals of the Basel church council. His Basel writings were rounded out by religious works, devotional writings, hymns, and poems to the Virgin. Brant gained Maximilian's attention when he wrote poems that praised the emperor, but he also sought to inspire Maximilian to stronger leadership over the German Empire.

While Brant was working in Basel, he wanted to reach a wider audience and began writing in German in addition to Latin. To this end, he began working with the printer Bergmann von Olpe in Basel, and they collaborated on many projects, including the first edition of *Das Narrenschiff*. Brant quickly became a literary advisor to other printers in Basel. The influence of *Das Narrenschiff* can be seen in Brant's composition of several German broadsides. It is interesting that one of the inspirations of these broadsides was Brant's extensive use of illustration. These pamphlets were often accompanied by woodcuts, probably added with Brant's suggestions on content, layout, and design. Brant took an active interest in the visual layout and presentation of *Das Narrenschiff*. Many artists furnished woodcuts for it; among these are substantial contributions from Dürer.

Das Narrenschiff was an immediate best-seller both locally and abroad. Six additional editions were produced in Brant's lifetime alone and with his active participation in revisions. Unauthorized versions quickly appeared, and a "protestation" against these imitations was inserted into subsequent authorized editions. *Das Narrenschiff* was published in several languages from 1507 on, including Latin, Low German, and French. A Flemish edition (1500) and an English adaptation (1508, *Barclay's Shyp of Folys*) followed. A satirical adaptation, *Cocke Lorelles Bote* (extant now only in a 414-line fragment), appeared in England around 1510. Brant's work proved to be particularly popular and long-lived in England. The themes and characters treated in *Das Narrenschiff* were adapted by several English authors through the seventeenth century, including John Skelton's *Boke of Three Fooles*, Robert Copland's *Hye Way to the Spyttle House* and *Twenty-Five Orders of Fools*, and Thomas Dekker's *Gul's Hornbooke*.

After Maximilan lost Basel to the Swiss Confederation, Brant returned to his hometown of Strassburg in 1501 and accepted a civil post as a legal advisor. He also continued work with a local printing house (Grüninger) and edited versions of Virgil, Terence's comedies, and several religious and legal works. Brant's professional responsibilities increased with his new post, and he was soon promoted to municipal secretary. Brant was summoned on at least two more occasions to give advice to the emperor. Brant's legal influence grew in the religious sphere in these later years of his career. He served as censor and as a mediator in a dispute over the Immaculate Conception.

As a defender of the Roman church as well as a humanist, Brant found himself in a difficult position late in life. He objected to a younger generation of humanist scholars who held different ideas about the nature of spiritual freedom, and who promoted the study of classical works for its own sake. For Brant, education was not an end in itself, but the preparation for a life of service. He saw his active role in the civic community as a means of strengthening and defending the Catholic faith both in the local community and abroad in the German Empire. As devoted as Brant was to teaching and scholarship, education for him was a path to spiritual wisdom, and Brant strove to make his life an example of his humanist ideals.

Bibliography: Sebastian Brant, *The Ship of Fools by Sebastian Brant*, trans. Edwin H. Zeydel, 1962; John Van Cleve, *Sebastian Brant's The Ship of Fools in Critical Perspective, 1800–1991*, 1993; Edwin H. Zeydel, *Sebastian Brant*, 1967.

Donna Bussell

Bridget of Sweden, Saint (c. 1303–73), (in Swedish, Birgitta), was a visionary, the foundress of an order, and an outspoken critic of prelates and princes. Known for her repeated calls for the return of the papacy to Rome after its long sojourn in Avignon, her fearless denunciations of immoral kings and bishops, and her frequent visions, Bridget was an important figure in fourteenth-century religious life.

Bridget was born around 1303 at Finstad. She was the daughter of Birger, governor or "lagman" (lawman) of Upland. Her devotion to the Virgin Mary and Jesus was manifest early. At age seven she had a vision in which the Virgin crowned her, and a few years later she experienced a vision of Christ after hearing a sermon on the Passion. She dutifully married Ulf Gudmarsson, the lagman of Nrke, in 1316 and bore eight children, one of whom was St. Katherine (or Karin) of Sweden.

Bridget entered the arena of Swedish political life when she became a lady-in-waiting to the twelve-year-old Blanche of Namur, wife of King Magnus II, in 1335. Finding the king and his court insufficiently devout, Bridget began her career as a critic and advocate of reform. Her religious vocation intensified at the Cistercian abbey of Alvastra after Ulf's death in 1344. Bridget remained a guest of the monks for four years and, experiencing visions with increased frequency, she was overwhelmed when at one point Christ named her his bride.

Bridget's political activities continued in tandem with her new life as a religious woman. She once criticized King Magnus for unjust taxation, offering to ransom her own sons to raise the necessary revenue. She experienced visions about the political life of Sweden and about the private lives of political and religious figures and, much to their annoyance, proclaimed many of these visions openly. She also intervened in international affairs, urging Pope *Clement VI to negotiate peace between the kings of England and France, who were engaged in the hostilities now known as the Hundred Years' War.

In 1346 Bridget convinced King Magnus to endow a monastery at Vadstena, where she intended to found an order in honor of the Holy Savior for sixty nuns and a brother house of thirteen priests (representing the twelve Apostles and St. Paul), four deacons (representing the Doctors of the Church), and eight lay brothers. The abbess was to represent the Virgin Mary, to whom Bridget had a particular devotion. Bridget's vision known as the *Sermo angelicus* served as the basis for the daily office of the order. Bridget left Sweden before construction of the monastery was completed, but her daughter Katherine returned after Bridget's death to establish the order and become its first abbess. The order and its rule, considered by many Bridget's most important contribution to medieval religious life, spread quickly after it was approved by Pope Urban V in 1370.

Bridget traveled to Rome in 1350 accompanied by her confessors, one the prior of the Cistercian monastery of Alvastra, named Peter Olavsson, and the other a theologian from Skänninge. She lived in the austere manner appropriate to a late medieval holy woman, dressing poorly, confessing frequently, and subjecting herself to penance. She founded a hospice for Swedish students and pilgrims, and she cared for the sick and the poor. She remained a fearless critic of religious and political leaders, believing herself to be God's chosen instrument of reform.

Her most prolonged, and perhaps least successful, endeavor was to persuade the Avignonese popes Clement VI and Urban V to return to Rome. Her letters to Pope Clement VI were ineffectual, and although Urban returned to Rome in 1367, he left again just three years later. Bridget followed as far as Montefiascone, where she predicted dire consequences if he returned to Avignon. In the audience was Cardinal Pierre Roger de Beaufort, the future Pope Gregory XI, who returned the papacy to Rome in 1376, largely at the urging of *Catherine of Siena.

Bridget traveled to the Holy Land in 1373. The vision that she had at the Nativity Grotto, in which Mary showed her the moment of Christ's birth, had a radical and lasting effect on the iconography of the Nativity. Bridget saw the birth as a sudden appearance of the Christ child on the ground in front of the Virgin, surrounded by light that outshone Joseph's candle.

Bridget sometimes wrote down her visions in Swedish and sometimes dictated them to her two spiritual advisors. They translated the texts into Latin, which Bridget checked diligently against the original. The visions were later compiled by Alphonsus of Pecha, former bishop of Jaen, who was Bridget's closest advisor in her last years. Bridget's *Revelations* range from the early visions she experienced in Sweden (books 1 and 2) to the long theological vision in the "Book of Questions" (book 5), the visions concerning the life of Mary and Christ experienced in Jerusalem (book 7), and the topical visions addressed to political figures (book 8). Additional visions not included in the *Revelations* were collected later and are known as the *Extravagantes*.

Bridget's writings were the subject of some controversy in the late Middle Ages. Prominent among her critics was *Jean Gerson, the chancellor of the University of Paris, who was skeptical of the growing authority accorded women visionaries. Her visions were formally questioned in 1433 at the Council of Basel; her writings were examined by Cardinal *Juan de Torquemada, who found them doctrinally sound.

Bridget died on 23 July 1373 at Rome, and her body was brought to Vadstena in 1374. A campaign for her canonization, spearheaded by her confessors and by her daughter Katherine, was eventually successful. She was canonized by Boniface IX on 7 October 1391, and her canonization was reconfirmed, despite the politics of the Great Schism, in 1414 and again in 1419.

Bibliography: Birgitta of Sweden, *Life and Selected Revelations*, trans. Albert Kezel, 1990; James Hogg, ed., *Studies in St. Birgitta and the Brigittine Order*, 1993; Barbara Obrist, "The Swedish Visionary: Saint Bridget," in *Medieval Women Writers*, ed. Katharina Wilson, 1984.

Catherine Sanok

Broederlam, Melchior (fl. 1378–99), was a Flemish painter who entered the employ of *Philip the Bold in 1378 as valet de chambre. Prior to Broederlam's appointment in the duke's household, he worked for his father-in-law, Louis de Male. He worked at Ypres and at the duke's castle at Hesdin, where his work included the designing and painting of banners, furniture, and flooring tiles. Little is known about his life, and there is only one known work by him, the painted wings of the *Retable de Champmol*, including the *Adoration of the Magi, Crucifixion*, and *Entombment*, in the Musée de la Ville, Dijon. The central panel was carved and gilded by Jacques de Baerze. Broederlam's painted scenes, the *Annunciation and Visitation* and the *Presentation and Flight into Egypt* from the *Infancy Cycles*, serve as an introduction to the Passion scenes of the carved central panel. The details of the landscape settings and building interiors and the handling of the figures in the two panels indicate an early blending of elements of the Flemish and Italian styles. The artist's juxtaposition of Romanesque and Gothic architectural elements, indicating the Old and New Testament traditions, the *hortus conclusus* (enclosed garden) with its flowers referring to the chastity of the Virgin, the presence of the Trinity, and incidents from the apocryphal Gospels of Pseudo-Matthew all permit the viewer a glimpse into the arena of the new fifteenth-century Flemish painting. Here, "disguised symbolism" (the presentation of spiritual ideas clothed in everyday objects and figures) combined with a long-established tradition for presenting these scenes to mark what would come. The depth of the landscape and its mountains indicate that Broederlam had access to the style of the Italo-Byzantine and Sienese artists of the south. He coupled their style with the naturalism of his own Flemish training. The maternal concern of the Virgin expressed toward the Christ child in the *Flight into Egypt* also shows the sense of naturalism significant in the work of the Flemish artists. Broederlam here produced an early example of the intermingling of the divine and the secular that would become a hallmark of Flemish fifteenth-century art.

Bibliography: E. Panofsky, *Early Netherlandish Painting*, 1971.

Marian Hollinger

Brunelleschi, Filippo (1377–1446), was a pioneer of early Renaissance architecture. He is most famous for applying scientific laws of perspective and for designing the dome, Il Duomo, on the Florentine Cathedral of Santa Maria della Fiore. He spent the bulk of his career in Florence, where, in addition to the cathedral's dome, he designed the Ospedale degli Innocenti, the sacristy and basilica of San Lorenzo, the Pazzi Chapel, and the Church of Santo Spirito.

Filippo Brunelleschi was born in 1377 in Florence, Italy. He was the second of three sons born to Ser Brunellesco di Lippo Lapi, who was a notary of some distinction. Brunelleschi's father had intended him to become a notary, but when his son demonstrated talents for mechanics, he placed the young Brunelleschi in the goldsmith's guild. Brunelleschi quickly became a skilled goldsmith and sculptor and in 1401 entered a competition to design the bronze reliefs for the doors of the baptistery of Florence. His entry depicted the scene from *The Sacrifice of Isaac* when the angel intervened to save the boy. Brunelleschi's relief was brilliantly original and naturalistic and represents the high point of his career as a sculptor. He lost the competition, however, to *Lorenzo Ghiberti, an accomplished painter and sculptor. In disgust, Brunelleschi gave up sculpture and turned his talents instead to architecture. He set out with *Donatello, perhaps the greatest sculptor of the quattrocento, for Rome to study the older classical style of architecture and sculpture, hoping to rediscover their proportions.

In 1407 Brunelleschi returned to Florence and soon thereafter (c. 1410) developed the principles of linear perspective, applying them to both painting and architecture. These principles had been known to the ancient Greeks and Romans, but had been forgotten during the Middle Ages in Europe. It is clear that Brunelleschi understood the principle of a single vanishing point, toward which all parallel lines on a plane appear to converge, and the relationship between distance and the diminution of objects. These principles enabled Renaissance artists to produce realistic works that represented three-dimensional space on two-dimensional surfaces.

In 1418 Brunelleschi once again competed against Ghiberti, this time to design the machines and technical devices for the construction of the Florence cathedral dome. The dome had been designed in the late Gothic period as an eight-sided vault without exterior buttresses. Brunelleschi's model demonstrated how, by using new machines and techniques, the dome could be constructed without the traditional wooden scaffolding, which accounted for much of the expense. His model was declared the winner in 1420, and he was named chief architect for the project. Work began in 1420 but was not completed until 1436, the same year in which Brunelleschi's design for the lantern that crowns the dome was approved.

Brunelleschi began his first major architectural commission in 1419, the Ospedale degli Innocenti. This building combined traditional Gothic and Romanesque architecture with many novel features. Brunelleschi introduced formal principles from classical art and architecture that offered a marked contrast to the medieval architecture mostly found in Florence. The most important of his innovations was the use of geometric proportions, symmetrical planning, and classical details; Brunelleschi's science of measure and proportion dominates the simplicity of the design. By the early 1420s Brunelleschi was the most prominent architect in Florence and attracted the attention and patronage of the Medici, Florence's most powerful family. Brunelleschi was commissioned to design both the sacristy, known as the Old Sacristy to distinguish it from Michelangelo's later one, and the basilica of San Lorenzo. Work began in 1421, and the sacristy was complete in 1428. Here again Brunelleschi employed a simple system of proportions and symmetry. Work on the basilica halted in 1428, resumed in 1441, and was completed in the 1460s. The conventional layout of the basilica stemmed from the control the Medici family exerted on the final plans. To this layout Brunelleschi added his own interpretation of classical designs for capitals, friezes, pilasters, columns, and a strict regularity and symmetry. Separate parts of the basilica corresponded to each other and represented mathematical relations that created a profound visual harmony.

Brunelleschi was commissioned by the powerful Pazzi family in 1429 to design a chapel. The plan of this chapel represented an amplification of the principles he had used for the sacristy of San Lorenzo. The central square, covered by a hemispherical dome, was extended on either side to form a rectangle, and to a third side of the central square was attached a square apse that contained the altar. The walls of the chapel were decorated with geometric patterns of dark gray stone.

Brunelleschi welcomed the opportunity to design the new Church of Santo Spirito in the 1430s. Santo Spirito, patronized by multiple Florentine families, allowed Brunelleschi freedom he had not enjoyed previously. With this structure he swept away all remnants of medieval architecture, complex vaulting systems, compound piers, and radiating chapels. He wanted to return to the simple three-aisled design of early Christian churches that he had studied in Rome. The entire structure and in particular the interior conformed to Brunelleschi's strict principles of proportion. To emphasize this proportionality and the relationships between parts of the structure, Brunelleschi devised a system of gray and white stone to decorate the interior of the church. Brunelleschi died in 1446, before Santo Spirito was completed in 1470.

Brunelleschi's influence was most strongly felt in his architecture, through his revival of the classical style and the restrained, simple elegance that became expressive of Renaissance taste. His achievements also included his advances in perspective and in engineering, often developed to support his architectural work.

Bibliography: Eugenio Battisti, *Filippo Brunelleschi: The Complete Work*, 1981; Antonio Manetti, *The Life of Brunelleschi*, ed. Howard Saalman, 1970; Frank D. Prager and Gustina Scaglia, *Brunelleschi: Studies of His Technology and Inventions*, 1970.

Darin Hayton

Bruni, Leonardo (1370–1444), was the most illustrious humanistic scholar of the first half of the Italian quattrocento. Although he engaged in a wide range of intellectual endeavors, his enduring fame and greatest scholastic reputation rest upon his Greek scholarship and its resulting influence upon the art of translation, his work in historiography, and his deep belief in what is often referred to as "civic humanism."

Bruni's memoirs, *Rerum suo tempore gestarum commentarius*, composed toward the end of his life, supply most of what is known about Bruni's youth. He was born in 1370 to a Guelf family of Arezzo, where his father was a grain merchant. In 1384 both Bruni and his father were seized and imprisoned by exiled Ghibellines who occupied Arezzo with the support of a French army.

Bruni tells us in his memoirs that the picture of *Francisco Petrarch in his prison room inflamed him with a passion for his studies. A year later the French sold the city to the Florentines, whom Bruni appears to have viewed as liberators.

Bruni's father died in 1386 and his mother in 1388. When he completed his Latin schooling at Arezzo, his closest familial ties gone, Bruni moved to Florence to attend university, where he was accepted under the personal mentorship of the chancellor, *Coluccio Salutati. In 1398, after spending two years in the school of liberal arts and four studying law, Bruni began to study Greek under the tutelage of *Manuel Chrysoloras, a Greek expatriate who offered lessons in his home to a number of students. Bruni was a most outstanding student when, in 1400, Chrysoloras was forced to leave Florence. During this period of intensive study, Bruni produced, among other things, his translations of Xenophons' *On Tyranny* and St. Basil's treatise on the value of Greek studies in education. His own *Laudatio* (1403/4), composed a few years after Chrysoloras's removal from Florence, was the first humanistic work to use a Greek model for a contemporary work, the *Panathenaicus* of Aelius Aristides.

Bruni began his papal service in 1405 when he accepted a lucrative position in the Curia of the Roman pope Innocent VII. He remained in almost continual papal employment for the next ten years. During this period he composed, among other things, the second part of his second dialogue, in which his principal character attacked the modern Florentine writers *Francesco Petrarch, *Dante, and *Giovanni Boccaccio as inferior to the ancients. In 1409 he left the Roman pope Gregory XII for Alexander V, the pope elected by the dissident cardinals of Rome and Avignon at Pisa. He remained with Alexander's successor John XXIII until 1414, when the Council of Constance deposed all three schismatic popes, at which time Bruni returned to Florence. He had married a Florentine woman in 1412 and became a Florentine citizen in 1416.

These years after his papal service proved to be some of Bruni's most prolific academically. After his return to Florence in 1415, he composed his life of Cicero. This landmark work of historical biography did not, like former biographies of Cicero, base itself upon Plutarch's *Lives*; rather, it presented a fresh assessment using many of the historical methods used today. In these first years after his return to Florence Bruni also composed the first book of his *History of the Florentine People*. The next five books were published over a span of years between 1419, when the second book came out, and 1429, when the sixth was published. During these years he also composed his translation of Aristotle's *Nichomachean Ethics* (1417), his introduction to humanist moral philosophy (*Isagoge to Moral Philosophy*, 1425), and *On the Study of Literature* (1424), which presented his model for the humanistic educational ideal.

In the years after 1427, during which he served as chancellor of the Republic of Florence, he also produced a number of important works. His *Oration for the Funeral of Nanni Strozzi* is considered the fullest expression of republicanism produced by the Italian quattrocento. In it he opined that the political freedom of Florence encouraged literary and artistic talent. During this period he also wrote his lives of Dante and Petrarch. Dante in particular he represented as a political figure, a citizen-poet. He also concentrated on his Greek studies, completing his translation of Aristotle's *Politics*, the final book of his Aristotelian trilogy that included *Ethics* and *Economics*, between 1418 and 1421. The last six books of his Florentine history were completed after 1427, as was his *Commentarius* upon his own life, mentioned earlier. Bruni died, still chancellor of his beloved Florence, in 1444.

Bruni's enduring reputation rests upon three major achievements: his influence upon the art of translation, his revolutionary approach to historiography, and his concept of what has come to be called "civic humanism." Although more modern translations and works have generally superseded Bruni's own writings, these new works largely are based upon Bruni's innovations.

When Bruni began his translating work, translations were generally word-for-word renderings of texts from Greek into Latin. Bruni rejected this mode of translation, which resulted, he claimed, in Greek prose written in Latin. Instead, Bruni translated *ad sententiam*, or according to the sense of the original work. He maintained that the sense of the Greek word should not only be rendered in Latin words, but in the stylistic manner of Cicero, in good classical Latin. This method not only required en excellent understanding of Latin prose form, for which Bruni is justly famous, but also a more profound understanding of Greek authors, their lives and prejudices, and their works than ever before.

Bruni's innovations in the field of historiography also relied on a personal understanding of the period and assessment of the events from a historical perspective. Rather than reproducing or rewriting earlier histories, Bruni searched for sources and sought the underlying causes of events. He tried to see events in a larger historical perspective and used critical judgment to evaluate the information at his disposal. Through this approach he became the first modern historian, introducing methods that form the basis for modern historical procedure. His *History of the Florentine People* is the landmark work of this type, for it explored the history of Florence with an emphasis on the democratic government as a force to nurture the pinnacle of human endeavor. His biographical efforts displayed this philosophy as well, grounded as they were in his careful research of available materials and assessing lives on the basis of his own evaluation of achievement.

Bruni, like Cicero, was a man who united scholastic endeavor with civic service. Bruni not only lived the *vita activa*, he argued for the importance, the crucial value, of the life marked by civic service as the culmination of the values learned by humanistic study. These values, as expressed by Bruni, marked a focus for the man of letters in the Italian quattrocento, even though a generation later they had largely faded from prominence and the *vita activa* had largely given way to the prominence of the contemplative life of the scholar.

Bibliography: Hans Baron, *From Petrarch to Leonardo Bruni: Studies in Humanistic and Political Literature*, 1968; Leonardo Bruni, *The Humanism of Leonardo Bruni: Selected Texts*, trans. Gordon Griffiths, James Hankins, and David Thompson, vol. 46 in

Medieval and Renaissance Texts and Studies, vol. 46, 1987; Benjamin G. Kohl, Ronald G. Witt, and Elizabeth B. Welles, eds., *The Earthly Republic: Italian Humanists on Government and Society*, 1978.

Laura McRae

Buridan, Jean (1295–1358), was a central figure in fourteenth-century natural philosophy and logic who dominated studies at the University of Paris long after his death. The period of his intellectual influence until the time of Galileo can truly be called the "age of Buridan." Buridan was one of the few Scholastic philosophers who retained his prominence into the seventeenth century. He is associated with the intellectual school of nominalism.

Buridan was born in Béthune, France, sometime before 1300. He became a master at the University of Paris in the 1320s but does not seem to have advanced to a degree in theology. He is recorded as rector of the university in 1328 and 1340 and last appeared in a document dated 1358.

Several legends about Buridan's thought and life have arisen. First, he is known today for the logical problem of "Buridan's ass," which, however, has not surfaced in any of his surviving writings. In this problem, an ass starves to death because it is unable to decide between two equal bales of hay. The question is, how does one make a rational, logical choice between two completely equivalent options? One solution involves the paradox that a random selection of either option would be a rational choice. Rationality, however, has been traditionally connected to intent, purpose, and measurement, in fact, everything that is the antithesis of randomness, and so the dilemma of Buridan's ass. In the second legend, *François Villon alleged that Buridan was thrown into the Seine in a sack because of an affair with the wife of Philip V of France.

Buridan made substantial contributions to logic, publishing his nine books of the *Summulae logicae*, which were inspired by Peter of Spain's standard work on logic. He also wrote the *Consequentiae* and *Sophismata*, exploring true-false statements, among other topics. Buridan investigated such questions as the liar paradox, a self-reference paradox (the statement "What I am now saying is false" appears logically only to be true if it is false). Buridan also produced important commentaries on Aristotle's physical and logical treatises, including *On Generation and Corruption, On the Soul, On Interpretation, Rhetoric, Categories, Prior Analytics*, and *Posterior Analytics*.

Buridan's influence on the methodology of early modern science was considerable, since he broke natural philosophy's dependence on theology. Nicholas d'Autrecourt had raised the question of the uncertainty of studying natural phenomena without consideration for metaphysical or theological laws because one could never know if an event were natural or caused by the intervention of God's will (i.e., supernaturally). Buridan rejected this objection, stating that hypothetical or conditional knowledge was sufficient for science. After Buridan, no longer would scientific knowledge be grounded solely in theology or Aristotelian metaphysics.

Buridan is best known among historians of science for the development of the impetus theory, a critique of the Aristotelian conception of motion. Aristotle believed that what kept projectiles in motion was the propulsion of the air. Franciscus de Marchia had earlier advanced a theory of a self-exhausting *virtus impressa* (impressed virtue) of an object. Buridan further extended this theory to his concept of impetus (*vis motiva*), a permanent motive force only diminished by the weight of the object and the resistance of the medium, an idea similar to the later concept of inertia. The power of impetus was proportional in Buridan's theory to an object's speed and mass. Buridan's impetus theory was communicated to Galileo through his teacher Buonamici. From 1474 to 1481, books with nominalist tendencies, including Buridan's works, were banned in France, but interest in Buridan's writings on logic and ethics continued into the seventeenth century, particularly in England.

Bibliography: Marshall Clagett, *The Science of Mechanics in the Middle Ages*, 1961.

Alan S. Weber

C

Cade, Jack (d. 1450), alias Mortimer, alias Amendalle, alias Aylemere, was the shadowy leader of the largest camp of rebels who rose in 1450 throughout the south and east of England. Cade's origins are lost in obscurity, though he may have been an artisan or merchant from Kent with ties to international trade. The government suspected that Cade was linked to the Mortimer faction, and therefore to the duke of York, because he may have been a smallholder on the Mortimer lands in Ireland. Other contemporary legends held that Cade was a necromancer in the service of Sir Thomas Dacre, a relative of the powerful northern lord; still others thought him a partisan of the French, while yet another story held Cade to be a physician. Despite his dubious past, Cade managed to rise rapidly to a position of prominence in the troubles of 1450, perhaps analogous to that of *Wat Tyler in 1381.

The troubles began around May 1450 when the duke of Suffolk was captured and brutally murdered by pirates off the southern coast of England, who cast his body on a Kentish beach. Suffolk, head of a faction influential with the weak *Henry VI, was much hated not only by rival aristocrats but also by the commonality. Soon rumors spread through Kent that the king intended to return the county to wild forest out of misguided vengeance. These fears were compounded by economic turmoil and the increasingly obvious military failures in France, with the attendant threat of enemy raids, which served in turn to heighten frustration at governmental corruption and weakness.

Around Whitsuntide 1450 rebellion broke out at the Rochester market and quickly spread throughout the county. By early June rebel camps gathered at meeting places and elected Jack Cade as their chief captain. On 8 June Cade failed to take Canterbury, but four days later the main rebel army had encamped at Blackheath, just south of London, at which point the gathering had probably been reinforced from Surrey and Sussex. On 15 June the king's delegation received Cade's terms, which demanded that Henry break with the Suffolk faction in favor of the duke of York. The rebels withdrew southward, but the royal forces sent in pursuit of them only succeeded in terrorizing the countryside and emboldening the rebels. By 25 June the king had abandoned London for Warwickshire as new risings were reported throughout the south. By 1 July the rebels had returned to plunder Southwark. When Cade broke through London's defenses a few days later, the rebel groups lost all discipline. Popular villains suffered execution even as prominent Londoners suffered pillage and looting. On 5 July the embittered city reorganized and fought back, ejecting the rebels across the Thames and disarming them with an offer of free pardon. Losing control of his army, Cade fled to Kent to seek reinforcements and a defensible position, but his bands dissolved with royal forces in pursuit. On 12 July Cade was captured but died of wounds before he could be brought to trial.

While Cade's rebellion shares many attributes with Wat Tyler's rising of 1381, it is clear that national and regional politics rather than social grievances served as the fundamental pretexts. Facing military disaster, politically conscious Englishmen cast about for scapegoats and settled on the corrupt and factious duke of Suffolk, an arrangement that inevitably led to questions concerning the king's worthiness and ability to rule. As such, Cade's rebellion might rightfully be seen as a prelude to the Wars of the Roses.

Bibliography: R. A. Griffiths, *The Reign of King Henry VI: The Exercise of Royal Authority, 1422–1461*, 1981; I.M.W. Harvey, *Jack Cade's Rebellion of 1450*, 1991.

James C. Owens

Campin, Robert (c. 1378–1444), was a painter of Tournai. Many scholars identify Campin as the Master of Flemalle, teacher of *Rogier van der Weyden and Jacques Daret, although there is still debate about this conflation of the artists. Documents of 1406 for Tournai named Campin as a master painter. By 1408 he owned a house there and became a citizen of the town in 1410. In 1423 there was a revolt of Tournai's guildsmen against the city's patriciate. From this event, Campin emerged as dean of the painters' guild and a member of one of the three city councils created by the new political order. In 1428, with the overthrow of this order, Campin retired from civic life. Despite two legal conflicts—one for "un-Tournaisian activities," the other for moral turpitude—Campin's workshop remained popular. The work of this artist is regarded as the initial phase of the development of fifteenth-century Flemish panel painting. Although early scholars of Netherlandish painting sought to arrange a strict chronology and relationship among their native painters, which are now known to be more complex than first thought, the works of Campin still must be considered antecedents for much of the rest of the century.

The debate concerning his identification with the Master of Flemalle aside, Campin's work does seem to foreshadow many of the subjects, compositional arrangements, and iconographical details that marked fifteenth-century Flemish painting. He was an early practitioner of the oil technique that was then rendering tempera techniques obsolete. Arguably, he was one of the earliest artists to incorporate "disguised symbolism" within his panels. Erwin Panofsky wrote at length about this idea: the notion, expressed by St. Thomas Aquinas, that physical objects are "corporal metaphors of things spiritual." In terms of the paintings, this meant that the middle-class Flemish interior, with all its minutiae of daily life, had hidden beneath its skin symbols of the Mariological and Christological traditions. Despite some contemporary scholars' arguments to the contrary, there is still much in these works that seems to be explained only by such an interpretation. The paintings continued, in some instances, compositional and symbolic themes found in manuscript illustration, but they expanded them. The combination of traditional subject matter and a greater use of naturalism in setting and gesture created a new sense of the contemplative aspect of the panels and, at the same time, drew the minds of the viewers into the central activity of the figures. Each work (many are triptychs or surviving panels from triptychs) became a small stage upon which the scriptural or hagiographical event was enacted, ever new, for the beholder. Among Campin's works are the *Entombment Triptych* now in London, the *Merode Altarpiece* in New York, the *Salting Madonna* in London, and the *Nativity* in Dijon.

Bibliography: E. Panofsky, *Early Netherlandish Painting*, 1971; P. H. Schabaker, "Notes on the Biography of Robert Campin," *Mededelingen van de Koninklijke Akademie voor Wetenschappen* 41, no. 2 (1980).

Marian Hollinger

Capistrano, John. *See* John Capistrano, Saint.

Casale, Ubertino da. *See* Ubertino da Casale.

Castagno, Andrea del (1419?–57), was born Andrea (or Andreino) di Bartolo di Bargilla. While he was praised by his contemporaries for his skill, especially in draftsmanship, this early Florentine painter has only relatively recently received the attention he deserves for his powerful, realistic frescos and tempera paintings of both secular and religious subjects. Except for a brief period in Venice in 1442, Castagno painted in Florence from the time he was "discovered" by Bernardetto de Medici as a young man. While his artistic training and education are disputed, his work was undoubtedly influenced by the graceful sculpture of *Donatello and the emotional intensity of *Masaccio's painting, especially evident in such pieces as his *Last Supper* and his series of *Famous Men and Women*.

Little is known of Andrea del Castagno's birth and early childhood; his birth date of 1419 has been determined by what is known about his adult life and is disputed. What is known from tax ledgers and other documents is that while he was still a young child, Castagno and his family fled his natal village to the nearby town of Corella to escape the ravages of a war between Florence and Milan that began in 1423 and was to last ten years. These documents also show that they returned to Castagno, and one can assume that the boy spent the remainder of his youth there.

Giorgio Vasari's damning account of Castagno in his treatise *Le vite del più eccellenti pittori, scultori, e architetti* (*Lives of the Most Eminent Painters, Sculptors, and Architects*), largely fictitious as a biography but valuable as a catalog of his works, was written approximately a century after the artist's death and is crucial to understanding the change in attitudes toward this otherwise-talented painter. According to Vasari, the orphaned Castagno, working as a shepherd, came upon a country painter at work and began drawing figures of animals on the wall of the tabernacle. Upon hearing of this child prodigy, the Florentine nobleman Bernardetto de Medici took the boy to Florence, where he was trained by a famous master whose name Vasari did not tell us. Castagno's fame and skill grew, but Vasari claimed that he was a vile and jealous man who betrayed and murdered a fellow painter, *Domenico Veneziano. Much of what Vasari wrote has been disproved. Castagno, never orphaned, was cleared of the murder charge when it was discovered in the late nineteenth century that he died four years before Veneziano, and the tale of the boy scratching out animals on rocks is a topos from classical antiquity that should be considered on the same level as a myth. Vasari's slander, in combination with changing tastes in art that turned away from the strong colors and realism that were essential characteristics of his work, all but removed Castagno's name from the lists of great Florentine quattrocento painters.

Castagno's artistic education has inspired lively debates and remains a mystery, but such eminent names as *Paolo Uccello and *Fra Filippo Lippi have been posited as the master who instructed Castagno, especially for their expertise in frescoes that was passed on to this talented pupil. Castagno's earliest known work of major importance was a fresco he was commissioned to paint on the facade of the Bargello in 1440, whose subject was the punishment of a group of rebels against the Florentine state and for which he earned the nickname "degli Impiccati" (of the hanged men). It has been speculated that the violence of this work, in addition to the realism, the use of strong, vivid colors, and the bold, sculptural quality of his figures, went far to establish Castagno's unfounded reputation as a brutal man. He died of the plague in Florence on 19 August 1457 after a brief but influential career, the results of which endure to this day as brilliant examples of Florentine Renaissance painting.

While sixteen extant works are attributed to Andrea del Castagno, only thirteen are generally accepted as being by his hand; many others attributed to him by Vasari and accounts of commissions have been lost. His remaining religious frescoes are characterized by his trademark realism, color, and solid figures. The celebrated *Last Supper*, considered by many to be his best work, exemplifies the sober emotional intensity that Castagno achieved with this powerful combination. The solemnity of his religious works is also seen in those of secular content, with the personages expressing heroic and contemplative moods that complement the severity of Castagno's style. Some of these, of a more civic nature, are among his most famous, such as the cycle of *Famous Men and Women* now in the Uffizi and the portrait of the eminent Florentine condottiere, Pippo Spano. As popular tastes shift back toward an appreciation of the bold style that was characteristic of Castagno's painting and his reputation is restored, Andrea del Castagno is once again known as one of the innovative masters of early Renaissance art.

Bibliography: Marita Horster, *Andrea del Castagno*, 1980; John R. Spencer, *Andrea del Castagno and His Patrons*, 1991.

Wendy Marie Hoofnagle

Catherine of Siena, Saint (1347–80).

In concert with Pope Gregory XI, Catherine of Siena helped to end the Babylonian Captivity of the papacy, thereby unwittingly giving rise to the Great Schism. Born Catherine Benincasa in the Italian republic of Siena, she appears to have been obsessed with piety from a very early age. She is popularly believed to have received her first mystical vision at the age of six and experienced such visions on a regular basis thereafter. At fifteen Catherine declared her intention to remain a virgin and to become a Dominican nun. After overcoming her family's objections, Catherine began a life of ascetic discipline that would compromise her health, but that underscored her growing reputation as a holy mystic. She coupled her spiritual devotion with a fierce intelligence, abundant charm, and a discernible gift for understanding politics.

Her early years were filled with caring for the poor and sick, and she took up the causes of condemned prisoners; in one case, she converted a prisoner, accompanied him to the scaffold, and caught his head when it fell from the block. Such acts confirmed Catherine's holy reputation, drawing around her a group of friends and disciples who shared her work. Three major mystical experiences marked her life. In 1366 she had a vision of herself as married to Christ, followed by another in 1370 in which she claimed that her heart was taken by the Lord. Finally, in 1375 Catherine announced that she had received the stigmata of Christ while she was in a fit of ecstasy.

At the same time that her spiritual life was reaching its height, Catherine, around 1372, began to involve herself in the reformation of the debased church and attempted a resolution of the political chaos in the Italian peninsula. Catherine felt that a return of the papacy to Rome from its subject status in Avignon, France, would achieve the reformation she sought. To that end, she began to implore Pope Gregory XI to return to Rome once and for all. Gregory proved susceptible to her entreaties, but he was also swayed by French influences. In many ways, Catherine's career was evocative of that of St. Bridget of Sweden, a holy visionary who had also worked for the reform of the church and the pope's return to Rome. Gregory had ignored Bridget, but her last predictions persuaded him that he should be more receptive to Catherine's appeals. She continued to perform miracles, curing plague victims in Siena, though, curiously, several of her relatives died from it.

Catherine was soon drawn into the Italian revolt against the papacy, and regardless of her failure to persuade Gregory to return to Rome, she saw such incidents as attempts to turn the ordinary people away from the church. She admonished the pope to be strong and install spiritual leaders who would reform the church and implored him to raise the standard for a crusade to regain the Holy Land. Gregory resorted instead to excommunication and interdict, and Catherine begged Florence to submit to his authority, but the city refused. She began to believe that only a return of the papacy to Rome would bring peace to Italy, and she offered her services as an intermediary to Florence; though she suffered attacks on her credibility, Catherine persevered, and Gregory finally made the decision to return to Rome.

Once the pope's return had been accomplished, Catherine continued her work for reform of the church and the calling of a crusade, but spent most of her remaining years establishing a convent just outside of Siena and launched into apostolic work in the region. Her health, never very good, began to deteriorate, and Catherine felt that the time had come to set down her views on paper. The result was the *Dialogue*, published in 1378.

Despite her other obligations, Catherine got more involved in the political chaos in Florence, which had devolved into factionalism. The violence was such that Catherine almost achieved martyrdom in one incident. The death of Gregory and the election of a new pope, *Urban VI, brought peace to Florence, but broke down the fragile consensus that had kept the papacy intact. The new pope's zeal led the college of cardinals to depose him, thus beginning the Great Schism. Catherine supported Urban VI and traveled to Rome to champion his cause. The schism was devolving into war, and Urban used Catherine as his liaison; she lobbied Naples, stating that submission to Urban meant a defense of the church.

Her health buckled under the strain, complicated by depression over her failure to end the schism. It was a blow from which she never recovered, and by February 1380 it was clear that she was approaching her end. She began to have mystical visions of her spirit leaving her body, and after eight weeks of illness she died on 29 April 1380. Her subsequent canonization emerged from the miraculous cures that occurred between her death and her burial. Her body did not deteriorate in death, and the stigmata of which she had spoken appeared clearly. Her head was eventually brought to rest in Siena, and she was formally declared a saint by the Catholic church in 1461, a martyr to her spiritual and political causes.

Bibliography: Michael de la Bedoyere, *Catherine, Saint of Siena*, 1947; Mary Ann Fatula, *Catherine of Siena's Way*, 1987; Sigrid Undset, *Catherine of Siena*, 1954.

Connie Evans

Cauchon, Pierre (1371–1442). Bishop of Beauvais and Lisieux, Pierre Cauchon was an ecclesiastic with strong ties to the Anglo-Burgundian party in France. Cauchon is best known for his crucial role in the trial and execution of *Joan of Arc. Throughout his career, Cauchon's actions were motivated by his political convictions.

Pierre Cauchon was born near Rheims, France, in 1371. He studied theology and canon law at the University of Paris and was involved there in debates over the Great Schism. As did the English and the Burgundians, Cauchon supported the pope in Rome and opposed the Avignon pope. This marked the beginning of Cauchon's involvement in the conflict between the French Crown and the Anglo-Burgundian alliance. Cauchon was given several official opportunities to advance his cause, first by attending the Parlement of Paris as a representative of the university and then by traveling to Avignon to convince *Benedict XIII to give up his claim to the papacy. Throughout his career, Cauchon was associated closely with the University of Paris, not only because of his political views, but also by his official service in offices such as rector of the university, which he held as early as 1403, and conservator of university privileges, which he held in 1419. Furthermore, the university was the center of the development of the theory of the double monarchy, which the Anglo-Burgundians used to support the unification of the Crowns of France and England in the person of the English king.

From his time at the University of Paris, Cauchon consistently allied himself with the Burgundians. He championed their cause during the Cabochiens' riots in 1413. Cauchon, who had been trained as a canon lawyer, also collaborated in the drafting of the Ordonnance Cabochienne on 25 May 1413. The Ordonnance was intended to promote royal reforms, especially financial reforms. After the Armagnacs returned to Paris in 1414, Cauchon left Paris and entered into service under two successive dukes of Burgundy, John the Fearless and Philip the Good. He also acted as an ambassador during the Council of Constance and as a negotiator for the Treaty of Troyes. As rewards for his service, he was named provost of Lille, archdeacon of Chartres, and chaplain to the duke of Burgundy. His main reward was his appointment as bishop of Beauvais in 1420. Beginning in 1422, Cauchon served the English directly as a counselor to *Henry VI and a servant of John Plantagenet, the duke of Bedford and the king's regent in France. He helped to expand Anglo-Burgundian holdings in northern France throughout the 1420s, and in 1424 he accepted the surrender of Vitry for Henry VI. The conflict between the Anglo-Burgundians and the French throne resulted in Cauchon's being forced out of Rheims and Beauvais by *Charles VII in 1429.

Cauchon's most famous act on behalf of the Anglo-Burgundian alliance was his role in the capture and pursuit of Joan of Arc. After Joan was captured in Compiègne on 24 May 1430, Cauchon offered a substantial ransom, a reward for her capture, and a hefty pension to her captor, John of Luxembourg. Cauchon also produced a summons from the University of Paris requesting that Joan be delivered to it to be tried for heresy. Cauchon's motivations for pursuing Joan were tied both to his political views and to his concern for his career. The theory of the double monarchy would be vindicated if Joan were found to be a heretic and not an instrument of God, while the empty bishopric of Rouen could be a fitting reward for Cauchon's service on behalf of the English king. Cauchon devoted a great deal of time and effort to the negotiations for Joan, whom he delivered to Rouen on 21 November 1430. Cauchon was then named as Joan's chief judge, and a special commission of territory enabled him to preside over the trial, which was held outside his diocese. Henry VI's regents and the theological faculty at the University of Paris were responsible for setting up Joan's trial, and the assessors and the judges, Cauchon and Jean Lemaître, were closely allied with the Anglo-Burgundian cause. Throughout the trial of condemnation, Cauchon was careful to act according to official inquisitorial procedure. He apparently made every effort to get Joan to confess in order to avoid her execution. However, because of his central role in the proceedings and his commitment to the Anglo-Burgundian cause, Cauchon today bears the main responsibility for Joan's execution. Cauchon was rewarded with the See of Lisieux in 1432, and until his death he continued to serve the Anglo-Burgundian cause.

Bibliography: Régine Pernoud, *Joan of Arc by Herself and Her Witnesses*, 1966/1982; Marina Warner, *Joan of Arc: The Image of Female Heroism*, 1981.

Kristine Lynn Rabberman

Caxton, William (c. 1421–91), is best known for establishing the first printing press in England. His early careers as a trader, diplomat, and translator provided the skills and political connections he needed in order to learn the new printing trade and establish his own presses in Flanders and England.

We know very little about Caxton's early life, partly because Caxton was a popular surname in fifteenth-century England and partly because Caxton himself provides no helpful information in his own writings. From what is known of his early career, we can assume that he was born sometime between 1415 and 1422, possibly in Kent, and that his father was possibly a mercer, a dealer in textiles such as velvet and silks.

Around 1438 Caxton was apprenticed to Robert Large as a mercer. He lived in his master's home in the Old Jewry in London, along with several other apprentices, and while he was serving Large, he soon joined the Mercers' Company, an important trade guild. Upon Large's death in 1441 Caxton moved to Bruges, the capital of Flanders and seat of the Burgundian government there. Bruges was a center of culture, manufacturing, and trade where English wool was imported and woven into fine Flemish cloth. Caxton joined the Merchant Adventurers, an overseas trading company that had grown out of the Mercers' Company. Eventually he was appointed governor of the English Nation of Merchant Adventurers in Bruges, negotiating trade treaties and supervising textile quality control. In Bruges, he became acquainted with *Charles the Bold, duke of Burgundy, because he had become friends with Charles's wife *Margaret of York, the sister of England's King *Edward IV. In 1469 the duchess hired him to procure and translate books, beginning with the *Recueil des histoires de Troyes*. There is some evidence that Caxton had traded in manuscripts in addition to textiles during his career as a mercer, and this experience would have suited him particularly well to assist the duchess.

After translating the *Recueil*, Caxton relinquished his position as governor and traveled to Cologne on a diplomatic mission. Cologne was the city closest to Bruges that had a printing press, and it was there that Caxton met Ulrich Zell, a priest from Mainz, the town in which *Johann Gutenberg had established the first printing press. It was Zell who established the first press in Cologne and most likely taught Caxton the printing trade.

After learning the printing trade, Caxton returned to Bruges, where he set up his own press under Margaret of York's patronage. He hired calligrapher, bookseller, and translator Colard Mansion, the dean of the Guild of St. John, an association of men employed in the printing trade. Together Caxton and Mansion printed *The History of Troy*, the first book printed in English (1474), and *The Game and the Play of Chess Moralized* (c. 1475). At this time Caxton continued his diplomatic missions while printing four or five more books.

Influenced by cooling relations between England and Burgundy, Caxton returned to England in 1476. He set up a press at Westminster, where he received help from Abbot John Esteney. Caxton printed nearly one hundred books, most notably *Geoffrey Chaucer's *Canterbury Tales* and *Troilus and Criseyde*, *John Gower's *Confessio Amantis*, John of Trevisa's *Polychronicon*, Jacobus de Voragine's *Golden Legend*, and Thomas Malory's *Morte d'Arthur*. He had eclectic tastes, printing saints' lives, fables, and chronicles, but he favored chivalric literature such as *Godfrey of Bouillon, The Ordre of Chyualry, Charles the Grete, Paris and Vienne*, and *The Fayttes of Armes and Chyualry*. Caxton translated his sources himself, supplied his own woodcuts, and wrote his own prologues and epilogues. Although the printer borrowed heavily from other works in his own writings, the prologues and epilogues continue to interest scholars not only because of the dedications that refer to English and Burgundian politics but also because of Caxton's explanations of his choices to print certain works. Caxton was assisted at Westminster by Wynken de Worde, whom he might have met in Cologne. De Worde printed Caxton's last work, *The Lives of Our Fathers*, after Caxton's death in 1491/92 and inherited the press, becoming an important printer in his own right.

Caxton's press influenced English literature long after his death. The romances, saints' lives, and manuals not only reflected public taste but also helped shape it. Although Caxton cannot be credited for Chaucer's critical success, for example, Caxton made Chaucer's work more readily available than it would have been otherwise, perhaps accelerating his influence on others, most notably the Scottish Chaucerians. Whatever his influence might have been on English literature, Caxton's corpus tells us much about the literary tastes of fifteenth-century England, and his printing endeavors helped pave the way for centuries of English publishers.

Bibliography: N. F. Blake, *Caxton and His World*, 1969; Edmund Childs, *William Caxton: A Portrait in a Background*, 1978.

Staci Bernard-Roth

Celtis, Conrad (1459–1508), also spelled Celtes, born Conrad Pickel, was a German scholar and Latin lyric poet who was the first German to be crowned poet laureate. Celtis was instrumental in spreading humanist learning throughout Europe, especially by his organization of sodalities, associations of humanists who supported each other's research and writing. Among his many writings, his love poetry was especially renowned, and one of his central themes was the celebration of German history and culture.

Conrad Celtis was born on 1 February 1459 at Wipfield, near Würzburg, Germany. His father, Hans Pickel, was a peasant who wanted Celtis to work in the family's vineyards. However, Celtis's interests in scholarship inspired him to run away to the University of Cologne in 1477 at the age of eighteen. Although Celtis was not able to pursue his interests in Latin and the classics, he received the baccalaureate on 1 December 1479. On 13 December 1484 Celtis matriculated in Heidelberg University, an early center of humanism in Germany. Celtis finally received his master's degree on 20 October 1485. While he was at Heidelberg, Celtis studied under *Rudolf Agricola, a noted humanist whose studies in Italian literature and music had a profound influence on Celtis.

Celtis left Heidelberg after Agricola's death in 1485. While he was at Leipzig, Celtis wrote *Ars versificandi et carminum* (1486), one of the first treatises on poetry in German literature, and produced editions of Seneca's *Hercules Furens* and *Thyestes* (1487). The *Ars versificandi* brought Celtis to the attention of Frederick the Wise of Saxony. At Frederick's urging, Holy Roman Emperor *Frederick III crowned Celtis poet laureate on 18 April 1487, when Celtis also was granted a doctorate of philosophy.

Shortly after receiving this honor, Celtis traveled to Italy, where he visited Rome, Florence, Ferrara, Padua, and Venice. In Italy, Celtis studied history, philology, grammar, and rhetoric. He also had contact with the Platonic Academy, which served as a model for his German sodalities. Eventually Celtis left Italy for Hungary, and he later arrived at Cracow University in the spring of 1489. At Cracow, Celtis studied natural science, mathematics, and astronomy under Albert Brudzewo, who later taught Nicolaus Copernicus. According to Celtis, in Poland he had a vision in which Phoebus appeared and ordered him to celebrate German history and culture in his writings. At Cracow, Celtis also met Hasilina von Rzytonic, with whom he fell in love. Hasilina served as the model for many of his symbolic female characters and was the subject of many of Celtis's love poems. Celtis returned to Germany in 1491; he continued to move from place to place throughout the remainder of his life, sometimes leaving in the middle of his teaching appointments. His longest tenure was at the University of Vienna, where he stayed from his appointment by *Maximilian I in 1497 until his death in 1508. There he established the College of Poets and Mathematicians.

As he traveled, Celtis contributed to the spread of humanism in Europe, a cause that was furthered by his establishing sodalities throughout Germany. The sodalities gave humanists places to meet other scholars, plan and publish collaborative works, and share ideas and discoveries of manuscripts. Although the Rhenish and Danubian sodalities were the most successful ones formed directly by Celtis, other loose associations of humanists were formed throughout Germany. Celtis hoped that the sodalities would contribute to *Germania illustrata*, a collaborative history of Germany, and he contributed two of his works, *Germania generalis* (1500) and *Norimberga* (1502), to this enterprise.

Although Celtis's wanderlust and lack of organization left many writings and projects unfinished, he also made important contributions to scholarship until his death in 1508. At Ingolstadt University, Celtis published *Epitoma in utramque Ciceronis rhetoricam* (1492), a guide to his lectures on Ciceronian rhetoric. On 31 August 1492 Celtis delivered his inaugural address, the *Oratio*, which served as his call both for educational reform and for a celebration of German patriotism in works of philosophy. In *Amores* (1502), his chief work, four female figures represented the four parts of Germany. His edition of Tacitus's *Germania* and his discoveries of the plays of the tenth-century nun Roswitha and of the medieval epic poem *Ligurinus* were important contributions to the development of romantic cultural nationalism in Germany. Among Celtis's other works were plays, including *Ludus Dianae* (1501) and *Rhapsodia* (1504), and a book of *Epigrams* (published in 1881). His *Odes* (published in 1513) provide good examples of the erotic nature of Celtis's love poetry.

Bibliography: Conrad Celtis, *Selections*, 1948; Lewis W. Spitz, *Conrad Celtis: The German Arch-Humanist*, 1957.

Kristine Lynn Rabberman

Charles VI, King of France (b. 1368, r. 1380–1422),

also known as Charles the Mad, remained largely a figurehead throughout his forty-two-year reign, first because he was only eleven years old when he inherited the throne from his father Charles V, and later because of his periodic fits of madness. His time on the throne coincided with a period of great upheaval in France, marked by bloody rivalries between members of the royal family and by a renewed claim to the French Crown by the English under King Henry V.

Upon ascending to the throne in September 1380, Charles fell under the tutelage of his uncles the dukes of Anjou, Berry, Burgundy, and Bourbon, who were only too eager to use their influence over the young king to further their own interests. During these early years his uncles, led by *Philip the Bold of Burgundy, took hold of the important offices of government, raided the royal treasury, and reestablished previously abolished taxes. This led to insurrections throughout northern France, which the dukes urged Charles to suppress severely. Philip, who had inherited the countship of Flanders, arranged the marriage of Charles to Isabeau of Bavaria (17 July 1385) because of his own desire to forge a German alliance to ward off English intervention in the region.

Charles declared his intent to rule alone in November 1388. At this time his uncles' political influence was supplanted by that of the former officials of Charles's father, a group derisively called the Marmousets ("little men," or up-starts), a mixture of nobles with military backgrounds and persons from the bourgeoisie. Among the policies they implemented were a reduction in the enor-mous tax burden on the French population, frugal management of royal re-sources, and the establishment of a three-year truce with England, which continued to be sporadically engaged in the seemingly interminable Hundred Years' War with France. This same desire for peace would later motivate the arrangement of a marriage between *Richard II of England and Charles's daugh-ter Isabelle in 1396.

In an effort to restore a degree of unity among the chivalric class of Europe and to find useful employment for the bands of mercenaries left with nothing to do but pillage the countryside after the truce of 1389, Charles envisioned a crusade. However, such an undertaking on behalf of Christendom seemed un-tenable without an end to the Papal Schism that divided the leadership of the church. Support for the Roman pope *Urban VI was so lukewarm that plans were under way for French military intervention in Italy to overthrow Urban and install Clement VII, the Avignon antipope, in Rome. Urban VI's death in 1389 was quickly followed by the election of Boniface IX as his successor. Boniface's greater popularity produced revitalized support of the Roman pope by the English. Boniface appealed to Richard II not to conclude peace with Charles without a promise by the French to stay out of Italy. Richard agreed, and after two years of diplomatic activity, the planned incursion into Italy was scrapped.

In August 1392 Charles became ill with a fever and convulsions, marking the onset of the periodic fits of madness that would plague him for the rest of his life. These attacks lasted from a few days to a few months and became more frequent as the years passed. During his episodes of madness, which may have been a form of schizophrenia, Charles destroyed his clothes and other household objects, suffered from persecutory delusions, failed to recognize the queen and his children, forgot who he himself was, and imagined that he was made of glass and would shatter if he moved. Yet his illness did not completely inca-pacitate him, and he was allowed to continue to rule with full authority whenever he was lucid.

As the king's mental stability deteriorated, the dukes of Burgundy and Orléans began to vie for power, and in 1407 the Burgundians arranged the murder of Louis, duke of Orléans. Starting in 1415, Henry V, now king of England, took advantage of the lack of a unified opposition and swept through northern France in a series of successful battles, including his defeat of the French at Agincourt. Charles's fifteen-year-old son, refusing to recognize his father's personal authority, declared himself regent in December 1418 and was implicated in the murder of the duke of Burgundy in September 1419. In January 1420 his father responded by disinheriting the dauphin of his claim to the throne. Five months later France and England signed the Treaty of Troyes, which arranged for the marriage of Charles's daughter Catherine to Henry V, who then became regent and heir to the French throne. When both Henry V and Charles VI died in 1422, the question of who had the rightful claim to rule France pitted the supporters of Charles's son, dubbed *Charles VII, against those of the young English king *Henry VI, and the war with England dragged on for many more years.

Bibliography: R. C. Famiglietti, *Royal Intrigue: Crisis at the Court of Charles VI, 1392–1420*, 1986; John Bell Henneman, *Olivier de Clisson and Political Society in France under Charles V and Charles VI*, 1996.

Susan Arvay

Charles VII, King of France (b. 1403, r. 1422–61), lived in a period of turmoil and crisis both internally at home and externally abroad. Accused of apathy, he constantly relied on encouragement from counselors, such as Yolande of Aragon, Richemont, *Joan of Arc, and his mistress Agnès Sorel, and he did exhibit a perennial innate indolence and shyness. But Charles VII, as we know him from history, came out at last, from a time of chaos, as one of the most important kings in the history of France precisely because of his enormous capacity for transforming situational disadvantages into advantages from which he was able to consolidate his royal domain, reconquer territory, rebuild his army, reform the French noble system, and settle accounts with the pope.

Charles VII was born in 1403, the eleventh child of King *Charles VI and his wife, Isabeau of Bavaria. He was brought up at the French court, where intrigue, a taste for the arts, extravagance, and profligacy prevailed. He also lived through a time punctuated by the frequent attacks of his father's derangement, which, together with his mother's promiscuity, cast doubts on his legitimacy. However, the successive deaths of his older brothers in 1415 and 1417 made Charles heir to the throne at age fourteen and dauphin at the moment when Henry V of England was systematically conquering northwestern France.

On the death of his father on 21 October 1422, Charles became the king of France. Although he was faced with the threat of the English, Charles's worst difficulties were financial. Finding it hard to cover his needs from taxes voted by the Representative Assembly, he had to mortgage his lands and borrow from financiers and nobles such as Georges de la Tremoille. The financial difficulties were compounded by a military setback when his army was repulsed at Verneuil in 1424. Consequently, in the eye of his English and pro-English Burgundians, he cut a poor figure of a lethargic and indecisive "King of Bourges" (his temporary capital) who failed to resist the English advance led by the duke of Bedford. On 12 October 1428 the English laid siege to Orléans when Charles was just twenty-five years old. For twelve years he had known only war; he could neither reconquer his kingdom nor conclude peace with the Burgundians. However, his fortune changed dramatically in 1429 when a peasant woman, Joan of Arc, whom he received in February of that year, persuaded him that the saints had called her to break the English siege of Orléans. She restored the confidence of the French army, which liberated Orléans. On 17 July 1429 Charles was crowned at Rheims after a relief expedition led by Joan of Arc marched through the town.

After his coronation, Charles strengthened his royal position by maneuvering skillfully in financial, military, and church affairs. In 1435, after protracted negotiations, Philip of Burgundy, who in 1419 had formed an alliance with the English against France, recognized Charles as his sovereign. From 1425 to 1439, gradually acquiring the permanent right to levy taxes, Charles finally gained financial independence. In 1438, with the signing of the Pragmatic Sanction, Charles sharply limited papal control of the French church. From 1437 onward Charles improved the discipline and recruitment of his army and in 1439 took control of the army for the first time since his coronation and returned to Paris, which had been retaken from the English the year before. In 1440, acting with skill and energy, he ruthlessly put down a rebellion spearheaded by his own son, the future *Louis XI. Finally, by the ordinances of 1439, 1445, and 1448. Charles established the regularly paid royal companies of heavy cavalry and bowmen. Thus he had at his service the best mercenary troops, which ultimately enabled Charles to expel the English in 1453.

By any standard, these were significant accomplishments; however, Charles still had the time to father eleven children with his wife and four with his mistress. Agnès Sorel, considered by some to have been the first royal mistress in the history of France. Charles also found time to patronize art, gathering around himself men of letters and intelligence, among them *Jean Fouquet, an important fifteenth-century artist who painted Charles's portrait. Charles died at Mehun-sur-Yèvre in 1461 at the age of fifty-eight after having reigned for thirty-eight years and eight months.

Bibliography: Michel Herubel, *Charles VII*, 1981; M.G.A. Vale, *Charles VII*, 1974.

Wentong Ma

Charles VIII, King of France (b. 1470, r. 1483–98),

was the last of the Valois line of the house of Capet. Born in 1470, Charles succeeded to the throne upon the death of his father, *Louis XI, in 1483. The eldest son of King Louis XI and Charlotte de Savoje, Charles VIII is little discussed or treated today due to his short life and reign—he died at the age of twenty-eight without issue after fifteen years of rule. He is best known for his invasion of Italy in 1494–95 and his consolidation of Brittany with other French-held territories.

Charles was thirteen when Louis XI died. In accordance with the wishes of the late king, Charles's elder sister *Anne Valois and her husband, *Pierre de Beaujeau, duc de Bourbon, were named as reagents.In 1488 François II, duke of Brittany, died, and the young king's sister and brother-in-law attempted to arrange a marriage between Charles and the duke's daughter, twelve-year-old Anne of Brittany. Such an alliance would have incorporated the Duchy of Brittany—long an independent province—into the French kingdom, but the Breton nobility sought to avoid this loss of autonomy by having Anne married by proxy to *Maximilian Habsburg, who was first in line to succeed as holy Roman emperor. After the Beaujeaus declared war on Brittany in 1491, Anne at last agreed to marry Charles. The couple had four children, all of whom died before the age of five.

Early in his reign Charles turned his attention to Italy, which had long been of concern to French monarchs, and to which Charles could legitimately make several dynastic claims. Although Charles's father, Louis XI, had been interested in maintaining the long-standing French claim to various Italian city-states, he had focused most of his energies during his reign on consolidating royal power within French borders and creating a stable realm. He had, however, acted as arbitrator in Italian disputes on several occasions, and thus the French connection to and interest in Italy was strong when Charles VII ascended the throne.

Italy at this time, it should be noted, was not a unified nation, but a collection of autonomous city-states that had become loosely associated in the second half of the fifteenth century by the Treaty of Lodi (1454–55), which allied longtime enemies Naples and Milan with Florence in anticipation of a potential Turkish invasion. In 1494 the peace established by the Treaty of Lodi was broken when Naples made ready to attack Milan at the urging of the Borgia pope *Alexander VI, who had also procured the support of Florence. *Ludovico Sforza, "Il Moro," a powerful ruler in Milan, turned to France for help in the face of Neapolitan hostilities, suggesting that Charles VIII enter Italy and revive France's claim to Naples, which from 1266 to 1435 had been ruled by French kings. It had been at the request of the papacy in 1266 that Charles, count of Anjou, had conquered the Neapolitan city-state, and the French had maintained control until they were driven out by Duke Alfonso of Sicily in 1435.

In contrast with his father, Charles VIII looked beyond France's borders, seeking to recapture Jerusalem and Constantinople for Christendom; Naples was the logical place to launch just such a project. Thus Charles was quick to accept Ludovico's invitation and quickly stormed through Italy, claiming not just Naples—weakened by the death of its ruler, *Ferrante I, in 1494—but Florence and the Papal States as well. Charles met little resistance, due in part to the efforts of the preacher *Girolamo Savonarola, who managed to convince a large portion of the Florentine populace that Charles's invasion of Italy was divine retribution for their immorality. Thus the Florentines welcomed Charles into their city, offering him Pisa in an attempt to spare their town from almost certain destruction at the hands of the well-organized and technologically superior French forces.

Ludovico Sforza, meanwhile, soon realized that the French invasion he had invited in order to subdue his enemy, Naples, might become a threat to his own rule over Milan—a city-state to which France also had dynastic claims—and joined the newly formed League of Venice. Alarmed at French activities in Italy, *Ferdinand of Aragon, also king of Sicily, created the league in March 1495, convincing the Papal States, Venice, and Holy Roman Emperor Maximilian I to stand with him against the French. Ludovico's alliance with the League of Venice sent Charles VIII into retreat by May 1495, but he continued to prepare for the reconquest of Italy, a project cut short by his early death in 1498. He was succeeded by the duke of Orléans, who, as Louis XII, married Charles's widow, Anne of Brittany, and resumed the French campaign in Italy with an attack on Milan in 1499.

Bibliography: David Abulafia, ed., *The French Descent into Renaissance Italy, 1494–95: Antecedents and Effects*, 1995; David Potter, *A History of France, 1460–1560: The Emergence of a Nation State*, 1995.

S. Dorsey Armstrong

Charles the Bold (b. 1433, r. 1467–77), Duke of Burgundy, Count of

Charolais and Knight of the Golden Fleece, ruled Burgundy and Flanders during the mid-fifteenth century. The last Valois duke of Burgundy, Charles is best known for his vast collection of books and illuminated manuscripts, his efforts to transform the duchy of Burgundy into a kingdom and his attempts to recreate the ancient kingdom of Lotharingia.

Charles was born in Dijon on 11 November 1433, the third and only surviving son of Philip the Good and his third wife, Isabella of Portugal. As a child Charles was studious and reserved, with few close friends or confidantes. His education was provided by tutors, notably Antoine Haneron, a prominent scholar from Arras and founder of the College of St. Donat at the University of Lorraine. Burgundian knights such as Jean de Rosimboz and the Lord of Auxy trained Charles in the use of weaponry and fighting.

Charles grew to be a tall, broad-shouldered man, inheriting his dark hair and swarthy complexion from his mother Isabella. In contrast to his father, Charles was chaste, impulsive, ambitious and proud. A hard worker who expected no less from those around him, Charles possessed a furious temper, and could often be impatient, cruel and vindictive. In fact, he was reprimanded by the Order of the Golden Fleece for his overly harsh treatment of servants and his inability to curb his temper, even toward other nobles.

A product of the Renaissance, Charles enjoyed music and art but especially literature. From his father he inherited one of the most renowned libraries of that period, containing more than 900 volumes, to which he added throughout his life. Charles was an avid reader. He chiefly enjoyed histories of ancient heroes such as Hercules, Pompey, Caesar and Hannibal. In particular he was fascinated by Alexander the Great, with whom he often compared himself (both had fathers named Philip). Court historian *Olivier de la Marche reported that Charles refused to sleep at night unless read to for at least two hours.

Charles inherited the duchy of Burgundy upon his father's death in 1467. At that time the duchy was split into two pieces of territory, Burgundy and Flanders, separated by an eighty-mile gap that included the lands of Alsace and Lorraine. From the beginning of Charles' reign his goal was to unite the two parts of his territory, solidifying his authority and establishing Burgundy as an independent kingdom.

In September 1473, at the height of his power, Charles met with the *Holy Roman Emperor Frederick III at Trier ostensibly to discuss the wedding of Charles' daughter Mary to the Emperor's son *Maximillian. However, the true purpose of the meeting was to negotiate a peace settlement between France and Burgundy, to organize a crusade against the Turks and, most importantly, to raise his duchy to the dignity of a kingdom. Charles' exorbitant demands were unacceptable to Frederick, who felt compelled to abandon the talks, secretly fleeing Trier in the middle of the night. Although this act infuriated Charles, it did not stop him from announcing in January 1474 at Dijon his ambitious intention to recreate the kingdom of Lotharingia.

Later on that year, Charles signed a treaty with his brother-in-law *Edward IV of England, which renewed the Anglo-Burgundian alliance. According to the treaty both rulers would commit 10,000 troops to the invasion of France; Charles would recognize Edward as king of France but would not be required to pay homage, thereby making Burgundy an independent state. However, when Edward landed at Calais in 1475, Charles was unable to fulfill his end of the bargain. His army was tied down in the east, attempting to put down a revolt in the territory of Alsace and dealing with a declaration of war made by René II of Lorraine.

Meanwhile, *Louis XI of France sent envoys to Edward proposing a truce in exchange for a lifetime annual payment of 50,000 crowns. Edward agreed to the settlement and promptly took his army back across the channel. Nevertheless, Charles was able to conquer the territory of Lorraine without his ally, and declared the capital of his future kingdom at the city of Nancy.

However, in October 1476 Nancy fell to René of Lorraine. Charles marched with a small army to meet him but was too late, so instead he chose to lay siege to the city. Finally, on 5 January 1477, René's forces, which numbered almost 15,000, attacked Charles' army of approximately 2,000 men, completely devastating the Burgundians. Charles himself was apparently killed by a massive blow to the head while attempting to jump a frozen stream on his horse. His men did not locate his barely identifiable body until two days after the battle when it was found at the bottom of the muddy stream, naked and mutilated by wolves.

After Charles the Bold's death, the duchy of Burgundy was largely occupied and dismantled by Louis XI and would never again achieve the state of power and influence that it had attained under his rule. Today the remnants of Charles' library reside in the Bibliothéque de Bourgogne in Brussels, permanently testifying to his love of the classics. Charles the Bold is remembered not only for his lofty political aspirations but also as a fearless military leader and a great patron of literature.

Bibliography: Christopher Cope, *The Lost Kingdom of Burgundy*, 1986; W. Prevenier and W. Blockmans, *The Burgundian Netherlands 1380–1530*, 1986; R. Vaughan, *Charles the Bold*, 1973.

Jaimie B. Hanson

Chartier, Alain (c. 1380–1430), was a French writer, moralist, and diplomat under *Charles VII of France. He wrote French and Latin prose, French lyric poetry (rondeaux and ballades), and political, moral, and didactic verse, with a predilection for first-person dialogue and debate. Evidence of his extraordinary appeal as a writer can be seen in the survival of his work in close to two hundred fifteenth- and early-sixteenth-century manuscripts. His most influential piece, *La belle dame sans mercy* (c. 1424), sparked a playful literary dispute—the so-called Quarrel of the *Belle dame sans mercy*—that lasted into the mid-sixteenth century.

Alain Chartier was born in Bayeux, France, presumably between 1380 and 1390. His activity as a royal notary, secretary, and diplomat at the French court fell primarily in the youth and early reign of Charles VII. He entered Charles's service sometime before 16 September 1417, having been previously employed by the prince's mother-in-law, Queen Yolanda of Aragon. In May 1418, when the Burgundians occupied Paris, Charles and his court were forced to retreat south into the secure regions of Berry and Touraine. Over the next ten years, a period of war and "doleful exile," Chartier remained a loyal servant to the French Crown and increased his reputation as a writer. As a diplomatic envoy, he delivered two orations before King *Sigismund of Hungary in 1425, requesting support for France's war against the Anglo-Burgundian coalition. A year later, in Bruges, he tried to detach the duke of Burgundy from his alliance with the English, but without success. In 1428 he helped negotiate a new alliance with *James I of Scotland.

Contemporaries greatly admired the sophistication of Chartier's work in French and Latin. His poetry and fictional prose, in particular, appealed to the tastes of his aristocratic patrons by combining the fashionable ideals of courtly love with traditional moral values and a nascent sense of patriotism. Conventional narrative frameworks, allegory, dialogue, courtly rhetoric, and the rich, pervasive rhyme of his verse were common hallmarks of his style. His longest poem, *Livre des quatre dames*, was typical in this respect. Written sometime after the defeat of the French army at Agincourt (25 October 1415), it lent voice to the anguish of four ladies, each of whom had lost a lover as a result of war. Other noteworthy texts in French are *Debat de réveille matin*, in which a poet-narrator overhears in a hostel the confession of a smitten lover's chagrin; *Bréviaire des nobles*, a moral-didactic digest of nobility's twelve cardinal virtues; and *Quadrilogue invectif* (1422), a political dialogue between Lady France, a knight, a cleric, and a peasant, the latter three representing the realm's three estates. Significant works in Latin prose included *De vita curiali*, a critique of life at court, and *Dialogus familiaris amici et sodalis*, an indictment of declining moral values—both appeared in English translation before the end of the century.

Of all his works, however, none has attained the lasting celebrity of *La belle dame sans mercy*, a narrative poem consisting of one hundred eight-line stanzas. It presents with wry humor and grace a knight's timeworn panoply of amorous entreaties and his failure to seduce the lady of his choice with its help. Her obduracy and insuperable wit reduce the knight to tears, and he soon dies of a broken heart. For this unusual display of "cruelty," Chartier was cited to appear before Issoudun's "Court of Love," a mock tribunal of friends and literati, to answer charges that he had violated the ethics of their society. Was not pity a lady's most essential quality? Chartier's response in *Excusacion aux dames* only spurred further debate concerning the lady's guilt or innocence, leading to such mimetic works as Baudet Herenc's *Parlement d'amours* and Achille Caulier's *Cruelle femme en amours* and *Ospital d'amours*. For the modern critic, *La belle dame sans mercy* not only illustrates the principal tenets and boundaries of courtly love, it also signals, as does much of Chartier's work, the demise of a culture founded on these tenets. Among the last pieces he wrote were the *Epistola de puella* (c. July–August 1429), describing *Joan of Arc's inspiring role in the war against England, and an unfinished *Traité de l'espérance* (begun c. 1428). The circumstances surrounding his death are not clear; however, information derived from a fifteenth-century epitaph suggests that he died in Avignon, perhaps while on a diplomatic mission, in 1430.

Bibliography: Alain Chartier, *The Poetical Works of Alain Chartier*, ed. J. C. Laidlaw, 1974; Leonard W. Johnson, " 'Je est un autre': Alain Chartier and the Game of Love and Death," in *Poets as Players: Theme and Variation in Late Medieval French Poetry*, 1990: 106–66.

Jan Pendergrass

Chastellain, Georges (c. 1415–75).

Historiographer and courtier, Georges Chastellain was as much a poet as a chronicler. He is best known for his *Chronique*, an official, commissioned history of the deeds of the Burgundian court.

Details of his youth are sketchy. While his epitaph indicates that Chastellain was born in 1405 in the county of Aalst in Flanders, biographical information drawn from his works places the date in 1415. He studied at the University of Louvain, graduating in 1432, and joined the court of Philip the Good in Burgundy. Following the Treaty of Arras, Chastellain served *Charles VII of France from 1439 to 1446 before rejoining the Burgundian court as a diplomat. His roles at the court of Burgundy were many and varied, though mostly ceremonial: diplomat, carver (*écuyer tranchant*), bread-store keeper (*panetier*), councilor, and finally chronicler (*indicaire*). Duke Philip endowed Chastellain with a considerable pension for this last service and set him up in the ducal Hôtel Salle-le-Comte in Valenciennes. He remained there, working on his immense *Chronique*, until his death in 1475.

The *Chronique*, widely renowed during Chastellain's lifetime, survives only in incomplete manuscript form. He began his work with the assassination of John the Fearless at Montereau in 1419 and left the work incomplete just before his death in 1475. However, only about one-third of the work covering these fifty-five years of Burgundian court history can be located today. Chastellain centered his account on the Franco-Burgundian conflict and on the acts of Charles the Timid and Duke Philip the Good. The *Chronique* treated most of fifteenth-century Europe in the process of making a hero of Duke Philip. Chastellain, a courtier of considerable reputation who spent most of his life at court, reports the intimate details of his surroundings. Thus his work is important to understanding the history of much of Europe as well as the social history of court intrigue and life in the fifteenth century.

Though Chastellain is best remembered for his historiography, his treatise on prosody and other works also deserve mention. He and his fellow Burgundian historians were the only chroniclers to have valued poetic rhetoric on an equal level with the historical account. His efforts brought him the honor of being named a knight of the Order of the Golden Fleece by Charles the Timid. Chastellain was later named chronicler of the order as well. His poetic works include *Douze dames de rhétorique* (Twelve ladies of rhetoric), a complex, multileveled "conversation" cowritten with Jean Castel. The *Temple de Boccace* honors *Giovanni Boccaccio while providing consolation to Margaret of Anjou for having lost her throne in the Wars of the Roses. He penned some courtly poetry, including rondeaux and the *Oultré d'amour*, in which a man debates whether he would remain a constant lover if he were to love again after the death of his first love. History and politics remained Chastellain's focus in a play, some poems, and a prose book on the peace treaties of Arras and Péronne. Finally, he wrote numerous poems and prose works in honor of the deaths of great men of his time, including Philip the Good, Charles VII, Pierre de Brézé, and Jacques de Lalaing.

Chastellain's considerable corpus attests to his popularity and success in his own day. His attention to rhetoric made him a model for his fellow *rhétoriqueurs*, French poets dedicated to exploring the possibilities of prosody and convinced of the dignity and importance of the poet. His student, Jean Molinet, continued Chastellain's own work on the *Chronique* and became one of the central *rhétoriqueurs* in his own right.

Bibliography: L. W. Johnson, "Prince of Princes? Fifteenth-Century Politics and Poetry," *French Review* 68 (1995): 421–30; Graeme Small, *George Chastelain and the Shaping of Valois Burgundy: Political and Historical Culture at Court in the Fifteenth Century*, 1997.

Lynn Ramey

Chaucer, Geoffrey (1341/43?–1400), was an influential poet best known for *The Canterbury Tales*, a cluster of interwoven stories told to beguile the time on pilgrimage. The narrators thus thrown together represent a cross-section of medieval professions and perspectives, from knight to monk, guildsman to plowman, or, among women, from prioress to wife. His other major achievement, *Troilus and Criseyde*, is an elaborate courtly love tale in five books, set in the latter days of the Trojan War. Additional works include *The Legend of Good Women*, ostensibly written to atone for "showing how women have done amiss" in *Troilus and Criseyde*, and *The Book of the Duchess, The House of Fame, Parliament of Fowls*, and numerous short poems like the humorous "Complaint of Chaucer to His Purse." Equally at ease at court or in the tavern, Chaucer was also an internationally traveled poet who translated *Giovanni Boccaccio, Boethius, and the *Roman de la Rose*. His burial in Westminster Abbey prompted the "poet's corner" to evolve around his tomb.

The son of John and Agnes Chaucer, Geoffrey was born into a family of prosperous wine merchants on Thames Street, London, in the area known as Vintry Ward. In 1347 John was appointed deputy in Southampton to the king's chief butler, leaving his business temporarily in the hands of his stepbrother. This meant that when the plague reached London in 1348, Geoffrey was in Southampton. Most of the family on both sides died in the months that followed, and the family returned to London in 1349 to inherit several properties. But the family also had connections at court, and in his teens Geoffrey was sent to the household of Elizabeth de Burgh, countess of Ulster (wife of Lionel, son of *Edward III), probably as a page. This episode of Chaucer's life became known when two pages of the household expense book were discovered in an old bookbinding, where they had been used as filler. After serving the countess for several years, Geoffrey followed Lionel to war on the Continent in 1359. There he was captured at Rethel, near Rheims, France, and ransomed by the king for sixteen pounds in March 1360.

Little is known of the seven intervening years, but Chaucer may have studied law at the Inns of Court. This would have been traditional for the king's esquires by the fifteenth century, and some scholars argue that Chaucer's later posts required legal experience. In addition, there is the evidence of Thomas Speght, who wrote in 1598 that "Master Buckley," keeper of the Inner Temple records, saw a fine of two shillings issued to "Geffrye Chaucer" for beating a "franciscane fryer in fletestreate"; the records themselves have disappeared in the centuries that followed. This incident, if true, would not only establish Chaucer's legal training; it would also colorfully foreshadow Chaucer's later, more literary attacks on the variously knavish churchmen satirized in *The Canterbury Tales*.

But Chaucer was also in the king's service, and in the years that followed he made numerous trips overseas in this capacity. In 1366, for instance, he traveled to Spain on business connected to the forthcoming war. By 1367 he had traveled to Milan with Lionel's wedding party, was sent home with messages, and then returned again. In 1370 he traveled on a brief mission, perhaps to Genoa, and by 1372 he was in Italy again for roughly six months, first in Genoa and then in Florence. The influence of *Dante, *Francesco Petrarch, and Boccaccio dates from this journey. In 1376 and 1377 peace negotiations took him to France; a year later French-war business took him to Milan, and it was on this trip that he probably acquired manuscripts of Boccaccio and Petrarch.

In 1366, either before or after his trip to Spain, Chaucer married "Philippa," then a "domicelle" of Queen Philippa and, probably, a daughter of Payne (Paon) de Roet. If so, she, too, served the Countess Elizabeth in her youth before leaving to serve first with the queen and then with the Duchess Constanza. Her sister Katherine was the mistress, and later the wife, of *John of Gaunt, son of Edward III. Upon their marriage, Philippa received ten marks a year for life from the Exchequer; a year later Chaucer received an annuity of twenty marks a year. Further annuities followed: ten pounds a year for Philippa in 1372, from John of Gaunt, ten pounds more in 1374, for Chaucer, and, in the same year, a daily pitcher of wine from the king (later commuted to twenty marks). Since Philippa continued to attend the countess, she seldom lived with her husband, but Chaucer collected her Exchequer annuity regularly every six months, and they had at least one son together, Thomas. Chaucer had a second son, Lewis, who was ten when his father addressed him in the prologue of his *Treatise on the Astrolabe*; whether Philippa was his mother has not been ascertained.

For at least two more years, in 1371–73, Chaucer was an esquire of the king's chamber. In 1374 he left the court permanently, accepting the post of controller of the wool custom and wool subsidy and of the petty custom in the port of London. The job paid sixteen pounds and, far from being a sinecure, was relatively onerous, for Chaucer had to keep all records in his own hand. At the same time, Chaucer was granted the lease for life, rent-free, of a large dwelling above the city gate at Aldgate, where people and business of all sorts passed under him daily. It was the perfect location for the author of *The Canterbury Tales*.

On 1 May 1380, a little before he began work on *Troilus and Criseyde*, one of the most puzzling documents of Chaucer's life was enrolled in the Court of Chancery and witnessed by his most influential friends. In it, Cecilie Champaigne (a baker's daughter) released Geoffrey Chaucer unconditionally from all actions concerning her rape ("raptus"). Later that month Richard Goodchild, a cutler, and John Grove, an armourer, released Chaucer from all actions of law they might have against him and, on the same day, were themselves released by Cecilie from legal action. Finally, on 2 July Grove, perhaps acting for Chaucer, acknowledged a debt of ten pounds to Cecilie (subsequently paid). In the months that followed, Chaucer called in his debts and otherwise raised money.

Since the matter never came to trial, Chaucer's guilt or innocence cannot be established, but the care he took to secure immunity from prosecution, together with the large sum paid to Cecilie, may imply guilt of some sort. Possibly the charge of rape was used as leverage and then dropped, once the desired compensation was achieved. Neglect or betrayal of promises seem more likely than violent rape.

In 1386, as the political crisis around *Richard II deepened, Chaucer distanced himself from the king by giving up his position, together with his lease at Aldgate, and moved to Kent. Two years later Chaucer completed the break by selling his Exchequer annuities as well. Later, in 1394, these annuities were replaced, but in the meantime Chaucer must have found himself in tightened circumstances. Other than his fifty-nine days as a member of Parliament in late 1386, Chaucer held few official positions for the next three years and probably began planning *The Canterbury Tales* during this period. However, on 12 July 1389 Chaucer was appointed clerk of the king's works. This was an arduous position, since it put him in charge of wages and materials for workmen, local deputies at major establishments, and some implementation of construction plans. Three times (once on 3 September 1390 and twice on 6 September) he was beaten and robbed of money due to workmen (losing, in addition, his own horse and other property). The following February an audit showed overspending by more than twenty pounds, which was charged to Chaucer, and in June 1391 he was instructed to give up his office. The last decade of his life was heavily occupied by writing *The Canterbury Tales*. Although individual tales were read or circulated among friends, Chaucer left the work incomplete at his death, and the tales were not collected into one text until three or four years after he died.

Bibliography: Geoffrey Chaucer, *The Riverside Chaucer*, ed. Larry D. Benson, 1987; Donald R. Howard, *Chaucer: His Life, His Works, His World*, 1987; Derek Pearsall, *The Life of Geoffrey Chaucer: A Critical Biography*, 1992.

Kathryn Jacobs

Chichele, Henry (c. 1362–1443), archbishop of Canterbury for his last twenty-nine years, served the church and the Crown in the Lancastrian age. His episcopate coincided with the end of the Great Schism and the early stages of the Conciliar Crisis. The archbishop also was a benefactor of his alma mater, Oxford University.

Chichele was born around 1362 at Higham Ferrers in Northamptonshire. His family was prominent in commerce and local government. Educated at Winchester, young Chichele went to New College, Oxford, where he received degrees in canon law in 1389 and 1396. By 1397 he was in the service of the bishop of Salisbury, but then he entered royal service and by 1404 was being employed on embassies to Rome. Gregory XII, the Roman claimant to the papal throne, provided him the See of Saint David's in Wales. Despite this promotion to a "foreign" see, Chichele was an English delegate to the Council of Pisa in 1409. Chichele was named to King *Henry IV's council in 1410, but he remained abroad representing the king until the next year.

When the archbishop of Canterbury died in 1414, young Henry V, whom Chichele had served, secured his translation to the archiepiscopal see, and John XXIII, the Pisan pope, confirmed the election. Being archbishop of Canterbury involved a great deal of legal and pastoral work, much of which had to be delegated to subordinates. Among these was the canonist *William Lyndwood. Chichele did conduct a visitation of the Diocese of Canterbury, but affairs of state occupied much of his time. In his political role, Chichele received Henry V upon his return from the Agincourt campaign (1415) and greeted *Sigismund of Luxembourg when he visited England during the next year. The archbishop led the opposition to Pope Martin V's effort to name *Henry Beaufort, bishop of Winchester and the king's uncle, both cardinal and legate. He also remained active in diplomacy, especially Anglo-French relations.

When Henry V died in 1422, Archbishop Chichele received his body at Dover. During the minority of *Henry VI, the archbishop was a prominent member of the regency council, negotiating between the divisive interests of Cardinal Beaufort and *Humphrey, duke of Gloucester. Chichele helped bring the duke of Bedford home from France at one juncture to reconcile the king's feuding kinsmen. Chichele also resisted Pope Martin V's efforts to expand papal control of the English church during the royal minority. Martin replied by suspending the archbishop's legatine powers, forcing him to plead in vain with the Crown for revocation of the Statute of Provisors, which had instituted the royal, rather than papal, appointment of prelates. Despite this period of tension, the archbishop supported the papal policy of waging war on the Hussites.

If Archbishop Chichele's relations with Martin V were difficult, the next pontificate, that of *Eugenius IV, proved even more strained. When the pope was in conflict with the Council of Basel, both pontiff and councilors began courting the English. Because of French influence at Basel, the English came to support Eugenius, and Chichele played a significant role in charting this course of action. When Eugenius transferred the council to Ferrara (1437), the archbishop directed English delegates at Basel to move to Italy. Any chance that the English might reconsider their Eugenian support came to an end when the Basel assembly decreed the deposition of the pope (1439).

Chichele's relations with Eugenius, however, were not always smooth. The archbishop successfully resisted papal efforts to assign the See of Ely *in commendam* to Louis of Luxembourg (the right of appointment would have been ceded to Louis of Luxembourg). He failed, however, in his effort to curb the pretensions of John Kemp, archbishop of York, whom Eugenius had named a cardinal in 1439. A case over precedence, pitting Archbishop Chichele against Cardinal Kemp, was resolved by Rome in the latter's favor.

The period of this lawsuit also saw the archbishop's health go into decline. Illness prevented him from paying continuous attention to business, and the Basel schism dragged on. Chichele began to contemplate his own memorial. He already had founded a collegiate church at Higham Ferrers along with the "Chichele Chest" at Oxford, but the archbishop also decided to found a new college at Oxford. After extensive preparations, All Souls College received its statutes on 2 April 1443, and only ten days later Henry Chichele died. He lies buried today in his cathedral church at Canterbury.

Bibliography: E. F. Jacob, *Archbishop Henry Chichele*, 1967; Walter Ullmann, "Eugenius IV, Cardinal Kemp, and Archbishop Chichele," in *Medieval Studies Presented to Aubrey Gwynn, S.J.*, 1961: 359–83.

Thomas M. Izbicki

Christine de Pizan (c. 1364–1431) was the most important French literary figure of her day, a champion of women and a patriot. Christine, born Christina da Pizzano in Venice around 1364, was the daughter of physician and astrologer Thommaso de Pizzano, a native of Bologna and graduate of its university. Summoned by King Charles V, Thommaso moved to Paris in 1365 and remained there until his death in 1388. His family, including young Christine, who vividly remembered the journey to France for the rest of her life, joined him in 1368. Christine had a happy childhood, though she later confessed that her father clearly wished that she had been a boy. Aged fifteen, she married scholar Étienne de Castel in 1380. The marriage was happy, and the pair had three children, though one did not survive to adulthood.

Christine's future seemed secure but for two strokes of "fortune." The first was the premature death in 1380 of Charles V, whose reign she later looked back upon as a golden age, effectively ending her father's court career. The second was even more serious, the death of her husband in 1390 at the age of thirty-four. Christine was only twenty-five and was left to cope with a widowed mother, children, and her husband's disorganized finances, with but little worldly experience.

For most of the next decade Christine was in highly straitened circumstances as much of the elite world she had known turned its back on her. Engaged in almost constant lawsuits to protect what she had left and recover what was hers, in the end, she had no choice but "to become a man," in her own words. Part of this "becoming a man" was learning to be a writer. She seems already to have become involved in book production before that time, but by the end of the fourteenth century she was beginning to take her trade as an author more seriously. She began to make a name for herself, at first as a poet of occasional verse, primarily ballades, rondeaux, and virelays, and then as an author of more serious poetic and then prose work. She was also engaged in a careful self-education, taking advantage of the libraries of the wealthy whose doors were opened to her by her courtly past and by her talent for poetry.

Christine continued to write, with increasing success, for more than twenty years and achieved a truly prodigious output. She also found time to help in the design of the manuscript editions of her works, over which she exercised close control. Some of her volumes were among the most beautifully balanced books of a time noted for its fine books. As conditions deteriorated in France after the Battle of Agincourt, Christine increasingly tired of her active life and in 1420 retired to a religious establishment. Her writing ceased, except for one remarkable work, precisely dated to 31 July 1429, the *Ditií de Jehanne d'Arc* (Song of *Joan of Arc), a stirring patriotic panegyric that is one of the few contemporary notices of Joan. After that work, Christine disappeared from view and probably died during or before 1431.

Christine's most famous work was her *La cité des dames* (City of ladies), a long allegory in defense of women, written about 1405. In it, she joined the great literary dispute of the age, the debate over the value of the misogynistic *Roman de la Rose*, a discourse in which Christine, still relatively unrecognized, was able to hold her own. Christine was also the author of delightful autobiographical or semiautobiographical sketches, including *Lavision* (Christine's vision), providing most of what we know about her early life. Other works included her *Le livre de la mutacion de fortune* (Book of the mutation of fortune), in which she both lamented her fate and counted her blessings, and *Le livre du dit de Poissy* (Tale of Poissy), about a journey to the cloister of Poissy, where her daughter was a nun. Christine also wrote one major historical work, *Le livré des fais et bonnes meurs du sage roi Charles V* (Book of the deeds and good character of King Charles V). Long neglected, this work is now highly regarded for its observant eyewitness testimony.

What most impresses modern readers in all of Christine's writings, except some early poems when she was still finding her way, is the stamp her personality indelibly put on everything she wrote. It was a personality breathing the new air of humanism, even if much of her work was rooted in the values of a past era.

Bibliography: Enid McLeod, *The Order of the Rose: The Life and Ideas of Christine de Pizan*, 1976; Christine de Pizan, *The Writings of Christine de Pizan*, ed. Charity C. Willard, 1994; Charity C. Willard, *Christine de Pizan, Her Life and Works*, 1984.

Paul D. Buell

Chrysoloras, Manuel (c. 1353–1415), is best known as a Greek scholar and teacher of Italian humanists who helped accelerate the humanist Renaissance in Europe. Chrysoloras was about the same age as the Byzantine emperor Manuel II Palaeologus, whom he befriended early in life. Manuel II sent him on numerous European missions, among them an unsuccessful trip to Italy to get help against the Ottoman Turks. On these trips in the 1390s Chrysoloras first came into contact with some renowned Florentines; in Venice he also mixed with Italian scholars. From 1394 to 1397 he traveled in Europe and accompanied Manuel II on his tour of various European states. While Chrysoloras was in Florence in 1397, *Coluccio Salutati, humanist and Florentine chancellor, sought him out and was a powerful force in having him named professor of Greek at the University of Florence that same year. He held the post the First European chair in Greek, for three years. During these years Chrysoloras was instrumental in introducing, preserving, and encouraging Greek studies in Italy. Some call Chrysoloras's arrival in Florence one of the great events of the Renaissance because he renewed interest in Greek studies. At Florence Chrysoloras propounded a clear, simple style of Greek that caught on with many of his students. His study of Greek and translations of Plato were important steps for the humanist movement in Italy.

Chrysoloras, himself a student of Demetrius Cydones, wielded strong influence as a teacher. His most prominent pupil was *Guarino da Verona (1384–1460), an Italian humanist and classical scholar and one of the pioneers of Greek studies in Renaissance western Europe. Chrysoloras also strongly influenced *Leonardo Bruni, whose history of Florence is considered one of the first modern works of historiography. Under Chrysoloras's guidance, by reproducing the sense of the Greek prose rather than following it word by word, Bruni produced Latin translations of Plato and Aristotle that broke with the medieval tradition. Others of Chrysoloras's humanist pupils included *Poggio Bracciolini, Francesco Barbaro, *Giannozzo Manetti, Carlo Marsuppini, and Ambroggio Traversari. Chrysoloras also lectured in Rome, Pavia, and Milan. His scholarship greatly increased European demand for Greek learning and manuscripts.

After Manuel's return to Constantinople in 1403, Chrysoloras remained for the most part in the West, primarily teaching Greek at Florence. He was known as a translator of Homer and Plato, and he wrote a textbook on grammar. He continued to undertake periodic missions to seek assistance for Byzantium against the Turks. In 1406 he was in Venice and Padua, and from 1407 to 1410 he traveled through Paris, London, Spain, and Bologna. He converted to Catholicism and spent two years (1411–13) in Rome attempting to negotiate the convocation of a general council to consider the union of the Greek and Latin churches. On 15 April 1415 he was on his way to the Council of Constance, having been chosen to represent the Greek church, when he died.

Chrysoloras's influence as a teacher on the humanist movement far outweighed his less prolific literary output. He left the *Erotemata* (Questions), a Greek grammar based on the question-and-answer method; some letters; the *Syncrisis, a comparison of old and new Rome*; and a Latin translation of Plato's *Republic*. He wrote his *Comparison of Old and New Rome* in the form of a letter to Emperor John VII Palaeologus in which he demonstrated his appreciation of the naturalism of antique art, which he found "philosophical"; he also marveled in his letters at the ancient ruins and Christian shrines of Rome. That did not prevent him, however, from concluding that Constantinople was superior because of its ideal location and its wondrous monuments such as Hagia Sophia. A 1414 discourse to Manuel II also survives in an autograph manuscript (Meteora, Metamorph. 154) in which he lamented the deceased despots Theodore I

Palaeologus and pressed for a renewed interest in the past and an intensified focus on education.

Bibliography: John W. Barker, *Manuel II Palaeologus (1391–1425): A Study in Late Byzantine Statesmanship,* 1969; Walter Ullmann, *Medieval Foundations of Renaissance Humanism,* 1977; Ronald G. Witt, *Hercules at the Crossroads: The Life, Works, and Thought of Coluccio Salutati,* 1983.

Clay Kinsner

Cisneros, Francisco Jiménez de. *See* Jiménez de Cisneros, Francisco.

Clavijo, Ruy González de. *See* González de Clavijo, Ruy.

Clement V, Pope (b. c. 1260, r. 1305–14), formerly Bertrand de Got, was the first of the Avignon popes. Clement V intended throughout his pontificate to return the papal court to Rome, but chronic illness and political instability prevented him from doing so. He conducted the controversial trial of the Knights Templars and struggled, often unsuccessfully, with France's *Philip IV to exert church superiority over secular rule. He was an expert in canon law; his *Clementiae* were added posthumously as a seventh book to the *Decretals.*

Bertrand de Got was born in Villandraut, Gironde, to a prominent Gascon family. He was educated at the convent of the Deffendi of the Order of Grandmont and studied law at Orléans and Bologna. After taking holy orders, he was a canon at Bordeaux, Agen, Tours, and Lyons before serving his brother Bérard, archbishop of Lyons, as vicar general. In 1295 he became bishop of Comminges, and in 1299 he was made archbishop of Bordeaux.

The death of Pope Benedict XI in Perugia in July 1304 left the college of cardinals sharply divided. None was able to attain the two-thirds majority required for election, and looking outside their conclave, the cardinals elected Bertrand de Got on 5 June 1305. The conclave approved of his conciliatory nature and his close ties with both the English and French kings; they hoped that he would bring peace to Aquitaine, perhaps as a precursor to an Eastern crusade.

Poor health—likely cancer of the stomach or bowel—prevented Clement from traveling to Italy, and he was instead crowned at Lyons in November 1305. He immediately created ten new cardinals, nine from France, and later promotions strengthened the French domination of the college. Clement suffered a serious, lengthy illness in 1306, during which he allowed only members of his family near him, to the consternation of his cardinals. Even when he settled the papal Curia at Avignon in 1309, he stayed there infrequently, spending much of his time in the surrounding countryside. He endured further attacks on his health in 1309 and 1313–14, and his long absences from court led to serious financial corruption.

Clement's relationship with Philip IV of France and the influence the king wielded over him colored many elements of his pontificate. Philip, keen to discredit the legacy of Pope Boniface VIII (d. 1303), with whom he had quarrelled bitterly, prompted Clement to revoke two of Boniface's most controversially theocratic bulls, *Unam sanctam* and *Clericis laicos*. Clement's *Rex gloriae* (1311) praised Philip's perseverance in investigating the merits of the dead pope's acts. Yet elsewhere Clement openly opposed Philip. He supported the candidacy of Henry of Luxembourg as king of the Romans, against Philip's wishes; his late bull *Pastoralis cura* reasserted Boniface VIII's theocratic insistence of the superiority of the church over secular power; and when in 1313 he capitulated to Philip's insistence that he canonize Celestine V, he did so as a confessor rather than a martyr, thus undermining Philip's promotion of the theory that Celestine had been murdered by Boniface VIII. Clement wrote to the French king expressing his dismay over the 1307 arrest of the Knights Templars, but his intervention arose less out of a belief in the innocence of the order than from concern over the king's meddling in what the pope considered a church matter. His decision to suspend the Council of Vienne when it appeared to be proceeding in favor of the order was motivated in equal parts by pressure from Philip, keen to have access to the order's resources, and Clement's own belief in the Templars' guilt.

The pope's lasting contribution to the church was his *Clementiae*, promulgated by *John XXII in 1317 as the seventh book of the *Decretals*. This work, begun by Gregory IX to compile a definitive account of ecclesiastical law, completed the *Corpus juris canonici*, the law of the church and the papacy, into the twentieth century. Other aspects of his pontificate confirm that Clement was an intelligent and peace-seeking pope and a pleasant though at times weak man who was prone to excesses of financial and bureaucratic nepotism. He encouraged the marriage of Edward, Prince of Wales (later Edward II of England) and Isabella, daughter of Philip IV of France. He founded a university at Perugia, established the statutes of the Faculty of Medicine at Montpellier, and created chairs of Hebrew, Syriac, and Arabic at Paris, Oxford, Bologna, and Salamanca. He also centralized the papal government, although as a consequence the pope's direct role in nominating and awarding recipients of benefices became somewhat burdensome. Among the cardinals he created, no fewer than five came from his own family. Although he raised considerable sums through unpopular taxation, he bequeathed only a small portion of his papal court's finances to his successor, the balance having been loaned to English and French kings or given for crusades or to his friends, family, and household. At his death the papal treasury was all but exhausted. He died on 20 April 1314 and was buried in Uzeste, in the parish church he built close to his birthplace.

Bibliography: Guillaume Mollat, *The Popes at Avignon, 1305–1378*, 1963; Yves Renouard, *The Avignon Papacy, 1305–1403*, 1970.

Andrew Bethune

Clement VI, Pope (b. 1290/91, r. 1342–52), formerly Pierre Roger, was derided by critics during his lifetime as a pontiff whose reign was corrupted by rampant nepotism and excessive luxury, but he nevertheless emerged as one of

the more adept diplomats to occupy the papal throne in Avignon, during a time of general political malaise in Europe. Within the church, Clement also proved himself to be an able and aggressive administrator who greatly increased the power of the papacy over the appointment of church officials and the distribution of ecclesiastical offices.

Pierre Roger was born in Maumont in Corráze, Limousin, in France at some point between May 1290 and May 1291. Pierre was the son of Guillaume Roger, a petty nobleman, and his wife, Guillemette de Maestre. As a child, young Pierre probably attended a nearby school administered by the Benedictines, who were instrumental in influencing Roger to pursue a religious vocation. In 1301, at the age of ten, Roger took his vows and was accepted into the Benedictine monastery at Chaise Dieu in the Diocese of Clermont. Six years later, in 1307, Roger departed for the University of Paris, where he studied the disciplines of philosophy and theology.

In 1316 Roger received his first position of authority within the church, the Priory of Saint Pantalçon de Lapleau in the Diocese of Limoges. That position also amounted to a significant social advance for Roger, since the post carried with it a position of recognized nobility within the French court. By 1323 Roger had completed his doctorate in theology and had been promoted to the Priory of St. Baudil in Nimes; he was later made an abbot in the Diocese of Rouen. However, Roger generally exercised these administrative duties as an absentee based in Paris, where he continued to serve as a professor of canon law.

In 1329 Pope *John XXII appointed Roger bishop of Arras. The following year Roger was once again promoted, this time to archbishop of Sens. By the following year the rising cleric had added the archbishopric of Rouen to his ecclesiastical résumé. Unable personally to attend to his growing list of responsibilities, Roger increasingly relied upon proxies and appointed delegates to administer his various flocks. Nevertheless, the archbishop's absenteeism did not slow his rise through the church hierarchy, and in 1338 Pope *Benedict XII appointed Roger to the Sacred College of Cardinals.

Meanwhile, Roger devoted most of his time and effort to serving as an emissary between the popes in Avignon and the French king Philip VI. In 1329 Roger played a prominent role in a dispute between Philip VI and the church over the boundaries between the civil jurisdictions of the church and the state and emerged having successfully defended the church's position. On the other hand, Roger could be as skilled in avoiding controversy as he was in engaging in it. Such was the case in 1331–32 when John XXII proclaimed, much to the theological chagrin of Philip VI, that the souls of the righteous would not be fully present with God until after the Day of Judgment. Ordered by the pope to persuade the royal household of a doctrine he himself rejected, Roger cleverly employed a strategic series of delays until the crisis was resolved by John's death. Thus Roger retained the favor of both the Crown and the papacy. The archbishop further enhanced his reputation with Philip by serving on several occasions as a mediator between the French king and *Edward III of England in the hope of forestalling what would become the Hundred Years' War.

Such ventures into high politics served Roger well when, in May 1342, he was elected by the Sacred College to succeed the recently deceased Benedict XII. Taking the name Clement VI, Roger declared that "my predecessor did not know how to be pope," and initiated a reign that would be characterized by lavish ceremony and wildly undisciplined spending, even to the extent of purchasing the whole city of Avignon from Queen Joanna of Naples. The new pontiff also immediately undertook a campaign to guarantee the church's prerogative in appointing officials and distributing offices, precipitating angry reprisals from Philip VI and Edward III, both of whom claimed similar rights. Clement also successfully deposed Holy Roman Emperor *Louis IV in 1346, replacing him with his former student Charles IV. Outside of Europe, Clement had always hoped to lead another crusade against the Turks; however, the idea never gained momentum, and the pope was forced to settle for a series of small naval raids instead.

Perhaps Clement's finest moment took place in 1348 when Avignon was stricken by the Black Death. Rather than fleeing the city, Clement and his Curia remained at their posts, overseeing care for the sick and burial of the dead. When many of the city's residents attempted to blame Avignon's Jewish population for the epidemic, Clement denounced such accusations and extended his personal protection to the Jewish community.

On 6 December 1352 Clement died in Avignon due to a hemorrhage from a ruptured tumor. Although Clement's generosity won him considerable support during his lifetime (he had been fond of the slogan "A pope should make his subjects happy"), by the end of his reign the papal treasury had been bankrupted and the church had been pushed further into financial peril.

The reputation of Clement VI in the centuries following his death has been somewhat mixed. His reputation for corruption and excess made him an easy target for later Protestants on the lookout for symbols of "Catholic" decadence; he was thus exhumed in 1562 by the Huguenots, who desecrated his tomb and incinerated his remains. Nevertheless, in recent years attention to his personal magnanimity and his diplomatic acumen has restored much of his lost prestige.

Bibliography: Yves Renouard, *The Avignon Papacy, 1305–1403*, 1970; John E. Wrigley, "Clement VI before His Pontificate: The Early Life of Pierre Roger, 1290/91–1342," *The Catholic Historical Review* 56 (October 1970): 433–73.

Timothy L. Wood

Coeur, Jacques (1395?–1456), was a merchant and argentier of France under *Charles VII. Jacques Coeur rose from the urban bourgeois to ennoblement and an important post in the royal court and oversaw the renewal of the French economy and French involvement in Mediterranean trade that marked the end of the Hundred Years' War. Coeur also discovered the fact that what the Crown and his own hard work raised up, royal disfavor could destroy in a few months, when he was suddenly imprisoned and ruined.

Born in Bourges, Coeur grew up with the expectation that he would establish himself as a merchant in that city. He married Macée de Léodépart, daughter of the provost of the city, in 1422, and a son was born the following year. He took charge of the local mint in 1427, and he and his partner Ravaut le Danois beat a charge of debasing the currency. A few years later, Coeur was shipwrecked off Corsica while returning from the Levant; he lost his cargo, but that trip established the connections necessary to expand French trade into the Mediterranean over the next decade.

Coeur came to royal attention around this time, and he took over the Paris Mint in 1435; Charles VII created the position of argentier for him in 1439, which led to his ennoblement. As argentier, Coeur handled the purchase of provisions and supplies for the court, the *argenterie* (a sort of pawnshop for the court), and many expenses of the Crown; charges that he exceeded the mercantile practices officially permitted may have merit. He also remained successful in business. His palace in Bourges is still a landmark, and he controlled mining and cloth manufacture, had offices all over Europe and the Levant, and owned France's largest fleet. Simply moving his primary export shipping to Montpellier generated an economic boom in that city.

Coeur's role in expanding French trade into the Mediterranean was pivotal in the French economic recovery of his time and at the same time made him a figure of international renown. Coeur gained permission from Pope *Eugenius IV to trade with Muslims, and he also sent an embassy to the sultan of Egypt, personally negotiated a treaty between the Knights of Rhodes and that sultan, and was an ambassador to Genoa and Rome. Although his role in royal finances made it difficult to separate Coeur's personal wealth from that of the Crown, personal loans to the Crown financed much of the campaign to take back Normandy from the English. These loans were probably a personal mistake, because a fundamental unwritten rule of medieval finance was never to lend money to a king who might feel obligated to pay it back.

After more than a decade demonstrating the motto of his arms, "A vaillant coeurs, rien d'impossible" ("to the brave, nothing is impossible"), and seeing his brother Nicholas become bishop of Luçon and his son Jean archbishop of Bourges, Coeur's rise abruptly ended with the loss of royal favor. He was arrested in 1451 on the charge of poisoning the king's mistress, Agnès Sorel. Though that charge was eventually dropped and his accusers, Jeanne de Vendôme and Jacques Collona, were arrested, the placement of Guillaume Gouffier, Otto Castellani, and Antoine de Chabannes on the royal commission trying Coeur guaranteed his demise, as all of them stood to gain substantially from his downfall.

Upon the failure of the poisoning charge, the commission found other charges; Coeur's powerful position and precipitous rise had left no shortage of witnesses against him. Adding to his misfortune, his wife and his brother both died while he was in prison. Despite intervention by Pope *Nicholas V and the archbishops of Poitiers and Bourges (his son), the commission found Coeur guilty on the very day of the fall of Constantinople and confiscated his goods and position; Coeur remained in prison until his daring escape in 1454.

After that escape, Coeur found refuge in Rome with Nicholas V. When Nicholas and his successor Calixtus III organized a crusade against the Turks, Coeur, the former fleet owner, took charge of the fleet. He died on the crusade and was buried on the island of Chios. Within a year Charles had restored what remained of the argentier's property to Coeur's sons, and so the Coeur family prospered under *Louis XI. While his conviction and posthumous exoneration leave questions about his guilt, Coeur is remembered largely for his demonstration of just how far a bourgeois could rise in fifteenth-century society and how fast one could fall.

Bibliography: Albert Boardman Kerr, *Jacques Coeur: Merchant Prince of the Middle Ages*, 1927; M.G.A. Yale, *Charles VII*, 1974.

Roger A. Ladd

Cola di Rienzo. *See* Rienzo, Cola di.

Colet, John (1467?–1519), was an English theologian and clergyman. A close friend of Desiderius Erasmus, Colet figures as one of the early Tudor humanists and pre-Reformers of the Catholic church. He is known for employing historical criticism on biblical writings and for his emphasis on the spread of Christianity exclusively by peaceful means. He was appointed dean of St. Paul's in 1504 and undertook the establishment of St. Paul's School in 1510. He both influenced and was influenced by Erasmus and, in all probability, influenced Sir Thomas More and William Tyndale.

John Colet was the firstborn son—and the only one of twenty-two siblings to survive childhood—of a wealthy London merchant. Sir Henry Colet had at various times been lord mayor of London and was held in high regard by *Henry VII and his court. John's future, therefore, appeared to hold high promise. He attended Magdalen College, Oxford, where he attained a master of arts degree, having successfully completed the usual course of study in Scholastic philosophy. However, shortly after earning the master's degree, he became interested in the knowledge being acquired through the Italian Renaissance. *William Grocyn and Thomas Linacre, both Oxford scholars, returned from Italy enthusiastic about the advent of Italian humanism and undoubtedly influenced Colet, who eagerly read Cicero, Plato, and Plotinus. Having decided to take orders in the church rather than to pursue a commercial career, he was soon given a parish in Suffolk and a prebend in Yorkshire. Although Colet was consistently dedicated to service in the church, at an early point in his career he decided to travel in Europe, stopping first in Paris and then going on to Italy, where he arrived in 1493. There he studied canon and civil law, Greek, philosophy, and the Holy Scriptures. He seems to have been favorably impressed by *Marsiglio Ficino, *Giovanni Pico della Mirandola, and other Italian humanists. In addition, he read the church fathers and came to prefer Origen, Ambrose, and Jerome to Augustine. His particular concern, however, was to prepare himself to preach the gospel of Christ. In Italy he would certainly have come in contact with the teachings of *Girolamo Savonarola if he visited Florence, as Linacre and Grocyn had done before him. In that case, he would have been challenged by a direct appeal for reforms in the church. In Paris during his return from Italy, Colet became acquainted with Erasmus's thinking and scholarship and was duly impressed, although he did not meet Erasmus himself. Quite some time after his return to England, Colet attended Oxford once more and this time earned a doctorate of divinity. It was a lengthy process (1483–1504), during which time he was reading Augustine and Peter Lombard and writing Bible commentaries. In 1496 he passed over lecturing on Lombard's *Sentences* and began a series of lectures on the Epistles of St. Paul.

In his lectures on Romans, Colet showed his break with Scholasticism and his arrival at a Christian-humanist view of the Bible and life. He sought to implement humanist historical criticism in place of the Scholastic approach. In doing so, he attempted to understand Paul's motives for writing by grasping the historical context in which the Apostle had written. He considered the Schoolmen to have mixed their own teachings with those of Christ. Therefore, he rejected as useless, even harmful, the debates of the Schoolmen on such topics as the ability of angels to be in more than one place at one time and the nature of man before and after the Fall. Colet considered that the simple truths of Christianity had been corrupted by the addition of the Schoolmen's theories. In this matter he had a significant influence on Erasmus, with whom he established a lifelong friendship in 1499, as he had also done with Thomas More, who was a few years behind Colet at Oxford. In these same lectures on Romans, Colet also presented a strong case for the spread of Christianity exclusively by peaceful means, thus breaking with the teachings of Ambrose, Augustine, and the Schoolmen that war is a just means of extending the faith. He also taught that justification by faith meant "simple consent to what was preached and taught about Christ." Later, however, he defined faith in light of a person's response to God's grace and his promises. Such souls believe that they can be justified by God's grace—a belief that would seem to place Colet close to the Lollards. But Colet asserted that there were necessary works of righteousness for acceptance by God, a seeming contradiction that has stirred some debate among students of his writings.

In 1512 Henry VIII waged war with France. In doing so, he reflected the typical attitude of sovereigns toward war and conquest. As he had done with Pope Julius II (who inspired Erasmus's *In Praise of Folly*), Emperor *Maximilian of Austria, and Louis XII of France, Colet condemned Henry's war efforts. In 1513, as Henry once again prepared to renew the war, Colet again preached against hostilities in the king's presence. Although there were courtiers and prelates who attempted to turn Henry and the archbishop of Canterbury against Colet on this and other occasions, he remained in their favor. When Colet, as dean of St. Paul's, founded the school for boys, he used much of his inherited wealth to provide adequate income for his schoolmasters. His concern for his students was that they not be overburdened with rules (the traditional educational approach), but that they read good books and have good models in their teachers. His generosity and his liberal educational views were consistent with his belief that God's people should perform works of righteousness.

Bibliography: Maria Dowling, *Humanism in the Age of Henry VIII*, 1986; John B. Gleason, *John Colet*, 1989; Peter Iver Kaufman, *Augustinian Piety and Catholic Reform*, 1982.

Paul Sheneman

Columbus, Christopher (c. 1451–1506). As much myth as man, Christopher Columbus fundamentally altered the world by discovering the route to lands that should not have existed. His crossing of the Atlantic Ocean opened the Western Hemisphere for European exploration and exploitation. The historical record of this legendary figure's life is blurred in many particulars, often betraying the bias, dissimulation, and blatant propaganda of his biographers. Columbus himself deliberately altered the events of his life, and even his own name, to fit his purposes.

Born near Genoa around 1451 to a family of weavers and tavern keepers, he became a seafaring merchant in the early 1470s. Widely traveled, even for a Genoese merchant, Columbus found new naval technologies, navigational techniques, and academic geography through his Portuguese contacts. He soon moved to Lisbon, married, and had Diego, his only legitimate son. Around 1480 Columbus hit upon the idea of traveling west to access the glorious mineral and agricultural riches of the Far East. A voracious but highly selective reader, he found support for his idea in two influential books, *Historia rerum ubique gestarum* by *Pius II and *Pierre d'Ailly's *Imago mundi*, but other geographers, including Ptolemy, argued that the great circumference of the earth made such a voyage untenable. Having failed to persuade the Portuguese king to support his venture, in 1485 he tried his luck in Spain. During seven years of frustrating meetings with academics and the Spanish court, Columbus attempted to convince the Spanish Crown of the feasibility of his plan and of the great profits for all should he succeed. Only after Granada fell, completing the Reconquista, did *Isabel, the queen of Castile, decide to take a chance on this persistent man.

Gathering money, ships, and men, Columbus sailed west in May 1492, using a combination of latitudinal sailing, sidereal navigation, and dead reckoning to keep his course. After some adversity, more from his fellow captains and crew than the elements, the admiral of this small fleet dropped anchor near a small Caribbean island on 12 October. In a carefully planned ceremony of dubious legality, Columbus took possession of the island in the name of the Spanish Crown. The natives of the island, primitive and strange beyond his expectations, welcomed the strangers and engaged in a trade of information and commodities. Unsure of what he had found, Columbus would try to convince himself and his patrons that he had discovered the western route to Asia, which was the most felicitous and profitable of possibilities. On Christmas Eve he left some men to start a colony on Hispaniola and set out for Spain. The Spanish court greeted him with royal acclaim and immediate plans for a second voyage. His success engendered a battle over geographic rights between the Spanish and Portuguese governments, leading to the famous 1494 Treaty of Tordesillas.

At the time of his return, Columbus found a massacred fort and fractious natives at Hispaniola. The dearth of food and profitable commodities and the difficulty of communication hampered the development of a new colony. Unable to control the situation, Columbus returned to the sea and discovered the islands of Jamaica and Cuba, claiming that the latter was the coast of China. Meanwhile, the colony at Hispaniola degenerated into bickering and warfare, with atrocities committed by all sides. In the spring of 1496 Columbus departed for Spain to defend his discoveries and his conduct. Lacking gold or spices, he brought several hundred enslaved natives to defray the cost of the expedition, but Isabel abhorred this abuse of her authority. Faced by an unsympathetic court, Columbus fled to his studies for two years to bolster his claims and his newfound status. In the summer of 1498 he received permission for a third voyage, in which he encountered the South American coast and another rebellion of the colonists. Faced with adversity, Columbus's accounts of this period became increasingly religious, culminating in a visitation by a celestial voice on Christmas Eve 1499. The following year, royal judges arrived to deal with the colonial problems and sent Columbus home in chains. As his political and economic fortunes declined, his interest in mysticism increased until he became convinced of a divine mandate for his actions. In 1501 he began writing his *Book of Prophecies* and took to signing his name as Christo-Ferens or (Christ bearer).

The Crown tried to deprive Columbus of the rights and privileges he had acquired, while he spent the rest of his life trying to preserve them. Finally, he was allowed to make a fourth and final voyage in 1502. Desperate to find a strait leading to China, he blundered into Central America instead. On the return trip, he and his crew spent a miserable year marooned in Jamaica. Through his knowledge of astronomy, Columbus used an eclipse to intimidate the angry natives into providing food for his crew. When he was rescued in 1504, he returned to Spain in disgrace to find that Isabel had died shortly before he reached the court. Without this powerful patron, his status at court steadily declined. He spent the next year and a half writing letters to *Ferdinand, the pope, the government of Genoa, and anyone else he thought could help him regain his coveted privileges. Christopher Columbus died a disturbed and bitter man on 20 May 1506. As in so many other aspects of this man's life, his exact burial place is unknown. Both the city of Sevill and the Cathedral of Santo Domingo claim to have his remains.

Columbus rose from the son of a tavern keeper to the Spanish Admiral of the Ocean Sea through his vision and persistence. His common birth embarrassed him and burdened him with the defensiveness of the parvenu. Over the course of his adult life, this self-educated man built an imposing, if disorganized, edifice of geographical theories and speculations to convince the experts and his patrons of a western route to Asia. A natural rhetorician, he carefully tailored his ideas, his motivations, and even the evidence to fit the desires of his audience. He spun grandiose tales of crusades to the Holy Land for a pious Isabel and dreams of gold and spices for a greedy Ferdinand. He exaggerated both the dangers and outcomes of his exploits to glorify himself. Hungry for titles and nobility to leave his heirs, Columbus proved unable to balance his personal ambition with the needs of his patrons. A better courtier and navigator than a leader of men, he vacillated between indecision and brutality when he was dealing with his subordinates and native peoples. While he certainly engaged in behavior considered reprehensible today, he did try to curb the excessive greed and cruelty of the Spanish colonists under his administration.

A stubborn and secretive man, Columbus became more bitter and strident in his claims as the world turned against him, though he found comfort in religion and mysticism. Ever since his first voyage, biographers and historians have made him into an icon of European colonization, as if his explorations made him somehow responsible for all that followed. Despite his flaws, Columbus achieved something unprecedented. Guided by a mixture of nautical experience, limited geographical knowledge, and wishful thinking, this forceful man crossed the impassable ocean and discovered the route to the Western Hemisphere, opening the way for the exploration of our world that continues to the present day.

Bibliography: Miles H. Davidson, *Columbus Then and Now: A Life Reexamined*, 1997; Felipe Fernández-Armesto, *Columbus*, 1991; Gianni Granzotto, *Christopher Columbus: The Dream and the Obsession*, 1985.

Brian G. Hudgins

Commynes, Philippe de (c. 1447–1511), was a diplomat and chronicler during the rule of the autocratic *Louis XI and the reckless *Charles VIII whose *Mémoires* endure as one of the foremost sources on the political environment of late-fifteenth-century France and Burgundy. His stark, psychologically revealing analysis of war, politics, and diplomacy has been compared to the work of Niccolò Machiavelli for its philosophy regarding the morality of princes. As a diplomat and advisor to Louis XI and Charles VIII, Commynes played a crucial role in the vast military campaigns and the power politics that were in constant evidence in Europe at the end of the medieval period.

Philippe de Commynes was born about 1447 at the castle of Renescure in Flanders, but both parents died while he was still a young child (his mother within a year of his birth), leaving him the heir of an estate plagued by debts. The boy Commynes was sent to his cousin Jean, lord of Commynes, when these estates were seized after his father's death in 1453; his later mercenary streak is often attributed to the straitened financial circumstances of his youth. His fortunes changed, however, when in 1464 he was brought to the court of his godfather, Philip the Good, and attached to the service of the duke's heir, Charles, then count of Charolais. Thus it was as an impressionable young man that Commynes learned firsthand of the intrigues of court, political maneuvering, royal rivalries, and the travails of war, and these lessons were to remain with him until the end of his days and become the main themes of his *Mémoires*.

Commynes has come under considerable criticism for his self-serving and mercenary tendencies, largely from a change of allegiance that was the pivotal political decision of his career. While he was *Charles the Bold's chamberlain and accompanying the duke on a savage campaign in northern France in August 1472, Commynes abandoned him and entered the service of Louis XI instead. His apparent excuse was his objection to the brutality of Charles's scorched-earth war tactics, the final insult of a long-term personal and political clash between the duke and his chamberlain. Commynes had many occasions to witness Louis XI in negotiations and to confer with him, and if his *Mémoires* are to be believed, Commynes admired Louis's shrewd intellect and political savvy. Critics believe that it was for money and influence that Commynes defected to Louis's court, but others counter that allegiance in the Middle Ages tended to center upon concrete personalities rather than abstract causes or ideals and that this kind of maneuvering was not uncommon. Certainly money and power held some sway over the younger Commynes, for while Charles immediately confiscated all his lands and possessions in Flanders, Louis rewarded Commynes with the principality of Talmont in the west of France and soon after with the lordship of Argenton through marriage to a wealthy Poitevin heiress, Hélène de Chambes.

Commynes's star continued to rise early in his career, and with Louis he became one of the most trusted royal counselors. The king would have most certainly relied on his intimate knowledge of Charles and his court during the struggle with the Burgundian duke. Among Commynes's political triumphs were his instrumental role in the negotiations for the Treaty of Picquigny in 1475, which assured *Edward IV's withdrawal from the failing Burgundian conflict, and the entrapment of Louis of Luxembourg, constable of France, who had conspired with Edward IV and Charles the Bold. When 1477 brought demise of Charles the Bold at the battle of Nancy, however, it seems that Commynes did not enjoy the same high favor with Louis as he had previously done after a disagreement of some kind with the monarch about strategy. For the next several years, until the last days of August 1483 when Louis lay dying, Commynes spent the majority of his time on diplomatic missions in Italy and out of the king's confidence.

Commynes's surprisingly bad political judgment continued when he made common cause with other dissidents regarding the regency of *Anne Valois, the king's elder sister, for the young Charles VIII. He was arrested at Amboise in January 1487 and spent six months in an iron cage at Loches Castle. He was freed in March 1489 but was fined a quarter of his goods and sentenced to internal exile on one of his estates at Dreux. It was during this time that he began to write his *Mémoires* for Angelo Cato, archbishop of Vienne, who was planning a history of Louis XI.

In the final decade of the century, the French political scene changed once again, and Charles VIII, now king, began planning in earnest an invasion of Italy and so needed Commynes's expertise. It seems, however, that Charles did not trust his father's former counselor implicitly, because Commynes was not granted as much power in policy making as he had briefly enjoyed in Louis XI's reign. Charles VIII's failed campaign in Italy in 1495 left Commynes once again out of the court's inner circle, and he did not receive any more important assignments. It was after this time that Commynes wrote the last two books of his *Mémoires*, which relate Charles VIII's reckless expedition and conclude with his death in 1498, and he spent the remainder of his life attending to his personal affairs and pleading for court favors until his death at Argenton on 18 October 1511.

Recent scholarship suggests that Commynes wrote his *Mémoires* to seek revenge on his enemies for his fall from grace at court and that his judgments and portrayals should be regarded with considerable suspicion. Whatever Commynes's purpose for writing the *Mémoires*, he remains one of the foremost authentic voices of the period, and virtually any study of late medieval France and Burgundy must turn to him for invaluable information regarding the personalities of its policy makers and for insight into the medieval mind.

Bibliography: Philippe de Commynes, *The Memoirs of Philippe de Commynes*, ed. Samuel Kinser, 1969; Philippe de Commynes, *Memoirs: The Reign of Louis XI, 1461–83*, trans. Michael Jones, 1972; Michael Jones, "Philippe de Commynes: A Courtly Middle-Man," *History Today* 39 (March 1989): 34–41.

Wendy Marie Hoofnagle

Conrad of Geinhausen (c. 1320–90) was a conciliarist at the time of the Great Schism. He was numbered among other German theologians who disputed the power of the papacy, such as Conrad of Megenburg, Leopold of Bebenburg, *Henry Heinbuche, Dietrich of Niem, and *Nicholas of Cusa. In his *Short Letter* of 1379, which requested that the French and German kings form a council to deal with the schism, Conrad produced the first formal set of conciliar declarations.

Conrad studied and taught at the University of Paris. In 1359 he became canon in Mainz and in 1361 procurator of the German nation at the University of Bologna. The occurrence of the Great Schism in 1378, establishing one pope in Rome and another at Avignon, not only divided the faithful in their allegiance and proved an embarrassment to the church, but also raised to the forefront the issue of final authority in church matters. In 1215 the Fourth Lateran Council, summoned by Pope Innocent III, had firmly established the pope as the supreme authority in the church and had claimed that because "every knee shall bow to Christ and his earthly representative," the pope was sovereign in the world as well. The schism brought that position into question. Conrad, having been influenced by *William of Ockham's *Dialogues* and perhaps by the writings of *Marsiglio of Padua and the efforts of the Spiritual Franciscans, argued that papal authority was not final. In the thirteenth century Cardinal Hostiensis had argued that the entire church held final authority. Conrad, working toward the same conclusion, offered the first important scholarly work of the conciliar movement, the *Epistola concordiae*, distinguishing between the universal church and the Roman church. He reasoned that the promise of Christ for guidance and protection could only apply to the entire church, not a local church, for even previous popes had erred. He also contended that the pope and cardinals could not constitute the universal church, for that would position the college of cardinals above the Apostles, who wavered in fear at the arrest and crucifixion of Christ. An extreme example of Conrad's views occurred in his statement that at the time of Christ's crucifixion only Mary held to the true faith, and that the supremacy of this one surviving member of the church was final. Conrad's appeal to the faithful as the final authority of the church was the heart of the conciliar movement, and it led to the position that authority bestowed on the representative of the church could be withdrawn by those who granted it, should the need arise. Conrad's inherent idea, and that of the other conciliarists, was that the pope is the servant of the church, not its master.

Conrad went to the University of Heidelberg, where he became its first chancellor. Although Conrad died in 1390, he and the other conciliarists appeared to prevail when the holy Roman emperor called a council to settle the dispute. The Council of Constance (1414–18) deposed two popes, the third resigned, and a conciliar pope, Martin V (1417–31), was elected to end the schism. However, he and his successors claimed absolute papal authority and frustrated the future efforts of the conciliarists. The conciliar movement was varied in its motives, some men challenging papal authority, some seeking church reform. They all agreed with Conrad, however, that the power of the church rested with the council of the bishops.

Bibliography: John C. Dwyer, *Church History: Twenty Centuries of Catholic Christianity*, 1985; Brian Tierney, *Foundations of the Conciliar Theory*, 1955.

Paul Sheneman

Córdoba, Leonor López de. See López de Córdoba, Leonor.

Corvinus, Matthias. See Matthias I Corvinus, King of Hungary.

Cresques, Abraham (c. 1325–87). Under the patronage of *Pedro IV of Aragon, Abraham Cresques created several world maps, possibly including the famous "Catalan Atlas," and operated at the center of the ground-breaking Majorcan cartographic school of the fourteenth century. After its incorporation into the Crown of Aragon in 1229, Mallorca had become a center of international trade and cultural exchange, including a succession of famous cartographers.

Abraham Cresques (also known as "Cresques the Jew") was born in 1325 or 1326 to a well-to-do Jewish family in Palma de Mallorca. The Cresques family had been established in Mallorca and in the royal service of Aragon for several generations at the time of Abraham's birth. Little is known about the life of Abraham Cresques, but his craft is not in doubt; a contemporary described him as "master of *mappaemundi* and compasses." Cresques was credited with the creation of several *mappaemundi*, or circular maps of the world, but only one survives, the so-called "Catalan Atlas," dated to 1375 by its accompanying perpetual calendar. Other Cresques maps appear in inventories from Spain and France dating as late as 1387, which is presumed to be Cresques's date of death. Cresques may have created the atlas together with his son and cartographic successor, Yehuda or Jaffuda Cresques, who converted to Christianity during the forced conversions of 1391. Under the name Jaime Riba (Jacobus Ribes), the younger Cresques became "master of navigational charts" at the Aragonese court in the 1390s. He may be the "Mestre Jacome de Malhorca" of a 1419 document who catalyzed the emerging school of Portuguese cartography at the court of *Henry the Navigator.

The "Catalan Atlas," which is currently held in the Bibliothèque Nationale in Paris, has been identified with the world map requested from the Aragonese court by envoys of the young *Charles VI of France in 1381. However, a description that fits the work also appears in a 1380 inventory of the library of Charles V of France. Whatever its date, the atlas has been described as "the zenith of medieval map-work." The "Catalan Atlas" is unique in being a multisheet world map in twelve half-sheets of vellum mounted on boards to fold like a screen. Four of the twelve half-sheets recount cosmographical and navigational information in Catalan; the other eight are a world map. The atlas includes elements derived from *mappaemundi*, information from thirteenth- and fourteenth-century travelers' accounts, including those of Marco Polo and Sir John Mandeville, and relatively accurate outlines of Mediterranean and western European coastlines derived from compass-based portolan charts. It is also the first map to depict a compass rose, probably based on the windroses of portolan charts. The atlas correctly places the Mongol territories within central Asia, describes the shape of the Indian peninsula more or less accurately, mentions some towns and rivers in China (most notably "Chambaleth," or Beijing), and defines the shores of northern Europe and North Africa with some inland rivers and towns, including "Tenbuch" (Timbuktu). Christian cities are marked with a cross, water is symbolized by wavy blue vertical lines, and the names of important ports are in red while less vital ones are in black. Like most medieval *mappaemundi*, however, the atlas is centered on Jerusalem; at the far west is a commentary on the mythical "Fortunate Islands" described by Pliny the Elder and Isidore of Seville and an illustration of the equally fabulous Island of Brazil. The atlas includes relatively few mythological characters in comparison to other *mappaemundi*, but it does feature Amazons, Sirens, and Pygmies battling storks along with such biblical standards as the queen of Sheba and Mount Ararat.

In its attention to the Far East and its precision in dealing with local coastlines, the "Catalan Atlas" heralds the increasing emphasis placed on trade and exploration throughout the Iberian Peninsula. From its evidence, Abraham Cresques may justly be counted an innovative master cartographer, combining information from old and new sources to come up with the best medieval guess at a map of the world.

Bibliography: Ella Campbell, "Introduction to the History of Cartography," In *Introducció General a la História de la Cartografia*, 1990; John Noble Wilford, *The Mapmakers*, 1981.

Wendy Love Anderson

Cueva, Beltran de la. *See* Beltran de la Cueva.

Cusa, Nicholas of. *See* Nicholas of Cusa.

D

da Gama, Vasco. *See* Gama, Vasco da.

D'Ailly, Pierre. *See* Ailly, Pierre d'.

D'Albarno, Montréal. *See* Albarno, Montréal d'.

D'Amboise, Georges. *See* Amboise, Georges d'.

Dante Alighieri (1265–1321), a famous Italian literary figure, is considered the father of Italian literature and also of the modern Italian language. He is best known for his *Divine Comedy*, an epic poem that combines history, philosophy, and religious doctrine with the author's own mission of defining Italian national identity and mapping its future. There is relatively little exact documentation concerning his life, and much of this has been pieced together using citations from his own works and *Giovanni Boccaccio's biography.

The Florence of Dante's birth was a city-state in turmoil. He was the son of Alighiero di Bellincone d'Alighiero, whose family, Dante himself stated, descended from the Roman founders of Florence and whose great-grandfather, Cacciaguida, was a warrior in the Crusades. Little is known of his mother except that she was probably a member of the Abati family. Regardless of the supposedly noble origins of Dante's family, his father was probably a moneylender or small businessman who left little to his children. Dante had three half brothers and perhaps also a full sister.

Dante's match to Gemma Donati was contracted by his father, and they were later married around 1294, but Dante did not mention her in his works, nor did she accompany him when he was later exiled from Florence. They had two sons and one daughter.

As a child and young man, Dante studied philosophy and the classics, and his teachers included the scholar Brunetto Latini. The closest of Dante's friends during his youth was the poet and political leader Guido Cavalcanti, and both experimented with the "sweet new style" (*dolce still nuovo*) of poetry in the vernacular.

Dante was of noble lineage and therefore aligned with the Guelf party, which was losing power in Florence, and which also favored the unification of the Italian states under one European emperor. During Dante's life, the city was under the rule of the Ghibelline party, that of the merchants, which supported the pope and was determined to remain independent of the empire. In 1289 a Guelf army, Dante included, fought and defeated the army of Aretino in the battle of Campaldino. Because of this victory and the nobles' increased arrogance, the Ghibelline government passed a law excluding all nobles from positions of power unless they were members of the professional guilds. Dante, always active in politics, joined the apothecaries' guild in 1295 in order to participate in city government. From November 1295 to April 1296 he was a member of the council of the Capitano del Popolo, and in December 1296 he was a member of the Consigli dei Savi (the Council of the Wisemen) to reach an agreement on the conditions for the elections of the new city priors. From May to September 1296 he also served on the Council of the One Hundred, a commission dealing with city fiscal matters.

The culmination of his political career came in 1300 when he was elected as one of the six priors from 13 June to 15 August. However, this apparent political success was actually the cause of his downfall and exile from Florence. In 1301 Prince Charles of Valois was marching toward Florence, supposedly to calm the conflict between two feuding factions of nobles, the White and Black parties. More probably he was sent by the pope to secure control of the city. Dante, while he was a prior, had concurred in the exile of the battling leaders of both parties even though these included his own best friend Cavalcanti. He also had continually favored the selection of advisors who would not favor pope Boniface VIII's bids to control Florence. Dante was sent on a political mission to the pope to safeguard Florentine independence in the face of Charles's advance, but in October 1301 Charles entered Florence with Corso Donati and the leaders of the Black party, which began to attack their old enemies, this time without fear of punishment. Their enemies included Dante, who was exiled from the city on 27 January 1302 and, upon refusing to face charges of political crimes, was sentenced to death should he ever return to Florence, on 10 May 1302.

While Dante continued to advocate the unification of Italy in an empire that could assure peace yet be free of papal control, he was never able to return to the city of his birth. He spent the rest of his life in the various courts of Italy, and even though he was on several occasions offered the opportunity to return to Florence, these offers came with humiliating conditions that he would not accept. In 1321, after being sent on a mission to a scientific conference in Venice by the regime of Guido Polenta, he died returning to the court in Ravenna on the night of September 14–15.

Dante's works are marked by two important occurrences in his life. One was his opportunity to study philosophy and the classics in the new Dominican school at Santa Maria Novella and the Franciscan school at Santa Croce. The other was his meeting with Bice (Beatrice), the daughter of Folco Portinari, supposedly at age nine, and whom he selected as the model for his studies on pure love and the perfect beloved.

His first book was the *Vita nuova* (New life), written around 1292, which was a combination of lyric poetry with a philosophical treatise on love. In this work, Dante demonstrated his years of study of philosophy, the classics, and religious doctrine. *De vulgari eloquentia* (1303–4) was the first scholarly treatise on the aesthetic validity of the vernacular. It was, in part, a linguistic study in which human speech was defined and the evolution of languages and dialects was explained. This work was also a defense of the adoption of the Florentine dialect as the national language of poetry and selected the most appropriate words, sounds, and ideas that should be included in the poetic language. *De monarchia*, written probably between 1312 and 1313, was Dante's treatise on civil government. It was an explanation of the importance of the world empire and a justification of its center in Rome. In this work, Dante also justified his belief in the necessity for the separation of power, the religious in the hands of the pope, and the political in the hands of the emperor.

The *Divine Comedy*, Dante's most famous work, was probably begun around 1307 and not finished until the very end of Dante's life. It was the culmination of his studies of the classics, religious doctrine, philosophy, and his mission to explain pure love completely. It contained one hundred cantos and was broken into the three nonwordly realms, the Inferno, the Purgatorio, and the Paradiso, in three almost equal sections. It is perhaps the most studied single work of Western literature. There are also fifty-four rhymes, ten letters, and other lesser works attributed to Dante.

Bibliography: Peter Dronke, *Dante and Medieval Latin Traditions*, 1986; Robin Kirkpatrick, *Dante, The Divine Comedy*, 1987; Alison Morgan, *Dante and the Medieval Other World*, 1990.

Timothy McGovern

da Vinci, Leonardo. *See* Leonardo da Vinci.

Deschamps, Eustace (c. 1346–c. 1406), is also known as Eustache Morel. Though he is not well known to students of English literature, the French poet Eustace Deschamps was a formidable poet in his own right. Perhaps overshadowed by the work of the legendary *Geoffrey Chaucer, Deschamps is known for his concern for lyricism, sincerity, and realism.

The exact date of Deschamp's birth is uncertain, but his birthplace of Vertus, Champagne, in France, has been verified. He was most likely the pupil of the more famous fourteenth-century French poet *Guillaume de Machaut, with whom he studied at Rheims. Deschamps did not plan to make a living as a poet; his education at the University of Orléans centered on the field of law. His studies permitted his entrance into the service of the duke of Orléans, as well as both Charles V and *Charles VI. In 1367 he was promoted to royal messenger, *chevaucheur*, and this experience fueled his desire to write. Often melancholy references to his experiences as a *chevaucheur* are evident in his poetry. His writing was further complicated by the destruction of his family home, Les Champs, by a fire in 1380. As a result, he referred to himself in his writing as "Brûlé des Champs," or "the burned-out former inhabitant of Les Champs."

Deschamps's body of work includes about 1,500 pieces, three-fourths of which are ballades. His writing style has been described as melodic even though it does not compare with the style of the master of melody, Guillaume de Machaut. Deschamps's masterpiece, *L'art de dictier* (1392), is representative of fourteenth-century French poetry. This was a commissioned piece, perhaps for the duke of Orléans, and its emphasis was on educating the reader on the composition of poetry. *L'art de dictier* explained what contemporary writers thought of poetry and, despite its disjointed nature, earned Deschamps's poetry its classification as "musical."

Since *L'art de dictier* was composed mostly of ballades and rondeaux, both of which contain underlying musical patterns, the poem naturally expressed rhyme and meter. This is known as *musique naturelle* (natural music), a technique that Deschamps preferred. Deschamps himself distinguished his style of poetry as *musique naturelle* from what he termed *musique artificielle*, that is, classical music. Deschamps's main concern, therefore, was with eloquence and the movement of the poetry rather than the song. His distinctions between *musique naturelle* and *musique artificielle* are very important to the comprehension of his poetry. *Musique artificielle* tends to express itself in other art forms, such as dance, while *musique naturelle* is communicated in poetry, as it was in that of Deschamps.

Deschamps's poetry was also narrative in form; he used the first person *je* as an expression of sincerity, as in the example of "Sui je, sui je, sui je belle" (Am I, am I, am I beautiful?), and he also wrote in the voice of the female in both the satiric and didactic traditions. Deschamps's language was surprisingly gritty, the physical descriptions were notably coarse, and few subjects were left untouched. Not only aging and sexuality, but also romance and nature, combined with a tone of ennui, were subject to tirades by Deschamps. The typical fourteenth-century motif, known to literary historians as the "ubi sunt" refrain, perhaps better expressed in English as "Where have all the heroes gone?" is a figurative expression evident in the former examples as well as elsewhere in Deschamps's poetry.

The concept of forgotten yesteryears (the "ubi sunt" refrain) and Deschamps's interest in *la musique naturelle* were both found not only in *L'art de dictier* but also in his other ballades. After the death of his mentor Guillaume de Machaut in 1377, Deschamps composed a eulogy entitled "Armes, amours, dames, chevalerie" in which he combined the elements for which Machaut had been famous and that he himself tried to emulate in the perfection of form, courtly manner-isms, and the expression of musicality. The "ubi sunt" refrain evident in this eulogy lent a certain poignancy to the piece.

By the time of his death in the early fifteenth century (c. 1406), Eustace Deschamps had authored 1,032 ballades and 110 rondeaux, as well as other forms of poems. He had described love and passion, old age and misery, and in so doing had ridiculed many of his contemporaries in his bawdy fashion, an expression of his *musique naturelle*.

Bibliography: Leonard W. Johnson, *Poets as Players: Theme and Variation in Late Medieval French Poetry*, 1990; Douglas Kelly, *Medieval Imagination: Rhetoric and the Poetry of Courtly Love*, 1978;

Jennifer L. Harrison

Dias, Bartolomeo (1450–1500), is best known as the first person to round the Cape of Good Hope, thereby opening a direct sea route between Europe and India and points east. Dias was born around 1450, but little is known of his early life; by the time of his African voyages, he had achieved the rank of squire of the royal household. Dias departed Lisbon in August of either 1486 or 1487, with the latter date being more likely, under orders to find the southern limit of the African continent. Dias commanded a fleet of three ships: his own *São Cristovao*, the *São Pantaleao* under João Infante, and a supply ship under his brother. Dias sailed directly along the coast, following the route established by earlier explorers such as Diogo Cão. Dias passed the Land of St. Barbara on 4 December, Walvis Bay on 8 December, and the Gulf of St. Stephen on 26 December. A gale forced Dias to sail south and away from the coast on 6 January, and when he turned east again, he found no land. By turning northeast, Dias sighted land on 3 February. The fleet landed on the east coast of Africa at Angra de São Bras (the Bay of St. Blaise, also known as the Bay of Cowherds). Dias had led the fleet around the southern tip of Africa without having seen the cape. While both the crew and Dias's officers wished to return home—the of-ficers recorded their votes—Dias convinced them to sail north for a few more days. The fleet turned back when they reached the estuary of the Rio do Infante, probably the modern Great Fish River, where one of his stone markers was found in 1938. Dias sighted the southern tip of Africa in May and named it Cabo Tormentoso (Cape of Storms); either Dom João or Dias himself later renamed it Cabo de Buena Esperanza (Cape of Good Hope). On his return to Lisbon, Dias stopped at the island of Principe, at the mouth of the Rio do Resgate, and at the Portuguese fortified trading post of Mina.

Little is known of Dias's return to or reception at Lisbon when he arrived in December 1488. While a follow-up journey seems to have been planned, no Portuguese navigator left for India until *Vasco da Gama nine years later. The delay may have been because of tensions between those who would have benefited from direct contact and trade with the East and those who currently prospered from trade with Muslim middlemen. At any rate, it was Dom João's successor *Manuel I who commissioned da Gama; Dias accompanied that fleet as far as Mina. After da Gama's return to Portugal in 1498, Dom Manuel organized a fleet of a dozen ships, heavily laden for trade and well armed, intended to impress the Indians and to open regular direct trade with the East. Dias was given command of one of the smaller ships, but the fleet was commanded by Pedro Alvares Cabral. This fleet took a considerably different route from that of Dias and his predecessors, following the route favored by da Gama. Dias's original journey down the African coast was successful largely because of the efforts of earlier explorers whom the Portuguese Crown had commissioned. They had played a game of nautical leapfrog. Each ship or fleet crept down the west coast of Africa and returned by the same route; the next followed the route laid out in the previous captain's logbook to a point further south. Thus, fleet by fleet, the Portuguese had slowly stretched down the coast. Da Gama, and Cabral after him, took radically different routes in order to take advantage of favorable winds and currents. The fleets sailed west into the Atlantic Ocean and then tacked southeast to land at the Cape of Good Hope. While da Gama's fleet had narrowly missed sighting the westernmost tip of Brazil, Cabral's fleet, and Dias with it, did sight it. Thinking it an island, they named it the Land of the True Cross. When the fleet reached the Cape of Good Hope, ever true to its original name, a squall sprang up that claimed Dias's life in December 1500.

Bibliography: Christopher Bell, *Portugal and the Quest for the Indies*, 1974; Bailey W. Diffie and George D. Winius, *Foundations of the Portuguese Empire, 1415–1580*, 1977; Sanjay Subrahmanyam, *Improvising Empire: Portuguese Trade and Settlement in the Bay of Bengal. 1500–1700*, 1990.

Tim Sullivan

Diaz, Andrés. *See* Escobar, Andrés de.

Diego de Valera. *See* Valera, Diego de.

Diego Hurtado de Mendoza. *See* Hurtado de Mendoza, Diego.

Domenico Veneziano (1405?–61) was a noted early quattrocento painter of the Italian Venetian school who strongly influenced the works of *Piero della Francesca and *Fra Filippo Lippi. Domenico's relatively few remaining paintings are attentive to detail and mathematical proportions and are notable for their graceful depiction of drapery and clothing. Domenico's distinctive use of color and lighting perhaps best distinguishes his work. His paintings appear influenced by manuscript paintings of artists such as the Limbourg brothers as well as by *Masaccio and *Fra Angelico.

Apparently born in Venice, Domenico was trained by Gentile da Fabriano in

Florence in the early 1420s. He lived in Rome between 1426 and 1432, receiving further instruction from Pisanello. Working first in Florence from 1432 to 1437 and then in Perugia from 1437 to 1438, Domenico resettled in Florence in 1439 and remained there for the rest of his life. There are few records of his personal life. Nothing is known of his Venetian works, and most of his other early works, such as a series of frescoes painted for the Florentine Church of Sant' Egidio in the Hospital of Santa Maria Nuova, have been lost. Giorgio Vasari claimed that Domenico was favored by Florentine patrons because of his expertise in oils, a technique previously unknown in Tuscany that he had learned from Antonello da Messina in Venice. Vasari described Domenico as being very friendly and generous to his fellow painters, a "good and affectionate fellow, fond of singing and devoted to playing on the lute," who eagerly shared his knowledge of painting with oils. Vasari claimed that the artist *Andrea de Castagno, infuriated by Domenico's success, beat him to death. This account was refuted much later by Gaetano Milanesi, who proved that Domenico died four years after Castagno.

Domenico's chief stylistic concern was the representation of color and light. The subject and technique found in Domenico's painting *Adoration of the Magi* (1435?) reveals the influence of Masaccio and Fra Angelico. Its circular, or tondo, shape was innovative for its time and was adopted extensively in quattrocento architecture and painting. The composition's many elaborately dressed figures, set against a highly detailed landscape background, underscored Domenico's preoccupation with overlapping gradations of light, shadows, and colors.

Domenico's principal extant work is *St. Lucy's Altarpiece* (1445–47), a painting for the high altar of the Church of Santa Lucia dei Magnoli in Florence. One panel presents images of the Madonna and Child with St. John the Baptist and Zenobius (the patron saints of Florence) in an architectural setting replete with colonnettes, capitals, arches, vaults, and inlaid steps and pavement. The scene is infused with sunlight, creating intricate shadowing in corners amid the folds of the clothing. The golds, pinks, whites, and greens of the painting have multiple variations. One can distinguish, for instance, the difference in lustre and color between the seed pearls and the larger pearls adorning the mitre of St. Zenobius. Emphasis on these same colors and shadows is seen again in another panel representing the Annunciation. Its setting is another, but less elaborate, colonnaded courtyard. The enclosed garden in the background, a symbol of Mary's virginity, has delicately painted foliage and roses. Another panel, *St. John the Baptist in the Desert*, indicates Domenico's interest in body form. The nude figure, set against a range of rugged mountains, is graceful and reflects the bright sunlight Domenico has cast over the entire picture. The saint's slightly melancholy and hesitating image marks a break from the trecento tradition of portraying John the Baptist as more vivacious.

Domenico's oft-cited 1438 letter to *Cosimo de Medici requesting a commission to paint the San Marco altarpiece carries historical and cultural importance. It forthrightly acknowledged Fra Filippo and Fra Angelico as the most important painters of that period. More significantly, the letter's obsequious tone reveals the degree of flattery required in quattrocento art patronage and requests for commissions. Domenico ultimately lost the job to Fra Angelico.

Bibliography: Jacob Burckhardt, *The Altarpiece in Renaissance Italy*, trans. and ed. Peter Humfrey, 1988; Frederick Hartt, *History of Italian Renaissance Art*, 2nd ed., 1979.

Margaret Harp

Donatello (1386–1466), originally Donato di Niccolò di Betto Bardi. Best known during his lifetime and throughout history by his nickname, Donatello, Donato di Niccolò di Betto Bardi was a key figure in late medieval and Renaissance art. This Florentine sculptor, along with his contemporaries *Lorenzo Ghiberti, *Filippo Brunelleschi, Michelozzo Michalozzi, and *Leon Battista Alberti, was one of a seminal group of Italian sculptors whose works marked the beginning of the humanist style. Like his contemporaries, Donatello continually adapted themes and styles of medieval sculpture even as he became increasingly interested in those of antiquity. His work, however, was unique even among his peers. Donatello brought a new vitality to the sculpted figure by combining innovative linear perspectives with meticulous attention to the human body, especially the relationship between the movement of the body and emotional expression. He defied contemporary practices of framing and symmetrical composition and, in doing so, used the space around the sculpture to bring the viewer into the affective space of the sculpted figures.

Donatello was the son of Niccolò di Betto di Bardo, a wool comber. His mother Orsa was about forty years old when Donatello was born. He had at least one older sister, and Donatello himself never married. There are numerous references to Donatello in Italian archives and many posthumous stories of varying degrees of credibility, including Giorgio Vasari's account of Donatello in the *Lives of the Most Eminent Painters, Sculptors, and Architects* (1568). According to several accounts, Donatello was a rough, often-gruff man who preferred a simple unpretentious life that allowed him the freedom to take assignments where and when he liked. He was generous to friends and to the poor—often to a fault—and had difficulty managing his financial affairs. Donatello, not unlike some of his Florentine contemporaries, was also quick tempered, witty, and tart tongued.

Donatello's talent and candor earned him the affectionate and loyal patronage of *Cosimo de Medici. However, Donatello's relationship with many of his corporate patrons, the guild, and civic groups that commissioned his works on behalf of the town or local church were often strained. One reason for these difficult associations was the changing nature of patron-artist relationships during the late Middle Ages and the Renaissance. There was a movement away from the corporate patronage of artisans, in which patrons maintained a high degree of control over the product they purchased, toward agreements between individual patrons and particular artists, in which the artist insisted on a greater degree of control over his work. In spite of these tensions, Donatello was a prolific sculptor whose work was in high demand during his lifetime.

Donatello first appears in Italian records as an assistant in the shop of Lorenzo Ghiberti (1404–7) while he was working on the bronze reliefs for the baptistery doors in Florence. He probably traveled with Brunelleschi to Rome before working in Ghiberti's studio. Donatello's rapid acquisition of important commissions shortly after his employment in Ghiberti's shop indicates that he was already quite skilled in his early twenties. He was registered with the Guild of St. Luke as a stone carver in 1412. Donatello worked in several kinds of media, including marble, terra-cotta, sandstone, bronze, wood, and stucco. A great deal of his work was done, and can still be seen, in Florence, where Donatello started and ended his career. He also accepted commissions throughout Italy, including Rome, Padua, Siena, Venice, Prato, and Pisa. Donatello lived for ten years in Padua (1443–53) and, for a short time before his death, in Siena (1457–59). He created sculptures of many sizes and numerous shallow relief carvings. His works also include a small medal bearing the likeness of Cosimo de Medici and an innovative glass mold, the *Chellini Madonna*, that Donatello gave as a payment to his physician. Donatello's sculpture adorns pulpits, tombs, baptistery fonts, doorways, and architectural structures of all kinds in churches. His work was also commissioned for civic spaces and private courtyards due to the increasing demand for sculpture in public works and private homes.

Donatello was much less interested in projecting a sense of harmony or majesty in his compositions, a stylistic focus evident in the works of many contemporaries, than in revealing the emotional heights, depths, and paradoxes in human experience. Excellent examples of this quality in Donatello's work are the *Christ in Purgatory* and *The Resurrection* reliefs of the Ascension Pulpit in San Lorenzo, Florence. The Christ of Donatello's *Resurrection* emerges wearily from Purgatory. He holds steadfastly to the banner of victory, his face sagging with fatigue, but must step past figures who wail and sink hopelessly back into the pit. Donatello used objects, architectural detail, and fabric drape (such as the pit and the gown sticking to Christ's straining leg muscles) to amplify the human drama. More than any other element in Donatello's work, however, it is the body that conveys the affective essence of humanity.

Donatello's sculptures abound in bodily motion. The putti of Donatello's Singing Gallery (Cantoria), arranged in two rows running in opposite directions, convey their joyful abandon in a dance of movement and countermovement with one another. In statues and reliefs, Donatello used the figures' stance to break through the two-dimensional plane that separated the viewer from the work. Donatello's innovations in this regard included new placements of arms and hands in front of the figures, and hips that were turned so that bodies moved forward and backward in a three-dimensional space. In the *Amor-Atys*, for example, the boy rocks back on one heel and raises his arms outward and upward in the direction of the viewer so that he appears to sway with delight. Donatello's understanding of the body's expressive power was also conveyed in more subtle postures. *The Pazzi Madonna*, for example, holds her holy infant high in front of her so that she pulls him close against her forehead and their eyes meet in a tender, intimate gaze. In his later works, such as the ascetic *St. Mary Magdalene*, Donatello conveyed the rawness of human experience so acutely in a single expression that many of Donatello's admirers, then and now, find these works deeply moving and profoundly disturbing. Donatello died in December 1466 and, at his request, was buried in the crypt of San Lorenzo near his lifelong friend and patron Cosimo de Medici.

Bibliography: Charles Avery, *Donatello: An Introduction*, 1994; Bonnie A. Bennett and David G. Wilkins, *Donatello*, 1984; Joachim Poeschke, *Donatello and His World: Sculpture of the Italian Renaissance*, 1993.

Donna Bussell

Douglas, Sir James, "The Black Douglas," Lord of Douglas (c. 1286–1330),

a notorious hero of Scottish independence, is remembered both in the epic poetry of his countrymen and in the chronicles of his English enemies. During his career he terrorized the English with his unorthodox methods of warfare, earning the name "Black Douglas" more for his dark deeds than for his swarthy complexion. He entered the war in the service of Robert the Bruce as a dispossessed stripling and ended his life as a close confidant of his king and one of the wealthiest lords in Scotland.

Born sometime between 1285 and 1287, James was the son of a minor Scottish nobleman who lost his life and lands fighting the English. In 1298 his family sent the young James to a safe haven in France to prevent his capture. He had just begun to learn the skills and chivalric codes of behavior proper to a gentleman when he entered a new life as a street urchin in the slums of Paris. The bishop of Lamberton, a shrewd and able politician, took James off the streets and employed him as a page. This unusual "education" and upbringing made him a flexible and unconventional man.

In 1306 James joined the rebellion of Robert the Bruce in order to regain his patrimony. The resourceful Douglas had a talent for the carefully planned ambush and the surprise raid deep into enemy territory. Always outnumbered and poorly equipped, this Scottish reiver avoided open battle unless the terrain was favorable. He preferred to inflict maximum material and psychological damage, then disappear before the English could respond. In the spring of 1307 he briefly captured his ancestral home with the help of two soldiers, a few poorly armed tenants, and his own wits. He left the beheaded bodies of the garrison inside the looted and ruined hulk of his home as a warning to the English. In the age of chivalry, when noblemen followed a rigid code of military conduct, James's unchivalrous tactics baffled his opponents.

His continual harassment of northern England brought Lord Douglas booty, truce money, respect, and fear. After the famous Battle of Bannockburn in 1314, when Scottish pikemen defeated a much larger English army, he harried the retreating army out of Scotland more on the strength of his reputation than by the number of his troops. By 1318 he had regained most of his ancestral territory and had become part of King Robert's intimate circle. The fact that Robert named James as regent of his infant heir over many other Scottish lords of higher status is a tribute to their friendship. James was as adept at diplomacy as he was in guerrilla warfare. He negotiated several truces with the English and led the delegation in 1328 that crafted a treaty that acknowledged Scottish independence.

A year later, King Robert, knowing that his own death was near, asked James to remove his heart and take it with him on crusade against the infidel. With Palestine in the hands of the Turks, James chose to battle the Muslim forces in Granada. His pious zeal and loyalty to his friends overcame his usual caution, and the Black Douglas died in battle on 26 August 1330. His compatriots buried him with the heart of his king in Douglasdale, in the Church of St. Bride, his patron saint.

James Douglas broke all the rules of medieval warfare, but he became a legendary hero in Scotland's colorful history. Terrifying in battle and charming with his friends, he was a loyal soldier and an excellent leader of men. Personally daring, he refused to endanger the lives of his men frivolously. In a world of rigid social hierarchy, the meteoric rise of the Black Douglas, from a landless youth to regent-designate of Scotland, gives powerful evidence of his military, diplomatic, and personal virtues.

Bibliography: I. M. Davis, *The Black Douglas*, 1974.

Brian G. Hudgins

Durand of Saint-Pourçain (c. 1275–1334). Nicknamed "doctor resolutissimus" or "doctor modernus," Durand of Saint-Pourçain was a Dominican Scholastic philosopher, theologian, and bishop, the author of various *Quaestiones*, sermons, and a commentary on the *Sentences* of Peter Lombard that was well known for its criticism of Thomas Aquinas. For his conviction that in extramental reality only individual entities exist, Durand can be seen, together with *Peter Aureoli and Henry of Harclay, as one of the precursors of *William of Ockham's nominalism.

Born in Saint-Pourçain-sur-Sioule in southern France, Durand entered the Dominican order in Clermont and later studied theology at the Dominican Convent of Saint-Jacques in Paris, where in 1307–8 he lectured on the *Sentences* of Peter Lombard. Most of his theological *Quaestiones* date from this period. He received his master's degree in theology in 1312, but meanwhile, his commentary on the *Sentences* had provoked the criticism of his fellow Dominicans, especially Hervaeus Natalis, because it disagreed with the views of Thomas Aquinas. Probably under the influence of the philosophy of James of Metz and John Duns Scotus, Durand had come to criticize Thomas's Aristotelianism in favor of a more

Platonist-Augustinian philosophy, in a period when Thomas was promoted as the official theological doctor of the Dominican order. A list of ninety-one supposed errors was drawn from Durand's work, and Durand had to defend himself in several quodlibetal *Quaestiones*. Despite this controversy, Pope *Clement V made Durand lecturer at the papal court in Avignon in 1313. Although Durand retracted some of his anti-Thomistic views in a second redaction of his *Sentences* commentary (1310/11), his position in the Dominican order continued to provoke cricism. The general chapter, held in Montpellier in 1316, installed a commission that found no less than 235 errors in Durand's work. In 1317 Durand was promoted to a bishopric (of Limoux, later of Le Puy), which freed him from direct obedience to the Dominican order. In the third redaction of his *Sentences* commentary (1327), after he had become bishop of Meaux (1326), he reintroduced some of his anti-Thomistic points of view, again provoking a fierce reaction from the Dominican theologian Durandellus. In 1329 Durand was part of the assembly of theologians summoned by King Philip VI called together at the royal palace in Vincennes to discuss the limits of papal and royal jurisdiction. This occasion prompted him to write a treatise on political theory, *De origine potestatum et jurisdictionum* (On the origin of powers and jurisdictions).

As a bishop, Durand continued to enjoy the favor of Pope *John XXII. He was asked to give his theological advice on several occasions: in 1322 on the question of Franciscan poverty; in 1326 on the errors in William of Ockham's own commentary on the *Sentences*; and finally, in 1333, on the Beatific Vision controversy. His treatise on the latter, however, this time provoked papal criticism. A list of supposed errors was drawn up, and several theologians were asked to give their opinion. Durand died on 10 September 1334 before a final decision on the Beatific Vision controversy exonerated him from suspicion of heresy.

Bibliography: Etienne Gilson, *History of Christian Philosophy in the Middle Ages*, 1955; David Knowles, *The Evolution of Medieval Thought*, 2nd ed., 1988.

Frans A. van Liere

E

Eannes, Gilberto (c. 1415–c. 1450?), also known as Gil Eannes or Gilianes, is best remembered as the fifteenth-century Portuguese explorer who succeeded in passing Cape Bojador. Very little is known of Eannes prior to his navigational service to Prince *Henry the Navigator. Eannes was born around 1415 (no one knows for sure) and grew up in Lagos in the southern Algarve region of Portugal. There is brief mention of Eannes's early service to Henry as a squire in his court, serving his household and once even setting out on a crusade under Henry's banner. There is a minor reference to his holding the title of princely shield bearer.

In 1433, despite Eannes's inexperience as a navigator or mariner, Henry sent him on a voyage south to try to get around Cape Bojador (which means "bulging cape"), the known southern limit of the Atlantic Ocean and the West African coast, just below twenty-seven degrees north. The cape projects twenty-five miles out from the mainland, causing violent waves and currents, capricious winds, and difficult passages to navigate. Sailors nicknamed it the "Green Sea of darkness." Before Eannes, there had been fifteen unsuccessful attempts by sailors who turned back—usually in fear—before rounding the cape. On his first trip, Eannes only got as far as Tenerife in the Canary Islands, where he took some captives and returned to Portugal after his frightened sailors reported seeing the fabled boiling waters. When Eannes returned to court with the prisoners, Henry was frustrated and immediately sent him out again the next year, admonishing him to go all the way this time. He encouraged Eannes to ignore the myths of monsters and appealed to Eannes's patriotic sensibilities. Eannes did in fact make it around the cape on the next trip and found the sea much less troublesome and fantastic than had been rumored. He landed on the coast in a small wooden boat, collected "Saint Mary's Roses," and returned to prove his accomplishment to his patron.

When he returned to Henry's court at Sagres, he was welcomed as something of a hero. On the surface, the act was one that helped inspire national unity and pride. Eannes had opened the door for explorers, breaking the psychological barrier of fear that the circulating tales had built up. Now Europeans would venture down the west coast of Africa without fear.

In 1435, with Alfonso Gonclavo Baldaya, Eannes set out again, landing about fifty leagues south of the cape. His purpose on this trip was to extend trade contacts with African people beyond the purview of the Muslims. There Baldaya and Eannes saw tracks of humans and camels but did not actually see anyone.

Records of Eannes's career after his rounding of the cape are spotty. He did command expeditions sponsored by the merchants of Lagos, Portugal, exploring as far south as the mouth of the Rio de Oro. On 10 August 1445 Eannes left in the great armada of fourteen caravels under the command of Admiral Lancarote to conquer the largely Muslim island of Tidra, off the coast of what is now Mauritania. A party of Portuguese sailors had been attacked there, and now they wanted revenge. Taking fifty-seven captives, the Portuguese won the battle. After this incident, Eannes disappeared from the historical record, but is presumed to have died at a young age around 1450.

Bibliography: P. E. Russell, *Portugal, Spain, and the African Atlantic, 1343–1490*, 1995; John Ure, *Prince Henry the Navigator*, 1977.

Clay Kinsner

Ebner, Margareta (1291–1351), was a mystic and author of the text of her revelations, the *Offenbarungen*. She knew and corresponded with several members of the Friends of God, a network of friars and laypeople interested in affective mysticism. Her primary correspondent was Heinrich von Nördlingen, who appears in her text as the "true friend of God," but never by name. His identification was made based upon a sixteenth-century collection of Heinrich's letters, now in the British Library. If these letters are genuine, they represent the oldest epistolary exchange in the vernacular.

Ebner was born around 1291 into the patrician Donauwörth branch of the Ebner family. She entered the Dominican Monastery of Maria Medingen near Dillingen-an-der-Donau at an early age. After a severe illness in 1312, Ebner experienced a type of conversion and devoted herself to the inward, mystical life. She first met the "true friend of God" in 1332, a visit that developed into an enduring friendship, surviving the upheavals of imperial and papal schisms, even though she remained loyal to Emperor *Louis IV, and he to Pope *John XXII. She began to record her mystical experiences in 1344 and was aided in this endeavor by Elsbeth Scheppach, according to the Nördlingen letters. Scheppach was elected prioress in 1345, and her continued support of Ebner's writing indicates official sanction, both within and outside the monastery, for this type of mystical narrative. Ebner died on 20 June 1351 and was buried in the chapter house of the monastery. Shortly thereafter, the chapter house was converted into a chapel honoring Ebner.

The *Offenbarungen* recorded Ebner's experiences of divine grace, beginning with her illness of 1312. After searching unsuccessfully for a cure, she surrendered herself to her illness and thereafter existed only to suffer and pray so that others might be eased through her pains. Her symptoms included not only physical pain and weakness, but also loud outcries similar to screams, and speaking episodes in which she repeated the name of Jesus Christ several hundred times. She also received visions. Ebner's symptoms and experiences were tied to the liturgical calendar, coming and going according to the liturgical chronology of Christ's life and reaching a fever pitch at Easter and the time of the crucifixion. Similar mystical episodes were experienced by *Margery Kempe of England.

Ebner was especially devoted to the Christ child and the crucifixion, the beginning and end points of Christ's life. She was given a Christ-child doll, a manger, and a crucifix during her lifetime; all of these items receive special mention in her revelations and served her as objects of contemplation and meditation. The doll and crucifix are enshrined within the Margareta Ebner Chapel in Maria Medingen. Although scholars have tended to emphasize Ebner's devotion to the Christ child, she also especially venerated Christ as divine judge of souls.

Bibliography: Margareta Ebner, *Major Works*, trans. Gertrud Jaron Lewis, 1993.

Rebecca L. R. Garber

Eckhart, Meister Johan (c. 1260–1328).

Probably the best-known mystic of the Middle Ages, Meister Johan Eckhart was also arguably the most important. He rivaled Pseudo-Dionysius as a spokesman for the tradition of negative theology, yet his doctrine also incorporated the Scholastic theologies of Thomas Aquinas and Albertius Magnus and the Trinitarianism of Augustine. His challenging and often-paradoxical investigations, undertaken both in learned treatises and in many sermons in both Latin and German, exerted tremendous influence, but also incurred the adverse judgment of the papal Curia, which in 1329 condemned a number of propositions drawn from his writings.

Johan Eckhart was born around 1260 in Hochheim, near Erfurt in Thuringia. He entered the Dominican order, which sent him to Paris about 1277 to study the arts. While Thomas Aquinas had died in 1274, Eckhart would have been thoroughly acquainted with the great Dominican doctor's work. He appears to have studied with Albertus Magnus, Thomas's own teacher, at the Dominican *studium generale* in Cologne, placing him there before 1280 (the year of Albert's death). Eckhart's Neoplatonism clearly reflected Albert's particular appropriation of Proclus and Pseudo-Dionysius.

Eckhart returned to Paris in 1293 and obtained the master's degree in theological studies. Between 1294 and 1300 Eckhart served as prior of the Dominican house at Erfurt and as the order's vicar in Thuringia. During his time there he composed the *Counsels on Discernment*, a compilation of advice to his charges. From 1302 to 1303 Eckhart occupied one of the two Dominican chairs at the University of Paris. In 1303 he was appointed provincial of the new Dominican province of Saxony, and in 1307 he also took the office of general vicar of Bohemia. At this time Eckhart wrote his most famous vernacular work, *The Book Benedictus*, a two-part work consisting of a speculative treatise, "The Book of Divine Consolation," and a long sermon, "On the Nobleman." In 1311 the order saw fit to return him to one of its two chairs in Paris, an indication that it esteemed his scholarship as highly as it did his administrative abilities. *The Parisian Questions* date from this period, as do the extant portions of his *Work in Three Parts*. Most of the latter work was probably never finished, and much of what was finished that has been lost, but the bulk of Eckhart's surviving Latin oeuvre, six exegetical treatises and fifty-six sermons, derives from this ambitious project's third part, the "Work of Commentaries."

Much of the rest of Eckhart's life was taken up with preaching. In 1314 he was in Strassburg, where he was responsible for the spiritual guidance of Dominican nuns and Beguines, to whom many of his eighty-six vernacular sermons would have been delivered. In 1323 he returned to the Dominican school in Cologne as the master for advanced students. Eventually his preaching drew the attention of Henry of Virneburg, the archbishop of Cologne, who early in 1326 instituted inquisitorial proceedings against Eckhart.

The details of Eckhart's two trials are not entirely clear, but a sketch of the major points is still possible. In September 1326 Eckhart responded in writing to a list of forty-nine suspect articles drawn from his work, and shortly thereafter to another list of fifty-nine. The committee was prepared to pronounce against him when, on 13 February 1327, Eckhart made a public profession of faith and appealed to Pope *John XXII for vindication. Sometime that spring he left for Avignon, where John XXII set up a commission of cardinals and court theologians to investigate the charges. This committee distilled the massive lists of the earlier trial to twenty-eight propositions, to which Eckhart again responded. He denied even teaching two of the propositions, while several others he admitted might be poorly expressed or even wrong. Sometime early in 1328 John XXII submitted the trial documents to the famed inquisitor, now cardinal, Jacques Fournier (later *Benedict XII), who was clearly very uncomfortable with the methods of the trial and complained that he would have preferred to see the articles in their contexts. In any event, Eckhart died before the conclusion of the proceedings, although exactly when or where remains unknown. John XXII wrote to Henry of Virneburg on 30 April 1328 that the investigation would proceed despite Eckhart's death. On 27 March 1329 the bull *In agro dominico* was promulgated, condemning as openly heretical fifteen of the articles Eckhart admitted to teaching; the other eleven it labeled suspect, but noted that with explanation these articles could be given a Catholic meaning. The text of the bull mentioned that on his deathbed Eckhart "revoked and also deplored" the condemned articles insofar as they might mislead or be misunderstood. This caveat was significant, and Eckhart seems to have maintained his earlier stance that, as he put it, "I am able to be in error, but I cannot be a heretic, for the first belongs to the intellect, the second to the will."

Eckhart was among the most challenging and creative mystical thinkers of the Middle Ages. As a negative theologian, he emphasized divine transcendence, but he also taught that the divine is immanent in the soul. Insofar as this tension was reconciled in Eckhart, it was only to the extent that Scholastic considerations of essence, existence, and knowledge formed the foundations of his mystical metaphysics, a metaphysics that grounded itself in the doctrine of the soul as *imago Dei* (image of God). Three key themes pervaded Eckhart's mysticism: first, the ideal of detachment, or spiritual poverty, by which the soul makes itself open to the will of God; second, the birth of the Son in the soul, which reflects God's immanence in creation, and which is in one sense made possible by detachment but is at the same time occurring perpetually in the eternal now of the Godhead; and finally, the contemplative's "breaking through" to the supreme deity, the "simple ground" that is identical in God and in the human soul and by which the soul is the image of God. Again, breaking through stands in a dynamic relationship with the birth of the Son in the soul; the soul, upon breaking through to that simple ground beyond itself and beyond the Trinity, also participates in the fundamentally Trinitarian activity of giving birth to the Son and so of giving birth to itself. The key difference here between the Son and the soul, Eckhart maintained, was that what occurred in the Trinity by its nature occurred in the soul by grace. Eckhart both drew on and contributed to women's spirituality in the later Middle Ages, and his influence is clearly discernible in his renowned disciples, *Heinrich Suso and *Johann Tauler, and in *Nicholas of Cusa.

Bibliography: John D. Caputo, "Fundamental Themes in Meister Eckhart's Mysticism," *The Thomist* 42 (1978): 197–225; Meister Eckhart, *Meister Eckhart: The Essential Sermons, Commentaries, Treatises, and Defense*, trans. Edmund College and Bernard McGinn, 1981; C. F. Kelley, *Meister Eckhart on Divine Knowledge*, 1977.

Jeffrey Fisher

Edward III, King of England (b. 1312, r. 1327–77).

Best known for his brilliant victories against the Scots and then the French during the early stages of the Hundred Years' War, Edward III also reigned during a period of constitutional development in England. Edward III was born at Windsor Castle on 13 November 1312, the eldest son of Edward II of England and Isabelle of France. One of Edward's greatest accomplishments as king was his ability to overcome the unfortunate governments of his father and later his mother and to restore prestige and authority to the English monarchy. Edward II was an incompetent

king who showered wealth and power on undeserving favorites, alienating many
of the great magnates of the realm. He was also a poor warrior, losing to Robert
the Bruce and the Scots in the humiliating Battle of Bannockburn in 1314. His
queen, Isabelle, was the daughter of King *Philip IV, "the Fair," of France and
an unhappy wife. In 1325 Isabelle, sent to France on a diplomatic mission to
her brother King Charles IV, began an affair, both political and romantic, with
an exiled English baron, Roger Mortimer of Wigmore. The two lovers invaded
England in September 1326 with a band of mercenaries mainly from Hainaut
in the Low Countries. Within a few months Edward II was captured, and in
January 1327 he formally abdicated his throne in favor of his fourteen-year-old
son, Edward of Windsor.

For the first three years of his reign, Edward III was king in name only. The
real rulers of England were Isabelle and Roger Mortimer. Their government was
little better than the one they had overthrown. Isabelle, Mortimer, and their
supporters enriched themselves at the expense of their fallen enemies, and they
were as inefficient as the former king in dealing with the Scots. They were
ruthless in eliminating their political enemies, most notably Edward II, who
probably was killed in captivity sometime in the fall of 1327, and his half
brother, Edmund, earl of Kent, who was beheaded in March 1330. By October
1330 the young king was eager to throw off his yoke and take the government
of England into his own hands. He had Mortimer arrested, tried, convicted, and
executed within six weeks; his mother was placed under luxurious house arrest
until her death in 1358.

The first decade of Edward III's reign was not successful either in domestic
or foreign policy. Though he fought a successful battle against the Scots in 1333
(the Battle of Halidon Hill), Edward's relationship with the new French king,
Philip VI of Valois, was deteriorating rapidly. Edward's position as a pretender
to the French throne (as the only surviving grandson of Philip the Fair), his
willingness to lend aid and comfort to *Robert of Artois, a French prince who
had been banished by Philip VI for the crimes of forgery and subornation of
testimony, and his status as duke of Aquitaine finally led the two kings into
armed hostilities after Philip confiscated Aquitaine in May 1337. Edward did
not acquit himself well in the early years of the conflict that would later be
known as the Hundred Years* War. His alliance system with states in the Low
Countries and the Holy Roman Empire was not helpful to his cause. A number
of abortive campaigns and his constant need for money via taxation did not
endear him to his English subjects or to his Parliament. Edward dismissed his
treasurer and chancellor, Bishop Stratford, who was accused of working against
his policies, and arrested five royal judges. A disgruntled Parliament, meeting
in 1341, refused to grant Edward's needed taxes unless some concessions were
approved, including a public auditing of the royal finances. Edward had no
choice but to agree.

The political crisis of 1340–41 appears to have been a turning point in Edward

III's career. For the next twenty-five years Edward enjoyed the favor of both his magnates and the commons. Much of this support came as a result of some outstanding military victories in the 1340s and 1350s. On 26 August 1346 Edward III's outnumbered English army solidly defeated the French at Crécy, a battle in which many of the great French nobles were killed. At the Battle of Neville's Cross in October 1346 an English army defeated the troublesome Scottish king David Bruce, who was captured and imprisoned. The important French port city of Calais fell to the English in the summer of 1347 after a successful siege. Finally, on 19 September 1356, during the Battle of Poitiers, the English forces led by King Edward's eldest son *Edward of Woodstock, known as the Black Prince, captured the French king John II. By 1360 French internal politics were in chaos. In the Treaty of Brétigny of May 1360, although Edward had to give up his claim to the French throne, he gained full sovereignty over Aquitaine, Calais, and other small territories. Edward III's power had never been greater.

The year 1360, however, marked the apex of Edward III's reign. Slowly the military advances in France of the two previous decades began to erode. Edward named his son the Black Prince as the resident lord of Aquitaine, a task that because of his temperament he was ill suited to perform. Domestically, now that the great military victories had ceased, Edward had an increasingly difficult time maintaining his popularity. The lords and commons were demanding, and usually receiving, more concessions from the Crown. In the last decade of Edward's life the memory of the great warrior king seemed very remote. Edward's devoted queen, Philippa of Hainaut, died in 1369, after which the king seemed to remove himself from public life. He surrounded himself with flatterers and an ambitious younger mistress, Alice Perrers. Edward's adult sons, particularly the unpopular *John of Gaunt, duke of Lancaster, began to take on more and more royal duties. The political community's complaints about the lack of effective leadership culminated in the so-called Good Parliament (1376). During this session a speaker was appointed to act as representative of the commons, and officials were impeached. The commons proceeded for the first time in English history to oust unpopular favorites at court and to attack the Crown itself. Although most of the Parliament's achievements had been reversed by the next year, a precedent had been set.

On 21 June 1377 Edward III died of a stroke at Sheen, to be succeeded by his grandson *Richard II, the Black Prince having died the year before. Historians have been divided over the significance of Edward III's reign. Nineteenth-century constitutional historians criticized Edward as a king, claiming that he gave over too much power to the lords and commons as a way of financing his military ventures. Historians today tend to see Edward III as a strong king who not only enjoyed military success, but who also was an astute politician able to navigate the treacherous political waters that his father had left for him.

Bibliography: W. M. Ormrod, *The Reign of Edward III*, 1990; Scott Waugh, *England in the Reign of Edward III*, 1991.

Dana L. Sample

Edward IV, King of England (b. 1442, r. 1461–83). Edward, duke of York, gained the throne of England after the deposition of *Henry VI in 1461 during the so-called Wars of the Roses. A claimant to the throne through his descent from the second son of *Edward III, Edward became the leader of the Yorkist faction following the death of his father at the Battle of Wakefield in 1460. The following year Edward was proclaimed king in London, a claim made real by his victory over the army of Henry VI at Towton.

Edward had great difficulty in establishing a stable monarchy; attempts to restore Henry in the early 1460s and in 1470–71, Edward's dependence on the earl of Warwick until the latter's death at the Battle of Barnet in 1471, and his patronage of his queen's family, the Woodvilles, which alienated the nobility, all worked against the establishment of a stable regime. The defeat and death of Warwick and the murder of Henry VI in 1471 were the preludes to a period of domestic calm until Edward's death in 1483.

The twelve years of peace in the latter half of the reign allowed Edward the opportunity to indulge in the sort of opulent artistic patronage that was expected of a fifteenth-century monarch. Arguably Edward's most lasting influence as a patron was his foundation of St. George's Chapel at Windsor Castle in 1473. The chapel was to be a monument and mausoleum for Edward's new Yorkist dynasty and the symbolic focal point of the Order of the Garter, which Edward promoted enthusiastically as a rival to the Order of the Golden Fleece in France.

By contrast, Edward attempted to run down the collegiate foundations of his predecessor Henry VI. All royal grants in favor of Eton College were revoked as part of the Act of Resumption passed by Edward's first parliament in 1461. A bull for the college's dissolution was obtained from the pope in 1463, but Edward had a change of heart, restoring Eton's lands and successfully petitioning for the revocation of the bull.

Henry's foundation at Cambridge University, King's College, also fell from royal favor and was ordered to pay all its revenues to the Exchequer. Edward's queen, Elizabeth Woodville, founded Queen's College, Cambridge, in 1475, reestablishing an earlier foundation of 1448 by Margaret of Anjou, wife of Henry VI. Queen Elizabeth's brother, Lionel Woodville, was appointed chancellor of Oxford University, where the king also founded a lectureship in divinity.

Edward IV was a notable bibliophile and has been credited as the first king to establish a permanent royal library in England. Many of these volumes were Flemish illuminated manuscripts, reflecting Edward's strong connections with the Burgundian lands. He was exiled in Flanders during the restoration of Henry VI to the throne in 1470–71, during which time he was a guest of Louis of Bruges, the lord of Gruthuyse, a great collector of books and literary patron.

This exposure to one of the great libraries of Europe led to the establishment of a library following Edward's return to England and defeat of the resurgent Lancastrians in 1470–71.

Edward's reign was notable for the introduction of printing into England with the establishment of *William Caxton's press at Westminster in 1477. Caxton dedicated his *Tully on Old Age* and *Godefroy of Bologne* to the king in 1481, but Edward does not seem to have been an active patron of Caxton, who enjoyed more favor from Edward's brother-in-law, Anthony, Earl Rivers. An edition of Rivers's *Dictes and Sayings of the Philosophers* printed by Caxton was presented to Edward and was the first book to be printed in England.

Despite the troubles of his times and the king's own relative lack of interest in the new learning, Edward's reign represented something of a political and cultural recovery after the disastrous rule of his predecessor. The printed works of Caxton and St. George's Chapel and Windsor stand as cultural memorials to the achievements of his age.

Bibliography: A. J. Pollard, ed., *The Wars of the Roses*, 1995; Charles Ross, *Edward IV*, 1974.

Michael Evans

Edward of Woodstock, "the Black Prince" (1330–76). Our knowledge of *Edward III's eldest son Edward of Woodstock, the Black Prince, comes to us largely through the influential contemporary accounts of *Jean Froissart, who was attached to the English court during the 1360s, and the herald of Sir John Chandos, one of the prince's closest advisors. Both Froissart's *Chronicles* and the Chandos herald's biography of Prince Edward are concerned with presenting the significant events of military history the authors had witnessed within the context of the chivalric virtues they championed.

The martial victories of the Hundred Years' War enjoyed by England under Edward III's rule were the stage upon which the prince played out his role as one of the heroic figures of the late fourteenth century. Edward III, who was to model the Order of the Garter on the legendary Round Table of King Arthur, claimed the throne when he was seventeen, a few months after the birth of the first child born to him and Queen Philippa of Hainaut at Woodstock in June 1330.

At sixteen years of age the prince fought alongside his father in the Battle of Crécy in 1346 and went on to achieve his own victory at Poitiers in 1356 when he defeated and captured King John II of France. This high point of English martial success around the middle of the century was also displayed in the spectacular tournaments hosted by the king, at which the prince played a primary role. Wealth and chivalric pride characterized the career of the Prince of Wales, who was also the earl of Chester and the duke of Cornwall, and who owned, in addition to his principal residence of Berkhamstead Castle, estates in several counties.

The volumes of the prince's household register attest to the lavishness of his lifestyle and reveal that constant efforts had to be made to collect revenues and rents from his landholdings. The Chandos herald's biography made much of the prince's chivalric generosity to his knights and retinue, but evidence for his behavior is also found in the register. For instance, on 31 July 1347 he doubled the wages of the servant who kept his wardrobe from three pence to six pence per day. Expenditures for luxuries did not abate during times that saw losses in revenue due largely to outbreaks of the plague. Thus during 1352–55 there were unpaid rents in Chester due to the wastage of land during the pestilence, while at the same time, in addition to money he spent on gambling, the prince bought (on 24 June 1352) an enameled gold cup as a New Year's gift for his father and a large brooch with three rubies and an emerald as a gift for his mother.

In 1361 Edward married his cousin Joan, the countess of Kent, and in 1362 he was made prince of Aquitaine. Although the elaborate entertainments of their court illustrated the liberality and courtesy of the prince, it was not long before he made mistakes that tarnished his image and led to his downfall. The Gascon lords whom he now ruled resented the taxation increases he imposed. In 1366 the prince agreed to support Pedro of Castile in his attempt to regain the throne from his half brother Henry Trastámara. Although the subsequent Battle of Ná-jera was a victory, the death toll in the prince's army was heavy, and he himself seems to have caught chronic dysentery, the disease that gradually weakened his health and eventually led to his death. After the siege of the rebellious Limoges in 1370, the prince's military career came to an end. Following the death of his oldest son Edward of Angoulême, he returned to England in 1371 with his wife and the son who would later become *Richard II.

Throughout his life the prince, like many other prominent knights in this period, had exhibited considerable piety as well as prowess. He generously supported the College of Boni Homines at Ashridge, Hertfordshire, and it is fitting that the final entry for his register records a grant to Agnes Paynell, a nun of the cell of Sopwell, to support her from the revenues of the prince's manor of Busshey. He is recorded as having died, as he was born, on Trinity Sunday, and his devotion to the Trinity was also attested by his establishment of a chantry chapel at Canterbury.

Before his death in 1376, the prince drew up a will in which he made plans for his funeral and entombment in Canterbury Cathedral. The tomb that he designed, with its bronze effigy in battle armor looking up at the image of the Trinity painted on the tester, invokes the chivalric ideals of piety, duty, and courage. Around the base of the tomb are carved his badges of war and peace with their respective mottoes, *houmont* (high courage) and *ich diene* (I serve). The tomb effectively signifies both the worldliness and the piety of knighthood in this time period. His achievements in battles and tournaments are displayed overhead, while inscribed along the edge of the tomb, under the heroic figure, are the popular *memento mori* verses from the early twelfth century *Disciplina clericalis* of Petrus Alfonsus. These lines direct the passerby to contemplate the decomposition of the prince's body after death and the transitory nature of earthly success and material wealth.

The name by which Edward of Woodstock has been remembered in history and legend, the Black Prince, survives in John Leland's sixteenth-century *Collectanea* and is notably preserved in a speech assigned to Charles VI in Shakespeare's *Henry V*. The meaning given there to the legendary name was repeated by John Weever in 1631 in his *Ancient Funeral Monuments within the united monarchie of Great Britain*, who stated that Edward was called "black" because of "his dreaded acts of battell."

Bibliography: Richard Barber, *Edward, Prince of Wales and Aquitaine: A Biography of the Black Prince*, 1978; Mildred K. Pope and Eleanor C. Lodge, eds., *Life of the Black Prince by the Herald of Sir John Chandos*, 1910; *Register of Edward, the Black Prince*, 4 vols., 1930–33.

Karen Arthur

Enrique IV, King of Castile (b. 1425, r. 1454–74). Enrique IV was one of history's most maligned monarchs. His reign was plagued by controversy, and the resulting chaos was blamed by his contemporaries, critics, and even later historians on his assumed impotence and rumored homosexuality. Recent historical scholarship, however, has sought to separate his accomplishments from the comments of his detractors, and the result has been an improved recognition of the achievements of his tenure on the throne.

Enrique was born in 1425. His relations with his father, *Juan II, were not always harmonious. As a young prince, he obtained control of the city of Segovia and created a base of power from which he often challenged the authority of Juan. In 1441, for example, he refused to come to his father's aid in an important battle against his upstart cousins, the infantes. The historical record offers little insight into the source of his alienation from his father. Throughout his career Enrique relied heavily on a trusted advisor, Juan de Pacheco.

Enrique acceded to the throne in 1454 upon the death of Juan II. The early years of his reign were marked by several successes. Early on, he pacified members of the nobility by offering them titles and other grants. He "promoted" members of the lower ranks of the nobility to positions of higher status in return for their loyalty. He also undertook to transform Castilian government in several ways. First, he began appointing university-trained *letrados* to administrative posts, a practice that his successors, *Isabel and *Ferdinand, would continue. He also extended the range of royal officials appointed to monitor affairs at the local level.

During the years 1455–58 he continued the medieval reconquest against Muslims in Spain, engaging in several campaigns designed to subdue the Islamic kingdom of Granada. His strategy was one of caution and negotiation, which frequently angered and frustrated the nobility, who wanted to engage in bloodier, more decisive campaigns as a means of enhancing their own honor and influence. He preferred diplomacy over destructive campaigns and waged an incremental campaign that was very unlike the earlier character of the reconquest. He fought short, more decisive battles and slowly secured several key regions. He was reluctant to take fortresses since he did not wish to provoke Muslim revenge or vest too much influence in the hands of the nobility, who would have received such fortifications as rewards for their contributions of money and troops.

As had been the case with his father, the greatest challenge facing Enrique was the Spanish nobles. Anxious to amass wealth and influence, they were a constant thorn in his side as he sought to assert his royal power. The nobility was never completely satisfied with Enrique as a ruler. The nobles were critical of his Granadan policy, and they distrusted his reliance on Pacheco. They were suspicious of his reliance on *conversos* (Jews who had converted to Christianity) and his perceived favor for Jews and Muslims. Ultimately, it was not just the nobility that challenged Enrique's power. Various noble factions began to rally around Enrique's half brother Alfonso, who, as the next of Juan II's male children, was the heir apparent. In 1462, however, Enrique's wife gave birth to a daughter, *Juana of Castile. Almost immediately rumors began circulating that Enrique was not the child's father and that the infant was instead the result of an adulterous union between the queen and one of Enrique's advisors, *Beltrán de la Cueva. This galvanized Alfonso's supporters, who waged civil war and who made their position brutally clear when they staged a mock dethronement of Enrique in 1465. Alfonso's death in 1468 raised the question of the political legitimacy of his sister, Isabel of Castile. At a historic meeting that year Enrique recognized Isabel as hereditary princess in return for her loyalty and promise to persuade her noble supporters to support Enrique. She continued, however, to consolidate her power behind the scenes, even marrying Ferdinand of Aragon against Enrique's wishes. In the end, her plotting served her well. With Enrique's death in 1474, a new civil war broke out between the supporters of Isabel and the supporters of Enrique's daughter, Juana.

Bibliography: Townsend Miller, *Henry IV of Castile,* 1972; William D. Phillips, Jr., *Enrique IV and the Crisis of Fifteenth-Century Castile, 1425–1480,* 1978; Nancy Rubin, *Isabella of Castile: The First Renaissance Queen,* 1991.

Elizabeth Lehfeldt

Escobar, Andrés (Andreas) de (1367–c. 1439), also known as Andrés Diaz or Andrés Didace, was a Benedictine who spent most of his ecclesiastical career in the papal Curia. Escobar wrote several widely read works on penance and the reform of the church, including an important treatise on conciliar theory. Portuguese by birth, Escobar studied theology at the University of Vienna, where he received his master's degree in 1393. Soon thereafter he began working in the Roman penitentiary (the papal office concerned with confession, penance, indulgences, and related matters), and in 1408 Pope Gregory XII made him the bishop of Cività in Sardinia.

Between 1408 and 1410 Escobar wrote two minor works on ecclesiastical reform and the problem of the papal schism, *Colles reflexi* (Necks bent) and *De schismatibus* (Concerning the schismatics). Escobar attended the Council of Constance and was present at the proclamation of the decree *Haec sancta*, which stated that the council had authority over the pope and could use that authority to end the Great Schism. In 1422 Pope Martin V translated Escobar to the bishopric of Ajaccio in Corsica, and in 1428 he was made bishop of the titular See of Megara. In addition to this series of bishoprics, Escobar was also abbot of the Benedictine house at Randuf (in Braga) and was granted use of the revenues of the monasteries of San Juan de Pendorada (in Oporto) and San Rosendo de Celanova (in Galacia) during abbatial vacancies in those two houses.

In 1429 Escobar wrote his first major work, *Lumen confessorum* (Light of confessors), a treatise on the theological and legal aspects of the sacrament of penance. This work proved popular during Escobar's lifetime and for several centuries thereafter. In 1431 Escobar attended the Council of Basel as a representative of Pope *Eugenius IV, but he appears not to have been an active participant in the council's deliberations. Between 1434 and 1437 he spent much of his time in Florence and Bologna on papal business, and he participated in the Council of Ferrara-Florence. Escobar wrote his last major work, *De Graecis errantibus* (Concerning the mistaken Greeks), in 1437 as part of the debates at the Council of Florence surrounding the possible reunion of the Greek and Roman churches. The exact date of Escobar's death is unknown, but he almost certainly died sometime before 1440.

Escobar's most important work was the treatise *Gubernaculum conciliorum* (The government of councils), which was written in 1434–35. Although Escobar was employed in the papal Curia and attended the Council of Basel as a papal representative, his treatise argued in favor of a conciliarist position. Escobar presented the ideal council as a republican institution, composed of clerics and laymen working together as equals to reform the church. In the more radical passages of this treatise, Escobar argued that a properly constituted council had the authority to rule the church, even to the point of deposing the pope and carrying out reforms on its own. Despite these conciliarist views, Escobar sided with Pope Eugenius IV in his disputes with the Council of Basel and argued in favor of papal primacy over the patriarch of Constantinople in *De Graecis errantibus*, perhaps in the hope that a strong papacy could better guarantee a lasting reunion of the Greek and Roman churches.

Bibliography: Antony Black, *Council and Commune: The Conciliar Movement and the Fifteenth-Century Heritage*, 1979.

Stephen A. Allen

Este, Beatrice d', Duchess of Milan (1475–97).

Under Beatrice d'Este, the Milanese ducal court represented the best in Renaissance values. Her influence shored up the fortunes of Milan in the fractious political world of the late fifteenth century. A daughter of the ruling house of Ferrara, Beatrice was well educated and was affianced to *Ludovico Sforza, the regent of the Duchy of Milan, in 1480. Ludovico, a true Renaissance politician and prince, became a patron of universities, artists, and poets, but proved to be less than adept as a ruler.

Married in January 1491, Beatrice soon came into her own as a princely consort. Ludovico adored his young bride and gave her free rein; she immediately drew the best and brightest minds to the Milanese court, with herself at the center. Beatrice enjoyed a good relationship with the titular duke of Milan and his wife, but she and Ludovico were acknowledged as the real power in the duchy. In 1491 Beatrice arranged a lavish reception for the French king, *Charles VIII, who had designs on the throne of Naples and wanted to establish an alliance with Milan. A treaty was signed, but 1492 was a year of peace, a year that saw the flowering of intellectual and artistic interests in Milan. Ludovico and Beatrice went forward with plans to revitalize the buildings and gardens of the city, and Beatrice in particular worked assiduously to make the court of Milan the cultural center of Europe and succeeded in doing so. Some of the greatest artists and poets of the day made their way to Milan, including *Leonardo da Vinci. An alliance was established between Pope *Alexander VI and Naples, but no hostilities erupted for the time being. In 1493 Beatrice gave birth to her first child, a son and heir. The birth spurred Ludovico in his quest to become ruler of Milan in name as well as in fact, and he began to seek alliances with the pope, Venice, and the holy Roman emperor. A triumphant visit to Ferrara by the couple in mid-1493 resulted in Ludovico naming Beatrice as his representative to Venice, where she charmed the Venetians as her husband's ambassador. When the king of Naples died in 1494, France made its claim, and Ludovico and Beatrice, as allies, welcomed the French king when the invasion began. The titular duke of Milan fell ill and died, and Ludovico wasted no time in having himself proclaimed the next duke. The French king's successes in the Italian peninsula frightened Ludovico, who feared for Milan, and as a result, he formed an alliance with Venice and the Holy Roman Empire. It was now believed by many that only Ludovico could save Italy from the French, and so the pope and Spain joined the alliance. Charles marched north to attack this "holy league," yet Ludovico was successful in expelling the French from Milan, despite a temporary loss of nerve on his part that led to the use of Beatrice as his liaison to the army. The combined forces of the league were brought against Charles, leading to an Italian victory, though not to a complete defeat of Charles. A treaty was negotiated between France and Milan, and this separate peace angered the other members of the league.

With Ludovico's title and hold on Milan no longer in doubt, he turned to aid Pisa against Florence. He enlisted the aid of Emperor *Maximilian I, who had been enchanted by Beatrice at a meeting to discuss this intervention. France was eventually pushed out of Italy completely, but the internal war against Florence did not go well for Milan. Swelled by his victory over the French, Ludovico overextended himself within the Italian peninsula, and the Venetians in particular were angered by his swaggering.

During these days Beatrice concentrated on her duties as duchess, wife, and mother, but she was troubled in late 1496 with the news that Ludovico had fallen in love with one of her ladies-in-waiting. In addition, a beloved daughter from Ludovico's first marriage died at about the same time, but the couple's mourning was cut short by a visit from Maximilian. Beatrice's grief and depression were evident to all, complicated by her recent pregnancy.

On 2 January 1497 she inexplicably fell ill, gave birth to a stillborn son, and passed away early the next morning. Despite his infidelities, Ludovico fell into deep mourning, and Milan shared his grief. Even by the standards of the day, the obsequies for Beatrice were excessive, and many feared for Ludovico's sanity. He built an elaborate tomb for Beatrice, became devoutly religious, and even cast off the mistress who had so troubled Beatrice. The ducal court of Milan lost its shining center, and Ludovico lost his bearings with Beatrice's death. His political acumen failed him, and he was eventually exiled from Milan by the French and ended his days in one of their prisons. The loss of Beatrice spelled ruin for the future of the house of Sforza.

Bibliography: Julia Cartwright, *Beatrice d'Este, Duchess of Milan*, 1903; Trevor Dean, *Land and Power in Late Medieval Ferrara*, 1988; W. L. Gundersheimer, *Ferrara: The Style of a Renaissance Despotism*, 1973.

Connie Evans

Este, Ercole I d', Duke of Ferrara (1431–1505), also ruler of Modena and Reggio, was born on 24 October 1431 to Niccolò III and Rizzarda da Saluzzo. He was Niccolò's third legitimate son and succeeded his two brothers, Leonello (r. 1441–50) and Borso (r. 1450–71) on the ducal throne. Little is known about his early youth. Knighted by the holy Roman emperor in 1433, he was sent by Leonello in 1443 to the court of Alfonso, king of Naple, (*Alfonso V of Aragon) where he remained for many years and became a knight of some repute. Later he fought under Bartolomeo Colleoni for the Venetians against Florence in 1466–67. A seasoned veteran, he became duke two months before the age of forty, and after putting down rebels who were hostile to his accession, he emerged an entirely new man. He married Eleonora of Aragon in 1473 and had seven children by her, plus two bastards, an impressive record of moderation by contemporary standards.

Like Borso, he was a lover of peace, an enthusiast for vernacular poetry, drama, and romance, and a patron of the arts. He was also a fine ruler, genuinely dedicated to Ferrara, and a brilliant diplomat who raised Ferrara, the smallest of the Italian Renaissance states, to a cultural eminence far beyond its size. His diplomatic skills were much sought after to mediate disputes between other states throughout the Italian peninsula. He was the first to actually implement city planning. His addition to Ferrara, or *addizione erculea*, engineered by Biagio Rossetti, was the first modern city based on a plan. He also raised the university in Ferrara, II Studio, to a first-class institution.

Ercole was also an innovator in theatre. The first performance of a classical humanist drama in a modern language was done in Ercole's new courtyard on 25 January 1486. The play was the *Menaechmi* by Plautus, and it was performed in Italian on a wide platform stage with five "houses" on it. The production abandoned the stiff rhetoric of the Latin style for a theatre of action and characterization. The material was prepared by scholars in II Studio by *Guarino da Verona, his son Battista, and Ludovico Carbone. The great humanist Peregrino Prisciani supervised the construction of the scenery, and Nicoletto appears to have been the painter. Ercole's theatre established trends followed by Renaissance dramatists all over Europe. It continued long after his death and produced the first perspective scenery in 1508, done by Peregrino da Udine. Ercole died on 25 January 1505 on the nineteenth anniversary of his first performance of Plautus's *Menaechmi*. His works in theatre are probably his most significant contribution to Western culture.

Bibliography: Trevor Dean, *Land and Power in Late Medieval Ferrara*, 1988; Edward Gardner, *Dukes and Poets in Ferrara*, 1968; W. L. Gundersheimer, *Ferrara: The Style of a Renaissance Despotism*, 1973.

C. Thomas Ault

Eugenius IV, Pope (b. 1383, r. 1431–47), chose to be named after Eugenius III, the disciple of Bernard of Clairvaux. His background was monastic, and he owned a copy of Bernard's *On Consideration*, which was addressed to his namesake. Eugenius IV, born into the age of the Great Schism, had a troubled pontificate that spanned the subsequent Conciliar Crisis.

Gabriel Condulmaro, was born into a Venetian noble family in 1383 and entered the Monastery of S. Giorgio in Alga at an early age. However, he was drawn into the public sphere when his uncle, Angelo Correr, became Pope Gregory XII in the Roman obedience during the schism. Gregory called his nephew to the Curia and made him bishop of Siena (1406); two years later, Gabriel became a cardinal. This promotion of a kinsman helped convince the Roman cardinals that the pope had no desire to end the schism, and they agreed to meet with the Curia of Avignon at the Council of Pisa in 1409. This council only succeeded in creating another obedience, that of Pisa, and so most of Gregory's followers deserted him. When the Council of Constance began in 1414, Gregory proved willing to abdicate on the condition that he be allowed to "convoke" the council. Cardinal Condulmaro went to Constance and there became a member of the college of cardinals under the pope of union, Martin V. During Martin's reign he concentrated on monastic reform and negotiations for the reunion of the Eastern and Western churches.

When Martin died in 1431, Condulmaro was elected to succeed him. Eugenius inherited a council scheduled to meet at Basel and a failed crusade against the Hussites. Eugenius, hearing that the assembly was poorly attended, announced its transfer to Bologna to meet with the Greeks. This set off protests from the delegates at Basel, which was negotiating with the Hussites in an effort to pacify central Europe. Eugenius, faced with the hostility of Milan and Naples, enemies of his native Venice, temporized. When he was driven from Rome, he took refuge in Florence. In exile, the pope extended grudging recognition to the Council of Basel.

This peace between Eugenius and Basel, however, did not last long. The council imposed the oath of incorporation on the presidents appointed by the pope, which means that they could not leave, and it set about reforming the Curia. In addition, the Basel assembly refused to move to a site in Italy acceptable to the Greeks. This decision split the council, and Eugenius was able to capitalize on this tactical error by agreeing to meet the Greeks in Ferrara. With the support of the Medici, the pope moved the council of union to Florence instead. There an agreement was made on the outstanding theological issues, and a bull of union was published in 1439. The Council of Basel replied by declaring conciliar supremacy a truth of the faith and then declared Eugenius deposed.

Eugenius, buoyed by his union success, replied with a condemnation of Basel's rulings. There ensued a diplomatic struggle across Europe in which envoys of the Roman pope and of Basel's chosen successor, Felix V, competed for the allegiance of the princes. England and Burgundy readily came to support Eugenius; and France and Castile eventually accepted him as well. The Italian princes also were won over to the Eugenian camp, so that only Germany remained outside the pope's reach. Here Eugenius's tactics often proved too clumsy to succeed, but eventually, in 1447, while the pope was mortally ill, the empire too acknowledged his authority.

Eugenius, meanwhile, had returned to Rome. There he continued negotiations for the reunion of the Eastern and Western churches. He commemorated his attempts at reunification by commissioning new doors for the Vatican basilica from Filarete. The fragility of this achievement, however, was underscored both by the reluctance of the Greeks to adhere to the terms of reunion and by the disastrous Crusade of Varna. More successful was Eugenius's effort to promote monastic reform. The Dominican and Franciscan Observants received his favor, and the Dominican reformer Antoninus was made archbishop of Florence, while the Camaldolese humanist Ambroggio Traversari was made general of his order. When Eugenius died in Rome in 1447, he chose to be buried next to Eugenius III, whose interest in monastic reform he had shared.

Bibliography: Joseph Gill, *Eugenius IV, Pope of Christian Union*, 1961; Joachim W. Stieber, *Pope Eugenius IV, the Council of Basel and the Secular and Ecclesiastical Authorities in the Empire*, 1978; Charles L. Stinger, *The Renaissance in Rome*, 1985.

Thomas M. Izbicki

Eyck, Hubert van (1366?–1426), was a painter of Ghent. Long considered the early master of fifteenth-century Flemish panel painting, Hubert van Eyck is, in fact, the most elusive figure of all the Flemish artists. There are only four records that mention such a man, and they are brief. Yet based upon these, one of the longest-running debates among scholars of Netherlandish painting has continued unabated. Documentary evidence indicates that Hubert was the elder brother of *Jan van Eyck, for whom a considerable number of works and a long bibliography exist. No works were signed by Hubert, nor is there any firm evidence to support which parts of the Ghent altarpiece (an inscription praising Hubert's work on it survives) might have been his. The pictures with which Hubert has been credited range from none, with the exception of some unidentified parts of the panels of the Ghent altarpiece, to six panels, part of the Ghent polyptych, two drawings, and a portion of the Turin *Hours*. Without greater documentary proof that Hubert received these commissions, his life and work will remain shadowy. Thus in 1424–25 Master Luberecht (Hubert) received six shillings for two designs for an altarpiece commissioned by the Ghent magistrates; in 1425–26 his apprentices received a half shilling on their visit to Hubert's workshop, presumably to help execute a commission; on 9 March 1426 Hubert had in his workshop an image of St. Anthony and some other works for an altarpiece commissioned by Robert Poortler and his wife for the Lady Chapel of St.-Sauveur; and, in the same year, inheritance taxes were paid on Hubert's property. Although the spelling of the name varied, as was often the case, it seems certain that these references were to one man.

The inscription that links this Hubert to Jan van Eyck and to the Ghent altarpiece is found on the frames of the altarpiece's wings. This, too, has provided material for debate among scholars, for they do not all translate the inscription similarly. However, most do agree that the inscription identified Hubert van Eyck as a painter whose brother Jan was "second in art" to him. Precisely what this meant is controversial: was Hubert the better or more famous painter, or was he merely the first or older brother? Whichever translation is accepted, most scholars agree that Hubert had some part in the design and/or execution of the polyptych. How much and which parts are vigorously debated. All of the attributions to Hubert are made on the basis of stylistic determination, and that is a style defined negatively: images that are not clearly Jan's works are attributed to Hubert. Works assigned to Hubert separate from the Ghent altarpiece include an *Annunciation to the Virgin* in New York; *The Three Women at the Sepulchre* in Rotterdam; two panels, *Crucifixion* and *Last Judgment* (wings of a diptych sometimes credited to Jan van Eyck) in New York; a *Crucifixion* in Berlin; *The Carrying of the Cross* in Budapest; drawings of the *Adoration of the Magi* and *Betrayal of Christ*, and folios in the Turin *Hours* manuscript identified as the work of "Hand G." Many of the panels were also assigned to "Hand G" of the Turin *Hours*. Otto Pächt attributes, albeit tentatively, all "Hand G" works to Hubert in his last publication, ascribing perhaps the largest body of work ever to Hubert, and by so doing has reawakened the controversy about the existence and work of Hubert van Eyck, a debate that will not soon be resolved.

Bibliography: Elisabeth Dhanens, *Hubert and Jan van Eyck*, 1980; Otto Pächt, *Van Eyck and the Founders of Early Netherlandish Painting*, 1994.

Marian Hollinger

Eyck, Jan van (c: 1380–1441). Few early modern European painters have provoked as much discussion as that which has centered on the Flemish painter Jan van Eyck, perhaps best known for his double portrait of Giovanni Arnolfini and his wife, *The Arnolfini Wedding*. Jan van Eyck's works displayed a commitment to detail as well as the use of vivid color schemes. His use of disguised symbolism, a technique by which the objects in the painting often bore a deeper religious meaning, established him as a forerunner of modern artistic techniques.

Little evidence exists to verify the date of birth of Jan van Eyck. His birth date was first proposed as around 1370 by the seventeenth-century historian Joachim von Sandrart, but has since been placed anywhere from 1380 to 1390. Tradition places van Eyck's birthplace as the province of Limburg in Old Netherlands, a region located near what today is Belgium. As the son of gentry, Jan was expected to enter service as an apprentice to the nobility. Little is known of his education beyond the assumption that he was educated in the very courts to which he was apprenticed. From 1422 to 1424 Jan served as court painter at The Hague for John of Bavaria, count of Holland, and it was there that he acquired a reputation as an excellent craftsman, fame that led him into service as a court painter and "varlet de chambre." From 1425 until his death in 1441, Jan van Eyck served Philip the Good, duke of Burgundy, in the capacity of court painter, and he was often asked to make confidential journeys on behalf of the duke in order to arrange marriage alliances. On one such mission in 1427, Jan was sent to Tournai to negotiate the marriage of Philip to Isabella of Urgel (which never took place), as well as to paint her portrait. Many of van Eyck's early paintings were commissioned in such a fashion, and it was the only way he could make a decent living. In 1428 Jan was sent on another diplomatic journey, this time to Portugal to arrange the marriage of Isabel, the daughter of the Spanish king Juan I, to Duke Philip, a ceremony planned for 1430. Other than details from works commissioned by royalty, little evidence exists to determine the historical background of van Eyck's early paintings. Paintings often had to be created according to the wishes of the patron, and so patronage was crucial to the understanding of the background of some paintings. Regardless, works such as *The Man in the Red Turban*, executed in 1433, the Ghent altarpiece, completed in 1432, and *The Arnolfini Wedding*, painted in 1434, provide pictorial testimony to the excellence and skill of Jan van Eyck.

Few other painters at the start of the fifteenth century captured the essence of early modern Europe as did van Eyck. His technique of self-inscription was unique among his peers. For example, his *Man in the Red Turban* contains his motto, *Als ich kan* (As I can), on the frame. In addition, the date found on another portrait of a young man known simply as *Timotheus*, "actum anno domini 1432. 10. die octobris," represents the authoritative language of legal formulas, thereby revealing van Eyck's level of education. Again, in *The Arnolfini Wedding*, Jan declared his presence in the depicted ceremony with the words "Johannes de Eyck fuit hic" (Jan van Eyck was here). Since the previous inscriptions were written in Latin, they also reflect the level of classical education attained by Jan van Eyck.

Not only his education, but also his marriage in 1433 to a woman known to us only as Margaret was a positive influence on van Eyck's art. It was in 1432 that he most likely completed the Ghent altarpiece, a painting probably begun by his brother, *Hubert van Eyck, and left unfinished at Hubert's death. This may also be the first painting by Jan van Eyck in which the date and the authorship were included on the surface of the painting itself. Altarpiece paintings are known as polyptychs, a term describing paintings made up of three or more separate panels joined together with hinges. This was an arrangement similar to the more familiar two-hinged diptych. The theme in this polyptych was religious, like much fifteenth-century art, and illustrated a combination of St. Augustine's *City of God* and the Book of Revelation from the Bible. The altarpiece contains such panels as the *Annunciation*, the *Adoration of the Lamb*, and portraits of saints.

Although van Eyck did not always paint portraits of saints or religious figures, his paintings almost always had a religious connotation. *The Arnolfini Wedding* is perhaps his best-known work because of the intimacy Jan established between the viewer and the subjects he portrayed. Despite the fact that Jan lived in a culture unaware of the printing press, his use of physical gestures and depth "tease" the viewer. His portrait of the young couple seems openly simplistic, merely a man and woman standing before the viewer preparing to take their vows. They appear not to acknowledge the presence of any observers, but their aloofness is deceiving, while a third dimension is introduced via the use of the dog standing at their feet. Through an understanding of the concept of disguised symbolism, the viewer then discovers by looking at the mirror directly above the dog that the couple is not alone. Reflected in the mirror is a second couple— two men who are also observing the scene. Such complexities were typical of van Eyck's work and forced the viewer to consider another realm of possibilities.

All of van Eyck's works appear to be deliberately symbolic; his meaning is not found just in the elements of the paintings but in an understanding of how certain details related to theology. Jan van Eyck's incredible use of detail and his ability to capture a fleeting moment in order to express the unique whole were what made him a master of European and, most certainly, early Flemish art.

Bibliography: Elisabeth Dhanens, *Hubert and Jan van Eyck*, 1980; Craig Harbison, *Jan van Eyck: The Play of Realism*, 1991.

Jennifer L. Harrison

Eymeric, Nicholas (c. 1320–99). A Catalonian theologian of the Dominican order, Nicholas Eymeric (also spelled Eimeric, Eymerich or Aimerich) was in-

quisitor general of Aragon. Best known for his *Directorium inquisitorum*. he was a prolific author of philosophy, theology, and biblical exegesis. He was also involved in several ecclesiastical disputes and was a supporter of the Avignon papacy.

Nicolás Eimerico (Nicolaus Eymericus in Latin) was born in Gerona, Catalonia, around 1320. He entered the order of Friars Preachers at the Geronese convent on 4 August 1334 and was the novice of Dalmace Moner. He spent one year, between 1351 and 1352, at Saint-Jacques in Paris and then became headmaster of students in the convent of Barcelona.

Named inquisitor general of the kingdom of Aragon in 1357, Eymeric became infamous for his zeal. His prosecution of alleged heretics and his vigorous inquisitorial methods gained him many enemies among his peers. In 1360 the general Dominican chapter of Perpignan ordered his transfer to Ferrara in order to avoid further discord. Though he was elected provincial prior of Aragon in 1362, his enemies influenced Pope Urban V to ban him from this post. Meanwhile, he began his prolific writing career.

Named inquisitor once again in 1366, Eymeric turned his attention to the disciples of the mystic Catalan poet *Ramon Llull. At the same time, he defended the Roman Catholic church's rights in a conflict between the archbishop of Tarragona and King *Pedro IV of Aragon. Both campaigns earned him the monarch's enmity, since Pedro also favored the Llullists. In 1371 Eymeric notified the Avignonese Pope Gregory XI that certain Aragonese monks, led by the Franciscan Pedro Bonageta, had a peculiar doctrine of eucharistic theology. Bonageta's teachings held that the Host ceased to be the body of Christ once it was placed in the mouth or if it was handled improperly. Gregory found this doctrine repugnant enough to forbid its preaching in Tarragona and Zaragoza. Thus when Eymeric was banned from Aragon by royal decree on 11 March 1375, he was in turn well received by the pontiff.

It was in Avignon that Eymeric wrote his *Directorium inquisitorum* (Inquisitors' manual) in 1376. Printed for the first time in Barcelona in 1503, the *Directorium* became a most influential handbook of inquisitorial procedure for centuries to come. Besides procedure, it also treated the history of religious doctrine and behavior, discussed the signs of heresy, and detailed the methods by which one might recognize and punish heretics. Much of its subsequent popularity was due to the annotated and largely expanded edition by Francisco Peña that was first published in 1578.

Eymeric accompanied Gregory XI to Rome in January 1377 and obtained from him strong support in his campaign against the Llullists. When *Urban VI was elected by Roman cardinals in September 1378, however, Eymeric continued to support the Avignon papacy. He wrote to the French cardinals, who had fled from Rome to Anagni, to support their choice of Clement VII. While this hardly improved his standing with Pedro IV, who supported Urban, Eymeric nevertheless was able to return to Aragon that same year.

Named inquisitor general again on 13 April 1387, Eymeric relaunched his pursuit of the Llullists. Though Pedro's son Juan I was a supporter of the Avignon papacy, the powerful Llullists had garnered his favor. Eymeric was thus exiled from Aragon again in 1393, and so he moved to Avignon. Ever faithful to the Avignon papacy, he supported the election of *Benedict XIII (Cardinal Pedro de Luna, whose confessor he had been) against the Paris conciliarists in 1395. Near the end of 1397 he returned to his convent in Gerona, where he continued writing treatises until he died on 4 January 1399.

Eymeric's writings, mostly unedited, fill eleven large volumes. Besides the *Directorium* and various other works on inquisitorial procedure and jurisdiction, he wrote numerous sermons and commentaries on three of the Pauline Epistles. His theological treatises largely concerned the divine nature and eucharistic theology. As for specific heresies, he composed separate treatises on demonology, astrology, alchemy, and divination. His *Elucidarium*, which he wrote during his exile in 1393, was a response to Honorius of Autun's work by the same name. Another notable work, the *Correctorium correctorii*, which he wrote at Avignon in 1396, was a response to the *De contemptu mundi* by Innocent III. Thirty-two of his works are extant, most of them preserved from the library of Pedro de Luna.

Bibliography: Henry Kamen, *Inquisition and Society in Spain in the Sixteenth and Seventeenth Centuries*, 1985; Edward M. Peters, "Editing Inquisitors' Manuals in the Sixteenth Century: Francisco Peña and the *Directorium inquisitorum* of Nicholas Eymeric," "Bibliographical Studies in Honor of Rudolf Hirsch," ed. William E. Miller et al., *Library Chronicle* 40, no. 1 (1975).

Michael Lindsey

F

Fébus, Gaston. *See* Gaston III, Count de Foix.

Ferdinand V, King of Aragon and Spain (b. 1452, r. 1474–1516), was known as "the Catholic" and was also king of Castile (1474–1504) with his wife *Isabel; king of Sicily (1468–1516) and Aragon (1479–1516) as Ferdinand II; and king of Naples (1504–16) as Ferdinand III. While he was an astute, dynamic ruler in many ways and was responsible, with his wife Isabel, for the unification of the area now known as Spain, the reign of Ferdinand V is most notable for its financial support of the ventures of *Christopher Columbus and the cruelties of the infamous Inquisition.

Ferdinand the Catholic was born in the small town of Sos in Aragon, a region of what is now Spain, on 10 March 1452, the son of Juan II of Aragon and his second wife, Juana Enriquez. The young life of the prince was unremarkable, his education similar to that of any young nobleman destined for a political career. When his older brother Carlos died suddenly in 1461, Ferdinand found himself the heir apparent to the powerful but turbulent kingdom of Aragon. At the urging of his shrewd father, in 1469 Ferdinand secretly married his second cousin, Isabel of Castile, who was the popular contender for the Castilian crown then held by her half brother, *Enrique IV. This union was fated to be one of the most cunning political maneuvers in all of Spanish history.

When Enrique died in 1474 without indicating a successor, Isabel proclaimed herself queen of Castile, an action that sparked a bitter war that lasted until 1479 and was decisively won by Isabel and Ferdinand. Ferdinand's father had died just months prior to this victory, and thus, after more than four centuries of separation, the kingdoms of Aragon and Castile were reunited. To safeguard this union, the monarchs, supported by the Cortes or parliament and the towns, severely restricted the power of the aristocracy by destroying their fortresses, depriving them of many semiroyal privileges, seizing command of the three orders of knighthood, and demanding the return of revenues appropriated by the nobles. Ferdinand also created the Santa Hermandad, or Holy Brotherhood, a police force controlled by the Crown and made up of men from every region in the kingdom, to uphold the law and ensure peace. Because it had the authority to try as well as arrest prisoners, the Santa Hermandad was instrumental in maintaining control of both the general populace and the aristocracy, thus reducing the influence of the nobles. With the support of the devout Isabel, Ferdinand reduced the power of the church, another political force to be reckoned with at that time, by reclaiming the right to make his own appointments. The king also initiated a large-scale reform of the church in Spain, thereby reducing the upheaval of the Protestant Reformation later in Spanish history.

With the strength and security of the two kingdoms restored, Ferdinand could divert his attentions and ambitions elsewhere. In the spirit of the earlier Crusades and the Reconquista, a holy war against the Moorish territories on the Iberian Peninsula began in earnest when, on 16 December 1481, King Mulay Hassan and his armies laid waste the Christian fortress of Zahara in Andalusia, killing any who resisted and enslaving the rest. With the wars of succession finished in Castile, Ferdinand used this opportunity to expand his territory in the name of religious zeal. In a merciless campaign of ten years that utilized slash-and-burn tactics and long sieges with heavy artillery to weaken Moorish resolve and demolish their formidable strongholds, Ferdinand conquered the kingdom of Granada in January 1492, a year that would prove to be the most significant of his reign.

Christopher Columbus had arrived at Ferdinand's court in 1486 with plans to find a western route by sea to Asia. Interested in this opportunity to increase his kingdom's wealth and glory, Ferdinand organized a commission to investigate Columbus's claims. Unfortunately, Ferdinand was also embroiled in the war with Granada at that time and so could not afford to finance this risky venture. It was not until the surrender of Granada early in 1492 that the monarchs were able to afford this investment, and they were amply rewarded for their faith and vision with extraordinary riches and a newly discovered territory that would eventually become a vast overseas empire.

The year 1492 is also infamous for the edict of 31 March that compelled every Jew in Spain to convert to Christianity or face exile. Because they were unable to take any gold or silver out of the country, the 150,000 Jews who fled were forced to sell their property for anything they could carry, allowing the Christian population to virtually confiscate Jewish property for next to nothing. While the edict was purportedly issued to establish Spanish unity, politically and religiously, it was really the culmination of the ravages of the notorious Inquisition on Spanish society. While relations between Christians and non-Christians in Spain were relatively close until the end of the thirteenth century, the fourteenth century saw these relationships deteriorate due in part to efforts of the clergy and in part to popular resentment against Jewish involvement in usury and tax collection. In addition, class rivalry between the Jews and the nobles increased as the Crown's financial dependence on the Jews (who were politically reliable) for tributes and tax collection grew. As a result of pressure from pogroms and oppressive legislation, many Jews converted to Christianity, and this new social class swelled in number and prestige as its members gained positions of authority in the court and society as a whole. By the end of the fifteenth century, the *conversos*, as these converted Jews were called, posed a serious threat to the established hierarchy based not on merit but on landed wealth and hereditary status.

The Inquisition was established in 1478 ostensibly to combat heresy, especially among those *conversos* who were practicing their Jewish faith in secret, but it quickly evolved into a weapon of racial persecution. Ferdinand was more reluctant to persecute the Moors still living in Spain because they were generally not as prominent as the Jews and were largely a valuable laboring class. While the edict forcing the Moors to choose baptism or exile was issued in Castile in 1502, it was not until 1525 that Ferdinand's successor did the same in his kingdom of Aragon.

Unfortunately, Ferdinand's policies regarding the Jews and *conversos* had far-reaching effects: the Inquisition and banishment significantly reduced the number of artisans and the crucial merchant and manufacturing class that sustained economic growth in society, which would later limit the impact of the Industrial Revolution in Spain. The bloom of the Renaissance that was flourishing elsewhere in Europe was severely withered in the suffocating atmosphere engendered by the Inquisition and the concomitant economic decay. In spite of this, the building of a new university and certain tax exemptions allowed for the growth of the printing industry and encouraged the influx of foreign scholars and humanists. The removal of duties on imported books, in combination with the strong printing industry, fostered learning not only among the nobility but also in the middle classes. As a result, there was a growth in the literary arts that included works in the vernacular, especially translations of the classical and Italian Renaissance writers.

When Isabel died in 1504, the Castilian Crown went to their daughter Juana and her husband *Philip I, archduke of Burgundy. When Philip died of a fever two months after arriving in Spain in 1506, Juana's insanity paved the way for Ferdinand to assume the throne once again as regent for her son, Charles V. With Spain reunified under his command, Ferdinand was able to turn his attention toward foreign conquest. The years 1508–9 saw the defeat of Oran and Tripoli on the North African coast, Moorish cities that harbored pirates who had frequently raided southern Spain. The unstable chaos of Italy, which was then a collection of independent and warring city-states, made it a natural target for an ambitious ruler. In 1496 and again in 1503 Ferdinand liberated Naples, a fief of the church, from the French in the name of Pope *Alexander VI. In doing so, he established Spain as a formidable military power and a leading kingdom in Europe, and his possession of Naples directly involved him in Italian politics. By joining the League of Cambrai with France, the Papal See, and Emperor

*Maximilian in 1508, Ferdinand acquired five new cities in Italy. He later formed a Holy League against France with the pope and the Venetian republic, which later included England and Maximilian, and defeated the French armies, taking control of France's Italian territories as well. In 1512 Ferdinand conquered the kingdom of Navarre, thus extending Spain's northern border the entire length of the Pyrenees Mountains, so he could move Spanish troops easily to the wars in Italy. Ferdinand died on 23 January 1516, having spent his life creating an empire that extended far beyond the borders of the kingdom of his birth and leaving a legacy of accomplishments that would reflect the best and the worst of medieval kingship.

Bibliography: Felipe Fernández-Armesto, *Ferdinand and Isabella*, 1975; Jean Hippolyte Mariéjol, *The Spain of Ferdinand and Isabella*, trans. Benjamin Keen, 1961; Nancy Rubin, *Isabella of Castile: The First Renaissance Queen*, 1991.

Wendy Marie Hoofnagle

Fernández de Madrigal, Alfonso Tostado. *See* Tostado, Alfonso.

Fernández de Palencia, Alfonso. *See* Palencia, Alfonso Fernández de.

Ferrante I, King of Naples (b. 1423, r. 1458–94), was the bastard son of *Alfonso V, "the Magnanimous," whose historical reputation for duplicity, cruelty, treachery, and greed is most likely the result of propaganda disseminated by the dukes of Anjou to support their own claims to the throne of Naples and justify their invasions of Italy. Ferrante swiftly and mercilessly consolidated his power in Naples after his coronation in 1458 through a systematic elimination of his enemies and the formation of strategic alliances both within Italy and elsewhere in western Europe. Once he had finally established peace within his kingdom, Ferrante's liberal economic policies strengthened a wide variety of enterprises in Naples and fostered other new crafts, such as printing, and important innovations in music, vernacular literature, and the law. Ferrante died in 1494, shortly before the invasion of Naples by *Charles VIII, the first in a series that destroyed the peace and growing prosperity that Ferrante had spent his life trying to achieve.

Few leaders have suffered from such extremely negative propaganda for as long as Ferrante I of Naples. Even well into the twentieth century, the image has been perpetuated of a Ferrante who was completely untrustworthy in his dealings with friends and enemies alike and sadistically cruel to the point that today one might consider his actions insane. This shocking, and largely false, reputation has its origins in the writings of the French chronicler *Philippe de Commynes, ambassador in Italy for Charles VIII, the duke of Anjou and king of France who also had a legitimate claim to the Neapolitan throne. It was probably Ferrante's questionable status as the illegitimate son of Alfonso V that spawned this vitriolic campaign to discredit him and, as a result, his right to the title of king of Naples.

Ferrante was born in Valencia on 2 June 1423, the illegitimate son of Alfonso the Magnanimous, then king of Aragon, Sicily, Valencia, and Sardinia and later also conqueror of Naples and southern Italy. His mother was most likely a Catalan gentlewoman named Gueraldona Carlina Reverdit. Even at a young age, malicious rumors surrounded Ferrante that his real father was a half-caste Spanish Moor or a converted Jew, vicious slanders at the time, considering the powerful pro-Christian forces emerging in Europe that eventually led to the infamous Inquisition. Alfonso sent for his son to come to Italy in 1438, where Ferrante was legitimized in 1440. In 1452 and 1453 Ferrante, as Alfonso's heir, took command of his father's forces as the determined Alfonso sought to extend his power over areas in central and northern Italy. It was Alfonso's aggressive policies that alienated Pope Calixtus III, an estrangement that nearly cost Ferrante his throne.

Alfonso died on 27 June 1458, and Ferrante assumed the throne despite lack of support from Calixtus. In fact, while encouraging other pretenders to the throne, Calixtus refused to invest Ferrante with the crown of Naples, which was a dependency of the Holy See, at a time when papal endorsement would have been crucial to a smooth succession. It was only with Calixtus's death six weeks later that Ferrante was able to avoid the first thorny challenge to his crown, and the pope's successor, *Pius II, quickly recognized Ferrante's claim in order to maintain peace in Italy while he pursued his own crusade against Constantinople.

Unfortunately, peace was more difficult to achieve than simply obtaining the papal blessing; the French dukes of Anjou, at the urging of Calixtus, were eyeing the peninsular kingdom greedily and fomented revolt among several important Neapolitan barons. In opposition to his father's ambitious policies, Ferrante won powerful support from some of Italy's key princes by claiming that his only goal was peace and stability in the peninsula, not new conquests.

The seeds for Ferrante's later reputation were sown following his victory in 1465 against the forces of Jean d'Anjou and his rebellious barons. In the guise of forgiveness and friendship, Ferrante invited several barons and their families to a reconciliatory celebration and imprisoned them, some unfortunates for as long as thirty years. Others did not even escape with their lives. A famous example is that of the mercenary captain Jacopo Piccinino, who was arrested at Ferrante's court after a month of feasting in his honor, whereupon he met his untimely demise by "falling" out of a window (a common Neapolitan method of eliminating enemies).

Once peace was established and he was secure on his throne, Ferrante instituted many liberal economic policies in order to encourage export trade and internal production, thereby increasing the wealth of his kingdom and his own coffers. Throughout his reign he lowered taxes on export trade, offered privileges to foreign merchants to stimulate the silk industry, maintained ships to advance trade as far as England, and limited cloth imports to bolster local production. Ferrante also welcomed the rush of Sicilian and Spanish Jews escaping the purges of the Inquisition. These wealthy financiers and master craftsmen, especially those in cloth and metals, were trusted to help revive the sagging Neapolitan economy. In return, the Jews received protection against overzealous Christians and the restoration of certain rights such as the formation of communities with synagogues. Other oppressive policies, such as the burden of wearing a distinguishing mark, were relaxed.

Ferrante exhibited a rather plebeian and practical interest in intellectual matters that varied greatly from the usual generous support for the more esoteric thought of the Italian humanists. Although the vernacular was considered only for the dull and uneducated, Ferrante commissioned some of Naples's most learned men to translate great works into Italian rather than Latin. During his reign he employed more than thirty scribes for the purpose of building his library and insisted on hiring only the finest copyists and miniaturists in spite of the cost. Because of his own interest in the law and his need for well-educated professional administrators, he reopened the Studio in 1465, the university of Naples that emphasized legal education. The Studio alone was largely responsible for the growth of the printing press in Naples because of the demand for student textbooks and law collections, and so Naples became an influential center for works published in Italian, Latin, and Hebrew. The printers themselves also enjoyed special privileges, such as citizenship and royal protection, in return for publishing political propaganda favoring Ferrante and his policies. He was also an ardent and generous supporter of music, attracting some of Europe's best musicians, composers, and musical theorists by offering extravagant salaries, which resulted in significant innovations in court music.

The order and prosperity that Ferrante established proved to be short-lived, however, when soon after his death early in 1494 Charles VIII descended upon Naples and took the city with barely a fight, starting a dynastic tug-of-war that lasted several years. Ferrante was indeed a merciless ruler when he was dealing with his enemies, namely, those who had betrayed him by participating in the revolts. Yet he was a pragmatic, generous, and forward-thinking king who sought not to expand his lands at the expense of peace and abundance, but to foster stability and economic growth through practical fiscal and cultural innovations and through strong alliances with powerful friends. His reputation as a vicious, bloodthirsty, and treacherous autocrat, promoted by Commynes's writings in support of the Angevin ducal claims to the throne, was largely undeserved. He was, in fact, a leader who encouraged new ideas and new immigration to better his kingdom, as evidenced by such unusual policies as the harboring of banished Jews, and was generally admired as one of the great political masters of his time.

Bibliography: David Abulafia, *Commerce and Conquest in the Mediterranean, 1100–1500*, 1993; David Abulatia, "Ferrante of Naples: The Statecraft of a Renaissance Prince," *History Today*, February 1995, 19–25; Jerry H. Bentley, *Politics and Culture in Renaissance Naples*, 1987.

Wendy Marie Hoofnagle

Ferrer, Vincent, Saint. *See* Vincent Ferrer, Saint.

Ficino, Marsiglio (1433–99), was a Florentine intellectual and priest who is credited with founding the Platonic Academy of Florence. Ficino revived the study of Plato and translated into Latin the works of Plato, Plotinus, and several other classical writers. Although he is mostly known for his work editing classical texts, Ficino was also a philosopher himself who wrote extensively on subjects like medicine, religion, art, and the immortality of the soul. Although he was affected by the humanist tradition, he was also influenced by Aristotelian logic and the medieval religious heritage. He was most famous for his articulation of Platonic philosophy, which exerted considerable influence on European literature and art until the seventeenth century.

Marsiglio Ficino was born on 19 October 1433 in Figline, near Florence. His father was a physician named Diotifeci. Little is known about his activities as a child, but he most likely received his early education at a Florentine public school. After studying grammar for several years, Ficino continued his studies at the University of Florence in philosophy and medicine. Although most of Ficino's early works have been lost, he began writing his first work in 1454. As a student in fifteenth-century Florence, Ficino would have received an education grounded in a humanist curriculum. It is clear that Ficino also encountered remnants of medieval Aristotelianism with which he later grappled in his writing. In 1452 Ficino developed a valuable friendship with *Cosimo de Medici, who later supported Ficino's efforts to revive the Platonic tradition. In 1462 Cosimo provided him with a villa at Careggi where the Platonic Academy was eventually created.

Troubled by Aristotle's rejection of the soul's immortality, Ficino dismissed secular Aristotelianism for the optimistic spirituality of Plato and the Neoplatonists. In 1463 Ficino began the mammoth task of translating Plato's works into Latin, and by 1464 he had translated ten dialogues. Although Ficino spent much of his life reviving the works of classical writers influenced by pagan traditions, he remained a devout Christian throughout his life and became a priest in 1473. After he was ordained, he received several benefices. In 1487 he accepted a post as a canon at the Cathedral of Florence.

Although he is most famous for his work as a translator and commentator, Ficino was also a writer and philosopher of some note. Between 1469 and 1474 he wrote his most important work of philosophy, the *Theologia Platonica*, which explained his reconciliation of Platonism with Christian theology. In 1474 he composed his major theological work, entitled *De Christiana religione*. In 1489 Ficino wrote a medical treatise, *De vita*, which discussed astrology, magic, and the role of the spirit. A collection of his letters that included smaller treatises was printed in 1495. Ficino also translated and wrote commentaries on the works of Plotinus, Porphyry, Proclus, and other Neoplatonists. The mystical wisdom of ancient Egypt also intrigued Ficino throughout his life and led him to translate the works of Hermes Trismegistus. Like his humanist contemporaries, Ficino also undertook the translation of Tuscan poetry, especially that of Dante, into Italian. In 1492 Ficino returned to the country, dismayed after *Lorenzo de Medici's death and the expulsion of the Medici family from Florence. Marsiglio Ficino died on 1 October 1499.

Throughout his lifetime Ficino not only held private discussions at the villa in Careggi, but also gave public lectures in Florence. In his lectures Ficino discussed his interpretation of Plato and explained a variety of philosophical issues. Ficino spent much of his time as leader of the Platonic Academy articulating his conception of the universe and the hierarchy of beings. For Ficino, Plato and other ancient philosophers provided a philosophical basis for Christian spirituality. Through Plato's writings, Ficino developed his conception of love, the divine, and causality. Ficino's discussion of Platonic love exerted considerable influence on Renaissance artists and scholars. Platonic love was a spiritual matter free from the constraints of the material body that permitted humans to leave everyday distractions for the eternal happiness of the spiritual world. Ficino's world derived from the Platonic doctrine of ideas. In a carefully ordered hierarchy of beings, the divine occupied the highest position while humans served as the intermediaries between the spiritual and material worlds. For Ficino, human nature was a powerful spiritual force. Through contemplation and rejection of the constraints of the material world, the immortal human soul could attain spiritual happiness and knowledge of the divine.

Two of Ficino's most famous pupils at the academy, Alamanno Amati and Francesco da Diacceto, eventually produced their own works of philosophy. Ficino's influence also spread throughout Europe and affected humanists like *John Colet and *Giovanni Pico della Mirandola. Although Ficino's work both affected and was affected by humanists, he was not a humanist himself, since he was equally influenced by the Scholastic tradition and the medieval religious heritage. Although he rejected Aristotle's notion of the mortality of the human soul, the logical reasoning of Aristotelianism influenced Ficino's writing, particularly in his youth. In reality, Ficino's philosophy appealed to only a small minority with the means to pursue a life of spiritual contemplation, but his influence on art, music, literature, and humanism was widespread. As a philosopher and scholar, Ficino's pioneering work reviving the Platonic tradition represented a fusion of humanism, Scholasticism, and Christian spirituality that exerted a powerful influence on European culture for many years after his death.

Bibliography: Michael J. B. Allen, *The Platonism of Marsilio Ficino*, 1984; Konrad Eisenbichler and Olga Zorzi Pugliese, eds., *Ficino and Renaissance Neoplatonism*, 1986; Paul Oskar Kristeller, *The Philosophy of Marsilio Ficino*, 1964.

Celeste Chamberland

Flüe, Nicholas of. *See* Nicholas of Flüe, Saint.

Foix, Gaston Fébus, Count of. *See* Gaston III, Count de Foix.

Fordun, John of (d. 1384–87?). John of Fordun's *Chronica gentis Scotorum*, as later redacted in its fifteenth-century continuation, Walter Bower's *Scotichronicon*, served as the prime source of Scottish history through the mid-twentieth century. Fordun's work also greatly fostered the idea of "Scotland" as a distinctive entity, with an antiquity and history all its own, deserving of independence from England and its kings.

Like that of many another medieval chronicler, John of Fordun's life is little known, and much of what we do know is provided by notes in fifteenth-century copies of either his *Chronica* or the *Scotichronicon*, which provide but dubious evidence for his life. The preface to *The Black Book of Paisley* referred to him as "capellanus ecclesiae Aberdonensis." Later in that manuscript he was referred to as "dominus Joannes Fordoun, presbyter." Bower recounted a conversation he had with a learned doctor of the law who stated that Fordun was a "simple man" (*homo simplex*), and not a university graduate. Finally, in the *Book of Coupar Angus*, he was described as a priest who, to repair the losses of Scottish history caused by the English invasions, wandered throughout Britain and Ireland collecting all the tales and information about Scotland's past that he could. William Skene, the editor of the 1871–72 edition of Fordun's *Chronica*, thus identified him as "a chantry priest in Aberdeen Cathedral," and most scholars since have not seen fit to question that identification. As the geographical locus of the *Chronica* can be seen in the detailed treatment given to events and persons from the Scottish lowlands of the Northeast (Fife, Angus, the Mearns, and Aberdeenshire), the identification of Fordun with Aberdeen rings true. Indeed, this regional bias probably lies behind the unfavorable portrayal of Robert the Steward and his family in the *Chronica*. The dating of Fordun's *Chronica* also remains at issue. Some scholars hold that internal evidence dates most of it to between 1363 and 1365; others, between 1365 and 1384, and still others, to 1384–87. The best that can be said is that Fordun wrote and compiled the work sometime between 1363 and 1387.

Fordun's *Chronica*, the first compilation of the entire history of "Scotland," promoted the idea of the Scots in a context designed to ensure not merely an antiquity far superior to that of England, but also Scotland's right to exist as an entity independent of all ties to its southern neighbor. As such, it was part of the process in the development of "Scottish" consciousness arising from English attempts to conquer the northern half of Britain from 1294 onwards. Thus, to counter English claims to superiority through antiquity, Fordun—presumably drawing upon Irish sources—traced the history of the Scots back to Gaythelos, one of the princes of Greece who had triumphed over Brutus and the Trojans, and his wife, Princess Scota of Egypt. Fordun also dismissed Arthurian claims to dominance over the island. He explained that the homages Scottish kings had rendered to English kings had only been for their lands in England proper, not for the kingdom itself, and he traced an unbroken line of succession of kings from Fergus in 330 B.C. Though modern historians give no credence to either of these histories, the English Brut legend served as a key element in English claims to Scotland from the time of Edward I down to the union in 1707. Fordun's work thus established a strong counter to English claims in the island's history and implied that Scotland was among the oldest kingdoms in Christendom, unbroken in conquest by Romans, Saxons, Danes, or Normans. As a result, Fordun's *Chronica* played a profound and fundamental role not merely in Scottish historiography, but also in forming a Scottish consciousness and "nation" out of what was, in reality, a land of divergent cultures, languages, and histories.

Bibliography: R. James Goldstein, *The Matter of Scotland: Historical Narrative in Medieval Scotland*, 1993; Roger A. Mason, "Scotching the Brut: Politics, History, and National Myth in Sixteenth-Century Britain," in *Scotland and England, 1286–1815*, ed. Roger A. Mason, 1987.

Jerome S. Arkenburg

Fortescue, Sir John (c. 1390–1476), was an Englishman who served as chief justice of the King's Bench for most of the two decades preceding 1460. He was also *Henry VI's chancellor and accompanied that king into exile, where he wrote several influential constitutional and legal works, defended his sovereign's royal claims, and established himself as the most eminent and popular constitutional theorist in late medieval Britain.

The second son and namesake of a Devonshire gentleman and the younger brother of the chief justice of the Common Pleas in Ireland, John Fortescue was educated at Exeter College, Oxford, and Lincoln's Inn, where he served many terms as governor. He became a justice of the peace in 1418, served on many royal commissions, and represented Devonshire in seven of the eight parliaments he attended. He was appointed a king's serjeant ten years after he received his serjeant-at-law degree in 1430. In 1436 he married the daughter of a Somerset gentleman and increased his involvement in government service. In 1442 he was named chief justice of the King's Bench and was knighted soon after. He was an extremely active judge, sat on many key royal commissions, and attained a degree of unpopularity for his loyalty to the Lancastrian cause.

Fortescue was present at the Battle of Towton in 1461 when *Edward IV drove King Henry into exile, and so he was among those attainted by the triumphant Yorkists. He lost his considerable properties in the southwest by the attainder while he accompanied the Lancastrian court during two years of exile in Scotland. He followed Queen Margaret of Anjou and her son to Flanders and lived there in poverty until 1471. In his writings during the early part of this period he claimed to be Henry's "chancellor" and was a most articulate and productive defender of the Lancastrian cause. He was the primary tutor to Prince Edward; two of Fortescue's main books may have begun as part of Edward's instruction.

When the earl of Warwick and Henry VI were victorious in the fall of 1470, Fortescue, Queen Margaret, and Prince Edward planned to return to England. On the day they landed in April 1471, Henry VI was again defeated by the

Yorkists at Barnet. Fortescue, who joined the Lancastrian forces, was captured at the Battle of Tewkesbury, where Prince Edward was killed and the queen was captured. With his cause doomed, Fortescue petitioned Edward IV for a revocation of his attainder, which was granted with the proviso that Fortescue refute his earlier defense of the Lancastrians. His "Declaration upon Certain Writings Sent Out from Scotland" brought not only a pardon and the restoration of his lands but a seat on Edward's council for four years. Fortescue spent his final years with his family at Ebrington, Devonshire, and is buried in the parish church.

Fortescue's eleven tracts in defense of Lancastrian claims are not unique, but his time in exile, his responsibilities to Prince Edward, and his devotion to Henry prompted Fortescue to speculate about the development of England's legal system and government in three works that made him famous. His *De natura legis naturae* (On the laws of nature) began with an examination of three rival claimants to the throne of a deceased ruler. In the work's first section, Fortescue explained the relevant natural law and its application within the English legal process. In the second part, "Justice," the rival claimants stated their arguments, while he denigrated the natural weakness of women and explained the legal process supporting the position of the deceased king's brother.

In *De laudibus legum Angliae* (In praise of English law), Fortescue depicted England as a "mixed" realm with features of absolute and constitutional monarchy and a balance of statute and common law that in turn provided both civil and criminal justice far better than any other system. *On the governance of England*, Fortescue broadened his description and proposed changes to increase royal revenues, expand the powers of the royal council, discourage popular discontent, and enhance the effectiveness of the royal patronage system.

Fortescue was the most prolific legal writer of his age and was probably the first to treat the corpus of parliamentary statutes as a constitutional framework. In addition, his ability to use his own experiences to explain to his elite audience both the legal theory and the processes used in his profession gave his works an unsurpassed influence and readership among his contemporaries that lasted for several centuries.

Bibliography: A. L. Brown, *The Governance of Late Medieval England, 1272–1461*, 1989; Sir John Fortescue, *The Governance of England*, ed. Charles Plummer, 1885; A. J. Pollard, *The Rule of England in the Time of Henry VI*, 1997.

Sheldon Hanft

Fouquet, Jean (1420–80), was a native of Tours, France. If a document discovered by Yves de Raulin is to be trusted, Fouquet was the illegitimate child of a priest and an unmarried woman. It is not known at which university Fouquet studied or where he learned his craft of painting, but it may be assumed that it was in Paris during the decade of the 1440s.

Fouquet's journey to Italy marked an important stage in his career. Already a master of his craft, he was there after 1445 and before February 1447, certainly before the death of Pope *Eugenius IV, whose portrait he painted. In Italy, Fouquet's fame was documented in the architectural treatise of Antonio Filarete, who in 1461 recommended to Duke *Francesco Storza of Milan the best masters of his time for a model. In addition, a much-traveled Florentine, Francesco Floro, who in 1467–77 paid a long visit to Tours, wrote that Fouquet surpassed not only contemporary but also all old masters. Fouquet's name was also mentioned in two writings by Jean Lemaire, who was a poet and archaeologist employed by Anne of Brittany and Margaret of Austria. When Fouquet left the Italian metropolis in 1448, he took away with him not only the new theories of Italian art, its new rhythm and lively images, but also the very breath of new life; he had discerned the new value of the individual that gave Italian art its universal character.

Upon his return to Tours, Fouquet created a new style combining the experiments of Italian painting with the exquisite precision of characterization and detail of Flemish art. For Étienne Chevalier, the royal secretary and lord treasurer, he executed between 1450 and 1460 his most famous works: a large book of hours with about sixty full-page miniatures, fourty of which are among the great treasures of the Château of Chantilly, and the diptych from Notre Dame at Melun with Chevalier's portrait on one panel and a Madonna with the features of Agnès Sorel, the king's mistress, on the other.

The years after Fouquet's stay in Italy gave him the happiest moments of his life. The years 1450–60, the first decade of peaceful reconstruction in France and the last years of *Charles VII's reign, witnessed in quick succession the production of Fouquet's most exuberant creations. It is clear from this output that Fouquet retained the privileged position he had enjoyed under Charles VII under the less art-loving *Louis XI. In 1474, when the king planned to erect a monumental tomb for himself, he ordered designs from Fouquet and the sculptor Michel Colombe. The highest proof of royal favor was bestowed on Fouquet in 1475 when he was granted the official title of *peintre du roy*. Thereafter he took up permanent employment in the royal household, was freed of taxes and various compulsory duties, and obtained other privileges that went with the appointment. At the beginning of his career, most of his works had been commissioned by members of the ennobled officials; now, at the height of his fame, he was patronized especially by the higher aristocracy. Fouquet was considered one of the geniuses (the other being *François Villon) who arose from the defeat of France in her war with England to found French pictorial style, a reincarnation of national awakening in art after the devastation of France in the Hundred Years' War.

Bibliography: Trenchard Cox, *Jehan Foucquet: Native of Tours*, 1931; James Snyder, *Northern Renaissance Art*, 1985; Paul Reinhold Wescher, *Jean Fouquet and His Time*, 1947.

Wentong Ma

Francisco Jiménes de Cisneros. *See* Jiménes de Cisneros, Francisco.

Frederick III, Holy Roman Emperor (b. 1415, r. 1452–93), Frederick
V as Duke of Styria, Carinthia, and Carniola. The first member of the Habsburg
dynasty to be crowned emperor in Rome, Frederick III was neither a strong nor
a decisive ruler. His concentration on dynastic matters at the expense of imperial
affairs weakened the Holy Roman Empire, but he was able to establish the
Habsburgs as one of the preeminent noble families in Germany.

Frederick was born in Linz on 21 September 1415, the son of Archduke Ernst
of Austria. Frederick's father died in 1424, and for the next eleven years he
lived under the guardianship of his uncle, Duke Frederick IV. In 1435 he
claimed his inheritance and became Duke Frederick V of Styria, Carinthia, and
Carniola (three provinces to the south and east of Vienna). Frederick IV died
in 1439, and so Frederick V became guardian of his son, Sigismund, thus gaining control of the Tyrol in western Austria. Later that same year Emperor Albrecht II died, allowing Frederick, who was his cousin, to gain control of a
number of additional duchies along the Danube. Frederick also became guardian
of Albrecht's son Ladislas, who was heir to the crowns of Hungary and Bohemia. Thus by 1440 Frederick directly or indirectly ruled over much of what is
now Austria, Hungary, and the Czech Republic. On 2 February 1440, five of
the seven German electors chose Frederick to succeed Albrecht II as king of
the Germans, the traditional first step toward becoming holy Roman emperor.
Frederick was crowned king in Aachen on 17 June 1442, but his coronation as
emperor did not take place until 19 March 1452. As king, and later as emperor,
he was known as Frederick III.

In the decade between his royal and imperial coronations, Frederick suffered
a series of setbacks. In 1442 he entangled the empire in a conflict between the
canton of Zurich and the Swiss Confederation. The Habsburgs had lost some of
their western lands to the Swiss in 1415, and Zurich promised to return these
lands in exchange for Frederick's assistance. Despite being king of the Germans
and emperor-elect, Frederick was unable to raise any support for Zurich within
the empire, and the canton suffered a series of military defeats. In 1446, bowing
to pressure from the Tyrolian nobility, Frederick gave up his guardianship over
Sigismund. In 1448 Frederick and representatives of Pope *Nicholas V concluded the Vienna Concordat, which greatly increased papal power over the
church within the empire. Although he faced domestic turmoil and opposition,
Frederick was still able to negotiate a favorable marriage with Eleanor, the
daughter of King Edward of Portugal. The two were wed by proxy in 1451 and
in person in Rome in 1452. Their first son, *Maximilian, was born in 1459.

Frederick's troubles continued after his imperial coronation. His guardianship
over Ladislas ended in 1452, leaving him in direct control of only a handful of
the Habsburg duchies. Although Frederick reclaimed Ladislas's Austrian lands
after the latter's death in 1457, the kingdoms of Bohemia and Hungary were

able to free themselves from Habsburg rule. *George of Podebrady, who had acted as governor on Ladislas's behalf, claimed the Bohemian throne in 1458, and in the same year *Matthias Corvinus was elected king of Hungary. Corvinus would eventually invade Austria, driving Frederick from Vienna in 1485, but the emperor was more successful in his dealings with his neighbors to the west. In 1475 he was able to arrange the marriage of Maximilian to Mary, the daughter of Charles the Bold of Burgundy. When Charles died in 1477, Frederick's son Maximilian claimed Burgundy as his own, although it took nearly fifteen years of fighting before the French acknowledged his claim. In 1486 Maximilian was elected king of the Germans, and until Frederick's death the two ruled jointly. Although his relations with Maximilian were frequently strained, Frederick was generally content to let his heir take the more active role in running the kingdom. Maximilian eventually drove the Hungarian forces from Austria after Corvinus's death in 1490, leaving Frederick free to return to Vienna, but the emperor instead retired to Linz, where he died in 1493.

Frederick's contemporaries generally described him as indolent and ineffectual. His political decisions frequently led to disaster, and he rarely enjoyed military success. Indeed, many of his lasting gains were the result simply of outliving his opponents. Nevertheless, by consolidating the Habsburg lands under his control and by arranging Maximilian's marriage to Mary of Burgundy, he was able to provide a solid foundation for later Habsburg greatness.

Bibliography: F.R.H. DuBoulay, *Germany in the Later Middle Ages*, 1983; Joachim Leuschner, *Germany in the Late Middle Ages*, 1980; Gerald Strauss, *Pre-Reformation Germany*, 1972.

Stephen A. Allen

Free, John (1430–65), was an eminent fifteenth-century English humanist, a scholar and physician well known in Italy. Reportedly born in Bristol, Free apparently spent his early years in London and then attended Balliol College, Oxford, receiving his bachelor of arts in 1449 and his master of arts in 1454. After leaving Oxford, he was the rector of St. Michael in Monte at Bristol. In 1456 he traveled to Italy in the company of John Gunthorpe in order to study at Ferrara at the expense of his patron, William Grey, bishop of Ely—both men were former Oxford colleagues. Free studied under *Guarino da Verona at Ferrara, acquiring a strong reputation for his command of Greek and Latin; he perhaps also began to study Hebrew at this time. Subsequently he lectured at the University of Padua in medicine, philosophy, and civil law, earning doctorate in medicine in 1461. In April 1459 he was made rector of Kelshall in Hertfordshire and held the position until his death. He remained an absentee in Italy, however, traveling to Florence and then to Rome in 1465. Under the patronage of John Tiptoft, he quickly gained favor with Pope Paul II, who made him bishop of Bath and Wells. However, Free died in Rome in September 1465 before he could return to England. It was rumored that he was poisoned, although this was never confirmed.

Along with John Tiptoft and John Gunthorpe, Free was an important English link to Italian humanism. He exemplified the growing interest in classical languages and texts in the fifteenth century. His own writings included a number of Latin poems (now lost) dedicated to Tiptoft, whom he probably served as a secretary; an epitaph for *Francesco Petrarch's tomb written at the request of a number of Italian scholars; an array of letters, including some to Grey asking for more money to continue his studies; and a collection of translated excepts from Pliny's *Natural History*. He translated several Greek texts into Latin, including Synesius of Cyrene's *Laus calvitii* and *De insomniis*, and collected a large number of books in both languages.

Bibliography: R. J. Mitchell, *John Free: From Bristol to Rome in the Fifteenth Century*, 1955.

Andrew Scheil

Froissart, Jean (c. 1338–c. 1404), was an important late medieval chronicler and poet. Froissart's *Chronicles of England, France, Spain, and the Adjoining Countries* is a major source for historians for events in Europe during the fourteenth century, and his work is especially useful in studying the Hundred Years' War between England and France. It is also a work of literature. Highly readable and full of interesting stories, it was a medieval "best-seller," and so many copies were commissioned by various nobles during the fourteenth and fifteenth centuries that more than one hundred manuscripts are still extant. With the invention of the printing press, it continued to be popular and in the quarter century after 1495 the *Chronicles* went through no less than ten editions.

Froissart was born at Valenciennes in the county of Hainaut. Although his family was not noble, there appears to have been some contact with the court of the count of Hainaut, whose daughter Philippa was married to King *Edward III of England; in 1361 Froissart traveled to England, where he presented his countrywoman with a book of his poetry. He remained attached to the English court for six years, traveling extensively and interviewing numerous people involved in affairs of state, including King John the Good of France and other French nobles who had been captured for ransom by the English at the Battle of Poitiers. He made extensive notes of his conversations and subsequently used the information in composing his *Chronicles*.

In 1368 Froissart traveled to Italy with an English diplomatic delegation (*Geoffrey Chaucer was also a member of the group). While he was in Italy, his patroness Queen Philippa died, and Froissart decided to return to his native Hainaut. Although he was officially a member of the clergy, for the rest of his life he worked primarily on his *Chronicles*, supported by various nobles, including Robert of Namur, Queen Philippa's nephew, and Guy de Blois, lord of Beaumont. He moved easily through the various courts of Europe, obtaining information from participants in historical events. In 1395, after an absence of twenty-seven years, he made a three-month visit to England, where he presented

King *Richard II with a volume of his poetry shortly before the tumultuous end of Richard's reign. His conversations with members of the English aristocracy during his visit added much interesting background to his subsequent account of Richard's overthrow.

Early in his life Froissart gained some fame as a poet, and Chaucer is believed to have modeled some of his early poetry on that of Froissart. However, he is best remembered today for the *Chronicles*, which cover roughly the period from 1329 to 1400. The first part of his work was based on the *Chronicles* of Jean Le Bel, also from Hainaut; Froissart's book was originally intended to be simply a continuation. However, based on his conversations with people during his English years, Froissart supplemented Le Bel's account of the Hundred Years' War. He soon developed his own style of writing, and the fact that he frequently obtained his information from eyewitnesses (or was present at many events himself) has caused him to be called "the first war correspondent." While historians have found numerous errors of fact in his work, which is true of most medieval chronicles, it appears that Froissart did attempt to report accurately what his sometimes-biased informants passed on to him. His account was also colored by the fact that he considered himself a chronicler of chivalry and the knightly tradition. He was unstinting in his praise of those he believed embodied the best of knighthood, while at the same time reporting, apparently without being conscious of inconsistency, actions that appear to modern eyes to be completely at odds with knightly virtue. Froissart completed his *Chronicles* in 1400, and it is believed that he died about 1404.

The *Chronicles* are divided into four books, the first two in several "redactions," or revisions, made by Froissart himself. Most of the manuscripts still extant are illustrated with illuminated paintings that make them superb examples of medieval art. Perhaps the most famous of these is that now at the Breslau Library in Germany, which was commissioned by Anthony of Burgundy and was produced in Bruges with 123 exquisite miniatures. Other particularly fine examples reside in the Vatican Library, the Bodleian Library, and the Bibliothèque Nationale in Paris.

Froissart's influence as a writer extended far beyond the Middle Ages, and it was not limited to historians. Sir Walter Scott acknowledged Froissart as his master and said that it was Froissart who inspired the historical novel. Arthur Conan Doyle based *The White Company* on events and knights described by Froissart, while Alexandre Dumas, père made extensive use of information from Froissart in some of his novels.

There are numerous editions of selections from Froissart's *Chronicles* in print, none of which contain more than a very small percentage of the whole. The only more or less complete translation in English is that of Thomas Johnes, first published in England in 1804. This was reprinted a number of times and is available in some of the larger university libraries.

Bibliography: Peter Ainsworth, *Jean Froissart and the Fabric of History*, 1990. J.J.N. Palmer, ed., *Froissart: Historian*, 1981; Peter E. Thompson, ed., *Contemporary Chronicles of the Hundred Years War*, 1966.

Dan Wages

Fust, Johann (c. 1400–1466), is best known for loaning *Johann Gutenberg funds for printing the Forty-two–Line or "Gutenberg" Bible. Yet Fust and his partner, *Peter Schöffer, were the printers who worked to make print a successful technology. Because they continued to produce exceptionally fine volumes after Gutenberg printed the Forty-two–line Bible, they were able to show that printing technology could consistently produce texts that equaled the quality of manuscripts.

No records of Fust's birth or early life exist; we know only that he was a merchant, goldsmith, and moneylender in Mainz. Fust and Gutenberg formed a partnership in 1449, and Fust loaned Gutenberg a sum of money so that he could buy equipment for the printing press. When Gutenberg began printing the Forty-two–line Bible in 1450, Fust loaned him more money in order to furnish a large workshop located in the Humbrechthof. Fust continued to make loans to Gutenberg in 1452 and 1453 for the "work of the books," and the Bible was completed in 1454. All the copies sold quickly, and Fust demanded repayment of the loans. A disagreement arose between the two men regarding both the payment of the interest and how Gutenberg had initially appropriated the money, for Fust accused Gutenberg of diverting some of the loans into private projects.

Fust successfully sued Gutenberg in 1455 and was able to seize both the workshop and the printing equipment. He began a new printing enterprise with his foster son, Peter Schöffer. Schöffer was a talented scribe and calligrapher who had worked with Gutenberg on the design and printing of the Forty-two–Line Bible. In 1457 Fust and Schöffer printed the Mainz *Psalter*, an artistic and typographic achievement equal to the Bible. Every item in the *Psalter* was printed, including the large illustrative initials, some of which were printed in two colors. When Fust and Schöffer printed the *Canon missae* in 1458 and a Forty-eight–Line Bible in 1462, they secured a reputation for high-quality printing and established themselves as suppliers of church literature.

During the conflict over the archbishopric of Mainz, Fust and Schöffer used their press to print eight broadsides, some supporting Adolf von Nassau, Pope *Pius II's choice for the office, and others supporting Diether von Isenburg, who had been elected by the cathedral chapter of Mainz. When Nassau's faction captured Mainz in 1462, all citizens of Mainz were expelled from the city and their properties seized. During this year Fust traveled to Paris in order to sell copies of the Forty-eight–Line Bible and successfully created a number of trade relationships there. Fust and Schöffer resumed printing in 1465, producing the *Decretals* of Boniface VIII and De officiis of Cicero; soon after, Fust returned to Paris in order to arrange for the distribution of these new books. It is believed that he died of the plague that was then devastating the city, since he was not mentioned in any record until 30 October 1466, when a mass was said for him at the Church of Saint Victor in Paris. Johann Gutenberg may have designed and manufactured the first printing press, but it was Johann Fust who enabled the printing of the Gutenberg Bible and helped establish printing as a technology appropriate for creating high-quality, beautifully designed texts.

Bibliography: Norma Levarie, "Fust and Schöffer," in *The Art and History of Books*, 1995; John Clyde Oswald, *A History of Printing: Its Development through Five Hundred Years*, 1928.

Kristin R. Hofer

G

Gaguin, Robert (c. 1425–1501), was a French diplomat and prior general of the Trinitarian order, but is best known as a significant figure in the humanist movement in Paris at the end of the fifteenth century. Born between 1420 and 1425 at Colline-Beaumont in the Pas-de-Calais, France, he joined the Trinitarians at Préavin, near Arras, at a young age. Sent to Paris for higher studies in 1457, he became a pupil of Guillaume Fichet, who exercised a great influence over him. He took his licentiate in canon law and eventually, because he was delayed by his other duties, his doctorate at the Sorbonne in 1480. He acted as assistant to Fichet, who taught rhetoric at the Trinitarian house and at the College of Navarre, before replacing him when Fichet left for Rome in 1472. He collaborated with Fichet in the establishment of the first printing press in Paris at the Sorbonne in 1470. From an early age, Gaguin strove to improve his knowledge of Latin, and, through Fichet, he was introduced to the writings of many classical authors. Gaguin's ideal was the learned Christian humanist, imbued with a love for literature and inspired by figures such as St. Augustine. His cherished aim was to revitalize theology and express it in the language of Cicero. This strong religious theme inspired many of the early humanists, and a number of Gaguin's friends entered religious life. At Paris, other literary friends included Philippe Béroualde, Guillaume Tardif, and the famous Desiderius Erasmus, who was one of his pupils.

Gaguin's leadership qualities were quickly recognized, and he was elected general of his order in 1473. However, he continued his association with the Sorbonne and maintained contact with his circle of friends. After 1480 he began giving lectures on canon law that had a wide influence. However, his time was increasingly occupied by diplomatic duties on behalf of his order and the king, *Charles VIII. He visited the Trinitarian houses in Spain in 1468–69 and went on a mission for the king to Germany in 1477 to seek the support of the German princes in opposing the marriage of Mary of Burgundy with *Maximilian of

Austria. In 1486 he served on another diplomatic mission to Rome and Naples, and in 1491 he was ambassador in England, where he probably met the young Thomas More, then serving in Archbishop *John Morton's household. During his journeys Gaguin took the opportunity to make the acquaintance of many leading humanist figures and to broaden his circle of friends. He died in Préavin on 22 May 1501.

Gaguin's own writings are varied, and he was interested in a wide range of subjects. His first work, *The Art of Writing Verse*, was published in 1473, and he later published a number of Latin poems. He produced translations into French of the works of Julius Caesar and Livy, but the major work for which he is best known was his *Compendium of the History and Acts of the Franks*, first printed in 1497 and reprinted many times thereafter. It was widely popular, being praised by Erasmus and others, but because of its partisanship, it led to Thomas More's comment, "Gaguin, who neither disparages the honour of the French nor broadcasts our honour." Gaguin's religious duties were not neglected, and he strove to reform and rekindle spiritual enthusiasm in his own order. Apart from addresses to chapters and other gatherings, he twice revised the rule and statutes of the order and composed a chronicle of the ministers general of the Trinitarians. He had a great devotion to the Virgin Mary and argued in support of the dogma of the Immaculate Conception, publishing several works on this theme, including a long poem and a letter addressed to his order. Surprisingly for a man of his ability, Gaguin appears to have suffered from a good deal of stress, and in addition to a poem he wrote on this problem, he translated *Giovanni Pico della Mirandola's *Useful Advice against the Worries and Tribulations of This World*.

In spite of his numerous interests and talents, Gaguin's own writings did not reach the heights of those of the more illustrious humanists with whom he was friendly; his main claim to fame lies more in his encouragement of the talents of others. He had a wide circle of friends, not only Parisians but also Italians such as Pico della Mirandola and *John Bessarion, writers in other religious orders such as the Benedictine abbot John Trithemius, and the Carmelites Arnold Bostius and Laurent Bureau, bishop of Sisteron. As with many others, Gaguin encouraged Erasmus, read some of his works in draft, and exchanged letters with him. The two volumes of Gaguin's letters give an idea of his wide range of contacts and his fluency in Latin (sadly, they are not translated); they are a valuable source for the study of the humanist movement in the late fifteenth century.

Bibliography: Peter G. Bietenholtz, ed., *Contemporaries of Erasmus: A Biographical Register of the Renaissance and Reformation*, vol. 2, 1986.

Richard Copsey

Galba, Joan Martí de (d. 1490), is the purported author of the last part of the most famous medieval chivalric romance in Catalan, *Tirant lo Blanc*. In recent years some prominent scholars have come to consider Galba's contribution to *Tirant* principally organizational, with *Joanot Martorell being indeed the only author. It is unknown when Galba was born, but there is evidence that his early life was spent in a castle known as Montnegre, in the Cataluña area of Spain. His father was the knight Mossén Guerau de Galba, and his mother was known as Elionor, her last name unmentioned in any records. The Galba family was of noble heritage, the family crest showing a windmill and millstone. In 1457 Galba married Catalina Celma, a wealthy woman of high social standing. They had no children, and Galba inherited Catalina's fortune when she died in 1482. From that time Galba lived luxuriously, inhabiting a palace in Valencia filled with antique and modern arms as well as other notable collectibles, including a sizable library. These books were willed to his nephew after Galba's death in April 1490.

His interest in books would seem to be Galba's principal involvement in literature. There is no evidence of his having written anything else. No one knows how Galba and Martorell came to know each other. The only reference to Galba in the voluminous *Tirant lo Blanc* comes at the end of the last chapter in an explanatory note. It states that because of Martorell's untimely death, he was unable to complete his translation and it was Galba, a *magnifico caballero*, who finished the last fourth of the book at the request of Doña Isabel de Lloris. Because Martorell died in 1468, it is unclear when Galba made his contribution to the book. He himself did not see the publication of *Tirant*, dying seven months before its publication in Valencia in November 1490.

Martorell's term "translation" poses the first problem concerning *Tirant*'s authorship. In 1460, the year he began the work, Martorell claimed in his dedication to Prince Ferdinand of Portugal that he was, at the king's request, translating an English tale into Portuguese and the "Valencian dialect," or Catalan. There is, however, no trace of such an English romance, nor does the Portuguese version exist, leading most scholars to conclude that the Catalan version was the original and that Martorell was engaging in artistic license by calling it a translation. Galba maintained this fiction by saying that he "translated" the fourth and last part of the work. Most confusing is that *Tirant* has no discernible fourth section. Martorell announced at the beginning of his work that there would be four parts but then immediately referred to the "seven sections of the first part." Whatever *Tirant*'s organization, the virtually identical spelling, vocabulary, and style found throughout the book place in doubt Galba's claim of composition. Indeed, as Joseph Vaeth has noted, it would not have occurred to a reader that a second author was involved in *Tirant* had Galba not been mentioned at the end of the work. Vaeth concludes that Galba probably prepared the manuscript for publication, and having done so, believed himself entitled to a claim of partial authorship. Vaeth also speculates that, due to its superfluous nature, the last brief chapter may have been written by Galba. Later scholars such as Martí de Riquer and Lola Badier have both provided evidence supporting Martorell as the sole author of *Tirant lo Blanc*. Although definitive proof is lacking, recent translations in Spanish and English nonetheless prominently list Galba as coauthor.

Bibliography: Joanot Martorell and Joan Martí de Galba, *Tirant lo Blanc*, trans. J. F. Vidal Jové, 1969; Joseph A. Vaeth, *Tirant lo Blanch: A Study of Its Authorship, Principal Sources, and Historical Setting*, 1918/1966.

Margaret Harp

Gama, Vasco da (1469?–1524), was the Portuguese navigator famed for opening the all-sea route from Europe to India in 1498. Da Gama was born in Sines, Alemtejo, in southern Portugal to a family of minor nobility. Little is known of his first twenty-five years, but his father, Estevão da Gama, was a ranking member of the Order of Santiago, a crusading order established in the twelfth century that later concentrated on mercantile ventures in southern Portugal and Castile; Vasco joined the order in his early teens. The first mention of Vasco comes in 1492 when King *João II commissioned him to retaliate against a group of French ships along the Moroccan coast, which he did successfully. In 1497 *Manuel I, the newly crowned king of Portugal, ordered da Gama to reach India by sea. Success meant finding a trade route to the east free of Muslim middlemen, a direct source of African gold, an alternate crusading route to the Levant and North Africa, and, possibly, the legendary Prester John.

There is some question as to why King Manuel chose a relatively unknown mariner and member of a rival court faction for such an important task. It is probable that some mercantile factions discouraged Manuel from investing fully in the trip since they disliked the idea of losing their monopoly on eastern trade and feared strengthening the royal hand, a growing concern for nobles and merchants alike. King Manuel also may have feared losing prestige if one of his own men failed.

Da Gama sailed from Lisbon with four ships in early July 1497, passing the estuary of the Tejo on 8 July. Da Gama himself commanded the *São Gabriel*; his brother Paulo, the *São Rafael*; and Nicolau Coelho, the *Berrio* the fourth, a smaller supply ship, did not reach India. After rounding the Cape of Good Hope on 19 November, da Gama spent more than four months exploring the trading cities of the East African coast. In March 1498 the fleet arrived at Moçambique Island. Contact at the city of Mozambique was tentative. The ruler and merchants of the city may have thought that da Gama and his crew of two hundred were Muslims, perhaps Ottomans, from the north; once they discovered that the Portuguese were Christians, relations may have soured. Difficulties acquiring fresh water led to open hostilities in late March, and after quelling resistance and filling their water barrels, the Portuguese left on 29 March. On 7 April 1498 they arrived at Mombasa and at Malindi on 16 April. Da Gama was suspicious and hesitant at both ports but spent nine days at Malindi, though he himself never set foot on land. The sailors' encounter with St. Thomas Christians from the Malabar city of Cranganore encouraged the belief that Christians ruled large parts of India. To assure the fleet's safe journey to Calicut, da Gama secured the services of a Gujarati pilot, sometimes confused with the famed Arab geographer Ahmad ibn-Majid, by taking the sultan of Malindi's ambassador hostage. The fleet departed Malindi on 24 April and arrived at Calicut on 20 May 1498.

Da Gama's East African experience influenced his approach at Calicut. Upon arrival, he waited for boats to approach from land rather than sending parties to the city. Da Gama himself chose not to be the first to land; rather, he sent João Nunes, a convicted felon, to the city. While there was no immediate confrontation upon the arrival of the Portuguese, they did not make a good impression. Their gifts of cloth, hats, coral, and agricultural products, they were told, were less than the lowest merchant from Mecca would have brought. A general air of distrust, including the taking of hostages and counterhostages, marred their official relations with the Samudri raja of Calicut.

The fleet departed Calicut on 29 August 1498. On the return voyage, da Gama lost more than fifty men to scurvy and had to abandon and burn the *São Rafael* south of Mombasa. Still, da Gama's voyage made real advances for King Manuel, who added the epithet "lord of the conquest, navigation, and commerce, of Ethiopia, Arabia, Persia, and India" to his titles. Manuel was now able to invest more resources into his Indian Ocean venture. Shortly after da Gama's return, the king sent Pedro Alvares Cabral to Calicut with a fleet of thirteen ships and a crew of over a thousand men with orders to establish a permanent Portuguese presence in India. In 1502 da Gama, with the new title of admiral of the Indies, was dispatched to continue Cabral's mission. Da Gama did not take his fleet directly to Calicut, but rather spent time reducing the other trading cities on the northern Malabar coast. After several more months of fighting and negotiation, da Gama established peace with Calicut as well as a permanent Portuguese presence in the Indian Ocean, and his negotiations at Cochin helped to establish the city as the center of Portuguese activities in India for nearly a decade. After collecting spices and other goods, he sailed back to Portugal, arriving in October 1503, where he was received as a hero. Da Gama did not see further active sea duty for twenty years. During these two decades he solidified his position at court, oversaw his land grants, and established his family. In 1519 King Manuel granted him the title of count of Vidigueira. In 1524 he was named viceroy of India and was sent to correct corruption at Cochin. Da Gama reached Cochin, but died three months later.

Bibliography: Sanjay Subrahmanyam, *The Career and Legend of Vasco da Gama*, 1997; Sanjay Subrahmanyam, *Improvising Empire: Portuguese Trade and Settlement in the Bay of Bengal, 1500–1700*, 1990.

Tim Sullivan

Gascoigne, Thomas (1403–58).

A theologian and longtime member and at times chancellor of the University of Oxford, Thomas Gascoigne is best known today for his ardent calls for church reform and his efforts to elevate the teachings of the church fathers as authorities in religious doctrine. His most famous work was his *Liber de veritatibus*, which contained much important commentary on the church and the university.

Thomas Gascoigne was born on 5 January 1403 at Hunslet, near Leeds, Yorkshire, to wealthy parents. Originally destined for a civilian career, he entered the church instead. Little is known of his youth before he proceeded to the University of Oxford as a member of Oriel College around 1420. Two years later he lost his father, but he was well provided for and was able to continue his studies at the university. In 1427 he was ordained, earned a bachelor of theology in 1434, and was awarded the doctorate in theology the following year. On 15 May 1442 Gascoigne was elected *cancellarius natus* (vice or first chancellor), a position he held until he became chancellor of the university on 14 March 1444. He resigned from this post in April 1445 but, due to his popularity and good reputation, was immediately reelected. He was reluctant to resume the duties and did not do so until 7 June 1445, and he resigned again in November that same year. Gascoigne, however, continued to play an important role at the university: in 1448 he was on the committee of ways and means for raising money to build new buildings in the Divinity School; in 1449 he was granted the use of his rooms rent-free in return for his services to Oriel College; in 1453 he was elected *cancellarius natus* again; and in 1456 he was asked to preach the university sermon to celebrate victory over the Turks at the Battle of Belgrade. Gascoigne was a generous benefactor to colleges throughout Oxford, and in all he gave more than thirty manuscripts to college libraries.

Gascoigne's real significance derives from his efforts to effect church reform, which showed most clearly in his attitude toward contemporary ecclesiastical practices, in his attacks on Bishop *Reginald Pecock, and in his *Liber de veritatibus*, composed between 1434 and 1457. Gascoigne denounced the commonplace practices of pluralism, nonresidence, and impropriation of tithes (monastic claims on tithe money in local parishes), and his actions bore witness to his observance of these convictions. In 1433 he was offered the rectory at Kirk Deighton, Yorkshire, but he resigned because he himself could not preach in the diocese. Likewise, in 1445 he was offered the rectory of St. Peter's, Cornhill, in London, but his ill health prevented his living and working in the city, so he resigned. He even declined the lucrative appointment in 1452 to the chancellorship of York Cathedral. Gascoigne's aversion to these practices stemmed from his conviction that friars, parish priests, and bishops had a duty to preach to the members of their diocese. This conviction was at the center of his attacks on Bishop Pecock, who had belittled the importance of preaching and had argued that the development of the parochial system had excused bishops from preaching. Gascoigne argued that the most important task of bishops was to preach the gospel. Gascoigne accused Pecock and other bishops who did not preach of worldliness and ignorance.

Although Gascoigne's attacks were directed personally at Pecock, they were aimed at what he perceived to be problems in the church as he knew it, including the sale of indulgences. In his most important work, *Liber de veritatbus*, Gascoigne argued for a conservative reform that would reinstate the authority and teachings of the church fathers into contemporary practices. He thus sought to reestablish the older, purer doctrine of the church. He compared the church of his day with that of St. Jerome; he contrasted the Augustinian doctrine of penance to the sale of indulgences; and he invoked the episcopal ideal put forward by Robert Grosseteste as a critique of the prelates of his own time. Gascoigne found the church too deficient in many ways and tried to establish an authoritative dogma based on the patristic writings. Gascoigne's emphasis on patristic sources contributed to a growth of interest in the church fathers at both the Universities of Oxford and Cambridge and to efforts to reform the church by bringing it into conformity with this older and purer tradition. Before he could bring about any reforms, Gascoigne died on 13 March 1458.

Bibliography: R. M. Ball, "The Opponents of Bishop Pecok," *Journal of Ecclesiastical History* 48 (1997): 230–62; R. N. Swanson, *Church and Society in Late Medieval England*, 1993

Darin Hayton

Gaston III, Count de Foix (1331–91),

also known as Gaston Fébus, was the most powerful prince in southwestern France during the fourteenth century. He was also viscount of Béarn, of Marsan, of Gabardan, of Nebouzan, of Lautrec, and of Lower Albigeois, and co-prince (with the bishop of Urgel) of Andorra. Although Gaston held most of his territories as fiefs from the king of France, Béarn was sovereign, a fact that allowed him considerable independence of action. He successfully defended Béarn's sovereignty against John the Good's attempts to claim overlordship of the territory, and it did not become part of France until 1620.

By all accounts, Gaston was an effective ruler and an exceptionally learned and cultivated man. The great wealth he accumulated through efficient administration of his territories enabled him to maintain the most magnificent court in southern France, and he was well known as a patron of art and literature. He himself wrote a book on hunting, *Le livre de la chasse*, which was copied so frequently that more than forty medieval manuscripts, a number of them exquisitely illuminated, still exist. He also wrote *Livre des oraisons* following the death of his son, a book of prayers that was widely copied. Gaston is largely remembered today through *Jean Froissart's account in book 3 of the *Chronicles*, in which the chronicler sojourned at the count's court at Orthez in 1388. Although Froissart admired him as the "perfect knight," Gaston could be extremely cruel and unscrupulous. The count himself chose the surname Fébus (or Phoebus, "Brilliant") when he was still a young man.

Gaston was born on 30 April 1331, the son of Gaston II and Elinor of Comminges. He succeeded to the title at age twelve upon the death of his father, his mother serving as regent until June 1345, when Gaston was fourteen. While little is known of his youth, he evidently was well instructed in French, Latin, and history as well as the knightly use of arms. Gaston received his baptism of fire in 1346 fighting for France at the Battle of Crécy. For most of his life, with the (English) Duchy of Aquitaine on his border, Gaston maintained a neutral stance in the Hundred Years' War, thus sparing his dominions from both sides in the conflict. Indeed, the fact that his court was frequented by knights from both the English and French sides, as well as by knights from Spain, was a major factor in attracting Froissart to his court.

In 1358 Gaston took part in the Teutonic order's crusade in Prussia and en route back to Béarn led an exploit that greatly enhanced his knightly reputation. The rebellion of the Jacquerie was in full swing, and Gaston rescued several hundred ladies of the French court, including the wife of the dauphin, who were in danger of being captured at Meaux by the rebels.

In 1349 Gaston married Agnès, sister of Charles the Bad of Navarre, but in 1362, shortly after the birth of their son Gaston, they became estranged, and Agnès returned to Navarre, where she was supported by her brother. Young Gaston visited his mother in Navarre in 1380 and there appears to have become involved, either wittingly or unwittingly, in a plot by Charles the Bad to poison Count Gaston. In any case, the count put his son in prison, where he died, possibly killed by Gaston himself.

Count Gaston de Foix died, possibly of apoplexy, in 1391 while he was engaged in a hunt, his favorite pastime. He was succeeded by a cousin, Matthew of Castelbon.

Bibliography: Jean Froissart, *Chronicles*, 1968; Pierre Tucoo-Chala, *Gaston Fébus, Prince des Pyrénées, 1331–1391*, 1993.

Dan Wages

Gaunt, John of. *See* John of Gaunt.

Geiler von Kaysersberg, Johan (1445–1510), counted as one of the orthodox precursors of the Reformation, is most notable for his vernacular sermon collections, which addressed contemporary social issues and institutional problems of the church. His other achievement was the translation and edition of major works of *Jean Gerson, the best known among them his *Ars moriendi*.

Johan Geiler von Kaysersberg was born on 16 March 1445 in Schaffhausen, Switzerland, where his father was assistant to a municipal scribe. Upon his father's promotion to scribe, the family moved to Ammerschwihr, where Geiler's father died one year later. The education of Geiler was entrusted to his grandfather, who sent him to the municipal school in Kaysersberg. On 28 June 1460 Geiler enrolled in the faculty of arts at Freiburg University and received the baccalaureats degree in 1462 and the master of arts in 1463 or 1464. On 28 December 1465 he joined the faculty of arts as an instructor and was appointed dean of the faculty of arts in the academic year 1469–70, while he was still working on his doctorate. After his consecration as priest in 1470, he continued his studies in 1471 at the faculty of theology at Basel University; there he was appointed dean of theology in 1474 and received his doctorate in theology in 1475. In 1476 Geiler returned to Freiburg University and was elected chancellor on 31 October, yet in the autumn of 1477 he left Freiburg and renounced his academic career. He subsequently went on a pilgrimage to Beaune and visited Lyons and Marseilles, as well as the Chartreuse house at Avignon, where he began to prepare the edition of the works of Jean Gerson, a task that was to take eleven years. Sometime after his return in 1477, Geiler rejected the offer of a lucrative post as preacher in the wealthy city of Würzburg and instead decided to settle in Strassburg, where he was appointed preacher and vice dean of the city cathedral. Apart from several brief visits to Augsburg, Geiler remained there until his death on 10 March 1510, preaching in local churches and nunneries and holding a number of administrative functions.

A number of Geiler's writings have survived, among these several letters and some sermons and treatises, as well as his edition and translation of Jean Gerson's writings, including the *Ars moriendi*. The works not edited by Geiler himself, the majority of his sermons, fall into two groups: editions of his Latin sermons that make use of his own manuscripts, unlike the editions of his German sermons, which are frequently based on the notes of listeners, and his Latin manuscripts found in his estate. These codicological problems compound a sometimes-questionable authenticity of some of the vernacular sermon collections attributed to Geiler.

Scholastic in method and thought, Geiler's theology has been described as a "pastoral nominalism" and was most clearly expressed in his claim that humans have to accept the full responsibility for their relationship with God. However, his careful avoidance of any controversial theological and dogmatic issue makes it difficult to assign him an outstanding place in late medieval Scholasticism. Despite his involvement with Gerson's work, it is doubtful whether Geiler can be placed in the intellectual and political tradition of this outspoken opponent of the Great Schism, who voiced his opinion at the Council of Constance (1414–18). Geiler was more widely known as a preacher than as a Scholastic, and his popularity rested predominantly on his intimate knowledge of worldly literature and the liberal use he made of it in his sermons. His biggest success was a sermon cycle on *Sebastian Brant's *Das Narrenschiff* (Ship of fools), which must have displeased the authorities, since he had to justify himself for these sermons in front of other theologians. Geiler's avoidance of Scholastic jargon, as well as the sermons' clear structure and his use of exempla, fables, and metaphors, is testimony to the preacher's capability and his sensitivity to his audience's intellectual and spiritual needs. Exemplary for his technique is his use of thematic cycles, based, for instance, on the fundamentals of the Christian faith, such as the Lord's Prayer and the Decalogue. Despite his reluctance to take sides in theoretical issues, his critique of the social and institutional conditions of his time, particularly the corruption in the church, was a recurring topic in a considerable number of his sermons. Often hailed as one of the precursors of the Reformation, Geiler stands in a tradition of orthodox critics of the church who in particular pilloried the abuses of the priest's office. Despite his authority and popularity as a preacher, Geiler was not convinced that his work could effect any significant change. Deeply pessimistic in the last years of his life, he remarked, "There is no hope that matters will improve, but things will deteriorate, and more evil will be heaped on a measure that is already full."

Bibliography: E. Jane Dempsey Douglass, *Justification in Late Medieval Preaching: A Study of John Geiler of Keisersberg*, 1966.

Martin Blum

Geinhausen, Conrad of. *See* Conrad of Geinhausen.

George of Podebrady, King of Bohemia (b. 1420, r. 1458–71). The first strong king of Bohemia after decades of civil unrest and religious wars, George (or Jirí) of Podebrady spent much of his reign trying to revive the authority of the Bohemian monarchy, reunite his country, and restore relations with the rest of Europe. George was born in 1420 to Victorin of Kunstát, a younger son of a major Moravian noble family. The Kunstáts had been early followers of the Czech reformer *Jan Hus, and George's father had fought under the great Hussite leader John Zizka. When Victorin died in 1427, George became a ward of his uncle Boček and then of his father's cousin, Heralt. In 1434 he took part in the Battle of Lipany, fighting on the side of the conservative Hussites against the radical Taborites. During the next decade George emerged as one of the leaders of the Utraquist, or conservative Hussite, party in Bohemia. Under George's leadership, the Utraquists made several attempts during the 1440s to reconcile themselves with Czech Catholics and with the papacy. These attempts, however, failed, and in 1447 George began to plan a conquest of the Czech dominions. His armies seized Prague in September 1448, and by 1450 the Utraquists were in firm control of Bohemia. In April 1452 George was elected regent over the minor king of Bohemia, Ladislas. As regent, George worked to restore royal authority and government in Bohemia and undo the damage done by the religious wars of the early fifteenth century. He also continued in his attempts to unite the Hussite and Catholic parties. In late 1452 George besieged and subjugated the city of Tabor, the major stronghold of the radical Hussites, and for the next decade Bohemia was relatively free of sectarian conflict. Ladislas died in 1457, and on 2 March 1458 George was elected king of Bohemia; he was crowned the following May.

At first, George's primary concern as king was the reconciliation of Bohemia with the papacy. The basis of his attempts at reconciliation was the Compacts of Basel, which were a version of the Four Articles, the basic statement of Hussite belief. In 1436 representatives of the Council of Basel had approved the

Compacts as the basis for peace between Catholics and Hussites in Bohemia, but the papacy had never accepted them. George hoped that he could convince Pope *Pius II to recognize the Compacts, thus removing the taint of heresy from the Czech people. His persecution of the more radical Hussite groups was part of this reconciliation attempt, and in 1461 he reinstated antiheretical legislation originally imposed by Emperor Charles IV. In March 1462, however, the pope rejected the Compacts and demanded that George abandon his Utraquist beliefs and enforce Catholic orthodoxy in Bohemia. George refused and soon abandoned his attempts at reconciliation in favor of an ambitious plan for a union of princes free from papal control. This union, which would have been led by the king of France and would have been dedicated to defending Europe against the Turks, never materialized, but George's diplomatic activities did lead to an alliance with King Casimir IV of Poland. In 1466 Pope Paul II excommunicated George and declared him deposed. A civil war soon erupted in Bohemia between George and an alliance of Catholic nobles. *Matthias Corvinus, the king of Hungary, soon entered the conflict, and in 1467 he invaded Moravia, ostensibly as the savior of the Czech Catholics. Although Corvinus enjoyed considerable military success in 1467 and 1468, George was able to retain his throne. A series of Hussite victories in 1469 and 1470 led Corvinus to propose peace, and even the papacy began to reconsider its rejection of the Compacts of Basel. George, however, died in March 1471 before any agreements could be concluded.

George combined considerable political acumen and military skill with a curious optimism that can be seen above all in his attempt to create a union of European princes. As the last native king of Bohemia, George became a hero to Czech nationalists in the nineteenth century, and his "Hussite kingdom" was seen as an early precursor of an independent Czech state.

Bibliography: Frederick G. Heymann, *George of Bohemia, King of Heretics*, 1965; Otakar Odlozilik, *The Hussite King: Bohemia in European Affairs, 1440–1471*, 1965.

Stephen A. Allen

Gerson, Jean (1363–1429). A noted conciliarist and mystic, Jean Gerson was one of the most important ecclesiastical figures of the fifteenth century. He played a key role in the survival and success of the Council of Constance and in that council's condemnations and executions of *Jan Hus and *Jerome of Prague. His mystical writings extended the tradition of Pseudo-Dionysius the Areopagite, his spiritual mentor, and thus Gerson defended the mystical tradition from what he regarded as potentially dangerous ideas, particularly those of *Jan Ruysbroek and *Ubertino da Casale. Gerson's substantial literary production, in both Latin and French, reflected the breadth of his interests and the scope of his influence. His corpus included mystical, theological, philosophical, and ecclesiological treatises, as well as exegetical works, poetry, letters, and a large number of sermons.

Gerson was born into a humble family in Gerson-les-Barby near Rethel in Champagne, the first of twelve children. Gerson matriculated at the University of Paris in 1377, one year before the Great Schism divided Christendom between two popes. He entered the College of Navarre under the tutelage of *Pierre d'Ailly and Gilles des Champs, receiving his master of arts in 1381 and his license in theology in 1392. Gerson was appointed dean of St. Donatien in Bruges in 1393 and in 1395 succeeded his mentor, Pierre d'Ailly, as chancellor of the university. Gerson argued vigorously against the withdrawal of obedience from *Benedict XIII, which, when it occurred in 1398, depressed him severely. He retreated to Bruges in the spring of 1399, weary of the political charades forced upon him as chancellor. Indeed, he attempted to resign, but his resignation was refused by his sponsor, the duke of Burgundy.

By the time Gerson returned to Paris in the fall of 1400, he had discovered the sense of mission to reform and renew the spiritual life of the church that would drive the rest of his career. His lecture "Contra vanam curiositatem" (Against idle curiosity) in 1402 signaled not only his dwindling patience with theological speculation, but also his commitment to offering in its place an articulated and accessible mysticism grounded in love rather than learning, a spirituality to unite the theologian and the lay believer. He fulfilled this commitment in two university courses issuing forth in his definitive works De mystica theologia speculativa (1402–3) and De mystica theologia practica (1407), published together in 1408. These treatieses revealed Gerson's early mystical theology, for which he depended not only on Pseudo-Dionysius but also on Scholastic commentators such as Bonaventure and Albertus Magnus and the Carthusian Hugh of Balma. He espoused an affective Dionysianism, criticizing the presumptuousness both of Scholasticism and of autotheistic mysticism such as he saw in the thought of Jan Ruysbroek.

Gerson's return to Paris also meant accepting his duties as chancellor, which he did within the framework of his desire for reform. Like most others, Gerson had been advocating the via cessionis (mutual abdication) as the means to resolve the papal schism. The reinstatement of obedience to Benedict XIII in 1403 was a first step toward that end, but with the failure of the convocation at Savona in 1407 Gerson instead backed the via concilii. While he was unable to attend the Council of Pisa in 1409, Gerson rejoiced in the selection there of Pope Alexander V. It was not long, however, before disappointment with Pisa resulted in John XXIII, Alexander's successor, calling the Council of Constance (1414–18). At that time Gerson was caught up in a struggle to condemn Jean Petit's defense of Duke John of Burgundy, who had assassinated the duke of Orléans in 1407. Gerson thus arrived late to Constance, his influence weakened by the battle with Burgundy. But when the council was thrown into confusion by John XXIII's sudden departure on 20 March 1415, Gerson's sermon three days later played a crucial role in preventing it from collapsing altogether. Gerson was also instrumental in attaining the council's condemnations of Jan Hus and Jerome of Prague and in defending the Brethren of the Common Life.

The Council of Constance was a turning point in Gerson's life in two ways. First, the continuing dispute over Jean Petit's defense of tyrannicide, which Gerson eventually won, also earned him the enmity of his one-time patron, the duke of Burgundy. Fearing for his safety, Gerson spent the next year in Austria and Bavaria, most notably in the Benedictine monastery at Melk. Second, Gerson's *Consolation of Theology* (1418), a recapitulation of Boethius's *Consolation of Philosophy*, also made it clear that his bout with Jan Hus had affected him deeply. Gerson's criticism of Hus arose from his concern that souls in this life should have some reassurance of their salvation. The *Consolation of Theology* articulated Gerson's reassessment of covenantal relations in view of this problem, offering a mystical doctrine that the believer fulfills his or her obligation by genuinely seeking the divine.

Gerson never did return to Paris, but in 1419 he joined his brother (also Jean) in the Celestine monastery at Lyons. He took over the diaconate at St. Paul's and spent the rest of his life there in contemplation, writing, and teaching. His mystical thought continued to develop in letters and treatises sent to his Carthusian friends at the Grande Charteuse. The key expressions of his later mysticism were the 1425 letter *In doctrinam Hubertini* (Against the teaching of Ubertino da Casale) and the 1429 *Anagogicum de verbo et hymno Gloriae* (A meditation on the word and the hymn Gloria), wherein he adopted a more apophatic Dionysianism, less mediated by affective commentators. Jean Gerson died in Lyons on 12 July 1429 at the age of sixty-six.

Gerson's sense of responsibility for *les simples gens*, uneducated lay believers, determined much of his work. His conciliarism and his largely affective mystical theology in many ways democratized Christian spirituality, while his deeply hierarchical and at times positivistic ecclesiology (including in this respect treatises on the discernment of spirits), designed to protect believers from "scandal," seems somewhat reactionary today. This conflict within Gerson, sometimes called his "conservative progressivism," in the end reflected the centrality of his pastoral theology to every aspect of his activity as a writer and teacher.

Bibliography: Mark Stephen Burrows, *Jean Gerson and De Consolatione Theologiae*, 1990; Jean Gerson, *Jean Gerson: Early Works*, Brian Patrick McGuire, trans., 1998; Louis Pascoe, *Jean Gerson: Principles of Church Reform*, 1973.

Jeffrey Fisher

Gersonides, Levi (1288–1344),

is also known today as Levi ben Gershon, Levi ben Gershom, or Leon de Bañols. Gersonides, a major medieval Jewish thinker, is remembered as a philosopher, mathematician, astronomer, Talmudic scholar, and Bible commentator. Working at a time when the Jews of his southern French county of Venaissin were facing expulsion, Gersonides began his astronomical observations in Orange, France, in 1320. He composed astronomical tables in 1321 at the request of important local Christians and completed his work in the same place in 1339–40. As an astronomer, Gersonides suggested alternatives to Ptolemy, supporting his arguments with his own observations, as he did on the lunar eclipse of Sukkoth in 1335. His astronomical works, which challenged contemporary theories, were greatly admired by many of his contemporaries, both Jews and Christians. Gersonides' major work of astronomy, part of his important treatise *Milchamot-Adonai* (Wars of the Lord), was later studied by Johannes Kepler. He designed "the staff of Jacob" (Baculus Jacob), which measured angles of light between two stars or two planets and was used in astronomy and especially navigation, and he improved the design of the camera obscura. His mathematical works included analyses of arithmetic, geometry (he wrote both a treatise and commentary after 1337), harmonic numbers, and trigonometry. Scholars have noted that his trigonometric studies, later expanded by *Regiomontanus in 1464, gave birth to many of the principles of modern trigonometry. His work on trigonometry was translated into Latin in 1342 and was dedicated to Pope *Clement VI of Avignon.

Gersonides is best known as a philosopher and is often considered by some the greatest Jewish philosopher after Maimonides. He was particularly admired for his work on Aristotelian philosophy, in which he focused on an Aristotelian rather than on a traditionally Jewish concept of God, whom he imagined as supreme thought rather than a personal deity. Using Hebrew translations of the texts, Gersonides wrote "supercommentaries" to Averroës' commentaries on Aristotle, composing them in 1337 at Avignon in the midst of an increasingly anti-Jewish climate that forbade, for instance, Christians to consult Jewish doctors (a law repealed four years later). His major work, the *Milchamot-Adonai* (sometimes known as *Milchamot ha-shem*), was written in six books that addressed the immortality of the soul, divination and prophecy, divine omnipotence (if God knows all things, how does he know them?), divine providence, astronomy (what forces drive celestial spheres into motion?), creation, and miracles. He worked on this text for twelve years, completing it in early 1329. He complained at that time of troubles that impeded his speculations, probably referring to continued acts of hostility against the Jews (including the wearing of "Jewish badges" imposed in 1326). Nevertheless, he presented this work as an enormous achievement and defended it as a book of science that proved its arguments through mathematics, physical science, and philosophy. The fifth part of the work, on astronomy, provided the heart of the book, and Gersonides in his conclusion called the knowledge of stars the fruit and goal of all other sciences. Celestial bodies demonstrated the entelechy of all physical things and provided a way of understanding the relations between the heavens and the earth. This long fifth part, however—136 chapters in itself—was usually not included in later editions of the *Milchamot* and has been preserved in separate manuscripts.

Gersonides' "rabbinic work" was eclectic but comparatively slight and included three poems, a confession, and a Purim parody. From 1325 to 1338 he composed many biblical commentaries, explicating, among other books, Job, Ecclesiastes, the Song of Songs, the Book of Esther, the Book of Ruth, Genesis, Exodus, Leviticus, and many books of the prophets. His commentary on the

Torah was later one of the first printed Hebrew books, directed at an educated public audience to whom he offered moral and philosophical insights.

Bibliography: Gad Freudenthal, ed., *Studies on Gersonides*, 1987.

Deborah S. Ellis

Ghiberti, Lorenzo (1378?–1455),

was a Florentine goldsmith and sculptor whose bronze doors for the baptistery in Florence, in addition to his writings and other contributions to quattrocento religious art, confirm him as one of the greatest early Renaissance artists. His classical handling of subjects and poetic refinement, combined with technical superiority, helped establish the foundation for the later High Renaissance and influenced such celebrated sculptors as *Donatello and *Paolo Uccello.

Lorenzo Ghiberti was born Lorenzo di Bartolo in Florence at a time when the great city was hovering on the brink of the cultural Renaissance. His date of birth was first listed as 1381, but later doubts cast on his legitimacy forced him to change his name and his birth date to 1378. While there remains some question concerning his true paternity, there seems little doubt that Ghiberti received his early artistic education in painting, sculpture, and goldsmithing in the workshop of his mother's second husband, the goldsmith Bartolo di Michele, called Bartoluccio. In 1400 Ghiberti fled with another painter to Pesaro to escape the plague that was sweeping through Florence, but he returned to Florence the following year to participate in the competition for the baptistery's new bronze door that would complement another designed by Andrea Pisano more than sixty years earlier. The contest was sponsored by the city's most important guild, the Arte di Calimala, with the winning artist's future professional eminence and material success virtually guaranteed. It was this major victory for Ghiberti that was destined to make him one of the best-known and influential sculptors of the early Renaissance.

The competition for the baptistery door is considered by many to have been one of the most momentous of the period because it brought together such illustrious sculptors as *Jacopo della Quercia and *Filippo Brunelleschi, all of whom were making significant and enduring changes in the world of art. Ghiberti's triumph is all the more startling when one considers that he was both the youngest contestant, being around the age of twenty, and the least experienced in the field, having only worked as a painter and possibly a goldsmith until this time. These factors were to be the cause of considerable bitterness among some of the competitors, which would curse Ghiberti and stain his reputation even beyond his death.

Ghiberti labored on the bronze door, which is made up of twenty-eight reliefs of New Testament scenes, for twenty-one years until it was finally put in place in 1424. During this time many sculptors were trained in his workshop who would later go on to make names for themselves, such as Donatello and Paolo Uccello, but Ghiberti's distinct personality and skill defined the eloquent late

Gothic reliefs. In them, one sees the artist striving toward a new form that illustrated an elegant French influence in its complex realism and a new lyricism that would later become one of the hallmarks of the High Renaissance.

While Ghiberti was working on the bronze door, his business flourished. He served as an architectural consultant to the *opera* (redesign and refurbishment) of the cathedral and used his skills as a painter to design cartoons for its stained-glass windows. In 1412 or 1413 the Calimala commissioned a bronze statue from him for the guild sanctuary at Or San Michele, which was followed by orders for two more statues from other important guilds; these statues occupied his workshop until 1428. In spite of this flurry of activity, Ghiberti left Florence in 1416 to begin work on two panels for the baptismal font at Siena, which were not completed until 1427, and he may possibly have contributed to its design as well. His goldsmith work was celebrated for its delicacy and attention to detail but has been lost entirely, including his famed jeweled papal mitres and morses.

After the placement of the first bronze door, the Calimala contracted a second door from Ghiberti. He began this new work in 1425, the theme of which was select scenes from the Old Testament depicted in ten panels, and did not complete it until 1452. It is this door that is regarded by many as Ghiberti's masterpiece and one of the major stepping-stones from Gothic to Renaissance art. Indeed, while the legend that the door was named by Michelangelo, who proclaimed it the "Gates of Paradise" because of its surpassing beauty, is largely considered apocryphal, it reflects the prevailing pride in and admiration for his marvelous accomplishment. The reliefs on this door took Ghiberti's earlier achievement with engaging narrative, graceful naturalism, and elaborate perspective to a higher level and demonstrated a rare command of these sculptural challenges that awed and inspired generations to come.

One of Ghiberti's last great works was not a piece of sculpture or gold, but a written treatise called the *Commentarii*, a book of three parts containing his ideas on art and art history and his autobiography, probably written in the winter of 1447–48. The treatise is valuable not only because Ghiberti was the sole fifteenth-century sculptor to leave a chronicle of his life and art, but also because of its second book, which is considered to be one of the period's most significant writings on art. While Ghiberti was hardly a scholar or an intellectual, his *Commentarii* maintained a humanist tone because of its historical scheme and theory of art; however, Ghiberti's voice can still be heard in his independence and refusal to rely on others' opinions of the artist's craft. It is a fitting example of the kind of artist that Ghiberti was, always striving toward a better understanding and perfection of art in his own way. It was this powerful and talented personality that helped bridge the worlds of Gothic and Renaissance art and left an enduring legacy of quattrocento bronze sculpture that will continue to inspire generations to come.

Bibliography: Richard Krautheimer, *Lorenzo Ghiberti*, 2 vols., 1970; Sarah Blake Wilk, *Fifteenth-Century Central Italian Sculpture*, 1986.

Wendy Marie Hoofnagle

Ghirlandaio, Domenico (1448/49–94). Although Domenico Ghirlandaio was a goldsmith and mosaicist as well, he is best known today as a painter. He was in business with his brothers, Benedetto (1458–97) and Davide (1452–1525), and their studio was one of the most successful and popular workshops in quattrocento Florence. Leaving administration to his brother Davide, Domenico was the creative genius behind the highly finished artistic product. He is notable for a documentary narrative style using an abundance of contemporary portraiture blended with antique decoration. His most famous works are the fresco cycles *Life of the Virgin* and *Life of St. John the Baptist* in the Tornabuoni Chapel, Santa Maria Novella, Florence.

Domenico was born in Florence around 1448/49 to a prosperous family of artisans and small businessmen and was admitted to the confraternity of S. Paolo in 1470. Prior to 1475 frescoes and panel paintings can only be attributed to Domenico on stylistic grounds. The earliest were the *Baptism* and the *Virgin and Child Enthroned with SS. Sebastian and Julian* in S. Andrea a Brozzi, outside Florence. These showed a bias toward the style of *Andrea del Verrocchio, revealing an awareness of the latest developments in Florentine art; however, his creative contribution lay in the rectilinear ordering of composition that unified the real and depicted space.

Eight lunettes, busts of the church fathers and classical philosophers now housed at the Biblioteca Latina in the Vatican Palace, in Rome, are his earliest documented works, dated 1475/76. This important commission reflected the high regard his workshop commanded. In Rome, Ghirlandaio incorporated Roman illusionistic wall decoration into his decorative vocabulary. In 1476 he set to work on the *Last Supper* at Badia in Passignano, developing his technique of using actual space to create a greater effect of depth and atmosphere and demonstrating a maturing ability to create a sense of monumentality. The frescoes of the S. Fina Chapel (1477), the *Last Supper*, and *St. Jerome in His Study* at the Ognissanti in Florence (1480) show his ability to create tense energy, using sharp angular forms defined with striking highlights and shadows, using the medium to create a finish that had become shiny and enamellike.

Ghirlandaio's most important work was done in the 1480s, during which he received his most prestigious commissions. In 1481/82 he returned to Rome to paint the *Calling of SS. Peter and Andrew* in the Sistine Chapel. In this work he mastered a proper balance of monumentality appropriate for the theme. The extensive use of gold, first employed here, reappeared in later works. Ghirlandaio freely used portraiture from life to illustrate loosely clustered groups of people. Portraits of *Sandro Botticelli, *Pietro Perugino, and Cosimo Rosselli, also working on the Sistine Chapel, appear in these groups. This work marks the successful collaboration of narrative intention with documentary tendency.

Ghirlandaio's highest achievement of this collaboration was in his *Life of St. Francis* in the Sassetti Chapel, Sta. Trinita in Florence, where the sacred, antique, and contemporary all coexisted in balanced form. Portraits of patrons such as the Medici, depicted in the haute couture of contemporary Florence, gave this cycle a realistic and worldly ambiance. The documentary aspect of his work made Ghirlandaio's shop prosperous, and throughout the 1480s his business was occupied with large commissions. His personal prosperity provided him with an understanding for, and the ability to satisfy the tastes and aspirations of his patrons.

The fresco cycles *Life of the Virgin* and *Life of St. John the Baptist* (1486–90) are Ghirlandaio's most famous works. Rich with imagery and Florentine portraiture, these frescoes represented the height of Ghirlandaio's synthesis of sacred narrative with personal contemporary documentary. The project, which took four years to complete, was not only his most ambitious monumental cycle, it also was his last major fresco commission.

Although popular demand for Domenico Ghirlandaio's frescoes waned in the 1490s, his workshop continued to produce mosaics. His corpus of work was not without influence; Raphael studied his work closely, and in 1488 Ghirlandaio apprenticed Michelangelo. Domenico Ghirlandaio died in Florence in January 1494.

Bibliography: J. Lauts, *Domenico Ghirlandaio*, 1943; E. Micheletti, *Domenico Ghirlandaio*, 1990.

Patricia Cossard

Giotto di Bondone (c. 1267–1337),

was a seminal Florentine artist who departed from the Byzantine models of his predecessors and developed a new, more naturalistic style of painting. Giotto was recognized by his contemporaries as a major innovator, and subsequent commentary has tended to regard him as the first "modern" painter, one who achieved his novel effects through bold experimentation with color, light, and the depiction of perspectival space, as well as through an insistent effort to capture the human, emotional, and dramatic aspects of the religious themes that he had inherited from medieval tradition.

Giotto was born to a peasant family in the village of Colle di Vespignano, just north of Florence, in either 1267 or 1276; the former date is accepted by most scholars. A legend recorded in Giorgio Vasari's *Lives of the Most Eminent Painters, Sculptors, and Architects* (1568) gives a charming version of his early training. While tending his father's flocks one day, the story goes, Giotto began drawing a sheep on a flat stone, for he was "drawn instinctively to the art of design, and was always sketching what he saw in nature." At just that moment, the famous Florentine artist Giovanni Cimabue happened to pass by and, recognizing the genius of the child, invited him to join his workshop. Though the veracity of this story is doubtful, it is likely that Giotto did receive his earliest training under Cimabue, supplementing this with a period of apprenticeship in

Rome. The robust, three-dimensional quality of his paintings also suggests that he was strongly influenced by three major Tuscan sculptors of his day, Nicola and Giovanni Pisano and Arnolfo di Cambio.

One of Giotto's first known works, his *Crucifix* (completed c. 1296) for the Church of Santa Maria Novella in Florence, provides a compelling illustration of his revolutionary approach. In the latter half of the thirteenth century certain Tuscan artists had attempted to imbue the scene of Christ's death with greater pathos by depicting his physical suffering in more realistic terms. But it was Giotto who first represented Christ's body as a fully human figure: the stylized, majestic Christ of previous iconography was replaced in Giotto's version with an image of a real human victim, one whose body slumped forward under the laws of gravity, whose muscles were rendered with anatomic accuracy, and whose skin was tinted with the greenish hue of death. The image implicitly attempted to evoke compassion from the viewer, and in doing so, it anticipated Giotto's subsequent works, which were to demonstrate an acute sensitivity not only to the physical position of the viewer in relation to the image, but to the emotional impact of the scene on the beholder as well.

The fresco cycle of the Arena Chapel in Padua (also called the Scrovegni Chapel after its wealthy patron) is widely considered to be Giotto's masterpiece. Completed in 1305/6, the cycle consists of a vivid, dramatic narrative of the life of Christ, preceded by scenes from the lives of the Virgin and her parents and accompanied by an ambitious *Last Judgment*. Many aspects of this cycle make it remarkable, including the innovative use of color, light, and perspective, the meaningful juxtaposition of various scenes, and the strong sense of narrative movement. Perhaps above all, this cycle manifests Giotto's gift for dramatizing human emotion and the realities of earthly existence while conveying the deeper spiritual meaning of the action. Through the language of gesture and an unprecedented attention to naturalistic facial expression, Giotto continually strove to portray the inner state of the human actors in the sacred narrative, whether this was the deep dejection of Joachim in the *Expulsion from the Temple*, the confident humility of the Virgin in the *Annunciation*, or the profound grief of John the Evangelist in the moving *Lamentation*.

Other works that can be attributed to Giotto with a good degree of certainty include fresco cycles of the lives of St. Francis, St. John the Baptist, and St. John the Evangelist in the Bardi and Peruzzi chapels at Santa Croce, Florence; the *Ognissanti Madonna*, now at the Uffizi Gallery; a number of crucifixes and panel paintings; and the *Navicella* mosaic at St. Peter's Basilica in Rome, which survives only in a fragmentary state. The most controversial question surrounding Giotto is the nature of his involvement in the frescoes of the Upper Basilica of St. Francis at Assisi. While Giotto has traditionally been credited with the famous cycle of the *Life of St. Francis*, the dramatic stylistic differences between this cycle and that of the Arena Chapel have cast serious doubt on Giotto's authorship of the Francis cycle. Scholars are also divided on the issue of whether or not Giotto painted the two scenes from the *Life of Isaac* in the Upper Basilica.

In the judgment of many, the Isaac scenes are superior to those of the *Life of St. Francis*; they were the work of a true genius who must be, if not Giotto, an unknown painter of equal significance in the history of art.

Though his fame rests on his religious art, Giotto is known to have painted frescoes on secular themes at the Palazzo della Ragione in Padua, the court of Robert of Anjou in Naples, and the palace of Azzone Visconti in Milan, though none of these works survive. He was also a talented architect who designed the campanile of the Duomo in Florence as well as the graceful Carraia Bridge, which was unfortunately destroyed in World War II. He died on 8 January 1337, and his fellow Florentines gave him the great honor of burial in the Duomo.

Bibliography: Moshe Barasch, *Giotto and the Language of Gesture*, 1987; Bruce Cole, *Giotto and Florentine Painting, 1280–1375*, 1976; Francesca Flores d'Arcais, *Giotto*, 1995.

Sarah McNamer

Goes, Hugo van der (fl. c. 1470–82), was a Flemish painter active in Bruges and in Ghent, where he was born. His late years and death are known from a report written by a religious confrere of Hugo's, Gaspar Ofhuys. According to this source, Hugo was a *converso* member of the Red Cloister, located outside Brussels and affiliated with the Windesheim Congregation. Although Hugo had retired from the world of the painters' guild, his abbot permitted him to continue to accept commissions and to associate with those who wished to hire him, both privileges remarkable for a man who had deliberately withdrawn from the secular world. That the artist suffered from some form of mental illness seems certain from Ofhuys's account. The writer identified the disease as either *frensis magna* or possession by demons, caused (he suggested) by "corrupt humors" or divine providence. Whatever the cause, it seems to have been a debilitating disease that left the artist in despair of finishing his numerous commissions. Historians offer this illness as a possible cause for the tension and disparity of scale in the artist's compositions.

Scholars have identified fifteen works by Hugo, all attributed on the basis of style, since none was signed by the artist. Although the attribution of some of these paintings has been disputed, the majority of the works are still considered his. By far the most important of his surviving works is the *Portinari Altarpiece*, completed in 1476. Its commissioner was Tommaso Portinari, the Medici family's representative in Bruges. The date of the triptych is determined by the number and ages of the Portinari children present in the wings of the altarpiece. In this and other works of Hugo, there was a reintroduction of disguised symbolism. With respect to this practice and many other aspects of Hugo's style, he looked back to his predecessors, rather than forward to his own contemporaries. The use of such medieval symbolism as he employed had run its course before Hugo's time. With the figures in his works, Hugo harkened back to the style of the slender, curly-haired angels of the *Ghent Altarpiece*, which Hugo had surely seen when he lived in Ghent. The painter established tension in his compositions by destroying the internal unity of the gaze, scale, and placement of the figures. It is in these anomalies of style and composition that scholars see an expression of his illness, but it is also possible to see these manipulations as a way for the artist and his viewer to move into the spiritual realm, for he created a space that is not of this world. Other works by van der Goes that illustrate these tendencies are the *Fall of Man* and the *Lamentation* diptych wings (c. 1470); the *Montforte Altarpiece* (c. 1472); *Portrait of a Man* (c. 1475); *Adoration of the Shepherds* (c. 1480); and *Dormition of the Virgin* (c. 1480).

Bibliography: E. Panofsky, *Early Netherlandish Painting*, 1971.

Marian Hollinger

Gonzaga, Ludovico, Marquis of Mantua (1412–78), was a sensitive

patron of the arts and an enlightened and just ruler. Like other Renaissance princes, he spent a part of the family fortune on luring the most famous Renaissance painters, architects, and philosophers to Mantua to work. Through Ludovico, Mantua became a city universally admired for its beauty and culture.

Ludovico was born into a battle-scarred family that had made the largest part of its fortune as condottieri, or leaders of mercenary armies that fought for other Italian cities. He was educated at the Mantuan court school of Vittorino da Feltre and so imbibed the principles that formed the just and well-educated man of the age. When Vittorino first encountered Ludovico, he was a fat and lazy boy of ten, but Vittorino trained him to curb his appetite and taught him to make himself fit for governing Mantua. Ludovico's father, Gianfrancesco, found Ludovico plain, physically slow, and awkward, and so he favored his second son, Carlo, as his heir. Ludovico, unsure of his future in Mantua, offered himself as a condottiere captain to the Sforza family in Milan. Gianfrancesco's criticism of Ludovico may have strengthened his son's determination to prove himself as a condottiere, for he did become a respected military leader and a highly skilled diplomat. As he grew older, Ludovico was often called upon to settle disputes, even outside Mantua. Upon the death of his father, with whom he had made an uneasy peace, Ludovico became the marquis of Mantua in 1445. In spite of Carlo's treachery in trying to succeed his father as marquis, Ludovico treated him more generously than was normal for the time.

In 1463 Ludovico resigned as condottiere in Milan because of a disputed marriage contract between Galeazzo Maria Sforza's son and one of his daughters. Ludovico was now able to concentrate on improving conditions within Mantua. Earlier, in 1459, Ludovico had played host to a conclave called by the pope to formulate a plan that would stop Turkish incursions into Europe. Ludovico had heard the participants' complaints about the mud in his streets, and so he now had the time and motivation to have them paved. He had mulberry trees planted to create a silk industry to complement Mantua's wool-weaving industry. Dikes were needed to hold back the flood waters of the Po River, and canals were needed to irrigate the mulberry trees and also a new crop, rice, which had recently been brought to northern Italy. Ludovico petitioned the Florentine government to allow *Filippo Brunelleschi, designer of the dome of Santa Maria del Fiore in Florence, to come to Mantua to design and build these dikes.

Although Ludovico was a condottiere, he was religious within the bounds of his position and was supportive of the Mantuan clergy's attempt to revive church attendance and to reinvigorate church sacraments such as confession and baptism. This led to renewed religious fervor that sparked the building of churches whose interiors in turn needed decorating. At Ludovico's request, the architect *Leon Battista Alberti came from Florence and designed the churches of Sant'Andrea and San Sebastiano, along with the Incoronata Chapel in the cathedral. Ludovico also established the Ospedale Maggiore for the care of the poor and feeble and supported it with government funds.

Ludovico's biggest coup was persuading *Andrea Mantegna, one of the most famous Renaissance painters, to come to Mantua in 1460 to live and work. Mantegna worked for Ludovico and the next two marquises painting the walls of their palaces, villas, and chapels. The only surviving examples of Mantegna's work in Mantua are the famous frescoes in the ducal palace. The Sala degli Sposi (the Hall of the Betrothed) was named and decorated in honor of the engagement of Ludovico's heir.

Ludovico collected an excellent library that boasted a manuscript copy of Virgil, his favorite poet, and miniaturists were employed to illustrate his *Aeneid*. There were illustrated editions of *Dante, *Francesco Petrarch, and *Giovanni Boccaccio, the founders of Italian literature. Several books dealt with the raising and care of horses, which was an important subject to condottieri. There were five volumes devoted to the animals of the earth that symbolized awakening interest in scientific knowledge. In conjunction with his growing library, Ludovico also established the first printing press in Mantua. Ludovico at varying times invited to his court many famous poets, scholars, and writers who enlivened the atmosphere with their vibrant ideas. *Angelo Poliziano, *Giovanni Pico della Mirandola, and Francesco Filelfo were just some who responded to Ludovico's invitation.

Before his death of the plague in 1478, Ludovico had turned Mantua into a rich and reasonably secure city. His court had entertained a steady stream of stimulating people, and his city had been decorated by some of the most famous Renaissance painters and architects. Ludovico's achievements were recognized in 1477 when the pope bestowed upon him the golden rose, a distinction usually reserved for European royalty.

Bibliography: Lauro Martines, *Power and Imagination: City-States in Renaissance Italy*, 1988; Kate Simon, *A Renaissance Tapestry: The Gonzaga of Mantua*, 1988.

Kathryn Kiff

González de Clavijo, Ruy (d. 1412), was a nobleman of Madrid, an ambassador to the court of Timur the Lame (Tamerlane) in Samarkand, and a chamberlain of King Enrique III of Castile. Although the date of Clavijo's birth is unknown, he served King Enrique III as chamberlain from his youth, and he was one of the witnesses to the king's will and testament. In service to Enrique, Clavijo was the chief envoy in a diplomatic embassy sent by the king to Timur in 1403, doubtless seeking an alliance with him against the Turks. The mission resulted from a friendly gesture by Timur, who had sent an escort bearing gifts and letters to Enrique III following the Mongol victory over the Turks at Angora (1402).

Clavijo's narrative of this journey, the *Embajada a Tamorlán*, consisted of firsthand observations, reports from and conversations with various persons, and ruminations upon the meaning of some of the events he witnessed. While the text has been attributed to Clavijo as author, he may have dictated the work to a scribe upon his return from the journey, based upon notes he made along the way. Clavijo described the nature of sea voyage and land travel, cities and ports and their condition, landscape and climate, non-Western peoples (the Chagatay), unusual animals such as giraffes and elephants, trade and merchandise along the Asian and Levantine routes, food and feasting customs, and customary behavior among and toward ambassadors. His description of Constantinople was detailed and reverential; and the loving attention he gave to the Church of Santa Sophia is all the more poignant when it is read today with the hindsight that it would soon be taken by Muslim forces.

Clavijo and his companions had embarked from Santa Maria (near Cádiz) on 22 May 1403, and they met Timur (by then almost seventy years old) in September 1404. Though the embassy was well received, and Clavijo described in detail the courts and banquets at Samarkand, the embassy was hurried in its departure because Timur was in ill health and his counselors did not want the news of his imminent death to spread too quickly. The embassy did not arrive home until 1406, after the death of the Mongol ruler.

Ruy González de Clavijo was the only Latin traveler of the early fifteenth century to see, for the last time, some of the sights in the declining Byzantine Empire. His is the only contemporary Western account of Timur the Lame and his court at Samarkand, demonstrating a skill for detailed, straightforward description separate from received knowledge about Eastern peoples. Clavijo was a reliable witness to the events and sights of his age and served as an invaluable source for the history of the fifteenth-century East and its relationship with the West.

After Enrique III's death in 1406, Clavijo retired from the court and arranged for the building of his sepulcher in a chapel he had founded in the Convent of San Francisco in Madrid. He was interred in that place in 1412, but his tomb was destroyed in the late fifteenth century in order to bury Juana of Portugal, the widow of King *Enrique IV.

Bibliography: Francisco López Estrada [Ruy González de Clavijo], *Embajada a Tamor-lán*, 1943; J. N. Hillgarth, *The Spanish Kingdoms 1250–1516*, 1976.

Rowena Hernández Múzquiz

González de Mendoza, Pedro (1428–95), cardinal, a Spanish politician and writer, was one of many sons of *Iñigo López de Mendoza, the marques de Santillana and was chosen for the priesthood from an early age. After his ordination, he served in his native city of Guadalajara for a while before moving to Salamanca to finish his studies. He became a member of the Aragonese court of King Juan II, and in 1454 the king named him bishop of Calahorra. Later he also became bishop of Siguenza and Osma. González de Mendoza was an energetic man, and this brought him many other honors; he rose to become archbishop of Seville and was eventually named a cardinal.

After the death of King *Juan II of Castile, González de Mendoza endured the times of intrigue and scandal brought about by the reign of *Enrique IV of Castile. During this time he wrote a long treatise defending the advice he gave to King Enrique against dealing with the king of Portugal. Sometimes the cardinal sided with the interests of the Catholic church, which was his primary duty, but he did try to help King Enrique in overcoming the many political problems he faced. When civil war broke out after the death of Enrique IV, he sided with the Catholic monarchs, *Ferdinand and *Isabel. Cardinal González de Mendoza distinguished himself during the Battle of Toro and the siege of Zamora with the aid of his family. As a prize for his assistance, the Catholic monarchs gave him the coveted episcopal see of Toledo. When the final push to drive the Moors from Granada started, he was sent to the frontier to fight and thus took part in the final phase of the Reconquista. Afterwards, González de Mendoza retired to his native city of Guadalajara, where he was visited by the Catholic monarchs as a show of their affection for him.

Even while he was involved in politics and warfare, Cardinal González de Mendoza was a prolific writer. Among his many works are the *Catecismo de la doctrina cristiana*, the *Poesias de Pero González*, and various letters, as well as translations of works by Virgil and Homer.

Bibliography: Helen Nader, *The Mendoza Family in the Spanish Renaissance, 1350 to 1550*, 1979; Nancy Rubin, *Isabella of Castile: The First Renaissance Queen*, 1991.

Peter E. Carr

Gower, John (1330?–1408), is probably best known for his authorship of *Confessio Amantis* and his friendship with *Geoffrey Chaucer. The *Confessio*, written in English and divided into eight books, was cast as a dialogue between a lover and his confessor. To keep the lover from indulging in the "sins of love" (Pride, Envy, Ire, and so on, each subdivided into sundry branches), the confessor told numerous tales of antiquity, each intended theoretically to illustrate the evils of the sin in question. Additional works of Gower include *Vox clamantis* (in Latin), *Mirour de l'omme* (French, and renamed the *Speculum meditatis*), *Traitie pour essampler les amants marietz* (French), *Cronica tripertita* (Latin), and *In Praise of Peace* (English).

The written record reveals very little of Gower's early life. In part, this is due to the popularity of the name "John Gower" in fourteenth-century England, which makes it impossible to disentangle the poet's birth, parentage, and upbringing from that of numerous others. Biographers, therefore, usually begin with the tomb celebrating his achievements. Gower's original tomb, according to John Stow's *Survey of London*, was located in the Church of St. Mary Overeys and included a sculpture of the poet with auburn curls, a small, pointed beard, and three of his own books beneath his head. By 1600, however, the hands and nose of the sculpture had been cut off, and the nearby wall painting had been washed out. Gower's popish reputation during the sixteenth century may be the culprit here; John Urry's *Life of Chaucer*, for instance, referred to Gower as "Bigot to the Church of Rome," while two manuscripts of the *Confessio Amantis* contain erasures of words like "pope," "papacy," and "purgatory."

The mutual commendations of Chaucer and Gower are also a matter of record. In *Confessio Amantis*, Venus compliments Chaucer (her "disciple") for eighteen lines; "to him in special / Above alle othre I am most holde." No other contemporary poet receives such praise. Perhaps Gower is responding to Chaucer, who had closed his *Troilus and Criseyde* with a direction to "moral Gower, this book I directe / To the, and to the, philosophical Strode, / To vouchen sauf, ther nede is, to correcte, / Of youre benignites and zeles goode." Such exchanges, in addition to linguistic parallels between the two poets, suggest that the poets exchanged manuscripts, and have thus encouraged readers to postulate a more personal relationship.

Those documents that can be tied with certainty to the poet date from the last decades of his life, rather than the first. By 1377 Gower had assisted with the restoring of St. Mary Overeys; the priory, where he lived by the time of his death, had access to the sort of library Gower's writing required. This, plus his association with Chaucer and the allusions to Southwark, the Thames, and the royal court, suggests a lengthy London residence. Yet as late as 1382 Gower was still described on the Close Rolls as "Esquire of Kent." During the same year Gower bought manors in Norfolk and Suffolk and leased them again almost immediately to a group headed by the parson of the church in Fettwell. These manors were later mentioned in his will. Some years after this, in 1398, Gower was granted a license to marry Agnes Groundolf in the oratory by his lodgings in the priory of St. Mary Overeys, without prior reading of banns. This, Gower's first marriage (as far as we can tell), was celebrated only after his physical state had deteriorated, or so Gower said in a letter to the archbishop of Canterbury accompanying a gift manuscript of the *Vox clamantis* in 1402. If, indeed, he was really as old, blind, decrepit, and totally miserable as he claimed ("Senex et, cecus, corpus et egrotum, vetus et, miserabils totum"), Gower may have married to secure an able nurse.

Sometime roughly contemporaneous with his move into the priory, Gower described in *Mirour de l'omme* a change of life and subject matter; instead of singing and dancing, "veine joye," and "foldelit" (foolish delight), Gower turned to prayer and self-examination. By the end of *Mirour*, however, Gower sounded patriotic and sharply political, even predicting something like the Peasants' Rebellion, "a mob of common people led by instigators, for they will not be stopped by reason nor discipline."

Certainly, as Gower grew older, he became steadily more involved in politics and a decided partisan of the new king *Henry IV. The changes made in Gower's dedications of colophons clearly reflected growing disaffection from *Richard II. The initial version of *Confessio* described a personal meeting with King Richard, who, he said, invited the poet into his barge and asked him to write the poem that followed. Similarly, the Epistle attached to the earliest version of the *Vox clamantis* pities the king's youth and exculpates him, blaming those who ruled in his name. But the later version of *Confessio* cuts the meeting and substitutes "a bok for Englondes sake" for "a bok for king Richardes sake." By the time of the *Cronica tripertita*, all trace of pity was gone; the king always had a hard heart ("Rex induratum cor semper habet").

Even before Henry of Lancaster deposed Richard II, Gower must have been cultivating the rising power. In 1393, after revising the dedication of *Confessio amantis* (which had previously been dedicated to Richard II), and while Henry was still duke, the latter paid for a collar to replace one given to "un Esquier John Gower." This collar resembles the one depicted on the effigy and in the portrait at the beginning of the Fairfax manuscript. A year later, just weeks after the coronation of Henry IV, Gower was granted two pipes of wine of Gascony yearly, at the port of London; probably this was Henry's appreciation of *Cronica tripertita*, which defended Henry's usurpation. Gower then acknowledged this gift with a complimentary poem. In the last years of his life, Gower enjoyed the favor of the new Lancastrian king. When he died, his will, proved on 24 October 1408, left one hundred pounds, household goods, and rents from at least two manors to his surviving wife.

Bibliography: J. A. Burrow, *Ricardian Poetry: Chaucer, Gower, Langland, and the Gawain Poet*, 1971; John H. Fisher, *John Gower: Moral Philosopher and Friend of Chaucer*, 1964; John Gower, *Complete Works*, 4 vols., 1968.

Kathryn Jacobs

Grocyn, William (1446?–1519) was recognized as the foremost classical scholar and teacher in England in the late fifteenth century even though he had no published works to his credit, though one of his letters to the Venetian printer *Aldus Manutius is extant. Grocyn is of interest because he was one of the first, if not the first, to teach Greek at Oxford. With the help of the leading scholars of his day, such as *John Colet, Thomas Linacre, and Sir Thomas More, the light of classical learning was spread throughout the university.

William Grocyn was born at Colerne, Wiltshire. Though little is known about his family, it is thought that his father was a copyhold farmer, or perhaps one who reads a manuscript aloud to a proofreader. Grocyn was admitted to Winchester College in 1463, and two years later he entered New College, Oxford, where he held a fellowship from 1467 to 1481. At Oxford Grocyn tutored William Warham, who later became the archbishop of Canterbury and who bestowed upon Grocyn the college church of Newton, Longuerville, in Buckinghamshire. This gift provided Grocyn with the means to make a living. Grocyn also accepted the office of divinity lecturer at Magdalen College and was ordained, though the exact date is uncertain. In 1483, while he was at Magdalen, he participated in a debate with three others before *Richard III and received a buck and a gift of money from the king. He became a prebendary of Lincoln Cathedral in 1485, thereby receiving a prebend or regular fixed income. In 1488 he resigned his post at Magdalen and went to Italy to study Greek.

Both George Liley, Grocyn's godson, and Desiderius Erasmus, who was to become Grocyn's close friend, maintained that he taught Greek at Oxford before his visit to Italy. It is known that Thomas Chaundler, warden of New College in Grocyn's day, had invited the Italian scholar Cornelio Vitelli, who was visiting Oxford, to lecture. Vitelli was probably a Greek scholar and could have tutored Grocyn in the Greek language. This exposure to Vitelli could have inspired Grocyn to further his knowledge of Greek, thus prompting his trip to Italy. Grocyn spent most of his time in Florence studying under *Angelo Poliziano, an Italian poet, and Chalcondyles, an Athenian teaching Greek in that city. He and his fellow scholar and friend Thomas Linacre, who had journeyed to Italy in 1485, met often to study together, and it was during this time that they both met Aldus Manutius. Upon his return to England, Grocyn gave daily public lectures in Greek, and though the work was done voluntarily, the most advanced students of the day thought it important enough to attend. When Erasmus arrived on his first visit to Oxford in 1497, he found Grocyn and his fellow scholars spreading the new learning throughout the university. Erasmus noted that although Grocyn was a devoted student of the Greek classical writers, he still studied the medieval Schoolmen, who were considered out of step with the new classical learning on the Continent. Grocyn also preferred Aristotle to Plato and appears to have held more conservative religious views than those of his fellow scholars. About 1499 Manutius printed a work by Linacre to which he attached a letter he had received from Grocyn. In his letter, Grocyn thanked Manutius for his kind treatment of their mutual friend Linacre and congratulated him on preparing an edition of Aristotle before one on Plato. Manutius, in return, praised Grocyn as a man of great skill and universal learning even in the Greek language.

In 1496 Grocyn became the rector of St. Lawrence Jewry in London. Grocyn's good friend Colet became dean of St. Paul's Cathedral in 1503, and upon his request Grocyn often preached there. During Colet's tenure Grocyn gave what is considered a remarkable series of lectures on the book *The Ecclesiastical Hierarchy of Dionysius*, a mystical account of early Christian doctrine. It was believed to be the work of Dionysius the Areopagite, who had been converted to Christianity by St. Paul. Grocyn contested that belief, thereby paving the way for an entirely new view concerning the authorship of this work. Grocyn's old friend Warham made him master of the collegiate church of All Hallows at Maidstone in 1506 and followed that with the rectories of Shepperton and East Peckham. An attack of paralysis in 1518 disabled Grocyn, and the following year he died.

Grocyn was greatly respected not only for his classical scholarship but also for his leadership in disseminating classical learning throughout Oxford. In a letter to Colet, who was traveling outside London, Sir Thomas More wrote that Grocyn had become the master of his life during Colet's absence. Such an acknowledgment from More was a tribute to the significance of Grocyn's scholarship and teaching, which allowed More and other young scholars to remain in England instead of traveling to Italy to study Greek.

Bibliography: Maria Dowling, *Humanism in the Age of Henry VIII*, 1986; Alistair Fox and John Guy, *Reassessing the Henrician Age: Humanism, Politics, and Reform, 1500–1550*, 1986.

Kathryn Kiff

Groote, Gerard (1340–84), was a Dutch ascetic and reform preacher, founder of the late medieval movement of spiritual reform known as the *devotio moderna*. Gerard Groote was born in 1340 in Deventer, a small Hanseatic town on the IJssel River in the Netherlands. His father, a devout and conscientious city magistrate, died in the Black Death in 1350, leaving Gerard a wealthy orphan under the care of his uncle. Groote studied in Paris and received his master's degree in liberal arts in 1358. After a brief return to Deventer and some academic trips to Cologne and Prague, Groote resumed his study in Paris in 1362 in the fields of theology and law. At the same time he applied for several benefices at the papal court in Avignon and was eventually rewarded with canonries in Aix-la-Chapelle and Utrecht. He seemed to be embarking on a successful ecclesiastical career until disease struck in 1372. With the illness came a severe crisis of conscience about his involvement in natural science and astrology, which he had developed during his time of study in Paris. He would later denounce these as "magic."

Groote's disease was a turning point; admonished by his friends, William de Salvarvilla and Henry Egher of Calcar (prior of the Carthusian monastery at Monnikhuizen near Arnhem), he repented of his former life and vowed to devote himself to God. He gave up his benefices in 1374 and signed away his parental mansion in Deventer for the use of people "who wish to serve God." The house was to become the first foundation of the Sisters of the Common Life, for which Groote wrote a rule in 1379. Groote himself spent three years, 1374–77, in the seclusion of the monastery at Monnikhuizen.

Although the contemplative life held a great appeal for him, Groote eventually chose to lead an active life as a reform preacher. To prepare himself for this task, he undertook a book-buying trip to Paris in 1379. The same year he was ordained as deacon in the Diocese of Utrecht (he considered himself unworthy of priesthood) and began preaching in the IJssel region. His main message was one of personal repentance and asceticism; he also attacked heresy (especially that of the Brethren of the Free Spirit) and clerical abuses like simony and priestly concubinage. His zeal for monastic reform eventually inspired the foundation of the Brethren of the Common Life. On Groote's advice, the Brethren chose a way of life between the cloister and the world guided by the Augustinian Rule, but the first foundations (Deventer, Agnietenberg, and Windesheim) were not established until after Groote's death by his disciple Florentius Radewijns (1350–1400).

Groote's career as a preacher culminated and came to an abrupt end in 1383 with a sermon preached before the assembled clergy at the bishop of Utrecht's residence. Groote urged a boycott of priests who had broken their vow of celibacy. The bishop of Utrecht, who at first had been supportive of Groote's mission, yielded to Groote's opponents among both the secular clergy and mendicant orders and issued a general prohibition against preaching by deacons in 1383. Groote appealed the decision, but shortly afterwards died in 1384, infected with the plague after a visit to a sick friend.

Groote's ideals were expressed in his various writings, especially in his letters and sermons. The most personal document of his surviving writings is his *Resolutions, Not Vows*, a personal statement composed around 1375 shortly after his conversion. His sermons included the *Sermo contra focaristas* (Sermon against concubinage), which he delivered before the assembled clergy at Utrecht in 1383, and the *De nativitate Domini*, an admonition to follow Christ's example in daily living. Groote's treatise on marriage, *De matrimonio*, surpassed its main source, St. Jerome, on the subject of misogyny. Groote's translation of the Book of Hours into middle Dutch became a best-seller and was preserved in more than eight hundred manuscripts.

Groote's influence on the resurgence of Christian ascetic spirituality was considerable; he can be considered the founder of the *devotio moderna*, the reform movement active in northern Europe on the eve of the Reformation. Although some scholars have seen this movement as an overture to the Reformation, it must be remembered that it offered no fundamental doctrinal reform, but rather a quiet, obedient, ascetic, and somewhat moralistic spirituality. The *devotio moderna* produced a large array of spiritual literature; the most influential book was perhaps *The Imitation of Christ*, sometimes falsely ascribed to Gerard Groote but probably written by *Thomas à Kempis, who also wrote Groote's major biography.

Bibliography: John Van Engen, trans., *Devotio moderna: Basic Writings*, 1988; Theodore P. Van Zijl, *Gerard Groote, Ascetic and Reformer (1340–1384)* in *Studies in Mediaeval History*, vol. 18 (1963).

Frans A. van Liere

Guarino da Verona (1384–1460), also called Guarino Veronese, first appears in Bologna as a student of Giovanni Conversino da Ravenna, where he became a notary. Having chosen the vocation of humanist, he went to Constantinople to study Greek under *Manuel Chrysoloras. Returning after five years, he began his career, teaching in Florence, Verona, and, finally, Ferrara, where he was called by Duke Niccolò III d'Este in 1429 to become the personal tutor of his son, Leonello, who would succeed him as duke in 1441. After seven years' tutelage of his noble pupil, he accepted the chair of eloquence and greek at the Studio, or university, of Ferrara, in 1436, where he remained for the rest of his life. Stimulated by Guarino's genial enthusiasm and by Marquis Leonello, Ferrara became one of the most cultured and learned cities of Italy. Scholars and artists frequented Ferrara, including the great architect *Leon Battista Alberti, who was an intimate of both Guarino and the marquis, and who designed the campanile for the cathedral. Matteo Boiardo was the court poet. The marquis's library itself grew to impressive size by contemporary standards, and an inventory of 1436 lists 297 manuscripts. A passionate researcher of codices, Guarino emended, among others, works by isocrates, Caesar, Gellius, and the two Plinys. He did the first translations of Herodotus, Plutarch, Lucian, Strabo, and Plautus into vernacular Italian. Of the latter, he wrote commentaries on eight comedies in the codex that was discovered at Colonia by Niccolò da Trier in 1428 and acquired for him by Leonello. The codex contained twelve plays thought lost. Guarino's son, Battista, translated some of them, preparing the ground for their revival and performance in Italian later under Duke *Ercole l d'Este. Guarino's contribution to pedagogy was also significant, because he abandoned the medieval trivium and quadrivium for a new approach to education employing an elementary course, a bipartite grammar, and rhetoric.

Bibliography: Edmund Gardner, *Dukes and Poets in Ferrara*, 1968.

C. Thomas Ault

Guesclin, Bertrand du (c. 1320–80), was lord of Broons and later count of Longueville, count of Trastámara, duke of Molina, and constable of France. Born in the castle of la Motte-Broons (near Dinan) into an impoverished noble Breton family, Bertrand du Guesclin became one of the most celebrated knights of the Hundred Years' War, fighting for his longtime friend and patron, King Charles V of France.

A man of renowned ugliness, Bertrand du Guesclin rose through the ranks to become the constable of France by serving the French king in several troublesome conflicts. He was instrumental in defeating the forces of the king of Navarre, Charles the Bad, whose long history of enmity with the Valois dynasty had culminated in a rebellion against his father-in-law, King John II, beginning in 1354. The ten-year conflict ended in May 1364 when a force led by du Guesclin soundly defeated the forces of Charles the Bad at Cocherel in Normandy. No longer would the king of Navarre be a serious threat to the authority of the French Crown.

Du Guesclin also participated in the battles for the succession of the Duchy of Brittany. After the death of Duke Jean III of Brittany in 1341, the inheritance was disputed between two parties: the late duke's half brother, Count Jean of Montfort, and his niece, Jeanne of Penthièvre, married to Charles of Blois. This dispute led to a civil war that raged for twenty-three years, involving not only the Bretons but also the English and the French, each taking a different side. Bertrand du Guesclin fought on the side of Charles of Blois, who, as nephew of the French king Philip VI, represented Valois interests in Brittany. This conflict, however, did not end as successfully as the Navarrese episode. In the battle of Auray on 29 September 1364, Charles of Blois was killed. Du Guesclin, taken prisoner by the English, was soon ransomed.

One of the greatest talents of du Guesclin was an ability to command groups of soldiers called *routiers*. The conclusions of the Navarrese and Breton conflicts left many soldiers unemployed, who then began ravaging and pillaging the French countryside. Through a combination of comradery, strict discipline, and authority, du Guesclin was able to control bands of *routiers* and to use them effectively in service to the king of France. Much to Charles V's relief, in 1365 du Guesclin led *routiers* to southern France and Spain to fight on behalf of the Spaniard Henry of Trastámara, a pretender to the throne of Castile. At first du Guesclin's campaigns with Henry were successful. The king of Castile, Peter the Cruel, fled, and Henry of Trastámara took the throne in his stead. Soon, however, Peter the Cruel allied himself with the celebrated English knight *Edward, the Black Prince, who led forces into Spain. In April 1367 the Battle of Nájera concluded with the defeat of Henry of Trastámara and the imprisonment, yet again, of Bertrand du Guesclin. *Jean Froissart relates an interesting story at this point in his narrative. The Black Prince, chatting with his prisoner, asked du Guesclin how he was faring. Du Guesclin replied that he felt like the most honored and valued knight in the world, since he knew that the prince did not dare set him free. The Black Prince retorted that it was not true, that he would happily liberate him for a set sum. In less than a month the king of France provided the ransom, and du Guesclin was freed. Another legend has du Guesclin bragging that every peasant woman in the kingdom of France would contribute to his ransom.

For a short time du Guesclin continued in the service of Henry of Trastámara, but in 1369 Charles V called him into his own service in order to fight the

English. In 1370 Charles did Bertrand du Guesclin great honor by naming him constable of France, an important office that gave him supreme command over the French fighting forces. In the final ten years of his life du Guesclin slowly began to take back for France areas that the French had lost in the Treaty of Brétigny (1360). Du Guesclin and the Breton lord Olivier de Clisson conquered Poitou and Saintonge in 1371–72, and one year later they took over Brittany, whose duke, Jean IV, had taken the English side. While besieging the town of Château-neuf-de-Randon, du Guesclin died, probably of dysentery, on 13 July 1380. Du Guesclin's death came as a shock to King Charles V. The king's regard for his constable was manifested by his burial at the Cathedral of St. Denis, among the tombs of earlier French kings and queens. No other French noble had ever been so honored for service to his king. Historians, however, have not always been so kind to Bertrand du Guesclin. He has sometimes been portrayed as a loser rather than a winner, a man who had more talent in his own personal public relations than skill in winning battles or successfully besieging towns. The contemporary view of him was the opposite, however; chroniclers extolled his martial talents, manuscript illuminators drew pictures of his successes, and a poet wrote an epic poem about him. For this reason, Bertrand du Guesclin remains the embodiment of the chivalrous knight of the era of the Hundred Years' War.

Bibliography: Christopher Allmand, *The Hundred Years War*, 1989; Edouard Perroy, *The Hundred Years War*, 1951.

Dana L. Sample

Gutenberg, Johann (1394 or 1404–68),

Gutenberg, Johann (1394 or 1404–68), designed and manufactured the first printing press as well as the typefaces used in the press and oversaw the design and composition of the first printed texts. His major achievement, the Forty-two-Line Bible, established printing as a way to produce high-quality texts more quickly and less expensively than hand copying, with results that were both accurate and beautiful.

Gutenberg's date of birth is uncertain. He was born in Mainz to Friele and Else Gensfleisch. In 1411 the Gensfleisch family, along with other patrician families, was forced to leave Mainz because of political conflicts between burghers and guild members. Although the family was allowed to return a few months later, it again left in 1413 and did not return during Friele Gensfleisch's lifetime. Nothing is known about Gutenberg's early life or schooling, although his knowledge of Latin may indicate a university education.

After the death of his father in 1419, Gutenberg returned to Mainz and began training as a metalworker. The family soon after gained the full title to a property in Mainz called the Gutenberghof and so took the name Gutenberg. In 1434 Gutenberg appears in Strassburg court records in a case concerning his annual annuity payments, and he apparently took up residence there around that time. In 1438 he went into partnership as a metalworker with a Strassburg citizen named Hans Riffe in order to produce metal holy mirrors for pilgrims traveling to a nearby shrine at Aachen. It was in Strassburg that the first indications of Gutenberg's interest in printing technology surfaced. In 1439 Gutenberg appeared in a court case with Jörg Dritzehn, who was suing Gutenberg on behalf of his dead brother Andreas, who had been Gutenberg's partner in the manufacture of the holy mirrors. There is also mention of a new metalworking enterprise, which may have been the manufacture of the printing press and the casting of typefaces. These court documents indicate that Gutenberg may have begun work on printing with movable type as early as 1438.

Strassburg, which saw the early developments of Gutenberg's printing-press technology, also may have been the place where Gutenberg first set up his print shop. The first texts Gutenberg printed, the *Fragment vom Weltgericht* and the *Donatus*, may date from 1440–44, which places Gutenberg in Strassburg. He did return to Mainz sometime between 1444 and 1448 and set up a printing shop in his family home, the Gutenberghof, where he continued to print editions of the *Donatus* in versions that were set in 26, 27, 28, and 30 lines per page. In 1449 he entered into a partnership with *Johann Fust, from whom he received a loan to set up a new press and manufacture a new typeface to print the Bible. The printing of the Bible may have been completed as early as 1454 and stands as Gutenberg's most important typographic achievement. The text of the Bible was printed on vellum and was set in double columns of forty-two lines per page. The text itself was rather simple and unadorned, printed in black ink with red headings (some printed but most handwritten), yet the Gutenberg Bible is printed text of very high quality—as a typographical document it was extremely well designed and executed. The printed Bible was very well received, and every copy of the first edition sold. However, Fust and Gutenberg disagreed on how the profits from the edition should be distributed and how Fust's loan to Gutenberg should be repaid. Fust successfully sued Gutenberg in 1455, and their partnership was dissolved. Fust, who essentially owned most of the printing operation, began to work exclusively with his son-in-law *Peter Schöffer to continue printing. Peter Schöffer was a talented clerk and calligrapher who had worked with Gutenberg since 1452, and the printing house of Fust and Schöffer continued the high-quality typographic work that Gutenberg had begun. They successfully produced such significant early printed documents such as the *Mainz Psalter* in 1457, the *Canon missae* in 1458, and the forty-eight-Line Bible in 1462.

Gutenberg, who still had a small printing operation in the Gutenberghof, continued to print, but on a reduced scale. While Fust and Schöffer focused on church documents and canon law, Gutenberg began to print calendars, indulgences, and the *Donatus*, all of which continued to bring in a solid income. Significant documents from Gutenberg's press during these years include the *Türkenkalender* for the year 1455, the *Türkenbulle* of Calixtus III in 1456, the *Aderlass und Laxierkalender* for the year 1457, and the *Astronomisches Kalender für 1458*, printed in 1457 or 1458. In 1458 Gutenberg entered into a new partnership with Dr. Konrad Humery in order to finance production of the *Catholicon* of Johann Balbus de Janua, a large Latin dictionary and grammar. This was a major textual project, and printing was completed in 1460. This was the last large work tentatively attributed to Gutenberg until the fall of Mainz in 1462, when Gutenberg and other citizens were expelled from the city due to a conflict over the Mainz archbishopric. Gutenberg's property was seized, and his printing operation was effectively dissolved. It is possible that Gutenberg may have settled in Eltville and collaborated with the printing shop of Heinrich and Nicolaus Bechtermünze, who produced such documents as the Indulgence for the Order of the Holy Trinity in 1464 and the *Vocabularius ex quo* in 1467. Gutenberg was able to return to Mainz in 1465, when he was appointed electoral courtier by the new archbishop, Adolf von Nassau. Gutenberg died three years later in Mainz on 3 February 1468.

The output of Gutenberg's presses was not large, but the quality of the texts he designed and produced set a high standard for early printing. Gutenberg's achievements in printing technology allowed written texts to become less expensive and more accessible to the reading public, causing major changes in the authorial profession, the shape of the European book trade, and private reading practices.

Bibliography: Janet Ing, *Johann Gutenberg and His Bible*, 1988; Albert Kapr, *Johann Gutenberg: The Man and His Invention*, 1996; Paul Needham, "Johann Gutenberg and the Catholicon Press," *Papers of the Bibliographical Society of America* 76 (1982): 395–456.

Kristin R. Hofer

H

Halevi (ha-Leví), Solomon (c. 1352–1435), was a rabbi in Burgos who became the most influential *converso* in the Kingdom of Castile. Solomon Halevi was the son of a prominent Jewish family of Burgos that held various governmental and financial posts in the kingdom. He received a distinguished education that included Jewish and Arabic philosophy, science (astronomy and physics), studies in Christian theology, and interaction with the outstanding Jewish scholars of his day. Solomon was not only a rabbi in Burgos, he also served as advocate for the Jews of the city. In one instance in 1388, Solomon led the Jews of Burgos in asserting their royal prerogative of exemption from provisioning and billeting the garrison from a nearby castle.

Solomon wed in 1378 and founded an extended family that became very active in both domestic and international affairs. The rabbi's renown and prestige increased during these years, as attested by Solomon ben Verga in *Sébet Yehudá*. This work told of Solomon Halevi's visit to the pope to appeal a judicial order against the Jews regarding usury. Verga's work also described his plea against the ordered demolition of a synagogue and his miraculous resurrection of a dead child by placing the name of God under the victim's tongue.

Solomon's most dramatic act, however, was his own conversion to Christianity. Although scholars dispute the exact date of this conversion, the evidence indicates that it took place sometime in the summer of 1390 (before the wave of pogroms that swept Castile the following year). His children (four sons and a daughter) converted with him, as did his three brothers, while his wife apparently followed suit a few years later. Solomon took the baptismal name of Pablo de Santa María, traveled to France to study and advance his ecclesiastical calling, and then moved to Avignon to serve Pope *Benedict XIII as legate (*a latere*/papal emissary) for four years. Pablo rose through the clerical ranks rather quickly, becoming archdeacon of Trevinno in 1396, bishop of Cartagena in 1403, and bishop of Burgos in 1415 (a post he held until his death). Pablo was also an important political figure, serving as *canciller mayor* (chancellor) of the kingdom under Enrique III as well as personal tutor to *Juan II. He was so highly regarded by the royal family that he was one of the four keepers of Enrique III's testament upon the king's death in 1406.

Pablo de Santa María proved himself a sincere *converso*, one who dedicated his life and work to his new calling in the Catholic church. To this end, he was responsible not only for his own Christian apologies addressed to both Christians and Jews, but also for sponsoring militant preachers such as *Vincent Ferrer in his diocese and for encouraging anti-Jewish legislation on the part of Juan I of Aragon.

Bishop Pablo was an accomplished writer, leaving behind a variety of works. These included the *Scrutinium scripturarum* (or *Dialogus [Sauli et Pauli] contra Judaeos*), completed in 1432, which clarified several points of Christian dogma for the benefit of a Jew being induced to convert, and the *Additiones ad postillam Magistri Nicolai Lyra* (Additions to the biblical commentary of Nicholas of Lyra), completed in 1429. He also composed the historical poem *Las siete edades del mundo* or *Edades trovadas*, dedicated to Queen Catalina, mother of Juan I, and the *Suma de las crónicas de España*, a history of Spain from the ancient period to 1412.

Two of Pablo's sons became bishops, and his brother, Alvar García de Santa María, became a royal secretary and chronicler. A third son, Pedro de Cartagena, became a leading noble in Burgos. The descendants of Pablo de Santa María achieved such prestige that King Felipe III awarded them the benefit of *limpieza de sangre* (untainted bloodline) in concert with a papal brief from Clement VIII in 1604.

Bibliography: Francisco Cantera Burgos, *Alvar García de Santa María y su familia de conversos*, 1952; Norman Roth, *Conversos, Inquisition, and the Expulsion of the Jews from Spain*, 1995.

Rowena Hernández Múzquiz

Hawkwood, Sir John (1320?–94). Calling himself Miles Anglicus, John Hawkwood was known throughout his long career as a mercenary knight in Italy as Giovanni Acuto (John the Sharp). Not much is known of Hawkwood's early life. The younger son of a tanner in the Essex parish of Sible Hedingham, he presumably began his military career in the campaigns of the Hundred Years' War. His name starts to appear in documents following the Treaty of Brétigny in 1360, at the time when many members of the disbanded armies formed themselves into free companies. The French countryside and its inhabitants suffered at the hands of these mercenary groups until Pope *Innocent VI paid them to leave for other parts of Europe.

Hawkwood went into Italy, and by 1364 he was the captain of the White Company, which had been hired by Pisa in 1363 to assist in its conflicts with Florence. Hawkwood carved out a respected career by fighting for hire and was at times engaged by more than one employer, his contract always including a clause stating that he would not fight against the king of England. He continued to be in the employ of Pisa after Giovanni Agnello became doge in 1364, and although by 1369 he was assisting Bernabò Visconti of Milan in his battles against Florence, in 1370 Bernabò agreed to let the doge of Pisa use Hawkwood's services. Attempting to regain power in Italy, Pope Gregory XI retained Hawkwood in 1372 to attack Milan and Florence. Hawkwood took his orders from Cardinal Count Robert of Geneva, who directed the massacre of Cesena in 1377. The church was slow to pay for Hawkwood's services, and while he was ostensibly invading Florentine territories in 1375, he accepted payment from the Florentines not to attack. He entered into similar contracts with a number of other cities and, in an effort to receive payment from the pope, kidnapped a cardinal in 1376. In lieu of payment, the church gave him two estates in Romagna.

In 1377 Hawkwood married Bernabò's illegitimate daughter, Donnina; possibly his second marriage, this alliance with the Visconti family illustrated the respect and power he had gained by this time. Hawkwood owned various estates throughout Italy but finally settled more permanently near Florence at San Donato in Polverosa. His work for Florence continued, and in addition to granting him an annual income, in 1390 the appreciative Florentines exempted him from paying taxes and assured his wife of a widow's pension. When he died in 1394, the Signoria of Florence paid for a funeral worthy of the soldier whom they admired for his courage and military leadership. Although his body was first placed in the Duomo, it was later sent at the request of *Richard II to England to its final resting place in the parish church of St. Peter in Sible Hedingham. The famous equestrian portrait of Hawkwood by *Paolo Uccello in the Duomo at Florence still celebrates his fame in Italy.

Bibliography: Michael Mallett, *Mercenaries and Their Masters*, 1974; Geoffrey Trease, *The Condottieri: Soldiers of Fortune*, 1971.

Karen Arthur

Hegius, Alexander (1438–98),

Hegius, Alexander (1438–98), was a gifted and influential pedagogue who, through the implementation of a rigorous and effective educational regimen in the classics at Deventer, helped promote humanism in northern Europe. By utilizing traditional Latin and Greek texts in a methodical and well-organized course of study, along with his meticulous attention to grammar, Hegius was able to develop the school into a flourishing center of humanistic thought, one that proved crucial in the intellectual and spiritual development of a number of important men of letters, most notably Desiderius Erasmus.

Alexander Hegius, according to Erasmus, was a learned, holy, and eloquent man, but one who because of his contempt for glory accomplished nothing great. Although the last remark is questionable, particularly coming from a well-known student, Erasmus's comment was insightful, particularly for understanding why there is relatively little known about a man of considerable importance. Hegius was born in Heek (hence Hegius), Westphalia, and commenced school at Zwolle, where he supposedly came under the instruction of *Thomas à Kempis. After an uncertain amount of formal education, Hegius joined the clergy, and in 1469 he entered his first position as schoolmaster at St. Willibrord's School in Wesel. In 1475 he took a similar position at St. Martin's School at Emmerich, where he made the acquaintance of Wessel Gansfort and more importantly *Rudolf Agricola, the "father of German humanism." The meeting between the two was highly profitable for Hegius; under the guidance of Agricola, not only did the schoolmaster acquire a decent proficiency in Greek, but he also developed a deep admiration for the classical language and concomitant culture as a source for genuine learning, a view that proved very important in the years to follow.

In 1483 Hegius took the position of headmaster at St. Lebwin in Deventer, a school erected under the auspices of the Brethren of the Common Life. Upon his arrival, Hegius immediately revitalized the school by fusing the moral and spiritual teachings that undergirded the Brethren's *devotio moderna* with a new pedagogy that promoted a classical education. One of Hegius's first objectives was to dispose of the current Latin texts used for teaching grammar, which he derided as barbarous and useless, harmless trash. He replaced these texts with works by such Latin masters as Virgil, Cicero, Livy, and Sallust, which he used to familiarize his students with the formal Latin employed in the New Testament and in the canonical texts of the church fathers. Equally important, Hegius introduced Greek to Deventer. In a poem entitled "On the Utility of the Greek Tongue," Hegius expressed his conviction that Greek was an indispensable ingredient for understanding grammar, rhetoric, philosophy, mathematics, poetry, art, and medicine. In order to assist him in initiating Greek in the curriculum as well as with implementing grammar reform, Hegius made much use of the printing press in Deventer, which between 1480 and 1500 was responsible for the exponential increase in the school's collection of humanistic literature. He also sought to restructure the way the courses were taught at St. Lebwin. Discarding the antiquated methods of Scholastic pedagogy, Hegius implemented a rather modern approach that divided the school into eight specialized classes, with each class being taught by a highly trained educator of Hegius's own choosing.

The result of Hegius's efforts at Deventer was extraordinary. In the thirteen years he served as schoolmaster, Hegius was able to transform the school into a vital source for humanist thought in Germany and Holland. He had over 2,200 students, many of whom went on to become successful men of letters responsible for fostering humanism north of the Alps. Some of his most distinguished students included Ortwinus Gratius, Gerald Geldenhouwer, Hermann Buschuis, and Herman von dem Busch. Hegius's greatest pupil, however, was Desiderius Erasmus. Although there is considerable disagreement as to what extent he actually influenced Erasmus's thought, it is plausible to suggest from the written praise that the pupil gave his mentor that his intellectual debt was considerable.

Hegius's legacy also included a number of writings, all of which were related to the pedagogical reforms initiated at Deventer. One of the works to be published during his lifetime was *Doctrinale* (1488), which was a simple commentary on the grammar of Alexandre de Villedieu. The other works, including *Invectiva in modos significandi, Carmina,* and the *Dialogi,* were published posthumously in 1503 by a devoted pupil, James Faber. In general, none of these works were of any significance outside Deventer, for Hegius's talent and efforts were not in writing but in teaching.

Bibliography: Anthony Goodman and Angus McKay, eds., *The Impact of Humanism on Western Europe,* 1990; John Matthews, "Alexander Hegius (ca. 1433–98): His Life, Philosophy, and Pedagogy," 1988.

Gregory E. Canada

Heinbuche, Henry, of Langenstein (1325–97),

also simply known as Henry of Langenstein and Henry of Hesse, was a German-born scholar of science and theology who taught at the University of Paris from 1363 to 1382 and the University of Vienna from 1384 until his death. Science was Henry's first love and the subject of all his writings until he received his doctorate in theology in 1376. His promising career within the church was blighted by the advent of the Great Schism (1378–1417). When the schism crisis began, he was selected as one of three representatives from the University of Paris to travel to Rome in order to represent the university's position. In the *Epistola pacis* (1379) and the *Epistola concilii pacis* (1381), Henry advocated holding a general church council to settle the problem. As the schism continued, Henry found it more and more difficult to remain at a French university, and in 1382 he and many of his German colleagues left Paris. Henry traveled to a Cistercian abbey at Eberbach, where he remained for a time with his friend and former colleague James of Eltville, the current abbot. Away from the political and academic pressures of the university, Henry turned to religious contemplation and produced a popular work of mysticism, *Speculum animae* (1382). During the following year, 1383, Henry accepted an invitation to join the faculty of the troubled University of Vienna, which was undergoing reorganization. He became a great asset to that university and there wrote and delivered the culminating work of his career, the *Lecturae super Genesim,* which combined his interests in science and theology.

Not much is known about the first thirty-eight years of Henry's life beyond the date and place of his birth, at Langenstein in the region of Hesse. He is first mentioned in the 1363 records of the University of Paris, in February and May of that year, as a student preparing for the degree of master of arts, and then as a graduate in July. While he taught at the university, Henry was also closely involved with the court of the French king Charles V. When a comet was sighted in 1368, Charles V requested that Henry write a scientific treatise dealing with the question of whether comets should be regarded as portents of future events.

Henry's response, found in *Quaestio de cometa*, was that they should not be so regarded. From 1376 onward, Henry was increasingly concerned with the affairs of the church. He became a leading figure in the fight to end the Great Schism, advocating the conciliarist position that was generally held at the University of Paris. When the duke of Anjou, regent for *Charles VI, rejected that position, however, most German scholars left Paris, and Henry was among them.

During the period he spent at Eberbach, Henry continued to write, producing several treatises in addition to *Speculum animae*. He remained closely interested in controversies over the schism and wrote several letters of advice to concerned German clerics. It is believed that while he was at the abbey, Henry reread the abbot's commentary on the *Sentences* of Peter Lombard. This work may have prompted Henry to contemplate the burning scholarly question of the day—whether or not Aristotle's system of logic was a reliable tool in the study of theology. At the time, Henry supported Aristotle's use in theological debates, a position also held by *William of Ockham.

The invitation from Duke Albert III of Austria, the patron of the University of Vienna, to take an administrative post at the school was an honor and also a challenge for Henry. He was considered a leading member of the faculty of theology from the beginning and was eventually named rector of the university in 1393. His *Lecturae super Genesim* began in 1385 and continued until 1392 or 1393, and the copied text of the lectures became a popular work of the day. Henry also continued his correspondence with clerics all over Europe on issues relating to the schism during his Vienna years, as well as developing his own philosophic thought. At this time he abandoned his earlier position on Aristotle, joining the school of thought of Thomas Aquinas, which advanced a vague Platonism as more appropriate to the study of Christian theology. Henry's willingness to adapt his views in this way was only one indication of the versatility of this scholar, who was respected as both a scientist and a mystic.

Bibliography: Nicholas H. Steneck, *Science and Creation in the Middle Ages: Henry of Langenstein (d. 1397) on Genesis*, 1976.

Angela B. Fulk

Henry IV, King of England (b. 1367, r. 1399–1413). Known early in life as Henry of Bolingbroke, he later became earl of Hereford, earl of Derby, duke of Lancaster, and eventually king of England. He was the only son of *John of Gaunt, duke of Lancaster, and his first wife Blanche. His date of birth is questionable due to a lack of detailed birth records, but this only contributes to the enigma of Henry IV. Known principally for the "revolution" of 1399, he usurped the power of the throne from the exiled king, his cousin, *Richard II, but his claim to the throne was shaky at best. Well educated, he wrote in both English and French and also exhibited a familiarity with Latin. In addition, he was both a skilled musician and a patron of the poets. History has recorded Henry IV as a somewhat inconsistent ruler, but this may have had something to do with the precarious position he inherited upon assuming control of the kingdom. In 1399 power was not concentrated in the hands of the king, but, rather, was distributed unevenly among a number of magnates. Henry IV also created no new peerage positions, unlike his two immediate predecessors, Richard II and *Edward III. However, he did accomplish what Richard II had been unable to do; by the time of his death in 1413, he had left a peaceful kingdom for his heir.

Nevertheless, the knowledge that he had usurped the royal power was detrimental to his rule and played a significant role in his precarious health and early death. He possessed many of the qualities beneficial to a ruler, specifically, bravery in battle and courage and diligence in leadership, but his brief reign was unremarkable, beset by contenders trying to overthrow the tenuous claim he had on the throne.

The poet Thomas Elmham said of him, "Calm and fearless, he excelled as knight, earl and duke; a king distinguished alike for his bodily vigour, mind and stature." Impressions such as these are all that remain of Henry IV's character. In 1399 he had charmed many with his promise as a great leader, but by his death, that promise had been extinguished. However, he did court acceptance among the artists of his era. He was also scrupulous in his observance of religion and his desire to unite Christendom under his own command by leading an army of Christian knights to the Holy Land. Unlike many would-be crusaders, he was a world traveler and had actually visited Jerusalem. When it came to the arts, he was a patron of *John Gower, *Thomas Hoccleve, and *Geoffrey Chaucer, although the latter was also related to Henry IV by marriage. Chaucer did not reap the full benefits of Henry's patronage, however, for he died a year after Henry's accession. Ironically, Henry IV had doubled Chaucer's pension upon assuming control of the throne. Neither Hoccleve nor Gower, however, appear in Henry IV's record books as ever having amassed financial benefit from their relationship with him. Gower had left King Richard II in the last year of his reign, writing, "I send unto myn owne Lord, / Which of Lancastre is Henry named," and had presented Henry with a new edition of *Confessio amantis*. He showered praise on Henry IV's learned capabilities: "Thus tellen thei which olde bookes canne / Whereof, my lord, y wot wel thou art learned." His fellow poet, Hoccleve, benefited from his relationship with Henry by working as a clerk in the privy seal office. Other than Hoccleve's civil service position, there is no record of either Gower or Hoccleve ever receiving any royal remuneration. Henry's interest in poetry, however, was second only to his passion for music. His minstrels accompanied him on his travels and remained with him at the court when he became king. It is probable that Henry IV even composed some fifteenth-century church hymns, including a version of *Gloria in excelsis*.

In the political realm, Henry is best remembered for the role he played in the development of Parliament. Members of Parliament were always quick to remind Henry that he had usurped the crown, and it could be easily removed again. Although Henry created few, if any, new peerages, he did grant special privileges for members of Parliament and their servants, thus ensuring that members could avoid arrest or any sort of public defamation. Instead of dominating his Parliament, however, Henry IV came to its members as a petitioner on numerous occasions. By 1408, just five years before his death, his health had begun to fail, and, with faith in his leadership abilities in question, he began to leave control of his affairs in the hands of either Archbishop Arundel or his son, Henry, Prince of Wales, the future Henry V. The discord between father and son was no secret, but the successes the future Henry V would have can partly be attributed to the peaceful state of affairs created during his father's reign.

Bibliography: Bryan Bevan, *Henry IV*, 1994; John Lavin Kirby, *Henry IV of England*, 1970; K. B. McFarlane, *Lancastrian Kings and Lollard Knights*, 1972.

                                                                                  Jennifer L. Harrison

Henry VI, King of England (1421–71, r. 1422–61, 1470–71), has two conflicting, but not mutually exclusive, posthumous reputations: as England's most incompetent king and as a saintly royal martyr. Never a very effective ruler at the best of times, Henry frequently suffered from bouts of severe mental illness that rendered him incapable of governing. His reign was characterized by defeat for English arms in France and political factionalism leading to the so-called Wars of the Roses at home. At the same time, Henry was an active patron of the church and of learning.

Henry was the son of Henry V of England and the French princess Catherine of Valois. The deaths of Henry V and *Charles VI of France in the same year made the infant Henry VI king in name of England and France under the terms of the Treaty of Troyes. However, much of France remained loyal to the dauphin *Charles (VII), and from 1429 the area controlled by Henry's government was steadily eroded until by 1453 only Calais remained in English hands.

Henry's reign in England, both before and after he attained his majority in 1437, was racked by factional disputes. The first half of the reign was dominated by rivalry between the king's uncle *Humphrey, duke of Gloucester, and his great-uncle Cardinal *Henry Beaufort, bishop of Winchester. King Henry was accused of being overly dependent on favored councilors, notably Beaufort and his relatives and William de la Pole, duke of Suffolk. In addition, his marriage to Margaret of Anjou in 1445, and her subsequent influence over royal policy, further alienated an already-restive English nobility by the next decade.

Discontent over favoritism at home and military setbacks in France led to crisis and war in the 1450s. Suffolk was impeached and then murdered in 1450. In 1453 Henry suffered his first attack of mental illness, and Richard, duke of York, who had opposed Suffolk and the Beauforts, was appointed protector for the duration of the king's incapacity. However, the birth of a son, Edward, strengthened the political position of the Lancastrian dynasty and of Queen Margaret.

Henry's recovery at Christmas 1454 removed power from York's hands, and the court's vindictiveness in removing Yorkist appointees led him to rebel. York's victory at St. Albans in May 1455 restored him to power, but the queen was able to establish an effective alternative power base on her own estates. York fled to Ireland in 1459, but the Yorkists regrouped, capturing the king at the Battle of Northampton in June 1460. York returned from exile, but baronial opposition prevented him from seizing the throne. Margaret launched an invasion from Scotland to regain her son's rights. York was defeated and killed at Wakefield in December 1460, his ally the earl of Warwick was defeated at St. Albans in February 1461, and Henry was reunited with his queen. However, London refused to admit Margaret and instead proclaimed York's son the earl of March as King *Edward IV. Margaret's retreating army was defeated at Towton. After a period of exile in Scotland, Henry was finally captured in Northumberland in 1465 and was confined to the Tower of London.

Edward's alienation of his most powerful supporter, the earl of Warwick, led to Henry's brief restoration to the throne in July 1470, with the aid of Warwick and *Louis XI of France. However, Edward returned to England in April 1471 and defeated and killed Warwick at Barnet, recapturing Henry before defeating Margaret at Tewkesbury in May, where their son Edward was killed. Henry was murdered in the Tower of London shortly afterwards.

Henry's activities in the cultural field are without doubt more impressive than those in politics. He was not known for the kind of extravagant artistic patronage that was popular at other courts, notably that of the dukes of Burgundy, and was criticized for his lack of regal bearing and display.

King Henry did, however, make two notable collegiate foundations. He founded Eton College in 1440, elevating the existing parish church to collegiate status, although the foundation was first envisaged in 1437 in celebration of Henry's assumption of personal rule after his minority. The original foundation in 1440 consisted of a provost, 10 priests, 4 clerks, 6 choristers, 25 poor scholars under a schoolmaster, and 25 paupers and "enfeebled men" who were to pray for the king's soul. This number was later increased to 70 to match the number at Winchester College, which had been founded in 1382.

Henry also founded King's College, Cambridge, in 1441. His commitment to education stemmed in part from a desire to raise the educational standard of clergymen, not least to help tackle the Lollard heresy. However, collegiate foundations (like the endowment of chantries, which was popular in the fifteenth century) were primarily intended to assist the patron's personal salvation. It is possible that King's and Eton were originally linked foundations. Politically, Henry's reign was one of the most disastrous of any English monarch, and it is therefore probably best to remember him for his collegiate foundations, both of which still flourish today.

Bibliography: Ralph A. Griffiths, *The Reign of King Henry VI: The Exercise of Royal Authority, 1422–1461*, 1981; J. L. Watts, *Henry VI and the Politics of Kingship*, 1996.

Michael Evans

Henry VII, King of England (b. 1457, r. 1485–1509), the first and most obscure Tudor king, ended the Wars of the Roses and founded a colorful dynasty that lasted more than a century. After decades of assassinations and civil wars, Henry's reign provided peace and prosperity to his exhausted kingdom. Under his careful guidance, England once more played a prominent role in European affairs.

Henry was born in 1457 to Edmund Tudor, the earl of Richmond, and *Margaret Beaufort; his royal blood was diluted and tainted by bastardy. The wars between the Yorkists and Lancastrians devoured the other claimants to the throne until even Henry Tudor's own minor place in the succession put him in danger. In 1471 Henry and his guardian William Herbert, the earl of Pembroke, fled their native Wales for the relative safety of Brittany and France. The heavy-handed administration of *Richard III forced many nobles to join Henry's court-in-exile, where he lived by the charity of others. Little is known about Henry in this period, but he seemed to acquire a fondness for the courtly life of music, tennis, chess, and hunting.

After a failed coup in 1483, Henry spent two years borrowing money, sending agents to foment rebellion in Wales, and attempting to suborn the remaining nobles of Richard's court. These activities bore fruit in 1485 at the Battle of Bosworth Field, where Henry took possession of England. Like other usurpers, Henry immediately began the arduous process of consolidating his royal claim. He proved himself generous to enemies as well as allies, hoping to thwart the inevitable rebellions. Less than a year after his victory he married *Edward IV's daughter Elizabeth of York, thus merging the two houses. To control his "overmighty subjects," he drastically reduced the legal number of retainers and took their children and family fortunes as hostages. He revived many defunct courts, thus bringing the rule of law back to England. Among them was the dreaded court of Star Chamber, which curbed the criminal excesses of the aristocracy. He pursued the favor of the church with legal and economic protections for its clerical members and properties.

Henry, notoriously avaricious, enriched himself at the expense of his wealthy subjects. Motivated more by prudence than greed, he reduced the risk of rebellion by keeping his potential rivals too poor to raise an army. The fact that he suffered only four rebellions gives testimony to the success of these measures. The first two, in 1486 and 1487, each headed by a young boy pretender who claimed to be the relative of Richard III, failed because Henry's supporters acted quickly and decisively. The third rebellion occurred in 1496, when Perkin Warbeck, another imposter, raised an army in Scotland. In the next year Cornish peasants, outraged at being taxed for the defense of the northern counties, revolted against Henry's rule. Henry's general popularity and reputation for fairness rallied his subjects against his enemies, and in the wake of these rebellions, he showed uncommon clemency in executing only a few of the leaders and extracting oaths of loyalty and immense funds from the rest.

Henry based his foreign policy on his desire for international recognition, respect, and trade. The 1489 Treaty of Medina del Campo, which culminated in the ill-fated marriage of Catherine of Aragon and his son Arthur, proved to the rest of Europe that a strong monarch held the throne of England. Unlike other rulers who gloried in war, Henry saw it as an expensive and hazardous waste of time, but this parsimonious king found ways to make it profitable. He forced Parliament to pay him to start a war against France, and *Charles VIII to end it. Henry also took great care to protect and expand the international rights and privileges of English merchants.

In domestic matters, Henry proved equally adept. To balance the inordinate power of the aristocracy, he appointed educated commoners to staff the reconstituted courts and councils. He enhanced the duties and powers of the justices of the peace in order to enforce the laws and extend his control to the local level. In contrast with his miserly reputation, Henry invested large sums of money in clothing, feasts, and court ceremonies to present a kingly image. He patronized the new humanist scholars, supporting such well-known figures as *John Colet, Thomas Linacre, Polydore Vergil, and Desiderius Erasmus of Rotterdam. He built the first drydock in England and subsidized the New World explorations of the Cabot family. Henry's life lost its lustre when his eldest son Arthur died in 1502, followed by his wife and mother in less than a year. After matching his second son Henry to Arthur's widow, Henry became a recluse, and his lavish court took on a monastic atmosphere. Henry's reputation as a greedy and ruthless monarch stems from these last grim years of his life. He died on 21 April 1509, rich and in bed, the master of his kingdom. His body was buried at Westminster Abbey in the chapel that he had built.

Not a pleasant or charming man, Henry lacked the grace, generosity, and military demeanor expected of a king. Diligent and pragmatic, he had a talent for choosing competent and loyal advisors and a penchant for hard work. Despite all the administrative and legal changes of his reign, Henry was no innovator. He merely revived old customs, prerogatives, and legislation to strengthen royal control of the government. Normally dour and taciturn, he could be surprisingly merciful to his enemies when it suited his purpose. This reserved and determined man ended decades of civil strife in England and left Henry VIII a wealthy treasury and a unified kingdom.

Bibliography: Michael Van Cleave Alexander, *The First of the Tudors: A Study of Henry VII and His Reign*, 1980; S. B. Chrimes, *Henry VII*, Rev. ed., 1999.

Brian G. Hudgins

Henry "the Navigator," Prince of Portugal (1394–1460), expanded

Europe's horizons of nautical and geographic knowledge and set his country on the path to a mercantile empire in India and the Far East. Nicknamed "the

Navigator" though he did little sailing himself, Prince Henry was more a patron and administrator than a scholar. Dedicated to outflanking the military and economic might of Islam, he gathered captains and savants from the entire known world in an effort to find the source of African gold and a route to the Indies. At Henry's court of Vila do Infante at Sagres, this symposium of scholars and seamen made important advances in cartography, navigation, and ship design, paving the way for the likes of *Christopher Columbus, *Vasco da Gama, and Ferdinand Magellan.

Born on 4 March 1394, the third son of João I and Philippa of Lancaster, Henry eagerly absorbed the ideals of knightly behavior that his mother, steeped in the chivalric traditions of England, brought to the Portuguese court. When the brothers came of age, they wanted to win their spurs properly, on the field of battle, against the North African Muslim city of Ceuta. Henry, who convinced his father to make a surprise attack, organized the shipbuilding in Oporto. For three years the royal brothers planned the assault, which took place in the summer of 1415. The city fell quickly, and the brothers became knights. Appointed governor, Henry hoped to control Ceuta's trade in gold and other commodities, but the Muslim merchants took their business to nearby Tangier. Thwarted, he returned home and plotted other ways to destroy the "infidel." He organized naval expeditions to harass Muslim shipping and chart the West African coast. Elected governor of the affluent Order of Christ, Henry sunk its wealth into exploration. His captains discovered and colonized Madeira and the Azores, which provided prisoners of war and important ports for further expeditions. In 1434 his squire, *Gilberto Eannes, passed the fabled Cape Bojador, which previous sailors had feared due to its supernatural and deadly reputation.

Despite these successes, Henry quickly abandoned further exploration when the king decided to attack Tangier. Ill prepared and lacking sufficient forces, Henry was defeated in 1437 and was forced by treaty to give his brother Fernando as hostage for the return of Ceuta to the Muslims. When the Berbers broke the terms of the truce, the outraged Henry refused to give up the trophy of his youth, and his brother languished in prison until his death. On Henry's return to Portugal, he exiled himself to Sagres, the southwestern tip of Portugal, and began construction of Vila do Infante. He gathered to his court seamen, astronomers, and navigators, of all nationalities, even despised Jews and Muslims, to find a sea route to the source of African gold.

Henry's lieutenants never found this route, but they did discover the extremely lucrative African slave trade, which greatly boosted Portugal's economy and Henry's career. Despite his uneasiness over the fact that his personal crusade had devolved into a demeaning trade in human beings, Henry enjoyed its profits and the royal monopoly he received in 1443. In the same year the prestigious English Order of the Garter welcomed him into its ranks. Acting on a pious desire to convert heathen souls, Henry obtained papal sanction for the slave trade in 1450. Captains and merchants flocked to Henry's court, begging to join his now-profitable expeditions, and the exploration and exploitation of Africa proceeded apace. With the revenue of this highly irregular "crusade," Henry endowed a chair of theology at the University of Lisbon and a mariners' chapel at Belem. He died on 13 November 1460 at Vila do Infante and was buried with his ancestors in the monastery at Batalha.

Essentially medieval in character, this forceful and persuasive prince patterned himself after the saintly knights of English myth, remaining chaste and abstaining from wine. He always tried to represent his questionable slaving practices in a noble and Christian light. Many biographers have tried to portray him as a devout scholar or a Renaissance visionary, which would have pleased this religious man who felt ambivalent about the mercantile turn of his chivalric endeavors. Under the patronage of this paradoxical man, the elements of classical geography, Arab naval technology, and Portuguese seamanship and drive merged to create the foundations of European expansion and hegemony during the next two centuries.

Bibliography: P. E. Russell, *Prince Henry the Navigator: The Rise and Fall of a Culture Hero*, 1984; John Ure, *Prince Henry the Navigator*, 1977.

Brian G. Hudgins

Henryson, Robert (c. 1425–c. 1505). A Scottish poet of the late 1400s, Robert Henryson is considered the best representative of a brief flowering of Middle Scots verse known today as the Golden Age of Scottish poetry, in which traditional alliterative verse was suppressed by a new poetry inspired by *Geoffrey Chaucer. The leader of the school of poetry known as the "Scottish Chaucerians," Henryson is remembered for his *Testament of Cresseid*, an alternate conclusion to Chaucer's *Troilus and Criseyde*. Henryson's poetry served as an inspiration for later Scots poets because he introduced into Scottish verse some of the best techniques and narratives of English literature, and his verse helped develop the Scottish language.

Robert Henryson was born in Scotland, and yet even this is only a probability, as the material for his biography is restricted to four references. First, a Robert Henryson was admitted on 10 September 1462 to the University of Glasgow. Second, in 1477–78 three land-grant deeds were signed in the chartulary of Dunfermline, and each deed lists a Robert Henryson as a witness and notary public. Third, the poet John Dunbar listed Robert Henryson among several recently dead poets, one of whom (Stobo) we are certain died in 1505. Fourth, on the title pages of the complete manuscripts of Henryson's *Fables*, Henryson was described as the "Schoolmaster of Dunfermling." From this evidence we may arrive at some sparse conclusions: Henryson in his *Fables* referred to his own old age, and this adds to the suggestion that the poet died in his late seventies. Henryson's poetry also suggests that he knew canon law, and the Glasgow reference supports this conclusion. A degree in canon law was required for a notary public, and scholars agree that notaries public were often schoolmasters. This evidence gives scholars only a vague notion of Henryson's biography, and therefore scholars have been forced to use the internal evidence of Henryson's poems for more information.

Henryson's poetry consists of three long and thirteen shorter poems, and of these the *Testament of Cresseid* is considered the best. The other two long poems are *Orpheus and Eurydice*, a retelling of the classical Orpheus tale, and the *Fables*, which share a thematic link in their championship of the peasant class. His thirteen shorter poems deal with love, religion, and social problems. From Henryson's poems a portrait of the poet becomes clearer. He was well educated in classical mythology, the medicine of his era, law, and agricultural practices, and he had read both widely and deeply in medieval English and continental literature. He is considered by some scholars to have been a humanist because of his focus on rationalism in theology and his use of classical learning and resources. Other scholars see Henryson simply as a man of excellent general knowledge, with an education that was solid but old-fashioned for his time, and who was a humanitarian observer of the mortal condition.

Henryson has been neglected since the sixteenth century for many reasons, one of which was early printers' inclusion of his *Testament of Cresseid* with Chaucer's *Troilus and Criseyde*, and readers mistaking Henryson's sequel as Chaucer's own. His reputation was revived in 1917 when full editions of Henryson's works were printed, and he is considered today to be a poet equal to, if not better than, Dunbar, Gawin Douglas, and David Lindsay. In this light, Henryson is considered a talented craftsman as well as an imaginative and original poet, and his genius has been a source of pride for later generations of Scottish poets.

Bibliography: Robert Henryson, *The Poems of Robert Henryson*, ed. Denton Fox, 1981; Marshall W. Stearns, *Robert Henryson*, 1949.

Dominique Tieman

Hereford, Nicholas (1355?–1420?),

was an Oxford theologian and Lollard heretic. He remains known today largely for his work in spreading Lollardy in the Midlands and for his translation of the bulk of the Lollard Old Testament. A year after the Peasants' Revolt of 1381, Hereford and the other Oxford Lollards came to prominence in the ferment over Wycliffite doctrines. In the midst of *John Wyclif's reform proposals presented to the May parliament of 1382, the new archbishop of Canterbury, William Courtenay, convened a synod at Blackfriars to inquire into Wyclif's doctrines. The synod, as expected by all involved, concluded that Wycliffism indeed constituted heresy. How then, the ecclesiastical authorities wondered, could they enforce orthodoxy upon the Oxford Lollards, who had, after all, papal privileges against archiepiscopal intrusion into academic affairs and disputes, as the Wycliffites characterized their preaching?

Although Nicholas Hereford is assumed to have come from Hereford (given his name), little evidence exists as to his life before he appeared in 1374 as bursar of Queen's College, Oxford. He graduated as doctor of divinity by the spring of 1382 and through Lent of that year preached Wycliffite doctrines at St. Mary's Church in Oxford. Indeed, one of the key sources of this period, the chronicler *Henry Knighton, called Hereford the first leader of Lollardy (presumably after Wyclif himself). Then Robert Rygg, the chancellor of the university, appointed him to preach the university sermon on the Feast of the Ascension (15 May) at St. Frideswide's Church in Oxford. This highly unusual event (given that normally only the chancellor of the university gave this sermon) on the most illustrious occasion of the university calendar in many eyes represented the high-water mark of Lollardy. In this sermon, Hereford not only preached and defended Wyclif's doctrines, he did so in English (unheard of at the time), asserted that Archbishop Simon Sudbury (killed during the course of the Peasants' Revolt) deserved death because of his desire to punish Wyclif for his ideas, and generally excited insurrection among the people.

Along with the other Oxford Lollards, Hereford continued his public preaching until 15 June, when Rygg, under threat of excommunication for heresy himself, published the sentence of suspension handed down by the Blackfriars synod against Hereford, *Philip Repyngdon, John Aston, Laurence Bedeman, and John Wyclif. Hereford, along with Repyngdon, immediately traveled to London and appealed to the king's uncle, *John of Gaunt, who had in the past served as Wyclif's protector. However, John chose not to interfere with the proceedings against them. Two days later, Hereford and the others received orders to reply to the accusations against them. All attempted to show conformity while stating the veracity of Wyclif's positions. On 20 June Hereford and Repyngdon presented written answers to the synod's twenty-four conclusions upon Wycliffism. Hereford accepted ten of these positions in their entirety, and the others with reservations, but both he and Repyngdon seemed insincere, perhaps even deceitful, because they refused to discuss their answers. Ordered to appear before the synod on 1 July, they did not, and as a result, the two received a sentence of excommunication. Both appealed to the pope, nailing copies of their appeals to the church doors of St. Paul's Cathedral and St. Mary of the Arches in London. While Repyngdon went into hiding in the Midlands, Hereford escaped arrest and made his way to Rome to present his appeal.

This appeal, in turn, proved unsuccessful, and Hereford escaped execution only due to papal efforts to broker a peace accord between England and France, then in the throes of the Hundred Years' War. Instead, he received a sentence of imprisonment for life, but he did not serve long. In 1385, during the chaos of the siege of Nocera by Charles of Durazzo, Hereford made his escape and returned to England. There he remained at large for a few years, presumably continuing to preach Wyclifism, even if covertly. The center of this activity seems to have been in the Lollard heartland, the three counties of Nottinghamshire, Derbyshire, and Leicestershire. There, in Nottingham, he was at last captured toward the end of January 1387. Remanded to the safekeeping of Sir

William Neville (a suspected Lollard, but the archbishop of York's brother and a friend of the king), Hereford spent most of the next few years in relative comfort at Shenley, a manor belonging to John Montagu, earl of Salisbury (another suspected Lollard).

In 1391, after Sir William Neville's death abroad, the king had Hereford turned over to Archbishop Courtenay, and imprisonment now meant close confinement at Saltwood Castle in Kent. After only a few months, Hereford recanted and received a grant of royal protection and an appointment as chancellor of Hereford Cathedral. While doubt exists today as to the sincerity of Hereford's recantation, he spent the remainder of his life building a reputation as a noted anti-Lollard preacher and persecutor. In 1397 he exchanged the post of chancellor for that of treasurer of Hereford Cathedral and held that post until 1417. In that year he took orders as a Carthusian monk, based at St. Anne's Charterhouse in Coventry, and he lived there until his death shortly afterwards.

Hereford's major extant work consists of his vernacular translation of the Old Testament in the Lollard Bible, which exists in two manuscripts, Bodleian MS. 959 and Bodleian Douce MS. 369. In both, Hereford's translation stopped in the midst of the Book of Baruch (at 3:20), presumably the point he had reached by June 1382. An extremely literal version and wholly unsuited as a popular Bible, this work seems either a first draft or a mere academic aid to understanding the Vulgate Bible. The second version of the Lollard Bible, a much more readable edition for the laity, completed in 1396, built upon Hereford's work. Though not the first translation of the Bible into English, the Lollard Bible, together with Hereford's evangelical work between 1382 and his apprehension in 1387 (and perhaps to 1391), contributed to the spread of Lollardy and its existence through the fifteenth century and thus prepared the way for the Anglican Reformation.

Bibliography: Anne Hudson, "Wycliffism in Oxford, 1381–1411," in *Wyclif in His Times*, ed. Anthony Kenny, 1986; K. B. McFarlane, *John Wycliffe and the Beginnings of English Non-Conformity*, 1952.

Jerome S. Arkenburg

Higden, Ranulf (1280?–1364). Though Ranulf Higden was a writer of several works, his main claim to fame, both now and then, rests on his authorship of the *Polychronicon*, a universal history in seven books that not only heavily influenced the style and substance of histories written through the sixteenth century, but also served as the source for much of English vernacular literature for the next two centuries. Born in the West Midlands, Higden first comes to notice in 1299, upon taking monastic vows at St. Werburgh's, a Benedictine house in Cheshire. Though little record exists of his work in that house, he may have served the monks as their librarian and head of the scriptorium. Despite the erudition of his work, no evidence exists that he spent any time at any university, nor, for that matter, that he journeyed much outside the Northwest. Thus, as is evident from his work, Cheshire, Shropshire, Derbyshire, and Lancashire constituted his sphere of direct knowledge. The one time he journeyed outside this region came in 1352, when *Edward III summoned him to court (along with his records and chronicles) for a purpose now unknown, though it was perhaps connected with the war in France. His death came on 12 March 1364, and his tomb still exists, in Chester Cathedral, by the gate of the south choir aisle.

Higden's most famous and influential work remains the *Polychronicon*. However, he wrote many other works that also had a wide contemporary appeal. These included the *Speculum curatorum*, a preacher's aid now at Balliol College in Oxford; the *Ars componendi sermones*, another aid to preachers for composing sermons, now in the Bodleian Library; the *Pedagogicon grammatices*, mentioned in library lists but no longer extant; the *Distinctiones theologicae*, housed today in Lambeth Palace Library; and the *Abbreviationes chronicorum* in the British Library in London. All of these demonstrated Higden's erudition and literary ability.

Nonetheless, Higden's fame rests upon his *Polychronicon*, a historical and literary masterpiece that also proved an instant and enduring best-seller. Few if any of the medieval chronicles popular with modern readers had any contemporary appeal. Indeed, few had any popularity outside their own region, much less their own monastic house. In contrast, by the mid-fourteenth century the *Polychronicon* had achieved kingdomwide popularity, even though Higden had yet to provide a finished version. The process by which this work became known outside St. Werburgh's remains unknown, but by 1350 Higden himself had already achieved some fame as the writer of the most popular history of the day, surpassed only by Bede and Geoffrey of Monmouth. All sorts of institutions—monastic houses, cathedral chapters, hospitals, and colleges—owned copies, as did individual clerks and a surprising number of the laity.

Presumably its popularity owed more to content and readability than marketing technique. Rejecting the old annalistic style of simple recitation of one event after another, Higden took a vast amount of material and reduced it to a cohesive whole in a tightly structured and highly readable narrative format. He began with an account of the geography of the known world (one of the most enduringly popular parts of the work) and traced the rise and fall of one empire and kingdom after another from the Creation to his own day. Particularly strong in its detailed history of Greece and Rome (heavily based on the Greek and Roman authors, of whom he had a detailed familiarity), it met a contemporary need for knowledge of antiquity and the beginnings of the several European states. It also provided information on all sorts of obscure yet interesting topics, persons, and places, which appealed not just to the antiquarian-minded laity, but also to preachers and storytellers seeking sources for sermons and tales. In other words, Higden's history, which had no rivals in its scope, provided a work that met the hitherto-unfilled needs and demands of both ecclesiastical and lay readers.

Influenced by Scholastic methods of compilation, the *Polychronicon* followed a rigid structure of seven books and sixty-four chapters, along with a detailed index of persons, places, and events. As is evident from Higden's autograph copy of the *Polychronicon*, now Huntington Library MS. 132, he wrote the work in several stages beginning in 1327 and continuing to his death in 1364. More than simply additions, in these continuations he not only added sections but revised and eliminated others. These changes derived not merely from a desire to bring the history up to date, but also from further research he evidently conducted. His authorities included Valerius Maximus, Pliny, Suetonius, Eutropius, Eusebius, Augustine, Orosius, Isidore of Seville, Bede, Florence of Worcester, William of Malmesbury, Geoffrey of Monmouth, Henry of Huntingdon, John of Salisbury, Alfred of Beverley, Gerald of Wales, and Vincent of Beauvais. He also cited many others he knew only from the florílegia of John of Wales and Bartholomew Anglicus. Higden also did not fail to express doubt and skepticism when appropriate, such as when the tales seemed too fantastic, or the inconsistencies too glaring. Though he was not a modern historian by any means, with little knowledge of the various ancillary disciplines taken for granted today, and no personal knowledge of the places he described, Higden's method of skeptical doubt paved the way for historians of later years.

The *Polychrnicon*—in either its various Latin or English versions—also heavily influenced other works of vernacular literature of the fourteenth and fifteenth centuries. Among these, the work of Thomas Usk, *Geoffrey Chaucer, and *John Lydgate, along with Richard Lavynham's *Litil Tretys on the Seven Deadly Sins*, *Mirk's Festial*, and the tracts *Stanzaic Life of Christ* and *Jacob's Well*, all mined it for stories. Higden's *Polychronicon* thus passed into English literature as a work of immense importance in its own right.

Higden's *Polychronicon* put an end to the old-style monastic chronicle. Its new style of historical reporting dried up demand for annalistic reporting, as seen in the style of later histories composed through the sixteenth century. Nearly all of these either purported to continue the *Polychronicon* to the present day, as seen in the histories of, for example, *Thomas of Walsingham, the *Westminster Chronicle*, Adam of Usk, *Henry Knighton, and the *Vita Ricardi Secundi*, or were modeled upon it, such as the medieval *Historia aurea*, the *Eulogium historiarum*, the *Speculum historiale*, the Scottish histories of *John of Fordun and *Andrew of Wyntoun, and the Tudor histories such as the *Cronycle of Fabyan*, John Stow's *Summarie of English Chronicles*, William Camden's *Rerum Anglicarum et Hibernicarum annales*, and Raphael Holinshed's *Chronicles of England, Scotland, and Ireland*. Only Sir Walter Releigh's *History of the World* finally replaced it as a model.

Bibliography: Antonia Gransden, *Historical Writing in England, vol. 2, C. 1307 to the Early Sixteenth Century*, 1996; John Taylor, *The Universal Chronicle of Ranulf Higden*, 1966.

Jerome S. Arkenburg

Hilton, Walter (d. 1395/96). A writer of mystical literature in both Latin and English, Walter Hilton occupies a central position in the small group of fourteenth-century religious writers commonly known as the Middle English Mystics, which included *Richard Rolle, the anonymous author of *The Cloud of Unknowing*, *Juliana of Norwich, and *Margery Kempe. Hilton's mystical system has been described as a simplification of that of Richard of St. Victor, and like Richard, Hilton humbly disclaimed any personal experience of the divine familiarity that he described, declaring that he had not the grace of contemplation himself "in feeling and in working, as I have it in talking." His writings, primarily focused on the many spiritual levels experienced by the individual soul in both the active and the contemplative life, were widely influential during the fifteenth century in England.

Little is known of the life of Walter Hilton apart from what can be gleaned from autobiographical references contained within his works and from contemporary manuscript ascriptions. The date and place of his birth are unknown. There is some evidence that he received formal academic training at Cambridge, as he is often referred to as "Magister" in the manuscripts, a title usually reserved for doctors of theology. It has also been suggested that he gave up a promising career as a lawyer to enter the priesthood, due to a unique manuscript reference describing him as *decretorum inceptoris*, which possibly implied a training in canon law. Other manuscripts described him as a Carthusian monk, but it is now accepted that he was probably an Augustinian canon of Thurgaton Priory near Southwell in Nottinghamshire. Three reliable manuscripts include references to a "Walteri Hylton quondam canonici in Thurgaton." His death is generally recorded as occurring on the Vigil of the Annunciation, 24 March 1395/96.

In the tradition of the English mystical writings, Hilton's works are considered among the finest. His most famous work, *The Scale of Perfection*, was written in the vernacular and provided the reader with a truly systematic theology of the contemplative life, describing the dynamics of the mystical experience in a manner both pastorally sensitive and psychologically acute. The material was separated into two books written at different times. The first book, addressed to a female recluse, was circulated as a complete work. The second book, probably written sometime after the first, complemented the material in the first, but there is an often-remarked-upon change of tone: the reticence of book 1 is absent from the imagistic structures that embodied his thought and insight in book two. An extremely popular text in fifteenth-century England, *The Scale of Perfection* was printed by Wynkyn de Worde in 1494 at the command of Lady *Margaret Beaufort, the mother of *Henry VII. It was also translated into Latin as *Speculum contemplationis*, or *Bacculum contemplationis*, by Thomas Fyslawe, a Carmelite.

Two other vernacular works attributable to Hilton offer spiritual counsel to a fellow religious and a worldly gentleman, respectively, highlighting the adaptability of Hilton's advice as occasion demanded. The first of these was an epistle, *De imagine peccati*, written to his friend Adam Horsley, a priest, who was an official of the Exchequer, encouraging him in his intention to become an anchorite. The treatise known as *The Epistle of Mixed Life*, or simply *Mixed Life*, gave advice to a wealthy businessman who also wished to create opportunities to cultivate his inner spiritual life. It is in this work that Hilton is considered to be the first English religious writer to explicitly recommend the reading of the Scriptures to the laity. Other works attributed to him included the mystical fragment *On Angels' Song*, which counseled the reader against too simple an understanding of Richard Rolle's notion of "canor" or song.

A tradition dating from manuscripts of the fifteenth century attributes to Hilton a treatise both in Latin and in English entitled *Musica ecclesiastica*, which was identical with the first three books of the popular work *De imitatione Christi*. For this reason, the latter work, now almost universally assigned to *Thomas à Kempis, was frequently ascribed to Hilton. At present, a large number of Hilton's works remain unpublished, but he was extremely popular in his day. His works are central to an understanding of Christian mysticism and the spiritual sensibility that informed the surge of lay devotion in late medieval England.

Bibliography: Marion Glasscoe, *English Medieval Mystics: Games of Faith*, 1993; Walter Hilton, *The Scale of Perfection*, ed. Evelyn Underhill, 1923.

Claire McIlroy

Hoccleve, Thomas (c. 1368–c. 1450). Although Thomas Hoccleve has long been classified as a minor writer known primarily for his admiration of *Geoffrey Chaucer, his works not only reflected the concerns of a poet and civil servant in the late Middle Ages, they also raised questions about the nature of autobiographical writing in this period. Hoccleve seems to have spent most of his life in London working as a clerk in the office of the privy seal. He began his career at the age of twenty and toiled as a scribe for about forty years, along the way writing some literary works that most likely came to the attention of a court circle that included *Henry IV, Henry V, and several dukes. The kinds of writing tasks that Hoccleve performed as a clerk can be seen in the compendium of model letters and warrants that comprise his *Formulary* (British Library MS. Additional 24062). His literary writing is notable for the complaints inserted throughout concerning late payment of monies owed to him by the king. He received an annuity of ten pounds in 1399 that was raised by about one-third in 1409, but the twice-yearly installments were often in arrears. He also received two corrodies (board and lodging at two religious houses), the first of which he seems to have converted to cash, while the second was granted not long before his death. Additional payments from the Exchequer are on record, and presumably he also received payment for additional scribal work.

Hoccleve wrote occasional poems; lyrics to Christ and the Virgin; translations of *The Letter of Cupid* and *Learn to Die*; two tales from the *Gesta Romanorum* that, along with his *Complaint, Dialogue with a Friend*, and *Learn to Die*, make up a linked group of poems called the *Series*; and notably a long (5,463 lines) mirror for princes, *The Regement of Princes*. His poems are significant for their references to contemporary events and persons. Hoccleve dedicated "The Compleynte of the Virgin before the Cross" to Sir *John Oldcastle, accusing him of heresy, lust, and cowardice. His concern over religious dissension and the Lollard movement inspired him to give a piece of counsel to Henry V in which he urged him to stop the religious disputes. In "La Male Regle de T. Hoccleve" he confessed his own sinfulness, describing how he had been "a mirour of riot and excesse." His *Letter to Cupid*, a translation of *Christine de Pizan's *Epistre au dieu d'amours*, employed the rhyme-royal stanza form and echoed the sentiments of Chaucer's *Legend of Good Women*. In his *Complaint* Hoccleve quoted the Wife of Bath, calling her an "auctrice," and declared that he was determined to become women's friend.

The Regement of Princes began with 2,000 lines of personal revelations in which Hoccleve complained of Lollardy, poverty, the trials of the life of a clerk, his disappointments in his career, his decision (a wise one, he added) to marry for love, the importance of being faithful, and the fact that lords only look after themselves. This long preamble to his main task of urging Henry to keep his promises as king and act wisely can be read as comic in parts, but an elegiac tone results in a complex work that was a remarkable tribute to Chaucer, whose death he lamented here.

Although the autobiographical references in Hoccleve's works can be called conventional, they convey an air of verisimilitude. For instance, his self-castigation over excessive carousing at local haunts contains his confession that he only kissed women, he did not "do the deed," and his revelation that he suffered some kind of mental illness during 1414 seems to express genuine anxiety. Moreover, his constant complaints concerning his annuity payments are borne out by the records. It is not difficult to sympathize with his concerns; in a poem addressed to Henry V, he sketched the scenario that he and three of his clerical colleagues faced, warning that if they did not soon receive the money they had earned, they would become indigent and would be forced to go to Newgate. If Hoccleve's use of the humility topos seems a bit stale at times, we are also reminded that he was comparing himself to Chaucer, "the flour of eloquence."

Bibliography: J. A. Burrow, *Thomas Hoccleve*, English Writers of the Late Middle Ages, 1994; Thomas Hoccleve, *Minor Poems I*, ed. F. J. Furnivall, 1892.

Karen Arthur

Hubert van Eyck. *See* Eyck, Hubert van.

Hugo van der Goes. *See* Goes, Hugo van der.

Huguet, Jaime (before 1414–92), was a late Gothic Aragonese artist remembered for his religious paintings. Huguet's work marks a stage of development in late Gothic art in Catalonia.

Jaime (sometimes spelled "Jaume") Huguet was born in the province of Tarragona and was raised by an uncle who was also a painter. Several of Huguet's brothers became priests. Huguet's uncle moved them to Barcelona by 1434. Huguet completed his earliest known works in the regions of Zaragoza (1434/ 35–45) and Tarragona, perhaps under the influence of the Gothic painter Bernardo Martorell. Moving to Tarragona in 1445, Huguet came under the influence of Luis Dalmaú. Huguet moved back to Barcelona in 1448, where he soon became the city's leading painter.

In 1453 Huguet designed with Miguel Nadal a group of tapestries for the Casa de Disputats in Barcelona. He was commissioned on 26 November 1455 by Abbot Bernat de Samosa of Ripoll to provide a predella and panels for the Blessed Virgin. His triptych of St. George dates before June 1461. Many of his works have been lost, although some details, according to art historian Benjamin Rowland, Jr., can be reconstructed from the surviving contracts. From 1459 until 1477 Huguet is regularly mentioned in the records of the Guild of Bridle Makers (Freners), for whom he did a retable of St. Stephen in 1462. From 1486 until his death in 1492, Huguet collaborated with painter Bartolomé Bermejo in Catalonia.

Scholars have observed that Huguet's style in its maturity was characterized by an "Italianate and tranquil linearism" and the rejection, especially in his painting of St. George, of "fluid luminosity of surface." Influenced by late medieval Flemish art, Huguet became interested in elongated form. His work was also characterized by "naturalistic detail, . . . gentle angularity, and a crowding of surfaces in an attempt to negate spatial depth." His work, however, rejected Flemish influence in its minimal use of perspective and chiaroscuro. To call Huguet's work Renaissance would be a misnomer, according to Rowland, because "there is never any interest in questions of form, of color, or of perspective for their own sakes. . . . Only in the last works, when the influence of Italy was communicated, perhaps by Bermejo, do we find any approximation of reality in contrast to the earlier naturalism."

Bibliography: Charles D. Cuttler, *Northern Painting from Pucelle to Bruegel*, 1968; Benjamin Rowland, Jr., *Jaime Huguet: A Study of Late Gothic Painting in Catalonia*, 1932.

Mark K. Fulk

Humphrey, Duke of Gloucester (1391–1447), was the youngest son of *Henry IV and a member of *Henry VI's regency council. Humphrey is best known not only as an important political figure during the early years of Henry VI's reign but also for his patronage of humanist scholarship, his generous manuscript donations to Oxford University and his own extensive literary holdings.

Born to Henry IV and his first wife Mary in either January or February 1391, Humphrey was the youngest of four sons who included the future Henry V, Thomas, Duke of Clarence and John, Duke of Bedford. Very little is known about Humphrey's early life, although it is believed that he was educated at Balliol College at Oxford.

Humphrey was created Earl of Pembroke and then Duke of Gloucester in 1414. The following year he accompanied his brother Henry V in his invasion of France. Although considered to be a poor strategist, Humphrey did command a squadron at the battle of Agincourt where he was wounded and thrown from his horse; he recovered quickly and later took part in the successful sieges of Harfleur and Cherbourg. However, his military career ended in 1419 when he was appointed "guardian and lieutenant of England." Henry V's death in 1422 left the throne of England to his nine-month-old son Henry VI. Members of the young kings' regency council included the Duke of Gloucester, his brother the Duke of Bedford and the Bishop of Winchester, *Henry Beaufort. Throughout his career on the council, Gloucester was at odds with the other members, especially with regard to the situation in France. His consistent opposition to peace with France made him popular with the common people as a champion of English interests there, but won him no friends on the council. Regardless, the Duke of Bedford's death in 1435 put Gloucester next in line to inherit the crown. A handsome man, Gloucester earned a reputation as a shameless womanizer, yet in 1422 he married Jacqueline of Bavaria. Although not a particularly attractive women, she did possess an enormous inheritance over which Gloucester hoped to gain control. Unfortunately, Philip of Burgundy was contesting that territory and in 1424, Gloucester brought an army of 4,000 men to Calais to assist Jacqueline in the defense of her lands. During the course of these events, Burgundy claimed that Gloucester had called him a liar and challenged him to a duel and, although Gloucester immediately agreed, the challenge was condemned by the pope and never took place.

Shortly thereafter Gloucester, who had tired of his wife's cause, left France on the pretense of preparing for his duel with Burgundy. On the journey home he became infatuated with a lady-in-waiting, Eleanor Cobham. By 1428 his marriage to Jacqueline had been annulled and sometime before 1431 he and Eleanor were married. The marriage was protested by a number of London housewives who shamed Gloucester for "abandoning his wife to her distress, while consoling himself with a harlot like Eleanor Cobham."

Humphrey of Gloucester's true claim to fame was his interest in literature. His library contained works on multiple subjects including theology, history, astrology, astronomy and medicine. He was particularly interested in the Italian scholarship of that period, and enlisted the services of several Italian scholars as his secretaries. In particular, these included Antonio di Beccaria, who was responsible for several translations of St. Athanasius' treatises, and Titus Livius of Ferrara, known as Gloucester's "poet and orator," who authored the first biography of Henry V. The Duke also served as patron to several other Italian authors such as Piero del Monte, Lapo da Castiglionchio and Pier Candido Decembrio, whose Latin translation of Plato's *Republic* was dedicated to Gloucester. Eventually his collection grew large enough that he was able to donate approximately 300 books to Oxford University.

In 1441 Gloucester's wife Eleanor, along with several accomplices, was charged with heresy, treason, witchcraft and necromancy. Specifically she was accused of making a wax doll of Henry VI and melting it slowly over a fire with the intention of causing the king's health to deteriorate. Eleanor's accomplices were executed, but she was imprisoned on the Isle of Man for the remainder of her life. During this time, Gloucester was powerless to help his wife and merely "took all things patiently and said little." Although Eleanor admitted to some of the heresies, it seems several of the charges were likely formulated in order to discredit her husband.

In 1447 Gloucester was summoned by Parliament to Bury St. Edmunds. Approximately one mile outside the town, he was met by two royal servants who informed the Duke that, due to the cold weather he should go directly to his lodgings rather than present himself at court. Later that evening, shortly after dinner was served, five noblemen came to the inn and placed the Duke under arrest. Less than five days later, on 23 February, Gloucester apparently suffered a stroke and died in prison. After his death it was rumored that the Duke had been murdered, perhaps by supporters of Margaret of Anjou, whose marriage to Henry VI he had opposed.

Humphrey, Duke of Gloucester was one of the most prominent English political figures of the fifteenth century—son, brother and uncle to kings—and yet he himself never truly wielded royal power. Certainly his greatest legacy lies in his many contributions to English humanism, and of course his library, which still exists today as the basis of the Bodleian library of Oxford University.

Bibliography: Rowena E. Archer, ed., *Crown, Government and the People in the Fifteenth Century*, 1995; G.L. Harriss, *Cardinal Beaufort*, 1988.

Jaimie B. Hanson

Hurtado de Mendoza, Diego (1365–1404),

was admiral of Castile and the eldest son of Pedro González de Mendoza and Aldonça de Ayala. The original home of the Mendoza was in Álava (one of the Basque provinces), where the family had an established, great lineage. They became active in Castilian society during the reign of Alfonso XI (1312–50). Diego was the product of two formerly feuding clans (the Mendoza and the Ayala) who reconciled their differences when they relocated in Castile.

The Mendoza supported the Trastámara lineage in its successful bid for the Castilian throne in the 1360s, and it was the events surrounding the Battle of Nájera (1367) that established the family both in political life and in artistic activity in the kingdom. The marriage alliances forged from this particular upheaval created an extended family network that separated the Mendoza from other noble families but entrenched them in the royal house itself. Modern historian Helen Nader notes that the Mendoza were the "pillars of the Trastámara dynasty."

Diego Hurtado de Mendoza was described by Fernándo Pérez de Guzmán in his *Generaciones y semblanzas* as pale in complexion, with a "Romish" nose, but graceful and strong for his (small) size. He was a reasonable and subtle man, but sometimes so daring in his speech that King Enrique III sometimes complained of it. This bold tendency served Diego well as admiral of Castile, as he gave his king a series of victories, particularly against Portugal. Diego served on the king's council during the same time as his uncles, *Pero López de Ayala and Juan Hurtado de Mendoza, and by 1395 Diego had received as a gift from the Crown the patronage of the city offices of Guadalajara. This city served as his base of operations, from which he built a considerable estate and fortune.

Diego's second marriage to Leonor de la Vega in 1387 brought extensive lands in Asturias, including sheep runs, salt mines, and seaports, into the Mendoza patrimony. The marriage also reinstated the former alliance that had existed between the Mendoza and the aristocracy supporting the Trastámara. Once Alfonso Enríquez (nephew of Enrique II) succeeded Diego Hurtado de Mendoza in his office, the admiralty of Castile became hereditary in the Enríquez family.

It seems that Diego's dynastic accomplishments were accompanied by complications in matters of the heart. He had several children by his second wife, since they kept separate households, he shared his with his cousin, Mencía de Ayala. The bitter feud between these two women cost the family some of its more distant territories. Diego's son, *Iñigo López de Mendoza (first marquis of Santillana, 1398–1458), was able to recover much of the family fortune as well as excel in the literary world. Diego's literary skills are attested in his extant poems, which appear in a manuscript in the Biblioteca de Palacio; they are all erotic verse.

Bibliography: Helen Nader, *The Mendoza Family in the Spanish Renaissance, 1350 to 1550*, 1979.

Rowena Hernández Múzquiz

Hus, Jan (c. 1373–1415), was a Czech religious reformer condemned for heresy by the Council of Constance and burned at the stake. His death ignited the Hussite revolt that defined Czech nationalism, inspired Martin Luther, and founded the Moravian church. Hus was born of peasant parents in Husinec in southern Bohemia, and after receiving a master's degree at the University of Prague in 1396, he became a professor of arts there, was ordained in 1400, and began studies in theology. Hus's teaching abilities were remarkable, and he was chosen to serve as preacher at Bethlehem Chapel, where his vernacular sermons calling for clerical reform brought him the respect of members of the nobility and of Prague's archbishop.

The late fourteenth century saw the genesis of a Czech nationalism centered in the Bohemian city of Prague as both university leaders and clerics defined themselves in the face of the Holy Roman Empire's German sovereignty. Earlier figures like Konrad of Waldhausen, *Jan Milič, and *Matthias of Janov combined pietist clerical reform with Bohemian nationalism into a widespread popular movement. At the same time, Prague intellectuals discovered the philosophy of *John Wyclif, whose realist metaphysics had been condemned along with his political and ecclesiastical thought in the last decade of the century. Wyclif's realism flew in the face of the nominalist thought universally accepted by German academics, and Czech intellectuals eagerly embraced it as definitive of their Bohemian identity. While Hus was by no means foremost among Prague's Wyclifftes, he became familiar with Wyclif's reformative ecclesiology and theology in pursuing his doctorate and incorporated some of the English reformer's revolutionary sentiment into his sermons.

The German academics at the University of Prague responded with a condemnation of Wycliffite writings in 1403, forcing prominent Czech intellectuals to recant or flee. This provided Hus with an opportunity for leadership, and he joined with *Jerome of Prague and others to create a new Czech nationalist movement among the remaining scholars and priests. The Great Schism also provided an opportunity for the growing movement. Bohemia's *Wenceslas IV had supported Pope Gregory XII until 1408, when he joined other princes in seeking conciliar resolution of the papal standoff. Archbishop Zbynik and the German academics at Prague remained united behind Gregory XII, and Wenceslas saw the utility of supporting the young Czech academics. In 1409 the Council of Pisa elected Alexander V in an attempt to end the schism, and Zbynik, angered by the heretical Wycliffism spreading through Prague, supported the new pope. This allowed him to begin to root out the dangerous anticlericalism that Wycliffism embodied, and Zbynik burned Wyclif's writings and commanded priests and scholars to cease spreading the heresy. Hus refused to comply, and in 1410 Zbynik excommunicated him, an act that was reinforced by papal excommunication in 1411.

The archbishop was understandably worried by the spread of Wycliffism. John Wyclif had argued that grace allowed Christians to regain natural Edenic *dominium* by living in apostolic poverty, and that it assigned certain civil lords the duty of protecting Christians in their poverty. Thus the entire church must be without material property, subject to the temporal powers of the grace-favored civil lords. Wyclif's realist metaphysics resulted in a determinism that led to a definition of the church as the body of those predestined to salvation, a de facto universal priesthood of grace-favored believers. Any cleric who owned property thereby demonstrated his lack of apostolic poverty and so could not be a true member of Christ's body. Finally, Wyclif had argued against transubstantiation later in his life and had stressed the importance of preaching and making Scripture available in the vernacular. Wyclif's writings, declared heresy during his own lifetime, had sparked Lollardy, an anticlerical English heretical movement.

Hus's movement was spreading through southern Bohemia, and his associates were preaching that the papal establishment was the body of Antichrist, as evidenced by the newly instituted papal indulgences for the crusade against the king of Naples. Wenceslas IV had supported the papal crusade and its indulgences and turned against Hus, condemning him in June 1412. The riots that erupted in Prague in response forced Hus to go into hiding, where he wrote his most important work, *De ecclesia*.

Hus's treatise incorporated none of Wyclif's *dominium*-centered philosophy and little of his antiproprietary theology into its argument that the Christian church was nothing more than the universal body of the predestinate. While many of Hus's arguments for clerical reform found their origin in Wyclif's *De ecclesia* and *De potestate papae*, the philosophical complexity that characterized Wyclif's work was absent from Hus. Arguments that Hus embodied a Bohemian incarnation of Wycliffism are overstated; at best, Hus used Wyclif's thought as an inspiration. Hus supported Utraquism, the belief that the communicant must take both bread and wine, but did not deny transubstantiation, as did Wyclif and later reformers. While Luther's exclamation on reading Hus's *De ecclesia*, "We are all Hussites without knowing it," is celebrated as evidence of Hus's proto-Reformation status, it is more accurate to view the treatise as the chief document of the phenomenon of Hussite revolution in fifteenth-century Bohemia.

In early 1414 Emperor *Sigismund and John XXIII called the Council of Constance to heal the schism, and Hus accepted Sigismund's offer of safe-conduct to explain his views to the assembled clergy. Expecting an opportunity for academic debate over the issues of reformation, Hus was arrested and tried for heresy. Among his persecutors were the leading nominalist theologians *Pierre d'Ailly and *Jean Gerson. Hus was repeatedly called upon to recant thirty alleged Wycliffite heresies culled from his writings, but he refused because he believed that the charges were inaccurate. On 6 July 1415 Hus was formally degraded from the priesthood and was burned. He reportedly died singing hymns.

The Hussite movement was to spread throughout Bohemia and Moravia, combining theological reform with Czech nationalist fervor. On a hill in southern Bohemia named Tabor, Hussites erected a fortress and militarized the revolt. These radical Hussites, called Taborites, developed a congregationalist socioecclesiastic structure similar to John Calvin's Geneva. The movement declined during the Council of Basel in the 1430s and was decisively defeated by Sigismund's army at Lipany in 1434.

Bibliography: Howard Kaminsky, *A History of the Hussite Revolution*, 1967; David Schaff, trans., *De Ecclesia: The Church, by John Hus*, 1915; Matthew Spinka, *John Hus: A Biography*, 1968.

Stephen E. Lahey

I

Inglés, Jorge (fl. c. 1455), was a painter in the new Flemish style in Spain. His origin, dates, biography, and death are not well known. Little is known about his name, which translates "George the Englishman." Whether he was given this name because of English heritage, such as an English father, or because his painting style was seen by his contemporaries as close to English style is unknown. He was certainly the painter of one work, and perhaps the painter of others as well.

The only work certainly painted by him was *The Retable of Angels* (1455?). Most of the pieces of this retable have survived well into the twentieth century. Inglés worked during the turbulent years of *Enrique IV of Spain (1425–74), a time when, due to civil and political strife, there was little painting done in Spain. The work was commissioned in a codicil to the will of *Iñigo López de Mendoza, the first marquis of Santillana, at a time when many Spanish lords had as much power and influence as did the king.

The work depicts twelve angels surrounding the Virgin and was meant to ornament Santillana's poem on the twelve joys of Mary. Depicted in portraiture are Santillana and his wife, Catalina Suárez de Figueroa, who are seen in prayer. The style of this painting, while not amateurish, is nowhere near those of the Flemish masters whom Inglés tried to imitate. Charles D. Cutler believes that it may date from the school of Tournal because of its "nicety of execution and a certain cramped mode of conception which demonstrate . . . that he was instructed by some miniaturist of this school." The retable thus "lacks . . . the ease and surety of draughtmanship that belong to a real master." Cutler also suggests that Inglés's work on the retable "shows a gradual loss of Flemish purity in its translation into Spanish, that is, a growth of decorative ornamentation at the expense of naturalism of setting, and an accentuated, almost exaggerated expression, gesture, and movement at the expense of lyrical balance." The retable nonetheless represented the first Castilian work in the new Flemish style finding its way to Spain at this time.

Chandler Rathfon Post suggests the possibility of three more works of art that may, but cannot conclusively, be linked to Inglés. The first are some miniatures done for a book belonging to Santillana, now housed at the Biblioteca Nacional in Madrid. The second is the retable of St. Jerome coming from the Hieronymite monastery of La Mejorda at Olmedo, housed at the Valladolid Museum, while the third is a representation of the bestowal of a chasuble upon St. Ildefonso.

Bibliography: Charles D. Cuttler, *Northern Painting from Pucelle to Bruegel*, 1968; Chandler Rathfon Post, *History of Spanish Painting*, vol. 4, 1933.

Mark K. Fulk

Iñigo López de Mendoza. *See* López de Mendoza, Iñigo.

Innocent VI, Pope (b. 1282, r. 1352–62), formerly Étienne Aubert, was the fifth Avignon pope. Innocent rejected the *Capitulatio* of the conclave that elected him, reformed the papal Curia at Avignon, and returned the Papal States to sovereignty under the pontiff. His rule, however, was marred by his inheritance of severely depleted finances, an aggressively self-interested college of cardinals, and strained relations with secular leaders successfully championing their superiority over the church.

Étienne Aubert was born in Les Monts, near Pompadour. He became a respected jurist and professor of canon law at Toulouse, where he was eventually made chief judge. In 1338 he was made bishop of Noyon, and two years later bishop of Clermont. *Clement VI made him a cardinal in 1342, cardinal bishop of Ostia a decade later, and finally grand penitentiary in Avignon. At Clement's death in 1352 the papal Curia in Avignon was severely hampered by the deceased pope's extravagance. The conclave that met to elect the new pope first reached an agreement that would limit the powers of the pontiff and considerably expand the interests and controls of the college. In electing Étienne Aubert— already seventy years old and in poor health—as Pope Innocent VI on 18 December 1352, the college hoped to choose a malleable pope who would adhere to their agreement and not hinder their desire to rule the papacy as an oligarchy. After his election, however, Innocent annulled the *Capitulatio*, arguing that it impinged upon the papal prerogatives.

Innocent continued the return of the Papal States to sovereignty under the pope and shrewdly appointed Cardinal Gil Alvarez Carillo Albornoz to this task. Despite difficulties in Bologna, under Albornoz's direction provincial laws were codified and simplified; the resultant *Aegidian Constitutions* formed the basis of Papal States law into the nineteenth century. Other areas of conflict, however, turned out less successfully for the pope; the Hundred Years' War, for example, provided a troubling backdrop to Innocent's pontificate. Although the pope and his cardinals were prominent in the negotiations leading to the 1360 Treaty of Calais, peace was often problematic. The Treaties of Bordeaux (1357) and Brétigny (1360) loosed roving bands of ravaging mercenaries from both armies upon Europe. In 1357 Arnaud de Cervole invaded Provence, and Innocent was required to broker peace. In 1360 bandits captured Pont St. Esprit, isolating Avignon. Once again the enemies were bought off before reaching the city, although their actions had grave consequences. Fear of the mercenaries in outlying areas sent the population flooding into Avignon, and 17,000 people, including 9 cardinals, died from famine and plague. Innocent's age and health had kept the papal court at Avignon, and the sieges of 1357–60 marked a strengthening of the ties between the pope and the city previously unknown during the papacy's residence there.

Crippling financial difficulties haunted Innocent throughout his reign. The papal treasury was drastically depleted, and Innocent trimmed the Curia, dismissed costly hangers-on and sycophants, and forced priests to return to their benefices. Intermittent periods of severe financial distress led to the sale of papal treasures. But the greatest challenge to Innocent's pontificate came from Charles of Moravia, who was elected king of the Romans in 1346 and was crowned emperor in 1355. Charles's *Golden Bull* of 1356 established the procedures to be followed in electing future kings of the Romans and pointedly omitted the need for papal confirmation of the election. Innocent, who required Charles's support against Bernabò Visconti in Bologna, did not protest. Three years later the pope's capitulation in the diplomatic battle against imperial power was made even more clear when he declared, at the insistence of Charles, that *Clement V's bulls that had championed papal superiority had not been intended to slight the legacy of Charles's grandfather, Henry VII. Innocent's statements contained no reference to papal superiority, a sign that implicitly acknowledged his recognition of the failing power of the papacy.

Innocent's weaknesses were the result of ill health, old age, and poor diplomacy, rather than corruption or willful disregard for the office of the pope. A scholar at heart, he established the College of St. Martial at Toulouse and a faculty of theology at Bologna. His death was likely hastened by his recognition that the goals to which he aspired—peace and stability—were obstructed by endemic disorder, and that his pontificate had witnessed the steady decline of papal influence over rising secular powers. He died on 12 September 1362 and was buried in the Charterhouse at Villeneuve that he had founded in 1356.

Bibliography: Guillaume Mollat, *The Popes at Avignon, 1305–1378*, 1963; Yves Renouard, *The Avignon Papacy, 1305–1403*, 1970.

Andrew Bethune

Innocent VIII, Pope (b. 1432, r. 1484–92), formerly Giovanni Battista Cibò, although not the worst of the early modern popes, was far from the best. His papacy was marred by political indecision and military failure. Although

Innocent did little to reform the church, he did act aggressively against the perceived enemies of Christianity, attempting to organize a crusade against the Turks, extending the persecution of witchcraft in Germany with his 1484 bull *Summis desiderantes affectibus*, and condemning the theses of the Platonist philosopher *Giovanni Pico della Mirandola in 1486.

Giovanni Battista Cibò was born in Genoa in 1432 and spent his early years at the court of *René of Anjou in Naples, where his father was a government official. He studied in Padua and Rome, although it appears that he did not originally intend to take holy orders and in fact fathered at least two illegitimate children: a son, Franceschetto, and a daughter, Teodorina. After taking orders, Cibò entered the service of Cardinal Calandrini, and through the cardinal's patronage he was made bishop of Savona in 1469. In 1472 Pope *Sixtus IV made Cibò bishop of Molfetta, and in 1473 the same pope made him a cardinal. After Sixtus's death in 1484, his nephew, the powerful Cardinal Giuliano della Rovere (later Pope Julius II), realizing that he did not have sufficient support to be made pope himself and looking for a candidate he could manipulate, settled on Cibò. After a night of intense negotiations and outright bribery, Cibò was formally elected on 29 August 1484.

Innocent inherited a nearly bankrupt papal treasury and a volatile political situation in Italy. To help alleviate the first problem, Innocent resorted to the traditional tactic of creating new curial offices and then selling them. Innocent also entered into an unprecedented arrangement with the Genoese banking house of Cicero and Sauli, and eight other Italian bankers. The bankers agreed to loan the papal treasury a total of 216,000 ducats over four years, and in exchange they were allowed to take over the collection of papal revenues for themselves. These expedients enabled Innocent to improve papal finances in the short run, although the gains he made did not long outlast his papacy.

Innocent was far less successful in the political arena. In 1485, influenced by Giuliano della Rovere, Innocent sided with a group of Neapolitan barons who had risen in revolt against King *Ferrante I. Faced with a lack of funds to hire mercenaries, opposition from Florence and Milan, and the prospect of a revolt in Rome, Innocent was forced to make peace with Ferrante in 1486. Realizing his weakness in Italy, Innocent made a pact with Venice in early 1487. A few months later, however, Innocent broke this pact and aligned himself with Florence and the Medici instead. This new alliance was sealed with a marriage between Innocent's son Franceschetto and *Lorenzo de Medici's daughter Maddelena. Innocent also made Lorenzo's son Giovanni (later Pope Leo X) a cardinal in 1488, even though he was only thirteen at the time. In 1487 Ferrante repudiated the treaty he had concluded with Rome, and in 1489 Innocent excommunicated Ferrante. Although Rome suffered a series of military setbacks, a treaty arranged between Innocent and Ferrante in 1492 was generally favorable to the papacy, in part because Ferrante feared that Innocent would support a French pretender to the throne of Naples.

Innocent did not have much more success in his attempts to organize a new crusade. He was able to convince several kingdoms to send envoys to Rome in 1490, and while these envoys did agree on tentative arrangements for an expedition against the Turks, renewed conflict between Holy Roman Emperor *Maximilian I and King *Charles VIII of France in the early 1490s ended all hope for a crusade within Innocent's lifetime. In 1489 Innocent agreed to keep Sultan Bayezid II's brother and rival, Djem, under papal guard in exchange for 40,000 ducats a year and the head of the Holy Lance. While this arrangement did give Innocent some leverage over Bayezid, it also undermined his calls for a crusade.

Innocent's contemporaries described him as kindly, good-natured, and easygoing, but also as easily influenced and temperamentally unsuited for the papacy. Although he showed himself capable of acting strongly in the religious sphere, his political actions were marked by uncertainty and the influence of powerful allies, such as Giuliano della Rovere and Lorenzo de Medici. As a result, his papacy has been overshadowed by those of his more forceful predecessors and successors.

Bibliography: Charles L. Stinger, *The Renaissance in Rome*, 1985; J.A.F. Thomson, *Popes and Princes, 1417–1517*, 1980.

Stephen A. Allen

Isabel, Queen of Castile (b. 1451, r. 1474–1504), jointly ruled the kingdom of Aragon with her husband *Ferdinand, whom she married in 1469. Her path to the throne of Castile, however, was an arduous one. Upon her birth, it was the son of her father *Juan II's first marriage, *Enrique IV, who sat on the throne of Castile. Isabel and her brother, Alfonso, were the children of Juan's second marriage. By 1464 various noble factions, dissatisfied with the perceived shortcomings of Enrique's regime, had rallied around Alfonso. They criticized the king for plunging Castile into a dark age of social disorder and crumbling Catholicism. They backed their sentiments with the force of arms and occasioned by 1466 a civil war in Castile. Yet in 1468 Alfonso died, and the partisans, whose strength had already begun to waver, lost their rallying point.

The death of Alfonso prompted a meeting between Enrique and Isabel. Enrique was anxious to resolve the issue of the succession, since by this time his second wife, Juana, had given birth to a daughter, *Juana of Castile. The daughter, however, had long been rumored to be the offspring of an adulterous affair between Juana and his advisor, *Beltrán de la Cueva. At a critical meeting in 1468 at a site outside of Ávila known as Toros de Guisando, Isabel and Enrique signed a pact. Enrique pardoned the rebels; Isabel was recognized as Enrique's legitimate heir, and she promised not to marry without Enrique's consent. All who had at one time taken an oath of allegiance to Enrique's daughter were then released from it.

From this point onward, however, Isabel proved herself to be a strong leader who moved quickly to consolidate her power. She began fashioning around her a royal household and administration, issuing orders and making appointments. She also had to settle the issue of her marriage. Her eventual inheritance of the Castilian throne was contingent in the minds of most on her willingness to marry and thereby create a "king" of Castile. Given the territory and title that she was due to inherit, her suitors were many. Enrique favored a match with the king of Portugal, a prospect that was less appealing to Isabel. She instead favored the young prince of Aragon, Ferdinand, and began negotiating secretly to wed him. In fact, the two were wed in private in 1469 in the city of Valladolid. Enrique was outraged at Isabel's blatant violation of the agreement at Toros de Guisando, but eventually recognized the union.

Isabel and Ferdinand immediately went to work to create the mechanisms of their joint administration and government. The two had signed a *capitulación* or agreement that specified the respective power and privileges of each in the realms of Castile and Aragon. Significantly, Isabel retained for herself important rights in Castile. She had the sole right to make various appointments, and even in cases where they would be made jointly, they had to come at her volition. She also maintained power over various forms of revenue. It was clear to many that Isabel was not going to take a back seat to Ferdinand in the administration of Castile. In fact, the two seem to have been highly compatible rulers, which enhanced their effectiveness as emerging monarchs.

The last significant battle that they would face on their road to the Castilian throne was precipitated by the death of Enrique in 1474. His death prompted the outbreak of another civil war between the partisans of Isabel and the partisans of his daughter, Juana. By 1477, however, Isabel and Ferdinand had been recognized throughout the realm as the legitimate rulers of Castile.

The achievements of the reign of Isabel were many. In the eyes of her contemporaries, she did achieve what her partisans had always predicted: she rescued Castile from the wayward rule of Enrique and restored it to glory as an ascendant world power that upheld the principles of Christianity.

One of her first accomplishments was to complete the Christian reconquest of the Iberian Peninsula begun in the eight century by recapturing the Muslim kingdom of Granada. Though it was Ferdinand who led the troops and marched into battle, many regarded the campaign as the "queen's war," and Isabel often camped near the army. It was a long campaign that was waged on and off for at least ten years. Finally, in 1492 the campaign was completed, and she and Ferdinand rode victoriously into the city of Granada. They underscored the significance of the city to the realm of Castile by reconsecrating mosques as churches and creating an *audiencia* or royal appellate court in the city.

Isabel also sought the return of Christian orthodoxy in more intolerant ways. Reversing centuries of coexistence (that was admittedly sometimes quite contentious) in 1492, she also ordered that all the Jews in Castile accept forced baptism and conversion to Christianity or be expelled. This was followed in 1502 by a similar expulsion decree directed at the remaining Muslim population, which was also directed to choose between conversion and expulsion.

To attack the perceived dilemma of Christian heresy, Isabel and Ferdinand petitioned the papacy for the right to administer a branch of the Holy Office or Inquisition. What was unique about their petition and its subsequent granting was the autonomy offered to the monarchs as part of the agreement. The papal bull issued in 1478 allowed them to administer independently many of the mechanisms of this institution, including the appointment of inquisitors. Much of the decision to create the Castilian branch of the Inquisition was fueled by suspicions regarding the practices of *conversos* (Jews who had converted to Christianity). Previous waves of forced and some sincere conversions in the late Middle Ages had created a substantial population of *conversos*. The sincerity of their conversions was often doubted, and many suspected them of reverting to the practice of Jewish rites and rituals. The initial target, then, of the Inquisition was this population, which was called upon to demonstrate its devotion to Christianity.

To answer the cry for the restoration of social order whose disruption had plagued the reign of Enrique, Isabel reaffirmed and emphasized the role of the *corregidores* and the *hermandades*. The *corregidores* were Crown-appointed officials who monitored affairs at the local level. The *hermandades* were local police forces that monitored criminal activity.

Finally, one of Isabel's most important legacies was her decision to fund in part the voyages of *Christopher Columbus. Isabel and Ferdinand were open to, if somewhat skeptical of, Columbus's proposals. In fact, some of their advisors suggested that his plans were ill founded. Columbus was nonetheless kept on retainer for a period of time, because Isabel was interested in developing Castile's interests in the Atlantic. Perhaps emboldened by their success in Granada, in 1492 the monarchs gave their final approval for Columbus's plans and drafted an agreement defining the rights and prerogatives of Columbus and the Crown in this expedition.

Isabel died in 1504, leaving the kingdom of Castile a significant legacy. She had remedied the perceived disorder created by her predecessor, Enrique IV. She had redefined Christian orthodoxy in the peninsula with the expulsion of its religious minorities. Finally, she had expanded the kingdom's horizons with exploration into the Atlantic.

Bibliography: Peggy K. Liss, *Isabel the Queen: Life and Times*, 1992; Marvin Lunenfeld, *Keepers of the City: The Corregidores of Isabella I of Castile*, 1987; Nancy Rubin, *Isabella of Castile: The First Renaissance Queen*, 1991.

Elizabeth Lehfeldt

Isabel de Villena. *See* Villena, Isabel de.

J

Jacob van Artevelde. *See* Artevelde, Jacob van.

Jacques de Molay. *See* Molay, Jacques de.

Jaime II, "the Just," King-Count of Aragon and Catalonia (b. 1267, r. 1291–1327), is best known for his Hohenstaufen-style administration and for making Aragon a leading Mediterranean power. He was called "Just" because of the respect he showed for traditional constitutions.

Jaime II was born on 10 August 1267 in Valencia, son of Pedro III (r. 1276–85). He was the grandson of Jaime I, "the Conqueror" (r. 1213–76), and he succeeded his brother Alphonse III (r. 1285–91). Prior to becoming king, Jaime had ruled Sicily (from 1283), which had been acquired after the revolt of the Sicilian Vespers.

Becoming king of a divided realm in 1291, Jaime moved quickly to assert his authority and resolve the conflicts that had brought his brother an early death. In August 1291, when Jaime sailed into Barcelona, his kingdom was technically at war with Naples, France, Navarre, and Castile and in the grips of a protracted struggle between recalcitrant Aragonese nobles and the Crown, whose power had been all but destroyed by the Cortes of 1283 and 1287. Jaime's first priority was to make peace with as many of his enemies as possible, including France, with which he signed the Treaty of Anagni on 20 June 1295. This treaty gave Jaime a free hand against Castile but weakened his position in Sicily, where his nephew Fadrique now ruled as his father's heir.

His throne momentarily secured, Jaime turned to reorganization. His most important reforms were fiscal, building upon those of his brother, and were designed to make him as independent of the Cortes as possible without provoking the open opposition of Aragonese nobles and others anxious to keep the royal regime weak. He accomplished his goals in part by personal participation in international trade and in part by introducing Norman-Hohenstaufen administrative practices as found in Sicily. Jaime also assembled about himself a retinue of "friends," loyal to himself above all, to fill the ranks of his new-style administration.

Having set his royal house in order, Jaime next prepared to restore the shaken authority of the Crown. In 1301 Jaime convened the Aragonese Cortes and proclaimed that since he as king had the right to assemble a Cortes as a legislative assembly, he held legislative authority even without the Cortes, thereby changing the balance of power in Aragon. In the showdown that followed, Jaime was able to isolate and suppress his opponents among the Aragonese *ricos ombres* through careful maneuvering and wisely marshalling Catalonian support. Jaime also gained from the Cortes the right to collect the salt tax, further strengthening his fiscal resources, although the Aragonese Cortes stopped short of granting the king the kind of taxation rights that he enjoyed in Catalonia. In the end, the conflicting parties agreed to be bound by the decisions of the Justicia of Aragon, subjecting all, including the king, in theory to the authority of the traditional constitution.

After 1301 Jaime continued to strengthen his hand in meetings with the various Cortes of his realm, attempting not only to settle outstanding issues and strengthen his growing power base, but also to gain support for foreign expansion. Jaime's first overseas endeavor, against his nephew in Sicily, was abortive, though Sicily remained firmly in the Aragonese orbit. The Balearic Islands also remained Aragonese under their own independent line, but Jaime was determined to acquire Sardinia for himself. On 31 May 1323 he sent off his fleet to conquer the island from the Pisans. Pisa finally agreed to give up its claims in June 1326, and the conquered island was subsequently ruled as a colony by Catalonian and Aragonese administrators, over the protests of the natives. A project to conquer Corsica as well went no farther than the planning stage, as did efforts to establish direct rule of the Balearic Islands. In Sicily Fadrique continued to rule more or less independently. Jaime died on 4 November 1327, having fortified the power of the monarchy and having inaugurated an era of Aragonese imperialism.

Jaime married four times. His first wife was the infant daughter of Sancho IV of Castile (r. 1284–95), repudiated for political reasons after Sancho's death. His second wife was Blanche of Naples (d. 1310), whom the king is said to have loved; the third was Marie de Lusignan, princess of Cyprus (d. 1319); and the fourth was the Catalonian Elicsenda de Montcada (d. 1364). His successor was Alfonso IV (r. 1327–36), his son by Blanche of Naples.

Bibliography: T. N. Bisson, *The Medieval Crown of Aragon: A Short History*, 1986; J. Lee Shneidman, *The Rise of the Aragonese-Catalan Empire, 1200–1350*, 1970.

Paul D. Buell

James I, King of Scotland (b. 1394, r. 1423–37). James I is best known as the first great Stewart monarch and as the possible author of *The King's*

Quair. Despite a long imprisonment in England, he reorganized Scotland's legislature and strengthened the economy, maintaining peace and stability for many years.

Born in 1394, James was the only surviving son of King Robert III and Queen Annabella. In 1402 James was made earl of Carrick, but in 1406 his father sent him to France, perhaps suspecting a plot against his heir. En route to France, James's ship was intercepted by English pirates, who turned over the young prince to King *Henry IV. Despite a truce between England and Scotland, Henry imprisoned James. James was named king after his father's death two months later but remained a prisoner for the next eighteen years, through the end of Henry IV's reign as well as that of Henry V.

In prison, James fell in love with Joan Beaufort, the daughter of John, duke of Somerset, and cousin to Henry V. It is said that during this time James wrote *The King's Quair*, a dream-vision about a man lost at sea who is taken prisoner and falls in love with a woman he sees outside his cell window. Despite possible references to James's own imprisonment and love for Joan, the actual authorship of the poem is in doubt, and if James indeed wrote it, he probably did so at some point after his release.

That release was realized in December 1423, soon after Henry V's death and problems with France left England weakened. According to the Treaty of London, Scotland was to reimburse England for James's room, board, and tuition, surrendering twenty-one hostages until the bill was paid. In addition, the Scots could not send more troops to France than they already had stationed there. On 13 February 1424 James married Joan Beaufort, and the couple was crowned on 2 May of that year.

After the death of Robert III, Scotland had been ruled first by the duke of Albany and then by Albany's son, Murdoch, a weak ruler who mismanaged funds and allowed crime to run rampant. When James returned, he recognized the urgent need for reform and thus the need to establish his authority swiftly. He arrested Murdoch's son Walter Stewart for attempting to send soldiers to France in violation of the Treaty of London (1424), and to secure his throne, he arrested and executed Murdoch and several members of his family (1425) and later suppressed two Highland uprisings (1428 and 1429).

James's reforms were many and varied. He was an innovative legislator who increased the power of the nonnoble members of Parliament and demanded that Scotland's laws apply equally to the Highlands and the Lowlands. He required members to attend Parliament and general councils in person and established a court that provided the poor with counsel and freed up Parliament to deal with other matters. James also implemented social reforms, prohibiting begging and requiring able-bodied men to find gainful employment. To improve his subjects' quality of life, he had wolves hunted and crows' nests destroyed. To ameliorate his country's economic problems, he reorganized the collection of revenues and attempted to replenish royal funds by levying taxes and by repossessing the lands of people who could not prove their entitlements. Similarly tenacious in his dealings with the church, James vehemently disagreed with Pope Martin V, whom he, unlike other Scots, had judiciously supported during the Great Schism, over whether the king or the pope should have the ultimate authority over the church in Scotland.

Although James's reforms and firm rule benefited most of his subjects, ultimately it was dissatisfied countrymen who were responsible for the king's death. In February 1437 a band of conspirators attacked the priory at Perth, where James and his household had remained after celebrating Christmas, and assassinated the king. After James's burial, the king's heart was taken on a pilgrimage to the Holy Land and back, and the conspirators were tortured and executed. One month later James's six-year-old son was crowned James II, continuing the Stewart line.

Bibliography: Caroline Bingham, *The Stewart Kingdom of Scotland, 1371–1603*, 1974; Gordon Donaldson, *Scottish Kings*, 2nd ed. 1977.

Staci Bernard-Roth

James III, King of Scotland (b. 1451, r. 1460–88), is best known today for his troubled reign. Habitually plagued by quarrels with both his nobles and his two brothers, James found himself in many untenable situations. Despite the many problems of his reign, however, his marriage to Margaret of Denmark proved successful, as their union added vast new lands to the Scottish Crown. Nevertheless, James's continuous confrontations with the nobility proved to have dire consequences when he lost his life in their rebellion against him.

James III was born on 10 July 1451 to James II of Scotland and Mary of Gueldres. He acceded to the Scottish throne in August 1460 at a mere nine years of age, and his early reign was subject to three regencies. His mother, Bishop James Kennedy of St. Andrews, and the Boyd family all attempted to control the Scottish Crown. After Bishop Kennedy's death in 1465, Thomas Boyd, the early of Arran, assumed the regency and kidnapped James in an effort to exploit the royal treasury. It was during Arran's regency that the much-coveted earldom of Ross was acquired by the Crown. After securing a marriage in 1468 between James and Margaret, princess of Denmark, Arran was dismissed by James, who then ruled in his own right.

The marriage of James to Margaret, daughter of King Christian I of Denmark and Norway, brought much fortune to Scotland. Short of currency to pay a full dowry, Christian pledged the royal estates of Orkney and Shetland as collateral. When in 1472 the balance of the dowry could not be paid, the Crown annexed the islands, which remain part of the United Kingdom today.

James's reign was filled with adversity. He frequently found himself at odds with his nobles because he tended to play favorites with some of the less powerful barons. This led to the alienation of his brothers, the earl of Mar and the duke of Albany, whom he imprisoned in 1479 for fear of their growing political influence. Mar died mysteriously in prison, but Albany managed a valiant escape to England, where he sought to enlist the help of the English king *Edward IV.

Thus began the conflict between the Crown and the barons that would dominate the remainder of his reign.

In 1482 Richard of Gloucester, later *Richard III, invaded Scotland with the intention of deposing James in favor of his brother Albany. Albany also enlisted the aid of many powerful nobles who were uneasy with the Crown's growing tendency to control and imprison them. They were insecure in James's aggressive assertion of power, and many thought that he was responsible for Mar's suspicious death. James's feudal army clashed with these nobles, led by Archibald Douglas, the earl of Angus, at Lauder in 1482. It was here that several of James's favorites were hanged on the bridge. The plot to depose James was unsuccessful; however, the nobles did escort him back to Edinburgh, where Albany briefly assumed the regency and reconciled with him. Much to the dismay of James, Gloucester was able to recapture the town and castle of Berwick. In September 1484 Gloucester entered into a three-year truce with James and even proposed marriage between the daughter of an influential family, Anne de la Tour, and James's son, the future *James IV, though the match was never made.

The Scottish nobles by 1488 had grown weary of what they viewed as James's incompetence as a ruler. He lacked interest in military affairs, preferring instead to pursue music, art, and architecture. He had also "wasted" large sums building a royal hall and chapel at Stirling despite a serious currency crisis. At a January parliament in Edinburgh, James tried to arrest a group of rebel nobles by enlisting the help of Archibald Douglas. Douglas refused and instead betrayed the king to his fellow lairds. James, fearing for his safety, fled to the north while Douglas then had James's teenaged heir proclaimed James IV, king of Scotland. After gathering an army of several thousand men, James III marched to Stirling, where tensions were briefly relieved by his concessions to the noble party. This hiatus, however, did not last long, and on 11 June 1488 James was killed in a battle on Beaton's Hill at Sauchieburn. Although there are many legends concerning his death, James was probably killed by an unknown cleric after being thrown off his horse. He was buried at Cambuskenneth.

Although James III is not generally looked upon favorably by historians, many significant developments occurred during his reign. In 1466 Parliament began keeping written records of its sessions. The evolution of the signet was also important, as it marked the beginning of the office of royal secretary. During this time the importance of the burghs also increased with their larger contributions to taxation revenue. In addition to the earldom of Ross and the royal isles of Orkney and Shetland, the lands of Arran and Bute were added to the patrimony of the Scottish Crown. Perhaps most important, Bishop Patrick Graham secured for the See of St. Andrews the archiepiscopal pallium, thus negating claims of supremacy by both the archbishop of York and the archbishop of Drontheim over the Scottish church. James III may not have been a particularly wise king, but he did preside over many important events and developments that ultimately had a great impact on the history of Scotland.

Bibliography: Norman MacDougall, *James III: A Political Study*, 1982; Leslie J. Mac-
farlane, *William Elphinstone and the Kingdom of Scotland, 1431–1514*, 1985.

Christina Brunson Defendi

James IV, King of Scotland (b. 1473. r. 1488–1513), brought stability

to his kingdom, supported education, extended civil justice, and expanded royal
power by his effort to pacify and exert control over the Highland and Island
clans. He made Scotland an important participant in international affairs through
alliances with England and France. The former led to his marriage to Margaret
Tudor, the daughter of *Henry VII, and to the accession of his grandson to the
English throne in 1603. The alliance with France led to his defeat at Flodden
in August 1513 and his subsequent death.

The firstborn son of James III and Margaret of Denmark on 17 March 1473,
the young prince developed into an intelligent, perceptive, and bold man who
possessed much confidence. When he grew suspicious of his father's intentions
at age fifteen, he joined the rebellion that overthrew and ended the life of James
III at Sauchieburn on 11 June 1488. After his coronation at Scone, James IV
took effective action to crush the 1489 rebellion led by Lennox, Lyle, and Forbes
and soon began the construction of a naval yard at Newhaven that produced a
well-armed fleet that included his flagship *Michael*. This powerful force was
used to intimidate his enemies at home and abroad, as well as to protect the
Scottish coast from raiders. He restored and strengthened fortifications and royal
castles in a style that featured pragmatic rather than Renaissance motifs.
Throughout his reign he pursued a broad strategy designed to enhance governmental power and prestige internally and externally. Recent assessments of
James's reign have noted that while he utilized selected contemporary technology, legal reforms, and educational advances, his actions were more consistent
with those of a traditional, rather than a "Renaissance," monarch.

Throughout his rule he introduced legal reforms to stabilize justice by fixing
tenures, appointing capable judges, and centralizing aspects of court administration and even accompanied expeditions to border areas to demonstrate his concern for matters of civil and criminal justice. He revoked many statutes that
were prejudicial to the interests of the church and the Crown, and he confirmed
borough privileges to assert royal authority. In a series of expeditions between
1493 and 1505 he ended the power of the lord of the Isles, suppressed the
rebellion of Donald Dubb, and exerted effective control over much of western
Scotland throughout the remainder of his reign. He supported the growth of
schools and the 1496 Education Act, both of which were aided by the introduction of the printing press and royal support for a diverse assortment of
"scholars." While James has been criticized for his "dabbling" in astrology, his
interest was shared by many of his contemporaries, including Nicolaus Copernicus.

As he increased his domestic power, he initially pursued an independent foreign policy. In 1491 he renewed Scotland's traditional alliance with France,

strongly opposed English expansionism, and recognized the Yorkist pretender Perkin Warbeck's claim to the English throne in 1495. He married Warbeck to Lady Katherine Gordon and mounted a futile raid in support of Warbeck in September 1496 before abandoning the pretender's cause after Warbeck departed Scotland in July 1497. As James turned his attention to the pacification of western Scotland and the Isles, relative tranquility evolved along the border that enabled James to negotiate a treaty of peace with England that was sealed by his marriage to Henry VII's daughter, Margaret, at Holyrood Abbey on 8 August 1503, a union often poetically called the "marriage of the thistle and the rose." James assisted the Danes in their war against the Hanseatic League in 1507–08 and maintained his English alliance despite its growing unpopularity and overtures from Louis XII of France.

The accession of Henry VIII to the English throne in 1509, some Anglo-Scottish naval incidents, a French invitation to join the League of Cambrai, and personal animosity between the Scottish and English monarchs combined to change James's policy. When the pope attempted to expel the French from northern Italy by forming a Holy League, James IV supported France, while Henry VIII joined the league in 1511. After renewing the Franco-Scottish alliance in 1512, Scottish naval forces assisted the French, while militia forces successfully raided the Northumbrian border. After Henry VIII mounted an invasion of France in June 1513, James summoned the nobility and led his forces across the Tweed in August. He was outmaneuvered by the smaller English army and suffered a disastrous defeat at Flodden. He died from his wounds on 9 September. He left behind an infant son to succeed him and a reputation as a prudent legislator, an effective diplomat, and a patron of education and letters.

Bibliography: Norman MacDougall, *James IV*, 1997; Robert L. Mackie, *King James IV of Scotland: A Brief Survey of His Life and Times*, 1958/1976.

Sheldon Hanft

Jandun, John of. *See* John of Jandun.

Janov, Matthias of. *See* Matthias of Janov.

Jan van Eyck. *See* Eyck, Jan van.

Jan van Ruysbroek. *See* Ruysbroek, Jan van.

Jean de Bondol. *See* Bondol, Jean de.

Jean Valois, Duke of Berry. *See* Valois, Jean, duc de Berry.

Jerome of Prague (c. 1375?–1416). Little is known about the early life of Jerome of Prague. In fact, there is still a good deal of controversy about how he spent the early years of his adulthood. While some scholars believe that Jerome and his contemporary, *Jan Hus, traveled to Oxford in 1398 and became acquainted with the works of *John Wyclif, others insist that there is no real evidence that either man was in England at that time. Whether he actually traveled to England or not, Jerome is considered, with Hus, to be a follower of the theology and reform that has historically been associated with Wyclif and the Lollards. Most scholars assume him to have been younger than Hus, who was born in approximately 1373. Jerome was certainly not born before this time. In fact, the earliest date that can be directly associated with him is 1403, at which time he traveled to Jerusalem. Within a few years he was involved publicly in the intellectual life in Prague, much of which was focused on resolution of the Great Schism. In 1408 Jerome and Hus were among the theologians who were summoned to Kuttenberg by King *Wenceslas IV to discuss the problem of the schism and its long-hoped-for resolution. Jerome and Hus, along with their countrymen, pledged their allegiance to Gregory XII, the pope who was backed by Rome. This choice of Jerome and his colleagues to support the papacy of Gregory XII was the beginning of their connection to heresy, and it was the first time they were threatened with execution.

Jerome's relationship with Jan Hus is another controversy associated with him. Some scholars argue that Jerome was a faithful and loyal follower of Hus who traveled with him to Constance knowing that the outcome of such a journey was likely to be his arrest and execution. Other critics have argued that Jerome was an unreliable and disloyal follower and colleague of Hus who recanted his "heretical" beliefs as soon as the possibility of his own death became a reality. The truth of the matter cannot now be determined; however, Jerome has been remembered in history more for his denials and recantations than his bravery in the face of the authority of the church.

Within a year or two of the council at Kuttenberg, Jerome was advised to quit Prague—his opinions and alleged "violence" had made him unpopular with the archbishop—and so he left the city. Lutzow describes the next few years of his life as wandering, first traveling to Hungary to the court of *Sigismund. While he was in Hungary, he was again denounced as a heretic and an adherent of Wycliffism and was briefly arrested. He left Hungary for Vienna, where he lectured at the university and again associated himself publicly with Wyclif. He was arrested in Vienna and was scheduled to appear (willingly, it seems) before a tribunal that had been formed to address his heretical teachings. Jerome promised to stay in Vienna for the tribunal, but instead he escaped, and his duplicity earned him the penalty of excommunication. After a short time in hiding, Jerome returned to Prague, where he preached and taught in open disagreement with the practice of selling indulgences. This again earned him disfavor in the Bohemian capital, and he was soon again in exile, this time to Poland, where he became associated with the Ruthenians. The Polish church officials rejected him as a result, but he was neither arrested nor expelled from Poland: he left willingly upon hearing the news of Hus's appearance before the

Council of Constance. Jerome appeared in Constance, ostensibly to stand before the council himself, in April 1415. Sensing the danger that he had put himself into, Jerome attempted to escape but was caught and imprisoned there in May of the same year.

Jerome's trial and death are similar in many ways to those of Jan Hus, although there are two major differences. First, Hus fully expected to be freed and assumed that the truth of his beliefs would be authenticated, and therefore, ultimately, he went willingly to the stake in support of those beliefs. Jerome, however, recanted his statements more than once, though ultimately he recanted his retraction as well. History has seen fit to focus on Jan Hus as the leader of the reform movement in Moravia at the time, and appropriately so. Most modern scholars see Jerome as a pale substitute for the holiness and integrity of Hus. However, the two men did suffer the same fate, and they were clearly well known to one another. In fact, Hus even mentioned Jerome in his letters, referring to him as his "dear brother." The second major distinction between the two men was that Hus believed that a denial or retraction of his writings and beliefs (or any admission of heresy) would damage the future of church reform. Thus not only did he refuse to retract his beliefs, but his final days also show him to have proudly reavowed the ideas that the church found to be heretical. Jerome, however, did retract his beliefs and, sadly, wrote in a letter to the Council of Constance that not only had he been wrong, but so too had his countryman, Jan Hus. In his famous letter of retraction, he agreed that Hus was rightly condemned and executed as a heretic. Here is where Jerome's history became unusual, to a certain degree. Within a few months of his retraction, he requested an audience with the council in which he claimed that he had been compelled to retract his beliefs by force. He also restated, most strongly, his belief in the teachings of both Hus and Wyclif. His appearance before the council was recorded by Theodoric de Vrie. At the council, Jerome declared "that he had never committed a greater sin and crime than when he wrote his recantation. Never also had he so greatly regretted any sin, as he now regretted having rejected the opinions of those holy men, John Wyclif and Jan Hus, and having expressed his approval of the death of those good men."

A contemporary witness to the council, *Poggio Bracciolini, wrote of Jerome at this time: "Not only not fearing, but even seeking death, he appeared as another Cato. He was indeed a man worthy of eternal memory in men's minds." Poggio was also a witness to Jerome's trial and execution, which occurred in quick succession. He recounted in his letter the presence of Jerome at the stake, singing a hymn and requesting that his executioner light the stake before his eyes. Poggio wrote of Jerome, "Socrates did not drink the poison as willingly as this man submitted himself to the flames."

Was Jerome a coward or a brave reformer? Or was he simply a victim of the time in which he lived? It was, after all, only the generation before him in which men like Wycliff and other early reformers had been accused of heresy but not put to death. It was his misfortune, perhaps, to have lived at a time when the church could not sustain further reform from within and closed its ranks upon those who dared to speak against its monolithic power. His retraction and later denial thereof serve as examples of how a man with the mind of a philosopher and reformer could find himself, and his beliefs, facing death and annihilation as the church flexed its muscles for the last time in the medieval world.

Bibliography: Francis Lutzow, *The Life and Times of Master John Hus*, 1909/1921; Frantisek Smahel, "Jan Hus—Heretic or Patriot?" *History Today* 5, no. 40 (April 1990): 27–33; Matthew Spinka, *John Hus and the Czech Reform*, 1966.

Susannah Chewning

Jiménez de Cisneros, Francisco, (1436–1517), cardinal, was a major ecclesiastical, humanist, and political figure of Spain. Originally named Gonzalo Jiménez de Cisneros, he was of noble birth. His studies began in Alcalá and continued later in Salamanca, where he studied theology and law. When his studies were completed, he taught privately for a while, but shortly thereafter he decided to go to Rome. Though this was normally an easy journey, he was twice robbed on his trip. After a time in Rome, he returned to Spain because of the death of his father. Upon his return Jiménez de Cisneros spent some time in prison when he refused to give in to Archbishop Alonso Carrillo de Acufia's instructions to vacate a lucrative benefice. However, the stubbornness of Jiménez de Cisneros finally led the archbishop to release him. Later he was named vicar general of Sigtienza by Bishop *Pedro González de Mendoza.

In 1484 he took the vows of the Franciscan order and went to live at the Convent of San Juan de los Reyes in Toledo. At this time he changed his name to Francisco, and he tried to live the life of a hermit and walked everywhere he was sent. However, his wisdom made his attempt at a secluded life almost impossible. This is evidenced by the fact that when he was fifty-six years of age, he was summoned to the court of Queen *Isabel to be interviewed as her possible new confessor. Jiménez de Cisneros was not happy to be chosen the queen's confessor and only accepted upon the order of Cardinal González de Mendoza. Even so, Jiménez de Cisneros insisted that he should be allowed to continue to live in the Franciscan convent.

After the death of Cardinal González de Mendoza, the Catholic monarchs wanted to name Jiménez de Cisneros archbishop of Toledo. In order to ensure their efforts, the king and queen solicited the help of the pope, who issued a brief ordering him to accept. Shortly thereafter, the pope, issued another brief that ordered him to try to live a less austere life to protect his health. Outwardly, Jiménez de Cisneros tried to live a less frugal life, but in reality his daily routines did not much change. He got up before the sun did, ate whatever was available, and walked barefoot wherever he went.

In 1499 he personally baptized several thousand Moors in Granada, but to the detriment of scholarship he ordered hundreds of Moorish manuscripts burned, though at least he saved those dealing with medicine. He founded the University of Alcalá de Henares with a humanist curriculum and had the Complutensian Polyglot Bible published with Hebrew, Greek, and Latin translations in comparative columns on facing pages.

After the deaths of the queen in 1504 and King *Philip I in 1506, Jiménez de Cisneros was named as governor-general of the kingdom. As his first duty, he wrote to King *Ferdinand, who was in Italy, urging him to return. This the king did, but it took him over a year, during which time Jiménez de Cisneros essentially ruled Spain. The king in his gratitude had him made a cardinal and named him inquisitor general. Jiménez de Cisneros aided the king in the conquest of northwest Africa by leading over 20,000 troops into battle, and in 1516 he was again named regent of Spain by the last will and testament of King Ferdinand. The cardinal made the most of his regency, holding fast against usurpers and plots. Time after time, he defeated attempts at revolt, repulsed an attempt by the French in the taking of Navarre, and increased the deposits in the treasury without increasing taxes. His administration of Spain is remembered as a golden age. Besides all his accomplishments in his duties as administrator of Spain and the church, Jiménez de Cisneros was a model of virtue and humility. In fact, at one time he was nominated for canonization as a saint.

Bibliography: Jeremy N. H. Lawrence, "Humanism in the Iberian Peninsula," in *The Impact of Humanism on Western Europe*, ed. Anthony Goodman and Angus MacKay, 1990; J.P.R. Lyell, *Cardinal Ximénes, Statesman, Ecclesiastic, Soldier, and Man of Letters*, 1917; Carlos G. Noreña, *Studies in Spanish Renaissance Thought*, 1975.

Peter E. Carr

Joan Martí de Galba. *See* Galba, Joan Martí de.

Joan of Arc (c. 1412–31) (Jeanne d'Arc or "La Pucelle"). Joan of Arc was a French country girl, soldier, and visionary who rallied the demoralized French army and contributed to French victories over the English at the end of the Hundred Years' War. Joan was born near the village of Domrémy in Lorraine, France, in 1412 or 1413 to Jacques d'Arc, a well-off farmer, later dean of Domrémy, and Isabelle Romée. The region in which she lived experienced much strife during the Hundred Years' War. In 1428 Domrémy was burned by Burgundian supporters, and Joan and her family fled to Neufchâteau. Joan was taught the traditional "female" arts of spinning, weaving, and sewing. Contrary to popular belief, she only guarded sheep when her village was in danger of attack. According to contemporary accounts, she was a devout Christian. Joan claimed that heavenly voices, accompanied by bright lights, first came to her when she was thirteen, in her father's garden, when the church bells were being rung. She claimed to hear the voice of St. Michael, and later those of Sts. Margaret and Catherine. These voices commanded her to raise an army and rally the French troops to victory in support of the Dauphin *Charles (VII). After hearing the voices, Joan decided to remain a virgin and refused to marry the man her parents had selected for her. In the winter of 1429, against the strong wishes of her parents, Joan went to Vaucouleurs to see its captain, Robert de Baudricort, and persuaded him to give her a horse, men's clothing, and an armed escort to take her to the dauphin at Chinon. At Chinon, Joan allegedly picked Charles out from behind a crowd of his courtiers, and he was impressed enough to give her a knight's retinue of a page, a squire, and some troops. He sent her to Tours to be examined by a tribunal of the exiled Parlement of Paris for three weeks. Joan then left for Blois with military reinforcements—contrary to popular belief, she was not given command of the army—to join Robert Dunois, the illegitimate son of Louis d'Orléans and the captain of the French forces. Together they marched on the city of Orléans, the gateway to the south of France, to break the English siege there. During this march Joan won Dunois to her side, and he gave her his support from then on. Joan rallied the dispirited soldiers, urging them to cease their blasphemous and licentious practices and exhorting them to unite against the English and win back France for the French. After fierce fighting, Joan led the French troops to victory at Orléans on 8 May 1429, and the surviving English were forced to retreat. Following the lifting of the siege, Joan was given the command of the French army and won further victories at Jargeau, Meung-sur-Loire, Beaugency, and Patay in June 1429. Joan became immensely popular with the French people, many of whom worshipped her as a saint, although against her wishes.

Joan then demanded that Charles be crowned in Rheims Cathedral, as was traditional for French kings. She believed that once Charles was anointed, his kingship would become sacred, and God would further weaken the power of the English. Joan swiftly accomplished her goal; after riding almost completely unchallenged though Burgundian territory, on 17 July 1429 Charles VII was crowned king of France in Rheims Cathedral. Charles's coronation was as important a victory for Joan and France as her military successes were; it legitimized his paternity, sanctified his kingship, and made him the head and the symbol of a unified France. After his coronation, however, Charles signed a treaty with the duke of Burgundy, retreated toward the Loire, and disbanded the army. Infuriated, Joan tried to take Paris on 8 September 1429, in defiance of the treaty, and failed, receiving serious wounds. Her power and popularity fell, and she had trouble raising money for an army. She took St. Pierre le Moustier in October 1429 and tried to win La Charité and Lagny, but failed. Charles VII ennobled her on 29 December 1429.

At a skirmish at Compiègne on 24 May 1430, Joan was captured by an archer serving the bastard of Wandomme and given to John of Luxembourg, a vassal of the duke of Burgundy. She was imprisoned in the Castle of Beaurevoir, where she tried to escape by jumping from the window. The duke eventually sold her to the English, who turned her over to the Inquisition, in the person of *Pierre Cauchon, bishop of Beauvais. Joan was brought to Rouen around January 1431 and put on trial by the Inquisitor's Court of the Catholic church on suspicion of heresy and witchcraft. The court asserted, among other claims, that Joan's wearing men's clothing defied the biblical commandment, and that her voices were either demonic or deliberate lies. The trial involved numerous influential members of the clergy. Joan at first refused to admit to the charges, maintaining that her voices were divine and believing that Charles or Dunois would come to her rescue. No one aided her, however, and Joan began to despair of being rescued. Faced with excommunication and burning, she recanted on 24 May 1431. Joan was received back into the church and condemned to perpetual, solitary imprisonment, but withdrew her recantation several days later. She was sentenced to be burned at the stake, and her execution was carried out on 30 May 1431 at Rouen.

In 1456 a retrial was held in which Joan was acquitted of heresy and witchcraft. The French people continued to revere her, and in 1920 she was canonized by the Roman Catholic church. Joan remains to this day a compelling figure and a powerful symbol of French unity. She was not the selfless, infallible heroine that many biographers paint her; we know from contemporary accounts that she was fond of fine clothing and often reckless in her military exploits. But she was also undeniably brave in challenging her many enemies: the English army, the inquisitors, and the restrictive social conventions for women of her day. Joan of Arc was determined, devout, and defiant; her most important victory was not military but rather her power, before and after her death, to ignite the spark of nationalism in a country long torn by war and opportunism.

Bibliography: Régine Pernoud and Marie-Véronique Clin, *Joan of Arc: Her Story*, 1998; Marina Warner, *Joan of Arc: The Image of Female Heroism*, 1981.

Miriam Rheingold Fuller

João II, King of Portugal (b. 1455, r. 1481–95).

Dubbed the "Perfect Prince" by contemporaries, João II is most renowned for his active role in the commercial exploration of coastal Africa and the Orient. Under his direction, Portuguese fleets continued to explore the African coast in hopes of rupturing the trade monopoly held by Muslim middlemen. While expeditions to Africa were intended primarily to unearth gold, spices, and slaves, the effects were much more far-reaching. These ventures, begun first in 1415 and enthusiastically continued under João II, inspired the extension of European influence throughout the world.

João II was born in 1455, son of *Alfonso V of Portugal. His youth was punctuated by his father's attempts to seize the throne of Castile in the face of Aragonese opposition from *Isabel and *Ferdinand. However, in 1477, on the verge of an alliance between Portugal, France, and the papacy, Alfonso was suddenly overcome by the vanity and egotism of human politics. In a letter to his son, Alfonso announced his intention to abdicate and join a monastic order. João had little choice but to immediately declare himself king. Meanwhile, Alfonso was soon convinced of the error of his ways and was persuaded to return to Portugal. Although Alfonso's title was restored to him, actual authority remained in the capable hands of João II. He did not come into power in his own right, however, until his father's death in 1481.

His first act as king was to effect political stability in Portugal by drastically reasserting royal supremacy. Not only did João impose a new form of oath on his subjects, by which all nobles were compelled to render a written promise of fealty, but he also eliminated all of his major rivals. Contemporaries rumored that one unfortunate opponent, the duke of Viseu, was stabbed by the king's own hand in the royal apartment. Having established himself as a formidable and unmerciful monarch, João then turned to the task of Portuguese expansion.

João was not the first Portuguese monarch to express interest in the African Atlantic coast. Portuguese ambitions inspired the famed papal bull *Romanus pontifex*, granted by *Nicholas V in 1455, which conceded to the Portuguese a monopoly over all navigation and trade in the African Atlantic, and which gave the monarch the right to conquer all lands, rulers, and peoples in this region, referred to under the blanket term of "Guinea." João was the first Portuguese king to give this matter serious personal attention, and he became the self-proclaimed lord of Guinea. While these expansionist activities were clearly motivated by economic interest, papal support lent a missionary appeal to the expeditions that now followed. Not only was João successful in establishing a strong hold on Atlantic trade, he also converted a number of important African leaders to Christianity. Perhaps his most auspicious achievement, however, was in the realization of a national dream, to find a route to India by sea. In 1488 this objective was attained by one of João's explorers, *Bartolomeo Dias, who voyaged around the Cape of Good Hope, so named for the promise it gave of finding India.

As the result of a serious domestic and dynastic dispute, João passed the final fifteen years of his life separated from his wife and cousin, Leonor. This bitter dispute arose from João's decision to bring his illegitimate son, Dom Jorge, into their household with the intention of rearing him to be his heir. His wife fiercely opposed this and was not reconciled with João until he was on his deathbed, when he agreed to recognize Leonor's brother Manuel, duke of Beja, as his successor. João died in October 1495.

During his time in power, João proved himself to be a man of two minds, at once brutal and tyrannical and yet an enlightened visionary. In many ways the fifteenth century was a time of ethnocentrism and cultural insularity. Nevertheless, in 1492, when the Jews were expelled from Spain, one-third of those exiles were accepted into Portugal as settlers. Further, in Portugal's African alliances, João commanded that his people treat the African leaders as they would any other Christian prince allied to the Portuguese Crown. Whether he was primarily motivated by economics or territorial interests, João demonstrated that he was ahead of his time in his easy acceptance of cultural and ethnic diversity.

Bibliography: H. V. Livermore, *A New History of Portugal*, 1966; P. E. Russell, "White Kings on Black Kings: Rui de Pina and the Problem of Black African Sovereignty," in

Medieval and Renaissance Studies in Honour of Robert Brian Tate, ed. Ian Michael and Richard A. Cardwell, 1986: 151–63.

Sara Butler

John XXII, Pope (b. 1244?, r. 1316–34), formerly Jacques Duèze, was the second Roman pontiff to rule from Avignon. John XXII proved a strong, some-times-headstrong ruler and able administrator. He reorganized church adminis-tration and finances and tried to restore the papacy to its central position in Latin Christendom. His pontificate was troubled by a long-lasting conflict with the German emperor-elect, *Louis of Bavaria, and the Franciscan order. The fierce opposition he provoked, together with his unbridled nepotism, made him one of the most controversial popes of the century.

Jacques Duèze, born in Cahors to a wealthy shoemaker, studied Roman and canon law at Montpellier. In 1300 he became bishop of Frĕjus. In 1308 he served as chancellor to Charles II of Anjou, king of Naples, and his successor Robert. In 1310 he became bishop of Avignon, in 1312, cardinal priest of San Vitale, and in 1313, cardinal bishop of Porto. On the death of his predecessor *Clement V, the cardinals took almost two years to choose a new pontiff. The aged Jacques Duèze was seen as a viable compromise because of his advanced age, but no one could predict that this small but energetic man would live to be ninety.

Faced with an empty treasury and a corrupt clergy, John XXII set out to reorganize the church both financially and spiritually. He created new bishoprics and reorganized old ones, instituted fiscal reforms, strengthened his grip on episcopal elections and the distribution of benefices, and condemned the accu-mulation of benefices among the clergy in his bull *Execrabills* of 1317.

In the same spirit of reorganization and reform, John tried to solve the internal conflicts between the more radical Spirituals and the moderate Conventuals in the Franciscan order. After his initial bull *Quorumdam exigit* in 1317 failed to bring the more radical groups back to obedience to the Holy See, a number of the Spirituals were captured by the Inquisition and burned at the stake in Avi-gnon. In 1317 and 1318 John condemned some of the more radical groups associated with the ideals of evangelical poverty, most prominent among them the Fraticelli. The condemned heretics promptly responded by denouncing John as the Antichrist and the Roman church as the "whore of Babylon." But the Franciscan order, led by its general Michael of Cesena, rather than submitting to the pope, continued to defend the condemned Spirituals. Most of the discus-sion focused on the question whether Christ, in his life on earth, had actually possessed the goods he used or not. If the absolute poverty of Christ could be proved, the Spirituals' point of view was defensible. The doctrine of Christ's absolute poverty was asserted by the chapter of the Franciscan order at Perugia in June 1322. John subsequently returned the ownership of the order's posses-sions, titularly vested in the Holy See, to the Franciscans in the bull *Ad con-*

ditorem canonum in 1322. This superseded two earlier papal bulls, *Exiit qui seminat* (1274) and *Exivi de paradiso* (1312), which permitted the Franciscans the use of unmovable goods that were in name property of the Holy See. This revocation stirred the Conventual Franciscans, and several theologians now started arguing that the earlier papal decisions were irrevocable, an idea that ultimately would lead to the doctrine of papal infallibility. John subsequently condemned the doctrine of Christ's absolute poverty in the bull *Cum inter non-nullos* (1323) and summoned the general of the order, Michael of Cesena, to Avignon to answer for himself. A schism in the Franciscan order ensued; the part of the Franciscan order loyal to John deposed Michael as general, while a large minority of the order, including Michael himself, who fled detention in Avignon in 1328, denounced John as a heretic and allied with John's main political rival, the German emperor-elect Louis of Bavaria.

Stubborn opposition to Louis of Bavaria characterized most of John's politics with regard to the Holy Roman Empire. In 1314, after the death of Henry VII, the imperial succession was disputed between Frederick of Austria and Louis of Bavaria. Claiming that the imperial throne was vacant, John asserted his right to take over the administration of the empire and confirmed Robert of Anjou's nomination as imperial vicar in Italy. After Frederick was defeated at the Battle of Mühldorf in 1322, Louis began to affirm his rights over the empire, appointed his own imperial vicar, and claimed his rights in Italy by supporting John's Ghibelline enemies there. The conflict heightened when John excommunicated Louis in 1324 and Louis denounced John as a heretic because of his position on Christ's poverty. In 1328 Louis made a triumphal entry into the city of Rome, had himself acclaimed emperor by the Roman populace, denounced "that priest Jacques Duèze, who calls himself Pope John XXII," and had him replaced with a Franciscan, Peter of Corbara, who chose the papal name Nicholas V. But Louis had reached the limits of his Italian power, and outbursts of Guelf violence forced him to retreat from Italy in 1330. The antipope Nicholas abdicated and humbly submitted himself to John's authority in Avignon, where he was eventually pardoned. The conflict between the papacy and Louis of Bavaria would not be resolved until 1346.

The main goal of John's Italian policy was to ensure a return of the papacy to Rome by establishing a strong Guelf alliance with Robert of Anjou and the city of Florence against the Ghibellines. He made Cardinal Bertrand du Poujet his mediator in Italian politics. His attempts to establish John of Bohemia as papal vassal over a Lombard kingdom in northern Italy ended in failure. Guelf and Ghibellines united against the pope, and eventually, in 1334, Bertrand du Poujet was chased from Bologna. As a return of the papacy to Rome became increasingly unlikely, John started to strengthen the position of Avignon as the papal see, enlarging the episcopal palace to suit his needs.

While John stimulated the role of the Inquisition in the fight against heresy (the condemnations of John of Pouilly in 1321, Peter John Olivi in 1326, and

*Meister Johann Eckhart in 1329 attest to this), his own orthodoxy was being increasingly questioned during the last years of his life. In a sermon on All Saints' Day 1331, and in several other sermons shortly thereafter, John denied that the souls of the saints in heaven were directly admitted to the beatific vision of the essence of God, and declared that the souls separated from the body could not enjoy the beatific vision before they received a glorified body at the Last Judgment. Toward the end of 1332 the subject was bitterly debated at the main European universities. The strongest opposition against John came from the Franciscans at the court of Louis of Bavaria and from the Dominican order, who defended the orthodoxy of Thomas Aquinas, whose theological opinions John here seemed to contradict. John died on 3 December 1334 before a final papal decision could be made to settle the conflict. His successor *Benedict XII ended the conflict with the bull *Benedictus Deus*, which rejected John's original opinion.

Bibliography: Guillaume Mollat, *The Popes at Avignon, 1305–1378*, 1963; Yves Renouard, *The Avignon Papacy, 1305–1403*, 1970.

Frans A. van Liere

John Capistrano, Saint (1385/86–1456),

was one of the "four pillars" of the Observant movement of the Order of Friars Minor along with St. *Bernardino of Siena, Albert of Sarteano, and St. James of the March. He also was instrumental in turning back Ottoman forces at Belgrade in 1456.

John was born into an aristocratic family in Capistrano on 24 June 1385 or 1386. He led an uneventful life through early adulthood as a lawyer and governor of Perugia, known for his integrity, intelligence, and fidelity to his patrons. His main weakness was vanity, primarily about his hair. The turning point of his life came in 1416. While he was imprisoned by forces at war with Perugia, he had two dreams of St. Francis calling him to join the Order of Friars Minor. In the second dream he accepted his fate and awoke with his once-magnificent hair shorn, and it was said that thereafter he never needed another tonsure. Soon after this conversion, John was released from prison. He had married that same year, but apparently the union had not been consummated, and so John obtained dispensation and took vows as a Franciscan Observant on 4 October 1416.

The Observance was a reform movement within the Order of Friars Minor. Observants believed that the vow of poverty and the mission to preach were the most important aspects of Francis's directives, and that the order, as represented by the Conventuals, had veered from that mission by becoming more concerned with property and doctrine. Conventuals believed that they were more obedient to the church, while Observants felt that they were truer to the ideals of Francis. Observants were usually more popular with the laity. They took pains to reach out to laypeople, their example of voluntary poverty had enormous appeal, and they boasted a number of charismatic preachers, including John Capistrano.

John traveled through much of Europe, preaching, writing, and establishing

Observant communities. He preached against the evils he perceived where he visited, and he often inspired the populace to make changes. He often used himself as an example of one who had reformed. His targets were not only corrupt officials, however; he also opposed Jews and Christians intermingling and urged that Jews be separated or expelled from communities. He wrote numerous treatises on dogma, canon law, theology, and issues surrounding the Franciscan order. Observants were often criticized for their lack of learning, and John sought to show that Observants could be both scholars and preachers. John became prominent in the Franciscan hierarchy for his efforts and often served as a diplomat in church matters.

In 1451 Holy Roman Emperor *Frederick III invited John to his realm. John spent about five years in northern and eastern Europe, preaching, establishing convents, and, in the last years of his life, crusading against Muslim invaders. After the fall of Constantinople, most Christian European territories were embroiled in other conflicts or were more concerned with protecting economic ties to the Ottomans. John thus had trouble finding crusading fighters, but he persisted. During Lent 1456, as the Ottomans under Mehmed II prepared to attack Belgrade, John preached daily in Buda and, when he felt that he had enough crusaders, led them to the battle scene. János Hunyadi, a Hungarian lord, had also been gathering forces, and so the two armies comprised the main defenders of Belgrade. When the battle was joined on 21 July, John accompanied the soldiers to urge them on. The Hungarian forces drove back the Ottomans, a victory that halted the Turkish advance into eastern Europe. John's biographers often credit him as the major force in the victory, but while his motivation was certainly crucial to his crusaders' success, Hunyadi's military skill was likely the more decisive factor. The victors paid a heavy price, however, as John and Hunyadi both fell victim to a plague that afflicted Belgrade. John lingered for more than two months before succumbing on 23 October 1456.

Though St. John Capistrano was intolerant toward nonbelievers, his commitment to his faith and abhorrence of hypocrisy inspired him to conduct his life in the same manner he urged others to follow. He made a vital contribution to the Observant cause with his preaching, his writings, and the houses he founded, and his participation in the defense of Belgrade was important in the balance of power in Europe.

Bibliography: John Hofer, *St. John Capistran: Reformer*, 1947; John Moorman, *A History of the Franciscan Order*, 1968.

Susanne Breckenridge

John of Fordun. *See* Fordun, John of.

John of Gaunt, (1340–99), duke of Lancaster and Aquitaine, earl of Derby, Lincoln, and Leicester, high seneschal of England, and titular sovereign of Castile and Léon, was the fourth and favorite son of King *Edward III of England

(r. 1327–77) and the uncle of *Richard II (r. 1377–99). The marriages and actions of his progeny by three wives made him the direct forefather and common ancestor of the future English (Lancastrian, Yorkist, and Tudor), Portuguese, and Spanish dynasties. Born in the town of Ghent (hence "Gaunt"), this intelligent and capable man, friend of *Geoffrey Chaucer and patron of *John Wyclif, loomed large in the politics of late-fourteenth-century western Europe.

Overshadowed in his youth by his eldest brother *Edward of Woodstock, the Black Prince of Wales (d. 1376), Lancaster spent much of his youth participating in the prince's campaigns in Aquitaine, Spain, and Calais. One such action occurred in 1370, when by his father's orders he took charge of affairs in Aquitaine in order to put down a rebellion and French invasion, sacking the city of Limoges in the process. A year earlier, the Black Prince's policies in Iberia had failed miserably when the English ally Pedro I, "the Cruel," had been assassinated by his illegitimate pro-French half brother Enrique of Trastámara, who proceeded to raid Gascony. To combat French control of Castile, Lancaster, whose first wife Blanche (the mother of Henry Bolingbroke, later *Henry IV) had died in 1369, agreed to marry Pedro's daughter and sole heir Constance in 1371, thereby elevating John of Gaunt to the thrones of Castile and León, albeit in exile. Lancaster's military exploits continued in 1373 with the so-called Grand Chevauchée, an incredible thousand-mile march from Calais to Bordeaux that inflicted great devastation across northern France. Still, because the French wisely refused to offer battle, it resulted in little military gain and indeed became a source of criticism among contemporaries who had expected glorious victories. After this experience, Lancaster, concluding that continued war with France was futile, began to support the idea of peace and later became one of the leading proponents of peace negotiations in 1374–75.

Meanwhile, in the 1370s John Wyclif (d. 1384), an Oxford theologian, entered Lancaster's service, later earning the duke a reputation for anticlericalism and tolerance of unorthodoxy. As the decade progressed, Wyclif grew increasingly radical and heterodox, ultimately condemning the church's wealth, papal authority, and the sacramental system, even as Lancaster became the political opponent of several powerful bishops, including *William of Wykeham of Winchester and William Courtenay of London. In 1377 Lancaster, angry at Wykeham, who had cultivated rumors questioning his legitimacy, protected Wyclif from the bishop's machinations. Yet it is certain that the duke did not agree with Wyclif's more extreme positions, and indeed he defended established institutions and repudiated the Lollards (Wyclif's followers) in 1383 despite the fact that he continued to shield the theologian from ecclesiastical justice. Ironically, the duke used Wyclif to humiliate the church, though the theologian himself called for renewed ecclesiastical strength and purity.

In the later 1370s Lancaster assumed the leading role in government as his father and brother began to experience health problems. Lancaster presided at the "Good" Parliament of 1376, becoming suddenly unpopular as he defended his father's policies. Stung by accusations of overweening ambition, bribery, and corruption, spread in part by the increasingly suspicious Black Prince, Lancaster avenged himself and his father by imprisoning some of the most outspoken critics. Embroiled in court politics following the death of the Black Prince in 1376, the duke held the reins of government, although he was countermanded by his ailing father on several occasions. While many contemporaries believed that he had designs on the Crown, Lancaster emphasized his loyalty to the ten-year-old Prince Richard. Meanwhile the "Packed" Parliament of 1377 met without securing the unity Lancaster sought, and he was later attacked by mobs in London, in part inspired by the growing enmity between the duke and the bishops. Despite this campaign of character assassination, Lancaster employed his power to bolster the position of his nephew when he might well have ambitiously fostered his own candidacy.

The death of Edward III meant the succession of Richard II, still a minor, in 1377. The duke, diminished in political stature and popularly reviled, continued to act as his nephew's protector. French raids on the Channel coastline prompted his erstwhile enemies to beseech his martial leadership, but Lancaster's minimal competence as a general ensured few positive results and even more unpopularity for himself. The Peasants' Revolt of 1381 revealed the full extent of Lancaster's unpopularity, for the commoners targeted and sacked his London palace and forced pilgrims in Kent to swear no allegiance to any king named John, yet few of the duke's own manors rebelled even as the duke fled to Scotland. Following the revolt, Lancaster withdrew from court politics as his relationship with Richard II grew increasingly tense, the young king having been influenced by court factions hoping to thwart the political power of his royal uncles. In 1386 the duke left England to pursue his ambitions in Iberia, leading a force partially funded by Parliament. Allying his house to Portugal through the marriage of his eldest daughter Philippa to King João I, Lancaster conquered Galicia but failed to defeat King Juan I of Castile. Abandoning his fruitless claims, Lancaster sealed a peace treaty by marrying his daughter Catherine to Juan's son and heir Enrique.

Meanwhile, Richard II faced a deepening crisis in Lancaster's absence in the form of parliamentary criticism and aristocratic rebellion. Having been defeated by the great magnates, Richard had no choice but to submit to the 1388 "Merciless" Parliament and the Lords Appellant, among whom was Lancaster's son Henry Bolingbroke. The duke returned to England at Richard's behest in the following year and helped to restore the young king's independence. In return for his aid, Lancaster received the Duchy of Aquitaine, but he faced stout Gascon resistance against tighter English rule. Despite his frequent military campaigns, the duke employed his renewed royal influence to involve himself in negotiations with France, finally securing peace in 1396 by Richard's marriage to *Charles VI's daughter Isabelle.

The events of 1397 sorely tested Lancaster's solid support for the king. The assassination of the duke of Gloucester and the arrest of other aristocrats were accompanied in 1398 by the banishment of Lancaster's son Henry Bolingbroke, a sentence that the duke himself as seneschal of England pronounced. Yet Lancaster secured from the unsteady king both the legitimation of the Beaufort line and Henry Bolingbroke's inheritance of the Lancastrian estate, which at that time amounted to nearly one-third of England. John of Gaunt's death in 1399 and Richard's subsequent seizure of the Lancastrian inheritance led to Henry Bolingbroke's invasion of England and the usurpation of the Crown, sowing the seeds of England's fifteenth-century dynastic turmoil. The duke of Lancaster proved himself an able and ambitious politician who, through his prolific marriages if not his martial prowess, exerted unquantifiable influence on the futures of several kingdoms.

Bibliography: Anthony Goodman, *John of Gaunt: The Exercise of Princely Power in Fourteenth-Century Europe*, 1992; Nigel Saul, *Richard II*, 1997; Simon Walker, *The Lancastrian Affinity, 1361–1399*, 1990.

James C. Owens

John of Jandun (c. 1285/89–1328). Often understood as a representative of "radical Aristotelianism" or "Latin Averroism," John of Jandun was among the most influential Aristotelian commentators of the later Middle Ages. Jandun's espousals of such doctrines as the *sensus agens*, the unity of the intellect, and the necessary immobility of the earth reflected less a slavish devotion to either Aristotle or Averroës than a dedication to solving philosophical problems philosophically, as much in line with faith as possible but without recourse to faith as an explanatory principle. Jandun is perhaps most famous for his association with his friend *Marsiglio of Padua's *Defensor pacis*, a radical challenge to papal authority, the publication of which forced them both to flee to the court of *Louis of Bavaria.

Little is known of Jandun's early life. He was born in the town of Jandun in Champagne and matriculated at the University of Paris in the first decade of the fourteenth century, receiving his *magisterium* (masters) in the arts in 1310. In the same year he produced his first work, *De sensu agente* (On the active principle of the sensitive soul), in which he argued for the unpopular position that human beings are able to perceive sensible objects by means of an active principle in the senses themselves (the *sensus agens*), rather than simply by receiving sensible species passively. In 1315 he was appointed a master of the new College of Navarre (later renowned for its "nominalism" and humanism), in the same year completing an investigation of Aristotle's *Physics*. By this time he had certainly made the acquaintance of Marsiglio of Padua, who was rector at Paris in 1313. In 1316 he received a canonry at Senlis from Pope *John XXII, primarily for financial support. Jandun continued writing, finishing a series of *quaestiones* on Aristotle's *De anima* in 1318 and his *In Praise of Paris* in 1323, among other works.

Jandun's life took a major turn with the publication of his friend Marsiglio of Padua's *Defensor pacis* in 1324. The treatise seriously undermined papal authority, subordinating the pope to the emperor. In 1326 Pope John XXII issued the first in a series of bulls attacking the work and its doctrines, whereupon Jandun and Marsiglio fled for protection to emperor-elect Louis of Bavaria. When in 1327 John XXII condemned and excommunicated Jandun and Marsiglio, Jandun had already become close to Louis, traveling as part of his retinue. In May 1328 Louis appointed Jandun bishop of Ferrara, and in July he received him formally into the court as a counselor. On 31 August 1328 John of Jandun died at Todi, probably en route to Ferrara.

Philosophically, Jandun was determined to understand Aristotle on his own terms, and he considered Averroës the best guide for doing so. Jandun's commentaries on Aristotle were highly influential, especially in northern Italy, and were still being read in the seventeenth century. Nevertheless, his dedication to the philosopher did not prevent him from filling in perceived gaps in Aristotle's system. Thus, following Averroës, Jandun argued for a separate, unified human intellect, through which particular human beings know universals. In an Aristotelian-Augustinian synthesis, Jandun also insisted that the soul must play an active part in sensation, which it does by means of the *sensus agens*, a power of the sensitive soul that renders potential sensible species actual. While Jandun, like Siger of Brabant, has been accused of espousing a "double-truth" theory, there are no grounds for believing Jandun to have held such a theory.

Bibliography: Stuart MacClintock, *Perversity and Error*, 1956; A. Pattin, *Pour l'histoire du sens agent: La controverse entre Barthélemy de Bruges et Jean de Jandun: Ses antécédents et son évolution*, 1988.

Jeffrey Fisher

John of Ragusa (d. 1443), born John Stojkovic, a native of Ragusa, entered the Dominican order early in life and went on to become a respected theologian. In 1420 he became master of theology at the University of Paris. Thereafter, John was very active in church politics. In 1423, when Pope Martin V was forced to assemble the Council of Pavia-Siena, John attended as the university's legate. After the required lapse of seven years, Martin V called the Council of Basel in 1431. Unfortunately, Martin died on 20 February 1431 before the council officially opened, leaving behind a vast agenda. Thus, when the council opened on 23 July 1431, chaos reigned as the delegates were faced with large and pressing issues such as church reform, the relationship between the pope and the council, the question of reunion with the Greek Orthodox church, and the Hussite wars. The new pope, *Eugenius IV, was kept out of most negotiations.

John was singled out for prominence during the Hussite negotiations. As a close confidant of the powerful cardinal Giuliano Cesarini, John, along with two other theologians, traveled to the court of King *Sigismund to ready him for an anticipated Hussite revolt. Furthermore, as a native Croatian who possessed an excellent knowledge of Hussite writings, John quickly became the council's expert on Hussite affairs.

John continued to be a major player in the Council of Basel. It was primarily due to his persistence and obstinacy that no concessions to the Hussites were even considered. Also at his urging, the council reorganized itself. Instead of the organization by nation that had been employed at the Council of Constance, the second session beginning on 15 February 1432 found four new divisions that represented all nations, and each of which concerned itself with a specific issue.

Although John was at first considered indispensable to the council, it was his failure to consider concessions that ruined the negotiations in 1431. As time passed, he grew more and more volatile. On 31 January 1432 John received his long-desired opportunity to respond to the continuing Hussite agitation. His initial speech was venomous, and his ensuing sermons became so vitriolic that other prominent theologians began avoiding them. Cardinal Cesarini protected him and used his influence to allow John to continue unchecked for four days; however, even the cardinal could not protect him forever. After four days the council finally succeeded in restraining him from further public speaking, and it was later admitted that his behavior had been highly improper. He was eventually replaced at the council by Juan Palomar of Spain.

After this disturbing sequence of events, John was sent to Constantinople to negotiate with the Greeks, where he appears to have been better placed. He was the official legate to the Council of Constantinople in 1435 and 1437. The remainder of John's career and life is indeterminate. Some accounts have him made bishop of Ardijsek in 1438 and raised to the cardinalate in 1440, both at the initiative of Felix V. Other accounts show him remaining faithful to Eugenius IV, who created him bishop of Argos.

Some of John's writings survive, including his incomplete history of the Council of Basel and a theological discourse, *De communione sub utraque specie*, against the Hussites. He was also responsible for the preservation of a large number of Greek manuscripts that he collected while he was in Constantinople and willed to the Dominicans at Basel.

Bibliography: F. M. Bartos, *The Hussite Revolution, 1424–1437*, 1986; Joachim W. Stieber, *Pope Eugenius IV, the Council of Basel and the Secular and Ecclesiastical Authorities in the Empire*, 1978.

Michelle M. Sauer

Juan II, King of Castile (b. 1406, r. 1419–54). Juan II was a member of the Trastámara dynasty that ruled Castile in the fourteenth and fifteenth centuries. He inherited the throne from his father, Enrique III (who died at the young age of twenty-seven), at the age of two. As a result, the rule of Spain fell to the coregency of his mother, Catherine of Lancaster, and his uncle Fernando.

When he came into his majority in 1419, Juan's reign was characterized by political intrigue, and he was besieged on all sides. The sons of his uncle, Fernando, known as the infantes, sought to control various parts of the peninsula throughout his rule. He also fought battles with the Castilian nobility, whose loyalties were constantly shifting. Finally, his own son, *Enrique IV, was an unreliable ally at best who frequently refused to come to his father's aid in conflicts involving the recalcitrant infantes.

Although the early years of the coregency were mostly quite peaceful, intrigue began to evolve when Fernando was elected king of Aragon. Having gained control of this significantly powerful region, Fernando and his children worked to expand their power base. By the time Juan achieved his majority, his cousins presented serious obstacles to his consolidation of power. When Fernando's son Alfonso (later *Alfonso V, known as "the Magnanimous") inherited his title in Aragon, for example, he worked assiduously to increase his influence and in due course acquired the throne of Naples. In Castile, Fernando's other sons, Juan and Enrique, were enormously powerful members of the nobility and, in rivalry with each other, challenged the young king's authority in Castile. In 1420 Enrique even stormed the royal palace and took the king prisoner, although Juan eventually escaped.

When Juan acceded to the throne in his own right, he entrusted much of the governance of Castile to his "favorite," Don *Álvaro de Luna. Luna seemingly counseled Juan to preserve the power and prerogatives of the monarch and to avoid dispensing too many of these among the nobility, who in the late medieval period always sought greater control of the instruments of government. In practice, this meant that Luna had considerable power since Juan was a notoriously weak-willed ruler who ceded many responsibilities to his trusted advisor. Luna's attacks against Alfonso and his brothers led to the declaration of a truce between Aragon and Castile in 1430. From here Luna moved on to campaigns against the Islamic kingdom in the south of Spain, which met with only limited success.

Luna, however, consistently attracted the criticism of the Castilian nobility, who disparaged his undue influence over the king. Beginning in 1439, under pressure from the infantes and the Castilian nobility, Juan banished Luna from the court several times. Each time, however, Luna retrenched and Juan's government faltered under his shaky leadership, resulting in Luna's return to service.

Ultimately, however, Luna could not overcome the machinations of two sets of rivals. The first was Juan's son, Enrique. Enrique had made a powerful alliance with his own "favorite," Juan Pacheco, and together they worked toward Luna's downfall. Additionally, Juan's second wife, Isabel of Portugal, was determined to undermine Luna's power. The combined force of these two factions and Luna's own unwillingness to retire until the conflict subsided led to his death in 1453. Juan had him arrested and tried as a traitor. He was found guilty of usurping royal power and acting as a tyrant. He was ordered beheaded, and in June 1453, in the main plaza of Valladolid, he was executed. Although it occurred under his orders, Juan was deeply disturbed by this event and died the next year.

Beyond the political intrigue of his reign, Juan II should be recognized for his unflinching support of the papacy during the conciliarist battles of the fifteenth century. He made *Rodrigo Sánchez de Arévalo his ambassador to the papacy and various Royal courts in this cause.

Bibliography: Jocelyn N. Hillgarth, *The Spanish Kingdoms, 1250–1516*, 1976; Joseph F. O'Callaghan, *A History of Medieval Spain*, 1983.

Elizabeth Lehfeldt

Juana of Castile (1462–1530), commonly called "La Beltraneja." The rightful heir to the Castilian throne in the late fifteenth century, Juana is best known for losing her inheritance to her more politically keen aunt, *Isabel I (later Isabel I of Spain, 1474–1504), one of the most notorious queens in Spanish history.

Juana of Castile was born to King *Enrique IV and Queen Juana in February 1462. Even before Enrique ("the Impotent") died, Isabel and her faithful supporters sought to raise doubts about Juana's birth. The legitimacy of her claim to the throne was publicly questioned as Isabel and her supporters insisted that Juana was not Enrique's own child but was instead the daughter of the king's principal minister, *Beltrán de la Cueva. Accordingly, she was saddled with the infamous nickname "la Beltraneja." Although Enrique had proclaimed her his sole heir to the throne of Castile, Juana saw her inheritance pass first to Enrique's half brother Alfonso (who died in 1468) before being snatched by Isabel.

At Enrique's death in 1474, Isabel forestalled Juana's accession to the Castilian throne by taking advantage of her niece's youth and lack of strong political support at court. After a hasty coronation with her consort, *Ferdinand of Aragon (later Ferdinand of Spain, 1474–1516), Isabel declared herself the rightful queen of Castile, shutting Juana off from her birthright. A civil war ensued between those who supported Juana and those who favored Isabel for the throne of Castile. Juana, only twelve years old at the time, managed to gain several powerful allies, including Afonso Carrillo (the archbishop of Toledo), Juan Pacheco (the marquis of Villena), and *Alfonso V of Portugal, whom she married in 1475. Juana also found support among important Castilian nobles who were wary of the Castilian-Aragonese alliance brought by Isabel's marriage to Ferdinand. Isabel commanded the greater support, however, finding allies across Old Castile, Andalusia, New Castile, and eventually even Portugal. Only Navarre, on the French border, and Granada, a Moorish stronghold, did not offer Isabel some assistance in her struggle to remain the queen of Castile permanently.

The civil war raged from 1474 to 1479. In this period Isabel, who had greater access to arms, wealth, and supplies than did Juana, steadily gained the upper hand. The war turned favorably for Isabel in 1476 when Ferdinand's army defeated the Portuguese forces commanded by Alfonso at the Battle of Toro in Extremadura. This defeat diminished support for Juana in Castile and lessened her viability as queen. Three years later the Treaty of Alcaçoras ended the civil war in 1479. The peace agreement reaffirmed the long-standing alliance between Portugal and Castile and forced Alfonso to recognize Isabel as queen of Castile officially and to deny his own wife's claim to that throne. The combined effects of her inexperienced youth, the aspersions cast on her legitimacy, and the strength of the factions arrayed against her ultimately cost Juana her rightful inheritance.

Soon after she was disinherited officially, Juana entered Santa Clara de Santarm, a Portuguese convent, in 1479. She took her vows a year later before Fray Fernando do Talavera, Isabel's favored confessor. For the remainder of her life Juana spent half her time in different convents and half in different Portuguese palaces. By some accounts, Juana never accepted her lost inheritance, still referring to herself as "Yo la Reina," or "I, the Queen," until she died in 1530.

Bibliography: Stephen Haliczer, *The "Comuneros" of Castile: The Forging of a Revolution, 1475–1521,* 1981; Nancy Rubin, *Isabella of Castile: The First Renaissance Queen,* 1991.

Susanna Calkins

Juan de Avignon. *See* Avignon, Juan de.

Juan de Mena. *See* Mena, Juan de.

Juan de Torquemada. *See* Torquemada, Juan de.

Juliana of Norwich (1343–c. 1416) was an important medieval mystic in fourteenth-century England. As an anchoress, Juliana experienced a series of sixteen revelations or "shewings," which were the foundation of her writings. Not much is known of Juliana of Norwich's early life. Her real name is not even known, but the name Juliana probably was chosen by her when she entered the anchorhold at St. Julian's Church in Norwich. She was even thought to have been a Benedictine nun. Not only is her original name unknown, her birth date is also obscure, although 1343 was likely the year of her birth. She referred to herself as someone who was "unlettered" (which meant that she did not know Latin) and "lewd" (ignorant), but she did have considerable knowledge of the Bible and some of the religious classics of her time.

The city of Norwich was considered an intellectual center in late medieval England, and this could have aided Juliana in her quest for knowledge. Juliana was born into an era that endured the ravages of the Black Death, experienced the schism of the papacy after 1377, and saw the material and social devastation of the Peasants' Revolt in 1381. Juliana also lived in a time when the Lollards, the followers of *John Wyclif, were preaching their heretical opinions across the kingdom. The Lollards wrote in English, not Latin, a practice followed by Juliana herself, but probably from ignorance of that learned tongue and not from adherence to Lollard teachings.

In 1373 Juliana experienced a series of sixteen revelations or "shewings" that proved to her that she was "blessed with a sequence of visions revealing God's love for humanity." The title of the book that emerged from these experiences was *Sixteen Revelations of Divine Love*. The revelations were based on the Passion of Christ and were seen by Juliana in a threefold sequence, including "a bodily vision followed by words formed in her understanding and thirdly by the means of a spiritual vision." There were different degrees of her "shewings," but they all acted as a "vehicle for spiritual content."

The recluse or anchoress was not something original in fourteenth-century England. In order to become an anchoress, a woman had to have permission from the bishop, and once she was enclosed, she was not permitted to leave her anchorhold. Such anchoresses had to offer almost continuous prayers and often acted as counselors to people who needed spiritual advice. One of Juliana's well-known visitors was *Margery Kempe, reputedly a mystic herself.

One of the main characteristics of the female mystics in England was the strange requirement for sickness, especially physical illness. For Juliana of Norwich, "the more spite, shame and reproof you suffer in this world, the greater is your merit in the eyes of God." When Juliana turned thirty years old on 8 May 1373, she had an experience that could have been attributed to a serious illness, for which she had been praying. She did not want to die from this illness, but she wanted to know what it was like to suffer and experience agony as had Christ. Along with the illness she had a vision, which proved to be the first in a series of mystical "shewings."

In the "shewings" she explained the three graces that she desired: (1) to have a recollection of Christ's Passion; (2) bodily sickness; and (3) three wounds. When she was explaining her desire for the first grace, she thought that she might imitate the divine sufferings of Jesus. When she desired bodily sickness, she was reminded that she was human and that she would come very close in such a vision to death. When she was wishing for the third grace, she sought to emulate St. Cecilia and her three fatal wounds, which corresponded to "the wound of contrition, the wound of compassion, and the wound of longing with my will for God." Soon after her initial visions in 1373 she began recording her experiences and then added to them over the course of the next twenty years.

Her writings focused on her mystical revelations and their meaning for her own spirituality and the religious experience of late medieval England. Dame Juliana of Norwich died around 1416 or 1417 at the age of seventy-three. She was never canonized, but a Juliana of Norwich Day was eventually entered into the Church of England calendar. Today, her works and ideas are considered important milestones in the female mystical tradition of medieval England.

Bibliography: Frances Beer, *Women and Mystical Experience in the Middle Ages*, 1992; Monica Furlong, *Visions and Longings: Medieval Women Mystics*, 1996.

Karen Holleran

K

Kaysersberg, Johan Geiler. *See* Geiler von Kaysersberg, Johan.

Kempe, Margery (c. 1373–1438), was an English mystic, pilgrim, author, and businesswoman. Margery Kempe is best known today for her *Book*, an autobiographical account of her spiritual life, and for her extremely unconventional manner of affective piety and religious enthusiasm.

Margery was born around 1373 in the city of King's Lynn in Norfolk, England, to John Burnham, a prosperous burgher, who was mayor of the city five times and a member of Parliament six times. Margery was married at about age twenty to John Kempe, also a prominent citizen of King's Lynn. She had a child in the first year of her marriage; the pregnancy was difficult, and the birth nearly killed her. Shortly thereafter, in fear for her immortal soul, she tried to confess a sin that she had had on her conscience for a long time, but was sharply chastised by the priest and was unable to confess. Her reaction to this led to a mental breakdown, lasting over half a year, from which she was cured by a vision of Christ, the first of many such visions. Margery resumed her domestic duties, resolving to serve God, but still showed many signs of pride and worldliness. She wore fine clothes, bragged about her family, and told her husband that her family was superior to his. She started two businesses, a brewery and a mill, both of which failed; she later attributed these failures to divine punishment for her pride.

Margery then experienced the conversion that led to the turning point in her spiritual career. While she was in bed with her husband, she heard a melody so sweet that she jumped out of bed, exclaiming, "It is full merry in Heaven." From that moment she abhorred sexual relations with her husband, although she continued to bear him children (fourteen in all), and she performed strict religious observances such as fasting, wearing a hairshirt, and rising early in the morning to attend church services. During this period she also began weeping copiously and loudly in sorrow for her own sins and those of others, as well as when she was contemplating Christ's Passion or the sorrows of the Virgin Mary. She was condemned for her piety, as well as for her loud weeping, and was accused variously of drunkenness, insanity, and hypocrisy, but she continued in her devotions, receiving assurances from Christ that he would exalt her more than others had despised her. Margery wrote in her *Book* that Christ also gave her instructions on how to live her life, commanding her to be a mirror for other Christians through her behavior and to save as many souls as possible through her weeping and praying for them. When she was about forty, Margery obtained her husband's consent to live chastely in return for her paying his debts and eating meat with him on Fridays. It was at about this time that Margery began visiting various clergymen and other religious figures to obtain spiritual counsel, and with a few exceptions, most of the higher clergy approved her meditations and her tears. *Philip Repyngdon, the bishop of Lincoln, urged her to write down her visions and gave her money to purchase white clothing and a silver ring, which Christ had instructed her to wear. *Juliana of Norwich approved her vocation of living piously within the world. Margery also obtained from the archbishop of Canterbury special permission to receive weekly Communion, an important privilege for a layperson that carried with it implicit approval of Margery's unconventional "vocation." Margery gave as well as received counsel, telling a number of clergymen that they (or their households) were living impious lives and needed to reform.

In 1413 Margery started on a pilgrimage to Jerusalem. Her companions were disturbed by her copious weeping and continual talk of the gospel and abandoned her several times; however, she received help from several church officials, including the papal legate of Constance. Margery arrived in Jerusalem in the spring or summer of 1414 and, while visiting Mount Calvary, first experienced the violent screaming and physical contortions that would visit her over the next ten years whenever she meditated on Christ's Passion or the Virgin's sorrows. Margery proceeded to Rome, where she was alternately reviled and reverenced for her piety and her frequent emotional outbursts. She returned to England in 1415 and in 1417 made a pilgrimage to St. James of Compostella in Spain.

Before and after this last pilgrimage, Margery was brought before several ecclesiastical courts, at Worcester, Leicester, and York, on charges of heresy and Lollardy, the latter charge probably arising because of her outspoken enthusiasm and love of the Scriptures. She was examined on the Articles of Faith and found innocent of the charges against her on each occasion, ostensibly because of her strict adherence to church doctrine, but possibly also because she was the daughter of such a prominent man. Her encounter with the archbishop of York is particularly noteworthy, as she defied his order to stop teaching in his district, upholding her right to practice her vocation. On her return home she suffered from various intestinal ailments for over eight years, though she continued to receive visions, teach, and experience ecstatic fits. Although many of her neighbors advised her to leave King's Lynn, others came to her for advice and asked her to pray for them. She began dictating her *Book* around 1430. In 1434 she journeyed to Germany and then to the Baltic, and she died in King's Lynn around 1438.

Margery Kempe, unconventional, often disturbing in the excesses of her devotion, presents a compelling alternative to the quiet, secluded piety of many medieval women mystics. Her candor, bravery, and spirit are refreshing and commendable. Her *Book*, the first autobiography in English, is an impressive legacy, giving us a striking account of Margery's life and her vivid visions, in which she participated in the events of Christ's and the Virgin's lives, and a firsthand account of late medieval urban life and pilgrimages.

Bibliography: Clarissa W. Atkinson, *Mystic and Pilgrim: The Book and the World of Margery Kempe*, 1983; Caroline Walker Bynum, *Jesus as Mother*, 1982; Margery Kempe, *The Book of Margery Kempe*, ed. Sanford B. Meech and Hope Emily Allen, 1940.

Miriam Rheingold Fuller

Kempis, Thomas à. *See* Thomas à Kempis.

Knighton, Henry (c. 1315–1396?). Not much is known about the life of the English Augustinian canon Henry Knighton, but his chronicle, written at St. Mary's Abbey in Leicester between approximately 1379 and 1396 provides a significant record of national and local events during the last quarter of the fourteenth century and was informed by the author's strong opinions. The chronicle survives in two manuscript copies in the British Library, Tiberius C. VII and Claudius E. III, neither of which has been established as authorial. Written in Latin, with French and English additions, it covers the period from just before the Norman Conquest up to 1396, incorporates various sources, and relies on other chronicles, most notably *Ranulf Higden's *Polychronicon*, for the earliest material.

Knighton was well placed to witness important events of the late fourteenth century. Leicestershire was a center of Lollard activity because of *John Wyclif's presence as the rector of Lutterworth. Although Knighton seems to have been a strong anti-Lollard, he was also quite scornful of the popular preacher William Swinderby, whose sermons, expressing a traditional denunciation of the female sex, incited local women to drive him out of town. Knighton was an unreserved admirer of William Clowne, abbot of St. Mary's from 1345 to 1377. Knighton praised him for his wisdom and virtue and for increasing the wealth of the abbey, noting that Clowne's famous hunting parties with *Edward III and his lords were an important means of gaining their support.

Since Leicester was the seat of the house of Lancaster, Knighton treated with considerable respect the able and pious Henry of Grosmont, earl and first duke of Lancaster, and his son-in-law, *John of Gaunt. The martial deeds of Henry received attention as Knighton recorded Edward III's progress in his campaigns in France during the Hundred Years' War. Knighton supported Edward's invasion of France, noting for 1346 that if Edward had not crossed the Channel, the French would have come to England. Always ready to admire Edward's strategy in individual battles, after giving a factual account of the Battle of Sluys (1340), Knighton proudly asserted that victory was due to English prowess as well as Christ's support. Knighton provided insight into the combination of pious idealism and pragmatic militarism of contemporary knighthood. Thus he recorded Henry accepting as a present from the king of France a thorn from Christ's crown, which he gave to the collegiate church he endowed at Newarke, Leicester. Knighton also recounted that when the siege of Toulouse was halted in 1350 because the enemy refused to fight, Henry inspired terror during the subsequent pillaging of the countryside.

Knighton attended to the peacetime exploits of chivalry, and even though he was shocked by the behavior of men and women at tournaments, he provided lively descriptions of such festivities. The year 1348 found Knighton denouncing the women who attended tournaments dressed as men, and he was pleased to add that God punished such loose behavior by sending violent storms wherever such strange sights appeared. Knighton's chronicle mentioned the usual portents and disasters. He noted, for example, a strange epidemic that struck in the summer of 1340 in which people experienced excruciating pain and cried like barking dogs. For the destruction caused by the plague in 1349 he had access to reports from different areas and recorded the number of deaths in such places as Southampton and Bristol and among the religious orders in France.

Knighton also kept track of mundane details such as the cost of provisions and other matters relating to the running of the abbey, including disputes over landholdings. When Edward III organized a large hunt in the forests of Rockingham, Cliffe, and Sherwood in 1362 to celebrate his fiftieth birthday, Knighton recorded the cost of this royal event. Drawing on oral reports, including local gossip, he described the sensational murder of the clerk John Allintheworld by his wife, Emma, and others and noted that after the deaths of Henry of Lancaster in 1361 and his daughter Maud in 1362 rumor suggested that she had been poisoned to avoid splitting the Lancastrian inheritance.

Knighton's chronicle is an important document of medieval England. The author's narration of events illustrated the influence of personal opinion and social context on those who record history.

Bibliography: Henry Knighton, *Knighton's Chronicle, 1337–1396*, ed. and trans. G. H. Martin, 1995; W. M. Ormrod, *The Reign of Edward III*, 1990; Scott Waugh, *England in the Reign of Edward III*, 1991.

Karen Arthur

Kraft, Adam (c. 1455/60–1509), also spelled Krafft, a late Gothic stone sculptor in the city of Nuremberg and a contemporary of Albrecht Dürer, is recognized as a meticulous craftsman and an artist sensitive to detail, though not an innovator. He is particularly admired for the poignant facial expressions of his human figures. Most of his work was done for civic buildings, churches, and private patrons in Nuremberg and may still be seen there.

Not much is known of Kraft's early life. It has been speculated that he may have journeyed to Swabia and the Upper Rhineland and there learned his craft. His important creative period, however, took place entirely within Nuremberg and dates from 1490 until his death in 1509. In 1490 the kirchenmeister, or superintendent, of St. Sebaldus, Sebald Schreyer, commissioned Kraft to carve the Schreyer-Landauer funerary monument. By 1492 Kraft had completed this series of three sandstone reliefs, the *Crucifixion, Entombment*, and *Resurrection*, located above the family tombs on the exterior of the choir. The monument stands eight feet high and almost twenty feet long. Many human figures are shown, among them images of both Kraft and his patron.

The Sacrament House that Kraft created for the Church of St. Lorenz was commissioned by Hans IV Imhoff in 1493 and finished in 1496. This receptacle for the storage of the Eucharist, placed near the main altar, towers sixty-one feet high, bending at its summit and decorated by a number of relief carvings. At its base is another self-portrait of Kraft, showing a man with a full curly beard, clad in a simple worker's smock, kneeling in respect before the Sacrament. He carries his hammer and chisel and looks up at the viewer with a serious expression.

Kraft's crowning work was a series of seven *Stations of the Cross*, commissioned by Bamburg knight Heinrich Marschalk von Rauheneck in 1505 and completed in 1508. These were sandstone carvings, measuring about four by five feet, set atop pillars and placed along a route leading from one of the city's northwestern gates to the St. Sebaldus parish cemetery west of town. At the cemetery itself were the final two stations, the life-size *Crucifixion* and *Entombment*. The first five stations are now in the Germanisches Nationalmuseum, and replicas stand in their places along the route. The *Crucifixion* originally contained more than half a dozen figures, but only those of Christ and the two thieves have survived. These now stand in the courtyard of the Hospital and Church of the Holy Spirit in Nuremberg. The final station, the *Entombment*, remains at the cemetery in a chapel dedicated to the works' patron.

Bibliography: Jeffrey Chipps Smith, *Nuremberg: A Renaissance City, 1500–1618*, 1983.

Angela B. Fulk

Krämer, Heinrich (c. 1430–1505), was a Dominican preacher and inquisitor best known for cowriting the *Malleus maleficarum*, the premier witch-hunting manual of early modern Europe. Krämer, also known as Henricus Institoris, was born in Schlettstadt in Lower Alsace, twenty-six miles southwest of Strassburg; he spent most of his life in this area as both student and inquisitor. Krämer entered the Order of St. Dominic at a young age and quickly rose to prominence, becoming the prior of the Dominican house in his hometown. He was appointed preacher general and master of sacred theology with high distinction and, before 1474, inquisitor for the Tyrol, Salzburg, Bohemia, and Moravia. Although he first focused his efforts on a search for heretics, by 1476 the main focus of Krämer's search was witches. Krämer's aptitude for his profession and the influence of friends at the papal court earned him papal recognition. On 9 December 1484 Pope *innocent VIII issued the bull *Summis desiderantes affectibus* (Wishing with the greatest concern) granting Krämer and his colleague *Jakob Sprenger broad inquisitorial powers in northern Germany and commanding the reluctant archbishop of Salzburg, Albrecht von Bayern, to lend them every assistance, including that of the secular arm, in their search for witches. The following year Krämer wrote a treatise on witchcraft that he subsequently expanded, with the aid of Sprenger, into the *Malleus maleficarum* (The hammer of witches) in 1486. Innocent's bull prefaced the *Malleus*, lending it an air of authority that brought it to most judicial benches throughout Europe shortly after its publication.

The *Malleus* became one of the most widely consulted and influential legal manuals in early modern Europe. Between 1487 and 1520 fourteen editions appeared, and sixteen more appeared during the time of the "witch-hunt" between 1574 and 1669. It was translated from its original Latin into German, French, Italian, and English, and most later witch-hunting manuals quoted from it extensively. It was divided into three sections: the first considered the nature of witchcraft; the second, the methods and practices of witches and their master, the devil; the third, proper judicial proceedings against witches. The authors lent their weight to such popular beliefs as the witches' pact with the devil, including sexual intercourse with the devil; the murder and use of unbaptized infants; the causing of impotence in men; flying through the air; the abuse of the Eucharist; and the creation of magical ointments. To these beliefs the Dominicans added renunciation of the Catholic faith and devotion of body and soul to evil.

More important, Krämer and Sprenger emphasized the feminine nature of the crime of witchcraft. While they based some of the *Malleus*'s exempla on the tales of contemporary men, each man was usually linked to a woman who had led him astray. Krämer and Sprenger supported their violent misogyny with pertinent passages from the Bible as well as from classical and medieval sources. Women, according to the *Malleus*, were more prone to lying, more superstitious, more impressionable, more wicked, more fickle, and lighter-headed than men. Most important, women became involved in witchcraft due to their naturally overabundant carnality; they were creatures of lust who must be supervised constantly. The *Malleus* recommended a careful search for witches, questioning witnesses, imprisoning any witch found, using torture to extract confessions, and possible use of trial by hot iron. Judges were to pronounce the appropriate sentence, including excommunication, force abjuration of suspected heresy, and put convicted witches to death by burning. Sprenger later repented, denouncing both Krämer and the *Malleus*.

While he is best known for the *Malleus*, Krämer did continue his career after its first appearance. Contemporaries respected his other published works, including a collection of sermons on the Eucharist (1496) and a tract defending papal supremacy against the claims of heretics (1500). The order condemned Krämer in 1490 for embezzlement and other crimes, but five years later, in 1495, the master general of the Dominicans, Joaquin de Torres, summoned him to Venice and invited him to lecture publicly on witchcraft and papal supremacy; among those in attendance was the patriarch of Venice. Krämer returned to Germany in 1497. Three years later Pope *Alexander VI appointed him nuncio and inquisitor of Bohemia and Moravia and ordered him to proceed against Waldensians and Picards as well as witches. Krämer died in Bohemia in 1505.

Bibliography: Heinrich Krämer and Jacob Sprenger, *The Malleus Maleficarum*, trans. Montague Summers, 1971; Brian Levack, *The Witch-Hunt in Early Modern Europe*, 2nd. ed., 1995.

Tim Sullivan

L

La Marche, Olivier de (1425–1502). Soldier, diplomat, writer, and maître d'hôtel for three successive dukes of Burgundy, Olivier de La Marche is known today largely for his *Mémoires*, an account of his life that chronicled more than five decades of Burgundian court life and military exploits. In addition to being a sagacious advisor and staunch, faithful soldier, La Marche was responsible for the court's fame for producing opulent, ceremonial affairs such as weddings and tournaments that surpassed all others in magnificence. He made several successful diplomatic missions to England, France, and Italy on behalf of the Burgundian dukes and remained active in the management of their courts until his death in Brussels in 1502.

Olivier de La Marche was born in 1425 in the Château de La Marche in Villegaudin, a small parish in the township of Saint-Martin in Bresse, Burgundy. He entered political service as a page to Philip the Good and was impressed by the pageantry of court life. Because of his position at court, from this time forward until his death in 1502, La Marche was involved in some capacity in every major event of Burgundy's turbulent history. The faithful soldier for much of his life, La Marche saw a great deal of action in his long military career, taking part in the battles of Villy, Ghent, and Neuss. On the day of the Battle of Montlery in 1465, he was knighted, and he served as *capitaine* for the last of the dukes of Burgundy, *Charles the Bold, in the Battle of Lorraine. La Marche was even taken captive at the Battle of Nancy in 1477, in which Charles the Bold was killed; he later rejoined Charles's daughter and heir, Mary of Burgundy, in Flanders after paying his ransom. She had married *Maximilian, duke of Austria and later emperor of Rome, in 1477, a few months after the Battle of Nancy. La Marche remained in their service, in time becoming the tutor, guardian, and even the premier maître d'hôtel for their son, Philip the Fair, later *Philip I of Spain.

As the maître d'hôtel for the Burgundian dukes, La Marche contributed to the fame of their courts by masterminding spectacular affairs that demonstrated and extolled the virtues of chivalry. It was this same code of knightly conduct that La Marche's contemporary and one-time compatriot, *Philippe de Commynes, criticized harshly in his own *Mémoires*, but even Commynes recognized the need for ceremony and display to project an aura of majesty, and La Marche was a master at staging royal entertainments. His accounts of tournaments, weddings, and funeral solemnities in his *Mémoires*, covering the period 1435–88, are filled with details that show the cost of these events. His description of one feast told of days of tournaments, banquets, plays, music, and a final lavish banquet whose opulent decorations and foods were the stuff of legends, such as a pastry that hid twenty-eight musicians. La Marche himself took part in the entertainment by composing an appeal for aid to a church in the Holy Land, which spurred all the nobility present to vow to go on a crusade. While La Marche's *Mémoires* are an invaluable account of the events that occurred in the court of late-fifteenth-century Burgundy, they are also a unique and personal look at the Burgundian fascination with chivalry and etiquette and the psychology of the dukes who fashioned their lives according to its code.

Although Olivier de La Marche was not a prolific writer, there is an interesting variety in the kinds of works attributed to him, which range from his *Mémoires* and treatises and epistles on the state of the Burgundian court to several short poems and even two longer allegorical pieces, *Le parement et triumphes des dames* and *Le chevalier délibéré*. The latter allegory, *Le chevalier délibéré*, was finished in 1483 and printed in Paris in 1488 and was a more complicated and influential piece than its urbane simplicity would lead one to believe at first. In addition to being read as a pseudoautobiography, an allegory of man's earthly struggle with death and spiritual salvation, and a poem in honor of Charles the Bold, *Le chevalier délibéré* was also an idealization of the Burgundian chivalric tradition as a political and moral ethos, a subject very close to La Marche's heart. There were twenty printed editions of the French version, and its subsequent translation into Dutch, Spanish, and English indicates the popularity of its romantically principled message; indeed, it was one of the most popular Burgundian literary works of its time.

Olivier de La Marche was the kind of historical figure whose name rarely occurs in current studies of Burgundian history. He was a seemingly quiet, unassuming man whose wisdom and dedication were invaluable assets to the last Burgundian dukes. Without La Marche, however, the Burgundian court would not have achieved the level of grandeur for which it was known throughout fifteenth-century Europe, and without his *Mémoires* and other literary works, our present understanding of chivalry and some of its major representatives would be considerably poorer.

Bibliography: Elizabeth Mongan, Introduction to *Le Chevalier Délibéré by Olivier de La Marche*, 1946; Malcolm Vale, "A Burgundian Funeral Ceremony: Olivier de La

Marche and the Obsequies of Adolf of Cleves, Lord of Ravenstein," *English Historical Review* 111 (September 1996): 920–38.

Wendy Marie Hoofnagle

Landini, Francesco (1325–97). Also known as Landino, Francesco Landini was the best-known and most important fourteenth-century Italian composer, a leading proponent of the Italian *ars nova*, which he more or less invented. Landini was born in Fiesole in 1325, four years after the death of *Dante, pointing up his links with the medieval rather than the early modern world. Landini was probably the son of the painter Jacopo del Casentino (d. 1358). Stricken with blindness due to a childhood attack of smallpox, Landini gained fame for his skills on the portative organ and other instruments, for his musical recitations and compositions, and for poetical talents, resulting in his becoming one of the most admired musicians and cultural figures of his day. In 1364 Landini was awarded a laurel wreath by the titular king of Cyprus for winning a literary contest in Venice and was patronized by some of the leading cultural and political figures of his time, including *Coluccio Salutati, the chancellor of the Republic of Florence, humanist Luigi Marsili, and poet Guido di Tommaso del Palagio.

Landini's more than five hundred compositions fall into three main categories: *ballate* or dance-songs celebrating courtly love, the vast majority of Landini's compositions; "madrigals," complex compositions that sound anything other than extemporized and share little more than a name with sixteenth-century equivalents; and a *caccia*, which celebrated hunting or, in Landini's case, fishing. Landini is best known for the sensuous and limpid beauty of his two- and three-part polyphonic compositions and highly ornamented style. These works were intended for a close interaction and harmony of singers and instruments in a way that was typically Italian and unique to Landini. Unlike *Guillaume de Machaut, the leading French expositor of the *ars nova*, there was a greater emphasis on lyricism in Landini's work and also a greater interest in the words of texts that were specifically intended to link high musical and high poetic achievement, a style particularly to be associated with Florence, where Landini spent most of his life.

Landini, for all his importance, found few imitators, and after his death the style that he had championed lapsed, in part because of social changes that gradually eroded the positions of the kinds of elites for whom he wrote his music. The reinvention of Italian music in the sixteenth century would be at the hands of the Flemish and other foreigners, who would create an entirely new art where late medieval composers like Landini had left off.

Landini died on 2 September 1397. His tombstone, with a now-worn bas-relief of the composer, his organ, and two angels hovering in the air playing a medieval violin and a lute, still exists in the Church of San Lorenzo in Florence. Unlike most early composers, the complete corpus of Landini's works still exists; they remain popular and are much recorded today.

Bibliography: Alfred Einstein, *The Italian Madrigal*, 1949; Francesco Landini, *The Works of Francesco Landini*, ed. Leonard Ellinwood, *Studies and Documents of the Medieval Academy of America*, 1939.

Paul D. Buell

Landino, Christoforo (1424–98), was one of the outstanding Florentine scholars of the middle and late quattrocento. He is primarily known for his literary endeavors: his commentaries on Virgil's *Aeneid* and more especially on *Dante were considered among the most important commentaries of Renaissance Florence, read by all educated Florentines of that time period. In addition to these vernacular literary commentaries, his *Disputationes Camaldulenses*, a debate on the active and contemplative lives, remains one of the great debate works of the Italian Renaissance.

Christoforo Landino was born in Florence to a noble family in 1424 and through an advantageous marriage allied himself with the prestigious Alberti family, one of whom would figure in the *Disputationes*. His early humanistic education concentrated on law and Greek. In 1458 he was appointed to the chair of rhetoric and poetry at the Florentine Studio, succeeding Cristoforo Marsuppini in this position. As a member of *Marsiglio Ficino's Platonic Academy, he formed a part of a group of Neoplatonic scholars influenced by Ficino. A few years older than Ficino, he was one of his tutors and served as an instructor for the house of Medici, tutoring *Lorenzo and his brother *Giuliano. He remained under Medici protection until his death in 1498 at the Borgo Collina, a gift of the Medici family.

Landino's fame rests primarily upon three works, his two vernacular commentaries on Virgil and Dante and his great philosophical dialogue, the *Disputationes Camaldulenses*. In addition to the renowned commentaries, he also published several vernacular translations during his lifetime, including Italian versions of Pliny's *Historia naturalis*. Despite his famous Latin philosophical work, his enduring body of work as a Florentine man of letters represents as well his commitment to the use of the vernacular.

The *Disputationes Camaldulenses*, one of three philosophical dialogues composed in Latin by Landino (his *De anima* was published in 1453 and the *De vera nobilitate* in 1469), was composed around 1474 and consisted of a dispute carried on by Landino with *Leon Battista Alberti, his father-in-law, Giuliano de Medici, and Marsiglio Ficino on the relative virtues of the active and contemplative lifestyles. Alberti, who in the framework of the dialogue supported the superiority of the contemplative life, finally carried the four-book debate. Despite this victory of the *vita contemplativa* over the *vita activa* in his philosophical discourse, however, Landino himself was far from a pure scholar divorced from the world. Rather, he was a citizen-humanist of *Leonardo Bruni's school, interested and involved in the activities of the city-state, and in 1467 he even served as the chancellor of the Guelf party.

The other element of Landino's fame, his vernacular literary commentaries, rounded out the figure of the quattrocento man of letters. As the scholar charged with the literary segment of Ficino's school, Landino applied Neoplatonic principles to poetry, describing a system of vernacular poetics based on a necessary grounding in classical language and literature. He demanded a thorough knowledge of classical language and literature as necessary prerequisites to vernacular composition. His approach to literary commentary was exegetical in nature, utilizing the tenets of Platonism and Neoplatonism to develop a system of hermeneutic tools designed to uncover hidden levels of meaning in literary works, following in the footsteps of Dante and others who espoused allegorical interpretive analysis. This system was exhibited in his famous commentary on Virgil, as well as his commentary on Dante, which not only followed his analytical precepts but also firmly placed the Florentine writer's vernacular work within the realm of the great literary epics with its classical predecessors.

Bibliography: Thomas H. Stahel, "Christoforo Landino's Allegorization of the Aeneid: Books III and IV of the Camaldolese Disputations." Ph.D. diss., Johns Hopkins University, 1968.

Laura McRae

Langenstein, Henry Heinbuche of. *See* Heinbuche, Henry, of Langenstein.

Langland, William (c. 1332–1400). A fourteenth-century English religious writer, William Langland is believed by many scholars to have been the author of the apocalyptic *Piers Plowman*, an epic poem considered to be a milestone in medieval literature both for its historical insight and artistic merits. Although little definitive information is available regarding the life of William Langland, it is believed that he was born either in the town of Cleobury Mortimer or Ledbury in Shropshire, England. Young William was the illegitimate son of Eustace de Rokayle, the lord of nearby Hanley Castle, and an unknown woman who was presumably either one of the servants at Hanley or the daughter of a local villager. Despite the humble circumstances of his birth, Langland did go on to receive a formal education, attending school at the priory at Great Malvern in Worcestershire. It is likely that Langland spent several years among the monks at Great Malvern, and it has been suggested that it was he who was ordained an acolyte under the name Willelmus de Colewell in December 1348 (Colewell was a parish that neighbored his hometown of Ledbury). Nevertheless, Langland ultimately decided against a religious vocation and never took his final vows. At some point later in his life Langland married and with his wife Kit and daughter Calotte took up residence in London, where he lived for a considerable portion of his life. Although it has been suggested that Langland suffered from some chronic ailment that limited his physical activities, he lived an exceptionally long life by the standards of his day, being nearly seventy years of age at the time of his death.

Langland's greatest (and his only known) contribution to English literature was his epic poem entitled *The Vision of William Concerning Piers the Plow-man*, which he kept under constant revision throughout his adult life. Conse-quently, the poem has come down to modern readers in three distinct versions, dubbed the A, B, and C texts. Each successive rendering of the poem expanded the work, with version A (c. 1362–73) containing twelve cantos (called passus) and a prologue, version B (c. 1377) having twenty passus plus the prologue, and version C (c. 1387–98) containing no prologue, but having twenty-three passus.

Piers Plowman offers the reader a number of interpretive possibilities. On one level, the poem was a work of social commentary in which Langland offered his opinion on such contemporary topics as the Black Death, the Hundred Years' War, the Great Schism, and the injustices implicit in England's highly stratified social system. On another level, Langland's work can be seen as an extended medieval sermon, designed to instruct its readers in the doctrine of Christian salvation. However, at its heart, the poem was a religious allegory, deeply steeped in symbolism. Langland effectively utilized the devices of poetry and metaphor to deliver a spiritual message containing multiple layers of meaning.

The basic structure of *Piers Plowman* was a vision in which the narrator, Will (who represents not only Langland personally, but also the inner will of all humankind), began a personal pilgrimage in search of salvation. Along the way, Will encountered a number of characters who personified various aspects of good and evil and attempted either to assist or derail his quest. By the end of the poem, the narrator had come to find his spiritual aspirations embodied in the person of Piers the Plowman, a Christlike figure who promised redemption to those who followed his ways.

The poem itself is divided into four major parts. In the first section, known as the "Visio," the narrator set the stage for his pilgrimage by describing the spiritual condition of medieval Christian society. Langland bemoaned the sin-fulness of fourteenth-century England and critiqued it as a society that had lost touch with the redemptive power of Christ. Thus persuaded of the inability of the secular world to provide the spiritual answers that he sought, the narrator undertook a quest for salvation that comprised the poem's next three sections, collectively known as the "Vita."

In the first section of the "Vita," known as "Do-wel," Langland explored the relationship of Christianity to the natural world, closely examining such issues as human will, rationality, education, natural law, and the problem of authority. In the next portion of the poem, known as "Do-bet," Langland addressed the topic of a human being's proper orientation toward Christ. In that context, Lang-land evaluated the merit of the traditional theological virtues and how these virtues contributed to the believer's quest for redemption. Langland discovered love to be the highest of these virtues, and Christ to be its embodiment. As Langland reflected in Passus XVIII (version B) concerning the redemptive death of Christ:

For I, that am lorde of lyf, loue is my drynke,
And for that drynke to-day,
I deyde upon erthe. I faughte so, me threstes yet, for mennes soule sake;
May no drynke me moiste, ne my thruste slake.

Thus in Langland's final section, called "Do-best," Will confronted the logical conclusion of the infusion of divine love into the hearts of individuals—the reordering of earthly society into the perfected Kingdom of God.

Some recent scholars have challenged Langland's authorship of *Piers Plowman* and have instead credited the A, B, and C versions of the text to as many as five different writers. However, most historians and literary critics have upheld Langland's claim to the work, seeing it as a long-term project that the author gradually refined over the course of his lifetime, always seeking ways to better illuminate the spiritual path that he dedicated his life to traveling.

Bibliography: John A. Alford, ed., *A Companion to Piers Plowman*, 1988; Morton W. Bloomfield, *Piers Plowman as a Fourteenth-Century Apocalypse*, 1962; Elizabeth Salter, *Piers Plowman: An Introduction*, 1962.

Timothy L. Wood

Langmann, Adelheid (1306–75), is known as an author and mystic. She recorded her mystical experiences in her text, *Offenbarungen* (Revelations). Her text was used by the Dominicans of the fifteenth century to further monastic reforms, particularly in women's houses. It exists today in three manuscripts, in Berlin, Munich, and Vienna.

Langmann was born in 1306 to a patrician family in Nuremberg. Although she was a pious child who showed a demonstrable religious vocation, her parents chose to marry her off instead. The groom died the day of the wedding, and so the thirteen-year-old Langmann overcame her family's objections and entered the nearby Dominican monastery at Engelthal, a well-known mystical center. Christine Ebner, another visionary mystic, was already in residence at Engelthal. There Langmann's extreme piety and mystical experiences were first met with skepticism, then with growing acceptance, and later with actual acclaim. Langmann proved adept at correctly identifying hidden sins, and people from outside the monastery sought her advice and blessing on their endeavors. She died on 21 October 1375.

Langmann's mysticism was unusual among women mystics: while most encountered the divine in a variety of ways, Langmann focused exclusively on participation in the *unio mystica*, the mystical marriage, and the image of herself as bride of Christ. While bridal mysticism appeared quite often in texts by contemporary male and female mystics, Langmann's bridal mysticism was extreme because it was almost completely asensual. This contrasted sharply with other mystics, who usually described the *unio mystica* in terms reminiscent of sexual intercourse.

Bibliography: Elizabeth Alvilda Petroff, ed., *Medieval Women's Visionary Literature*, 1986; Emilie Zum Brunn and Georgette Epiney-Burgard, *Women Mystics in Medieval Europe*, 1989.

Rebecca L. R. Garber

La Sale, Antoine de (c. 1385–1460).

An adventurer and soldier of fortune, Antoine de La Sale is best remembered for his literary endeavors. Combining history, geography, and pure invention in a unique mix, Antoine used his works to please and instruct those who received them.

Antoine was born the illegitimate son of Perrinette Damendel and Bernard de La Sale in 1385 or 1386. His father, a member of the minor nobility, made his living as a soldier-for-hire and became locally renowned for having married an illegitimate daughter of Bernabò Visconti. He later served as leader of the mercenary troops of Popes Gregory XI and Clement VII. Bernard eventually died in the service of the dukes of Anjou in 1391. Antoine followed in his father's footsteps, starting out as a squire to the house of Anjou at the age of fourteen. Because of the Sicilian-Anjou interests in Italy, Antoine's early exploits took him far and wide: Messina and the Lipari Isles (1407), Roccasecca (1411), Ceuta in Morocco for a crusade against the Moors (1415), Montemonaco (1420), and Pouzzoles (1425). In Naples in 1439, Antoine met and married a fifteen-year-old girl in the service of Marie de Bourbon.

Many of the locations Antoine visited in his years of travel appeared in his later literary works. According to some accounts, Antoine saw a tapestry belonging to the mother of Marie de Bourbon depicting the lake mountains of Sibylle. Upon viewing the tapestry, Antoine promised to tell the story of the queen of Sibylle, and he kept his promise in 1442 when he wrote *Le paradis de la reine Sibylle*. This fantastic tale told of a knight who managed to travel to the region ruled by the woman-monster and return again. The knight had to choose whether to stay in the perverted sexual paradise at the peril of his immortal soul or return to the outside world without hope of ever reentering the apparently idyllic realm. This story was followed by the *Excursion aux îles Lipari* and a geography of the world in the manuscript presented to Agnès de Bourbon; he called the compendium of these three works *Salade* (1442–44). Antoine became preceptor to Jean de Calabre and wrote several edifying works for the boy. He reworked his *Salade* and added to it considerations on good government, behavior, and part of Jean's genealogy. After Jean grew up, Antoine continued to work as a tutor for the children of Louis of Luxembourg, count of Saint-Pol. His writings included the *Sale* (1451), an allegorical room whose foundations were constructed on Prudence, the walls made of Justice, and the like. For Louis's brother, the formidable knight Jacques, Antoine penned the treatise *Des anciens tournois et faits d'armes* (1459). The *Reconfort de madame du Fresne* (1457) was destined for Catherine of Neuville, wife of Jacques of Fresne, to console her for the loss of her oldest son. The story focused on the inner strength of two women who, like Catherine, lost their sons in battle.

Antoine's most famous work was the *Petit Jean de Saintré* (1456), dedicated once again to his former student, Jean de Calabre. It told of the coming of age of a young boy who was initiated into the mysteries of manhood and chivalry by an older woman. In the end, the boy lost her affections to a lusty cleric. This odd combination of didactic literature and bawdy tale may well have been the basis for attributing *Cent nouvelles nouvelles* and the *Quinze joies de mariage* to Antoine de La Sale, though both works are now generally believed to have been written by another author.

Antoine de La Sale remains particularly noteworthy for his ability to mix genres, teaching history and geography while entering the realm of the fantastic and imaginative. His stories, told from the perspective of an intelligent and well-traveled man of the world, make their moral points without overwhelming the reader with didacticism.

Bibliography: C. A. Knudson, "The Prussian Expedition in Jehan de Saintré," in *Étupes de Langue et de littérature du Moyen Age, Offertes à Félix Lecoy*, 1973: 271–77; Karl D. Uitti, "Renewal and Undermining of the Old French Romance: Jehan de Saintré," in *Romance: Generic Transformation from Chrétien de Troyes to Cervantes*, ed. Kevin Brownlee and Marina Brownlee, 1985: 135–54.

Lynn Ramey

Leonardo da Vinci (1452–1519)

Leonardo da Vinci (1452–1519) was responsible for some of the world's greatest works of art. He is credited not only with the lovely *Annunciation* and *Virgin of the Rocks*, the breathtaking *Last Supper*, and the ageless *Mona Lisa*, but also the first known Western plans for a flying machine, the most thorough sketches of human anatomy of his time, and the invention of the bicycle. Some recent scholars have even identified Leonardo with the creation of the Shroud of Turin, which he may have created while experimenting with the camera obscura. Leonardo da Vinci was the quintessential Renaissance man, his work represents not merely the best of his own time, but of all time.

Leonardo was the illegitimate son of Ser Piero da Vinci, both men sharing the name of the village in which they were born. Because Leonardo's mother, Caterina, was of a lower class than Leonardo's father, she was not permitted to marry him. However, perhaps because of his gender, Leonardo was welcomed into the household of his father for a time. His separation from his mother may have had a significant effect upon Leonardo, since his work often depicts maternal feminine figures holding children or searching wistfully beyond their surroundings into the distant unknown. Some scholars have used Freud to analyze Leonardo's motives and behaviors; one does not need Freud, however, to understand that an isolated child made more isolated by an early separation from his mother might be affected throughout his life by longing and melancholy.

Eventually, Piero da Vinci's household moved to Florence, and when he was seventeen, Leonardo was sent to serve as an apprentice to the great artist *Andrea del Verrocchio. In Verrocchio's studio, Leonardo met other great artists who would one day serve as competitors for both public and political favor, such as *Sandro Botticelli. During Leonardo da Vinci's lifetime Florence was ruled by the Medici, a powerful yet surprisingly artistic family that spent a great deal of time and money in patronizing the arts. Leonardo would spend much of his life winning and losing the favor of the Medici, as well as that of another influential family of patrons, the Borgias, and their influence is clearly felt in many of his works.

One clue to the kind of man Leonardo was may be seen in an unusual event from his youth: he (with several other pupils from Verrocchio's studio) was arrested and threatened with the death penalty for "sodomy," which scholars interpret as an accusation of homosexuality. The accusation was not proven and the charges were dropped; however, the question of Leonardo's sexuality has remained, for five hundred years, just that: a question. He lived for a long time with a particular man, although the nature of their relationship is still unclear. His sexuality seems not to have affected his work to a degree that scholars have pursued it, but, like the separation from his mother, it could explain what some have seen as a sense of isolation and exile in a number of his works. It may also have compelled his innovative, almost subversive artistic pursuits. One has merely to look into the vast enigmatic stare of the *Mona Lisa* to get a sense of this characteristic of otherness in Leonardo's personality.

Leonardo da Vinci remained in Verrocchio's studio for at least ten years and during that time developed a reputation as a fine Florentine artist. In 1482 he traveled to Milan, where he lived and worked for another twenty years and where he completed some of his best-known works. In 1490 Leonardo adopted the child Salai, who would become his most beloved pupil. For the next few years he traveled extensively around Italy, working often for the Borgias, sometimes with his contemporary Niccolò Machiavelli, and continuing to build his great reputation. For part of this time, between 1502 and 1512, he lived in the Vatican in a private studio while he worked on the *Mona Lisa* and *Leda and the Swan*. He moved permanently to Rome in late 1513 but continued to travel throughout Europe. His now-famous notebooks are filled with his reactions to his travels, to both the people and the places that he came to know in his later years. Late in 1516 Leonardo and his two companions, Salai and Francesco Melzi, traveled to France and lived for a time in the royal castle of Ambroise, where he wrote, sketched, and designed buildings for the royal family. He recorded his will in April 1519 and died in Ambroise soon thereafter. His papers were collected, transcribed, and eventually made public by his longtime friend, Francesco Melzi.

The chronology of Leonardo's most important works reads like a catalog of the world's great museums: the *Annunciation* and the *Baptism of Christ* (1475); *St. Jerome* (1480); *Adoration of the Magi* (1481); the *Virgin of the Rocks* (1486); the *Last Supper* (1498); the *Mona Lisa* (1505); *Leda and the Swan* (1506); *St. Anne* (1510); the anatomical studies (1510); the *Self-Portrait* (1512); and *St.*

John the Baptist (1516). Although Leonardo da Vinci is considered a Renaissance artist due to his imaginative style and the striking originality of his use of color, light, and form, the subject matter of his paintings was predominantly Christian and/or biblical; thus most of his works were, in subject matter, more medieval than Renaissance. By comparison, one could look at the work of Botticelli, which focused predominantly upon classical subjects and included the *Primavera* (1477) and his most famous *Birth of Venus* (1484). It is sometimes assumed that Leonardo was himself a devout Christian, but there is little evidence for this. It is more likely that although Leonardo was clearly the most gifted artist of his time, his beliefs and ideals may have been ahead of his time. It is, after all, not merely his painting that proves him to have been so talented. Leonardo da Vinci's greatness was clear in his painting, but also in his writings, his sketches, his ink drawings, his knowledge and use of science, and his devotion to the creation of art for its own sake. Leonardo was a painter, a writer, a scientist, and a teacher, and yet his impact goes far beyond any of his specific actions or works.

Sometime after 1490 and before 1519, Leonardo began composing his *Treatise on Painting*. He believed that great painting could be taught, and he was, by all accounts, an excellent teacher. In his *Treatise*, however, he did more than explain the craft of painting; he also explained his philosophy of art, his impressions of many of his contemporaries, and his feelings about beauty, creativity, and talent. He wrote: "The painter can call into being the essences of animals of all kinds, of plants, fruits, landscapes, rolling plains, crumbling mountains . . . places sweet and delightful with meadows of many-colored flowers bent by the gentle motion of the wind which turns back to look at them as it floats on." These are the words of an artist and a naturalist, of one whose artistic creations reflected his devotion to the pure and simple beauty and minute detail of the natural world. His sketches, too, reflected this attention to the simple yet complex details of life—he drew and studied muscles, for example, not only at their peak of strength in youth but also in old age and decline.

Leonardo da Vinci was an artist, a scholar, a physicist, a biologist, an inventor, a machinist, a musician, an architect, and a writer. In his writing he explained his craft, his beliefs, and his genius. He lived his life fully and reveled in the moment and in life experiences. He once wrote, "My subjects require for their expression not the words of others but experience, the mistress of all who write well. I have taken her as my mistress and will not cease to state it" (Reti, 293). Leonardo lived from 1452 to 1519, but the years are unimportant. The great fact of his life is simply that Leonardo da Vinci lived; he shared that life and his love for it with posterity, and for that the Western world is richer.

Bibliography: Serge Bramley, *Leonardo: Discovering the Life of Leonardo da Vinci*, 1991; David Alan Brown, *Leonardo da Vinci: Origins of a Genius*, 1998; Bradley Collins, *Leonardo, Psychoanalysis, and Art History: A Critical Study of Psychobiographical*

Approaches to Leonardo da Vinci, 1997; Alessandro Vezzosi, *Leonardo da Vinci: The Mind of the Renaissance*, 1997.

Susannah Chewning

Leonor López de Córdoba. *See* López de Córdoba, Leonor.

LeRoy, Guillaume (c. 1450–c. 1529). Early modern Europe's first printer to specialize in publishing in the vernacular, Guillaume LeRoy is most famous for his printing of Jean de Vignay's translation of Jacobus de Voragine's *Legenda aurea*, the first printed book in French. He was active from 1473 until 1529 and concentrated on making books available to a more general reading public.

He was born in Liège, Belgium, and went to Venice, Italy, to learn his craft, where he worked with the Speier brothers. Venice was the center of printing in Italy, and it was there that John and Wendel of Speier established the first press in Italy. They were so fortunate as to obtain a monopoly over printing in the city-state that did not expire until John's death in 1470, and they were responsible for the printing of the first book in Italian, a volume of *Francesco Petrarch's *Canzoniere*. LeRoy moved from Venice to Lyons, where he set up his own business with the financial backing of the rich merchant Barthelémy Buyer. It was in Buyer's house that the press was established, and it is Buyer's name that appears on the colophons. He handled the commercial side of the venture, establishing a depot in Toulouse and sending salesmen to Paris. Buyer died in July 1483.

LeRoy's was the first printing press in Lyons, and the first volume he produced was Innocent III's *Compendium breve* on 17 September 1473. During Buyer's lifetime LeRoy's name was mentioned only three times, in 1473, 1477, and 1482. The contribution of LeRoy and Lyons to printing is that his press was marked by a strong provincialism. Printing had been introduced to France in 1470 by two professors of the Sorbonne who catered to university demands by printing volumes in Latin. In contrast to this, LeRoy's output was by and large in French, possibly inspired by his training with the Speier brothers. On 18 April 1476 he completed his imprint of Jean de Vignay's translation of the *Legenda aurea*. This was followed by another innovation, *Le Gui'don* by Guy de Chauliac, a classic text for surgeons. The other difference between LeRoy's volumes and those produced in Paris was that he published a wide variety of material, including popular legends, histories, and romances. He printed works that included *Fier-à-Bras, Le Bible en Français* (1480), the *Confessionale: Defecerunt, cum titulo de restitutionibus* by S. Antonio (c. 1485), Bartholomaeus Anglicus's *Des propriétés des choses* (translated into French by Jean Corbicher in 1485/86), Bernardus Parmensis's *Casus longi super quinque libros Decretalium* (c. 1485), *De consolatione philosophiae* by Boethius with *De disciplina scholarium cum commentario Thomae de Aquino* (1484–85), and Cicero's *De officiis* (c. 1485). He was interested in illustrated books and printed the third edition of the *Roman de la Rose*, the earliest illustrated book in France. In fact, he is known as "le Maître au nombril" (the master of the eye) because it was his trademark to produce elaborate frontispieces and vignettes. It was he who carried out for Jean Lemaire the *Illustrations de Gaule* with woodcuts. Lyons was an excellent choice of location for such printing activities because it was one of the wealthiest of French cities, situated on the important commercial route between the Île-de-France, Burgundy, and the Mediterranean countries. It also held a fair four times a year during the period 1463–84 (revived in 1498) where books could be sold. Guillaume LeRoy was at the heart of the dichotomy of Renaissance and medieval cultures present in Lyons. His importance lies in his focus on a more general reading public, making texts available in the ver-nacular.

Bibliography: Colin Clair, *A History of European Printing*, 1976; John Lewis, *Anatomy of Printing: The Influences of Art and History on its Design*, 1970.

Bonnie Millar

Lippi, Fra Filippo (c. 1406–69), was a narrative painter known today as one of the most artistically talented and socially notorious figures of the fifteenth century. His frescoes were harbingers of humanist thought, because he was the pioneer of painting the human expression with liveliness and emotion, ranging from the tender *Madonna* to the energetic *Daughter of Herodias*. The unity, attractiveness, and workmanship of Lippi's frescoes in the Prato and Spoleto cathedrals were an exceptional artistic leap forward in skill, beauty, and psy-chological sensitivity.

Filippo Lippi was born around 1406 in Florence, Italy; his father was Tomasso de Lippi, a butcher. His parents died soon after, and Lippi was placed in a Carmelite monastery around 1414. By 1420 he was admitted to the novitiate and became a Carmelite friar on 8 June 1421 at the age of fifteen. He began training as a painter in 1426, a common-enough apprenticeship for a friar, as the paintings of the age were all of religious subjects. He was considered a qualified painter by 1430 and was permitted to leave the monastery in 1431 in order to paint professionally. He was taken into the Medici household under *Cosimo de Medici, and in 1434 he began his career with a large commission to paint a fresco for the high altar of Sant' Ambroggio. In 1442 Lippi was appointed rector and abbot of the parish of San Quirico, near Florence, an hon-orific post due to the favor of Cosimo de Medici. He fell into a scandalous lawsuit in 1450, was imprisoned and tortured, and confessed to cheating his student Giovanni de Rovezzano of a year's pay, largely because Lippi himself had not been paid for his own work. He was soon released, and from 1452 onward he began his greatest work, the frescoes in the Cathedral of Prato. The effect of this lawsuit carried over for several years, and in 1455 Lippi was deprived of his benefice at San Quirico. This caused no hardship for Lippi, because in 1452 he had been appointed chaplain to the monastery of San Niccolò de Frieri in Florence, and in 1456 he was appointed chaplain to the nuns of Santa Margherita in Prato.

This appointment was the beginning of the most notorious and artistically creative part of Fra Filippo Lippi's life. Lippi was commissioned to depict the Madonna on a panel for the high altar of the convent's church, and the fifty-year old artist became romantically involved with his model, a twenty-three–year-old nun named Lucrezia Buti. This affair resulted in the birth of their son, Filippino, in 1457. Their romance could not be kept secret for long, and in May 1461 a *tamburazione* or secret accusation was made against Lippi, creating another scandal. But Lippi managed to avoid catastrophe again, because Cosimo de Medici convinced Pope *Pius II to grant them a special dispensation. This released Lippi and Lucrezia from the observance of their vows, allowing them to marry. He finished his masterpiece frescoes in Prato Cathedral in 1465 and tried to retire with his wife and family. He was invited, however, to paint the principal chapel of the Cathedral of Spoleto in 1467, and the birth of his daughter Alessandra in 1465 compelled him to agree to do the work. From 1467 to 1469 Lippi worked on his last frescoes, and on 9 October 1469 he died, rumored to have been poisoned as the result of yet another amorous intrigue.

Scholars have claimed that Lippi's artistic merits derived from a "healthy interpretation of sentiment, robustness of conception and execution, and unfailing good humor" combined with an "undeniable superiority of technique." He was trained in the classical methods of *Donatello and is considered the successor to *Giotto. Lippi was the predecessor of Michelangelo and precursor to Raphael, and his most distinguished student was *Sandro Botticelli. Lippi was the father to Filippino Lippi, who was an exceptional artist in his own right.

Fra Filippo Lippi is important in the history of fifteenth-century art because he opened new horizons and brought forth fresh possibilities to painters. He boldly shook off conventionalism in painting and gave a human interpretation to heavenly themes. He replaced the forbidding fourteenth-century Madonna and somber Christ child with a new human mother and a laughing baby. This is the heart of Fra Filippo Lippi's contribution: in simply painting his beloved Lucrezia as the Madonna, he translated the abstract ideal female into the real human woman, breathing life and affection into fifteenth-century art.

Bibliography: A. J. Anderson, *The Joyous Friar: The Story of Fra Filippo Lippi*, 1927; Charles M. Rosenberg, ed., *Art and Politics in Late Medieval and Early Renaissance Italy, 1250–1500*, 1990.

Dominique Tieman

Llull, Ramon, "the Blessed" (c. 1232–1316), also called Lull, Lully, or Lullius, wrote close to three hundred religious exhortations, poems, prose novels, and encyclopedias primarily for the conversion of nonbelievers to Christianity. He also developed a semimechanical system of logic, called his "Art," which he used to demonstrate rationally the truths of Christian revelation. He traveled extensively lecturing on his Art throughout France, Italy, Spain, and North Africa after a series of divine visions impelled him to abandon his troubadour lifestyle. He never took holy orders, but was associated with both the Dominicans and Franciscans. The Catholic church has refused his canonization, although he has been beatified and is venerated on Majorca, the island of his birth.

At the time of Llull's birth, Majorca, situated in the Mediterranean halfway between northern Africa and Spain and Provence to the north, had recently been annexed from the Moors by Jaime I, "the Conqueror," king of Aragon. Ramon maintained a lifelong friendship with the Conqueror's grandson, Jaime II, whose seneschal he became around 1257. Also around this date he married Blanca Picany. Our main source of information on Llull is his autobiographical *Contemporary Life*, dictated at Paris toward the end of his life. Llull castigated his youthful life of vanity and lust until he was visited by a vision of Christ crucified while composing a love lyric. In imitation of St. Francis, he sold all his possessions, and a vision on Mount Randa provided him with the outlines of the "books that he had in mind against the errors of the infidels." All of Llull's subsequent writings must be placed in the context of these visions and his missionary designs.

After his visions and a period of study, Llull campaigned among kings and popes for financial assistance for building missionary colleges and recapturing the Holy Land, but his only major success along these lines occurred at the Council of Vienne (1311), at which chairs for the study of Arabic, Hebrew, and Chaldean were established at major European universities. Llull himself wrote works in Arabic (now lost), Latin, and his native Catalan. He aided in the development of Catalan, a romance language related to Castilian Spanish and Provençale, as a literary language. His prose novels *Felix* (a thinly disguised encyclopedia) and *Blanquerna*, a tale of a Christian utopia, were among the earliest prose vernacular works written in Europe.

Llull's fame rests on his "Art," a series of works beginning with the *Ars compendiosa inveniendi veritatis* (1274), which has been variously described as a logic machine, a forerunner of the modern digital computer, "the syllogism represented in diagrams," and a "thinking machine" (by Friedrich Hegel). The Art went through several changes throughout Llull's career, with the appearance of an *Ars demonstrativa* (c. 1283), *Arbor scientiae* (1295–96), *Liber de praedictione* (1304), and the *Ars brevis* (1308). Some of the primary features of Llull's Art include (1) the nine (originally sixteen) Dignities or absolute principles of God, from which all creation proceeds—Goodness, Greatness, Eternity, Power, Wisdom, Will, Virtue, Truth, and Glory; (2) nine relative principles—Difference, Concordance, Contrariety, Beginning, Middle, End, Majority, Equality, and Minority; and (3) an alphabetic shorthand for these principles (the Dignities are labeled BCDEFGHIK, with God as A). These symbols were placed by Llull on concentrically rotating wheels that generated all possible combinations of the letters. The letter combinations were then explained in accordance with Llull's "necessary reasons" to answer specific theological, medical, scientific, and spiritual questions. Llull's purpose was to construct a device that would logically and rationally prove Christian revelation to theologians and natural philosophers of Islam and Judaism by reference to the very structure of physical reality, the same for all cultures and hence scientifically irrefutable. Llull therefore included in his system a relationship between the four Aristotelian elements of Air, Fire, Water, and Earth and the Dignities since God created the world of the elements by impressing his attributes upon material nature. Llull may have borrowed these ideas from Arabic writers, the Jewish Cabala, or Neoplatonic emanationism; he was apparently self-educated outside of the Scholastic universities and their Aristotelian curricula.

Llull's name was affixed to a large number of alchemical works after his death, although none of these works can be confidently assigned to him, especially in light of the negative attitudes toward alchemy expressed in his legitimate works. His Art, on the other hand, retained its currency into the seventeenth century, influencing Gottfried Leibniz's universal-language scheme.

Bibliography: Mark D. Johnston, *The Spiritual Logic of Ramon Llull*, 1987; Ramon Llull, *Selected Works of Ramón Llull (1232–1316)*, 2 vols., ed. and trans. Anthony Bonner, 1985.

Alan S. Weber

Lochner, Stephan (c. 1410–51). A key figure in the transition from the late medieval period to the Renaissance in German painting, Stephan Lochner was instrumental in combining the traditional Gothic elements of medieval art with a new realism and an innovative use of color. Lochner was born in Meersburg on the coast of Lake Constance in the Holy Roman Empire, the child of Georg and Alhet Lochner. At an early age Lochner's artistic talents were recognized, and he spent much of his youth in the Netherlands serving as an apprentice to the painter *Robert Campin. During these formative years Lochner was also deeply influenced by the work of the Dutch painter *Jan van Eyck. In 1442 Lochner, along with his wife Lisbeth, moved to the German city of Cologne, where he had been commissioned by the city council to undertake a number of artistic projects. However, Lochner sought to contribute more than just his artistic talents to his community, and in 1447 and 1450 he was elected to serve on Cologne's city council. Nevertheless, an outbreak of the plague in the early 1450s cut both Lochner's artistic and political careers short. Sometime between 22 September 1451 and 7 January 1452 the eminent artist succumbed to the disease and died in Cologne soon thereafter.

Artistically, Lochner emerged as the preeminent figure in the movement known as the school of Cologne. The Cologne school of painting has been described by John Rowlands as a style of art "closely bound up with the Gothic aesthetic system," characterized by "its precise, somewhat prosaically decorative drawing, abstract, gold backgrounds, [and] calligraphic silhouettes." Into that artistic environment Lochner injected a new sense of realism, creating scenes characterized by a "spontaneous and unaffected" grace. Even though his work was sometimes overwhelmingly elaborate, Lochner was still highly influential in the development of German art by being both a prominent practitioner of the new, "modern" techniques of his craft and by introducing stylistic ele-aments borrowed from Flemish painting into the German artistic scene. How-ever, Lochner was significant to the Cologne movement not as an object of direct imitation (for few subsequent painters slavishly copied his style), but instead because his works inspired other artists to break with the stale conven-tions of medieval painting and creatively inject an element of their own person-alities into their art.

Lochner left behind a number of prominent works. His earliest pieces from the 1420s and 1430s, such as *St. Jerome in His Cell*, still heavily reflected the influence of the Dutch artistic schools and his mentor, Campin. Many of Loch-ner's works not only exhibit a high degree of technical proficiency and aesthetic merit, but also serve as valuable portholes into the Renaissance world view of Lochner and many of his contemporaries. In the *Altar of the Patron Saints* (c. 1440), considered to be Cologne's most important panel painting, Lochner in-corporated a group of Cologne's most venerated religious heroes into a scene depicting the birth of the Christ child. In *The Last Judgment* (c. 1440), Lochner drew upon the traditions of late medieval German mysticism in depicting the struggle between ultimate good and evil in the hearts of all people. Lochner portrayed Christ, the Virgin Mary, and John the Baptist presiding over the forces of good as they battled their demonic adversaries on the Day of Judgment. Again, in *The Virgin in the Rose Bower* (c. 1450), Lochner employed both biblical symbolism and popular folklore to emphasize Mary's purity and inno-cence while he also used geometric patterns and the nuances of color to suggest perfection and eternity. Some of Lochner's other major works include *Virgin with the Violet* (c. 1440), two different pieces both entitled *Presentation in the Temple* (c. 1445 and 1447), and *Adoration of the Child* (1445).

Although Lochner behind no prominent students to build upon his legacy, his work still emerged as an important landmark in German painting's transition from the Middle Ages to the Renaissance. In fact, Lochner's creativity and innovative technique continued to be influential long past his premature death, inspiring other artists to break with convention and explore new ways of ex-pressing themselves through painting. Such was Lochner's reputation that almost a century later he was mentioned in the travel dairy of the renowned German artist Albrecht Dürer. The famed engraver reported that while he was touring Cologne in the early sixteenth century, his guide successfully bargained for a larger tip before allowing him to view Lochner's *Altar of the Patron Saints*, testifying to the value and durability of the Cologne master's art.

Bibliography: John Rowlands, *The Age of Dürer and Holbein: German Drawings, 1400–1550*, 1988; James Snyder, *Northern Renaissance Art*, 1985.

Timothy L. Wood

Lopes, Fernão (c. 1380–c. 1460). Known as the "father of Portuguese history," Fernão Lopes chronicled the reigns of the first ten kings of Portugal conscientiously and skillfully. His impact on Portuguese prose, as well as his legacy for Portuguese history, is considerable.

Fernão (or Fernam) Lopes was born around 1380, probably of humble parents; although he wrote that his father fought with Nuno Álvares on behalf of the eventual João I when Lopes was a child, very little is known about these early years of Lopes's life. In 1418 he was appointed keeper of the documents in Lisbon's State Archives under King João I, who named him his secretary the following year. In 1422 he was private secretary to the infante Fernando, João's son. In 1434 King Duarte assigned him the task of writing the chronicles of the kings of Portugal in exchange for a salary of 14,000 reis, later raised to 20,000 reis with the accession of *Alfonso V in 1449. He retired from his post as chronicler sometime between 1452 and 1454. Lopes's private life is largely unknown, although he did have a son, Martinho, who died in 1443. Martinho's illegitimate son, Nuno, was barred from inheriting his grandfather's possessions in a 1459 document that marked Fernão Lopes's last appearance in the historical record.

Lopes wrote accounts of all ten kings of Portugal up to his day, but only three remain: the short *Crónica del Rei Dom Pedro* [I], the *Crónica del Rei Dom Fernando* [I], and the two-part *Crónica del Rei Dom Joam de boa memoria* [João I]. In these works, Lopes drew heavily on the escalating arguments over the nature of kingship in the high Middle Ages, including those of Giles of Rome. Lopes detailed the abuses of justice and power by the foreign (largely Castilian) oligarchy established after the death of Fernando I, arguing that these factors justified setting aside the hereditary rights of Fernando's daughter Beatriz, who had married Juan I of Castile. The eventual succession of João I of Avis to the Portuguese throne, supported by the common people and the Cortes of Portugal, became part of a providential design under which the new king was identified with the Christ of the New Testament (a rival faction, Lopes noted, actually called him the "Messiah of Lisbon"). Thus the accession of the House of Avis was justified on political and religious grounds alike.

Although Lopes borrowed material from other medieval chroniclers, he was unusually concerned with establishing historical truth and accuracy, frequently critiquing earlier historians on those grounds. From Lopes's position in the archives, he traveled widely and culled documents from Portuguese churches and convents as well as from the neighboring kingdom of Castile. However, Lopes's attention to detail seems not to have hampered his storytelling genius: entire speeches attributed to various actors, including (at one point) the city of Lisbon, appear in his works alongside vibrant portraits of kings, queens, bishops, nobles, and the occasional commoner. At various points in his works, he asserted that his chronicles should be "well ordered" and "keeping to the rules of philosophy" while presenting facts "in a good and clear style." In fact, Lopes is considered to have been one of the greatest stylists of early Portuguese prose. By treating ideas such as Portuguese nationalism, divinely ordained kingship, and source-oriented history, Lopes characterized the fusion of so-called medieval and modern concepts that is often seen in gifted thinkers of his age.

Bibliography: L. de Sousa Rebelo, "The Idea of Kingship in the Chronicles of Fernão Lopes," in *Medieval and Renaissance Studies on Spain and Portugal in Honour of P. E. Russell*, 1981.

Wendy Love Anderson

López de Ayala, Pero (1332–1407), was one of the most important political figures in Castile during the early years of the Trastámara dynasty and a pivotal character in the intellectual life of the kingdom. He is sometimes considered Spain's first humanist because his literary works reflected much that was new at the turn of the fourteenth century. His life spanned the reigns of five Castilian kings, whose history he recorded as an eyewitness. In his seventy-five years he was able to remain politically viable despite his loyalty to a despotic king for sixteen years and his subsequent change in allegiance to a rival faction. Both during his official career and after his retirement to a Jeronimite monastery, Ayala produced masterworks in a variety of genres and provided a shining example of political savvy harmonized with intellectual acumen.

Pero López de Ayala was born in the province of Álava, son of Don Fernando López de Ayala and Doña Elvira Alvarez de Ceballos. Theirs was an ancient Basque family that by this period had become members of the wealthy nobility. His early education was supervised by his great-uncle, Cardinal Pedro Gómez Barroso, in Avignon. Ayala received a benefice in the Cathedral of Toledo, but when Cardinal Barroso died in the plague of 1348, the young Pero López returned to Castile and gave up his clerical career for the life of a *caballero* (knight).

Ayala's military and political career was under way by 1359, when he commanded a galley in a naval expedition for King Pedro I. He was appointed *alguacil mayor* of the city of Toledo as a reward. Pero López de Ayala and his family received many of the *mercedes reales* during the reign of Enrique II. As ambassador for this king, Ayala by his diplomacy averted warfare between Castile and Aragon, and his success in this venue earned him further assignments to negotiate a continuing alliance with the French monarchy (1378–80). During the reign of Juan I, Ayala had become royal counselor and ambassador to France. For his assistance in suppressing the Flemish revolt against their count and king (1382), *Charles VI of France granted Ayala a permanent salary. His influence and position continued to grow in the following reign, when he served as a member of the regency council for Enrique III. When that king began his personal rule, Ayala retired to Álava and dedicated himself to scholarly pursuits, but in 1399 Enrique III named him high chancellor of the realm. Among his titles and offices, Pero López de Ayala counted *merino mayor* of Guipúzcoa, *alcalde mayor* of Vittoria, *merino* of Álava, and lord of Salvatierra.

In spite of his active military and political life, Ayala was a prolific author. His literary works may be divided into four groups. The first included poetic works, the most distinguished of which was the *Rimado de palacio*, a lengthy poetry collection (2,150 stanzas written mostly in the style known as *cuaderna vía*), which was a moral treatise incorporating the Ten Commandments, the Seven Deadly Sins, the cardinal virtues, sections of the *Moralia in Job* by St. Gregory the Great, and an exposé of the corruption and dishonesty of his contemporaries. Another group included minor prose works such as the *Libro de la caça de las aves* (on hunting). A third group featured translations of a variety of works into Spanish, including Livy's *Decadas*, *Giovanni Boccaccio's *De casibus virorum illustrium*, and St. Gregory's *Moralia in Job*. His fourth group comprised major historical works in prose, such as *Crónicas de los reyes de Castilla* and *Crónica del Rey Don Pedro*, arguably his most important contributions to the scholarly work of this period.

Pero López de Ayala wrote his chronicles of the reigns of Pedro I (the Cruel), Enrique II, Juan I, and Enrique III with an attention to detail gleaned from years of personal experience in these royal courts. In addition to recording the biographies and events of these reigns, Ayala was concerned with providing information necessary to make sound moral and political judgments. He understood that his work as a historian could influence the future of Castile by affecting the hearts and minds of his readers. In his *Crónica del Rey Don Pedro* (which historian Helen Nader considers the rhetorical model and the political bible of the Castilian Renaissance), Ayala explained why he remained loyal for so long to a king so bloodthirsty that he ordered Ayala to participate in the demise of some of his own relatives. Ayala then described and analyzed the later events that led to his change of loyalty to the illegitimate Trastámara lineage, and to the ultimate demise of the cruel king. In each of his chronicles, Ayala approached his sources critically, in a strikingly "modern" style, to produce an accurate work of scholarship. It is this quality, along with his erudite writing and probing analyses, that warrants his reputation as "the first and greatest of the *caballero* historians."

Bibliography: Pero López de Ayala, *Crónicas*, ed. José-Luis Martín, 1991; Helen Nader, *The Mendoza Family in the Spanish Renaissance, 1350 to 1550*, 1979.

                                                              Rowena Hernández Múzquiz

López de Córdoba, Leonor (c. 1362–c. 1412).

The life of the Castilian noblewoman Leonor López de Córdoba is known to us primarily because she chose to record episodes from her life in one of the earliest examples of female autobiography, *Las memorias*. The text, which was probably written near the end of her life, provides a stirring insight into the tumultuous events and highly charged political climate of fourteenth-century Castile. The work is also noteworthy for its very personal tone; Doña Leonor narrated signal occurrences in late medieval Castile, but her individual suffering on account of these changes is painfully clear.

Leonor's family was caught in the middle of a fourteenth-century Castilian civil war that pitted King Pedro I against his illegitimate half brother, Enrique II of Trastámara. In 1369 Enrique II won the civil war he had launched against his brother and so claimed the throne as his own. As a loyal supporter of Pedro, Leonor's father was beheaded. Ultimately, in the aftermath of the civil war, Leonor, her husband, her siblings, and other members of the family were imprisoned for approximately nine years. While they were in prison, a plague epidemic broke out, claiming all of Leonor's family except her husband. With the death of Enrique in 1379, Leonor and her husband were freed from prison. Their overwhelming concern at this point was to reclaim their fortune and status. Leonor went to live with her aunt while her husband sought to restore their estate. He quickly discovered, however, that such a mission was doomed to failure, and he returned to Leonor. They lived an impoverished life, haunted as much by their lost honor as their lost wealth.

Recurrent outbreaks of plague assailed Leonor in the years that followed. While she was taking refuge from the plague in Córdoba in the town of Aguilar, Leonor adopted a young boy, Alfonso, who may have been either Jewish or Muslim. Plague soon came to Aguilar, and Leonor sent Alfonso to Ecija. He later returned to her in Aguilar, however, already suffering from plague. Leonor drafted various friends and family to help nurse him, yet these thirteen individuals all also died of plague, one of whom was Leonor's biological son. These deaths aroused feelings of profound guilt and despair in Leonor. Perhaps anxious to distance herself from this catastrophe, her aunt used these deaths as an excuse for abruptly ending the charity that she had extended to Leonor previously.

Leonor's autobiography ended at this point, but we know that she temporarily landed on her feet. The accounts of royal chroniclers reveal that she eventually became a lady courtier and counselor to the queen regent, Catalina de Lancaster. Here she appears to have occupied a prominent position, advising the queen in various affairs—the chroniclers suggest that the queen made no decisions without Leonor's approval. Yet her political career echoed that of her father. She fell from the queen's good graces, probably as a result of jealous court rumors, and Catalina expelled her. From this point forward we know little of her life except that she died around 1412.

Bibliography: Amy Katz Kaminsky and Elaine Dorough Johnson, "To Restore Honor and Fortune: 'The Autobiography of Leonor López de Córdoba,' " in *The Female Autograph: Theory and Practice of Autobiography from the Tenth to the Twentieth Century*, ed. Donna C. Stanton, 1987.

Elizabeth Lehfeldt

López de Mendoza, Iñigo (1398–1458), better known as the marquis of
Santillana, was born on 19 August 1398 to *Diego Hurtado de Mendoza and
his second wife, Leonor de la Vega, of the Asturias de Santillana family. His
elder brother and father succumbed during his early childhood, and his mother
had to fight to protect his patrimony from incursions by relatives. Leonor arranged a politically advantageous union for him with Catalina de Figueroa in
1408; they married in 1416 and apparently lived happily, giving birth to five
sons and three daughters. During his youth Iñigo frequented the court of Aragon,
meeting many great poets, including Enrique de Villena, *Ausias March, and
Jordi de Sant Jordi, and developing the military skills that served him well in
the interminable internecine struggles that characterized Castilian politics during
the fifteenth century. In Castile, Don Iñigo participated actively in the partisan
struggles against *Álvaro de Luna, *Juan II's favorite and the constable of Castile, whose power was so great he was widely considered the effectual ruler. In
1420 Iñigo backed Enrique of Aragon's imprisonment of Luna. With Luna's
escape and reassumption of power in 1422, Don Iñigo withdrew from court to
his fortress in Guadalajara to escape Luna's revenge and to compose literary
works. When Enrique attempted to exile Luna in 1427, Iñigo again supported
his efforts. Since his primary interests lay with Juan II, however, Don Iñigo
soon took up arms against the Aragonese to defend the Castilian border of
Agreda in 1429, where a few of his *serranillas* are set. During this campaign
Don Iñigo fought bravely in the Battle of Araviana and was amply rewarded by
Juan. The king recognized Don Iñigo's learning by asking him to compose
Proverbs (*Proverbios*) for his son, the future *Enrique IV of Castile. Don Iñigo
also participated in Juan's campaign against the Moors, capturing Huelma in
1438. When Álvaro de Luna moved against him, giving Iñigo's holdings in
Guadalajara to Prince Enrique in 1440, Don Iñigo took arms against the prince's
troops and occupied Alcalá de Henares, a conflict that culminated in Luna's
exile in 1441 and Iñigo's regaining Guadalajara. Two years later, when Luna
was recalled to Castile, Don Iñigo fought by his side to liberate Juan II from
the Aragonese; his noteworthy participation in the famous Battle of Olmedo in
1445 earned him the title of marquis of Santillana and count of Real de Man-
zanares. However, the marquis was soon openly conspiring against Luna, who
had imprisoned his cousin, the count of Alba, for whom he wrote his philosophical dialogue, *Bias versus Fortune* (*Bias contra fortuna*). Luna was finally
captured and decapitated in 1452, inspiring the marquis's satiric *The Confidants'
Manual* (*Doctrinal de privados*). After Luna's fall, the marquis gained influence
at court, but Juan II's death in 1454 and the deaths of his wife and son in 1455
encouraged him to retire to Guadalajara, where he died on 25 March 1458.

   Aside from his achievements in battle and his political role during this turbulent period of Castilian history, the marquis of Santillana is best known for
his literary works, especially for his Petrarchan sonnets that reflected the wider
European adoption of the Italian Renaissance. In his youth he studied Latin and

Italian letters as well as Galician-Portuguese poetry, and his work reflects his attempts to blend these earlier styles with Renaissance themes in Castilian language. One of many illustrious poets who frequented Juan II's court, he distinguished himself by cultivating many poetic styles, both lyric and allegorical, as well as producing prose texts. These included the didactic *Proverbs*, the philosophical *Bias versus Fortune*, and the theoretical *Prologue and Letter . . . to the Constable of Portugal* (*Prohemio é carta . . . al condestable de Portugal*), in which he discussed the science of poetry. In the breadth of his production, the marquis represents the height of the literary achievements of fifteenth-century Castile.

Bibliography: Helen Nader, *The Mendoza Family in the Spanish Renaissance, 1350 to 1550*, 1979; Rogelio Pérez-Bustamante, *El Marqués de Santillana: Biografía y documentación*, 1983.

Denise K. Filios

Louis I, "the Great," King of Hungary and Poland (b. 1326, r. 1342–82).

Revered as one of Hungary's greatest kings, Louis I ruled there from 1342 and in Poland from 1370, expanding the Hungarian domain and the monarchy's power to their maximum extent and actively supporting both the church and the arts. He was the son of Charles I Robert, first Angevin king of Hungary, who ended the anarchy following the Arpad dynasty's demise in 1301, and Elizabeth, daughter of Wladislaw I and sister of Casimir III (the Great) of Poland. Louis became prince of Transylvania in 1338 and king of Hungary at age sixteen. His second wife, Elizabeth of Bosnia, bore him three daughters, Catherine, Mary, and Hedviga.

Unlike his cautious, statesmanlike father, upon whose work his success was built, Louis was a soldier who idolized the warlike St. Ladislas and personally led his armies into battle, and whose foreign policy gratified the nobility and won him the title "the Great." In the Balkans Louis reestablished Hungarian control over Croatia in 1345 but elsewhere settled for creating vassal states (and looting) with multiple campaigns against Bosnia, Bulgaria, Serbia (aided by Stephen Dustin's death), Moldavia, and Wallachia. After suffering defeat against Venice at Zara in 1346, Louis acquired all of Dalmatia, including Ragusa (Dubrovnik), in his second Venetian war in 1355–58, consolidated by his third in 1372–81, in which his ally Genoa did most of the fighting. He conquered Naples in 1347 after Queen Joanna, who enjoyed the Avignon papacy's support, murdered her husband Andrew, Louis's brother, in 1345. He took the title "king of Sicily and Jerusalem," retreated before the plague in 1348, but returned to suppress opposition in 1350. Louis was forced to abandon the kingdom in 1352, but in 1381 he installed on the throne his adopted son Charles of Durazzo, who had Johanna strangled. Louis won Hungary's first battle against the Ottoman Turks in 1367 and defeated them in 1377 after they temporarily asserted control over Bosnia, Serbia, and Wallachia. He joined Casimir's wars against the Lithuanians and the Mongols, ending their encroachments on Hungarian and Polish territory.

According to his father's 1339 agreement with Casimir, Louis inherited the Polish throne on the latter's death in 1370, though he spent little time in Poland, relying heavily on his mother's presence there. At the Diet of Kassa in 1374, he confirmed the Polish nobility's privileges in return for recognition of his daughters' right to inherit that throne. Though he wished his eldest surviving daughter Mary and her betrothed, *Sigismund (Emperor Charles IV's son), to inherit both kingdoms, the Poles instead elected Hedviga following his death, and there was a protracted succession crisis in Hungary.

Modern estimates of Louis vary, many emphasizing his greatness, others the enormous cost of acquiring his vast but ephemeral domain. His kingdoms remained on Europe's periphery, and westernization was superficial, largely the work of clergy and Germans living in the cities. Cities grew, notably Buda, but major trade routes no longer ran through Hungary, and it was the kingdom's prolific gold mines, so important before discovery of the New World, that attracted traders. Louis's legal code of 1351 confirmed and expanded the rights given the nobility in Andrew II's Golden Bull of 1222, giving all the same freedoms, and it provided protection for peasants. True feudalism did not exist in Hungary, though western ideas of knighthood were popular during his reign. Louis actively propagated Catholicism throughout his realm and combated the resurgent Bogomil heresy in the Balkans, though outside Hungary proper he was tolerant of Orthodox Christians; however, he expelled the Jews after failing to convert them. Louis brought French and Italian artists and architects and thus early Renaissance influences to his kingdom, though Hungarian elements remained dominant. He built a grand palace at Buda, numerous churches, and other buildings; commissioned the beautiful illuminated *Chronicle*, a history of Hungary; and founded the University of Pécs in 1367. Much great sculpture was later destroyed, though the Kolozsvár brothers' statue of St. George survives in Prague. The growth of literacy in the fourteenth century was reflected in the proliferation of government documents, though western influence on literature was minimal, and comparatively little is extant. Notable exceptions are a bardic account of Nicholas Toldi, one of Louis's knights, and a history of his reign by János Kukullei.

Bibliography: Anthony Endrey, *Hungarian History*, 1982; Pál Engel, "The Age of the Angevines, 1301–1382," in *A History of Hungary*, ed. Peter F. Sugar, Péter Hanák, and Tibor Frank, 1990; Domokos Varga, *Hungary in Greatness and Decline: The 14th and 15th Centuries*, 1982.

William B. Robison

Louis IV, "the Bavarian," King of the Germans and Holy Roman Emperor (b. 1287, r. 1314–47).

Louis IV (also known as Lewis or Ludwig)

ruled the Holy Roman Empire from 1314 to 1347, conducted the last great medieval struggle between the empire and the papacy, and patronized several important political theorists. Son of the Wittelsbach Louis II, count palatine and ruler of Upper Bavaria (d. 1294), and Mathilda, daughter of the Habsburg emperor Rudolf I, Louis married Beatrice of Silesia-Glogau in 1309 and gradually gained control of Upper and Lower Bavaria. Following Emperor Henry VII's unexpected death in 1313, divisions among the German electors led to a double election in 1314 wherein the Habsburgs and Louis's brother Rudolf (his rival for Wittelsbach lands) elected Frederick I (the Fair), duke of Austria, while Archbishops Baldwin of Trier and Peter of Mainz and the Luxembourg party elected Louis. War resulted, lasting until Louis's victory at Mühldorf in 1322. By then he faced opposition from the aged French pope *John XXII (1316–34), ally of Robert of Naples and successive kings of France. In 1324 John excommunicated Louis, whom he derisively labeled Ludovicus Bavarus, for assuming the title "king of the Romans" without papal approbation. Louis responded by attacking papal abuses in the Appeal of Sachsenhausen, and John placed Germany under interdict. Louis strengthened his hand in Germany by marrying Margaret of Holland in 1324, compromising with the Habsburgs in 1325, obtaining the margravate of Brandenburg for his eldest son Louis in 1328, and consolidating Wittelsbach lands in 1329. Allied with the Ghibellines and Frederick of Sicily, he challenged Pope John in Italy, crossed the Alps in 1327, obtained the iron crown of Lombardy in Milan, conquered Pisa, received the imperial crown from Sciarra Colonna in Rome, deposed John (who was in Avignon), and elected a Spiritual Franciscan antipope, Nicholas V. However, a subsequent campaign against Robert of Naples failed, Rome became disenchanted, additional imperial allies were not forthcoming, and in 1330 Louis returned to Germany and Nicholas abdicated.

In the 1330s Louis faced new enemies in Pope *Benedict XII (1334–42) and Philip VI of France and a rival for the imperial throne in John of Bohemia. In 1337 he allied with *Edward III of England at the outset of the Hundred Years' War. In 1338 the electors asserted at Rhens that their chosen candidate might rightfully rule the empire with the title of king without papal approbation. Shortly after, at the Diet of Frankfurt, Louis extended this principle to the imperial election with the law *licet iuris*. However, Louis failed to capitalize on nascent German nationalism, and in 1341 his alliance with Edward ended. In 1342, following *William of Ockham's advice, he antagonized Germans by dissolving Margaret Maultasch of Tyrol's marriage to John of Bohemia's son John Henry, marrying her to his son Louis instead, and annexing Tyrol to Brandenburg. Pope *Clement VI (1342–52) excommunicated Louis again in 1343, and in 1346 a majority of electors deposed Louis and elected another of John of Bohemia's sons as Charles IV. Louis died of a stroke while hunting bears on 11 October 1347, sparing Germany further conflict.

Louis's Munich was a thriving intellectual center. *Marsiglio of Padua (c. 1275/80–c. 1342), a University of Paris professor whose *Defensor pacis* (1324) provoked John XXII to excommunicate him in 1326, sought Louis's protection, accompanied him to Italy, and lived at his court. *Defensor pacis* provided theoretical justification for Louis in his struggle with the papacy, just as *Dante's De monarchia* had done for Henry VII, though it is uncertain how well Louis understood its implications. Marsiglio's political theory, often described as the most innovative of the medieval era, espoused popular sovereignty, argued that the state's coercive power must be used for the common good, identified the emperor as the defender of peace and thus of justice, labeled the church as the enemy of peace, denied divine sanction for the ecclesiastical hierarchy and papal claims for *plenitudo potestatis* (supreme power), and regarded a general council as superior to the pope. Louis himself conducted an extensive propaganda war with the Avignon popes, lodging numerous appeals against them, including a call for a general council. The Spiritual Franciscans strongly supported Louis, led by philosopher/theologian Ockham and Michael of Cesena, general of the order. Their calls for apostolic poverty led John XXII to declare them heretics. In 1328 Ockham, Cesena, and others fled from Avignon to Louis's court. Ockham abandoned philosophy and theology and devoted himself to political works. Another Franciscan, Bonagratia of Bergamo, produced a manifesto justifying universal empire. Regrettably, many intellectuals in Germany succumbed to the Black Death, which reached Europe the same year that Louis died.

Bibliography: Joachim Leuschner, *Germany in the Late Middle Ages*, 1980; H. S. Offler, "Empire and Papacy: The Last Struggle," *Transactions of the Royal Historical Society*, ser. 5, vol. 6 (1965): 21–47; William Stubbs, *Germany in the Later Middle Ages, 1200–1500*, rpt., 1971.

William B. Robison

Louis XI, King of France (b. 1423, r. 1461–83).

Louis XI, the son of *Charles VII of France and Marie of Anjou, made a name for himself both as a fierce warrior and as a cunning negotiator. He came to be known as the "Universal Spider" for his ability to weave together alliances and agreements that benefited his kingdom without constant resort to warfare. By the time of his death, the territory ruled by the French Crown had vastly expanded, and the government of this domain had become centralized under his rule.

When Louis was two years old, his politically beleaguered father sent him to the Castle of Loches in Touraine, where he remained until he was ten, to protect him from Anglo-Burgundian enemies. He married Margaret, daughter of *James I of Scotland, in 1436; the next year, only fourteen years old, he led a successful assault against an English garrison along the Seine. Two years later his father made him lieutenant general in Languedoc, where his talent for restoring order through diplomacy first made itself apparent. In 1440 a league of princes of the realm convinced Louis to join them in a revolt against his father's own government. Their attempt to take over the government (called the "Praguerie" after similar uprisings in Bohemia) quickly failed. Charles pardoned his son and, recognizing in him a headstrong desire to rule, gave him partial control of Dauphiné.

Louis early distinguished himself as a military man. He served in his father's campaigns against the English, forcing them to raise the siege of Dieppe in 1443. The Anglo-French truce of 1444 unfortunately left large numbers of mercenaries unoccupied. To keep them from pillaging in France, Louis led them in a successful offensive against Basel in support of the German king Frederick V in his quarrel with the Swiss Confederation.

Louis's wife Margaret died suddenly in 1445. At this time Charles VII fell under the influence of Pierre de Brézé, his first minister. Louis, feeling his ambitions thwarted by Brézé, plotted unsuccessfully for his removal from court. Now estranged from his father, Louis removed himself to Dauphiné, where he promoted trade and agriculture, founded the University of Valence, established a parliament, and instituted the first government postal service in Europe. He married his second wife, Charlotte, daughter of the duke de Savoie, in 1451 against his father's wishes. When Charles, denouncing his son's "foolish enterprises," showed up on his borders in 1456 with an army and demanded that Louis submit to his will, Louis fled to the court of Philip the Good, duke of Burgundy. He stayed there until his father's death in 1461.

As king, Louis's main problem rested with nobles who were ready to form alliances with each other or with England in order to appropriate some of his power for themselves. In 1465 a coalition of feudal lords headed by *Charles the Bold, son of the duke of Burgundy, and including Louis's brother Charles, duke of Berry, formed the League of the Public Weal, whose alleged purpose was to sweep away injustices and reduce the tax burden on the populace. After engaging the armies of the league in an indecisive battle at Montlhéry on 16 July 1465 and enduring their siege of Paris, Louis agreed to grant Normandy to his brother and to give Charles the Bold all royal territories north of the Somme. By September 1468, however, Louis's forces had compelled the duke of Brittany to renounce his alliance with the duke of Burgundy, and the duke of Berry to give up his claim to Normandy.

Louis then proposed a summit with Charles the Bold at Péronne in October 1468. During the negotiations, news leaked out that agents of the king had been fomenting rebellion among Charles's subjects in Liège. Charles compelled Louis to participate in the suppression of the revolt and to offer the region of Champagne to the duke of Berry before letting him return to France.

Louis's greatest diplomatic triumph followed in 1475. *Edward IV of England landed an army at Calais that summer, ostensibly intending to seize the Crown of France. Louis's extensive intelligence network informed him that though they had invaded France, the English were not fully committed to all-out war. With the help of *Philippe de Commynes, Louis's chief counselor, who had deserted the Burgundian camp three years earlier and later became the king's biographer, Louis engaged in negotiations with the English that resulted in the Treaty of Picquigny in 1475. In return for peace with the English, Louis agreed to pay an annual subsidy of 50,000 crowns and open up free trade between England and France. Louis managed to accomplish, with no loss of life, what his predecessors had not been able to do through years of warfare.

Meanwhile, Charles the Bold began to act on his expansionist plans by attacking the Swiss and the region of Lorraine. He underestimated his foes, suffered resounding defeats at Grandson (March 1476) and Morat (June 1476), and was killed at Nancy (January 1477). Louis's troops now occupied Franche-Comté in an attempt to claim Charles's lands for France. But Charles's daughter, Mary, soon married *Maximilian of Habsburg, son of Emperor *Frederick III, and Louis found himself embroiled for five years in a war for the possession of Burgundy. After Mary died in 1482, Louis and Maximilian agreed to the Treaty of Arras (1482), which ultimately brought the Duchy of Burgundy, Picardy, the Boulonnais, and later Franche-Comté and Artois under French control. Louis extended the lands controlled by the French Crown by "inheriting" several additional regions, including Guyenne (upon the death of the duke of Berry), Anjou (upon the death of King *René of Naples, duke of Anjou) and Provence and Maine (upon the death of the count of Maine).

The end of warfare with England and Burgundy allowed for progress in agriculture and industry and the development of commerce. Among Louis's other achievements, he centralized the government of the kingdom, founded the knightly Order of Saint Michael, and fostered printing at the Sorbonne, which helped to establish the northern dialect of French as the national linguistic standard. After suffering from ill health and a series of strokes over the course of two years, Louis died on 30 August 1483 at his château at Plessis-les-Tours.

Bibliography: Paul Murray Kendall, *Louis XI: The Universal Spider*, 1971; Emmanuel Le Roy Ladurie, *The Royal French State, 1460–1610*, 1994; David Potter, *A History of France, 1460–1560: The Emergence of a Nation State*, 1995.

Susan Arvay

Luder, Peter (1415–74), was an influential wandering professor who, along with other such notables as *Rudolf Agricola and Samuel Karoch, played a significant role in spreading Renaissance thought to the northern regions of the Holy Roman Empire in the late fifteenth century. During his years as a nomadic lecturer, Luder moved throughout much of central Europe successfully promoting humanistic studies, which, in the centuries to follow, proved crucial in shaping the religious and intellectual landscape of modern Europe.

Peter Luder was born in Kislua in Franconia. Early in his life he became a member of the clergy, which provided him the occasion to make a sojourn to Rome. During his stay Luder undertook many travels about Italy that enabled him to absorb much, both intellectually and spiritually, from the cultural revolution then sweeping the peninsula. It was also during his short travels from Rome that Luder landed in the company of a group of German students in Padua. As part of Germany's campaign to import Renaissance thought and culture, these students had been sent to Italy in order to receive the finest education in the classics from the leading Latin and Greek scholars. By becoming a member of this entourage, Luder was not only able to share in the learning of these students, but, like many of his companions, he was subsequently called upon to assist in the German effort to carry the Italian Renaissance over the Alps.

In 1456 Count Palatine Frederick I summoned Luder to occupy a newly established position as the lecturer in classical languages and literature at the University of Heidelberg. With enthusiasm Luder accepted the appointed task, which he launched by delivering his monumental Heidelberg Address. In this ground-breaking public lecture, Luder valorized the *studia humanitatis* as the learning "worthy of a free man" and insisted that poetry, classical rhetoric, and, most important, history be included in the university's Scholastically oriented curriculum. During the next four years Luder was successful in establishing the humanistic liberal arts at Heidelberg. His success was in large parts due to the advent of the printing press, but it was also the result of Luder's assertive personality, which later became the grounds for his dismissal in 1460. Before departing from Heidelberg, however, Luder had one of his most distinguished students, Stephan Hoest, appointed as his successor to ensure the survival of liberal humanism at the university.

In the years that followed, Luder continued to trumpet the cause of the new learning by initiating similar programs at neighboring universities. He spent time at both the University of Erfurt and the University of Leipzig before making his way to the University of Vienna in 1470. There Luder was able to establish a chair of rhetoric and poetry, a position that was subsequently occupied (and expanded) by the German "archhumanist" *Conrad Celtis. After his stay in Austria, Luder migrated to the University of Basel, where he ended his career and life.

As was the case with other pioneers of humanism in the Holy Roman Empire, Peter Luder had a significant impact on defining the intellectual and religious terrain of Europe in the succeeding centuries. By successfully advancing the *studia humanitatis* at many of Europe's finest universities, Luder helped provide the humanistic underpinning that continues to support much of the philosophy and theology in the modern age. Moreover, by stressing the importance of the study of history, Luder contributed significantly to the development of the Protestant tradition as well as to the historicism that evolved from it.

Bibliography: Frank Baron, "The Beginnings of German Humanism: The Life and Work of the Wandering Humanist Peter Luder," Ph.D. diss., University of California at Berkeley, 1966; James Overfield, *Humanism and Scholasticism in Late Medieval Germany*, 1984.

Gregory E. Canada

Lullus, Ramond. *See* Llull, Ramon, "the Blessed."

Luna, Álvaro de (c. 1388–1453), was the most powerful uncrowned leader in the history of medieval Spain. The *privado* (favorite) of *Juan II of Castile,

Álvaro de Luna not only attained the position of constable of Castile but also became grand master of the Order of Santiago, the dominant military order in the peninsula. He is probably best known for his spectacular fall from grace in 1453, an event that occasioned a wide range of responses. Yet his life and career had been dedicated to developing and strengthening the kingdom of Castile, of which he was de facto ruler. Luna was a formidable courtier whose contributions to the history of Spain include literary as well as political accomplishments. His story has all the elements of a Greek tragedy: great characters, fatal flaws, the fall from a great height, and universal lessons to be learned.

Álvaro de Luna was born sometime between 1388 and 1394. He was a bastard son of Don Álvaro de Luna, lord of Cañete, Jubera, and Cornado, *copero mayor*, or chief cupbearer, to Enrique III of Castile, and Maria de Cañete, a commoner. Álvaro's birth name had been Pedro de Luna, but the pope renamed him Álvaro at his confirmation at age seven. The young Álvaro de Luna was raised in Rome by his uncle, Juan Martínez de Luna, and was tutored by Ramiro de Tamayo.

When his uncle, Pedro de Luna, became archbishop of Toledo, his connections with Juan II's tutor (Gómez Carillo de Cuenca) provided an opportunity for Álvaro (age eighteen) to enter the household of the king of Castile. Juan II had begun his reign at the age of twenty-two months, with his mother (Queen Catherine, daughter of *John of Gaunt, duke of Lancaster) and his uncle (the infante Fernando) as regents. Juan II's reign began in and was marred by conflicts between the infantes of Aragon, his cousins (Juan, Enrique, Pedro, Maria, and Leonora). In this volatile milieu, Álvaro de Luna was able to establish a relationship of genuine affection as well as powerful influence with King Juan.

In 1410 Álvaro de Luna became Juan II's page. By 1414 Álvaro had become head chamberlain to the king, and the young Juan II was extremely distraught when Álvaro had to be away from the court. By this time Álvaro de Luna had established himself as a model courtier whose prowess on the tournament field was matched by his musical and poetic skills. His graciousness and good looks had won him many admirers among the ladies as well as considerable envy among his competitors. By 6 March 1419, when Juan II was recognized in his legal majority, Álvaro de Luna was already a force to be reckoned with. The hostility between the infantes over control of the kingdom through their influence on the king was becoming a scandal, and tensions erupted the following year.

The events of 1420 were a turning point in the relationship between Juan II and Álvaro de Luna when the infante Enrique sequestered the king in Tordesillas. In order to ameliorate the king's anger, the infante praised Álvaro de Luna (who had remained with the king through this ordeal), and Álvaro became a member of the king's council. When the infante Enrique set out for Andalusia with the king, they stopped in Talavera, where Luna married Elvira Portocarrero and received from the king the towns of Jubera and Cornado, which had belonged to his father, Don Álvaro de Luna. Álvaro plotted the king's escape by devising a plan to go hunting, and ultimately the king and his men arrived at the castle of Montalvan. It was here that the infante Enrique and the constable Ruy López Dávalos besieged the king and his forces. Álvaro de Luna negotiated the king's release, and as a reward Luna received San Esteban de Gormaz (with its comital title) and Ayllón.

Don Álvaro's role in rescuing the king from the clutches of the infantes earned him the king's trust as never before. The infante Enrique was arrested and placed in Luna's custody in 1422. When Ruy López Dávalos learned about Enrique's imprisonment, he fled Castile, whereupon Juan II revoked his title and possessions. On 10 December 1423 the king named Álvaro de Luna constable of the kingdoms of Castile and Leon, which conferred upon him the staff of justice and the command of all the kingdom's armies.

Although Álvaro de Luna eventually secured the infante Enrique's release from custody, renewed intrigue among the nobility (fueled by resentment over Álvaro's growing power and influence) resulted in Luna's banishment from the court in 1427. The uproar and disorder caused by this action caused the king to revoke this decision in 1428. During this time Álvaro's diplomatic skill was called upon when *Joan of Arc sent ambassadors to Juan II requesting his aid in the siege of La Rochelle. The constable, a great admirer of La Poucelle, ensured that she received some thirty-five ships supplied with men and arms to assist her efforts. The subsequent victory of these combined forces earned Castile great renown in France.

In 1429 the infantes Enrique and Pedro invaded and despoiled various areas of the kingdom, including lands that belonged to the Order of Santiago. One of the outcomes of these incidents was that Juan II delegated the administration of the Order of Santiago to Álvaro de Luna. By 1430 a peace treaty had been signed that expelled the infantes of Aragon from Castile. That same year Don Álvaro, by then a widower, married Juana Pimentel, daughter of the count of Benavente.

Once again, in 1438, the nobles rebelled and the infantes Juan and Enrique returned to the kingdom, and once again Álvaro retreated to his villa of Ayllón while Juan II was reduced to a humiliatingly subservient position for a time. However, when the infantes Juan and Enrique resorted to armed rebellion against the king, they found themselves confronted by the constable himself at the Battle of Olmedo in 1445. The constable was victorious, the infante Juan retired to his lands in Navarre, and the infante Enrique died from battle wounds.

That same year saw another turning point for Álvaro de Luna with the death of Juan II's queen, Maria of Aragon. Don Álvaro secretly arranged a marriage for Juan II with the infanta Isabel of Portugal, which the king did not dare refuse. Thinking that the young queen would be grateful to him for his arrangement, Luna soon learned that scheming nobles had turned her against him. She eventually put pressure on Juan II to order a judgment against the *privado*. Álvaro de Luna was arrested, and the judges declared him guilty of usurping the royal power, appropriating the rents of the Crown, and bewitching the king in order to control him.

Álvaro de Luna was executed in Valladolid on 2 June 1453, opening a twenty-year period of feuding and anarchy for the next weak king, *Enrique IV, whose *privado* was not nearly as effective at protecting royal authority as Luna had been. Álvaro de Luna and his widow Juana Pimentel are buried in Luna's chapel (Capilla de Santiago) in the Cathedral of Toledo.

Álvaro de Luna accomplished the reform of Castilian bureaucracy after the disruptive years of the first Trastámara conflict during the reign of Pedro I. During that time the nobility had gained enormous privilege and control of offices, which the constable reduced considerably through his method of appointments by selection or merit. His chief concern was increasing royal authority at the expense of seigneurial privilege, and the codes of law that he was responsible for generating reflected these interests. He is considered the actual ruler of the kingdom during the reign of Juan II, and his loyalty to the king was not only what made him but also what destroyed him.

Luna was a man of letters as well as the king's chief minister. He was an accomplished poet whose works are included in the *Cancionero de Baena* (completed in 1445), and he wrote a courtly treatise on women, the *Libro de las virtuosas e claras mugeres*, in 1446. His dramatic rise and meteoric fall also inspired his contemporaries (both sympathetic and antagonistic) to produce major works such as the *Crónica de Don Álvaro de Luna* attributed to Gonzalo Chacón, the *Laberinto de fortuna* of *Juan de Mena, and the *Doctrinal de privados* by *Iñigo López de Mendoza, marquis of Santillana.

Bibliography: Didier T. Jaen, *John II of Castile and the Grand Master Alvaro de Luna*, 1978; Nicholas Round, *The Greatest Man Uncrowned: A Study of the Fall of Don Alvaro de Luna*, 1986.

Rowena Hernández Múzquiz

Luna, Pedro de. *See* Benedict XIII, Anti-pope.

Lydgate, John (c. 1370–1449), is considered one of the most prolific of all English poets, with over 145,000 lines of verse. In his own day and through the seventeenth century he was highly admired and imitated, and his name was linked with *John Gower and *Geoffrey Chaucer as equals among poets. Today his reputation has considerably fallen, as his style of poetry generally holds little excitement for the modern reader. Nevertheless, Lydgate's writings are worthy of study because they are very representative of the tastes and expectations of the medieval mind.

John Lydgate was most likely born in the village of Lydgate in Suffolk and entered the monastery at Bury St. Edmunds in 1385 at the age of fifteen. He was ordained a Benedictine priest in 1397 and studied at Oxford between 1406 and 1408. His literary abilities attracted attention early, and he was commissioned in 1412 by the Prince of Wales (later Henry V) to translate *The Troy Book* into English from Guido delle Colonne's *Historia destructionis*. Lydgate's next project was *The Siege of Thebes*, written in 1420–21 as a continuation of Chaucer's *Canterbury Tales*. Lydgate's longest work, *The Fall of Princes*, was written from 1431 to 1438 and was a rendering of the French prose translation of *Giovanni Boccaccio's *De casibus virorum illustrium*. In addition to his long poems, Lydgate wrote many short poems on a variety of subjects. His better-known efforts reflect heavy Chaucerian influence: *The Complaint of the Black Knight* is modeled on *The Book of the Duchess: The Temple of Glas* imitates *The House of Fame*; and *The Floure of Courtesy* is a Valentine's Day poem like *The Parliament of Fowls*. Lydgate's shorter poems are considered superior to his longer ones because of their lack of bulk and the variety of their subject matter. Lydgate lived in Paris from 1426 to 1429, working in the official entourage of the duke of Bedford in the capacity of court poet. He then returned to the monastery at Bury St. Edmunds and continued working prodigiously until his death in 1449 at the age of seventy-nine, leaving work in midtranslation when he died.

As a poet and an author, Lydgate is best considered an introduction to Chaucer and to medieval literature as a whole. His most important literary role is that of the creator and transmitter of the Chaucerian tradition, in that he popularized Chaucer's style, subjects, and materials. Lydgate, however, never followed Chaucer's innovations and creativity, choosing instead to reassert the depth of tradition that made up the medieval milieu and ignoring any transition or suggestion of the Renaissance. His most notorious characteristic was his flagrant imitation of Chaucer, using rhetorical amplification and expanding his original on a massive scale. Lydgate's opening sentence in *The Siege of Thebes*, for example, imitated the opening sentence to the prologue of *The Canterbury Tales*, but expanded Chaucer's eighteen original lines to Lydgate's sixty-five lines. This technique of elaboration, added to the fifteenth century's tradition of putting all important works into poetry (this tradition ranged from cookbooks to encyclopedias to medical guides), has earned him the reputation today of being wordy and common. But in many ways Lydgate was not a poet at all, for he never played with language or made his readers look at words in the new ways that we expect of modern poets. He was instead more of a rhetorician, a professional writer who kept to the basics in method and form and did not use experimentation, ambiguity, or deep eloquence. Despite our modern conceptions of poetry, Lydgate was the most popular poet of the fifteenth century, and his legacy is the profound rhetorical influence of his Chaucerian style on the writers and poets of the sixteenth and seventeenth centuries.

Bibliography: Derek Pearsall, *John Lydgate*, 1970; Walter F. Schirmer, *John Lydgate: A Study in the Culture of the XVth Century*, 1961.

Dominique Tieman

Lyndwood, William (c. 1375–1446),

was the most prominent English canon lawyer of the later Middle Ages. He also distinguished himself as an administrator and diplomat. Born in Lincolnshire, he was educated at Cambridge and Oxford, took holy orders, and in August 1414 became Archbishop *Henry Chichele's official at the court of Canterbury. In this role he was active in opposing the Lollards. By 1426 Lyndwood was dean of the Arches and thus head of the most important ecclesiastical court in England.

In his Canterbury period Lyndwood began work on his *Provinciale*, a collection of the synodal statutes of the province of Canterbury from the time of Stephen Langton in the early thirteenth century to his own day, a compilation he dedicated to Archbishop Chichele. The compiler's intent was to provide an orderly and trustworthy collection of texts that often were badly copied, prolix, or even circulated without a proper attribution. The *Provinciale*, finished by March 1422, was modeled on five books of the Gregorian *Decretals*. Superseded or trivial texts were omitted, and others were abridged. Many copies of this collection are accompanied by Lyndwood's commentary, which he completed in 1430. Both the full collection and abridgements were printed, some without the apparatus, in the late fifteenth and early sixteenth centuries. The legatine constitutions of Cardinals Otho and Othobonus, with the gloss by John of Acton, often appeared with the *Provinciale*.

By 1417 Lyndwood was in royal service, serving in the office of the privy seal and going abroad on many diplomatic missions. One of the most important of these missions sent him to the Congress of Arras (1435), at which the English strove in vain to preserve their alliance with Philip the Good of Burgundy. By 1432–33 Lyndwood was keeper of the privy seal and a royal counselor. In 1430–31 he substituted for the ailing chancellor, John Kemp, at the opening of Parliament. Although he proved unable to reconcile the opposing interests of Richard, duke of York, and the Beauforts, Lyndwood otherwise was an able servant of the Crown during the reign of *Henry VI. Lyndwood also was active in opposing the antipapal efforts of the Council of Basel. In 1442 *Eugenius IV, whose cause Lyndwood had favored, named him bishop of Saint David's. During the following year he helped frame the statutes for Henry VI's foundation of King's College at Cambridge, since he already had helped in the founding of Eton College. Shortly before his death on 21 October 1446, Lyndwood relinquished the office of keeper of the privy seal. His will directed his burial in Saint Stephen's Chapel, Westminster, where a chained copy of the *Provinciale* was to be available for consultation.

The *Provinciale* remains Lyndwood's monument. There are, of course, problems with the texts that he transmitted. Some are wrongly attributed, and others were not truly provincial in scope. Some of this reflects the complicated body of material that the canonist inherited, but he also made errors in judgment. Rarely, however, did he pervert the sense of the texts themselves. His ability to balance the common law of the church with local custom is notable. Lyndwood even felt free to criticize the laws contained in his collection. His authority was accepted not only in the province of Canterbury but in that of York, wherever it did not contradict local constitutions. Lyndwood remained an authority down to 1557, but no copies of the *Provinciale* were printed for more than a century thereafter. The Reformation made his work of lesser importance, although antiquaries and lawyers still consulted it. Lyndwood's work was one bone of contention in the debates of Stubbs and Maitland over English constitutional history.

Bibliography: Christopher Cheney, "William Lyndwood's *Provinciale*," in *Medieval Texts and Studies*, 1973; 158–84; John Ferguson, *English Diplomacy, 1422–1461*, 1972.

Thomas M. Izbicki

M

Machaut, Guillaume de (1300–1377). Guillaume de Machaut was the foremost French poet and composer of the fourteenth century. He wrote numerous lyrics and love poems, among them *Le voir dit* and *La fontaine amoureuse*, and composed one of the first polyphonic settings of the Ordinary of the Mass, *La Messe de Nostre Dame*. His friends and patrons were among the most powerful and illustrious people in Europe.

Guillaume de Machaut was born in 1300 near the town of Machault in Ardennes, France. He attended the University of Paris and received a master of arts degree, but did not take orders. Around 1323 he entered the service of John of Luxembourg, king of Bohemia. King John traveled extensively throughout Europe on his campaigns, and Machaut accompanied him and sometime in the 1330s wrote the long narrative *dit* in John's honor, *Le jugement dou roy de Behaingne*. In 1337, probably due to John's influence, Machaut was made a lifetime canon of Rheims and settled there around 1340. He composed the famous *Messe de Nostre Dame*, his only significant piece of sacred music, around 1346. Machaut was the foremost composer of the French *ars nova* school, which used polyphonic notation, allowing different rhythms to be used for each part. The church was suspicious of the *ars nova* and issued strict regulations as to the use of polyphonic principles in composing sacred music. It is a tribute to Machaut's genius—and diplomacy—that he was able to compose a piece of sacred music using polyphonic principles without offending the church's sensibilities. Before Machaut, the different parts of the Ordinary were treated as separate compositions; Machaut made the five parts of the Ordinary into a unified musical whole. John of Bohemia died in 1346, and Machaut served Bonne of Luxembourg, later the wife of King Jean II of France, then turned to Charles II ("the Bad") of Navarre for patronage. After about ten years, however, Charles allied himself with the English, and Machaut, who was loyal to the French royal house, left his service. His subsequent patrons included the duke of Savoy,

Charles V, and *Jean Valois, duc de Berry, the noted bibliophile, in whose library were preserved the most elaborate editions of Machaut's works.

Machaut was a prolific and versatile artist. His works included fourteen *dits* or narrative poems, twenty-three motets, several monophonic virelays, and a variety of lyrics. His musical and literary compositions showed a remarkable range of subject, tone, and flexibility of technique. He took great care in his work, personally overseeing the organization of several manuscripts of his poetry, which he presented to various patrons. Much of Machaut's love poetry was allegorical, exploring the lover's tribulations and detailing the typical course of a courtly love affair. Machaut introduced into literature the figure of the inexperienced, awkward lover who was also the narrator. The most famous of Machaut's narrative poems, *Le voir dit*, written when Machaut was in his sixties, infirm and blind in one eye, purported to be the true chronicle of a love between Machaut and a young noblewoman who fell in love with him through his poetry. Although some scholars have identified the lady as Péronne d'Armentières, it is not certain that she ever had a relationship with the poet. Machaut died in Rheims in 1377. He was mourned by many European aristocrats and intellectuals, including the king of France and *Geoffrey Chaucer, many of whose works were influenced by Machaut.

Machaut's genius and range of style and theme easily made him the most prominent and influential of fourteenth-century French poets and composers. His works showed a realism and sensitivity to amatory, political, and religious matters that few of his contemporaries attained. His *Jugement dou roy de Navarre*, with its vivid images of plague, war, and fire, showed that he was profoundly affected by the calamities and political upheavals of his time, but we find in his works an equal capacity for delight in the beauties of nature and the joys and sorrows of love. Machaut's diverse works, whether musical or literary, sacred or secular, expressed and informed the aesthetic, intellectual, and emotional spirit of fourteenth-century France.

Bibliography: Peter Dronke, *The Medieval Poet and His World*, 1984; Armand Machabey, *Guillaume de Machault, 130?–1377: La vie et l'oeuvre musical*, 2 vols., 1955.

Miriam Rheingold Fuller

Madrigal, Alfonso Fernández de. *See* Tostado, Alfonso.

Malory, Sir Thomas (c. 1416–71). Sir Thomas Malory is best known as the compiler of the *Morte d'Arthur*, the best-known and most influential work of Middle English Arthuriana. Composing this book (or collection of books) detailing the adventures of King Arthur and the knights of the Round Table seems an unlikely project for a man with so ignoble a past as Malory, but despite the numerous criminal charges leveled against its author, the *Morte* has provided models of chivalry and warnings against corruption for centuries.

Passages in the *Morte d'Arthur* tell us that the book was written by a man named "Thomas Maleore," but they do not tell us which one. There were several men named Thomas Malory living at about the time the *Morte* was composed, and identifying the work's author has not been a simple enterprise. It is now generally, although not unanimously, believed that the author of the *Morte* was Thomas Malory of Newbold Revel, Warwickshire. We know from references within the *Morte* that Malory was a knight and a prisoner, and that he was alive during the 1460s. Thomas Malory of Newbold Revel is the only one who fits this bill.

Malory was born around 1416, the son of John and Philippa Malory. He had three sisters and perhaps other siblings, and his uncle Robert was a Knight Hospitaller. Malory's early adulthood was by all accounts respectable; he fought for *Richard Beauchamp at Calais in 1443 and became a member of Parliament in 1445.

Shortly thereafter, however, Malory's reputation began to falter. Although false accusations were not uncommon in times of political upheaval, the number and variety of charges against Malory suggest that he did lead a life of crime. In 1450 he was a member of a group of men who ambushed the duke of Buckingham in an assassination attempt. Later that year he broke into the home of Hugh Smith and raped Smith's wife Joan. Although in Middle English "rape" could mean "kidnapping," it appears that Malory probably raped the woman in the modern sense. Three months later Malory returned to the Smith home, stealing property and again raping Joan. At about this time he also extorted money from three people. He was arrested the next year but was soon released on bail and proceeded to steal cattle. He was imprisoned again but escaped, only to rob a Cistercian monastery twice in two days. Malory was in and out of jail for the next twelve years for stealing cattle and other property. It was apparently in jail that he composed the *Morte d'Arthur*, finishing his ambitious project in 1469 or 1470. He died about a year later, possibly from plague, and in 1485 *William Caxton printed the *Morte*. Caxton's edition was the only known version until 1934, when a manuscript version was discovered at Winchester College. Although it was at first assumed that this manuscript was Caxton's source, it now seems that both versions descend from a lost original.

Malory did not write the *Morte d'Arthur* himself, but rather synthesized it from French and English works, untangling the sources, interlacing structures, and abridging long sections to produce a straightforward narrative. The *Morte* begins before Arthur's birth and follows the rise and fall of the kingdom of Camelot through Arthur's death at the hands of his nephew (and son) Mordred; included are Arthur's campaign against the Roman emperor Lucius and the adventures of individual knights such as Lancelot of the Lake, Gareth of Orkeney, and Tristram of Lyonesse, as well as the ethereal quest for the Holy Grail. These adventures fail to conceal or suppress the moral and spiritual corruption that pervaded Arthur's court; early in the work Arthur fathered Mordred by his own sister, and as the story progresses, the adulterous relationship between Sir Lancelot and Queen Guinevere leads to the deaths of innocent knights, dividing the kingdom and giving rise to the tragic final battle on Salisbury Plain.

Malory's *Morte d'Arthur* is noteworthy not only in itself and in relation to its sources but also in terms of its impact on English Arthuriana. Alfred, Lord Tennyson's *Idylls of the King* and T. H. White's *The Once and Future King*, as well as the paintings of the Pre-Raphaelites and contemporary novels and films, all reworked Malory's version of the Arthurian legend to express the aspirations and challenges of later ages. Despite Malory's disturbing career and his bleak depiction of the fall of Camelot, his name has continued to evoke the ideals of chivalry and romance for generations of writers, artists, and readers.

Bibliography: P.J.C. Field, *The Life and Times of Sir Thomas Malory*, 1993; Thomas Malory, *The Works of Sir Thomas Malory*, ed. Eugène Vinaver, 3 vols., 1973.

Staci Bernard-Roth

Manetti, Giannozzo (1396–1459), was a Florentine citizen-humanist, statesman, translator, historian, and biographer. He is probably best known today for his dialogues, especially that of the *Dialogus in symposio*. He was well known in his day for his piety and biblical scholarship, which resulted in several translations of both the Old and New Testaments and two religious treatises on early Christianity. Manetti attempted to relate vernacular literature and humanism through his biographies of *Dante, *Francesco Petrarch, and *Giovanni Boccaccio. His dedication to Aristotelian philosophy can be seen in his numerous translations of Aristotle and in his own loyal service to the city of Florence, demonstrating human greatness through the magnificence of man's works on earth.

Because Giannozzo Manetti lacks a modern biographer, it is difficult to obtain reliable information regarding his youth and education, and therefore one must turn to letters, tax records, and other official documents to divine clues. Manetti was born in 1396 in Florence; his father, Bernardo, was a merchant and a moneylender who, over the course of his life, expanded the family fortune to such a great extent that the Manetti clan would become the tenth wealthiest in the city, thus leaving Giannozzo and his brother with a considerable inheritance. Unlike his father or his brother, Manetti used this influence to enjoy a career in politics and built a reputation as a brilliant humanist and statesman, eventually obtaining such powerful positions as ambassador and territorial governor for his city-state.

While his father was opposed to Giannozzo's pursuit of literary and religious studies in his youth, we know that Manetti was a student of Ambroggio Traversari, the early humanist famed for his expertise on Christian Greek and his translations of the Greek church fathers. Traversari's influence on Manetti is evident in his fascination with biblical studies and his translations of the New Testament from a Greek text, which he began following his appointment in Rome as apostolic secretary from 1453 to 1455, where he served Pope *Nicholas V. Manetti was forced to leave Florence entirely in 1455 because his enemies in the oligarchy were taxing him so heavily that the expense threatened to leave him destitute, a not-uncommon predatory practice in Florentine politics at the time. Just prior to his self-imposed exile, Manetti began diverting some of his business investments out of Florence and founded a series of wool companies in Naples. In 1455 King *Alfonso "the Magnanimous" of Naples took him into his royal council, and he presided over the court of the Sommaria. He was also given a palace and a large staff, and to demonstrate his gratitude to the king, Manetti composed a work on earthquakes at the king's request and dedicated his Psalms translation and his *Apologeticus* to him. Manetti was a prolific writer in his three years with Alfonso: in addition to the works for his royal patron, he completed his translation of the New Testament, translated three texts by Aristotle, and revised and enlarged one of his previous works, the *Contra ludeos et Gentes*, which examined the evidence in the New Testament supporting Christ as the true Son of God.

Traversari may have also been the person who persuaded Manetti to pursue Hebraic and Old Testament studies, an area in which Manetti demonstrated an especially enlightened attitude, considering that his devoted scholarship contradicted contemporary views that the study of Hebrew letters was worthless. His interest may have been sparked around 1435, when Manetti was approximately forty years old, because at that time he had a young Jewish scholar living in his house as a tutor and later as a member of his family, whom he even converted to Christianity. In addition, beginning in November 1442, Manetti studied the Old Testament with a scholar called Manuello in return for philosophy lessons. During this time he built up a library of Hebraic manuscripts, a considerable number of which have survived and are now housed in the Vatican Library. Unfortunately, Manetti died in 1459 before he was able to complete his translation of the Old Testament, an endeavor that came under great criticism as "useless" and even "arrogant" when he finished translating the Psalter from the original Hebrew. This criticism prompted him to write his *Apologeticus*, his last work, which is more a treatise on biblical history and criticism than it is a defense in the traditional sense.

Giannozzo Manetti was an enlightened statesman and humanist whose piety and dedication to his ideals inspired his contemporaries. His vigorous participation in politics is evidence that he regarded human greatness as manifest in earthly works, in the building of modern human society and its trappings, according to his belief in Aristotelian principles. A student of the classics, Hebrew, and early Christianity, Manetti brought his vast knowledge and experience together in his translations, biographies, and treatises in an attempt to achieve a greater understanding of the nature of man and his destiny.

Bibliography: David Marsh, "Boccaccio in the Quattrocento: Manetti's *Dialogus in symposio*," *Renaissance Quarterly* 33, no. 3 (1980): 337–50; Charles Trinkaus, *In Our Image and Likeness: Humanity and Dignity in Italian Humanist Thought*, 2 vols., 1970.

Wendy Marie Hoofnagle

Manrique, Jorge (1440–79), is remembered as a Spanish lyric poet of the late Middle Ages and is best known for his 1476 elegy *Coplas por la muerte de su padre don Rodrigo el maestre de Santiago*. Born sometime in 1440, Manrique was the newest member of a family of prestigious Castilian lineage. His great-uncle was *Iñigo Lōpez de Mendoza, marquis of the Santillana, and Manrique's uncle, Gómez Manrique, was a poet himself, although he is not as well known as his nephew. Manrique's father was the count of Paredes, Rodrigo Manrique, grand master of the Military Order of Santiago and a general of some distinction. Manrique followed in his father's professional footsteps, becoming a soldier and fighting for *Isabel and *Ferdinand. Like his father, he sided with the infante Don Alfonso against *Enrique IV; after the death of Alfonso, he fought for Isabel. He contended at Calatrava against the marques de Villena and helped to lift the siege of Uclés with his father. After the death of his father, Manrique continued to fight for Isabel and Ferdinand in a quest to end the civil war.

Manrique is best remembered, however, for the legacy of his poetry. Manrique wrote many conventional love lyrics and is well represented in the *Cancionero general*. There are approximately fifty of these poems, which adhered to the courtly traditional styles. Much of the language was that of feudalism and Christian devotion. Perhaps most significantly, the theme of these poems treated many of the social concerns of his day. Although his melancholic explorations of death distinguished these poems as more memorable than the typical occasional verse of his day, Manrique's contemporaries thought of him as one of Spain's best love poets.

His best-known work, however, is the 1476 lyric elegy *Coplas por la muerte de su padre don Rodrigo, el maestre de Santiago*. written immediately after the death of his father but not published until 1494 in Seville. While the *Coplas* is little known in the English-speaking canon, it is a famous source of national pride for Spaniards. Written about his father, Manrique's verse continued in his uncle's tradition of writing great poetry about Manrique family members. The long elegy is at once extremely personal in its expression of a son's grief at the death of his father and strikingly universal in its articulation of humanity's sorrow in the inevitable presence of death. The verse celebrated the life of his father in lines that warned against the brevity of human existence and the selfish conceit of men. For example, one recurring metaphor is that of man as an exile and life as a pilgrimage. Life in these lines is temporal, while the rewards for the good Christian on earth and in heaven are everlasting. Some scholars see Manrique as a transitional figure between the Middle Ages and the Renaissance due to the complexity of his seemingly contradictory themes: the simultaneous expression of the vanity of quotidian life and the elevation of worldly glory. Manrique's theme was not original, but his expression of death and life's vanity struck a popular chord then and throughout the centuries.

While Manrique was fighting against Villena in 1479, he died in front of the castle of Garci-Munoz, Cuenca, as a result of his wounds. His influence has inspired writers such as Lope de Vega, José de Espronceda, and Pedro Salinas. The *Coplas'* impact stretches for centuries; most notable is Henry Wadsworth Longfellow's translation of the *Coplas* in 1833 that preserved much of the beauty, depth, and imagery of the original.

Bibliography: Frank A. Dominguez, *Love and Remembrance: The Poetry of Jorge Manrique*, 1988.

Clay Kinsner

Mantegna, Andrea (1431?–1506), was an Italian painter, draftsman, engraver, and sculptor who was a master in the representation of perspective and human anatomy. His use of Roman lettering and inscriptions aided in the development of printing. In the quattrocento he was considered the greatest artist outside of Venice.

Born of humble origins in Isola di Cartura, near Padua, Mantegna was the adopted son and student of the noted Paduan educator and collector of ancient art Francesco Squarcione. Mantegna first gained recognition at the age of eighteen for the frescoes he painted for the Ovetari Chapel of the Eremitani in Padua. Against Squarcione's wishes, Mantegna married Niccolosia Bellini in 1453, the daughter of the multitalented Venetian painter Jacopo Bellini, and so entered into an artistic dynasty. In 1459 he became court painter to the Gonzaga in Mantua and maintained this position for forty-seven years until his death in 1506. He dominated Mantua artistically during this time, earning a reputation as a difficult and irascible resident. The generations of Gonzaga for whom he worked all indulged his temperament due to his excellent, if slow, artistic creations. Portraits of the family, more realistic than flattering, were intriguing and ennobling.

In the 1480s Mantegna, inspired by ancient Rome, created nine large canvas panels depicting the triumph of Julius Caesar. Designed to evoke the triumphs of the Gonzaga, the panels reveal Mantegna's erudition and attention to historical accuracy. Mantegna stayed at the Vatican between 1488 and 1490 painting a chapel for Pope *Innocent VIII that included a fresco of the *Baptism of Christ by St. John the Baptist*, surrounded by allegorical figures representing the Virtues. Most scholars consider the *Madonna of the Victory* from 1493 to be Mantegna's best later work due to its attention to detail and linear accuracy. Despite generous and steady commissions, Mantegna remained in debt much of his life because of his continual purchases of antiquities. Fellow artists were particularly affected by his death; Albrecht Dürer said that visiting Mantegna on his deathbed was the saddest day of his life. Mantegna purchased and decorated his own memorial chapel in the Church of Sant' Andrea. It includes a bust, presumably his self-portrait, that features an unflattering image of an angry elderly man.

Despite the variety of media, all of Mantegna's work demonstrated a keen knowledge and appreciation of antique influences. At times his human figures resemble statuary more than living beings. Because of his fidelity to the standards of antiquity, Mantegna considered his art the most authentic among that of his contemporaries. Vasari included him among the masters who "sought with great efforts to do the impossible in art by means of labor, particularly in foreshortenings and in things unpleasant to the eye, which were as painful to see as they were difficult for them to execute." This comment could apply to Mantegna's fresco *Martyrdom of St. James*, painted for the Ovetari Chapel, in which the head of the saint appears outside the picture plane, ready to roll into the chapel once the executioner has struck with his blade. Vasari's description was also singularly fitting for Mantegna's startling painting *Dead Christ*, executed in 1466. This composition on canvas shows Christ's body laid out with his feet in the foreground. His torso and hands are arranged such that Christ's five wounds are on prominent display. It is a masterful study of both perspective and the human physique, and one that Mantegna himself apparently cherished since he refused to sell it even when pressured by many debts.

Mantegna's skill in perspective is perhaps best seen, however, in his decoration of the Camera degli Sposi in a tower of the Gonzaga castle in Mantua. Completed between 1465 and 1474, the paintings cover two of the room's four walls and the ceiling. The center of the ceiling is a prime example of trompe l'oeil, appearing as an opening into the sky. A painted circular parapet, seemingly adorned with marble relief sculpture, serves as a rail for the faces of putti and ladies-in-waiting who peer in and laugh at the room's inhabitants. A heavy planter appears to teeter on the edge. It is a whimsical but artful creation, suitable for a newlywed suite. Less renowned than Dürer and *Leonardo da Vinci, Mantegna nonetheless has had his influence. Indisputable links between the style of foreshortening found in some of Edgar Degas's paintings and those of Mantegna have been determined recently.

Bibliography: Frederick Hartt, *History of Italian Renaissance Art*, 2nd ed., 1979; John T. Paoletti and Gary M. Radke, *Art in Renaissance Italy*, 1997.

Margaret Harp

Manuel I, King of Portugal (b. 1469, r. 1495–1521). Called the "Fortunate" because his reign marked the golden age of Portuguese exploration and empire building, Manuel I was also fortunate in his choice of subordinates, including Francisco de Almeida and Afonso de Albuquerque, his capable viceroys in India. Manuel was born on 31 May 1469 in Alcochete, the last of six sons and three daughters of Infante Fernando (1433–70), paternal uncle of King *João II (r. 1481–95). At the time of his birth, Manuel was ninth in line for succession to the throne, but by the time King João, who took upon himself the protection of his late uncle's family, came to the throne in 1481, only two of Fernando's children, Diogo, duke of Viseu, and Manuel himself, remained. Young Manuel was now third in line, after Crown Prince Alfonso (1475–91) and Diogo. But Alfonso died in an accident, predeceasing his father, and Diogo plotted against the Crown and was executed, leaving Manuel to become king.

Manuel came to the throne just as many decades of Portuguese exploration down the west coast of Africa and out into the Atlantic came to fruition. *Bartolomeo Dias had returned from the Cape of Good Hope in 1488, and during much of the next decade, although most of the voyages are shrouded in silence, the Portuguese had improved on Dias's achievement by sailing even farther into the Atlantic, pioneering new routes that would ultimately lead them to India. In 1497 the final step was taken, and *Vasco da Gama, who is said to have prayed in the small chapel that still exists on the hill looking down on Belem and its tower, was dispatched to India, with Manuel and his entire court to see him off. His arrival there, after doubling the cape in 1498, was an achievement that stood the world economic system on its head and was quickly followed up by a flurry of other voyages. The Portuguese empire in the East quickly took shape. In September 1503 Albuquerque built a fortress at Cochin, the first Portuguese stronghold in India. Within a decade places all up and down the Indian coast and beyond were in Portuguese control, including Goa, conquered on 25 November 1510. An attempt by the Mamluks to beat back the Portuguese interlopers was crushed at Chaul in January 1508. During the same period the Portuguese also secured new bases on the East African coast and prepared to expand far beyond India, seizing the critical Malacca Strait in August 1511. By 1513 they had reached China, while, in another direction, Brazil was "officially" discovered on 3 May 1500 by Pedro Cabral on his way to India.

At home, Manuel and his kingdom enjoyed the good life as boatload after boatload of Indian pepper and other commodities landed in Lisbon. Except for a frightful massacre of Lisbon *novos Christãos* (converted Jews), blamed for an outbreak of plague in 1506, Manuel's reign witnessed few adverse political events at home. Much of the new wealth went into the pockets of the Italian city-states, and that helped to finance trade and redistributed imports. Lisbon itself, however, witnessed the florescence of a new, highly ornate art style known as *Manuelina*. Two of its monuments, the Tower of Belem and the Jeronomos Abbey, both located not far from where Manuel and his court said goodbye to Vasco da Gama, still stand.

King Manuel was married four times. His first wife, the infanta Isabel, daughter of the Castilian queen *Isabel, died in childbirth in 1498. His second wife, the infanta Maria, sister of Isabel, died in 1517. His third was Leonor, sister of the Emperor Charles V. Manuel, died on 13 December 1521, and was survived by his last queen and was succeeded by his son João III.

Bibliography: Elaine Sanceau, *The Reign of the Fortunate King, 1495–1521*, 1969; George D. Winius, ed., *Portugal the Pathfinder: Journeys from the Medieval toward the Modern World, 1300–ca. 1600*, 1995.

Paul D. Buell

Manuel, Juan, Prince of Castile and Adelantado of Murcia (1282–1348),

was also the author of political, didactic, and historical works. The grandson of Ferdinand III and nephew of Alfonso X, Juan Manuel suffered the fate of younger sons; himself never eligible for the throne, he engaged in struggles with two kings of Castile in order to protect and increase his personal power and wealth. Don Juan Manuel became politically active in 1294 at the age of twelve, engaging in war against the Moors who had invaded his holdings in Murcia, the frontier between Moorish Andalucía and the Christian kingdoms. Don Juan soon lost these lands in the struggle over succession after Sancho IV's death and, as the pretender to the Castilian throne, ceded Elche to Aragon in return for its support. Don Juan regained these lands in 1303 by contracting marriage with Constanza, the very young daughter of *Jaime II of Aragon; the two then allied against Ferdinand IV of Castile, who at one point ordered Don Juan's death. Although Castile and Aragon also allied against the Moors in 1309, Don Juan, not wanting Ferdinand to succeed, broke with the allied forces and engaged in raids in León. Don Juan finally married Constanza of Aragon in 1312, the same year in which Ferdinand IV died and his infant son Alfonso XI was elevated to the throne.

In 1319 Don Juan became one of the coregents of Castile, the most powerful position he was ever to hold. For the next six years anarchy reigned as the coregents battled each other, enabling Don Juan to exercise almost complete control of the Crown. When Alfonso assumed the throne in 1325 at the age of fourteen, he appointed two of Don Juan's enemies as his closest advisors. Meanwhile, Don Juan had begun to form alliances against Alfonso when the young king proposed marriage to Juan's daughter Constanza. Don Juan agreed, turned on his anti-Alfonso allies, and strongly supported the king until 1327, when Alfonso renounced his engagement, imprisoned Constanza, and contracted marriage with the king of Portugal's daughter instead. Enraged and humiliated, Don Juan formed an alliance with the Moors in Granada and engaged in open warfare with Alfonso. The conflict between Juan Manuel and Alfonso continued despite the arrival of a Moroccan invasion force in 1333 and Don Juan's loss of support from his Moorish allies. He turned next to Aragon and Portugal, contracting a marriage between his daughter Constanza and the heir to the Portuguese throne in 1336. When Alfonso withheld safe-conduct for Constanza to travel to Portugal, Don Juan mustered his allies to attack; however, Alfonso managed to defeat the allies in several encounters. Finally, in 1340 Don Juan and Alfonso settled their grievances. With the Pact of Seville, Constanza was allowed to travel to Portugal, and Don Juan took up arms against the Moors alongside Alfonso XI, participating in the Battle at the Salado. At the fall of Algeciras in 1344, Don Juan led the victorious Castilian army into the town, his last official act. Soon after, he retired to the monastery he had founded in Peñafiel, where he died in 1348.

Despite his active life of political intrigue, Don Juan is best known for his prose works, especially *Count Lucanor* (*El conde Lucanor*), a collection of exemplary tales told by Patronio, a servant-tutor, to Lucanor, illustrating proper personal and political conduct. Despite their didactic purpose, many of these tales were fantastic farces derived from Eastern (probably oral) sources and reflect the sort of practical morality Don Juan exemplified. Many scholars today consider Don Juan Manuel a precursor of both *Geoffrey Chaucer and Niccolò Machiavelli.

Bibliography: Reinaldo Ayerbe-Chaux, *Yo, don Juan Manuel: Apología de una vida*, 1993; Joseph F. O'Callaghan, *A History of Medieval Spain*, 1983.

Denise K. Filios

Manutius, Aldus (c. 1451–1515), is the best known of the early Venetian "humanist scholar" printers. He printed classical Greek and Latin texts as well as contemporary Latin texts from 1495 until his death in 1515. Although he was not the first printer to produce texts in Greek, Manutius successfully printed so many important Greek texts that his Greek typeface became the trade standard. He is also associated with popularizing both the italic font and the octavo size for printed literature, enabling printed books to be cheaper and more portable.

Although the exact year of his birth is not known, Aldus Manutius was most likely born in Bassiano, Italy, in 1451 or 1452. Nothing is known of his childhood or young adult life except what he himself asserted in the prefaces to his printed volumes. He did receive humanistic schooling in Rome from Gaspare da Verona and was influenced by the lectures of Dominizio Caldrini in Rome and of Battista Guarino at the University of Ferrara. This type of education emphasized the importance of studying classical Greek and Latin literature and laid the foundation of Manutius's interest in printing such texts as well as revealing the need for Greek editions, which were not widely available at that time.

In 1480 Manutius was named tutor to Alberto and Lionello Pio, the princes of Carpi. Through employment with this family, Manutius became part of an intellectual circle that included Alberto Pio and his uncle, *Giovanni Pico della Mirandola, as well as Ermolao Barbaro and *Angelo Poliziano, who were friends and colleagues of Pico. This intellectual circle later provided both financial and intellectual support for the Aldine Press. In this decade Manutius wrote a didactic pamphlet known as the *Musarum panegyris*, later printed by Baptista de Tortis, and a Latin grammar that was printed by Andrea Torresani in 1493.

During the period 1490–95 Manutius worked to acquire copies of Greek and Latin manuscripts and to coordinate financial backing for his first printed edition. Preparing for the enterprise of printing texts in Greek, Manutius applied for and received the exclusive twenty-year privilege of printing Greek texts from the Venetian senate. Andrea Torresani (the printer of Manutius's Latin grammar) and Pierfrancesco Barbarigo were the two initial investors in the Aldine Press; the first edition of the press was the *Erotemata* of Constantine Lascaris, a Greek grammar. Printed in 1495, the *Erotemata* included supplementary material on the Greek alphabet and introductory readings that included the Lord's Prayer and the opening of the Gospel of John. The grammar itself was printed with a facing translation in Latin to assist those who wished to use the grammar to learn Greek.

The Lascaris edition was a collaborative effort. Manutius worked with master engraver Francesco Griffo and Greek scholars such as Thomas Linacre, Marcus Musurus, and Aristobulus Apostolis in order to design the Greek font, gather and prepare manuscripts, and correct proofs. The collaboration continued through the next major achievement of the press, which was a collection of Aristotelian texts in five separate volumes issued between 1495 and 1498. In the second volume, Manutius specifically named Linacre, Francesco Caballi, Niccolò Leoniceno, and Lorenzo Maioli as having provided important assistance in the production of the Aristotelian editions. While Aristotle provided the backbone of Manutius's textual production in Greek, he also printed other important Greek authors, including Theocritus, Hesiod, and Aristophanes. Because the market for these Greek texts was an academic one, the Aldine Press also printed many Greek grammars in addition to that of Lascaris, and Latin texts that were meant to support the study of Greek. In the period from 1495 to 1500, Manutius also printed many texts by his contemporaries, many of whom were either associated with the press itself or were members of Manutius's intellectual circle. Such authors included Lorenzo Maioli, Niccolò Leoniceno, Pietro Bembo, and Angelo Poliziano. The most successful and popular book of this type was the *Hypnerotomachia Poliphili*, an illustrated romance written by Francesco Colonna and commissioned by Leonardo Crasso.

The next phase of the Aldine Press, from 1501 to 1504, saw a movement away from Greek and an increase in the printing of classical Latin authors such as Virgil, Horace, Martial, Ovid, and Cicero. During this period Manutius became associated with two very significant developments in early printing culture: the use of both the italic font and the octavo size for printed literature. This combination became the standard for printing humanist texts and was used not only for classical Latin authors but also for Italian humanist authors such as *Francesco Petrarch and Bembo. Manutius's textual style was popular with readers of early printed books because the small size allowed the volumes to be portable and less costly than quarto editions, and the font was an indication that the text was "classical" as opposed to "Gothic." Unfortunately, this type of text was so popular that other continental printers copied the Aldine editions and were able to produce them more cheaply, and these practices drove the Aldine Press into severe financial difficulties. Although Manutius had a copyright for his italic font and could have prosecuted piracy, it was difficult to enforce such copyright violations in his day.

The press gained new energy, however, from Manutius's marriage to Maria Torresani, the daughter of his financial backer, and a request by Desiderius

Erasmus that the Aldine Press print his translations of Euripides' *Hecuba* and *Iphigeneia in Aulis*. This volume was printed in 1507 and was soon followed by Erasmus's edition of the *Adagia* in 1508. When the League of Cambrai, which included the armies of France, Spain, and the papacy, declared war on Venice in 1509, however, the press had to suspend all activities until 1512. When Manutius began printing again, he continued to print humanist texts, but the circle of scholars who had supported his press was no longer intact, and the press's output was reduced mostly to texts that had been prepared prior to 1509. When Manutius died on 6 February 1515, he left the press to his sons and his father-in-law, Torresani, who continued the humanist printing enterprise.

Aldus Manutius's printing practice consisted of supplying humanist scholarly texts to a growing market. The Aldine Press solidified the look, shape, and content of humanist books and was responsible for enabling most of the important classical Greek texts to become available on the print market. The manner in which he chose, edited, and printed humanist texts was in large part a reflection of the needs of the Italian intellectual community. Yet Manutius also made works of classical and contemporary literature desirable to a larger body of readers and helped strengthen the practice of casual reading in Renaissance culture.

Bibliography: Nicolas Barker, *Aldus Manutius and the Development of Greek Script and Type in the Fifteenth Century*, 2nd ed., 1992; Martin Davies, *Aldus Manutius: Printer and Publisher of Renaissance Venice*, 1995; Martin Lowry, *The World of Aldus Manutius: Business and Scholarship in Renaissance Venice*, 1979.

Kristin R. Hofer

Marcel, Étienne (d. 1358),

was a reformer and later a rebel, the leader of the Parisian urban uprising against the government of the dauphin Charles in 1356–58 who was killed in 1358. Étienne Marcel, a rich draper, became provost of the Merchants of Paris in 1355. Following the capture of King Jean II at the Battle of Poitiers in 1356, the dauphin Charles (the future Charles V) convoked a meeting of the Estates-General of the Language d'Oïl to answer the growing clamor for reform. As leader of the Parisian bourgeoisie, Marcel emerged as the chief spokesman for the Third Estate and forged an alliance with Robert Le Coq, bishop of Laon. Marcel armed the artisans of Paris and persuaded the city fathers to resist the efforts of the dauphin to tax the citizens for royal ransom money.

However, Marcel's mobilization of the people in arms alienated much of his support among the nobility and clergy, allowing Charles to dissolve the council of commissioners in August 1357. A new meeting of the Estates called in January 1358 was unable to agree on a common course of action. From this point on, Marcel moved from reform to revolution. On 28 February an armed band of artisans attacked the dauphin's palace, killing two of his unpopular ministers before his eyes in his chamber.

In the summer of 1358 Marcel was presented with two potential sources of support. The peasant Jacquerie broke out in the Île-de-France in protest against taxation and the depredations of war, and one of its leaders, Guillaume Carle, approached Marcel for support. Charles the Bad, king of Navarre and a claimant to the French throne, emerged as another potential ally after his release from royal captivity and was acclaimed captain of the Parisians. However, the different class interests of the peasant Jacquerie prevented Marcel from making effective use of this new support, and so an opportunity to further the cause of reform was lost.

On 22 July Marcel allowed a group of Navarrese troops to enter Paris, a move that alienated many of his bourgeois supporters, as Navarre's troops were known for their rapacity and on this occasion included many Englishmen. Fighting broke out between the Parisians and the soldiers, who were forced to withdraw to the fortress of the Louvre.

On the night of 31 July–1 August 1358 Marcel's supporters planned to open the city gates, allowing Navarre's forces to enter Paris. However, many Parisians feared Navarre's armies or the reprisals that might be visited upon them if the dauphin were to take the city. Jean Maillart, a former ally, led the opposition to Marcel. A group of Maillart's supporters, led by Pierre des Essarts, killed Marcel as he attempted to open the Porte St.-Antoine, and leading supporters of Marcel were subsequently lynched by the crowd. Marcel, as the leader of the wealthiest merchants of Paris, was perhaps an unlikely rebel, but (at least initially) he represented the resentment of the bourgeoisie against taxation and inflation. However, his inability or unwillingness to construct a stable antigovernment alliance doomed his uprising to failure.

Bibliography: M. Mollat and P. Wolff, *The Popular Revolutions of the Late Middle Ages*, 1973.

Michael Evans

March, Ausias (c. 1397–1459) was born in Gandia, Valencia, to the recently ennobled Pere March family. March became the first major poet to write exclusively in Catalan and is now known as one of the greatest poets ever in that language.

Beginning in 1418, March fought in Sicily, Sardinia, Corsica, and Djerba under *Alfonso V of Aragon. Around 1425 he abandoned his military career to supervise the royal falconry at Albufera. He married Isabel, the sister of *Joanot Martorell, in 1437, but she died only two years later. In 1443 he married Joana Scorna, who died in 1454. One cannot overestimate the impact of these two untimely deaths on the poet's later work.

As an artist, March was prolific, writing over 128 poems—about 10,000 verses—which derive largely from the Provençal tradition. March usually adhered to the rules of versification created by the earlier thirteenth-century Catalan troubadour Ramon Vidal.

The themes of love and morality dominated March's work. In fact, over 75 percent of his poems concerned some aspect of love. His primary innovation, though, was in writing the poems in Catalan without mixing in any Provençal, distancing his poems from the courtly tradition.

March's work climaxed a renewed interest in the Catalan language, coming in the midst of the great period of Catalan poetry. In the fifteenth century the previously strong foreign influence on Catalan had been fully discarded, and a robust period of purely Catalan poetry emerged. March's *Cants d'amor* and *Cants de mort* (Songs of love and Songs of death) have been called the finest verses ever written in Catalan, even influencing literature in sixteenth-century Castile. His use of the earthier Catalan tongue underscored his focus on substance and often complemented the anguish and pain evident in the poet's voice and meaning.

March is primarily remembered for his poems that explored the psychological dimensions of love, commonly considered expressions of his own inner conflicts. March's approach—to explore the motif of sensuality versus idealism—differed from the standard courtly approach of his day. More specifically, March's works were the meeting ground for the battle between his carnal love and his ardent idealism. The lesson seems to be that when spiritual and physical love intersect, the result is carnal victory. The *Cants de mort* XCII–XCVII were likely influenced by the deaths of his wives, but most of his poems were addressed to the married Bou, whom he calls "plena de seny" (intelligent woman) and "llir entre cards" (lily among thorns). His poems, most fully published in 1543, were by convention divided into *Cants d'amor* and *Cants de mort* before and after his mistress's death. The main conflict in these poems is that since they were addressed to a dead mistress instead of a wife, he feared that she could not be in heaven due to his sin; if she were in hell, he felt, it was surely through his own sin.

March's strength may be more in the intellectual nature of his poems than in the poetry itself. He replaced the contemporary focus on sound with an energetic development of meaning. Most of his imagery occurred in the first person, exerting an energy and expressing a passion that had been absent or at best half-present in previous Catalan and Spanish verse. His more memorable images were of containment and inevitable bad fortune, as seen in his sailor besieged by storms, a sick man on his deathbed, or a prisoner in his cell.

His other group of poems is known as the *Cants morals* (Moral songs) and the great *Cant espiritual* (Spiritual song), in which he at last attained a measure of serenity in the face of death. In this poem, he confessed that he feared God more than he loved him. He was torn between the realization that his hope of salvation was weak without adequate love of God, although he wished to die without committing more sins.

March had a sudden and contemporary impact on the Spanish literary scene. One can see March's influence in the work of Cetina, Garcilaso, Herrera, Jorge de Montemayor, and Pere Serafi.

Bibliography: Robert Archer, *The Pervasive Image: The Role of Analogy in the Poetry of Ausias March*, 1985; Ausias March, *Selected Poems*, ed. and trans., Arthur Terry, 1976.

Clay Kinsner

Marche, Olivier de La. *See* La Marche, Olivier de.

Margaret I, Queen of Denmark, Norway, and Sweden (b. 1353, r. 1387–1412). Queen Margaret I is best known for establishing the Kalmar Union, which united the kingdoms of Denmark, Norway, and Sweden. Upon creating this union, one of the largest empires in Europe, she became queen of the three realms, ruling them until her death in 1412. The union lasted for only a short time after Margaret's death, eventually dissolving when her grandnephew Eric was unable to keep the three countries together.

Born in 1353, Margaret was the daughter of *Valdemar IV (also Waldemar), king of Denmark, and Queen Helvig. She was betrothed at age six to marry King Haakon of Norway, son of King Magnus VII of Sweden. In 1363, she married him, becoming queen of Norway and Sweden at the tender age of ten. The year of her marriage, Margaret's only brother Christoffer died, leaving Valdemar without a male heir. His throne in Denmark was to go either to Margaret, her older sister Ingeborg, or one of their sons. By Christmas 1370 Margaret gave birth to her only son, Olaf, who was now heir to the Crown of Norway and Sweden. During this period there were ongoing conflicts between Denmark and Sweden. For a short time Albrekt of Mecklenburg (Germany) ruled Sweden as king, rather than Haakon or Margaret, although Margaret and Haakon continued to claim the Crown and were recognized by some as the rulers of the region.

Five years after Olaf's birth, on 24 October 1375, Margaret's father King Valdemar died, and so Danish and Swedish officials had to decide whom to choose as king of Denmark: Olaf or Ingeborg's son, Albrekt. Margaret and Haakon persuaded the Swedish electors to choose Olaf over Albrekt, and the Danes elected Olaf as their king in May 1376. Only four years old, Olaf V, already heir to the throne of Norway, ruled Denmark under his parents' regency. Margaret was regent for her son Olaf in Denmark while Haakon ruled in Norway. In 1380 King Haakon died, and so young Olaf V now succeeded to his third throne. Olaf came of age in 1385, but Margaret retained authority as regent, and on 3 August 1387, when Olaf suddenly died, Margaret continued to rule Denmark and Norway as queen regnant.

The same year she was urged to lead opposition against Albrekt of Mecklenburg by some influential Swedes, who were discontented with his usurped regime. When in 1388 the greatest landowner in Sweden, Bo Jonsson, died, the executors of his will recognized Margaret as the regent of Sweden and gave Jonsson's patrimony to her. The gain of these vast estates helped Margaret defeat and capture Albrekt in 1389 near Falkoping, Sweden. She then persuaded the Danish, Norwegian, and Swedish parliaments to accept her grandnephew, Eric of Pomerania, as king of Sweden. In 1397 Eric was crowned king of Denmark and Norway at Kalmar, thus making him ruler of all three kingdoms. At the same time a tentative act of union of the three kingdoms was drawn up, establishing the Kalmar Union. Although Eric held the title of king, Margaret remained the actual ruler of all three kingdoms until her death in 1412.

Bibliography: Philip Pulsiana, ed., *Medieval Scandinavia: An Encyclopedia*, 1993; Birgit Sawyer and Peter Sawyer, *Medieval Scandinavia: From Conversion to Reformation, Circa 800–1500*, 1993.

Sigrid Kelsey

Margaret of York, Duchess of Burgundy (1446–1503),

was the sister of *Edward IV of England and the wife of *Charles the Bold, duke of Burgundy. Both her brother Edward and her father, Richard, duke of York, were major protagonists in the infamous Wars of the Roses. Her marriage to Charles the Bold, which joined together the houses of York and Burgundy, proved to be a significant factor in Edward's victorious reclamation of the English throne in 1471. But Margaret was an important figure in her own right in her relationship with the English printer *William Caxton, her business ventures in Flanders, and her plotting against the Tudor king *Henry VII.

Margaret was born on 3 May 1446 at Fotheringay Castle in Northamptonshire, England, to Richard, duke of York, and Cecily Neville. In 1460 her father was killed at Wakefield, and her brother, the earl of March, shortly thereafter declared himself Edward IV. Consequently, Edward was able in March 1465 to bestow upon her an annuity valued at four hundred marks, an amount later increased to four hundred pounds sterling.

On 1 October 1467, despite the French king *Louis XI's efforts to marry her to Philibert, prince of Savoy, Margaret announced her own engagement to Charles the Bold, duke of Burgundy, at a council held in Kingston-upon-Thames. Eight months later, on 3 July 1468, Margaret and Charles were married, thus bringing together the houses of York and Burgundy. The union was celebrated with nine days of lavish festivals, said at the time to have been rivaled only by those of the mythic King Arthur. Margaret's marriage to Charles the Bold proved its political usefulness when, in 1470, the Lancastrian king *Henry VI was restored to the throne of England, and Edward IV was forced to flee the country. Charles provided refuge to his brother-in-law and aided in his seizure of the throne once more in 1471. But this was not the end of political conflicts between Margaret's family and the house of Lancaster, for Margaret herself would soon make trouble for Henry VII.

While little is known about the marital relationship between Margaret and Charles, Margaret has been connected to William Caxton, who, because of the mass printing of his translation of *Lefèvre's recueíl des histoires de Troyes*, has been credited with a subsequent increase in the influence of the English language. Caxton resigned from his position as governor of the Merchant Adventurers at Bruges to join Margaret's household. She seems to have been particularly fond of him and showed him much attention and favor, but whether or not her relationship with Caxton interfered with her marriage is not known. When Duke Charles died at the Battle of Nancy in 1477, Margaret was childless. In 1480 she traveled to England to visit her brother Edward. Her visit proved quite fruitful when Edward granted her licenses both to export oxen and sheep to Flanders and to do so free of customs duties. Margaret thus proved herself a capable businesswoman, despite the fact that she spent the remainder of her life periodically feuding with the Flemish on account of her business interests there.

When Henry VII came to the English throne in 1485, the dowry Edward had given Margaret was reclaimed by the Tudor monarchy. It was for this reason that she incessantly conspired against the king. She lent her support to Lambert Simnel, who claimed to be the son of Edward IV's estranged brother, George of Clarence. She also supported the impersonator Perkin Warbeck and welcomed him as her nephew Richard, the younger duke of York. She tried to win him favor by writing to other governments on his behalf. By 1499, however, Margaret was forced to apologize to Henry for her behavior after both Simnel and Warbeck had been defeated.

Margaret, because of her bloodlines, lived a life founded upon political conflict. Her marriage was one of political convenience and was important to the house of York when it helped Edward reclaim his throne in 1471. Her prominent position in two regnal families made it possible for her to cause trouble for the last Lancastrian hope, the Tudor king Henry VII, yet she also witnessed the end of the bloody battles between the houses of York and Lancaster in her native England. She died in 1503 at Mechlin and was buried at the Church of the Cordeliers.

Bibliography: C.A.J. Armstrong, *England, France, and Burgundy in the Fifteenth Century*, 1983; Christine Weightman, *Margaret of York, Duchess of Burgundy, 1446–1503*, 1989.

Christina Brunson Defendi

Marigny, Enguerran de (c. 1275–1315),

was the financial minister of *Philip IV, "the Fair," of France. Marigny is best known for his firm control over the French government's financial institutions in the last years of the reign of Philip the Fair, becoming in essence the king's prime minister.

The career of Enguerran de Marigny is an excellent case study of how young, ambitious men were introduced into and thrived in royal service via patronage and ability in the early fourteenth century. He was born in Normandy, the son of a nobleman who was also a royal official. He had other relatives in high office as well. The archbishop of Rouen, Guillaume de Flavacourt (later cardinal), almost certainly introduced Marigny to Jeanne of Navarre, the wife of Philip the Fair. She took a liking to the young man, gave him a position in her household, and eventually married him to one of her goddaughters. By 1304 he had risen to become one of the king's chamberlains.

Marigny became one of Philip the Fair's royal councilors before May 1308 and performed several important assignments, such as governing the Louvre and directing the restoration of the royal palace in Paris. Marigny's greatest strengths, however, were in diplomacy and finance. In diplomacy, he succeeded in avoiding another costly war with Flanders from 1312 to 1314 and, by so doing, obtained the Flemish cities Lille, Douai, and Béthune for France in 1312. The Conventions of Marquette (3 September 1314), for which Marigny was primarily responsible, deflected war and provided favorable benefits to Philip. His troublesome vassals Robert of Béthune, count of Flanders, and his brother Louis of Nevers, asked for pardon for their rebellious activities; the cession of Lille, Douai, and Béthune was ratified; and an indemnity of 20,000 *livres tournois* was promised. Marigny also conducted negotiations with the pope. He played a role, for example, in persuading *Clement V to suppress the order of the Templars in 1312.

In 1314 Philip the Fair gave complete control over the kingdom's finances to Enguerran de Marigny. He became the king's primary councilor, with more power than any of his predecessors. He dominated the treasury, the Chambre des comptes (the royal chamber of accounts), banking institutions, and foreign exchange until Philip the Fair's death in November 1314. This power, however, also gained him many powerful enemies, chief among them the king's brother, Charles of Valois, who may have been jealous of his close relationship with Philip the Fair. After the king's death, Marigny's previous successes became reasons for his downfall at the hands of Charles, who had great influence over the new king, his nephew Louis X. Because he had attained such control over the finances of the kingdom, Marigny was accused of robbing the king. It was indeed true that Marigny had become enormously rich in the king's service, owning, for example, a great estate in Normandy. Marigny was also charged with treason; the Conventions of Marquette were popularly seen as evidence that the Flemings had successfully bribed Marigny to avoid war. Other accusations, such as necromancy and sorcery, were less easy to substantiate but served to blacken Marigny's character even more. Marigny was condemned by Louis X and his court to death, and he was executed by hanging on 30 April 1315.

Marigny's unpopularity remained legendary. Almost fifteen years after his death his name appeared in the suborned testimony of the case of *Robert of Artois, where it was claimed that Marigny had conspired with Thierry d' Hireçon, the primary councilor of Countess Mahaut of Artois, to destroy official letters granting the county of Artois to Mahaut's nephew Robert. Marigny was also vilified in one of the most famous French literary works of the early fourteenth century, *Le Roman de Fauvel*, probably written by Gervais du Bus, Marigny's chaplain, and completed shortly after the death of Philip the Fair. Fauvel, depicted as a horse, represented the Antichrist and was the epitome of evil. Fauvel was very rich, corrupt, and power hungry, exactly the characteristics most people believed that Marigny had possessed. Many scholars believe that Marigny was the model for Fauvel, and the allegorical verse a disguised account of the horrors that besieged France as a result of his power.

Bibliography: Joseph Strayer, *The Reign of Philip the Fair*, 1980.

Dana L. Sample

Marsiglio of Padua (1275/80–c. 1342) was also known as Marsilius, Menandrinus, or Marsiglio dei Mainardini. Marsiglio was one of the most innovative and controversial political theorists of the Middle Ages, and his ideas have been the subject of debate from the fourteenth century to the present day. In a series of works, above all in the monumental *Defensor pacis* (Defender of the peace), Marsiglio argued against papal claims of authority over secular rulers.

Marsiglio was born into the prominent Mainardini family of Padua sometime between 1275 and 1280. Very little is known about his early life beyond the fact that he studied medicine, presumably at the University of Padua. At some point, probably around the turn of the century, Marsiglio moved to Paris. In a charter dated 12 March 1313, Marsiglio was described as rector of the University of Paris, and he may also have written several short treatises on natural philosophy during his years in France. He returned to Italy by October 1316, where he was appointed a canon of the cathedrall at Padua. A letter written by Pope *John XXII in 1319 mentioned Marsiglio as an emissary of Can Grande della Scala and Matteo Visconti. It is likely that Marsiglio began writing the *Defensor pacis* during these years, although he did not finish this work until 24 June 1324, by which time he had returned to Paris.

The *Defensor pacis* is a sprawling, complex work that drew upon sources as varied as Aristotle, the Bible, Cicero, Bernard of Clairvaux, and Thomas Aquinas. In the first part of the *Defensor pacis*, Marsiglio discussed the ideal secular state. For Marsiglio, the purpose of the state was to ensure a well-ordered society in which the citizens were able to live a "sufficient life." The state was composed of various "parts," the artisan, the judicial, the warrior, the priestly, and so forth. When these parts worked together, each performing its proper tasks and not interfering with the others, the state was considered to be at peace, which was a necessary condition for the state to fulfill its purpose. This peace was ensured by the government of the state, which received its authority from the "human legislator," defined by Marsiglio as "the whole body of citizens or the weightier part thereof." For the state to be at peace, there could be only one government. Unfortunately, Marsiglio argued, this ideal was undermined by the papacy's claims to civil authority. The papacy, in effect, was attempting to set itself up as a second government whose authority was derived from God, not from the human legislator. As long as the papacy continued to act on its claims, the peace of the state was at risk. Marsiglio thus concentrated on the proper position of the priesthood within the state in the second, longer part of the *Defensor pacis*. Here he used biblical texts to support the arguments put forth in the first section—that the priesthood, even the papacy, should be subordinate to the government of the state. The priesthood, Marsiglio argued, was one of the parts of the state, and as such, it must obey the government, just as the other parts of the state must similarly obey. The priesthood did have a certain, God-given authority, in that it was responsible for teaching revealed truths and administering the sacraments, but obedience to this authority was voluntary, while obedience to the government was subject to coercion. Marsiglio further argued that the church itself was a human institution whose hierarchy was created and maintained by human, and not divine, activity. Thus, like the state, the church, from the lowest parish priest up to the pope himself, was governed by the will of its own "human legislator," that is, the body of the faithful. The final section of the *Defensor pacis* contained a brief summary of the main arguments of the work.

At first, the *Defensor pacis* was issued anonymously, but in 1326 Marsiglio's authorship was revealed. By 1326 Marsiglio had also probably finished his second major work, *De translatione imperii* (On the transfer of the empire), in which he argued that the authority of the holy Roman emperor was rooted in historical developments and was not the result of papal intervention. Fearing retribution from supporters of the papacy, Marsiglio fled to the court of the German king, *Louis IV, in Nuremberg. At the time, Louis was involved in a struggle with the pope over the king's claim to the throne of the Holy Roman Empire, and he was thus inclined to offer Marsiglio his protection. Marsiglio joined a group of influential thinkers, including *William of Ockham, who were active in supporting Louis's claims against the papacy. When Louis traveled to northern Italy in early 1327 to assert his imperial claims, Marsiglio accompanied him and may have been involved in organizing the king's itinerary. In October 1327, partly in response to Louis's Italian expedition, Pope John XXII declared the *Defensor pacis* heretical and condemned Marsiglio. Louis entered Rome in January 1328 and appointed Marsiglio the spiritual vicar of the city. Louis returned to Germany in 1329, and once again Marsiglio accompanied him. Little is known of Marsiglio's activities in the 1330s, and he appears to have fallen out of favor with Louis, who even offered to withdraw his protection from Marsiglio as part of his negotiations with the papacy. Around 1340, however, Louis consulted Marsiglio on the question of whether papal approval was needed to dissolve a marriage or legitimize a marriage between blood relations. Marsiglio replied with a short treatise, *De matrimonio* (On marriage), which argued that marriage was essentially a secular institution. During this same period Marsiglio composed the *Defensor minor*, in which he summarized the main arguments of the *Defensor pacis* and refuted some of the objections that had been raised against the earlier work. Marsiglio's death is mentioned in a papal document dated 10 April 1343, and it is likely that he died near the end of 1342.

Bibliography: Marsiglio of Padua, *The Defensor pacis*, vol. 2, trans. Alan Gewirth, 1956; Marsiglio of Padua, *Writings on the Empire: Defensor minor and De translatione imperii*, ed. and trans. Cary J. Nederman, 1993; Cary J. Nederman, *Community and Consent: The Secular Political Theory of Marsiglio of Padua's Defensor Pacis*, 1995.

Stephen A. Allen

Martí de Galba, Joan. *See* Galba, Joan Martí de.

Martin I, "the Humanist," King of Aragon (b. 1356, r. 1396–1410).

The last of the able counts of Barcelona who held the Crown of Aragon for three centuries, Martin I ruled from 1396 to 1410, renowned for his piety and humanism. Martin was the son of *Pedro IV, "the Ceremonious" (1336–87), and his third wife, Eleanor, the sister of Frederick III of Sicily. His older brother was Juan I (1387–96). In 1372 Martin married Marie de Luna, who bore four children, but only the eldest, Martin the younger, survived. Juan and Martin disliked Pedro's unpopular fourth wife, Sibilla de Fortia, and avoided her coronation in 1381. Pedro made Martin seneschal of Catalonia in 1368 and his lieutenant in Valencia in 1378. When Frederick III died in 1377, leaving Sicily to his daughter Maria, Pedro claimed the inheritance himself, sailed there with a large fleet, and made Martin, now count of Ejérica and Luna, his viceroy. Martin led expeditions to Sicily between 1378 and 1384, but resistance to Aragonese annexation persisted. Following his accession, Juan made Martin duke of Montblanc and entrusted him with capturing the fugitive Sibilla and defending Majorca against Bernard of Armagnac. In 1390 Martin the younger married Maria of Sicily, and in 1392 Juan sent the elder Martin to establish their control of the island. Though he captured Trapani and Palermo, revolts erupted in 1393 that occupied him for the remainder of his brother's reign.

At Juan's death Martin was proclaimed king in preference to his brother's wife, Yolande of Bar, and their daughters. Marie de Luna was regent until his return from Sicily in 1397, defeated Count Mathieu de Foix's attempt to seize the throne for his wife Juana (Juan's daughter), and punished corruption among Juan's advisors. Journeying home, Martin visited at Avignon with his wife's relative, Pope *Benedict XIII (Pedro de Luna of Aragon), whom he supported in the Papal Schism against his Sicilian enemies, who in turn backed the rival Roman popes. Once he was in the Iberian Peninsula, Martin made a point of spending time and convoking the Cortes in each of his realms of Aragon, Catalonia, and Valencia. After several months in Barcelona, he was in Aragon for two years, but plague prevented his entry into Valencia until 1402. While confirming his subjects' privileges, he suppressed aristocratic disorder and restored the fiscal resources dissipated by Pedro and Juan. Benedict XIII's backing turned Martin's campaigns against the Moors in 1398–1400 into "crusades," Aragonese soldiers defended the pope at Avignon, and Martin gave him refuge after the Council of Pisa deposed him and elected Alexander V in 1409. Martin made peace with Navarre in 1399, arranged Martin the younger's second marriage to Blanche of Navarre in 1402, and made treaties with France and Castile in 1406 and 1409, respectively. Though Martin reinforced his position in Sardinia in 1396–97, rebels there enjoyed considerable success, receiving aid from Genoa even after he had made peace with that city in 1402; resistance stiffened under Brancaleo de Oria and Guilhem of Narbonne in 1408. Martin the younger, who established firmer control in Sicily despite Maria's death in 1401 and continued

baronial opposition, defeated the Sardinian rebels in 1409 but died shortly
thereafter, leaving his father without an heir. Marie having died in 1406, Martin
hastily married Margarita de Prades in 1409 but died himself on 31 May 1410,
provoking a succession crisis that brought the Trastámaras to power in Aragon.

Like his father and brother, Martin was a well-educated patron of the arts,
the most "humanistic" of the three. At his Cortes of Perpignan in 1406, described
as the most brilliant in Catalan history and the high point of his reign, he delivered a brilliant oration filled with classical and scriptural references. He knew
the history and was sensitive to the concerns of his three peninsular realms. He
supported the University of Lérida, attempted to set up faculties in Barcelona,
patronized poets and the Consistori de la Gaya Sciensa, and encouraged study
of the brilliant Catalan thinkers *Ramon Llull (c. 1232–1316) and Francesch
Eiximenis (c. 1340–1409). A dedicated Christian who arrived from Avignon in
1397 with a piece of the True Cross, Martin sought to alleviate peasant suffering
and was a follower of the Dominican St. *Vincent Ferrer, a defender of Iberian
churches, and a patron of religious orders.

Bibliography: T. N. Bisson, *The Medieval Crown of Aragon*, 1986; James F. O'Callaghan,
A History of Medieval Spain, 1983.

William B. Robison

Martorell, Joanot (1413?–68), was the principal author of *Tirant lo Blanc*,
the most significant *libro de caballería*, or chivalric romance, in Catalan. He
was a frequent traveler and soldier, and it is believed that he based several of
the novel's episodes on his own experiences. Martorell was born in Gandia in
either 1413 or 1414 to an aristocratic and well-respected family. His parents
were Francesco Martorell, chamberlain to King Martin the Humanist and a magistrate in Valencia, and Damiata de Montpalau. Joanot had six siblings: Gal-
ceran, Jofre, Jaume, Isabel (the first wife of the distinguished fifteenth-century
Catalan poet *Ausias March), Aldonça, and Damiata. The latter's affair with a
second cousin, Joan de Montalau, led to a long, convoluted, and public dispute
between Mantorell and Montalau. Mantorell's dogged pursuit of his adversary
led to Damiata's disgrace, and she died unmarried. Mantorell's zealous attempts
to defend his family's honor reveal how seriously he took his role as a member
of Valencia's warrior nobility. It also suggests that Martorell had an argumentative and bombastic personality. Knowledge of the quarrel and of the resultant
travels for Mantorell comes from the numerous cartels of defiance exchanged
between him and Montalau beginning in 1437. Declaring that by refusing to
marry Damiata, Montpalau had stolen the honor of both him and his sister,
Martorell challenged him to any type of duel observed by an impartial judge.
Montalau accepted three days later, and numerous letters concerning the conditions of the duel were exchanged. By 1438 Martorell had traveled to London
to find an appropriate judge and stayed there at least eleven months awaiting
Montalau. The duel never took place, and the argument was ultimately resolved

by Queen Mary of Castile, who ordered that Montalau pay four thousand florins to Damiata.

Other details of Martorell's life are sketchy. There is evidence of an arrest warrant issued against him in 1440 along with calls for duels with three fellow Valencian knights. He at one point lived at the Portuguese court, but at what date is unknown. Martorell began *Tirant lo Blanc* in 1460 but died before completing the novel, a job left to *Joan Martí de Galba. The romance was only published in 1490. *William of Warwick* is Martorell's only other known literary work. It is virtually identical to the first thirty-nine chapters of *Tirant lo Blanc*, both of which were based on the thirteenth-century Anglo-Norman romance *Guy of Warwick*. Martorell never married and left no known heirs.

Composed in Catalan rather than Spanish, *Tirant lo Blanc* is well known but little read and is generally excluded from the canon of Renaissance literature. Cervantes immortalized *Tirant lo Blanc* by having a priest in *Don Quixote*'s famous book-burning episode describe it as "the best book of its kind in the world" (part I, chapter 6). Martorell today garners respect for his composition. The Peruvian author Mario Vargas Llosa has described Martorell as "the first of that lineage of God-supplanters—Fielding, Balzac, Dickens, Flaubert, Tolstoy, Joyce, Faulkner—who try to create in their novels an all-encompassing reality." It is the vivid realism of the text's language, characters, and subject matter that most distinguishes *Tirant lo Blanc*. A tale of 487 chapters recounting the adventures of Tirant the White, a "prince and caesar of Constantinople," the romance offers an idealistic view of chivalric behavior while also detailing a soldier's expertise and daily routine. The scenes of war appear sufficiently authentic to warrant the assumption that Martorell himself engaged in warfare and not just private duels. Martorell incorporated a rich variety of parlance in his narrative, from the verbose and flowery speech of Valencian aristocrats to the awkward and bawdy expressions of soldiers and adolescents. Numerous episodes irrelevant to the principal chivalric romance at times overwhelm the reader but presage the modern novel. Martorell presented social, sexual, and wartime realities absent in most other medieval chivalric romances. Martorell never seems to have recognized the value of his literary skills and successes and saw himself first and foremost as a knight. In his final cartel to Montpalau he declared that writing "is unworthy of knights and gentlemen and suitable only to women, and jurists, whose sole defenses are their tongues and pens."

Bibliography: Joanot Martorell and Joan Martí de Galba, *Tirant lo Blanc*, trans. David H. Rosenthal, 1984; Kathleen McNerney, *Tirant lo Blanc Revisited: A Critical Study*, 1983; Mario Vargas Llosa, *MVL: A Collection of Critical Essays*, 1980.

Margaret Harp

Masaccio (1401–c. 1428) was born Tommaso di Ser Giovanni di Mone Cassai and was a Florentine painter today considered the father of Renaissance painting. He applied to painting the system of linear perspective developed by *Filippo Brunelleschi and the realistic human grandeur of *Donatello's sculpture. He based the monumentality of his works upon *Giotto, but animated them in a dramatically secular pictorial space through the innovative use of a single constant light source. His short life left a small but revolutionary corpus, including *Virgin and Child Enthroned* (1426, National Gallery, London), *Trinity* (1425/27, S. Maria Novella, Florence), and *Tribute Money* and *Expulsion from Paradise* (c. 1427, Brancacci Chapel, S. Maria del Carmine, Florence).

Tommaso di Ser Giovanni di Mone Cassai was born a notary's son on 21 December 1401 in San Giovanni Val d'Arno. He came to be known as Masaccio, "Thomas the slob," perhaps to differentiate him from his frequent collaborator, Masolino. In 1422 he was listed as a member of the Florentine painters' guild, Arte de' Medici e Speziali, and by 1424 he joined the professional association, Compagnia di S. Luca.

The *Virgin and Child Enthroned* was originally the central panel of a chapel polyptych altarpiece commissioned by Giuliano di Colino degli Scarsi da San Giusto in S. Maria del Carmine in Pisa. The influence of Donatello is evident in Masaccio's experimentation with perspective and modeling, accentuating contrasts and frequently stressing contours with light. Using traditional late medieval formulas, Masaccio innovatively introduced space surrounding the throne. Angels were caught in a moment of actual time, made convincing by the use of a single source of light whose highlight and shadow gave depth to their figures.

The *Trinity* marks the introduction of a completely "Western" icon. Heavily influenced by Brunelleschi, Masaccio expressed the essence of traditional Trinitarian themes in radically different terms. The triumph over death was repeated three times, the eternal, the actual, and the potential. First, the Father supporting his crucified human Son, joined by the Holy Spirit, was presented within a Brunelleschian triumphal arch over a sepulche. Second, Christ was shown in a traditional crucifixion scene, with the Virgin and St. John at its feet. Finally, Christ was shown resurrected by his Father, savior to the waiting world represented by the two donors between whom lie the remains of Adam, with this warning: "As you are now, I once was, as I am now, so too you will be." Masaccio revolutionized the mechanism of icons with the use of central perspective that acted to draw the audience toward infinity, later developed by *Pietro Perugino and Raphael. Basing his work on Brunelleschi's use of the circular plan to symbolize God's grace mathematically emanating from the center of the perfect form of the circle, Masaccio placed the Father at the center of a semicircular arc. This device was also developed in *Tribute Money*.

Expulsion from Paradise achieved realistic figures in motion using the laws of dimension based on natural observation. The figures of Adam and Eve are independent of the picture plane, and the setting is sparing but has a remarkable illusion of depth. Eve's gestures were likely based on the nude figure of Prudence by Giovanni Pisano at the base of the Pisa Cathedral pulpit. Masaccio succeeded in portraying the figures as conscious individuals with full emotional intensity confronting the profound weight of the moral moment. Placing it at the entrance to the chapel opposite Masolino's *Temptation of Adam and Eve* represented the relation of original sinners expelled from paradise to redeemed sinner and embodiment of the church, gatekeeper to paradise.

Tribute Money was a development of Brunelleschi's influence, set against a landscape background with a center perspective. Placed at the center of the semicircular arc of Apostles, Christ was represented mathematically as the point of Grace. Although the audience is drawn to Christ, Masaccio's Christ does not dominate the scene; he stands equal to his companions and is depicted as a human being himself. Figures in Eastern icons look up, leading the viewer upward to God. Masaccio revolutionized this mechanism by drawing the viewer inward to identify with the humanity of the subjects, then moving toward Christ and beyond to infinity through the focus of a central vanishing point just behind Christ's head.

Masaccio died unexpectedly in Rome some time before June 1428, leaving Masolino to continue working on the chapel until 1434, when the patron was forced into exile. Ultimately it was finished by Filippino Lippi between 1481 and 1485. The Brancacci Chapel is indisputably significant to the importance of the Florentine school. Numerous masters, including *Leonardo da Vinci, Michelangelo, and Raphael, studied its frescoes. Surviving drawings by Michelangelo copied *Tribute Money* and *Expulsion from Paradise*.

Bibliography: B. Cole, *Masaccio and the Art of Early Renaissance Florence*, 1980; R. Longhi, *Three Studies*, 1995; U. Procacci, *All the Paintings of Masaccio*, 1962.

Patricia Cossard

Matthias I Corvinus, King of Hungary (b. 1443, r. 1458–90), ruled

during Hungary's period of greatest imperial power. Corvinus's three-decade reign was marked by incredible military advances against European nations to the west, but a neglect of the troubled frontier on the south. Known as both a humanist and a prototype Renaissance monarch, Corvinus offers the Hungarian people a legendary folk hero in the golden age of Hungary, as well as a ruthless imperialist who often sacrificed the common good in his quest to rule over a reunited Holy Roman Empire.

Matthias I Corvinus (known in Hungary as Matyas Corvin, born Matyas Hunyadi) was born on 24 February 1443 in Kolozsvár, Transylvania, to a wealthy, landed father, János Hunyadi. Hunyadi (1407–56) was a national hero and military leader who achieved success against the Turks, with whom Hungary continued to have an antagonistic relationship. Corvinus came to the throne in 1458 and reigned there until his death in 1490.

Corvinus was considered by many to be the second Attila the Hun, a name he cultivated and one that would come to symbolize both his greatness and his imperialistic ambitions. He attempted to establish a more modern governmental bureaucracy that, along with other reforms, sought to centralize his power away from the landed lords, often forcing these lords to labor against their own best interests. He also used as his advisers and rulers *familiares*, those men retained by great lords for their professional expertise. While Corvinus supported the arts, he did not support urban growth and thus often opposed the emerging bourgeoisie. Corvinus focused the military on campaigns into Europe, neglecting the southern frontier and the continuing wars with the Turks. He also taxed heavily, and his reign ended with debts totaling around two million florins, with revenues reaching not even half as much.

As part of Corvinus's move to make Hungary a more centralized kingdom, he supported scholars and artists in order to create a national identity. Corvinus continued to promote a cult of Attila around himself, and he commissioned Antonio Bonfini in 1486 to write a history of Hungary and the Huns. Entitled *Rerum Hungaricum decades libri XLV*, and edited by Johannes Sambucus, this narrative remained one of the standards for Hungarian history through the eighteenth century. Corvinus also filled his court with humanists.

Corvinus's westward expansion began with the seizure of Czech lands under the pretense of suppressing the Hussite heretics and then continued against Austria in 1477 until its conquest in 1485. The pope refused to comment either for or against the Hussite wars, and *Frederick III of Austria tacitly supported the Czechs. Corvinus was a constant threat not only to Austria but also to Bohemia, Venice, and Poland. His military campaigns, his neglect of his people and the southern frontier, and his increasing taxation led to a slow erosion of support among the nobility. The lesser nobles, supported by his father János Hunyadi before his death, organized against Corvinus in 1467. In 1470 János Pannonius (1434–72), once Corvinus's favorite court poet, wrote against him a noteworthy pacifist poem entitled "Pleading with Mars for Peace." In it, Pannonius, born in Croatia and raised by association with Corvinus to the wealthy position of bishop of Pécs, described Corvinus as a "waster of plowland, destroyer of towns, the world's depopulator, filler of Hell," and "drunk on human blood," and begged him to spare the country and the people of Europe from more spoilage and war. Pannonius, along with his uncle, Primate Johannes Vitéz, in 1471 became involved in a plot to dethrone Corvinus and raise Casimir of Poland into his place. The plan failed, and Pannonius died on his flight to Venice to seek new support against Corvinus, while Vitéz died under house arrest.

Corvinus sought revenge for both the plot against him by Pannonius and the 1467 plot by the lesser nobles. He exacted revenge from those who opposed him in his own country after they thought they were safe. Corvinus now turned against Hungarian humanists and replaced them at his court with humanists who did not have interests in Hungary, including Galeotto Marzio, Antonio Bonfini, and Pietro Ranzano. With his marriage to Beatrix of Naples, Corvinus's court became increasingly Italian in culture. In 1485 Marzio wrote a work of praise in honor of Corvinus entitled *De egregie sapienter jocose dictis ac factis regis Matthiae*. During the same decade, however, Callimachus Experiens (ambassador from Cracow, who spent 1483–84 in Hungary and worked to foil a Hungarian alliance with Austria and Poland and to isolate Corvinus) wrote his work *Attila*, which labeled Corvinus as "flagellum Del" (the scourge of God).

Corvinus's later reign was marked by continued successes at westward expansion, but also increased resistance and debt at home. The cost of this westward expansion was increased vulnerability to the Turks. He launched a surprise attack against Frederick III's son *Maximilian I while Maximilian was at war with France over Burgundy. Corvinus offered peace if Maximilian would marry his daughter to Corvinus's son Johannes Corvinus, but the Hungarian king died on 6 April 1490 before these negotiations were resolved. Within a few years after his death, Hungary had lost all the regions he conquered.

Bibliography: Marianna D. Birnbaum, *The Orb and the Pen: Janus Pannonius, Matthias Corvinus, and the Buda Court*, 1996; Tibor Klaniczay and Jozsef Jankovics, eds., *Matthias Corvinus and the Late Humanism in Central Europe*, 1994.

Mark K. Fulk

Matthias of Janov (c. 1350–94). Matthias of Janov was born to an aristocratic family, although the details of his birth and childhood are uncertain. Matthias traveled to Prague, probably fairly early in his life, where he studied the works of *Jan Milic of Kromeric and where he probably met and worked with Konrad of Waldhausen. It was perhaps his aristocratic background and his experiences with the growing intellectual movements in Bohemia that led him from his home in Bohemia to Paris, where he studied for nine years, probably during 1373–81. Around that time the name Magister Parisiensis was attached to him, a name by which he was usually known to his contemporaries. In Paris in 1376 he became master of the free arts, although the main focus of his study remained theology. He was ordained to the priesthood in 1378 and soon traveled to Rome, where he attempted to receive a papal provision due to his great poverty. Unfortunately, he did not at first receive the provision, which embittered him toward the church. This may explain some of his later writing, much of which has been identified with the early Reformation. He finally received his provision in 1381 when Pope *Urban VI conferred on him the "expectancy of a canonry" at the Cathedral of Prague. He returned to Prague at that time, although he did not ever become canon of the cathedral. Instead, he was granted the office of penitentiary of the archbishop. He also became a preacher at the Cathedral Church of St. Vitus that year. He did not find an end to his financial worries until later, when he became parish priest at Velika-Ves.

Matthias is perhaps best known as a forerunner of *Jan Hus, although his direct influence upon Hus was, according to most scholars, negligible. It is not known, in fact, if Hus even read Matthias's work or heard his sermons. However, some of Matthias's beliefs certainly reached Hus, and Matthias's attitudes toward church corruption and particularly the practice of Communion foreshadowed much of that for which Hus would later be persecuted. Matthias's most controversial idea was that lay Christians should be allowed to receive Communion each day, something the medieval church strongly rejected. This contentious belief, combined with his ongoing mistrust of the corrupt clergy, a corruption he had observed firsthand in Paris and Rome, caused him to be distrusted by the clergy in Prague. In 1388 proceedings were brought against Matthias when a decree of the Synod of Prague declared that laypersons should not participate in the Mass more than once a month. In 1389 Matthias was asked to retract his views on the subject by the archiepiscopal court. His punishment was that he was no longer allowed to celebrate the Mass anywhere except his own parish church at Velika-Ves. Matthias did recant his views in 1389 and on other occasions, but the rest of his career was marked by a consistent return to controversy and unpopular views, all of which are clearly laid out in his greatest work, the *Regulae Veteris et Novi Testamenti*. His willingness to buckle under the influence of the ecclesiastical system is part of the reason he has often been overlooked by scholars—he appears to be inconsistent, and that lack of consistency has made him seem unreliable. Throughout the rest of his career Matthias was often brought before the ecclesiastical court, and each time he appears to have recanted, although some scholars argue that he did this as a means of preserving his professional livelihood rather than submitting intellectually to the power of the church. Ultimately, he was relegated to serving his parish at Velika-Ves, where he died in 1394.

The *Regulae Veteris et Novi Testamenti* is a work in five chapters, and its completion occupied much of Matthias's adult life. His subtle use of language reveals in his thinking an overall condemnation of church corruption. The first chapter contains two treatises, one distinguishing between true and false prophets and the other explaining the sacrament of Holy Communion. It was here that, among other issues, Matthias argued for daily Communion among laymen and women, whom he found to be equal in their devotion and spiritual fervor to men. The second chapter contains two treatises: "De hypocrisi," in which Matthias railed against the corruption he found among the clergy, and "De distincta veritate," which is no longer extant. Chapter three contains six treatises, in which he again referred to daily Communion and the corruption of the clergy and outlined his Christ-centered theology. His most famous work, the fifth treatise of this chapter, entitled "De Antichristo," has mystical elements and described, in these terms, his vision of the Antichrist. The sixth treatise further outlined Matthias's disapproval of the church and its corruption. The fourth and fifth chapters again dealt with daily Communion and read like a Socratic dialogue, in which Matthias explained his opinion on the issue and attacked the clergy for being elitist and ignorant in denying lay Christians daily Communion.

Matthias has been underappreciated by modern church historians. This is always unfortunate, but particularly in Matthias's case. When his work is closely scrutinized, one can find in Matthias an excellent example of the tensions inherent in ecclesiastical life in late medieval Europe. The Reformation was, for many modern scholars, inevitable, and as such, the ideas that informed the great

Reformers of the fifteenth and sixteenth centuries must have had influence in the later Middle Ages. Matthias, like many of his contemporaries, seems to have wrestled with the problems he saw in the church: corruption, poor leadership, greed and elitism, and others. The fact that Matthias attempted to remain within the church, submitting to its sanctions against him when he dared to speak out, tells us that he tried to work within and preserve the system of which he was a part. He did not take the great heroic stands of the men who would be executed as heretics in the century following his death. He was, however, an influence upon these men, particularly Hus and *Jerome of Prague. His life as one who tried to maintain order within the tempestuous late medieval church marks him as not only an important predecessor of those who would live (and die) to reform the church, but also an important thinker and minor reformer within his own time.

Bibliography: Johann Loserth, *Wiclif and Hus*, 1884/1980; Matthew Spinka, *John Hus: A Biography*, 1968.

Susannah Chewning

Maximilian I, Holy Roman Emperor (b. 1459, r. 1493–1519), was born on 22 March 1459, the eldest son of Emperor *Frederick III and Eleanor of Portugal. During his life he held the titles archduke of Austria, king of Germany, and holy Roman emperor. He led his family to dominance in Europe, adding vast lands to traditional Habsburg holdings in Austria. He secured the Netherlands by marriage, Hungary and Bohemia through treaty and military pressure, and Spain and the Spanish Empire through an excellent marriage for his son *Philip I of Spain. He fought a series of wars, mostly in Italy, against the French, and upon his death on 12 January 1519, his grandson succeeded to the vast Habsburg realms and the imperial crown as Charles V.

In 1477 Maximilian married Mary, daughter of *Charles the Bold, duke of Burgundy. With this marriage Maximilian acquired Burgundian holdings in the Netherlands and along the eastern frontier of France. He was required to defend his new domains against incursions by *Louis XI of France. Mary died in 1482, and, bending to pressure from the Netherlands, Maximilian agreed to allow the States General of the Netherlands to act as regent for his son Philip. Quickly becoming dissatisfied with this arrangement, however, Maximilian defeated the States General in war and in 1485 regained control of his son's regency. To achieve peace in his French holdings, Maximilian then signed the Treaty of Arras in 1482 and was forced to consent to the betrothal of his daughter Margaret of Austria to *Charles VIII of France.

Maximilian was elected king of the Germans and crowned at Aachen on 9 April 1486. With military help from Brittany, England, and Spain, Maximilian continued to battle France and the Netherlands. Hoping to strenghten his position against France by controlling the surrounding territories, he married Duchess Anne of Brittany by proxy in 1490, but he could not prevent a French invasion of Brittany shortly thereafter. Charles VIII sent his fiancee Margaret back to

Maximilian and demanded that Anne sever her marriage to the German king and become queen of France instead.

Back in Austria, Maximilian managed to regain control of most of his family's traditional possessions that had been seized by Hungary. He then became a candidate for the Hungarian Crown. Vladislav II was elected instead, and Maximilian waged a successful campaign against the new Hungarian king that resulted in the Treaty of Pressburg in 1491. The terms of this treaty placed succession to the thrones of Bohemia and Hungary in the hands of the Habsburgs if Vladislav left no male heirs.

War with France and the Netherlands ended in 1493 with the Treaty of Senlis, leaving the Duchy of Burgundy and the Low Countries under Habsburg control. Frederick III died that same year, leaving Maximilian as sole ruler of Germany and head of the house of Habsburg, and he was named holy Roman emperor–elect. Maximilian then drove the Turks from the southeastern borders of Hungary and married Bianca Maria Sforza of Milan in 1494. He passed control of the Low Countries to his son, reserving the right of joint rule; the flourishing culture of the Low Countries influenced literature, art, government, politics, and military methods in all Habsburg possessions.

Charles VIII's invasion of Italy in 1494 upset the balance of power in Europe. The following year Maximilian allied himself with the papacy, Spain, Venice, and Milan in the Holy League to drive the French from the peninsula. The Holy League succeeded in ousting the French, but Maximilian gained very little from this alliance for himself. However, excellent marriages for his children profited the Habsburg family greatly. His son Philip married Juana (the Mad) of Spain, and his daughter Margaret married the Spanish crown prince in 1497. These marriages assured him of a Habsburg succession in Spain and control of the Spanish colonies as well.

The Imperial Diet of Worms was held in 1495 to try to resolve the tension growing between Maximilian and the German princes. The ambitious Maximilian wanted to strengthen his empire, and laws were proposed to reform the Reichskammergericht, or Imperial Chamber. No reconciliation occurred, and as the princes continued to resist any strengthening of imperial power, Maximilian established his own judicial and financial commissions to thwart opposition. All his attempts to centralize the administration of his empire and ensure reliable funding for his military ultimately failed.

Maximilian did not manage to subjugate the Swiss and was forced to recognize their independence in the Peace of Basil on 22 September 1499. Also, France once again moved into Italy and, in cooperation with Spain, occupied the imperial fief of Milan. Maximilian was also beset by domestic troubles. In 1500 the imperial princes met at the Reichstad in Augsburg and withdrew their remaining support from Maximilian. They considered deposing him, but his countermeasures were sufficient to prevent this. He made credit arrangements with prominent south German business firms that assured him of ready funds for his needs. His campaign against Hungary in 1506 also strengthened the Habsburg claim to the Hungarian throne.

In 1508 Maximilian was finally named holy Roman emperor by Pope Julius II, but he was unable to go to Rome because of a threat from hostile Venetians, and so he never actually received papal confirmation of his title. Maximilian spent the remainder of his reign attempting to effect both the diplomatic and military isolation of France, and a favorable settlement of the contested Polish succession, before his death from illness on 12 January 1519.

Emperor Maximilian I is considered one of the great Renaissance patrons of culture, learning, painting, and music. He was also an accomplished author in his own right and is credited with several treatises on architecture, history, and botany. His best-known works include *Geheimes Jagdbuch*, an instructional manual on hunting; the *Weisskunig* or "white king," an autobiographical treatment of his early reign; the *Freydal*, an account of his jousting exploits as a youth; and *Der Weisen Könige Stammbaum*, a history of the Habsburg dynasty. He had a monumental tomb built for himself in a Franciscan church at Innsbruck, but it was not completed until long after his death, and he is not buried there. Maximilian was instead buried in the Chapel of Saint George in Wiener Neustadt in 1519.

Bibliography: Gerhard Benecke, *Maximilian (1459–1519)*, 1982; Glenn Elwood Waas, *The Legendary Character of Kaiser Maximilian*, 1966.

John D. Grosskopf

Medici, Cosimo de (1389–1464), was the true architect of the Medici family fortune, which, begun with profits from the manufacture and sale of textiles, was grounded in the banking industry. However, Medici control extended beyond the financial world, and they were successful in the political arena as well. The Medici rose to seize power in Florence under Cosimo in 1434. Medici family power in both Florence and the papacy would last for another two centuries.

Florentine banking in the late Middle Ages was dominated by two important families, the Bardi and the Medici. It was *Giovanni de Medici "di Bicci" who primarily increased the wealth of the Medici family in the late fourteenth century. Not only did Giovanni do business in Italy, he established branch offices of his business in France and other European kingdoms, and he served the financial needs of the papacy when opportunities permitted. Upon his death, he passed his fortune and business down to his son Cosimo. He in turn saw that the family remained powerful in the banking world, but in addition, he helped make Florence one of the most important political states and cultural centers in Italy.

Not much is known about Cosimo's personal life, except that he was married to *Contessina Bardi, a match that was arranged by his father Giovanni. He had two sons: *Piero "the Gouty," who died five years after his father, and Giovanni. He also fathered an illegitimate child named Carlo by a *femme bestiali* or purchased servant, a practice not uncommon in wealthy households in Italy.

Cosimo never held high political office in Florence—he was never officially anything more than *gonfaloniere*, or official flag-bearer—but he nevertheless ruled Florence with an iron hand for thirty years, mostly through his control of patronage in the form of bank loans, city offices, and favorable marriage arrangements. Cosimo led Florence to prominence in foreign affairs as well and helped broker a balance-of-power alliance system between Italian city-states with the Peace of Lodi in 1454.

Cosimo de Medici was not a well-educated man, yet one of his interests was manuscript and book collecting, especially those dealing with aspects of Neoplatonic philosophy and metaphysics. As an enthusiast of the "new learning" of humanism, Cosimo was the founder of the Medici Library, later known as the Laurentian Library, in Florence. Cosimo utilized a goodly portion of his wealth to aid humanistic endeavors to a significant degree. He purchased texts for the scholar and translator Niccolò Niccoli and ensured that his manuscript works would be preserved. He rectified the debts of the satirist *Poggio Bracciolini and, helping to finance the Platonic Academy, was responsible for bringing the seminal Neoplatonic thinker *Marsiglio Ficino to Florence. The great humanist *Leon Battista Alberti lived and worked in Cosimo's city and praised the Medici ruler as a man of wisdom, generosity, and culture.

In addition to the literature of the age, Cosimo de Medici was also interested in the fine arts. His favorite sculptor was *Donatello, and that artist's sculptures of *David* and *Judith* first attracted attention when they were displayed at the Medici palace. Important Renaissance painters such as *Fra Angelico, *Paolo Uccello, and *Tommaso Masaccio all achieved great masterpieces and much fame in the stimulating cultural climate of Cosimo's Florence. Cosimo was particularly interested in architecture and was responsible for the planning and construction of a new Medici palace, the Church of San Lorenzo, and the Monastery of San Marco. Encouraging the architectural work of *Filippo Brunelleschi and *Lorenzo Ghiberti, Cosimo once wrote that "a most famous man builds now private homes, now sacred buildings, now monasteries, inside and outside the city, at such expense that they seem to equal the magnificence of ancient kings and emperors." Cosimo's interest in the arts was just that: interest. Although his true talent was in finance and banking, his ability to provide patronage for masters in the fine arts helped to make Florence the cultural center of all Italy. Cosimo de Medici died on 1 August 1464 and was buried in San Lorenzo in a tomb bearing the inscription "Pater Patriae" (Father of his country).

Bibliography: Gene Brucker, *The Civic World of Early Renaissance Florence*, 1977; J. R. Hale, *Florence and the Medici: The Pattern of Control*, 1977.

Karen Holleran

Medici, Giovanni de, "di Bicci" (1360–1429),

began the rise of the great Medici family while assisting the great outburst of Florentine art between the years 1400 and 1428 led by *Lorenzo Ghiberti, *Filippo Brunelleschi, *Donatello, and *Masaccio. His unwavering character established the family as both a political force and a paternal influence in Florence, known for its generosity and courtesy to all people and classes.

The Medici family itself began as a normal middle-class family in Florence. The family members, with various branches and riddled with illegitimate lines, were bankers and cloth and silk merchants. Giovanni became the head of the family's most famous branch. His father, Averado de Medici, had acquired the nickname "Bicci." To distinguish Giovanni's place in the long history of the family and the recurrence of names within it, he is known as Giovanni di Bicci (Giovanni, the son of Bicci). The family into which Giovanni was born had distinguished itself as a leader in the struggle against the nobles; at the age of eighteen, Giovanni witnessed a distant cousin begin the riot of the Ciompi against the nobles, while yet another cousin pacified the rebellion. The family had a history of championing the cause of the people against the nobility in Florence, and Giovanni and his descendants would eventually extend that influence beyond the politics of that city.

Giovanni di Bicci and his wife, Piccarda Bueri, with their sons, *Cosimo and Lorenzo, lived in Piazza del Duomo and daily witnessed the growing walls and dome of the Florence Cathedral. Giovanni was a shrewd businessman, and by 1400 he was a man in middle age who had inherited the family and banking operations and had distinguished himself as a prudent and generous financier. His public image was estimable as he continued to champion the popular cause against the nobles and spent liberally for public benefit, though not on the magnitude of the Albizzi oligarchy, the leading family of Florence. In 1401, when the plague again returned, Florence prepared to place a costly votive offering in San Giovanni Battista in the form of two large and elaborate pairs of bronze doors. Giovanni, as a leading citizen, was appointed a judge of the international competition to choose an artist, and Ghiberti was chosen to create the great works of art. Giovanni continued to support struggling artists, having the walls of his house decorated with frescoes, typically reserved for churches, and going against the customary style of housing and life in Florence. As a businessman, his concentration was focused more on banking than on merchandising, and he gradually amassed a vast fortune. His rise in public opinion and office continued when in 1402 he was elected by his bankers' guild as prior, which made him a member of the government. He was again elected in 1408 and 1417, and in 1421 he was promoted to the highest office in the republic, *gonfaloniere* (flag bearer). He remained aloof from the politics of the day, and it is recorded that these honors were forced upon him, unsought. In 1418 Giovanni, in conjunction with a party of nobles, achieved the release of the deposed and imprisoned Pope John XXIII, with Giovanni's payment of 38,000 ducats as ransom; Giovanni gave the deposed pope refuge and erected a monument to the pontiff at his death the following year. In 1419 Giovanni paid for the erection and endowment of the Foundling Hospital of Florence, which still stands today, selecting Brunelleschi to design and construct the structure. In 1426 Giovanni achieved the passing of his celebrated *catasto*, a property tax that replaced a poll tax and thus lessened the burden on the lower classes. Though this increased the tax that Giovanni himself had to pay, he went against the wishes of the nobility in favor of the humble *populo* of Florence. In 1427 Giovanni foiled an attempt by a group of nobles, notably Rinaldo degli Albizzi and Niccolò da Uzzano, to reduce the participation of the people in their own government. In this last act as defender of the commons, Giovanni increased his popularity with the people of Florence but further alienated the powerful Albizzi family.

Giovanni died in 1429, leaving an immense fortune to his two sons, Cosimo and Lorenzo. He died respected by his people, loved by the indigent citizens of Florence, remembered by the struggling artists whom he supported, and respected as an honorable adversary by the nobles he opposed. Niccolò Machiavelli, describing his character, wrote: "He never sought the honours of government, yet enjoyed them all. When holding high office he was courteous to all. Not a man of great eloquence, but of an extraordinary prudence."

Bibliography: Gene Brucker, *The Civic World of Early Renaissance Florence*, 1977; J. R. Hale, *Florence and the Medici: The Pattern of Control*, 1977.

Kristopher Bell

Medici, Giuliano de (1453–78). Born into the influential Medici family, Giuliano, *Lorenzo de Medici's younger brother by four years, was the darling of Florence. He was carefully raised by an adoring mother, who never tired of having her handsome son's likeness reproduced by the leading artists of the city. Giuliano won his place in history, not for financial or political acumen, but for his affable nature and masculine beauty, along with an untimely and violent death, though it can be fairly said that his death at such an early age left him reasonably untried. Well built, handsome, and charming, unlike his unattractive older brother Lorenzo, Giuliano was accustomed to having his features replicated on canvas, and he was immortalized in several important artworks by artists such as *Sandro Botticelli and Bronzino. Indeed, he was a favorite of Botticelli's and appeared in several works along with Simonetta Vespucci, Botticelli's model for *The Birth of Venus*. Simonetta ("la Bella"), who was lovely (but married) and celebrated by her peers, is reported by many modern scholars to have been Giuliano's lover. The pair were romanticized by Florentine society as an almost mythical couple and were the models for Botticelli's works *Primavera* and *Venus and Mars*. Interestingly, Giuliano had been intended for a cardinalate; thus publicly his attentions to Simonetta were officially promoted as platonic.

Giuliano, easily skilled in athletics, participated in tournaments, one of which was a famous contest organized in 1475 as a fête to his patrician looks and agile ability. He appeared in silver armor, carrying a standard and graced by a flag that bore the likeness of Simonetta, painted by Botticelli. His appearance usually eclipsed the others who entered into the contests, causing his participation to be romanticized and the attention he paid to Simonetta to be seen as the ultimate courtly gesture to a great beauty of the age.

Over two years after this popular tournament, Giuliano died in 1478 at the hands of his family's enemies, falling victim to a plot conceived by Francesco de Pazzi and Girolamo Riario. The former two were joined by the archbishop of Pisa, who happily participated in the conspiracy and, like the others involved, stood to benefit from the overthrow of Giuliano, Lorenzo, and the powerful Medici family. With the approval of the archbishop, the plan was to kill the brothers during a high mass at the Cathedral of S. Maria della Fiore. It was agreed that the archbishop would leave the sanctuary just before the Consecration of the Host, a sign to the would-be assassins that the plot should go forward. Separated from each other in the church, Giuliano and Lorenzo were stabbed by their designated assassins. When the attack was over, Giuliano, who was attacked by two priests, lay dead, his body pierced by nineteen stab wounds; however, Lorenzo, who had been immediately surrounded by family and friends, survived the onslaught with only a superficial wound in his neck. Escorted home by a heavy guard that carefully circumvented his brother's mutilated corpse, Lorenzo learned of his brother's death soon after. A crowd quickly gathered outside and viciously attacked the conspirators, who were hanged from windows or thrown down to the pavement below, left to be robbed of their valuables by those on the street who were loyal to the Medici family. Later, the members of the Pazzi family were forced to change their name, their coat of arms was smashed when it was found, and they were prevented from holding any sort of office again.

In the aftermath of the attack, the family and city grieved alike. Throngs of inconsolable, weeping citizens gathered to witness Giuliano's burial on Ascension Day at the Church of San Lorenzo. A son he had by a young girl from simple circumstances was taken into the family to be raised and would later become Pope Clement VII. Clement, who was a great admirer of Michelangelo, commissioned a sepulcher, completed in 1524, that would house the remains of Giuliano and another family member. Although Giuliano's likeness was available to him in many artworks, Michelangelo made no attempt to re-create it on the representative sculpture of the young man who still lies within. He is said to have remarked, "Who will care, a thousand years from now, whether or not these are their features?"

Bibliography: Gene Brucker, *Renaissance Florence*, 1983; Carol Bresnahan Menning, *Charity and State in Late Renaissance Italy*, 1993; George Pottinger, *The Court of the Medici*, 1978.

Susan Perry

Medici, Lorenzo de, "il Magnifico" (1449–92).

The elder son of *Piero de Medici, "the Gouty," Lorenzo lived a short, although memorable, life. He was given the epithet "il Magnifico," as many other notables and members of his family of the time would be, but the label stayed with him into history as an honor many thought that he alone had earned. Lorenzo is considered by most scholars to have been the most remarkable of the Medici line. His considerable intellectual capacity gave his Florence enhanced exposure to philosophy and the arts, the spectacle of great wealth lavished on leisure pursuits and astute political rule.

The Medici, including Lorenzo, had a strong family tradition of love for the arts; indeed, their interest in the arts extended to passion, and they were knowledgeable about them as well. Lorenzo's interest and patronage touched all three branches of art and included music, plastic art, and written works. He was patron to the best and most influential artists of his time, including *Leonardo da Vinci, Michelangelo, and *Sandro Botticelli. His patronage provided such glorious, lasting gifts as the *Primavera* and *The Birth of Venus* of Botticelli to the citizens of Florence and to ensuing ages.

Fervent about literature as well, Lorenzo wished to build a great library, a desire that was still unfulfilled at the time of his death. The Medici collected manuscripts for generations, as well as books newly produced from the printing press, and it was his great wish to house the extensive collection of his family in a magnificent library. It is said that on his deathbed, he lamented this unfinished task with great emotion.

Although Lorenzo was classically educated, he received the most important elements of his training by helping his father in his study, learning financial affairs, and by acquiring the ability to write poetry from his mother. He went on in early adulthood to pen his own poetry, mostly secular, including many sonnets (*Caccia col Falcone* and *Ambra* are examples), all possessing a variation of style that was well regarded in fifteenth-century literature. His rather limited contribution to sacred poetry included works such as *Laude*.

Additionally, his love of music led Lorenzo to employ many instrumentalists and to attend numerous recitals and musical performances. It is said that he encouraged even his servants to join him in song. His patronage of music influenced Florence commercially since his organist, Squarcialupi, drew admirers from all over Europe. Lorenzo's major influence on music involved development of the first madrigal and the setting of poetry to music. He encouraged budding artists who, while they were in his employ, experimented with the use of polyphonic sounds. This patronage allowed musicians such as Heinrich Isaak to gain skills they would later exhibit as great secular musicians.

All of these interests were a natural result of the lavish lifestyle Lorenzo enjoyed, byproducts of the great wealth his family had amassed during its climb to prominence. Further, Lorenzo and his family, including his younger brother *Giuliano, found themselves in the enviable position of providing opulent feasts and spectacles for the citizens of Florence to enjoy. Giuliano, lacking in political acumen, had the ability to assemble great fêtes, and Lorenzo happily left him to perform the tasks at which he excelled. His own interests were focused on the enhancement of his family's fortune and the growth and political stability of Florence.

Representing himself as "solely a citizen of Florence," Lorenzo was its unofficial ruler. He had somewhat of a dual nature and could be both kind and cruel, the latter doing nothing to diminish his popularity with the citizens of his city. His great strength lay in his political ability, and the city flourished under his guidance largely because his interests were in furthering the Medici interests. But it was his statesmanship that the people of Florence recognized and appreciated. So aligned with the well-being of Florence was his family that their prosperity ran parallel with that of the city.

His skill at diplomacy and his abilities helped him control Florence until his untimely death at age forty-two. Lorenzo's two greatest challenges were the Pazzi conspiracy of 1478 and the Florentine war against Pope *Sixtus IV and King *Ferrante of Naples. Both trials left him weakened, with the Pazzi conspiracy taking his beloved brother Giuliano's life and the Florentine war requiring him to go in person to the Neapolitan ruler to seek and gain favorable peace terms. However, he emerged from the war as the undisputed ruler of Florence, enjoying a reign that boasted a level of glory unequaled by others who preceded or followed him.

Toward the end of his life Lorenzo suffered from gout, a family affliction he inherited from his father, who was known as "the Gouty." As the disease advanced, he found himself unable to ward off the mounting problems presented by *Girolamo Savonarola, a powerful friar who was determined to unseat the Medici from power. As Lorenzo lay near death, a legend disseminated by Savonarola himself suggested that Lorenzo refused his offer of absolution, leaving him to die in spiritual agony. Modern scholarship rejects this myth; it is now known that Lorenzo had been given absolution and died peacefully, unburdened of the constant pain he endured from the disease that ended his life. The entire population of Florence attended his funeral as a tribute to the man who had ruled their city as a benevolent tyrant and who was, and still is, regarded as the greatest contributor to the growth of Florentine culture during the quattrocento.

Of his three sons with his wife *Clarice Orsini, *Piero, Giovanni, and Giuliano, Piero succeeded him. Known as Piero the Unfortunate, Lorenzo's eldest son was unsuited to take his father's place (he was more inept than unfortunate) and ruled poorly, causing his family to be driven from Florence and inaugurating a time of Medici misfortune and decline. Giovanni, the youngest son, later became Pope Leo X. Interestingly, Lorenzo died just as Europe began to reach out in the age of exploration, and *Christopher Columbus reached the "New World" only six months after his death.

Bibliography: Anthony Cummings, *The Politicized Muse*, 1992; Judith Hook, *Lorenzo de' Medici: An Historical Biography*, 1984; Hugh Ross Williamson, *Lorenzo the Magnificent*, 1974.

Susan Perry

Medici, Piero de, "the Gouty" (1414–69).

Piero di Cosimo de Medici was the first son born to *Cosimo and *Contessina (Bardi) de Medici, in approximately 1414. He became the leader of the Medici family in 1464 when his father died. Piero was plagued throughout his life with disfiguring illnesses, including gout (from which his nickname is derived), eczema, and arthritis. Despite his painful physical existence, most sources credit him with having been a kind, honorable man who was respected by his peers.

Piero may have been physically impaired, but he was by all accounts an intelligent, sincere, and effective ruler. He was a scrupulous businessman and a gifted diplomat. The lack of attention that he has received from scholars is caused by his placement within history and, to some degree, by bad luck. His father, Cosimo, a noted patron of great artists such as *Donatello and *Fra Angelico, was larger than life and was greatly loved and respected by his people. Piero's son *Lorenzo, called "il Magnifico," clearly made more of an impact on history and the life of Florence itself than his father or even his grandfather. Even his brother, Giovanni, who died suddenly in 1463, had been his father's most loved son and had showed a great deal of promise as a young man. Piero was, therefore, a less influential leader and patron, but he was very important to the overall history of the Medici, as well as to the specific history and political controversies of mid-fifteenth-century Florence.

Piero made his mark on the politics of quattrocento Florence because of a coup that took place from late 1465 to mid-1466. Cosimo's great rival, Lucca Pitti, attempted to take control almost as soon as Cosimo had died. Two other men, Agnolo Acciauoli and Dietisalvi Neroni, joined forces with Pitti and formed "the Party of the Hill," a group of conspirators who opposed the Medici in Florence. The group that opposed these agitators was called "the Party of the Plain" and was composed of faithful supporters of the Medici, and specifically of Piero. The merchant class supported the opposition "Hill" faction and helped to seek Piero's deposition. Another supporter of the Party of the Hill was Niccolò Soderini, a rhetorician and self-proclaimed social reformer. Because of his eloquence and the growing support in Florence of the Party of the Hill, Soderini was elected *gonfaloniere* (flag bearer) in November 1465.

Soderini was unable to effect change successfully while he was in office and was forced out within a few short months. By January 1466 the remaining members of the Party of the Hill began working toward an armed rebellion against the Medici. The center of their dispute was Florence's long-term alliance with Milan: the Medici favored a Milanese alliance, while the rebels urged an association with Venice. When the time came for action, Piero, weak and bedridden, was yet able to overcome the conspirators with diplomacy and presence of mind. By August 1466 Lucca Pitti was shocked to find the people reaffirming the power of the Medici, and he begged Piero's forgiveness. At the next election in September Piero saw to it that the Signoria was firmly controlled by those with pro-Medici sentiments. Soderini, Dietisalvi, and Acciauoli were banished, but they attempted another rebellion a year later with supporters in Venice. Piero's army, backed by supporters from Milan and Naples, defeated the conspirators totally, and Medici power was fully confirmed.

Piero is well known for his diplomacy and the systematic defeat of his enemies, but he is perhaps best known for his family life and for his devotion to the arts and, specifically, to artists. He married the religious and artistic *Lucrezia Tornabuoni, the daughter of a historic and prosperous Florentine family. With Lucrezia, Piero raised five children: Maria, Bianca, Lucrezia, *Giuliano, and Lorenzo. The three daughters married well, and the two sons became notable and well-respected men in their own right. As a patron, Piero is well remembered. His most famous relationships with artists included his friendships and patronage of Luca della Robbia, Paolo di Doni, Antonio Pollaiuolo, *Andrea del Verrocchio, and *Sandro Botticelli. Botticelli's most productive era of work, during which his great *Birth of Venus* (c. 1480) was completed, took place during the lifetime and reign of Lorenzo de Medici, but he began his great work during the era of Piero. Of this period, his most famous works are the *Madonna of the Magnificat* and *The Adoration of the Magi*. In the latter Botticelli portrayed the members of the Medici family, including Cosimo, Giuliano, Lorenzo, and Piero's brother, Giovanni. Piero was also represented, although the center of the piece is clearly Lorenzo. Piero was more centralized in another of Botticelli's paintings, *Fortitude*, one of six panels commissioned from various artists of the period.

The presence of Piero in these important paintings as a patron and humble Christian proves him to have been a well-respected and honored man, both by those whom he patronized and those whom he ruled. He died in 1469, having been ill for almost a year. Up to the end of his life he was a keeper of the peace, suppressing rioters and extortionists who claimed to be acting on his authority. His tomb in the Church of San Lorenzo was ornamented by the artists he had befriended during his relatively short life. Piero di Cosimo de Medici may not be the most famous man to have ruled his city or to have borne his name, but he was a great diplomat and strategist, and a collector and supportive patron of works of art and a great friend of artists. He is perhaps best remembered as a fair and popular leader, serving, one might guess, as an excellent role model for his son, Lorenzo the Magnificent.

Bibliography: Christopher Hibbert, *The House of Medici: Its Rise and Fall*, 1975; Dale Kent, *The Rise of the Medici: Faction in Florence, 1426–1434*, 1978.

Susannah Chewning

Medici, Piero de, "the Unfortunate" (1472–1503),

eldest son of *Lorenzo the Magnificent. In 1494, just two years after his father's death, Piero betrayed Florence through an alliance with *Charles VIII of France. As a result, Piero and his family were banished from Florence. Their banishment and the destruction that followed ended seventy years of the powerful Medici family dynasty. Thus Piero, who did not possess the governing power or the political ability of his father, received his nickname "the Unfortunate."

Piero de Medici was born in 1472 to Lorenzo the Magnificent and *Clarice Orsini. Piero married Alfonsina Orsini, and they had two children: Lorenzo, who later became duke of Urbino, and a daughter, Clarice. It was Lorenzo's daughter Catherine de Medici who, through her marriage to Henri II, later became queen of France. As the eldest son, Piero was destined to succeed his father as the ruler of Florence. Piero's introduction to the world of diplomacy began at an early age when Lorenzo sent the twelve-year-old to Rome as part of an official mission to congratulate Pope *Innocent VIII on his election. Two years later Piero was again sent to Rome to seek a cardinal's hat for his brother Giovanni. When Lorenzo died in 1492, Piero was only twenty years old. Although he had been schooled by his father, Piero was ill equipped to handle the complexities of governing Florence during a time of political instability, and it was Piero's political fate that earned him the nickname "the Unfortunate."

In 1494 Charles VIII invaded Italy, and by fall he had reached Tuscany. On 31 October Piero secretly fled Florence and met with Charles. This meeting was to be disastrous not only for Florence, but for Piero himself. During their meeting Piero agreed to give Charles free passage through northern Tuscany, possession of several fortresses, and the cities of Pisa and Livorno. In addition, Piero agreed to pay Charles two hundred thousand gold florins and gave him permission to enter Florence itself. Piero's only request was security for himself and the members of his family. When word of Piero's betrayal reached Florence, the Signoria officially banished him, and Florentine citizens took to the streets tearing down emblems of the Medici family from public buildings. Piero, however, did succeed in reentering the city on 9 November, but he was met with such a hostile reaction that he fled the city, first going to Bologna and then finally finding refuge in Venice. It was left to the friar *Girolamo Savonarola to meet with Charles and negotiate better terms for the city. On 17 November 1494 Charles entered Florence and stayed in the city for eleven days. The night before the French left, they vandalized the Palazzo Medici, taking or destroying many of the paintings in the magnificent Medici art collection.

After his banishment from Florence, Piero was taken under Charles's protection. When Charles left Italy, Piero went to Rome, where he continued to concoct schemes to regain his position and power in Florence. Reports from Rome described Piero's life as one spent gambling and carousing, which resulted in Piero having to pawn many of the family's valuables. In one last effort to regain his power, Piero departed from Rome on 20 April 1497 with a force of two thousand mercenaries. When he reached Florence eight days later, he found the citizens armed and ready to defend the city, and so he retreated and returned to Rome. Piero died in 1503 while fighting for the French against the Spanish. The Medici family did not return to Florence until 1512.

Bibliography: Rachel Erlanger, *The Unarmed Prophet: Savonarola in Florence*, 1988, Eugenio Pucci, *The Medici: Glory of the World*, 1980.

Patricia Worrall

Memling, Hans (c. 1430–94), was born in Seligenstadt on the Main. There is evidence that on at least one occasion he traveled to Cologne, but his training took place in the Low Countries, where he moved around 1459–60. The case that Memling worked in the atelier of *Rogier van der Weyden in Brussels has been sustained for the better part of a century based upon the number of his works that bear the iconographical, stylistic, and compositional style of the older master. From Brussels, Memling moved to Bruges, where he became a citizen in 1465. The Bruges records indicate that his career of nearly thirty years was successful, for Memling owned substantial property and supervised several apprentices during that time.

He has to his credit the largest corpus of works attributed to any fifteenth-century Flemish painter. The reputation of the artist has, to a remarkable degree, unfortunately suffered from the personal taste of his modern critics; he has been described as "divine" and "insipid" along with a range of more moderate adjectives. Memling's style recalls that of his teacher, and also that of *Jan van Eyck and *Hugo van der Goes. His figures were slender, sometimes beautifully garbed, and often apparently emotionless. In this regard, his panels suggest Dina Bouts's figures. However, Memling was never merely a copyist, borrowing from obvious sources without adaptation. The history of Flemish panel painting gives evidence of a degree of continuation of style and iconography throughout the fifteenth century that is typical for a period when model books were still in use in the painters' workshops. It was the modification of these similarities that created the distinctions in the various artists' works, and Memling was surpassed by few in his ability to transmute ideas and make them identifiably his own. This practice is visible in his triptychs of *The Last Judgement* (1467–71) and *Adoration of the Magi* (c. 1470–72), in which he has clearly alluded to van der Weyden. One of Memling's important contributions to the art of his age was his use of landscape to unite the panels of a triptych and to establish the context for the subjects within his compositions. He took the tradition of landscape setting already important to Flemish painting and expanded both its horizon and its particularized nature. In *The Shrine of St. Ursula*, scenes of Cologne, delineated in considerable detail, were the setting for the story. He used landscape in *Joys of the Virgin* to link the separate scenes and to lead the eye of the viewer through the intricate composition without. In the many portraits that survive from his workshop, he illustrated an ability to depict character and physiognomy somewhere between the extreme detail of Jan van Eyck and the more generalized portrayal of van der Weyden. Memling possessed a lucid touch with the details of skin, eyes, and costume in his panels. He was an agile painter whose deftness in no way connotes mere glib repetition of his craft. His was one of the largest studios in the Low Countries in the fifteenth century. Close examination of his carefully constructed works with their delicate colors, various textures, and clearly presented narratives permits the viewer to understand why that was so.

Bibliography: Shirley Neilsen Blum, *Early Netherlandish Triptychs: A Study in Patronage*, 1969; Dirk De Vos, *Hans Memling: The Complete Works*, 1994.

Marian Hollinger

Mena, Juan de (1411?–56), was a court poet for King *Juan II of Castile. He was the author of the *Laberinto de fortuna*, arguably the most important of the poems of fifteenth-century Spanish literature, which celebrated the coming unification of Spain as a result of the Reconquista, a war that would terminate during the reign of Juan II's daughter, *Isabel the Catholic.

Juan de Mena was born in Córdoba, probably after Christmas in 1411. Little is known about him. His father, Ruy Fernández de Peñalosa y Mena, seems to have been an honorary official in the local government, called the Veinticuatro (Twenty-four) of Córdoba (i.e., he was one of twenty-four members of a council of local citizens). Juan de Mena's parents died while he was young. While some scholars have conjectured that Mena was a *converso*, there seems little evidence to prove such a hypothesis. The background of his education is unclear, but he seems to have studied in Córdoba, in Salamanca, and then in Rome. Although most of his contemporaries would have begun their advanced schooling at the age of fifteen, Mena did not start his studies until the age of twenty-three. He probably studied in Rome during the years 1433–34 and seems to have enjoyed the support of Cardinal Juan de Cervantes. Cervantes was a great humanist and knew Aeneas Sylvius, the future *Pius II, and such influences would also have affected Mena. By 1450 Mena was appointed a court secretary to Juan II of Castile. He also served on the Veinticuatro of Córdoba, as his father had done before. He died at Torrelaguna in 1456.

Much of the body of Mena's poetry was religious. His *Coplas de los siete peccados mortales* (Couplets on mortal sins) consisted of a debate between reason and free will. A number of his works also celebrated the monarchy, notably poems like *Rey umano, poderoso* (Human, powerful king) and *Rey virtud, rey vençedor* (Virtuous, conquering king).

Bibliography: Ottis H. Green, *The Literary Mind of Medieval and Renaissance Spain*, 1970; Florence Street, "La Vida de Juan de Mena," *Bulletin Hispanique* 55, no. 2 (1953): 149–73.

John Donovan

Mendoza, Diego Hurtado de. *See* Hurtado de Mendoza, Diego.

Mendoza, Iñigo López de. *See* López de Mendoza, Iñigo.

Mendoza, Pedro Gonzáles de. *See* Gonzáles de Mendoza, Pedro.

Metge, Bernat (1340?–1413), was a Catalan humanist best known for *Lo somni* (The dream). Born in Barcelona to Guillem Metge, a pharmacist who occasionally attended *Pedro IV of Aragon, Metge was educated in Latin letters and gained a position in the royal chancellery due to the influence of Ferrer

Sayol, his stepfather, himself a pronotary in the court. Metge began his career in 1371 as a notary to Queen Eleonor of Sicily. After her death in 1375, he transferred to the court of John, duke of Gerona, whom he continued to serve throughout his reign as Juan I of Aragon (1387–96). In the chancellery, Metge developed his excellent prose style in the letters he composed for royal business and in his literary works, including a most elegant Catalan rendition of *Francesco Petrarch's *Griseldis*. Metge's influence at court resulted in an unusually generous remuneration, which may have provoked legal proceedings against him in 1388, perhaps as part of a general crackdown on corruption. These proceedings did not keep King Juan from making Metge his secretary in 1390. In this position, Metge was in constant attendance upon the king and privy to the Crown's most sensitive business. Metge became administrator of the papal tithes Clement VII conceded to the Crown of Aragon to finance an expedition to quell rebellion in Sardinia. When this expedition failed to materialize, popular opinion accused Juan's advisors of financial misappropriation and other abuses of power. These rumors caused a crisis in April 1396 when the city council of Barcelona formally accused Juan's advisors of isolating the king to prevent him from exercising justice and to allow themselves freedom to practice corruption, including seizing property, channeling the Crown's income to themselves, and otherwise despoiling the Crown's holdings (Martín de Riquer, in his carefully researched biography of Metge, argues that these accusations were true). Metge was in Barcelona investigating these charges, actually interrogating the accusers in order to force them to recant, when Juan died suddenly on 19 May 1396. In the absence of the new king, *Martin I (1396–1410), the queen, Maria de Luna, opened proceedings against forty of Juan's closest advisors, including Bernat Metge, who was apparently incarcerated sometime between July 1396 and May 1397. Despite the serious charges against the former advisors, most eventually regained their posts in the court of King Martin. Metge himself made a most literate appeal to Martin in the form of *Lo somni* (1399) and was once again accepted into royal service, becoming Martin's secretary in 1405 and holding this position until Martin's death in 1410. During the interregnum, Metge supported Diego of Aragon, the count of Urgell; upon the election of Ferdinand of Castile to the throne in 1412, Metge was dismissed from royal service. He died the following year.

Metge demonstrated his humanist bent by using both classical and contemporary Latin letters, especially Petrarch's work, as source material for his own compositions in Catalan. *Lo somni*, his final and most developed work, can be read cynically as a political appeal to Martin I, since Metge presented the former sovereign and Martin's older brother, Juan I, come from Purgatory to console the imprisoned Metge and to instruct him on the immortality of the soul, to save Metge from eternal damnation. Juan not only declared Metge innocent of the corruption charges, but showed heaven's support for the Avignon papacy and the Immaculate Conception, two issues very important to Martin "the Ecclesiast." In *Lo somni*, Metge produced a sort of encyclopedia of humanism, drawing upon Ovid's *Metamorphoses*, Cicero's *Somnium Scipionis* and *De amicitia*, *Dante's *Commedia*, Petrarch's *Secretum*, and *Giovanni Boccaccio's *Corbaccio*, showcasing his learning as well as his elevated Catalan prose style. Metge's contribution to humanism was recognized in 1923 by the establishment in Barcelona of the Fundació Bernat Metge, which published a series of Greek and Latin authors with Catalan translations.

Bibliography: Carlos G. Noreña, *Studies in Spanish Renaissance Thought*, 1975; Giuseppe Tavani, "Prologue," in *Lo somni*, by Bernat Metge, 3rd ed., 1989.

Denise K. Filios

Milič, Jan (d. 1374), was the first and most influential of the Bohemian forerunners of *Jan Hus. Little considered today, Milič exerted considerable influence in Bohemia on the reformation of the church. He was a biblical realist and an effective preacher. His sermons, coupled with the writings of *Matthias of Janov, whom he greatly influenced, affected an entire generation of reformers near the end of the fourteenth century.

In 1360 Milič was attached to the court of Charles IV and was archdeacon at the Cathedral of Prague. However, around 1363 he decided to devote himself to full-time preaching of the gospel. He addressed scholars in Latin (although he was never a member of any university), the laity in their native Czech (as did Hus later) or in German, which he learned for these sermons. He founded a hospice for repentant harlots called "Jerusalem," which was later given over to the Cistercians in 1374 and became a college of the University of Prague. The laity considered Milič saintly and mystical. He was conspicuous for his apostolic poverty, a deliberate choice that turned the mendicant triars against him.

As a philosophical and theological realist, Milič held the medieval nominalists in contempt. He declared them avaricious liars, men who denied the freedom of the will and the biblical account of Creation. Milič wrote that the nominalists with all their doctrines were sinking down to hell, while the uneducated were speaking in new tongues and reaching heaven. He insisted on divine revelation as necessary for understanding Scripture, as opposed to the necessity of the physics and logic of Aristotle, which the nominalists embraced. He believed that only the humble can correctly understand theology, using the example of Augustine, who, in his pride, could not understand the Scriptures in spite of his great learning, but who obtained understanding after he became humble. Milič categorized the nominalists as too proud in their learning to understand theological truth accurately. His realism probably owed nothing to the English realists at Oxford and Paris, and he has been compared to St. *Bridget of Sweden and St. *Catherine of Siena in being completely at odds with the German nominalists. The realism of Milič was rooted in Augustine, Ambrose, and Chrysostom, in the Gospels, and in the Hebrew prophets. The Bible, then, was of critical importance to Milič, and it was said that he knew it almost by heart.

Milič was morally zealous, ascetic, and filled with apocalyptic fervor. In his asceticism and desire for reform he was a disciple of Konrad of Waldhausen, who had been summoned to Prague by Charles IV and the archbishop. Milič was continually occupied with eternal matters, although his hospice for converted harlots illustrated his earthly care for individuals as well as his concern for their souls. In his apocalyptic zeal and his desire for reform, Milič identified Charles IV with the Antichrist, whom he considered to be a living individual described in Scripture, rather than an idea or a wicked spirit. He preached that wars, divisions, plagues, greed, and the self-indulgence of both clergy and laity were indicative of the presence of the abomination of desolation standing in the holy place, that the Antichrist and the year of the prophet Daniel had come. He believed that the only way to cure the evils of the day was through repentance, personal virtue, and the frequent participation of the laity in the Eucharist. He was convinced that only a general council of the church offered a way to reformation. Milič traveled to Rome in 1367 to declare his apocalyptic views; however, he was arrested and imprisoned there by the Inquisition. It was during this time in prison that he wrote *Libellus de Antichristo* and urged Pope Urban V to convene a general council. Urban ordered Milič's release, upon which he returned to Prague, where he preached daily in the Teyn Church. In 1374 Milič was summoned to the papal court at Avignon to answer changes of heresy, but he died there shortly after he was found innocent. Two volumes of Milič's sermons, *Abortivus* and *Gratiae dei*, are extant, as are some Latin and Czech devotionals and his *Lectiones quadragesimalcs*.

Bibliography: Heiko Oberman, *Forerunners of the Reformation*, 1981; Steven Ozment, *The Age of Reform (1250–1550)*, 1980.

Paul Sheneman

Molay, Jacques de (c. 1243–1314),

last grand master of the Order of the Knights of the Temple, was a tireless advocate for continuing the Crusades in the Holy Land at a time when crusading fervor was dying in western Europe, but he is best remembered today for presiding over the Templars when *Philip IV of France decided to abolish, and demolish, the medieval crusading order. Jacques de Molay was probably Burgundian, perhaps having been born in the small village of Molay in Franche-Comte in either 1243 or 1244. Little is known about his family or his early life. In 1265 at Beaune Jacques joined the Order of the Temple. The Templars were an old crusading order, established in 1119 to defend the Christians and fight the Muslims in the Holy Land. In the succeeding centuries, the Temple became a very rich organization that participated in the financial affairs of European monarchs. By the end of the thirteenth century, however, the Templars had lost their primary function as a group of monastic knights and were about to lose their secondary role as bankers as well.

Jacques de Molay missed the great crusading age of the twelfth century, but as a young Templar he fought in Syria and in Cyprus, where in 1291 the Templars had sent their assets after being ousted from the Holy Land by the Muslims. In Cyprus, where he remained most of the time between 1291 and 1306, Jacques was elected grand master of the order, probably in 1292 or 1293. He participated in the futile defense of Cyprus against Egyptian forces and likely was a supporter of Amaury de Lusignan in his attempt to depose his brother King Henry II of Cyprus in 1306.

Above all else, however, Jacques de Molay was dedicated to the cause of liberating the Holy Land. On 6 June 1306 the new pope, *Clement V, summoned the grand masters of the Templars and the Hospitallers to appear before him to discuss the possibility of a union between the two orders. Jacques brought a document that he had written rejecting the notion of union because, in his words, "it would not be honorable to unite such ancient orders." His real agenda, though, was to persuade the pope to call a general crusade, which, at least on the surface, Clement seemed to support. Clement V, however, had other problems to consider regarding the Templars that prevented the calling of a new crusade. Rumors that the Templars were immoral and heretical had been rampant, and by 1308 the pope had no choice but to address these charges in a formal manner.

The driving force behind the necessity for a papal inquiry seems to have come primarily from the French king, Philip the Fair. On Friday, 13 October 1307, Philip had all the Templars in his kingdom arrested and their assets confiscated. This turn of events came as a great shock to Jacques de Molay, who just the day before his arrest had attended and participated in the funeral of Catherine, the sister-in-law of Philip the Fair. On 25 October 1307 Jacques suffered the first of the many excruciating examinations he would undergo before royal and papal commissioners prior to his death in 1314. This first deposition proved, in the end, to be his undoing. No doubt confused, nervous, agitated, and very frightened, the old grand master confessed to some of the charges against him and the other Templars. Jacques claimed that on the day he was inducted into the order, he was told to deny Christ and spit on the cross. He staunchly denied any accusations of homosexual activity in this first confession, but other Templars eventually revealed that Jacques had pursued homosexual affairs throughout his career, particularly with his valet. Jacques's first confession, which he recanted several times in later years, remained to haunt him. He tried to explain it away to later papal commissions as the result of torture, but little evidence exists that he was actually tortured. The best explanation for his first confession is probably his age, confusion, and imprisonment in poor conditions.

For years the papal and royal inquiry into the accusations of the Templars continued, resulting in the imprisonment and deaths of many. Jacques himself was finally sentenced to life imprisonment in March 1314. By this time, hardened by his experiences and remorseful over his failure to save the Templars, he refused to accept his fate. He stated categorically that all the charges leveled against the order were false and malicious, and he once again retracted his first confession. Philip the Fair decided to burn Jacques de Molay as a lapsed heretic, and the grand master met that fate on 19 March 1314.

Bibliography: Malcolm Barber, "James of Molay, the Last Grand Master of the Order of the Temple," *Studia Monastica* 14 (1972); Malcolm Barber, *The Trial of the Templars*, 1978.

Dana L. Sample

Montefeltro, Federigo da (1422–82), was the luminous son and scion of the Montefeltro family that had controlled Urbino since the thirteenth century. Born illegitimate and raised in Venice, he was later moved to Mantua, where he obtained a liberal education. As a young man, he was soon off commanding mercenary troops, thus beginning forty-four years as a successful condottiere until his death in 1482. When his father died, power passed to Federigo's younger legitimate brother Oddantonio, who was so unpopular that he was assassinated. Federigo was asked to succeed him and did, promising a humanistic approach to government and initiating a "golden age" for Urbino. Profiting from the turbulent times, he was hired by the dominant rival states of northern Italy, such as Florence and Milan, but he also commanded forces for Naples, the church, and other clients. One of his lifelong rivals was his neighbor, Sigismondo Malatesta, whom he eventually survived. Federigo's large income was used for the benefit of Urbino by promoting culture and keeping the taxes low. In the 1460s he took as his second wife Battista Sforza, twenty-three years his junior, who bore all his children and his only son, *Guidobaldo. About the time of this second marriage, he commissioned one of the finest palaces built in the fifteenth century and employed thirty-four scribes to transcribe the famous ageless works in his library, the largest and most complete in Italy. He operated a very humane court, treated his subjects as equals, and liked to discuss art, books, and politics with his close friends. He attracted many famous painters to his court, such as *Leon Battista Alberti, Justus Ghent, and *Piero della Francesca, who painted the famous portraits of himself and his second wife that now hang in the Uffizi in Florence. Federigo's court, library, and humanistic patronage provided legacies that have endured through the centuries.

The third by that name to rule Urbino, Federigo da Montefeltro was born in Urbino in 1422, the illegitimate son of Guidantonio Montefeltro and an unknown townswoman. In his preteen years he was sent as a political pawn to Venice to demonstrate his father's support for that republic, and there Federigo won the favors of the doge and gained numerous friends because of his outgoing personality. When plague broke out in Venice, Federigo was transferred to Mantua, where the ruling Gonzagas had hired one of the great teachers of the age, Vittorino da Feltre, to establish a school there for the children of the nobility.

At Vittorino's school, Federigo was introduced to a semimonastic regimen of simple living, religious devotion, and a host of disciplines to develop the body, mind, and soul. Students were trained in fencing and horsemanship and studied the classical works of Virgil, Homer, Cicero, and Demosthenes in Greek and Latin. His two years in Mantua helped over the years to shape Federigo into the ideal Renaissance man—*l'uomo universale.*

Not long after returning home from Mantua, Federigo was married in 1437 at age fifteen to Gentile Brancaleone, whose deceased father Bartolomeo Brancaleone had left her the fief of Mercatello and some other small townships, which she brought as a dowry into the marriage. Within a year Federigo was hired by the famous captain Niccolò Piccinino to command four hundred troops in the Milanese assault on Brescia. He served out the rest of his apprenticeship fighting in Lombardy against condottieri such as Gattamelata, Bartolomeo Colleoni, and *Francesco Sforza. It was while he was in Lombardy that his neighbor Sigismondo Malatesta of Rimini began his encroachments against Urbino; so Federigo returned home to confront the aggressor. In retaking the small town of San Leo, Federigo helped spark the feud with Sigismondo that went on for the rest of their lives. Interestingly enough, one of Federigo's daughters eventually married Sigismondo's son, Robert.

Shortly afterwards, Federigo's father died around 1441, when Federigo was almost twenty. His younger legitimate brother Oddantonio succeeded their father, but was so insufferable that a plot was hatched against him, and he and his supporters were assassinated. In mid-1444 the people of Urbino asked Federigo, then only twenty-two, to assume control in exchange for some progressive changes that he was quite willing to make. Federigo agreed to lower taxes, governmental reforms, the establishment of health services, and some degree of elementary schooling for the people of Urbino. Thus began the "golden age" of Urbino; Federigo retained the affection of his people throughout his life, walked through the town unarmed and unprotected, and would often stop and talk with people in the street. In his later years he banned the custom of carrying swords, and toward the end of his life, when he was asked what it took to rule a kingdom, Federigo replied, "To be human."

Almost immediately after he succeeded to power, Federigo's military services were in demand, and he spent nearly the next thirty-eight years as a condottiere. Between 1444 and 1447 he commanded Francesco Sforza's troops in Milan. For five years between 1447 and 1451 he served the Medici of Florence. By 1460 he had gone south to Naples, where he won the Battle of San Fabiano d'Ascoli for Ferdinand I against the French under Jean d'Anjou. Three years later, in 1463, he was in Rome defeating Sigismondo Malatesta for Pope *Pius II, who named Federigo "vicar of the Church" for his successes.

In 1457 Federigo's first wife of twenty years died with no issue. Around 1460, when he was thirty-seven, he married the fourteen-year-old Battista Sforza, daughter of Alessandro Sforza and niece of Francesco Sforza, who is said to have suggested the betrothal the year before. Battista's cultured background brought a sense of direction to the court, helping it to become one of the most famous throughout Europe. About this same time Piero della Francesca painted the portraits of Battista and Federigo, perhaps as a marriage commemoration. Federigo, as in all his portraits, was in left profile to hide the damage to his right eye and the top of his nose from a sword slash.

In 1468, after his rival Sigismondo Malatesta died, Federigo commissioned the construction of his palace. Four stories high and consisting of seventy-five well-proportioned rooms, it has been described as the ideal princely residence. It has distinctively sculpted fireplaces, doorways, and friezes and contains a four-story arcaded courtyard in the center. Most of the windows look out onto wonderful vistas, while the entrance to the palace is flanked by two towers. The palace contained one of the largest libraries in Europe, and Federigo kept thirty-four transcribers busy for decades. Books were handwritten on vellum and bound in crimson leather with silver clasps. Urbino became one of the earliest centers of Greek studies in Europe when Federigo hired scholars who were fleeing from Constantinople. As an intellectual who enjoyed discussing the arts and letters with his friends and as a patron of writers and artists at his palace, Federigo created a court that in his later years and under his son became the ideal model for all Europe. Baldassare Castiglione of Mantua described this court in his work *Il cortegiano* (The book of the courtier).

In 1472 Federigo's wife gave birth to his only son and sixth child, Guido-baldo, but five months later Battista died of a fever. In August of that year Pope *Sixtus IV invited Federigo to Rome, where he bestowed on him the title of duke and pronounced him captain general. In 1482, in his sixtieth year, Federigo was given a three-year contract to defend Ferrara with a force of men from Florence, Naples, Milan, Mantua, and Bologna. The opposing forces of Venice and Pope Sixtus IV were led by Roberto Malatesta, his son-in-law. Occupying the fortress of Stellata on the Po River, Federigo's forces were decimated by fever, and Federigo himself came down with the malady. He and Roberto Malatesta died about the same time, giving his daughter unbelievable news, which sent her to a nunnery for the rest of her life.

When Federigo died, he bequeathed a humanistic legacy not only to Urbino, but to Western civilization as well. Being the strongest and shrewdest general of his time, he secured long-lasting peace and protection for Urbino. In his pursuit of the arts, Federigo created in his city an extraordinary environment not only for native-born artists such as *Donato Bramante and Raphael, but also for those, such as Piero della Francesca, Justus van Ghent, Pedro Berruguete, *Paolo Uccello, and Melozzo da Forli, who came there as beneficiaries of his patronage. The gracious court of the Montefeltros continued under the guidance of Guidobaldo until 1508 and was immortalized by Castiglione in *Il cortegiano*. Federigo's famous library eventually passed into possession of the Vatican. The most famous condottiere of his time, Federigo has not been incorporated into the general histories of western Europe as he probably should have been. Two contemporaries, Giovanni Santi, Raphael's father, and Francesco Filelfo, recorded his life and times.

Bibliography: Maria Grazia Pernis and Laurie Schneider Adams, *Federico da Montefeltro and Sigismondo Malatesta: The Eagle and the Elephant*, Studies in Italian Culture–Literature in History 20, 1997; Geoffrey Trease, *The Condottieri: Soldiers of Fortune*, 1971.

James Proctor Brown III

Montefeltro, Guidobaldo da (1472–1508), formerly Guido Paolo Ubaldo da Montefeltro, was the duke of Urbino from 1482 until his death in 1508. Guidobaldo was a condottiere, but a combination of poor health, bad luck, and strategic miscalculations contributed to his many defeats. His most famous conflicts were with Cesare Borgia, who captured Urbino on two occasions. A man of great learning, Guidobaldo, along with his wife Elizabetta Gonzaga, continued to shape the court at Urbino into a gathering place for leading scholars, literary figures, and politicians. Baldassare Castiglione later described their court in *Il cortegiano.*

Guidobaldo was born to *Federigo da Montefeltro and Battista Sforza on 24 January 1472. Federigo was a noted military commander whose martial and political victories greatly increased the size of the Duchy of Urbino. As a, child Guidobaldo was a gifted athlete and scholar, studying Latin, Greek, philosophy, literature, and history under Ludovico Odasio. When he was still young, he was afflicted with gout, which incapacitated him throughout his life.

On 10 September 1482 Guidobaldo became the duke of Urbino after the death of Federigo. At this time, Guidobaldo officially assumed command of the armies of Naples, Florence, and Milan in defense of Ferrara, although his cousin, Ottaviano Ubaldini, was the de facto commander. This was the first of many occasions when Guidobaldo accepted a contract in return for military service. However, Guidobaldo was not a successful military commander. As a supporter of Pope *Alexander VI, Guidobaldo fought against the Orsini, but he was wounded and captured on 23 January 1497. He was held at the castle of Soriano until he had raised 40,000 ducats for his own ransom. In 1498, while he was serving Venice, Guidobaldo was fighting Florence when he and his troops were surrounded in Bibbiena. They remained trapped in the mountains until Paolo Vitelli gave the ailing Guidobaldo permission to return to Urbino.

Guidobaldo's most important military struggles came when he was embroiled in a prolonged conflict with Cesare Borgia. After Guidobaldo politely refused Cesare's request for troops to fight Florence, Cesare invaded Urbino in June 1502. Guidobaldo was warned of the invasion and managed to escape from Cesare's forces on 20 June 1502. A confederation, including nobles from Urbino, Siena, and Bologna, formed to oppose Cesare, and thanks to their efforts, Guidobaldo made a brief return to Urbino in October 1502. However, he was forced to flee from Cesare again in December 1502, when Cesare recaptured Urbino and plundered the palace. Guidobaldo lived in exile in Mantua and Venice until Cesare's fortunes turned after the death of his father, Pope Alexander, in August 1503. As Cesare was losing his political and military power, Guidobaldo was restored to Urbino on 28 August 1503. After being named captain general of the church by Pope Julius II, Guidobaldo immediately secured the surrender of Cesena and Forlì.

Although Guidobaldo was not a successful military commander, he was an able administrator and ruler. Contemporary accounts emphasized the love and respect that his subjects had for him, and Niccolò Machiavelli used him as an example of a prince whose subjects loved him in *The Prince*. He was also influential in papal politics and was a frequent visitor to Julius II's court during the last years of his life. Guidobaldo's ties to Julius II were cemented by his naming the pope's nephew, Francesco Maria della Rovere, his heir when he was sure that he would never have children. Francesco, who was also the son of Guidobaldo's sister Giovanna da Montefeltro, lived at Urbino after he was named Guidobaldo's heir. Francesco was the first member of the della Rovere dynasty after Guidobaldo's death on 11 April 1508.

Guidobaldo was supported throughout his life by his wife, Elizabetta Gonzaga, whom he married in October 1489. An intelligent and able woman known for her beauty, Elizabetta ruled the duchy when Guidobaldo was absent and was a central figure at the court of Urbino. Guidobaldo's greatest accomplishment was in the field of culture and scholarship; his and Elizabetta's love for learning and intelligent conversation helped make the court at Urbino a model for Renaissance Europe. Among the visitors and residents at their court were scholars, such as Pietro Bembo and Bernardo Accolti, and members of the Italian nobility, such as *Giuliano de Medici and Cesare Gonzaga.

Bibliography: Cecil H. Clough, *The Duchy of Urbino in the Renaissance*, 1981; Lauro Martines, *Power and Imagination*, 1988.

Kristine Lynn Rabberman

Morton, John (1420?–1500), archbishop of Canterbury, began his church career as bishop of Ely and later emerged as the most important ecclesiastical and political figure in England in the late fifteenth century. By virtue of his training in civil law and his sponsorship by important patrons, he was a key player during and following the Wars of the Roses.

John Morton was probably born in 1420 to Richard Morton and Elizabeth Turburville. The eldest of five sons, he was educated by Benedictines at Cerne Abbey, where his uncle was a member of the community. He attended Balliol College (Oxford), was probably ordained a priest in 1448 or 1449, and was awarded his doctorate in law in 1451.

Morton moved to London, where he became an ecclesiastical lawyer. There he caught the attention of *Thomas Cardinal Bourchier, who insisted that Morton be appointed to the royal council of King *Henry VI. In September 1447 Morton was named chancellor to the infant Prince of Wales. Morton's training in civil law aided in his rise, and in March 1472 he became the first master of rolls who had been so trained; his successors would thus ever after require schooling in law. Two years later Morton did some diplomatic work, attempting to help restore Normandy and Bordeaux to England.

During the Wars of the Roses Morton supported the house of Lancaster—he was twice captured by the Yorkists after the battles of Towton and Tewkes-bury—and he later shifted his allegiance to *Henry (VII) Tudor. Together with Lord Hastings, Archbishop Thomas Rotherham of York, and Oliver King, Morton was arrested by King *Richard III on 13 June 1483. While Hastings was beheaded, Morton was imprisoned in the Tower of London and then at the request of the duke of Buckingham was moved to Brecknock Castle. He escaped and fled to Flanders to join Henry VII in exile. With the help of the French and other English Lancastrians, Henry defeated Richard at Bosworth Field on 22 August 1485. Morton remained in France until November, when he returned to England to join the new Tudor king.

Morton was made archbishop of Canterbury in October 1486 after Bourchier's death, and the following March he was named chancellor of Jesus College (Cambridge). He also attempted to enact reforms of the clergy. Morton's name has come to be connected with "Morton's Fork," an attitude toward taxation that assumed that the rich could afford to pay high taxes, while the poor could also pay their share because their wealth was really hidden. In fact, this sort of policy dated from the time of *Edward IV. Morton may actually have tried to ease the tax obligation. He remained vigorous in old age, even opening Parliament with a long speech in 1496.

An effort was made to make Morton a cardinal during the pontificate of Innocent VII. That pope declined to do so, but at Henry's request Pope *Alexander VI later made Morton a cardinal in 1493. Despite his advanced age, Morton served as chancellor of both Oxford and Cambridge universities. In July 1498 the Spanish envoy reported to King *Ferdinand and Queen *Isabel that Morton was the second most influential advisor to the king, the first being the king's mother, Lady *Margaret Beaufort. Morton died on 12 October 1500. His grave was broken into and his bones were stolen, and so his skull is now at the Jesuit College in Lancashire. R. I. Woodhouse published a brief biography of Morton in 1895, but a more thorough biography of him has yet to be written.

Francis Bacon wrote of Morton that "he was a wise man and an eloquent [one], but in his nature harsh and haughty, much accepted by the king, but envied by the nobility, and hated of the people." Some supporters of Richard III see Morton as an opportunist who shifted sides to advance his own career. However, Sir Thomas More, who worked as a page for Morton in the years 1490–1492, wrote more highly of him. In his *History of King Richard III*, he wrote, "The bishop was a man of great natural wit, very well learned, and honorable in behavior, lacking no wise ways to win favor." Some scholars speculate that much of More's *History of Richard III* may in fact have been written by Morton. In *Utopia*, More wrote that Morton was "[a] man . . . who deserved respect as much for his prudence and virtue as for his authority. . . . His countenance inspired respect rather than fear. In conversation, he was agreeable, though serious and dignified."

Bibliography: C.S.L. Davies, "Bishop John Morton, the Holy See, and the Accession of Henry VII," *English Historical Review* 102, no. 402 (January 1987): 2–30; V. B. Lamb, *The Betrayal of Richard III*, rev. ed., 1991.

John Donovan

Moulins, Jean Perréal, Maître de. *See* Perréal, Jean, Maître de Moulins.

Müller, Johann. *See* Regiomontanus (Johann Müller).

N

Nebrija, Antonio de (1444?–1522), the greatest Spanish humanist of his generation, is best known for his work in grammar and philology and for his biblical studies. Nebrija published a widely circulated schoolbook for Latin grammar, the *Introductiones grammaticae*, promoting humanistic ideas of grammar, as well as the first grammar of a vernacular language published in Europe, of the Castilian language. His biblical studies urged systematic grammatical and philological editing of the Bible, using both Greek and Latin manuscripts as textual sources.

Antonio de Nebrija was born Antonio Martinez, probably in 1444 (though possibly in 1441), in the Andalusian village of Nebrija, to small landowners Juan Martinez de Cala e Hinojosa and Catalina de Xarama y Oja. He later adopted the name of Aelius Antonius Nebrissensis as a symbolic claim to classical ancestry. At fourteen he entered the University of Salamanca. Between roughly 1460 and 1470 Nebrija studied in Italy at the University of Bologna, where he developed the humanistic tenets that were to characterize his later work. After his return to Spain in 1470 at the invitation of Alonso de Fonseca, archbishop of Seville, under whose patronage he worked until the archbishop's death in 1473, Nebrija became a lecturer at the University of Salamanca. Over the next thirty years Nebrija lectured at Salamanca, where he soon occupied a chair, and occasionally at Seville while he was studying under private patronage. During this period he was appointed one of the royal historians for King *Ferdinand (1509) and began to work on his history of the reign of Ferdinand and *Isabel. Also during this span Nebrija came to the attention of the inquisitor general of Spain, Diego de Deza, who confiscated papers containing Nebrija's philological work on the text of the Bible (1505/6), although he was never tried for heresy. Cardinal *Francisco Jiménez de Cisneros replaced Deza as inquisitor in 1507 and appears to have become a patron of sorts to Nebrija, who addressed an *Apologia* in his treatise on biblical editing to him when it was published in

1507. At Jiménez's invitation, Nebrija left Salamanca for the University of Alcalá in 1513 to accept a chair at the trilingual College of San Ildéfonso and to assist in the completion of the Complutensian Polyglot Bible, a trilingual edition of the Old and New Testaments, from which project he later resigned for its failure to adhere to humanist principles of editing. He was buried at the college after his death in 1522.

Although Nebrija published extensively during his lifetime, his enduring fame rests upon a tripod of work: his Latin grammar, his work in vernacular grammar, and his biblical scholarship. All of these endeavors bore the mark of his overarching determination to overcome barbarism (*la barbarie*) wherever he might encounter it; by "barbarism" he appears to have meant postclassical nonhumanistic scholarship. He believed that grammatical and philological knowledge constituted the most authoritative attributes of the scholar, superseding the authority of even theologians on religious matters, creating in the grammarian the "expert of final recourse" in all matters.

Nebrija's *Introductiones latinae* was published in 1481 at Salamanca. This influential teaching text was revised, expanded, and reprinted, eventually traveling all over Europe. A translation of the Spanish version prepared for Queen Isabel of Spain was published in England in 1631, entitled *A Briefe Introduction to Syntax*. Nebrija brought his views on grammatical usage to his 1492 publication, the *Gramáticca castellana*, the first vernacular grammar published in Europe.

Even above these achievements, Nebrija is known for his biblical scholarship, in which he followed ideals earlier detailed by *Lorenzo Valla and later utilized by Desiderius Erasmus in his edition of the Bible. Nebrija's ideals of biblical philological criticism were laid out in his *Apologia*, published in 1507 at Logroño. The text defended the grammarian's responsibility to scrutinize the text of Scripture using philological methodology. The companion volume, his *Tertia quinquagena* (The third fifty, 1507), contains forty-nine (a numbering error was made) biblical editing problems resolved by the methods outlined in the *Apologia*.

Bibliography: Jeremy N. H. Lawrence, "Humanism in the Iberian Peninsula," in *The Impact of Humanism on Western Europe*, ed. Anthony Goodman and Angus MacKay, 1990; Carlos G. Noreña, *Studies in Spanish Renaissance Thought*, 1975.

Laura McRae

Netter, Thomas (1372–1430), an English inquisitor and opponent of the Lollards, was born in Saffron Walden, Essex, in 1372. Netter entered the Carmelite order at Lincoln Convent in London and then studied at Oxford, graduating as a doctor of divinity in 1409. He acquired a reputation for learning and found a patron in Stephen Patrington, the provincial prior of the Carmelites in England. In 1408 he journeyed to the Council of Pisa and in 1415 probably attended the Council of Constance. Netter was an inquisitor of many of the early

Lollards, including John Badby in 1410 and Sir *John Oldcastle in 1413. He criticized Henry V for his tepid response to a Lollard sermon preached at St. Paul's Cross and subsequently became the confessor of the king. In 1414 the order elected Netter as the twenty-third prior provincial of the English Carmelites, a position he held until his death in 1430. Netter's orthodoxy influenced the king's views, and Henry reportedly died in his confessor's arms. Netter preached the sermon at the king's death and served as confessor to the young *Henry VI. In 1419 Henry V sent Netter as an ambassador to eastern Europe; he was the envoy to Vladislav, king of Poland, Alexander, duke of Lithuania, and Michael, grand master of the Teutonic Knights. Netter is credited with establishing the Carmelite order in eastern Europe and with the institution of the Carmelite nuns in England. He died on a trip to France in 1430 with Henry VI and was buried at Rouen.

Although Netter never knew *John Wyclif personally, the Carmelite prior devoted a great deal of energy to refuting the doctrines of the Lollards. His major work was the large tract *Doctrinale antiquitatum fidei catholicae ecclesiae*, published in three volumes from 1421 to 1428. The work was a defense of the church against Wycliffite charges of corruption. Henry V encouraged Netter to begin the work, and it was dedicated to Pope Martin V. Volume 1 consisted of four books: (1) *De capite ecclesiae Jesu Christo*; (2) *De corpore Christi quod est ecclesia*; (3) *De religiosis perfectis in lege Christi*; and (4) *Quomodo religiosi in ecclesia Dei*. Volume 2 consisted of one book, *De sacramentis*, and Volume 3 also contained one book, *De sacramentalibus*. Netter planned a fourth volume but never completed it. Netter's strategy in the *Doctrinale* comprised extensive quotations from Wyclif, commentary, and thorough counterarguments based on patristic sources. The *Doctrinale* was used extensively in the early Reformation period, both in England and on the Continent, as an orthodox weapon against heresy.

Bibliography: Anne Hudson, *The Premature Reformation: Wycliffite Texts and Lollard History*, 1988; Kirk Stevan Smith, "An English Conciliarist? Thomas Netter of Walden," in *Popes, Teachers, and Canon Law in the Middle Ages*, ed. James Ross Sweeney and Stanley Chodorow, 1989: 290–99.

Andrew Scheil

Nicholas V, Pope (b. 1397, r. 1447–55), is best remembered as the most generous cultural patron to occupy the See of St. Peter during the early Renaissance. His largess contrasts vividly with the poverty in which Tommaso Parentucelli was raised. He was born in 1397, apparently in Sarzana, Italy. His father, a physician, died young, and Tommaso, despite his scholarly aptitude, was unable to afford university studies, so he worked as a tutor to the children of prominent Florentine families until he earned enough money to attend the University of Bologna. In Bologna, Tommaso attracted the attention of the bishop, Niccolò Albergati, who eventually became a cardinal while Tommaso became the *majordomo* of Albergati's household. This connection brought him a wide acquaintance with the larger world of prelates and princes during the upheavals surrounding the Council of Basel.

When Albergati died in 1443, Parentucelli emerged as a prominent member of the Curia in his own right. He also succeeded his patron as bishop of Bologna (1444) and became one of Pope *Eugenius IV's envoys to the German princes. His role in the successful effort to win the empire's allegiance led to Tommaso's elevation to the college of cardinals in 1446. During the next year, when German envoys were treating for a final agreement with the pope, the cardinal of Bologna played a prominent role. Eugenius died shortly thereafter, and when the conclave reached deadlock, the cardinals turned to Tommaso, who chose to reign as Nicholas V, a tribute to his deceased mentor, Albergati.

As pope, Nicholas proved himself both pliable and generous. The most positive aspect of his character was revealed by his negotiations to end the Basel schism. Felix V was permitted to abdicate, and the rump of the Council of Basel was allowed to dissolve itself. Nicholas also received a few of Felix's cardinals into the Sacred College. The king of the Romans, *Frederick III, was richly rewarded for his role in this pacification, both by his receipt of extensive patronage powers and by being crowned emperor in Rome (1452). A more negative aspect was a lack of firm purpose in dealing with princes. *Alfonso V of Aragon, the king of Naples, was able to bend Nicholas to his will. Likewise, the pope backed away from his condemnation of the attack by rebels in Toledo (1449) on converts from Judaism as heretics when *Juan II of Castile applied diplomatic pressure. The same trait can be seen in Nicholas's refusal to uphold the actions of his legate in Germany, *Nicholas of Cusa.

Nicholas was more firm in his dealings with the Greeks, insisting that they fully implement the union decree of the Council of Florence (1439) before he would send assistance. This firmness, however, contributed to the weakness of Constantinople when Mehmed II launched his final assault in 1453. The remaining years of the pontificate were marked by failed efforts to launch a crusade. Nicholas played a role in keeping Italy at peace, but peace did not prevail at Rome, where Stefano Porcari, a humanist of republican sentiments, conspired unsuccessfully to kill the pope.

This upheaval contrasts with Nicholas's efforts to rebuild Rome after the civil discords of Eugenius's reign. The exact role of the humanist *Leon Battista Alberti in this effort is difficult to determine, but plans for the renewal of the city outstripped results. The projects completed, however, were expensive, but the jubilee year (1450) helped fill the pope's coffers, and many Germans decided that revenue, not a crusade, reform, or salvation of souls, lay behind papal policy.

The pope's benefactions to scholars were legion, supporting pagan as well as Christian, Greek as well as Latin, letters. Numerous translations from Greek to Latin were underwritten, and scholars were rewarded for producing original work. The Curia, moreover, included many other learned men, such as the scholarly cardinals *John Bessarion, *Juan de Torquemada, and Nicholas of Cusa. The pope also became the founder of the Vatican Library, which now houses some of the books commissioned by or presented to him. *Fra Angelico was invited to decorate the pope's private chapel with scenes from the lives of Sts. Stephen and Lawrence.

Even before Porcari's conspiracy was uncovered, the pope was ailing with gout. The strain of the conspiracy, followed by the terrible news of the fall of Constantinople, further undermined his health, but still Nicholas V survived until 1455. Humanists and artists would regard his reign as a golden age, all the more since his successor, the Borgia pope Calixtus III, was more interested in nepotism and the crusade than in learning.

Bibliography: Anthony Grafton, ed., *Rome Reborn: The Vatican Library and Renaissance Culture, 1993*; Carroll Westfall, *In This Most Perfect Paradise: Alberti, Nicholas V. and the Invention of Conscious Urban Planning in Rome, 1447–55*, 1974.

Thomas M. Izbicki

Nicholas of Cusa (1401–64) was an important fifteenth-century philosopher, ecclesiastical statesman, mathematician, canon lawyer, and papal diplomat. Also known as Niclas Krebs and Nicolaus Cusanus, he was born in 1401 in the German town of Cues (now known as Bernkastel-Cues) on the bank of the Moselle River. His father, Johann Krebs (or Cryfts), was a relatively wealthy man, carving out a prosperous middle-class living as a shipowner and merchant; Nicholas's mother was Catherina Roemer. Legend has it that Nicholas attended the school of the Brethren of the Common Life at Deventer, the famous alma mater of both Desiderius Erasmus and *Thomas à Kempis, but there is no direct evidence for Nicholas's early education. In 1416 he enrolled in the University of Heidelberg for his basic education in the liberal arts, and in 1417 he went to the University of Padua, where he studied with Giuliano Cesarini. He graduated from the university in 1423 as a doctor of canon law at the age of twenty-two. During his time in Italy, Nicholas delved into mathematics, philosophy, and other aspects of Italian humanism accelerated by the Greek revival there. He enrolled in the University of Cologne in 1425, where he deepened his study of philosophy and theology and probably lectured on canon law. It was here that he studied the philosophy of *Ramon Llull and Pseudo-Dionysius the Areopagite, both important influences on his own thinking.

At Cologne, Nicholas moved into diplomatic work, and in 1427 Otto of Ziegenhaim, the archbishop of Trier, named Nicholas his secretary. He collected a substantial personal library and in 1428 discovered some lost plays of Plautus. His reputation as a scholar grew, but he turned down a teaching position in law at the University of Louvain in 1428 and 1435. At some point in the late 1420s or early 1430s Nicholas was ordained, and he rose to prominence as an important figure in the conciliar movement. His role in the affairs of the Council of Basel produced his first work, *De concordantia catholica*, which he presented to the council in 1433. Although he originally sided with the council in ecclesiastical matters, he eventually emerged as a staunch papal advocate. Nicholas's transfer of loyalty has been much debated: was he simply an ambitious cleric, or did he truly favor the papacy's constructive attitude to the union of the Eastern and Western churches, in contrast to the council's ambivalence? For whatever reason, Nicholas worked diligently under Pope *Eugenius IV to bring about the union of the Eastern and Western churches. He was one of a three-member escort sent to Constantinople in 1437 in order to bring the Byzantine delegation to the Council of Ferrara-Florence. The decree of union in 1439 secured his reputation.

For Nicholas's efforts, Pope Eugenius IV raised him to the rank of cardinal in 1446. However, Eugenius died soon after, leaving Pope *Nicholas V to complete Nicholas's elevation in 1448. In 1450 Nicholas assumed the office of bishop of Brixen in Austria and formally took up the post in 1452. As a papal legate, Nicholas traveled throughout Germany and Austria in 1451 as an instrument of reform, working hard among the German nobility to secure their support for the pope. However, in trying to administer his diocese, he clashed continually with Archduke Sigismund, a formidable opponent of Nicholas's reforms. When Aeneas Sylvius, an old friend of Nicholas, rose to the papacy as *Pius II, he encouraged Nicholas to return to Rome. Nicholas died while traveling in the town of Todi, Italy, on 11 August 1464. After his death his heart was placed in a shrine in a hospice at Cues endowed by his own hand.

Nicholas of Cusa's early works concentrated mainly on canon law, and *De concordantia catholica* was a defense of conciliar theory steeped in the intricacles of canon law and patristic learning. In it Nicholas stressed the unity and concordance of the church community and argued that the collective unity of the faithful was the source of all authority in the church. His primary goal was to establish the union of discordant elements. Nicholas' later works comprised intricate and difficult texts of speculative philosophy. His most important was *De docta ignorantia*, completed in 1440 and dedicated to Cardinal Cesarini. *De docta ignorantia* exhibited the pervasive influence of Pseudo-Dionysius the Areopagite on Nicholas's thought. Pseudo-Dionysius's *via negativa*, or theological doctrine that God is ultimately unknowable, had a clear relationship to Nicholas's concept of learned ignorance. Nicholas argued that only by acknowledging the absolute inscrutability of God to human faculties could humanity begin to approach some sort of apprehension of the unknowable. Through the use of mathematical symbolism, among other techniques, Nicholas demonstrated that once one admitted that God could not be known, one indeed reached a type of understanding. Nicholas thus understood knowledge as a process of mystical and speculative thinking proceeding through a gradual acceptance of the contours of ignorance. Only with the acceptance of ignorance could true knowledge be approached through symbolism, especially mathematical and geometric symbolism. Metaphysically speaking, in *De docta ignorantia*, Nicholas opened up his theology to charges of pantheism, especially in his discussion of infinity, in which he compared God to a sphere whose center was everywhere and whose circumference was nowhere. He thus implied that God remains present in every thing as the essence of all things. Nicholas denied this charge, and although controversy remains, he is generally now not seen as a pantheist philosopher. Nicholas was an intricate thinker, combining the theological mysticism of the late Middle Ages with the inquisitive, scientific spirit of the Renaissance.

Bibliography: Henry Bett, *Nicholas of Cusa*, 1932/1976; Jasper Hopkins, *A Concise Introduction to the Philosophy of Nicholas of Cusa*, 1978; Jasper Hopkins, *Nicholas of Cusa on Learned Ignorance: A Translation and an Appraisal of De Docta Ignorantia*, 1981.

Andrew Scheil

Nicholas of Flüe, Saint (1417–87), or Nickolaus von Flüe, was also affectionately known as Bruder Klaus. The life of Nicholas of Flüe still commands the interest and admiration of the Swiss people. In the year 1917, the five hundredth anniversary of his birth, the people of Switzerland celebrated Nicholas as a religious and spiritual figure. This renewed interest in him prompted the publication of a number of books and articles examining his life and contributions. The memory of Nicholas is closely associated with a simple, three-stanza prayer attributed to him asking for God's help to remove the barriers between himself and God. Nicholas actively attempted to remove all that distanced him from God by adopting an ascetic, contemplative lifestyle that resulted in his elevation to the status of saint, especially among the Swiss people. He was canonized St. Nicholas in 1947.

Nicholas was born into a family of farmers near Sachseln in Unterwalden, Switzerland, in 1417. He was raised as a member of a Catholic society called the Friends of God or Gottesfreunde that promoted a simple, spiritual life as a means for achieving a closer communion with God. The practices of the Friends included special devotions and meditations on the Passion and death of Christ. In his early adult years, Nicholas assumed a role in public life. He fought in the war with Zurich in 1439 and later, as a captain, in the occupation of Thurgau in 1453. Based on his leadership in battle, Nicholas was appointed a magistrate and a judge and functioned as deputy for Obwalden at councils and meetings. He was offered the position of governor or *landamman* repeatedly, but he refused it. He continued the strong religious practices fostered in his childhood and married a religious woman, Dorothea Wissling, with whom he had ten children.

At the age of about fifty Nicholas began the second phase of his adult life, during which he left his wife, his children, and his public post and became a hermit. In 1467 Nicholas set out apparently for the headquarters of the Friends near Strassburg. According to one account, his journey was thwarted by his meeting with a peasant who encouraged him to remain in Switzerland, warning him that the view of the Swiss as a rustic, backward people would prevent him from finding peace abroad. Nicholas spent the night with the peasant and received a sign during a thunderstorm that seemed to him to confirm the peasant's advice. Nicholas was next found by hunters on the pasture land of the Klüster, living under a rough shelter of branches. His brother Peter and other friends convinced him to move to Ranft, where he occupied a hermit's cell built for him by the people of Obwalden.

Nicholas spent his mornings immersed in prayer and met with visitors in the afternoons. Remarkably, he appeared to live without food and drink. In an attempt to confirm this report, the cantonal magistrates ordered all approaches to his cell to be watched for a month; however, no human source for his sustenance could be identified. During this time the Swiss Confederation achieved independence, and Nicholas, though he was a hermit, was called upon again to participate in public affairs. In 1481 the Edict of Stans was drafted to resolve the internal differences of the new confederation. The members of the Stans Council could not agree on how to incorporate the areas of Fribourg and Soleure into the confederation and were about to terminate negotiations when a parish priest from Stans encouraged them to seek the advice of Nicholas of Flüe. As reported by the chronicler Diebold Schilling, the council reached unanimous agreement in one hour after hearing the priest recount Nicholas's response, and the admission of Fribourg and Soleure was successfully completed. Letters drafted by the Stans Council thanking Nicholas for his services attest to the significance of his contributions. Nicholas became ill in 1487 and died at the age of seventy.

The prayer associated with Nicholas survives in two versions in at least eight manuscripts. Because Nicholas was unable to read and write, the manuscripts preserve an oral text, and no consensus exists concerning the authenticity of either version. That it survives in numerous manuscripts further attests to its ability to move and inspire. According to Planzer, the prayer's concern with achieving a simplicity of lifestyle and closeness to God epitomizes the principles by which Nicholas lived his life and for which he is remembered today.

Bibliography: Charles Trinkaus and Heiko Oberman, eds., *The Pursuit of Holiness in Late Medieval and Renaissance Religion*, 1974; Donald Weinstein and Rudolph M. Bell, *Saints and Society*, 1986.

Colleen A. Reilly

Nogarola, Isotta (1416–66). An exceptionally learned member of a distinguished family of Verona, Italy, Isottia Nogarola was noted for her eloquent epistles written in Latin and exchanged with the first generation of leading quattrocento humanists. She is best remembered for her epistolary debate with Ludovico Foscarini concerning the relative culpability of Eve.

Nogarola was born in Verona in 1416 to Bianca Borromeo and Leonardo Nogarola. Her aunt Angela was noted for her Latin poems and letters. Nogarola and her sisters Ginevra and Angela were taught Latin and Greek by Martino

Rizzoni, a pupil of the renowned teacher and humanist *Guarino da Verona. At the age of eighteen Isotta and Ginevra pursued their intellectual interests by corresponding in Latin with leading humanists and dignitaries, including Guarino's son Girolamo and the son of the Venetian doge, Giacomo Foscari. The sisters' letters, made public, were widely admired for their learning and eloquence and were praised by Guarino himself. Their letters followed principally the classical forms for congratulatory and consolatory messages. When Nogarola wrote an enthusiastic epistole directly to Guarino, he refused to answer her, implicitly suggesting that she was behaving unsuitably for a woman. Nogarola was roundly ridiculed for having written to Guarino. It was only after writing to him a second time, complaining of his unjust disdain, that she received a conciliatory and laudatory letter from him urging her to continue her studies.

It is clear that Nogarola did maintain a course of study, but one in isolation. Within two years of her initial correspondence with Guarino, she was no longer exchanging letters with humanists. Three events in 1438 most likely led to this decision. First, anonymous letters publicly distributed accused Nogarola of incest with her brother, claiming that "an eloquent woman is never chaste; and the behavior of many learned women also confirms its truth." Also, Ginevra married, consequently giving up her humanist studies and leaving Isotta without her closest intellectual ally. Lastly, Nogarola was obliged to move to Venice in order to escape the plague. She remained there for three years, apparently undecided as to her future goals. By the time of her return to Verona in 1441, Nogarola had chosen, despite many requests, never to marry and, most striking for her society, not to enter a religious community either. She appears to have fully grasped the nearly insurmountable social restrictions against her becoming an active humanist. In her letters Nogarola complained of "men's denigrations in word and fact." Any praise Nogarola received emphasized that although her erudition surpassed that of other women, it was not equal to that of male humanists. She lived at home with her mother, pursuing sacred studies, for the next twenty-five years. Nogarola's frequent religious vigils, however, eventually undermined her health.

Between 1451 and 1453 Nogarola was able to come out of her intellectual isolation by corresponding with the Venetian humanist Ludovico Foscarini. He appears to have lent her needed moral support, championing her choice of chastity for the sake of learning and devotion to Christ. When she contemplated a marriage proposal in 1453, Foscarini adamantly advised against it. It is significant that Foscarini, also a lawyer and diplomat, himself refused a life of religious retreat, claiming instead to "serve Caesar."

The Nogarola/Foscarini letters are noted today for their lively intellectual rigor. Her dialogue with him on the role of Eve in the downfall of Man became a veritable "battle of the sexes." Revealing her thorough knowledge of the Bible as well as of St. Augustine's writings, Nogarola ultimately offered a self-defeating argument; she claimed that Eve was less responsible for Adam's sins because she was the weaker sex. She noted that Eve was created imperfect while

Adam was created perfect, and that God had told Adam, not Eve, to avoid fruit from the Tree of Knowledge. Margaret King has astutely observed that Nogarola, knowing that she could not refute higher authorities, was reduced to pointing out their inconsistencies. Nogarola, while continuing her upper-class family's tradition of intellectual pursuits, created a unique role for herself by making them her principal occupation. In recent years critics have acknowledged her as much for this unorthodox stance as for her intellectual prowess. Her correspondence presaged the humanist activity of the following two generations of quattrocento women writers. Laura Cereta (1469–99) later cited Nogarola as proof that men and women share the same human nature.

Bibliography: Margaret L. King, "The Religious Retreat of Isotta Nogarola: Sexism and Its Consequences in the Fifteenth Century," *Signs* 3 (1978): 807–22; Margaret L. King and Albert Rabil, Jr., *Her Immaculate Hand: Selected Works by and about the Women Humanists of Quattrocento Italy*, 1983.

Margaret Harp

Norwich, Juliana of. *See* Juliana of Norwich.

O

Ockham, William of (c. 1285–1349), was an Oxford theologian and philosopher known as the "Venerable Inceptor," definer of the *via moderna*, the most influential movement in late Scholasticism. Ockham was born in Surrey, entered the Franciscans while he was still young, and began theological study at Oxford in 1307. He completed his lectures on Peter Lombard's *Sentences* in 1319, was acknowledged an "inceptor" or bachelor of theology, and served as lector in philosophy with the Franciscans in London until 1324. He spent the next four years in Avignon defending himself against accusations of heresy. There he became involved in the Franciscan poverty controversy, taking the side of Michael of Cesena against Pope *John XXII, and was forced to flee to the protection of King *Louis IV of Bavaria in Munich, where he remained for two decades. He died of plague on 10 April 1349. Ockham's writings fall into two general groups: he composed his chief philosophical works, including his *Sentences* commentary (*Ordinatio*), *Summa logicae*, and *Quodlibeta septem*, between 1317 and 1327, and his polemical/political writings, including the *Opus nonaginta dierum, Dialogus*, and *Breviloquium de principatu tyrannico*, while he was in Munich.

Despite his reputation as a harbinger of modern anti-Aristotelianism, Ockham believed himself to have been the most dedicated of Christian Aristotelians. His theological-philosophical synthesis was predicated on the belief that Aristotle had absolutely rejected Platonism, and so unlike the earlier thought of Thomas Aquinas and John Duns Scotus, all evidence of residual Platonic realism is absent from Ockham's philosophical theology. Two general principles directed Ockham's approach. The first was theological, that God's power is absolute, limited by nothing in or out of creation, and all created occurrences are wholly contingent. The second was philosophical, that nothing exists save individual substances and their qualities, which are the building blocks of human experience in creation. This rested on the Aristotelian principle of parsimony, which has become famous as Ockham's razor: "It is useless to do with more what can be done with fewer." Welded together by a philosophic mind of uncompromising rigor, these principles founded the *via moderna* that defined Western thought for 250 years thereafter. Ockham's genius is most evident in his writings on logic, theology, and political theory.

Ockham is often called a "nominalist" because of his analysis of statements about the world. Earlier ontologies had held that universal or common natures existed in members of the same species, that the statement "Socrates is human" was true because "humanity" was some real entity in Socrates contributing to his essential nature or identity. Ockham argued that while words can be understood to describe this arrangement, it does not follow that the world is arranged that way. His "terminist" logic, with which he carefully analyzed the signification and use of words in sentences, provided the tools to show that universals like "humanity" are nothing more than concepts, mental acts, naturally signifying the ideas formed by our perceptions of objects in the world. The objects are individual substances and their qualities; we perceive similarities existing between them and construct concepts to explain our perceptions.

While Ockham's approach was empiricist, it was distinctly medieval because his epistemology allowed for direct, certain perception of objects. This was called "intuitive cognition" and represented an important change from standing Aristotelian epistemology, which held that the agent intellect abstracted intelligible species from the sensible species presented by the perceived object. Ockham's elimination of the need for talk of intelligible and sensible species in epistemology was an innovation highly suspect to fellow Franciscans as well as to other Scholastic theorists.

Ockham's theology, sometimes mentioned only to illustrate his philosophical approach, was his chief concern; he rarely turned his philosophical abilities to issues that did not have theological significance. The problem of God's knowledge of future contingent statements had long haunted Christian theologians. Ockham's approach was to frame the issue in terms of describing the differences between God's knowing and human knowledge, arguing that many truths are known unchangeably by God that are not necessary but simply contingent. Ockham's followers, among them the Dominican Robert Holcot, continued to develop related arguments, engendering heated debate on Pelagianism at Oxford and Paris with opponents like *Thomas Bradwardine.

Similarly revolutionary was Ockham's contention that natural, scientific theology is impossible, given the impossibility of our intuitive cognition of God. From this he reasoned that causal arguments for God's existence were impossible. Ockham's position on the Eucharist was the basis for early accusations of heresy. He argued that God's absolute power made possible the inherence of the qualities of bread and wine not in the quantity of the elements, but in nothing, supported by God alone. This effectively denied the long-standing Aristotelian position that substance and accidents are inseparable.

Ockham's innovations, however, were not restricted to theoretical theology.

In the early 1320s John XXII had condemned the Franciscan doctrine of the pure poverty of Christ and the Apostles, flying in the face of Nicholas III's earlier approval and threatening the existence of the order. Ockham became the Friars' principal spokesman, carefully defining and explaining the increasingly important notions of ownership, possession, and use. His explanations of the origin of property and its implications for ecclesiology were important not only for their immediate consequences, which included Ockham's excommunication, but also because they featured the first philosophically sustained arguments using the concept of a natural right.

At Oxford, Ockham had written extensively on ethical and psychological issues, notably on the relation of enjoyment and love of God and of earthly pleasures, showing great sensitivity to classical Augustinian thought on the will. The protection of Louis afforded him an opportunity to continue in this practical vein, widening his scope to the political arena. His arguments for the separation of the two spheres of the temporal and spiritual realms were, with those of *Marsiglio of Padua, representative of a growing impatience among political theorists with arguments for papal sovereignty. Ockham's Aristotelian arguments for the legitimacy of certain kinds of pagan government and his belief that consent of the governed was sufficient for just rule characterized proimperial monarchist arguments that exceeded mere polemic, a landmark in the history of political thought.

Bibliography: Marilyn McCord Adams, *William Ockham*, 1987; Anne Hudson and Michael Wilks, eds., *From Ockham to Wyclif*, 1987; A. S. McGrade, *The Political Thought of William of Ockham*, 1974.

Stephen E. Lahey

Oldcastle, Sir John (d. 1417), Lord Cobham, was a loyal English knight who, upon conviction for Lollard sympathies, unsuccessfully conspired to overthrow Henry V. Born along the Welsh border to an obscure family, Oldcastle entered royal service around 1400, campaigning in Scotland, Wales, and France. He secured his rise to moderate prominence and wealth by his election to the Parliament of 1404 and by his marriage to Lady Cobham in 1408. In a military capacity, Oldcastle served under the Prince of Wales in the war against Owen Glyndwr and became one of Henry's most trusted captains, demonstrated in 1411 when Oldcastle took part in the successful expedition against the Armagnac faction in France. His friendship with the prince might have secured advancement upon Henry's accession in early 1413 but for the revelation and exhibition of Oldcastle's religious views.

Perhaps as early as 1410 Archbishop Arundel had noticed the Lollard sympathies of one of Oldcastle's chaplains, but it was not until the summer and early autumn of 1413 that the archbishop, at the behest of Convocation, acted against the king's trusted knight. Apparently wishing to avoid offending the young king with an indictment against one of his boon companions, the archbishop approached Henry concerning Oldcastle's religious heterodoxy. In September Oldcastle was charged with heresy; at his trial he revealed himself sympathetic to Lollard views on the Sacrament and the priesthood. Following his condemnation, Oldcastle was sentenced to death with a forty days' reprieve granted by the monarch, but the unrepentant knight took the opportunity to escape from the Tower. Not content with a life of outlawry, Oldcastle and his allies hatched a plot to kidnap and murder the king and his entourage on Twelfth Night 1414 at Fickett's Field, calling upon his Lollard compatriots for aid. While the plot failed miserably, Oldcastle managed to escape the debacle, remaining free until 1417, when he was captured near Welshpool and suffered his long-delayed execution by fire.

While the plot remains absurd for its sheer audacity, its political ramifications were quite significant. Despite the formal condemnation of Lollardy, many scholars now believe that the church and state made at best periodic and listless efforts against the spread of heresy under *Richard II and *Henry IV. As a result, the Lollard sect grew increasingly organized, and overt recruiting drives by sympathetic preachers were not unknown. Thomas Ile, a friend and ally of Oldcastle, conducted such efforts throughout the Midlands. Indeed, Lollardy apparently had permeated the ruling classes, though certainly in a form more polite and less revolutionary than its ambitious poorer cousin. So successful was the sect that quite open connections existed with the government, and indeed, many of Henry V's own associates had ties to the organization. The Lollard knights proved themselves loyal if perhaps heterodox, and their chief heresy, subordinating the ecclesiastical under the secular, was of a kind to endear them to the central government.

Oldcastle's revolt must be understood in this context. Before the fifth Henry's accession in 1413, the government had done little to persecute the Lollard knights in its midst, but the accusation against Oldcastle and his response transformed the situation significantly. Despite Henry's lenience, including his pleas for Oldcastle to recant, his reprieve of forty days, and his offer of a limited pardon, Oldcastle nevertheless continued with his doomed course of action. The conspiracy brought home the threat to the government and permanently besmirched Lollardy with the stain of treason and social revolution, later compounded by the lesson of the Bohemian nobles. After Oldcastle's deeds, the government embarked on a more vigorous persecution of the heretics within its midst, while the upper ranks of society withdrew from *John Wyclif's ideas in an attempt to disassociate themselves from the taint of heresy and treason. Thereafter Lollardy was doomed as an organized movement because it lacked representatives among the natural leaders of society. The sect, barely surviving as a loose collection of faint beliefs among the common ranks of society, possessed little organization or coherent ideology. It is probably significant that later rebellions were associated with Lollardy, yet we cannot be sure whether this was an indication of rebel belief or aristocratic fears. Only a century after Oldcastle's rising, the Protestant Reformation in England returned Lollard ideas to the intellectual forefront, though the survival of old stereotypes was revealed when Henry VIII, during the suppression of the monasteries, was called a Lollard king.

Bibliography: G. L. Harris, ed., *Henry V: The Practice of Kingship*, 1985; K. B. McFarlane, *Lancastrian Kings and Lollard Knights*, 1972; Peter McNiven, *Heresy and Politics in the Reign of Henry IV*, 1987.

James C. Owens

Olivier de La Marche. *See* La Marche, Olivier de.

Oresme, Nicole (c. 1320–82). One of the brilliant scientific minds of the Middle Ages, Nicole Oresme anticipated many of the discoveries of modern science, including the law of falling bodies, the diurnal rotation of the earth, the use of coordinates, and the proportionality of space and time. His writings on politics, economics, and the nature of money also prefigured the discipline of political economy.

Very little is known of Nicole Oresme's early life. He was born in the Diocese of Bayeux, near Caen, around 1320. In Paris no later than 1348, he probably studied with *Jean Buridan. Oresme received the master's of theology in 1355 or 1356 and shortly thereafter was appointed grand master of the College of Navarre, a post he held until 1361. During this time he wrote his *Tractatus de configurationibus qualitatum et motuum*, in which he explored the geometric representation of variations in qualities, resulting in an understanding of movement anticipating Galileo's mean-speed theorem. Oresme then received appointments as canon of Rouen in 1362, canon of Sainte Chapelle in Paris in 1363, and finally dean of Rouen in 1364.

Oresme maintained close relations with the French court of John II, including teaching the dauphin, later Charles V. He translated four treatises of Aristotle, including the *Politics* and *Ethics*, from Latin into French for John. As a reward for this work, he received the bishopric of Lisieux in 1377. Nicole Oresme died on 11 July 1382.

Oresme concerned himself primarily with the conflict between natural philosophy and faith, endeavoring to prove the uncertainty of natural scientific investigation by establishing the plausibility of contradictory theses. Left with no means by which to adjudicate between such positions, Oresme believed that we are left with faith as the only source of certain knowledge.

One of Oresme's most important scientific works, his French *Traité du ciel et du monde* (Treatise on the heavens and the earth), deployed brilliant reasoning on the diurnal rotation of the earth toward precisely this end of demonstrating the impotence of scientific investigation. Aristotle had argued, against Plato, that the earth was necessarily immobile at the center of the cosmos, with the heavens rotating around it. Many Schoolmen in the medieval universities continued to hold Aristotle's position, which was also that of Ptolemy. From Ptolemy came the best-known argument in favor of the immobility of the earth, which was that if the earth rotates, everything above the surface of the earth (including clouds, birds, and so on) should appear to move rapidly westward. Similarly, a stone thrown straight up into the air should come to earth far to the west, but observation shows that the stone comes straight back down. Oresme hypothesized that everything on the earth (including the air surrounding it) shared the motion of the earth. Thus a stone thrown straight into the air will continue to move just as the earth does, and so it will appear to have only vertical motion, even though in fact it continues to move horizontally through space along with the rotating earth. Oresme marshalled these and other arguments to show that Aristotle's theory of the necessary immobility of the earth could not be sustained. He did not conclude from this, however, that the earth rotates. Rather, he considered the argument undecidable according to experience and held on faith that the earth is in fact immobile.

While it cannot be shown that Nikolaus Copernicus read Oresme, it seems probable that Galileo read his treatise on configurations, which was widely available in Italy. In this treatise, Oresme showed that a body accelerating at a uniform rate will cover the same distance in the same amount of time as a body traveling constantly at the mean speed of the accelerating body. In other words, the formula $d = rt$ applies equally to bodies traveling at a constant speed and to bodies accelerating at a uniform rate. Galileo's proof was strikingly similar to Oresme's, even using the same geometric figure. Galileo's originality was not significantly mitigated by Oresme's work, but it did highlight his indebtedness to the anti-Aristotelian natural philosophers and mathematicians of the Middle Ages, and especially to Nicole Oresme.

Bibliography: Nicole Oresme, *The Medieval Geometry of Qualities and Motions*, ed. and trans., Marshall Clagett, 1968.

Jeffrey Fisher

Orsini, Clarice (c. 1450–88), has received little attention from historians, who instead have concentrated their efforts on her better-known mother-in-law, *Lucrezia Tornabuoni, and even more on Clarice's famous husband, *Lorenzo de Medici, "the Magnificent." The Orsini were a powerful and noble Roman family. Clarice's father, Jacopo, came from the Monte Rotondo branch of the Orsini, and her mother, Maddalena, from another. One of Clarice's brothers was a cleric who was close to the pope and later became archbishop of Florence, while another was a mercenary soldier. The choice of Clarice as Lorenzo's bride was made in 1467 after Lucrezia Tornabuoni visited her in Rome. The lavish wedding festivities took place in June 1469 in Florence. The Orsini nobility, military prowess, and connections beyond Florence were the main reasons for this choice. Lorenzo's marriage to a non-Florentine was much remarked upon by contemporaries, marking as it did a significant departure from usual Florentine (and Medici) practice of the time. Clarice bore seven surviving children:

Lucrezia (1470–1553), *Piero, "the Unfortunate" (1472–1503), Maddalena (1473–1519), Giovanni (1475–1521), Contessina (1476–1515), Luisa (1477–88), and Giuliano (1479–1516). She also suffered a miscarriage of twin boys in 1471.

Lorenzo's and Clarice's marriage was a difficult one. Clarice was often in poor health and spent much time at the Medici villa of Cafaggiolo outside Florence. In spring 1479 a major quarrel erupted between them over Clarice's decision to dismiss the humanist poet, *Angelo Poliziano, from his post as the tutor of her sons Piero and Giovanni. Poliziano wished them to have a humanist education, while Clarice wanted her boys to have one based on the study of the Scriptures. Lorenzo was furious at his wife's treatment of Poliziano. A compromise was finally reached in which Poliziano returned to teach Piero. On the other hand, Giovanni, who later became Pope Leo X, was taught by Martino della Commedia, the man of Clarice's choice.

This quarrel did not, however, epitomize their whole relationship. Clarice exercised a great deal of influence with Lorenzo, something of which she and many others were well aware. Clarice received letters from her Orsini relatives and many others asking for favors and requesting that Clarice speak to Lorenzo on their behalf. Many of them were successful. Before the quarrel, Poliziano had provided Clarice with information about Lorenzo's activities, as did other Medici employees.

Clarice visited several towns during trips to Rome in 1472 and 1485. This provided the townsfolk with the opportunity to press their case for favors with her. She was seen as another Lorenzo, a substitute for her husband and a conduit to him on these occasions.

Apart from Angelo Poliziano, Clarice's contact with members of her husband's literary and intellectual circle was limited. However, she did ask the celebrated Neoplatonic philosopher *Marsiglio Ficino to translate St. Jerome's Psalter into Italian for her. Luigi Pulci, too, received sympathy from Clarice at the time of his quarrel with the other members of Lorenzo's circle, despite his suspect religious views. Niccolò Michelozzi, Lorenzo's influential secretary, was a particular favorite of Clarice's who kept her informed of Lorenzo's activities, acted as her scribe (as he did for other Medici), and assisted her to fulfill requests from clients and friends.

Clarice's patronage was of a solely religious nature. She helped the defenseless poor and gave donations to nuns, and she commissioned a book containing an Office of the Dead from the Benedictine Convent of Le Murate, well known for its production of illuminated manuscripts. Clarice also funded convent building works, namely, S. Onofrio, called Foligno, and possibly the building works at the Dominican Convent of Santa Lucia.

Clarice died in late July 1488, most probably from tuberculosis. Lorenzo was absent from the funeral, ostensibly because he was at a spa bath seeking relief from his gout and could not return in time. Clarice's death was not accorded the importance that Lucrezia Tornabuoni's death some six years earlier had received by either Lorenzo or his contemporaries. The ambassador of Ferrara, for example, failed to mention it in his dispatches for several days afterwards. Clarice's contribution to the Medici family's seigneurial ambitions was, however, later implicitly acknowledged at Cardinal Giulio de Medici's investiture celebrations in 1514 when she was portrayed on a float as a goddess standing between the gods of the Arno River in Florence and the Tiber River in Rome.

Bibliography: Y. Maguire, *The Women of the Medici*, 1927; George Pottinger, *The Court of the Medici*, 1978.

Natalie Tomas

P

Pacher, Michael (fl. 1469–98), was born near Brixen in the southern Tyrolean Alps. From 1469 to 1496 Pacher resided in Bruneck, and it is presumed that he died in Salzburg. He was renowned as both a painter and a sculptor, combining both talents in single pieces as well as in separate paintings and sculptures. It has been suggested that he received his training in the Upper Rhine, although there is no direct evidence for his apprenticeship. His most complex surviving work is the *St. Wolfgang Altarpiece*, for which Pacher provided both carved and painted sections.

This altarpiece was commissioned for Abbot Benedict Eck of Mondsee in 1471. It was completed in 1481 and is today in the church for which it was designed, the Church of St. Wolfgang on the Abersee in Austria. The work is a polyptych with two sets of wings that can be closed across the central panel, the carved, painted, and gilded *Coronation of the Virgin*. The outer wings, closed, contain four scenes from the life of St. Wolfgang, but when they are open, they illustrate eight scenes from the life of Christ. The inner panels of the second wings contain scenes from the life of the Virgin: left, *The Nativity* and *The Circumcision*; right, *The Presentation in the Temple* and *The Death of the Virgin*. These flank, when they are open, the central *Coronation*, which features the Virgin, Christ, tiny angels, and the figures of Sts. Wolfgang and Benedict. The architectural frame for the central panel and for the altarpiece as a whole reflects the popularity of the Flamboyant Gothic. The altarpiece, from the predella to the top of the frame, measures over forty feet in height and twenty feet in breadth. An existing contract for this altarpiece indicates that Pacher was to provide the drawings and measurements and that he was to be the supervisor for the entire program of painting and sculpture. It is clear from the various clauses of the contract that the plan was already agreed upon between the artist and the abbot, with the contract spelling out in considerable detail the provisions to be made for the artist and for the work.

In 1483–84 Pacher also designed the *Altarpiece of the Church Fathers* for the Collegiate Church at Neustift in the Alto Adige, commissioned by the dean, Leonard Pacher. Of the original framed work, only the four central panels remain, together with wings that bear scenes from the life of St. Wolfgang.

Bibliography: N. Rasmo, *Michael Pacher*, 1971.

Marian Hollinger

Pacioli, Luca (c. 1445–1515). A noted mathematician and bookkeeper educated in Venice under Domenico Bragadino, Luca Pacioli is best known for writing *Summa de arithmetica, geometria, proportioni, et proportionalita*, along with his mathematical treatise *Divina proportione*. Although the *Summa*, published in 1494, did not make original contributions to mathematics, it provided scholars at the time with a compendium of known mathematical principles. Furthermore, because it was written in the vernacular, it made such writings accessible to those who were not schooled in Latin, thus providing a catalyst for major progress in mathematics in Europe shortly thereafter. In 1509 Pacioli published a Latin translation of Euclid's *Elements*, the first printed edition of Euclid's work. In addition, Pacioli wrote three other treatises on mathematics, only one of which has been preserved. Pacioli also invented and wrote a treatise on double-entry-system bookkeeping.

Luca Pacioli was born around 1445 in Borgo San Sepolcro (also Sansepolcro), Italy, to a modest family. He probably received his early education under *Piero della Francesca, an artist, whose writings influenced him, but he received the majority of his education in Venice under Domenico Bragadino, a Venetian aristocrat. Pacioli moved to Venice as a young man and lived with Rompiasi, a Venetian merchant, while tutoring Rompiasi's three sons. During this time Pacioli in turn was the student of Bragadino. In 1470 Pacioli dedicated his first works on mathematics to Rompiasi's sons, whose father had passed away by this time.

Sometime between 1470 and 1477 Pacioli became a Franciscan friar. His membership in the order allowed him to travel with almost the same freedom as a layman. During 1477–80 he taught mathematics at the University of Perugia and published his first treatise on arithmetic in 1478. He continued to teach mathematics around Italy and in 1489–90 returned to his birthplace. In 1491 Pacioli had some conflicts with his religious order, but nonetheless remained a friar and conducted the Lenten services there in 1493. There is speculation that the trouble arose from jealousy on the part of other members of the order. In 1494 his major work, *Summa de arithmetica, geometria, proportion, et proportionalita*, was ready for printing, and so Pacioli went to Venice to supervise its publication. The *Summa* was dedicated to *Guidobaldo da Montefeltro, the duke of Urbino and possibly Pacioli's student.

Pacioli was invited to the court of *Ludovico Sforza, duke of Milan, in 1497 to teach geometry, where he met *Leonardo da Vinci. Here the first part of

Divina proportione was written and was illustrated by Leonardo. Pacioli and Leonardo left Milan in 1499 and went to Florence, where they lived together. Pacioli taught at the University of Pisa, now in Florence, during 1500–1506. Also during this time (1505) he was elected the superior of his order and was accepted into the Santa Croce Monastery in Florence. At the same time he was a lecturer at the University of Bologna (1501–2). In 1509 two more of Pacioli's major works, the Latin edition of Euclid and *Divina Proportione*, were published. Little is known about Pacioli's death except that he was at the University of Rome in 1514, but his name is not on the death records for 1515.

Bibliography: Frank J. Swetz, *Capitalism and Arithmetic: The New Math of the 15th Century*, 1987; R. Emmett Taylor, *No Royal Road: Luca Pacioli and His Times*, 1942.

Sigrid Kelsey

Padua, Marsiglio of. *See* Marsiglio of Padua.

Palencia, Alfonso Fernández de (1423–93?), was a Spanish chronicler and author, known by his second surname instead of his first, Fernández. Though his exact place of birth is unknown, some suppose that it was the city of Palencia whose name he bore; however, no concrete evidence for this has ever come to light. He was educated in the house of the illustrious Alfonso de Santa Maria in Burgos, so other historians have suggested that he was perhaps born in Burgos.

When he was about seventeen years of age, he started his education in letters and science. Palencia traveled to Italy, where he lived with family members of Cardinal *John Bessarion in Rome. Upon his return to Spain, Palencia became involved in the intrigue and scandal that enveloped the Castilian court of King *Enrique IV. De Palencia sided with those who supported the infante Alfonso as king and traveled to Rome to inform the pope of the occurrences at the Spanish court. However, due to the premature death of Alfonso, his trip was in vain. After the infante's death, he switched his allegiances to Enrique IV's sister, *Isabel of Castile. He was influential in negotiating the marriage of Isabel with *Ferdinand of Aragon. This marriage would lead to the unification of Aragon and Castile and the beginning of modern Spain and its role as a worldwide power.

De Palencia reveled in his triumph in helping to arrange the marriage of Ferdinand and Isabel, and for his part in it, he was allowed to frequent the Spanish court. He attained service with the duke of Medina Sidonia and was part of his household in Seville, where he lived during the last years of his life. Fearing that his death was near in 1480, de Palencia made a request from the *cabildo* of Seville and the dean of the cathedral to allow him to construct his tomb within the cathedral. In return, he offered to leave his library of books and manuscripts to the church. The last that is known of de Palencia's life dates from 1492, so it is supposed that he died shortly thereafter. However, because of repairs made to the cathedral of Seville in the eighteenth century, his remains were not interred where he had wished.

His many literary works include *Antiquitates Hispaniae gentis*, volume 10 of the *Opus synonimorum* (1472); the *Mores et ritus indolatrici incolarum Fortunatarum, quas Canarias appellant*; the *Vita Beatissimi Ildefonsi*; and many others. He is best known for his chronicles, especially those of Enrique IV, in which he detailed the decadence of the court and its members. Toward the end of his life de Palencia also translated various works from Italian and Greek into Spanish, including Flavius Josephus's *Jewish War*. The Biblioteca Nacional of Spain in Madrid has in its care nineteen manuscripts of de Palencia. These include items about the history of Spain and the war in Granada, as well as various chronicles of the reign of Enrique IV.

Bibliography: Alan Deyermond and Ian Macpherson, eds., *The Age of the Catholic Monarchs, 1474–1516*, 1989; William D. Phillips, Jr., *Enrique IV and the Crisis of Fifteenth-Century Castile, 1425–1480*, 1978.

Peter E. Carr

Paston, John (1421–66), was the patriarch of the Paston family, a fifteenth-century gentry clan from Norfolk, and is best known as the principal author of the Paston Letters. Discovered in 1735, these letters include personal dialogues, legal documents such as wills and petitions, and other correspondence. Most of the collection, consisting of more than one thousand pieces, is now in the British Library.

Most of the letters in the collection are addressed either to John Paston or to his wife or were authored by John or Margaret Paston themselves. Providing insight into everyday life at the time, the letters are of great importance to historical and linguistic scholars. Not only do the letters contain information about the social life of the Pastons and others in their circle, they also shed light on other aspects of life in fifteenth-century England such as education, letter couriers, monetary transactions, land claims, and the like. The letters were composed in a mix of Middle and Early Modern English, a fact that has attracted the attention of linguists interested in the evolution of the late medieval English language.

Born on 10 October 1421, John Paston was the son of William Paston I, a lawyer and a justice of the court of Common Pleas. The earliest surviving letter of the Pastons was written by William Paston I in 1425, four years after John's birth. John Paston married Margaret Mautby in November 1440, and most of the Paston Letters consist of the correspondence between John and Margaret. John Paston, like his father, became a justice of the peace in 1447, and he was also a lawyer.

John and Margaret had two sons, both named John, born in 1442 and 1444, a daughter, Margery (1448?), and another son, Edmund, born in 1450. As a lawyer, John Paston's most prominent client was Sir John Fastolf, who was a cousin of Margaret's father. Many of the Paston Letters dealt with Fastolf and the legal battles concerning his land, both before and after his death. The Pastons themselves engaged over time in a heated argument with Lord Moleyns, who claimed a right to their manor at Gresham, which John Paston had occupied after his father's death. This argument featured many threats and even attacks against the Pastons. In 1450 Moleyns sued Paston for trespassing, but Paston was able to recover Gresham in 1451. The language in the Paston Letters describing this dispute is detailed and descriptive.

Throughout his career John Paston continued to serve Sir John Fastolf and contended with Sir Philip Wentworth in 1455 over the wardship of Thomas Fastolf. In fact, the senior Fastolf at one point suggested a strengthening of the bond between the two families, proposing a marriage between Thomas Fastolf and John Paston's daughter Margery, though the marriage never took place. Sir John Fastolf died on 4 November 1459, leaving a vast estate and John Paston executor of his will.

Fastolf's will engaged Paston in further legal battles. In 1465 Paston missed several court sessions to which he was summoned, probably because of failing health. Usually this was not a punishable offense, but his enemies managed to have him arrested and imprisoned in Fleet Prison in June 1465. He was released in January 1466 and died the same year on 22 May 1466. John Paston provided through his correspondence a looking glass into the litigious world of gentry property and class values in a time of civil war and increasing social flux in fifteenth-century England.

Bibliography: James Gairdner, ed. *The Paston Letters*, 1973; Frances Gies and Joseph Gies, *A Medieval Family: The Pastons of Fifteenth-Century England*, 1998.

Sigrid Kelsey

Pecock, Reginald (c. 1395–c. 1460), was the talented bishop of Chichester whose own impetuous personality and lack of political awareness led to his eventual downfall. Born in Wales, he studied at Oxford, where he was elected a fellow of Oriel College in 1415 and was ordained a priest on 8 March 1421. By 1425 he had earned his baccalaureate in theology when he decided to leave the university for service at the royal court.

On 19 July 1431 Pecock was presented to the mastership of Whittington College in London, and it was there that he began his literary career. Lollard beliefs were still rampant and the traditional church was under severe criticism, so he began writing works, mostly in English, to explain the faith simply to the clergy and laity. His first two works, *The Reule of Crysten Religioun* and *The Poore Mennis Myrrour*, were followed by a third more popular composition, *Donet*, which took the form of a dialogue between a father and son, intentionally short so that everyone could afford a copy. Such works were not formally published but circulated among his friends.

Pecock's career prospered, and he was consecrated bishop of St. Asaph's in Wales on 14 June 1444 and, the same year, received his doctorate in theology from Oxford. In 1447 he preached at St. Paul's Cross, where his sermon marked a turning point in his fortunes. Firmly aligned with the Lancastrian party and conscious that he and his fellow bishops were under criticism for concentrating on their political careers rather than their pastoral duties, he sought in his sermon to justify absentee bishops or those who did not preach. However, his approach offended both the conservatives and those in favor of reform. Undaunted, he distributed the sermon among his friends and sent a copy to the archbishop of Canterbury. Subsequently, he modified his views, arguing that bishops were excused not from the traditional method of preaching but from the modern fashion of "pulpit-bawling" as practiced by the friars. His arguments were developed further in his best-known work, *The Repressor of Over Much Blaming of the Clergy*, written in 1449. This book is one of the early examples of serious theological argument being conducted in the English language.

On 23 March 1450, under the patronage of William de la Pole, duke of Suffolk, Pecock was translated to the Diocese of Chichester and joined the privy council. However, the death of Suffolk in 1451 left Pecock without a patron and linked to the failing Lancastrian party. In 1456 he completed his *Book of Faith*, in which he sought to use rational arguments for bringing people back to the church, but his choice of arguments provoked further opposition, especially his implied criticism of Aristotle and the church fathers, the placing of reason above Scripture, and his composing of his own version of the Apostles' Creed.

Matters began to come to a head when he wrote to Thomas Canning, mayor of London, warning of political disturbances. The letter was promptly forwarded to the king and gave excuse for his enemies to act. The archbishop of Canterbury cited Pecock to appear before him on 11 November 1457 with all his writings. However, Pecock refused to answer for any works issued more than three years previously because he claimed that they were only privately circulated and lacked his final corrections. The nine works that he produced were submitted to a commission of twenty-four doctors of theology who found a series of faults with them. On 12 November Pecock was expelled from the privy council, and the archbishop condemned his version of the creed. On 21 November he was confronted with the choice of a public recantation or being handed over to the secular authorities. However, he had no desire to set his own views against those of the church, and so he chose to make a public profession before a large crowd at St. Paul's Cross before handing over his books to be burnt.

Subsequently he appealed to Rome, and Calixtus III ordered him to be rehabilitated, but the pope's death in August 1458 dashed any lingering hopes. After resigning his see, he was confined in a single room at Thorney Abbey with no writing materials and no books except a missal, a psalter, lives of the saints, and a Bible. He died there in 1460 or 1461.

Bibliography: C. W. Brockwell, Jr., *Bishop Reginald Pecock and the Lancastrian Church*, Texts and Studies in Religion 25, 1985; E. F. Jacob, "Reynold Pecock, Bishop of Chichester," in *Essays in Later Medieval History*, 1968.

Richard Copsey

Pedro IV, "the Ceremonious," King of Aragon and Catalonia (b. 1319, r. 1336–87).

During the reign of Pedro IV the Crown of Aragon reached its peak both culturally and as a Mediterranean federal state that included Aragon, Catalonia, and Valencia in the Iberian Peninsula, the islands of Majorca, Sardinia, and Sicily, and the Catalan duchies in Greece. Pedro or Peter (Pere IV in Catalonia) was born at Balaguer, Catalonia, on 5 September 1319 to the future Alfonso IV (1327–36) and Teresa of Entença (d. 1327). Reared apart from his father, he quarreled with his stepmother, Leonor of Castile, who endowed her own sons with lands within the dominions of Aragon. Aged sixteen, Pedro succeeded to the throne on 25 January 1336 and crowned himself at Zaragoza, symbolically denying subservience to the church. In 1343–44 he took the Majorcan crown from his troublesome brother-in-law Diego III, annexing Cerdagne, Rousillon, and all the Balearic Islands. Assisted by his minister Bernat de Cabrera, he subdued his half brothers Jaume and Ferdinand and the Uniónes of Aragon and Valencia in 1347–48. His first wife, María of Navarre, whose only surviving children were daughters, died in 1347, and his second, Leonor of Portugal, in 1348. In 1349 he married Eleanor of Sicily, who bore Juan I (1387–96) in 1350 and *Martin I (1396–1410) in 1356. Sardinia and Sicily, as grain suppliers, were essential to Pedro's Mediterranean strategy. Thus, allying with Venice, he defeated Genoa in 1353–54 in a war to secure Sardinia, though trouble there continued. He established control over Sicily by making Martin viceroy in 1378 and defeating a further challenge from Milan in 1382. He assumed protection of the Catalan duchies in 1379–80. The Castillan War begun by Pedro the Cruel in 1356 was a struggle for Iberian supremacy, during which the Hundred Years' War spilled into the peninsula (the French supporting Aragon, England and its allies supporting Castile), court intrigues plagued Aragon, and civil war erupted in Castile. With the Treaties of Almazán (1374) and Lérida (1375) Pedro exchanged territory with Enrique II for an indemnity and secure borders. After Eleanor died (1375), Pedro married Sibilla de Fortia (1377), whose behavior incited virtual civil war with Count Juan of Emporda. At his jubilee (1386) Pedro found himself abandoned by the nobility, his plans to annex Sicily in ruins, Sardinia in turmoil, the duchies in Greece collapsing, and his family split over the Papal Schism. The financial demands of war had compelled him to concede considerable authority to the Cortes of Aragon and the Cortes of Catalonia, alienating much of the royal patrimony. Despite his authoritarian and sometimes brutal style, Pedro's real power declined.

Nevertheless, Pedro has an impressive legacy. A hard worker, he expanded the bureaucracy and left one of the most extensive secular archives of the Middle

Ages. The principal cultural influences on his realm were French, Eastern, and (eventually) classical. Consciousness of his image led to his *Chronicle* (the last of the four great medieval Catalan chronicles), an elaborate dynastic mausoleum at Poblet, appeals to history in his speeches, and other forms of pageantry (hence the nickname "Ceremonious"). Like Alfonso X (the Wise) of Castile (1252–84), he patronized Christian, Jewish, and Islamic scholarship in astrology/astronomy, cartography, history, law, literature, medicine, science, and theology, including Franciscan theologian Francesch Eiximenis and Dominican historians Jaume Domènech and Antoni de Ginebreda. He established a theological faculty at the University of Lérida, new universities at Perpignan (1350) and Huesca (1354), a huge library, and higher standards for the Catalan tongue. King Pedro encouraged original works and translations from numerous languages, including Alfonso X's *Siete partidas*, Diego III's *Leges palatinae*, Guido delle Colonne's *Historia destructionis Troiae*, the Koran, Moses Maimonides' works, and others. He attempted to revive the troubadour tradition and wrote poetry himself, issued ordinances for the chancery and royal household (1344), updated the *Libre del Consolat de mar* (maritime law), had astronomers revise Alfonso's *Tablas alfonsíes*, authorized a chronicle of the kings of Aragon and the counts of Barcelona down to 1336 (in Aragonese, Catalan, and Latin), constructed walls at Barcelona and Valencia, rebuilt palaces there and at Zaragoza, and commissioned numerous sculptures and other works of art.

Bibliography: T. N. Bisson, *The Medieval Crown of Aragon*, 1986; J. N. Hillgarth, *The Spanish Kingdoms, 1250–1516*, 1976; Pere III of Catalonia (Pedro IV of Aragon), *Chronicle*, ed. J. N. and Mary Hillgarth, 2 vols., 1980.

William B. Robison

Pedro de Luna. *See* Benedict XIII.

Pedro Gonzáles de Mendoza. *See* Gonzáles de Mendoza, Pedro.

Perréal, Jean, Maître de Moulins (fl. c. 1480–1505). The Maître de Moulins is the name given to a painter of late-fifteenth-century France so called for the famous triptych in the Moulins Cathedral of the Madonna, *Pierre de Beaujeau, duke of Bourbon, and *Anne Valois. Several portraits of donors with their patron saints are also attributed to this painter, whose major influence was the Flemish artist *Hugo van der Goes. The celebrated triptych of the Virgin in the Moulins Cathedral has been called one of the last great paintings of the era. The grace of the Virgin, head bowed in pensive devotion to the Christ child on her lap, and the benign solemnity of the adoring angels give an inspirational expression to medieval religious painting. The exquisite ethereal quality of the angels surrounding Mary have also earned the painter the nickname of "Master of the Angels." Flanking the center panel are portraits of Pierre de Beaujeau, duke of Bourbon, and Anne Valois and her daughter; each donor, kneeling in prayer, is being presented to the glorified Virgin by a respectful patron saint. The influence of the Flemish painter Hugo van der Goes, can be seen in the objectivity of the portraits, but the Moulins master attempted a lifelike naturalism in their appearances despite the ceremonial costumes and grave expressions. Because of the number of Bourbon portraits like those of the Moulins triptych attributed to the Maître, he has also been called the "painter of the Bourbons."

Earlier paintings by the Maître de Moulins also exhibit his unique inventiveness in the use of complex scenes, portraits, and landscapes. The oldest extant work attributed to him is the *Nativity* at the Cathedral of Autun, painted no later than 1482, a delightful work with a pastoral quality in the Bourbonnais landscape visible through a wide back door and the shepherds leaning in to catch a glimpse of the Christ child. While this work lacks the elegance of the Maître's later Virgin in Moulins Cathedral, the gentle naïveté of the Madonna and the lifelike rendering of the Christ child in the manger give this painting a tender, engaging charm that his other works seem to miss.

No study of the Maître de Moulins would be complete without the critics' pondering the identity of this painter, and thus far, three names have emerged from these studies: Jean Hey, Jean Prévost, and Jean Perréal. The latter figure, Jean Perréal (or Jean de Paris), has the most critical support for several reasons, both historical and stylistic. For one, Perréal would have been approximately twenty-eight years old when the *Nativity* at Autun was painted, a reasonable age to have completed a work such as that. As the celebrated court painter to *Charles VIII, Louis XII, and François I, Perréal also painted portraits of such Bourbon figures as the Cardinal Charles de Bourbon; so did the Maître de Moulins, whose own portrait of the cardinal is at Chantilly. In addition, the two painters are stylistically similar: generally, they both exhibited a natural, realistic approach to portraiture, as opposed to the objectivity of their contemporaries that idealized their subjects; more specifically, the kind of headdress known as a "balloon" coif that was peculiar to the Maître de Moulins (such as those found on St. Anna in the Moulins triptych and on the Magdalen in a portrait now in the Louvre) is also exactly like that found on the statue of Temperance that was designed by Perréal for the tomb of the duke of Brittany at Nantes. Perréal, who was held in high esteem by his contemporaries and was even called "a second Apelles in painting," would have had the kind of reputation that might have earned commissions in such places as the Moulins Cathedral, and his position at court would have brought him into contact with those painters who influenced the Maître, especially the Flemish and Italian masters.

The Maître de Moulins has been considered one of the last brilliant painters of the French medieval period. One can see a progression in style and spirit from the tender naïveté of the *Nativity* at Autun to the awesome solemnity of the Virgin triptych at Moulins Cathedral, and the realism of his portraits offers unconventional glimpses of some of the important figures of his time that do not emerge from the typically stylized paintings of his contemporaries. The sophistication of his work, from the original use of Bourbonnais landscapes to the bluntness of his portrayals of the French aristocracy, gives the Maître de Moulins an extraordinary position in medieval history as both an artist and a visual historian whose individuality was the apex of French art of the fifteenth century.

Bibliography: P. A. Lemoisne, *Gothic Painting in France: Fourteenth and Fifteenth Centuries*, 1931/1973; William Wells, "Abbot Nicaise Delorme and Jean Perréal: Glasgow's Master of Moulins Reconsidered," *Apollo* 113 (September 1981): 148–55; William Wells, "French Fifteenth-Century Miniature Painting, a New Hypothesis: Jean Perréal: From the René to the Bourbon Master," *Apollo* 124 (July 1986): 11–21.

Wendy Marie Hoofnagle

Perugino, Pietro (1450–1523), was born Pietro di Cristoforo Vannucci. He was an independent Italian painter active in Rome, Florence, and Perugia, whence came his name. His significant innovation was the synthesis of Florentine figural style with Umbrian spatial vision. His works attained a contemplative aura by opening up defined space to infinity through the use of perspective. His important works include *Christ Giving the Keys to St. Peter* (1480/82, Sistine Chapel, Rome), *Vision of St. Bernard* (1491, Alte Pinakothek, Munich), and frescoes in the Sala della Udienza (1497–1500, Collegio del Cambio, Perugia).

Pietro di Cristoforo Vannucci was born in 1450 to a respected landowner and town-council member of Città della Pieve. Apprenticed first to *Andrea del Verrocchio, through whom he was in contact with both *Leonardo da Vinci and *Sandro Botticelli, and later to *Piero della Francesca, Perugino was listed as a member of the Compagnia di S. Luca in 1472. By 1479 he was in Rome painting *Virgin and Child with Angels* (Cappella della Concezione, Old St. Peter's) for Pope *Sixtus IV.

Following this success, he was commissioned in 1480 to coordinate the frescoes of the completed Sistine Chapel. Joined by *Domenico Ghirlandaio, Botticelli, and Cosimo Rosselli, Perugino made the main contribution. He was responsible for the Neoplatonic program of parallel scenes from the lives of Moses and Christ, showing the fulfillment of the Old Testament in the New. Perugino's painting of the altar wall included portraits of the first four popes, the *Nativity*, the *Finding of Moses*, and the *Assumption of the Virgin*. Ultimately these works were covered by Michelangelo's *Last Judgment* (1535/41). The program, extended throughout the chapel, divided each wall into five sections, including two papal portraits, a narrative scene, and a painted drapery below.

The *Circumcision of Moses* and the *Baptism of Christ* have both been attributed to Perugino, although they were executed by Pintoricchio, a member of Perugino's workshop. In *Christ Giving the Keys to St. Peter* Perugino revealed his mastery of spatial treatment with the use of perspective. He posed a row of foreground figures at an angle with each other to form a central symmetry for the background buildings that are the real protagonists of the composition.

Having achieved fame through working on the Sistine Chapel, Perugino was extremely successful but reluctant to turn down any commission offered. He maintained a shop in both Florence and Perugia. In 1493 he married Chiara Fancelli, daughter of the architect Luca Fancelli, and made his main residence in Florence. He joined a second guild, the Arte de Medici e Speziali. He joined Botticelli in consulting on the installation of Michelangelo's *David*. In 1491 Perugino completed the *Vision of St. Bernard*. A clearly defined architectural setting creates the symmetry for the central arch that opens to infinity beyond an Umbrian landscape. Using luminous colors in harmonious tones, Perugino set a tone of contemplative otherworldliness. Figures in derived antique poses deployed gracefully against an interior reduced to essentials were carefully placed in calculated spaces heightening the sense of infinity through the center arch. It was in this period that Raphael was apprenticed to Perugino.

In 1496 Perugino was commissioned to decorate the Sala della Udienza. Perugino's visual attempt to reconcile the *antico* with the *nuovo*, pagan with Christian, is the basis for the allegorical program of the cardinal/classical virtues and the Christian virtues, represented by the incarnation of Christ, whose nativity is announced by both the prophets and the sibyls. He was heavily influenced by the poetry of Perugian humanist Francesco Maturanzio, whose couplets were featured throughout. The plan was implemented in simple forms on a large scale, with monumental figures ranged against a landscape only roughly sketched in, and was completed in 1500. Perugino considered it his most monumental work, devoting his full attention to it and achieving the most successful unified decorative schemes of the Renaissance.

After 1500 Perugino's life centered on Perugia. He was rewarded for returning to Perugia by being appointed *priore* in 1500 and was made a citizen of Città della Pieve. Until 1523, when Perugino died from plague, he found it profitable to copy earlier compositions. Until his death he remained popular with an increasingly provincial clientele.

Bibliography: Paul Hills, *The Light of Early Italian Painting*, 1987; P. Scarpellini, *Perugino*, 1984.

Patricia Cossard

Petrarch, Francesco (1304–74), or Petrarca, as he is known in Italian, was recognized as an eminent scholar and intellectual figure of his day who was both an author and a rhetorician. He collected the writings of classical authors such as Cicero, and by the time of his death he had established one of the most renowned libraries of the Latin classics anywhere. But it was his abilities as a poet and the new dimension he brought to poetry that made Petrarch exceptional.

Petrarch's family was living in exile in Arezzo when he was born on 20 July

1304. His father had been on the losing side in one of the many political feuds that kept the city of Florence in turmoil and had been exiled by the victors. By 1312 Petrarch's father had given up hope of returning to Florence and had moved his family to Provence, where the papacy was now established in Avignon. Petrarch's father was a notary, a transcriber of documents and legal records, and so he felt that chances for his employment would be greater near the papal court. Because of his father's appreciation of fine writing and poetry, Petrarch received an early introduction to the two classical authors who would be his favorites, Cicero and Virgil. When Petrarch was twelve, his father sent him first to Montpellier and then on to Bologna to receive a legal education. The law, however, did not appeal to Petrarch, and he spent most of his time reading the Latin classics. Upon the death of his father, Petrarch abandoned his law studies and returned to Provence, where he, along with his brother, led a life of dissolution, spending their father's estate on fashionable clothes and having their hair curled. When the money began to run low, Petrarch decided that he needed a profession, and since neither law nor medicine appealed to him, he decided upon the church. It was at this time, in 1327, that Petrarch first saw his beloved Laura in church. It could have been her refusal that kept her beyond reach, but whatever the reason, Petrarch's feelings for Laura had a profound effect upon his poetry. The frivolous light verse he had been accustomed to writing would no longer suffice, for it could not express the sweet agonies of love. For Petrarch, poetry now became infused with passion. Its dimensions expanded as he contrasted the bitter with the sweet, anguish with ecstasy. Laura was the inspiration for Petrarch's *Canzoniere*, a collection of 366 lyric poems of various subjects and poetic forms. After Laura died of the plague in 1348, Petrarch wrote a commemorative poem on the anniversary of her death for the next ten years.

Petrarch searched for a clerical position within the church that would provide him with an income but would also allow him time to write. He had met Giacomo Colonna at the University of Bologna, and through Giacomo, whose brother was a cardinal, Petrarch entered the cardinal's service as a chaplain. In the following years Petrarch received additional sinecures that brought financial independence and enough freedom to pursue his scholarly endeavors. As time passed, he began to write more of his works in Latin and eventually gave up writing in Italian altogether.

By the 1350s Petrarch had become quite famous. He had been writing poetry since his early twenties, and it was his fourteen-line sonnets in Italian that made the people of his day recognize him as the heir of *Dante. His work as editor of Livy, collector of classical writers (especially Cicero), and author of a series of brief biographies of Roman heroes also added to his fame. In ancient Rome, the custom had been to hold a poetry competition every five years and crown the winner with a wreath. This tradition had been revived in Italy, and Petrarch very much wanted a wreath. He campaigned for the honor and eventually received one invitation from Rome and one from Paris. Petrarch chose Rome's invitation and received his wreath from the Roman Senate on 8 April 1341.

Petrarch deplored the turbulent political strife and the wars that raged, especially in his beloved Italy. He felt that proper moral education was needed to ameliorate these problems, and that the church was a poor example because of the corruption and materialism rife in Avignon. Petrarch felt that the only proper models were to be found in the Roman classics that had been written when Rome, now in sorry decline, had ruled the world. Clearly the virtues displayed by Roman authors such as Cicero were to be emulated. Petrarch therefore called for the rebirth of classical learning. In response, many of Petrarch's friends and followers searched Europe, uncovering the long-forgotten manuscripts of Greek and Roman authors whose writings were the essential elements in this revival. As a rhetorician, Petrarch was adept in the use of language, and so he received diplomatic assignments as well. For him, the art of the rhetorician was communicating the moral examples of the classical writers and touching the inner spirit of men.

Petrarch set the stage for the cultural, learned image of the Renaissance man and for the modern "divisions" of history. Until Petrarch's time, history was reckoned from the birth of Christ, either before or after. With Petrarch's call for a rebirth of classical learning came the need to define the period between the end of the Roman Empire and his own time. He called those years the dark period or the Middle Ages, thereby dividing history into three distinct parts and setting in motion the modern sense of history and the idea of the Renaissance of learning and culture that characterized his own age. Petrarch also embodied two aspects of life that together comprised the Renaissance ideal, the active and the contemplative. The combination of his active political life with his life of the mind as a writer and his emphasis on the importance of the individual in society brought about the humanist movement.

Although Petrarch's thought and example set in motion the idea of the Renaissance, his reputation is based upon his writings. His works in Latin reflected his efforts to revive classical learning, and his Italian poems, especially the *Canzoniere*, represented his wish to explore and understand the human condition. Petrarch's stylish, elegant love poetry became the model for countless poets such as *Geoffrey Chaucer, Edmund Spenser, William Shakespeare, and John Milton. His invention of a universal poetical language continues to inspire and entertain poets and readers today.

Bibliography: Peter Hainsworth, *Petrarch the Poet*, 1988; Nicholas Mann, *Petrarch*, 1984; Theodore K. Rabb, *Renaissance Lives: Portraits of an Age*, 1993.

Kathryn Kiff

Philip I, King of Spain (b. 1478, r. 1506), also known as Philip the Fair or Handsome, or, in Spanish, Felipe el Hermoso, is most famous for his marriage to Juana "the Mad," daughter of the great Catholic monarchs *Ferdinand of Aragon and *Isabel of Castile, and his descendants. His eldest son, Charles I of Spain, became Holy Roman Emperor Charles V. Even though his reign as king of Castile was brief, just a few weeks in 1506, Philip founded the Habsburg dynasty of Spain, which ruled that country for some two hundred years. Philip died from fever in Burgos, Spain, on 25 September 1506.

Philip was born in Bruges in Flanders on 22 July 1478. His father was *Maximilian I (1459–1519), holy Roman emperor and German king. His mother, Mary of Burgundy (1457–82), was the daughter of the powerful Burgundian duke *Charles the Bold and was his sole heir. The duke of Burgundy controlled vast territories covering eastern and northeastern France and the Low Countries, in direct opposition to the expansionist ambitions of the French Crown. At the death of Charles the Bold in 1477, *Louis XI of France seized half of Mary's inheritance, but in that same year Maximillan married Mary. Showing his own expansionist ambitions, he reclaimed some of her territories. Young Philip was caught in this web and became hostage of the Burgundian city of Ghent at the death of his mother in 1482. Ghent refused to accept the regency of Maximillian during the minority of the young duke, now heir to his mother's possessions. Philip was released in 1485, but Maximilian labored until 1493 to assert the rights of his son in the Low Countries.

Philip's tumultuous youth did not prevent him from living in the gilded cage of the European elite. The Burgundian court was a paragon of decorum, pomp, and feasts, and, accordingly, Philip was educated for the needs of his class. He was a good dancer and conversationalist, a tennis player, and a valiant knight. He also enjoyed the pleasures of his rank, chases and tournaments, sometimes using the amusements to veil political intrigues.

In 1496 the eighteen-year-old heir to the house of Austria, candidate for the imperial throne, duke of Burgundy, and count of Flanders and Artois married Juana, daughter of the great Catholic monarchs of Spain. From his court in Brussels, Philip could dream of extending the Habsburg lands to southern Europe and through Spain to the newly discovered continent. On 22 August 1496 his sixteen-year-old bride-to-be left Laredo for the Netherlands, and on 18 October the wedding took place in Lierre. The couple resided in the Netherlands, but the Spanish monarchs insisted on attracting Philip to Spain. Philip always vacillated between Spanish and French interests, but a trip to Spain would incline his spirit to his country of adoption. On 25 February 1500 Juana gave birth to a son, Charles. That son became of prime importance when in July Michael, heir to the thrones of Castile, Aragon, and Portugal died. Juana, her husband, and her son were now next in the line of succession. In 1501 a treaty allying Burgundy, France, and Austria was signed, and since France and Spain were at war for the kingdom of Naples, the Catholic monarchs had to bring Philip on their side.

On 4 November 1501 Philip and Juana left the Low Countries for Spain, choosing against royal wishes a land route through France in order for Philip to renew his friendship with its king. From late April 1502 until February 1503 Philip toured Spain, falling sick with the measles at Oleas in April 1502. Still, he and his wife received homage as heirs to the throne from the Cortes in Toledo and Zaragoza. In February 1503 Philip traveled north again, leaving his wife a virtual prisoner of her parents. She joined him in May 1504, a few months before her mother's death in November. Isabel's hesitations at the end of her life had set the stage for the coming events. In a codicil amending her will, she shifted the burden of rule from Juana and Philip to Ferdinand, perhaps because she had read Martin de Maxica's diary, countersigned by Philip, describing Juana's tantrum and fit of jealous madness at the infidelity of her husband. In Brussels, Philip and Juana proclaimed themselves queen and king, while in Spain, Ferdinand ruled Castile. In November 1505 the Treaty of Salamanca recognized the joint rule of the three parties, and in order to expedite matters, Philip decided to travel to Spain. After a stormy voyage and a halt in England, Philip and Juana landed at Corunna in April 1506. The majority of the Castilian nobility chose Philip (who was young, a foreigner, and easily manipulated) over Ferdinand. The Treaty of Villafafila, signed on 27 June 1506, incapacitated Juana and made Philip sole ruler of Castile, with his father-in-law's consent. On 25 September 1506 Philip died. Ten years later, on 23 January 1516, Ferdinand died, and so Charles, son of Philip and Juana was recognized as king of Castile and Aragon. The Habsburg dynasty was thus born.

Bibliography: Amarie Dennis, *Seek the Darkness: The Story of Juana la Loca*, 1956; Henry Kamen, *Spain, 1469–1714*, 2nd ed., 1991; Ludwig Pfandl, *Juana la Loca*, 1984.

Joelle Rollo-Koster

Philip IV, King of France (b. 1268, r. 1285–1314).

Commonly known as Philip the Fair, King Philip IV of France was the last great king of the Capetian dynasty. During his rule royal power was extended in France, both geographically and institutionally. His reign is also notable for his conflicts with the papacy and the Knights of the Temple.

Philip was born between April and June 1268 to the future king Philip III and his wife, Isabelle of Aragon. Philip became heir to the French throne in 1276 when his elder brother Louis died, poisoned, it was suspected, by his stepmother Marie of Brabant. In February 1285 Philip married the greatest heiress of the day, Jeanne of Champagne and Navarre. In Jeanne, Philip found the love for which he had apparently been looking most of his life, and he remained devoted to her or her memory for the rest of his life, never remarrying when she died prematurely in 1305.

Also in 1285 Philip's father died in Perpignan during the retreat of an abortive crusade against the Aragonese, who were supporting the Sicilian rebellion against Charles of Anjou. The new king had no desire to continue his father's policies toward Aragon, but he soon proved himself willing and eager to pursue policies designed to expand his power and jurisdiction not only in France, but in neighboring provinces as well. This led him into conflicts with two of his most important vassals, the duke of Aquitaine (also the king of England) and the count of Flanders. The war with Edward I, the so-called Gascon War, was precipitated in 1294 by Philip's desire to extend his jurisdiction into English Aquitaine and ended in 1303 with no great gains by either side. The Flemish conflict, begun around 1300, was responsible for the one great disaster of Philip the Fair's reign, the humiliating defeat at the Battle of Courtrai in July 1302. Nonetheless, Philip was able to occupy most of Flanders and imprison its count, Guy of Dampierre, and his two sons. For a while Flanders was subdued, but harsh treaty conditions caused the Flemish to rebel again in 1312 and 1313, and while negotiation cooled tempers for a time, Philip's successor Louis X inherited a problem that his father had never been able to solve.

The wars were tremendously expensive, causing Philip to seek out extraordinary financial resources on a regular basis. Philip's taxation and monetary policies had the result of consolidating and expanding the kingdom's financial institutions, developing, for example, a new department of the auditing of accounts, the Chambre des comptes. They also caused him many problems. Attempts to tax the French clergy brought down the wrath of the new pope Boniface VIII, whose bull *Clericis laicos* (1296) forbade all monetary contributions to secular governments. While perhaps not a direct reaction to the bull, Philip's ordinance of August 1296 to ban the export of arms, horses, and money out of France did not endear him to the intellectually brilliant but short-tempered pontiff. Occasional conflicts continued between king and pope, culminating in the affair of Bernard Saisset, bishop of Pamiers, who was arrested by Philip for treason in 1301. The furious Boniface issued two famous papal bulls in response, *Ausculta fili* (1302), which listed Philip's misdeeds, and *Unam sanctam* (1302), which stated the superiority of the spiritual over the temporal authority in the strongest terms. After consulting with an assembly of prelates, nobles, and bourgeois, Philip denounced Boniface as a heretic. The king's councilor Guillaume de Nogaret and the pope's enemies the Colonnas forced their way into Boniface's palace at Anagni in September 1303, kidnapping the pope and abusing him physically and verbally. Within a few days, the people of Anagni had rescued him, but the pope, now a broken man, died within a month. This sordid affair has long been considered one of the turning points of the relationship between church and state in the Middle Ages, generating among its long-term consequences the Avignon papacy and the Great Schism.

Philip's need for money may also have contributed to two other notorious events during his reign: the expulsion of the Jews in 1306 and the suppression of the order of the Templars, also beginning in 1306. Policies against Jews were not uncommon in western Europe in this period (Edward I had expelled his Jews in 1290), but the attack on the Templars appears to have been Philip's scheme. The Templars, founded in the twelfth century to protect pilgrims and fight the infidel, had become very rich by the fourteenth century. Philip the Fair, who seems to have been motivated as much by morality as by financial need, issued orders on 13 October 1307 to arrest all Templars in France and to confiscate their estates. He encouraged his son-in-law, Edward II of England, to do the same. The Templars were accused of immorality, obscenity, and heresy; they confessed to many of these charges through the judicial use of torture. Although Philip's attack on the Temple strained relations with the French pope *Clement V, in March 1312 Clement bowed to Philip's wishes and abolished the order. Many Templars, including the grand master, *Jacques de Molay, were burned at the stake at the end of Philip's reign, some repudiating their forced confessions at the last moment.

Philip died in November 1314 after a year of serious problems and scandals. The Flemings had erupted in revolt again in 1312, and terms favorable to Philip, the Conventions of Marquette, were not sealed until September 1314. Also in 1314 leagues of nobles and bourgeois began to form to protest the king's taxation policies. This problem was left for Philip's son, Louis X, to address. Finally, a most peculiar scandal rocked the French court in 1314. Philip's daughters-in-law Marguerite of Burgundy, Jeanne of Burgundy, and Blanche of Burgundy, the wives of his sons Louis of Navarre, Philip of Poitiers, and Charles of La Marche, respectively, were arrested on suspicion of adultery. The knights with whom they were accused were put to death in a public spectacle, and the three women were imprisoned. Only Jeanne was eventually freed, due to lack of evidence. The public denouncement and imprisonment of his sons' wives were partly responsible for the lack of male heirs suffered by Philip's sons; the doubt cast on the legitimacy of the daughter of Louis and Marguerite killed her chances (and perhaps those of all other women) of becoming queen when Louis died without male heirs in 1316.

Why Philip would have exposed his dynasty to such scandal is not clear; in fact, Philip the Fair's character and abilities have been the subject of much debate among historians and remain enigmatic to this day. In his own day Bishop Saisset (who admittedly had reason to hate Philip) compared the king with an owl: "The handsomest of birds which is worth nothing . . . such is our king of France, who is the handsomest man in the world and who can do nothing except to stare at men." Such comments have caused historians in the past to assume that Philip was a weak king controlled by his councilors. The general consensus today, however, is that Philip IV was the master of his own policy, a king whose goal it was to extend royal power in France, and who, to a great extent, succeeded.

Bibliography: Elizabeth A. R. Brown, *Politics and Institutions in Capetian France*, 1991; Jean Favier, *Philippe le Bel*, 1978; Joseph Strayer, *The Reign of Philip the Fair*, 1980.

Dana L. Sample

Philip the Bold, Duke of Burgundy (1342–1404).

The first Valois duke of Burgundy, Philip was one of the most influential and powerful princes in Western Christendom during the late fourteenth century. The youngest son of King John the Good of France, Philip earned his sobriquet "the Bold" at the age of fourteen, defending his father at the Battle of Poitiers. He accompanied his father and other French nobles in captivity to England, where they were held for ransom following the French defeat.

In 1364 the Capetian duke of Burgundy died without an heir, and the duchy reverted to the French Crown. King John granted the duchy to Philip on terms that made Burgundy essentially independent, although it was nominally a French fief. Four years later Philip married Margaret of Male, the daughter and heiress of Louis, count of Flanders—a marriage that set the stage for the expansion of the house of Burgundy into the Low Countries. When Louis died in 1384, Margaret inherited Flanders, Artois, Nevers, Rechel, and the county of Burgundy (Franche-Comté). Through advantageous marriages of Philip's children and Margaret's family relationships, by the middle of the fifteenth century the dukes of Burgundy controlled most of what is now Belgium, the Netherlands, and Luxembourg; and since Flanders was far more advanced economically, commercially, and culturally than Burgundy, throughout the Valois dukes' reign their court was more often in Bruges or Brussels than in Dijon.

Philip the Bold himself frequently held court in Paris. Although he was the duke of Burgundy, Philip was still a "prince of the blood" in France. Upon the death of John the Good in 1364, Philip's oldest brother Charles V became king, and upon his death in 1382 his heir, *Charles VI, was only fourteen years old. Although in theory he shared the regency with Charles's other uncles, the duke of Berry and the duke of Anjou, Philip the Bold was far stronger and more assertive than his brothers. As Charles VI in the early 1390s began having fits of madness that were to plague him the rest of his life, it is only a slight exaggeration to say that Philip was the real ruler of France for most of the period from 1382 until his death. As such, he always put the interests of the house of Burgundy first and never hesitated to use the power and money of France to advance these interests. For example, in 1382 the Flemings revolted against Philip's father-in-law, Louis, count of Flanders, endangering his wife's inheritance. Philip acceded to Louis's request to send French troops to put down the rebellion. The Franco-Burgundian force won a decisive victory over the rebels at Roosebeke, although Philip had to contend with further uprisings later in the decade.

A later military expedition in which Philip was involved was not as successful. In the early 1390s, during a long truce between France and England, the two countries agreed to mount an international crusade against the Turks. The sultan, Bayezid I, had expanded his conquests alarmingly in the Balkans and boasted that he would soon bring his armies to France. The crusade was originally scheduled for 1395, and Philip was to lead the Burgundian forces and *John of Gaunt the English, with numerous knights included from other countries as well. In the event the crusading army was not sent until 1396, under the leadership of Philip's son and heir, John of Nevers, and of John of Gaunt's illegitimate son, John Beaufort. The crusading army mounted a poorly conceived and disastrous attack against Bayezid's forces at Nicopolis; thousands were killed, and the remainder of the army, including John of Nevers, was captured and held for ransom. The ransom Philip paid for his son, the future John the Fearless, was said to exceed 100,000 pounds.

Philip the Bold was a patron of the arts who commissioned many illuminated manuscripts for inclusion in his extensive library. It was he who originally employed the Limbourg brothers, who, after his death, produced for *Jean Valois, duke of Berry, the famous *Tres Riches Heures de Duc de Berri*, and he brought to Dijon the sculptor Klaus Sluter. Philip died in 1404. His tomb, designed and executed by Sluter, is now in the museum in the Hôtel de Ville in Dijon.

Bibliography: J.J.N. Palmer, *England, France, and Christendom, 1377–99*, 1972; William R. Tyler, *Dijon and the Valois Dukes of Burgundy*, 1971; Richard Vaughan, *Philip the Bold*, 1962.

Dan Wages

Philippe de Commynes. *See* Commynes, Philippe de.

Philippe de Vitry. *See* Vitry, Philippe de.

Pico della Mirandola, Giovanni (1463–94), was an Italian humanist and philosopher whose writing reflected both the Scholasticism of the Middle Ages and an interest in Islamic and Jewish thought more characteristic of the Renaissance. Pico's work focused on the role of human beings in creation, but he also asserted that man's role in the cosmos was divinely ordained.

Giovanni Pico della Mirandola was born on 24 February 1463 in Mirandola. His father died when he was quite young, so his mother took charge of his education, hoping that he would aspire toward a career in the church. At the age of fourteen he was sent to study canon law in Bologna, but two years later he undertook studies of Platonic philosophy under *Marsiglio Ficino (1433–99) in Florence. He read Aristotelian philosophy at the University of Padua, then returned to Florence to learn Greek. Around 1479 he befriended the noted Dominican preacher *Girolamo Savonarola (1452–98), who, like Pico's mother, hoped that the promising young scholar would pursue an ecclesiastical calling. However, Pico was more drawn to education in a secular state, and in 1485 he went to study Scholastic philosophy and theology in Paris.

Some controversy surrounded Pico on both a personal and a professional level. In the spring of 1486 he was en route to Rome to engage in a debate and stopped to spend the night in Arezzo. There he met Margherita de Medici, the wife of Giuliano di Mariotto de Medici, a relative of *Lorenzo de Medici (1449–92). Margherita and Pico seem to have fallen in love, and she departed with Pico and his companions, though it is unclear whether or not she departed willingly. An armed band left in pursuit of Pico, and a fight broke out. When some of the men in Pico's escort were killed, Margherita claimed to have been taken against her will, and Pico was subsequently imprisoned. He was released through the intercession of Lorenzo de Medici, but Pico understandably deferred his plan to participate in the Roman debate.

On a professional level, Pico's writings came under scrutiny from authorities in Rome. He intended to publish a treatise containing seven hundred theses, but the number swelled to nine hundred. After Pico's death, they came to be known as the *Oratio de hominis dignitate* (or simply the *Oratio*), but Pico did not apply that title to the work. The theses were finally published in Rome on 7 December 1486, and Pico offered to debate his work with critics. Several Roman Scholastic theologians attacked the *Oratio* and then denounced it to Pope *Innocent VIII. On 20 February 1487 Innocent canceled the proposed debate and instead ordered an investigation of Pico's work. The commission objected to thirteen of the nine hundred theses; among them were Pico's notions that Christ did not truly descend into hell (as declared at the Council of Nicaea), that a mortal sin did not deserve eternal punishment, and that it was logical to conclude that Origen (c. 184–c. 254) was not damned. More recent observers also have suggested that Pico's writing contained elements of Pelagianism (or at least semi-Pelagianism), a heretical notion arguing that there was no grace or original sin, and that human beings earned their salvation through their own efforts. Pico wrote an *Apologia* in defense of his work (which he dedicated to his friend Lorenzo de Medici), but on 4 August 1487 Innocent condemned his writings as heretical. Following his brief imprisonment after the Margherita debacle, Pico turned his attention to the study of Arabic, Aramaic, and Hebrew. His study of Hebrew would assist in analyzing the Cabala, the mystical writings of Judaism. The arrest over the abduction/elopement with Margherita was resolved, but now Pico was to be arrested once more for heresy. He fled to France but was captured and again imprisoned. He was released and brought to Florence, again under the protection of the Medici family, and at Lorenzo's insistence, Pico was permitted to remain at a Benedictine monastery in Fiesole. In 1492 Pope *Alexander VI absolved Pico of the charges of heresy that had followed him for years.

In the meantime, Pico continued writing. His *Heptaplus*, like the *Apologia*, was dedicated to his friend and protector Lorenzo de Medici and studied the first twenty-six verses of the Book of Genesis. In 1491 he attempted to reconcile the work of Plato and Aristotle in *De ente et uno*, but in 1494 Pico died at the age of thirty-one. During the last two years of his life Pico worked on a treatise attacking astrology, which he saw as detrimental to concepts of human dignity, liberty, and reason. His nephew Gianfrancesco later edited and published the manuscript and also wrote a biography of his uncle that Sir Thomas More translated into English and published in 1510.

Pico della Mirandola's work defies easy categories. Although he is thought of as a Renaissance humanist and philosopher, some of his writings seem more suited to the Middle Ages. Early and modern commentators have argued that his work went through stages that included Scholasticism, Neoplatonism, humanism, cabalism, and others.

Bibliography: William Craven, *Giovanni Pico della Mirandola: Symbol of His Age*, 1981; Arthur Field, *The Origins of the Platonic Academy of Florence*, 1988.

John Donovan

Piero della Francesca (1406–92), born Piero di Benedetto da Borgo San Sepolcro, was a Tuscan painter from Borgo San Sepolcro. He apparently traveled quite a bit, but Florence appears to have been where he learned his style. He is said to have been a student of *Domenico Veneziano in San Egidio around 1439. In Piero's polyptych of the *Madonna della Misericordia*, commissioned for Borgo San Sepolcro in 1445, but not finished until considerably later, scholars find influences of many Florentine artists, particularly *Masaccio. More than any other artist of his day, Piero believed in scientific perspective. In his treatise on perspective he demonstrated how it applied to all shapes, including human form. His figures took on a mathematical clarity as compounds of spheres, cones, and cylinders more at ease as monumental sculpture than as flesh-and-bone mortals. Piero's work was not bloodless, however, but was more concerned with clarity and order where geometry was the means to form in all things, animate and inanimate alike. These qualities are best seen in his mural at St. Francesco in Arezzo, *The Legend of the Cross* (c. 1455–c. 1465), which was his most important work. His *Resurrection* (1460), at the Palazzo del Comune, Borgo San Sepolcro, is a splendid example of his geometric composition. The glowing figure of Christ, banner in hand, stands triumphant over death at the apex of a triangular composition where shady, drowsy soldiers lie at his feet. He is backed by a rustic landscape and luminescent sky. Piero's drawing was precise, his colors cool and crystalline. Other important works were his portraits of *Federigo da Montefeltro, duke of Urbino, and his second wife (1465?), now at the Uffizi Gallery in Florence, and his altarpieces, now at the National Gallery in London, *The Baptism* (1442) and *The Nativity* (c. 1472). Though Piero was regarded by his contemporaries in Florence as rather provincial due to his strict adherence to Masaccio's geometric perspective, and he was long unnoticed by historians and critics, he was "rediscovered" and is now highly regarded as perhaps the best painter of the fifteenth century.

Bibliography: Carlo Ginzburg, *The Enigma of Piero: Piero della Francesca*, 1985; R. Lightbown, *Piero della Francesca*, 1992.

C. Thomas Ault

Pierre de Beaujeau. *See* Beaujeau, Pierre de.

Pius II, Pope (b. 1405, r. 1458–64), formerly Aeneas Sylvius Piccolomini. Early modern Europe's most famous humanist pontiff, Pius II is best known today for his novels, plays, and histories, his *Commentaries* on the nature of the fifteenth-century papacy, and his insistent calls for and sincere commitment to the dying notion of holy crusade against the Ottoman Turks. Pius was pope from 1458 to 1464. His most important papal bull, *Execrabilis*, formally reaffirmed the authority of the Roman popes over church councils in the wake of the late medieval Great Papal Schism.

Aeneas Sylvius (or Enea Silvio) Piccolomini was born on 18 October 1405 at Corsignano (later rebuilt by Pius II as Pienza) near Siena, Italy, to parents of the minor nobility. He grew up tending his family's fields and then studied humanist letters first at Siena and then at Florence under the teacher Francesco Filelfo before entering the service of Bishop Domenico Capranica of Fermo as a secretary. Piccolomini went with Capranica to the Council of Basel in 1432, where he remained for a few years moving up the ladder of prelatial patronage. By the mid-1430s he was serving Cardinal Niccolò Albergati on diplomatic missions to places such as England and even Scotland, whose damp climates later left him in rather fragile health. Making his oratorical mark on the continuing Council of Basel and relocating with it to Florence in 1436, Piccolomini was appointed secretary to the antipope Felix V late in 1439 and was eventually sent by him as a representative to the imperial diet at Frankfurt in 1442. There Piccolomini met and entered the service of King *Frederick III (later Holy Roman Emperor) as secretary and poet laureate; he also made the acquaintance in those years of the imperial chancellor Caspar Schlick, whose lustful exploits apparently inspired Piccolomini's popular novel *De duobus amantibus Eurialo et Lucresia* and his bawdy comedy *Chrysis*. Then the champion of imperial rights and enemy of the Roman popes (in particular *Eugenius IV), Piccolomini finally took holy orders following a serious illness in 1446 and then reconciled himself politically to Pope Eugenius and morally to the demands of his new calling, giving up the lascivious life that had produced several illegitimate children. For his now-vigorous support of the Roman councils and papacy against schismatic pretenders, Piccolomini was successively made bishop of Trieste (1447) and then of Siena (1450) by Pope *Nicholas V and, after authoring his *History of the Emperor Frederick*, was awarded a cardinal's hat by Calixtus III in 1456. Upon the death of that short-lived pontiff in 1458, Cardinal Piccolomini was himself elevated to the papal throne in a contentious, intrigue-ridden conclave that he later immortalized in his autobiographical *Commentaries*. Piccolomini took the name Pius II as pope in humanistic tribute to the hero "pius Aeneas" in Virgil's *Aeneid*.

Pius enjoyed a short but eventful pontificate. Appalled by the fall of Constantinople to the Muslim Turks in 1453, the new pope almost immediately issued a call to crusade and then tried to organize the effort at a congress that opened in the autumn of 1459 at Mantua. The meeting was practically boycotted by the French king *Charles VII, whose kinsman *René of Anjou, claimant to the throne of Naples, had been spurned by Pius in favor of the Aragonese claimant *Ferrante I. Since Holy Roman Emperor Frederick III was also slow to take up the cross, the Mantua congress fell apart, but Pius remained committed to his crusade until the very end of his life. Early in 1460 he issued the bull *Execrabilis et in pristinis temporibus inauditus*, which finally laid to rest the schismatic discord of the previous century by declaring heretical the belief that councils enjoyed higher ecclesiastical authority than did the Roman popes. There was discord aplenty in southern Italy in 1460, however, and so Pius returned to Rome to reinforce his opposition to the Neapolitan pretensions of René of Anjou, which in turn moved the new French king *Louis XI to reassert the old Gallic independence of the French church from papal control. In the empire, Pius quarreled with the Bohemian king *George of Podebrady over that ruler's claims to imperial lordship (versus Emperor Frederick) and his wish to include conservative Hussites within the doctrinal orthodoxy of the Roman church. In these busy years Pius somehow found the time to begin his *Commentarii rerum memorabilium quae temporibus suis contigerunt*, or *Commentaries*, and to author his *Historia rerum ubique gestarum*, an unfinished geographical and cosmological work that was later closely consulted by explorer *Christopher Columbus. Pius's abiding interest in his cherished crusade against the Turks led in 1462 to the preparation of his famous "Letter to Sultan Mehmed II," which sought, rather naïvely, to convert that Muslim conqueror to Christianity. The letter was never sent, but, undaunted, Pius renewed his call for crusade and then took up the cross himself despite ill health in June 1464 to set an example for reticent Christian kings. With the promise of German and Hungarian troops and a Venetian fleet to transport them to the Holy Land, Pius went to Ancona to await the arrival of his crusading force. There he contracted a fever and, in a moment celebrated by artist Bernardino Pinturicchio in a fresco at the Piccolomini Library in Siena, died on 15 August 1464 just as the first Venetian vessels were pulling into view.

Pope Pius II fused the humanistic ideals of quattrocento Italy with the powerful geopolitical influence of Europe's early modern papacy. He was a vain man, for in his autobiographical *Commentaries* we learn that he was a selfless servant of God and an engagingly brilliant speaker. Still, we are at the same time drawn to his other, more endearing human qualities, such as his delight in idyllic natural settings or his appreciation of the playfulness of his grandnephew and his puppy Musetta. He was a competent humanist scholar in his own right. Pius's most lasting legacy must remain his *Commentaries*, a work that affords us a unique insider's glimpse into the complex and often-mysterious world of the Renaissance papacy.

Bibliography: R. J. Mitchell, *The Laurels and the Tiara: Pope Pius II, 1458–1464*, 1963; Pius II, *Memoirs of a Renaissance Pope: The Commentaries of Aeneas Sylvius Piccolomini Pius II*, ed. Leona C. Gabel and trans. Florence A. Gragg, 1959/1988.

Clayton J. Drees

Pizan, Christine de. *See* Christine de Pizan.

Podebrady, George of, King of Bohemia. *See* George of Podebrady, King of Bohemia.

Poliziano, Angelo (1454–94), was the outstanding classical scholar of his

Poliziano, Angelo (1454–94), was the outstanding classical scholar of his age. During his lifetime he composed a large body of Latin poetry, as well as his acclaimed vernacular *Stanze*, and the first Italian drama, *Orfeo*. Also highly regarded are his translations of various Greek classics. His greatest achievement, however, was his *Miscellaneorum centuria* or *Miscellanea* (published in 1489), a collection of one hundred expanded philological notes that laid down his principles of editing, many of which are central to editorial practice today.

Angelo Poliziano was born Angelo Ambrogini on 14 July 1454. He later took the name Poliziano from Montepolitianus, the Tuscan region of his birth and early childhood. In 1464, after the death of his father in a local feud, Poliziano came to Florence, where he engaged first in the study of Latin and then in the study of Greek at the Studio, the Florentine university. By 1470 he had already translated part of the *Iliad* from Greek into Latin hexameters. A few years later he entered *Lorenzo de Medici's household as his protégé and later as the tutor of his sons. Unfortunately, this arrangement was countermanded due to his differences with Lorenzo's wife *Clarice Orsini, who preferred a more religious education for her sons. After a brief hiatus away from Florence, he returned to instruct only the eldest Medici son and accepted a post as lecturer at the Studio, where he remained until his death on 9 September 1494. During this time he became a minor friar, in which habit he was buried after his death.

Although Poliziano's influence was widespread and his achievements in editing, translating, and composing, particularly in Latin, were many, his fame rests primarily upon a tripod of achievements, his *Stanze*, the *Orfeo*, and his *Miscellanea*. His vernacular poem *Stanze per la giostra di *Giuliano de Medici* (Stanzas about the joust of Giuliano de Medici) remained unfinished at the death in 1478 of Lorenzo de Medici's younger brother, to whom the verses were dedicated. Likewise in the vernacular, his drama *Orfeo* represents the first drama in Italian written for the Italian stage. The play was performed at Mantua during the state visit of Duke Galeazzo Maria Sforza to that city. This work is considered to be one of the precursors of modern opera. Both the *Stanze* and *Orfeo* are examples of Poliziano's firmly held opinions on the subject of composition, which placed a premium upon the use of a wide and educated palette of classical allusions to produce works original and erudite, and, at least in his own case, usually based on more minor classical models rather than the venerated and heavily used Homer and Virgil.

However, his great achievement as a humanist lies in his exploration of the issues surrounding the editing of classical texts. Over the course of his academic career, Poliziano was the first scholar to make thorough collations of ancient manuscripts. Unlike his predecessors, he identified the manuscripts that he used in his editions, usually by symbols, referring to the owner of the manuscript and recording the details of its history and appearance—a practice continued today. His strictures on the editing of manuscripts were much more rigorous than those of his predecessors and contemporaries, and today they form the basis of modern editorial process. His *Miscellanea* laid down these strictures in a new form based on discrete examples rather than the line-by-line examination of a classical work. He insisted in this and other works on a meticulous approach to editing and collating manuscripts, demanding a rigorous and educated use of families of texts and other early witnesses in making editorial decisions.

A great classical scholar and humanist of his day, Poliziano differed markedly from earlier humanists in the focus of his scholarship. Unlike the earlier Italian humanists, Poliziano did not see classical scholarship as a preparation for a responsible public life or as a means to better himself as a human being. He viewed humanistic scholarship as an endeavor of a small group of pure scholastics able to engage the expertise he himself brought to each text or work. Thus he put classical learning back into a historical setting, ignoring the model of contemporary relevance nurtured by his predecessors as the ultimate purpose of such erudition.

Bibliography: Louis E. Lord, trans., *A Translation of the Orpheus of Angelo Politian and the Aminta of Torquato Tasso*, 1931/1979; Angelo Poliziano, *The Stanze of Angelo Poliziano*, trans. David Quint, 1979; Albert Rabil, Jr., ed., *Renaissance Humanism: Foundations, Forms, and Legacy*, 1988.

Laura McRae

Pontano, Giovanni (1426–1503), was the foremost humanist of fifteenth-century Naples. Renowned for his Ciceronian style, Pontano composed numerous poems, satiric dialogues, moral treatises, and historical works during his lifetime. He also directed the Pontanian Academy, so called after himself as its second, and most illustrious, director.

Pontano was born in Cerreto in Umbria in May 1426. At the death of his father he was sent to study at Perugia, where his uncle was the chancellor of the local commune. In 1447 he joined the court of King *Alfonso the Magnanimous of Naples, where he became a member of the literary circle, the Academy. Here he studied the usual humanistic subjects, including astrology and Greek. In 1471 he became a citizen of Naples and also became the second head of the Academy that was to bear his name, the Pontanian Academy. During these years in Naples, then under the rule of the Aragonese kings, he also participated in government as a statesman for his adopted city. When the Aragonese ruling house was conquered by *Charles VIII of France in 1495, Pontano, perhaps expecting the political change to be a long-lasting one, wrote and presented a positive oration on the French ascent to power, criticizing the Aragonese rulers under whom he had previously served. Such a move might have been expected to ensure his flourishing under the new rule. Unfortunately for Pontano, the Aragonese dynasty returned within the year, and he was removed from public service. His last years were committed to his literary endeavours, and he died in 1503.

As a poet, Pontano was generally skilled in all the various poetical forms of the age. His interest in poetry appears to have been directed to literary form rather than the grammatical study so popular with earlier humanists. Pontano composed several collections of love poetry, as well as a georgic on the subject of his adopted city and other pastorals, funerary poems, and religious compositions. He also took an interest in more scientific topics and published his meteorological treatise, *Meteora*, in the 1490s, as well as an astrological work, *Urania*, around 1500.

Although Pontano's work is generally considered derivative, scholars are coming to appreciate his expression of the problems facing contemporary society. Although Pontano was most cited by his contemporaries as a poet, a large portion of his work was comprised of satiric dialogues and treatises examining social problems and moral questions. Among other treatises, he composed a series of works on money and proper spending. He also composed a guidebook for rulers, *De principe*, in the "mirror of princes" tradition, and a companion work, *De obedientia*, outlining the comportment of the subjects of the ruler. His late treatises, *De fortuna* and *De prudentia*, were both composed after his retirement from civic duty. These philosophical compositions, *De prudentia* in particular with its discussion of the importance of prudence in controlling the individual's conduct in private and public life, were important documents of the "doctrine of prudence" prominent in Neapolitan culture.

Bibliography: Mario Santoro, "Humanism in Naples," in *Renaissance Humanism, Foundations, Forms, and Legacy*, ed. Albert Rabil, Jr., 1988.

Laura McRae

Prague, Jerome of. *See* Jerome of Prague.

Purvey, John (1353?–1428?), of Lathbury, a Lollard heretic, was admitted to the priesthood in 1377/78, according to a Lincoln episcopal register. He was a man of learning, but the exact nature of his education remains unclear; tradition maintains that he studied at Oxford, but there is no evidence for his attendance. Later chroniclers (e.g., *Henry Knighton) assert that Purvey lived with *John Wyclif at Lutterworth until Wyclif's death in 1384, and scholarly tradition depicts him as the secretary, confidant, collaborator, and devoted disciple of Wyclif. However, direct evidence for such a close association with Wyclif is slim, and it is perhaps best to think of Purvey as simply a prominent Lollard who may or may not have had a close relationship with Wyclif.

After Wyclif's death, Purvey dwelt in Bristol, and again it is difficult to ascertain the degree of influence Purvey had in making Bristol a Lollard center. Purvey probably preached in various parts of the country, and around 1387 he emerged as a prominent Lollard, associated with a circle of heretics including *Nicholas Hereford and John Aston. In August 1387 he was banned from preaching in the Worcester Diocese, and soon after, the bishops of Worcester, Hereford, and Salisbury granted authorization to seize his books. Authorities arrested Purvey and confined him to the prison of the archbishop of Canterbury at Saltwood Castle, Kent. According to an episcopal register of Archbishop Arundel, on 28 February 1401 Purvey stood trial and recanted his heretical views in St. Paul's Cathedral, London. He confessed his heresy on seven separate points of doctrine concerning the Eucharist, confession, holy orders, clergy, preaching, chastity, and the papacy. His recantation was acknowledged, and in August 1401 he became rector of West Hythe, Kent. He subsequently resigned this benefice in 1403 and generally disappeared from view until 1413, when he turned up in connection with the trial of *Sir John Oldcastle. During these years he presumably had declined in importance as a Lollard preacher, and it is not known to what extent he continued these activities.

Like his personal relationship with Wyclif, Purvey's influence on the Lollard Bible is unsubstantiated. He has been credited with translating and revising large portions of the English Wycliffite Bible and other heretical writings, but modern scholarship takes a very cautious view in assigning him any direct role in the composition. Purvey was certainly important as a public proponent of Lollard doctrine, but his role as a man of letters remains unclear.

Bibliography: Anne Hudson, *Lollards and Their Books*, 1985; K. B. McFarlane, *John Wycliffe and the Beginnings of English Non-Conformity*, 1952.

Andrew Scheil

Q

Quercia, Jacopo della (1374?–1438), was a Sienese artist who is considered one of the great quattrocento sculptors and is classed with such illustrious Tuscan contemporaries as *Donatello, *Lorenzo Ghiberti, and *Filippo Brunelleschi. His passionate and innovative work influenced later masters such as Michelangelo through its skillful emulation of nature and unusual subjects that predicted the signature classicism of the High Renaissance.

So little is known about the life of the influential yet enigmatic Jacopo della Quercia that the most elemental facts about him, such as his birth and artistic training, continue to be the subjects of much debate among art historians. According to Giorgio Vasari's account of the sculptor's life and art in the 1568 edition of his *Lives*, Jacopo was sixty-four years old when he died, "exhausted by fatigues and by continuous labor" but praised by the entire city of Siena, his birthplace. While the birth year calculated from this age, 1374, has been criticized, it is possible that Vasari found this number on Jacopo's tomb marker and that it is legitimate; at the very least, most contemporary authorities believe that he was born within a few years, in either direction, of this date.

Because of the geographic location of his early life, more than any other reason, Jacopo has been traditionally linked with the Sienese school of early Italian art for lack of a better classification of his style. Studies of his work uncover a determinedly individualistic artist who drew upon certain elements of several different styles in a concerted effort to more closely imitate nature. This focus diverged sharply from the heavier, more solemn approach of some of his late Gothic contemporaries and places Jacopo more firmly in the early Renaissance movement. His innovations were admired by many, not the least of whom was the great Florentine master, Michelangelo. It is claimed by some experts that Jacopo's powerful designs influenced Michelangelo's work on the Sistine Chapel ceiling; indeed, even the preservation of his Porta Magna of San Petronio is likely to have been the result of Michelangelo's intervention.

Jacopo's artistic training is widely disputed as well, but it is generally accepted that he received his early education at the feet of his father, Maestro Piero d'Angelo, who was a Sienese goldsmith and woodcarver. While there is no documented evidence of any later training in Florence, it is conceivable that Jacopo spent some time there before entering into the famous competition for the Florentine baptistery doors in 1401–3 with other such illustrious artists as Brunelleschi and Ghiberti. While he ultimately was not selected for this commission, Jacopo's reputation was already such that in 1403 he was chosen by the bishop to execute the Silvestri Altar in Ferrara. It was during work on this famous *Madonna* that Jacopo was retained for what is possibly one of his most celebrated pieces, the tomb of Ilaria del Carretto in Lucca. This delicate, sensuous sculpture superbly demonstrated, in the realism of the subject's face and hands, the undulating folds of her gown, and the animation of the winged putti flanking each corner, the artist's striving toward a more natural style that was later to become a signature Renaissance trait.

Jacopo's artistic career was fraught with delays and complications partly due to the fact that on several occasions, he accepted concurrent commissions and was unable to complete any one piece at once. This practice would even cost him work, as when one of the narrative reliefs for the baptistery in Siena that had been assigned to him was later transferred to Donatello. These same delays marked the progress of Jacopo's most illustrious work, the Fonte Gaia in Siena, which took ten years to complete. In spite of the postponements, the finished sculpture is praised even today for its fluidity and exhilarating adaptation of the antique, which demonstrated an inspired new direction for all of Tuscan sculpture.

Jacopo's personal life was marked with the same mix of notoriety and esteem that plagued his professional life. While it is unclear to what degree he was involved, Jacopo, along with his assistant, was accused of theft, rape, and sodomy when a love affair was discovered with the wife of a wealthy merchant-citizen in Lucca. Conversely, he was elected to public office in Siena on several occasions and was even made overseer of the Sienese Duomo, a position that also conferred upon him the honor of knighthood. He remained active both in public service and in his art until his death in Siena on 20 October 1438. His memory was revered not only in Siena but by later Renaissance masters who applauded him as an artistic prophet. His masterpieces have awed artist and layman alike with their gracefulness, subject choice, and attempts to imitate the perfection of the human form.

Bibliography: James Beck, *Jacopo della Quercia*, 1991; Charles Seymour, Jr., *Jacopo della Quercia, Sculptor*, 1973.

Wendy Marie Hoofnagle

R

Ragusa, John of. *See* John of Ragusa.

Regiomontanus (Johann Müller) (1436–76) was one of the foremost pre-Copernican astronomers and mathematicians who participated in the fifteenth-century revival of Greek scientific learning. He made significant contributions to trigonometry, the accuracy of celestial calculations, and the dissemination of scientific knowledge through his translations and short-lived printing press. Thus he laid the foundations for the later astronomical achievements of Nicolaus Copernicus, Tycho Brahe, and Johannes Kepler.

Regiomontanus (the name is a Latinization of his birthplace Königsberg in Franconia) was born to a family of prosperous millers in 1436. He enrolled at the University of Leipzig in 1447 and then proceeded to the University of Vienna in 1450. There he became closely associated with Georg Peuerbach, author of the *Theoricae novae planetarum*, a standard Renaissance textbook of Ptolemaic planetary theory. In 1457 Regiomontanus joined the faculty as a master of the University of Vienna.

When Cardinal *John Bessarion, the leading patron of Greek scholarship in the West, arrived in Vienna in 1460, he encouraged the study of original Greek astronomy and mathematics texts among his students. Regiomontanus was invited to Italy by Bessarion and, under the patronage of the cardinal, was able to travel to Venice and Padua, where he lectured on the Arabic astronomer al-Farghani. Regiomontanus probably perfected his knowledge of Greek under Bessarion and was able to complete a condensed version of Ptolemy's *Mathematical Syntaxis* (better known under its Arabic title, the *Almagest*), commissioned by Bessarion and begun by Peuerbach before his death in 1461. This *Epitome of the Almagest* was published in 1496, twenty years after Regiomontanus's death, and was later used by Copernicus.

The Copernican revolution in astronomy is often popularly characterized as the triumph of Copernicus's heliocentric model over the old earth-centered Aristotelian-Ptolemaic cosmology, but this development could not have occurred without Copernicus's thorough understanding of the Ptolemaic system, and Regiomontanus's studies helped introduce western European astronomers to the intricate mathematics of Ptolemy's cosmological works. Regiomontanus also clearly recognized the errors and discrepancies in Ptolemy's planetary theories and therefore indirectly inspired later astronomers to develop more accurate models that could be verified by actual observations.

Regiomontanus was the first to separate spherical trigonometry from the study of astronomy in his *De triangulis omnimodis* (On all kinds of triangles, published in 1533), and he established the modern study of that branch of mathematics. He was also widely known for his *Ephemerides*, an almanac listing planetary positions for the years 1475–1506. *Christopher Columbus carried Regiomontanus's *Ephemerides* with him on his voyages and may have used it to help predict an eclipse to frighten the natives of Jamaica in 1504. The planetary positions available in the *Ephemerides* were essential for casting horoscopes, making astrological predictions, and determining safe times for phlebotomy (bloodletting). Thus Regiomontanus was a believer in astrology along with the majority of his contemporaries, who nearly unanimously admitted to celestial influence on earthly bodies. In Vienna, Regiomontanus cast the horoscope of Eleonora of Portugal, the bride of *Frederick III.

In 1467 Regiomontanus was recruited by King *Matthias Corvinus of Hungary to teach at the newly established University of Pressburg. In Hungary he completed his *Tabulae directionum et profectionum* in (published in 1490), a work useful for calculating the boundaries of the twelve houses that divide the zodiac. In 1471 Regiomontanus settled in Nuremberg, where he hoped to improve the knowledge of planetary motions by direct observation, using those data to calculate revised and more accurate ephemerides.

In addition to his work in computation, he also throughout his lifetime designed and built observational instruments for measuring the stars and planets. In Nuremberg he established a permanent site for his observations, thereby founding one of the first European astronomical observatories, although Tycho Brahe's Uraniborg later superseded it.

In his efforts to further scientific learning, Regiomontanus established his own printing press to publish books on mathematics, geometry, and astronomy. The first work to appear was the *Theoricae novae* of his former master Peuerbach, probably in 1472. The press ceased operation at Regiomontanus's death and issued a total of only nine books, including calendars, the *Ephemerides*, Manilius's *Astronomicon*, and Regiomontanus's *Disputationes contra Cremonensia in planetarum theoricas deliramenta*, in which he attacked Gherardo da Sabbioneta's work on the *Almagest*.

Regiomontanus was apparently called to Rome by Pope *Sixtus IV in 1475 to help reform the church calendar. Regiomontanus would have been the most knowledgeable candidate for carrying out a revision of the Julian calendar, whose defects were widely recognized by church officials. He probably died in that city the following year during an outbreak of the plague. An unsubstantiated rumor arose after Regiomontanus's death that he had been poisoned by the sons of George of Trapezountios, who had been an intellectual opponent of Bessarion.

Bibliography: Ernst Zinner, *Regiomontanus: His Life and Work*, trans. Ezra Brown, 1990.

Alan S. Weber

René, Duke of Anjou (1409–80),

was also count of Provence, titular king of Sicily, and the father of Margaret of Anjou, queen of England through her marriage to *Henry VI. He was also a painter and writer of note and a patron of the arts. René's impressive list of royal and noble titles was not, however, matched by his wealth, and his political schemes invariably ended in disaster.

The son of Louis II, duke of Anjou and count of Provence, René was also adopted as heir to the Duchy of Bar by his great-uncle Cardinal Louis of Bar in 1419 and came into this inheritance in 1430. In 1420 he married Isabelle, daughter and heiress of Charles II of Lorraine, with whom he was to have four children. His sister Marie married King *Charles VII of France. René was heavily involved in the campaigns of his brother-in-law Charles VII against the English and Burgundians during the Hundred Years' War. He was present at Nancy in 1428 when *Joan of Arc sought the assistance of René's father-in-law Charles of Lorraine, and at the coronation of Charles VII in Rheims, the Battle of Senlis, and the siege of Paris the following year.

In 1431 Charles of Lorraine died, and René asserted his claim to the duchy in his wife's name. However, he was defeated and captured by his wife's uncle Antoine de Vaudemont and handed over to Philip, duke of Burgundy. While René was imprisoned at Dijon, have learned to paint miniatures on glass. He was released in 1437 after agreeing to marry his daughter Yolande to Antoine's heir Ferry, and on the payment of a ransom of 400,000 *écus d'or*.

On his release René rejoined Isabelle in Italy, where he attempted to make good his claim to the throne of Naples, which had been bequeathed to him on the death of Queen Joanna II. He arrived in Naples in 1438 but was unable to make good his claim, and the failure of this venture left René in poverty. He returned to France in 1442 and was involved in the reconquest of Normandy for Charles VII in 1449. In 1444 his daughter Margaret was married to Henry VI of England in a short-lived peace initiative. This exalted match, while serving Charles's diplomatic interests, brought no lasting benefit to England or to René.

With Anjou freed from the threat of English invasion by Charles VII's victories, René's court at Angers became a major cultural center and was strongly influenced by Italian art and scholarship. He was also drawn to the cult of chivalry popular at European courts at this time and founded the Order of the Crescent in 1448, the statutes of which included the recording of its members' chivalric deeds in a "Book of Adventures."

Isabelle died in 1453, and René married Jeanne de Laval, daughter of Count Guy XIV of Laval, the following year. It was around this time that René wrote many of his major literary works. His *Regnault et Jeanneton*, a 10,000-verse pastoral love ode written for his new wife, was criticized for its long-windedness by *François Villon. He also wrote *Le Cavalier Coeur d'Amour*, a satire on courtly love. Other works included *Mortifiement de vaine plaisance* (1455) and *Le livre du ouer d'amours espris* (1457).

René was proclaimed king in 1466 by the Catalans rebelling against Aragonese rule. His son John of Calabria went to Spain to pursue his father's cause, but was killed in 1470 at Barcelona. Due to his succession of ambitious but failed military and dynastic projects, René faced increasing hardship in his last years and was forced to hand over much of his patrimony to the French Crown, including Provence, which was ceded to *Louis XI. He died in this, his former county, in 1480.

The cultured, unfortunate René enjoyed a considerable posthumous reputation as "le bon Roi René." Much admired by the romantic movement of the nineteenth century, René and Isabelle are depicted in Dante Gabriel Rossetti's *The Kiss*.

Bibliography: Leonard W. Johnson, *Poets as Players: Theme and Variation in Late Medieval French Poetry*, 1990; Douglas Kelly, *Medieval Imagination: Rhetoric and the Poetry of Courtly Love*, 1978.

Michael Evans

Repyngdon, Philip (1360?–1424), cardinal and bishop of Lincoln. Philip

Repyngdon (or Repyngton or Repton), among the most eminent of the Oxford Wycliffites and a key propagator of Lollardy, afterwards recanted and later rose to the rank of bishop of Lincoln and cardinal of the church. Though he was known after his recantation as a zealous persecutor of Lollardy, the sincerity of both his recantation and his persecutions remains in question.

A year after the Peasants' Revolt of 1381, Repyngdon came to prominence in the ferment over Wycliffism, then widely blamed for the revolt. While *John Wyclif and his followers, including *Nicholas Hereford and Repyngdon, defended Wycliffism and propounded new reforms to the first postrevolt parliament in 1382, the new archbishop of Canterbury, William Courtenay, convened a synod at Blackfriars to examine and condemn Wyclif and his doctrines. The question then turned to Oxford University, the center of Wycliffism, the theologians who preached and taught there, and how to suppress this heresy in a setting that, after all, had papal safeguards against archiepiscopal intrusion into academic affairs and disputes, which included Wycliffism.

Repyngdon, likely of Repton, Derbyshire, came to prominence as an Austin canon of St. Mary de Pré in Leicester. Educated at Broadgates Hall, Oxford, he became a noted supporter of Wyclif, preaching the Wycliffite doctrine of the Eucharist first in a sermon at Brackley in Northamptonshire and thereafter at

Oxford, where he incepted as doctor of divinity on 10 June 1382. On 5 June, the Feast of Corpus Christi (the great feast of the Eucharist), instead of the university chancellor, Repyngdon preached the university sermon at St. Frideswide's. In it he defended not only the Wycliffite doctrine of transubstantiation but Wycliffism as a whole and claimed that these doctrines had the support of *John of Gaunt, the king's uncle and regent. Two days later, at a public *disputatio*, he continued praising Wyclif and urged adoption of Wyclif's reform program.

Meanwhile, at the Blackfriars synod, Archbishop Courtenay sent out orders to Oxford's chancellor, Robert Rygg, to suspend Repyngdon from all preaching and academic affairs, along with the most notorious of the Oxford Lollards, Nicholas Hereford, John Aston, Laurence Bedeman, and John Wyclif himself. After a few days of wrangling and obstruction, and only after being threatened with a sentence of heresy for his recalcitrance, Rygg reluctantly published the sentences of suspension on 15 June. Repyngdon, along with Hereford, then journeyed to London to appeal to John of Gaunt (Wyclif's protector), but without success. Summoned before the Blackfriars synod, Repyngdon and the other academics asked for time to prepare a considered response to the twenty-four anti-Wycliffite conclusions that the synod had propounded. On 20 June Repyngdon and Hereford then presented their written answers. They accepted ten conclusions wholly, and the others conditionally, but seemed insincere, perhaps even deceitful, when they refused to discuss their answers. Ordered to appear before the synod again on 1 July, they did not, and as a result, both Repyngdon and Hereford received a sentence of excommunication. The two then appealed to the pope, nailing copies of their appeals to the church doors of St. Paul's Cathedral and St. Mary of the Arches in London. While Hereford escaped arrest and made his way to Rome to appeal to the pope, Repyngdon went into hiding in the Midlands, though it seems that he continued his preaching.

However, after a few months of this covert existence, Repyngdon recanted, but he failed to issue a public abjuration as Courtenay had ordered, presumably because by November 1382 his enthusiasm to recant had waned. Repyngdon and the other academics (except Hereford, who remained at large until 1387) in the end received treatment not as common heretics, but as scholars who had merely strayed a bit too far beyond orthodoxy. Once he had publicly acknowledged his errors, Repyngdon returned to academic life and resumed his education and career. Of all the Oxford Lollards, Repyngdon suffered least and gained the most.

Repyngdon remained out of public notice for the next twelve years, but in 1394 he received the appointment as abbot of St. Mary de Pré in Leicester, and in 1397 he became chancellor of Oxford University, which office he again held from 1400 to 1402. At some point he came to the notice of Henry of Bolingbroke, perhaps through his Wycliffite connections with the latter's father, John of Gaunt. This connection proved beneficial to Repyngdon, for soon after Bolingbroke's accession as *Henry IV, he became the king's chaplain. On

29 March 1405 Archbishop Arundel consecrated him bishop of Lincoln. Repyngdon's connection with Henry IV paid its highest dividend in 1408 when Repyngdon received the cardinal's hat from Pope Gregory XII. Unfortunately for Repyngdon, Gregory XII was one of the schismatic popes. In 1409, at the Council of Pisa, Gregory was deposed and all his acts after May 1408 were annulled. Repyngdon, though, in the end received recognition of his cardinalate at the 1414 Council of Constance when, upon Gregory XII's final resignation, the council lifted the sentence of annulment against his acts, including Repyngdon's appointment as cardinal.

Thereafter active in both sacred and secular affairs, Repyngdon surprisingly resigned from his bishopric effective 1 February 1420. No further notice of Repyngdon then occurs, at least until the probation of his will on 1 August 1424. Though his exact date of death remains unknown, presumably it occurred a few days previously. Despite his wishes for a simple funeral and burial in St. Margaret's churchyard, he lies next to Bishop Robert Grosseteste in Lincoln Cathedral.

The language of his will has supported a supposition of Repyngdon's covert Lollard sympathies, for it echoes that of noted Lollards of the time. Additionally, though the noted Lollard William Thorpe and Archbishop Arundel both referred to Repyngdon's zeal in persecuting Lollardy, little evidence of actual persecuting zealotry exists in the records. Indeed, Repyngdon treated many heretics with noted gentleness, when he did not downright ignore them. The language of his will stated the three cardinal doctrines of Lollardy: one's wretchedness as a sinner, the fitness of one's body only for worm meat, and a desire for a plain, simple funeral in a plain, simple grave. This suggests the insincerity of his original recantation and, perhaps, covert support for Lollard doctrines during his reign as bishop, all of which must have contributed to the continued existence of Lollardy down through the fifteenth century. On the other hand, the language found in his will exists, too, in the testaments of known non-Lollards of the time, including Archbishop Arundel and Henry IV, and today one might identify it as a sign of someone in the throes of severe depression. Unfortunately, all too little evidence exists concerning Repyngdon's life and motivations, so that in the end, the sincerity of his recantation, his suppression of Lollardy, and the possible role that he played in the survival of Lollardy into the fifteenth century undoubtedly will remain a mystery.

Bibliography: Anne Hudson, "Wycliffism in Oxford, 1381–1411," in *Wyclif in His Times*, ed., Anthony Kenny, 1986; K. B. McFarlane, *John Wycliffe and the Beginnings of English Non-Conformity*, 1952.

Jerome S. Arkenburg

Reuchlin, Johann (1455–1522),

was, among other things, an educator, a judge, and a diplomat. He is known best, however, as a pioneer of German humanism whose interest and subsequent scholarship in Hebraic and classical studies not only paved the way for the migration of Renaissance thought and culture into northern Europe, but precipitated a controversy that ultimately altered the cultural underpinnings of early modern Europe.

An apotheosis of high literary art, Johann Reuchlin's life was defined by the Christian humanist conviction that reverence for God was made explicit through intellectual pursuits, particularly those in classical literature. At an early age Reuchlin commenced his education with Latin studies at the Dominican monastery school in Pforzheim, where his father was an official. He continued his studies in the classics at the University of Freiburg, but moved shortly thereafter to the University of Paris, where he was formally introduced to Greek under the supervision of John à Lapide. It was also here that Reuchlin made the acquaintance of *Rudolf Agricola, considered by many as the "father of German humanism." Reuchlin's interests in the classics took him to Basel, where he received both his baccalaureate and master's degrees in Greek and where, in 1477, he began his pedagogical career as a public lecturer on Greek language and Aristotelian philosophy.

After a brief stay in Paris, where he continued his studies in Greek, Reuchlin made his way to the University of Orléans and pursued an education in law. Within two years Reuchlin had acquired a degree there and in 1481 was appointed licentiate of law at the University of Poitiers. Continuing his studies in law the following year at the University of Tübingen, Reuchlin was requested by Eberhard, duke of Württemberg, to become his personal secretary and confidant. Not only did this newfound position afford him the time to acquire a doctorate of law in 1484, it required him to accompany his patron on diplomatic sojourns that, on four separate occasions, gave Reuchlin the opportunity to visit Florence and Rome, two of Renaissance Europe's most distinguished centers of intellectual activity. In Florence, Reuchlin attended the Medicean Academy, where he continued his studies in Greek and, more significantly, made the acquaintance of *Giovanni Pico della Mirandola, who, among other things, was a one of the foremost Renaissance scholars of cabalism, a system of Jewish theosophy and mysticism. The meeting with Pico, coupled with a preexisting love of the Old Testament, fueled Reuchlin's interest in learning Hebrew. For the next nine years Reuchlin concentrated his efforts on Hebraic studies, which he saw both as a means of ascertaining the divine truth behind the Old and New Testaments and as a means by which he would be exposed to the mystical insights of the Cabala. In 1492 Reuchlin undertook a mission to Linz, where he continued his studies in Hebrew under the instruction of a court physician and learned Jew, Jacob Jehiel Loans. Within two years Reuchlin's education in Hebrew, which had become increasingly focused on the cabalistic literature, came to fruition with the publication of *De verbo mirifico*, a project that attempted to extend cabalistic theosophy to Christian teaching.

Upon the death of his patron in 1496, Reuchlin was dismissed from his duties at the court of Württemberg. He relocated to Heidelberg and acquired a similar position under Elector Philip, but due to the unstable political situation there he soon returned to Württemberg, where he secured an important judgeship until 1512. During this time Reuchlin continued his pursuits in Hebrew and in 1506 published *De rudimentis Hebraicis*, a Hebrew lexicon and grammar intended for philological investigation of original Judeo-Christian Scripture. However, what the book as well as the rest of Reuchlin's intellectual enterprise actually did was inadvertently land him in the middle of a famous controversy that bears the stamp of his name. In 1509 a movement was initiated by the Cologne Dominicans to ban all Hebrew literature (with the exception of the Old Testament), with the hopes of homogenizing both the faith and the thought of fellow Christians. Heralded ironically by a reformed Jew, Johann Pfefferkorn, the provincial movement inspired much disapproval from Reuchlin, who took the matter to the emperor and the pope. As both the secular and religious authorities debated their positions on the issue, the controversy increased in both intensity and magnitude. The papacy eventually sided with Pfefferkorn and the Thomists of Cologne; Reuchlin, on the other hand, was warmly received by the humanists, who, in viewing the Scholastic movement as a threat to their own values of free thought and learning, published in Reuchlin's defense the *Epistolae obscurorum virorum* (Letters of obscure men), a polemic that showered derision on both the Schoolmen of Cologne and the intellectual and spiritual hegemony of Scholasticism. The ensuing antagonism between humanism and Scholasticism that developed in Reuchlin's name consequently set the stage for further invective against established manifestations of theological thought, which included attacks made by Reuchlin's nephew Philip Melanchthon and his passionate mentor, Martin Luther.

As the two supporters of Reuchlin changed both the scope and objective of the controversy, Reuchlin, who did not sympathize with the radical nature of their views, receded further and further into the background of the incipient crisis. He continued litigation against the censorship of Hebrew texts until 1520, but lived rather quietly on the fringes of the tempest himself. After his departure as judge in 1512, Reuchlin devoted his efforts to his endeavors in Hebrew and Greek, which, in 1517, produced the last of his major works, *De arte cabalistica*, a continuation of his attempt to blend the mystical elements of Judaism with the Christian tradition. Three years later Reuchlin took up a position as professor of Greek and Hebrew at Ingolstadt and a year later, during the last year of his life, at the University of Tübingen.

Johann Reuchlin died as one of Germany's most gifted humanists and accomplished scholars. Through his scholarship and his pedagogy, he provided a conduit through which the cultural Renaissance of Italy could pass to the lands north of the Alps. Such a role, however, was hazardous: Reuchlin's progressive interests in humanism, particularly Hebrew, resulted in a struggle with the conservative intellectual and religious forces of medieval Germany. This confrontation, which was bound to happen, inadvertently placed Reuchlin in another role: a catalyst for a crisis that ultimately reshaped the cultural structure of early modern Europe.

Bibliography: Eckhard Bernstein, *German Humanism*, 1983; James H. Overfield, *Humanism and Scholasticism in Late Medieval Germany*, 1984.

Gregory E. Canada

Richard II, King of England (1367–1400, r. 1377–99).

The life and career of Richard II have long fascinated historians; he acceded to the throne at the age of ten after the death of his father, *Edward the Black Prince, and his grandfather, King *Edward III. His accession ushered in a new era, but Richard's career was marred by political controversy and ensuing power struggles, an inability to sire a male heir, and, ultimately, a tragic dénouement. At his deposition and death only a few commentators paused to record any notice of his passing, and the few who made any remarks attributed his downfall to his incredible hubris, an aspect of Richard's personality adopted by William Shakespeare in one of the latter's more powerful history plays, *Richard II*. A mixture of imagination and historic fact, this play has been much maligned by historians, but it is in a sense a tribute to Richard II's cultural achievements.

His coronation, and specifically his oath, set the tone for the new reign. While previous kings had taken the oath after their presentation to the congregation in Westminster, Richard II took his oath before his presentation to the public, thus emphasizing the people's allegiance to their king. There were signs of trouble almost immediately, particularly in his ostentatious style, extravagant spending, and refusal to rely on the advice of older, more experienced counselors. Although it is difficult to portray Richard II as a cultural leader, western Europe looked to his example by virtue of his position as king of England. In terms of commissions for artwork and buildings, only one can be positively attributed to Richard II, namely, the restoration of the great hall at Westminster, which had begun to show signs of wear by the mid-fourteenth century. Built three hundred years earlier by King William Rufus, the east wall was strengthened by Richard's architects with flying buttresses, and by the time of Richard's death in 1400, the great hall at Westminster had been transformed into a showplace of secular architecture.

Although Richard II is known only for one architectural project, he is best remembered for his patronage and taste for all things French. He was trained from his youth in the French language, an interest that he never forsook. By the late fourteenth century the French and English courts were most certainly trying to outdo one another in splendor. In a collection of tracts written around this time, the compiler depicted Richard II as "the most noble king of the realms of England and France, who governs in sublime fashion not so much by force of arms as by philosophy and the two laws." This depiction of Richard II as philosopher king was perhaps unwarranted; much of the existing evidence points to the fact that Richard had little or no ambition to be a patron of learning.

However, his administration relied more heavily on published statutes and civil law than had his predecessors. He did cultivate a small gathering of literati, including *Geoffrey Chaucer, *John Gower, who wrote in English, Latin, and

French, and a chamber knight, Sir John Montagu, whose works have not survived but whose reputation was known in the court. Richard II commissioned at least two books, a collection of pseudoscientific advice tracts, the *Libellus geomancie* (Bodley MS. 581), and the St. John's College book of statutes, the last of which was followed rather closely by Richard II in his governance of England. It is likely that Richard II commissioned John Gower to write a poem for him in his *Confessio Amantis*. In the prologue to the *Confessio*, Gower referred to his poem as "a bok for king Richardes sake," thus giving the impression that it had been commissioned by the king. Richard also owned copies of a collection of recipes written for him by his master chef, *The Forme of Cury*, and Roger Dymmok's *Liber contra duodecim errores*, a polemic against Lollard heresies. However, these are the only existing examples of his literary patronage; no contemporary writer ever praised the assistance Richard II gave to scholars, thus implying that such support was nonexistent. The literary interest, however, can be traced to an increased literacy among the members of the king's court. The role of Richard II as a patron was less developed than that of his French contemporary, Charles V. Judging from his exchequer rolls and wardrobe books, however, Richard II was a pious leader with a variety of interests ranging from religious and dynastic concerns to astrology, hunting, and hawking. He took a leading role in the suppression of heresy; in fact, the epitaph on his tomb aptly summarizes his life and his penchant for "suppressing the heretics and scattering their friends."

Bibliography: Nigel Saul, *Richard II*, 1997; V. J. Scattergood and J. W. Sherborne, eds., *English Court Culture in the Later Middle Ages*, 1983.

Jennifer L. Harrison

Richard III, King of England (b. 1452, r. 1483–85), ruled England for a brief twenty-six months and was only thirty-three when he was killed at Bosworth-Field defending his throne. Despite his short life and reign, he is one of the best-known English kings because of William Shakespeare's characterization of him as an evil, deformed monster and because of the heinous crimes of which he has been accused. Not only is he accused of having his nephews murdered in the Tower of London, but also of murdering his brother George of Clarence, his wife Anne, and several political rivals. This evil portrait is so dominating that it overshadows Richard's accomplishments as king and his place in the cultural life of England.

When Richard was born on 2 October 1452, his father Richard, duke of York, was trying to wrest the throne from the Lancastrian supporters of *Henry VI. In 1460 the duke was killed in battle, and so his son Edward of March resumed the family's contention for the throne and was declared king in 1461. Not much is known of Richard's childhood until 1465, when he was placed in the care of his cousin Richard Neville, earl of Warwick. Richard then lived mainly in the north of England, and here he met his future wife Anne, the youngest daughter of the earl, a very powerful man. The earl supported *Edward IV's claim to the throne and acted as his advisor. When Edward began to formulate his own policy without consulting the earl, their relationship fell apart, and in 1469 Edward recalled Richard to London. For the next two years Richard remained at Edward's side, sharing his exile to Bruges when the earl secured the upper hand in the struggle for power. Richard played an active part in the last two major battles in the struggle for the Crown, acquitting himself well on the field. In the Battle of Barnet, the earl was killed, and in the Battle of Tewkesbury, the Lancastrian forces were defeated. The results of both battles helped to secure Edward's kingship, while Richard now turned his attention to Anne and marriage.

Richard and Anne were married in 1472 and went north to live. Marriage to Anne was politically advantageous for Richard because it gained him acceptance in the very clannish northern society from which he built his base of power, and over the next ten years he earned and received the loyalty of the people there. Anne was also heir to her father's estates, but Richard's brother George was married to the earl's oldest daughter and did not want to share the wealth with his younger sibling. Edward negotiated between the brothers, and Richard eventually received Middleham Castle and other northern holdings of the earl. In June 1471 Edward bestowed on Richard several royal offices held by the earl and in particular appointed him chief steward of the Duchy of Lancaster, also a northern territory. Richard was now empowered to exercise royal authority in the north of England, and as virtual king of this area he became known as "lord of the north." He used his power to resolve old conflicts between the Neville and Percy families and promoted justice in all levels of society. In some instances, he even upheld the law against men loyal to himself and thus brought peace and justice to a once-lawless region.

In April 1483 Edward IV died. Edward's queen, Elizabeth Woodville, had a large family whose members had benefited greatly from her position, and they wasted no time in trying to secure the power to rule in the name of the young king Edward V. Evidence suggests that Edward IV had intended for Richard to be the protector of the young king, who had until his father's death been surrounded by the Woodvilles. Richard now stood to lose his considerable power, and so control of the young king was of major importance to him. On 29 April he met up with the young king's retinue on its way to London. He arrested the members of Edward's household—they were to be executed in June on Richard's orders—and brought the young prince to London. No one knows when Richard decided to make himself king, but on Sunday, 22 June 1483 his claim to the throne was established on the grounds that his nephew was illegitimate: the marriage of Edward IV to Elizabeth was invalid, for Edward had been precontracted to marry another. Richard's coronation took place on Sunday, 6 July.

As king, Richard emphasized the establishment of justice throughout his realm. In 1485 he convened a conference of senior judges to discuss difficult points of law, and he instituted a system of legal aid for the poor. Richard's only parliament convened in January 1484 and served as a forum for legislation that would reform some of the ills of the realm. This parliament simplified land law that had become overcomplicated. Persons arrested on suspicion of a crime were to be allowed bail. Parliament also abolished the hated benevolence tax or demand for free gifts of money. Richard also proved to be a good friend to the church, which reflected his own religious devotion. He continuously distributed money to a variety of religious institutions, mainly while on his royal progresses throughout England.

Promotion of education and learned men were important to Richard. To King's and Queen's colleges in Cambridge he gave considerable sums provided they recognized Queen Anne as a founder of the college. He surrounded himself with scholars and preferred Cambridge men to those from Oxford. The men Richard promoted or placed in government and church offices were not only Cambridge graduates but were also familiar with the humanistic movement taking place in Italy. Some of Richard's appointees, such as John Shirwood, had even studied in Italy. It was clear that humanistic scholarship was becoming a qualification for high government office. Music was another area of great interest to Richard. Under Edward IV, the Yorkist court had gained an international reputation for the quality of its music, and Richard continued that tradition.

The termination of Richard's brief reign ended any further impact he might have had on English life. He had made a promising start as king, and only a longer reign would have allowed a fair assessment of his accomplishments. He lived in a very violent period of English history when a man was often forced to do all in his power to defend himself, his house, and his possessions. Under the young king Edward with Woodville backing, Richard stood to lose everything. But whether or not he had his nephews murdered, it is important to understand that the men of Richard's day believed that he had. If he had reigned for a longer period of time, the truth about his nephews and his character might have been revealed.

Bibliography: A. J. Pollard, *Richard III and the Princes in the Tower*, 1991; Charles Ross, *Richard III*, 1981.

Kathryn Kiff

Rienzo, Cola di (1314–54), was a Roman orator, revolutionary, and close friend of the poet *Francesco Petrarch. Rienzo rose through his sensitivity to the needs of the poor and working class to prominent power in a newly formed Roman republic, but power corrupted him, and he became a victim of both his own tyranny and the people's revenge. From the center of power, Rienzo fell and was put on trial for heresy, although eventually he was exonerated. He was beginning his political ascent once more when the people revolted and revenged themselves on him, beheading him on the steps of his beloved Roman Capitoline on his return. Rienzo came to represent the rise and fall of the sympathetic person corrupted by power, as shown in the Victorian-era play and novel based on his life.

Cola di Rienzo (his birth name was Nicholas Laurentii; Rienzo is the Roman nickname used by most historians) was born in the spring of 1314 in the Regiola section of Rome, just below the Capitoline near the Tiber Island. Rienzo's parents were lower middle class; his father Lorenzo Laurentii was an innkeeper and his mother Matalena was a washerwoman and water bearer. Rienzo lived some of his life among his peasant relatives in Anagni on the Campagna, where he developed an appreciation for their political and economic concerns. Rienzo at his own initiative read widely in both pagan and Christian classics. He also became a good friend of the Italian poet Francesco Petrarch, whose correspondence with him survives. In 1333 the self-trained Rienzo became an orator and an interpreter of ancient inscriptions in Rome, where he began his lifelong opposition to the nobles, particularly the Colonna, Orsini, and Savelli families. The revolt of the "Thirteen Good Men" overthrew the nobles' reign, and Rienzo was sent to Pope *Clement VI in Avignon to obtain his sanction of the new republican government. Clement VI appointed him notary of the City Chamber.

Rienzo built support for his political ambitions among the poor and working classes, merchants, and some of the lower nobility. During the absence of the Colonnas, Rienzo led a revolution. After midnight on 20 May 1347, Rienzo marched with the people and papal vicar Raymond of Chameyrac up the Capitoline, restoring the Roman republic and announcing himself the tribune of the people. However, Rienzo's rule quickly turned to tyranny, and from May until December 1347 his control of the republic was brutal. He childishly insulted high officials such as Cardinal Bertrand de Deaulx, and he publicly drowned two hounds he had named after the Orsini family. Although he had the support of King *Louis I of Hungary and the city perfect Giovanni di Vico, he resigned as tribune on 15 December 1347.

After wandering in Italy and attending the court of Emperor Charles IV at Prague, a disillusioned Rienzo was imprisoned at the papal court and tried for heresy in 1352. During his wanderings Rienzo spent time as a monk at Monte Maiella. He was arrested in the court of Charles IV and charged with heresy by Cardinal Bertrand de Deaulx and Bishop Annibaldo di Ceccano of Tusculum. He was accused of belonging to the Patarines, an orthodox but revolutionary group that had pushed for the moral reform of the clergy and had boycotted clergy living in sin. Rienzo was cleared of the charges and ironically became the papal agent to Rome in 1354 in an attempt to restore public order. Rienzo died in that attempt on 8 October 1354, on the steps of the Capitoline, beheaded by Cecco del Vecchio, who was supported by the people of Rome.

Bibliography: Francesco Petrarch, *The Revolution of Cola di Rienzo*, 3rd ed., ed. Mario Emilio Cosenza, 1996.

Mark K. Fulk

Robert of Artois (1287–1342) was count of Beaumont-le-Roger. During the first three years of the reign of Philip VI Robert was the most powerful

noble in France, but he soon became the most infamous, accused of suborning perjury, commissioning forgeries, and contracting the assassination of the king and his family. Robert's legal difficulties in the 1330s led to his eventual banishment from France and to a fateful encounter with the English king *Edward III, believed by contemporaries to have resulted in the beginning of the Hundred Years' War.

Robert of Artois was born in 1287, the only son of Philippe of Artois and Blanche of Brittany. Robert was born into an illustrious noble family; his paternal grandfather was Count Robert II of Artois (1250–1302), the son of King Louis IX's younger brother Robert I; his maternal grandfather was Jean II, duke of Brittany (1238–1305). After his father's death in 1297 at the Battle of Furnes and Count Robert II's death at the Battle of Courtral in 1302, Robert of Artois was brought up at the court of *Philip IV, "the Fair," in the company of the French king's sons. In the meantime, in the decision that was to haunt Robert of Artois all his life, Philip the Fair granted the county of Artois to Robert's aunt, Mahaut of Artois, the only surviving legitimate child of Count Robert II of Artois. When the young Robert reached the age of majority in 1308, he began judicial proceedings to claim the county of Artois for himself. Philip the Fair again concurred with Mahaut (the mother-in-law of two of the king's sons) and awarded her the county on 9 October 1309. Eventually Robert of Artois was recompensed with landed income and the title to a lesser county, Beaumont-le-Roger.

In 1314 the nobles of Artois entered into a rebellion against the government of their countess, Mahaut, and her primary advisor, Thierry d'Hireçon, who was widely hated. In the fall of 1316 Robert of Artois took over the leadership of the rebellion and invaded Artois. The new king of France, Philip V, took quick action to quash the invasion, and Robert was imprisoned for a few months. Robert promised to surrender castles in Artois, and Philip promised to hear Robert's claims again in court. But in May 1318 Philip V, the son-in-law of Mahaut of Artois, upheld his father's decision of 1309, and Robert was forced to swear in writing that he would no longer pursue his claims for the county of Artois.

For ten years Robert kept his promise. In 1328, however, politics in France took a turn in his favor. Philip V had died in 1322 without male heirs, his brother Charles IV also died without sons in 1328, and there were no more younger brothers. The new king was Philippe of Valois, the nephew of Philip the Fair and the brother-in-law and close friend of Robert of Artois. Robert played an important role as advisor to the new king Philip VI, who elevated Robert's county of Beaumont-le-Roger to a peerage. Robert also persuaded King Philip to listen to his claims for the county of Artois.

This time, Robert of Artois was determined to succeed. Councilors commissioned by Philip VI heard testimony from fifty-four witnesses in the summer of 1329, many of whom claimed that Count Robert II of Artois had left letters naming his son Philippe, and failing him, his heir, as the rightful ruler of Artois.

Two such letters were presented to Philip VI in December 1330, in addition to two others also concerning the disposition of Artois. Unfortunately for Robert, however, these four letters were soon proved forgeries and much of the testimony of 1329 subornations. Despite initial hesitation, Philip VI upheld the decisions of Philip the Fair and Philip V, and furthermore, he summoned Robert of Artois to court to answer these charges, the first subpoena being delivered in August 1331.

Robert never appeared in court, though he was subpoenaed four times. He fled France, first to the Low Countries, from where he allegedly sent assassins to kill Philip VI, his queen, Jeanne of Burgundy (whom Robert hated with a passion), and their son, Jean, duke of Normandy. Probably in the spring of 1334 Robert arrived in England, where he was welcomed in the court of his cousin, the young king *Edward III. At first Philip VI did little, but as tensions heightened between the two kings, the French king began to send letters to Edward III demanding the return of Robert of Artois. In March 1337 Philip VI issued a letter declaring Robert of Artois a mortal enemy of France and proclaiming that those who had done homage to him should not receive, aid, or comfort his mortal enemies. In May 1337 Philip confiscated Gascony, citing Edward's reception of Robert of Artois as a primary reason. After this, war between England and France was inevitable.

In the contemporary chronicles, Robert of Artois was often blamed as the initiator of the war, and a famous poem, *The Vow of the Heron*, probably written by one of Robert's supporters around 1340, emphasized the role Robert played in provoking the English monarch into war against France. Robert of Artois participated in the early battles of the Hundred Years' War, fighting at Edward's side. During the siege of Vannes in November 1342, Robert received a wound from which he soon died. He never achieved his goal of becoming the count of Artois, an obsession that colored his entire life and exacerbated the already-strained relationship between France and England.

Bibliography: Dana L. Sample, "The Case of Robert of Artois," Ph.D. diss., 1996; Jonathan Sumption, *The Hundred Years' War: Trial by Battle*, 1992.

Dana L. Sample

Rodrigo Sánchez de Arévalo. *See* Sánchez de Arévalo, Rodrigo.

Rogier van der Weyden. *See* Weyden, Rogier van der.

Rolle, Richard (1300?–1349), of Hampole, was one of late medieval England's earliest and best-known practitioners of mysticism and was the prolific author of many devotional works in both Latin and the vernacular English. He is remembered today for his poem *Pricke of Conscience*, which considered the nature of life, death, and the hereafter, and his *Incendium amoris* or *Fire of*

Love, an effusive and often-rambling reflection upon his own mystical experiences.

Richard Rolle was the son of William Rolle and was probably born around 1300 in Thornton-le-Dale in Richmondshire in the Diocese of York. The "legenda," a collection of stories about Rolle compiled after his death, tells us that young Richard was educated early by his parents and was then sent to study at Oxford by Thomas Neville, archdeacon of Durham. At age nineteen, after enjoying some success at his studies, Rolle seems to have decided against the secular religious path he was following at university in favor of an eremitical vocation of solitude. He left Oxford to take up residence in the woods near his father's home and, lacking the proper attire of an ascetic recluse, asked his family for and was given two old gowns and a rain hood. These he tried clumsily to fashion into a rough habit, but he appeared so ridiculous to his family and fellow villagers that he fled their derision to take up a life of wandering piety. According to the "legenda," Rolle next appeared at prayer in a private chapel in a village near Thornton, possibly Dalton or Pickering, where he seems to have kept vigil through the night and then preached a moving sermon at mass on the Feast of the Assumption the following day. One of his auditors happened to be the local gentleman John de Dalton, who was so impressed with the holy man that he outfitted him with more appropriate clothing and soon became his patron. Thus favored, Rolle commenced a life of contemplative prayer, mystical spirituality, and devotional writing, at times penning his thoughts with such concentration and speed that he was reportedly able to write and speak with visitors at the same time without interruption. Later in life he took to wandering again, and eventually arriving in Hampole, near Doncaster, he became the spiritual director of a small house of Cistercian nuns and of an anchoress named Margaret Kirkby in nearby Anderby. He is believed to have died on Michaelmas Day, 29 September 1349, possibly of the Black Death. Rolle's reputation for piety and posthumous miracles won such immediate fame after his death that a cult honoring "St. Richard Hermit" soon emerged, while the Cistercian sisters of Hampole compiled an "office" of prayers and hymns and a "legenda" of supporting stories in the hope that he would someday be canonized a saint. He never was.

Richard Rolle was the first of England's five great fourteenth- and early-fifteenth-century mystics, a group that included *Walter Hilton, the anonymous author of the *Cloud of Unknowing*, Dame *Juliana of Norwich, and *Margery Kempe. In *Incendium amoris*, Rolle struggled to describe his mystical progress toward and ultimate union with the divine, but his stages of "warmth, sweetness and melody" and his "melting" unitive raptures, though exuberant, were nonetheless obscure and often impenetrable. Rolle also authored a great many other works in Latin, including the partially autobiographical *Melos amoris* and his commentaries on the Psalms; several of these he subsequently translated into a Northumbrian dialect of Middle English. Of his many purely English writings, the best known has long been the *Pricke of Conscience*, possibly written to instruct Rolle's anchoritic student Margaret Kirkby. A meandering poem of nearly ten thousand lines, *Pricke* contains a prologue and seven books that discuss life and its tribulations on earth, death, and the various fates that await Christians in the world to come. Some modern scholars have been tempted to designate Rolle the real father of English literature, an honor that probably belongs more properly to *Geoffrey Chaucer, but Rolle was certainly an English-language pioneer and, perhaps more important, did much to initiate the mystical tradition that flourished in late medieval England.

Bibliography: Richard Rolle, *The Fire of Love*, ed. and trans. Clifton Wolters, 1972; Nicholas Watson, *Richard Rolle and the Invention of Authority*, 1991.

Clayton J. Drees

Ruiz, Juan (d. 1350). Juan Ruiz is the name of the first-person narrator and supposed author of *The Book of Good Love* (*Libro de buen amor*), also known as *The Book of the Archpriest of Hita* (*Libro del arcipreste de Hita*), an often-obscene account of the archpriest's frustrated search for a lady friend. The three extant manuscripts contain two different versions of the text, one dated 1330, the other, longer version dated 1343 (the source for most printed editions). Much scholarly debate has raged around the question of Ruiz's identity; the traditional position that Ruiz was a well-educated cleric who served in Hita, a small town in the province of Guadalajara, has most recently been defended by Francisco J. Hernández, who published a 1330 document that listed the name of the "venerabilis Johannes Roderici, archiprestiber de Fita." Other scholars have argued that the name Juan Ruiz, or more formally Juan Rodriguez, is simply too common for any documentary evidence to confirm unequivocally the identity of our author. Others have argued that Juan Ruiz is a fictive name assumed by many different minstrels who composed and performed bawdy, goliardic songs. In support of this position, scholars have pointed to the two manuscript traditions, suggesting that they represent not just earlier and later versions of the text, but two performance traditions of the materials associated with the name Juan Ruiz. The debate over Ruiz's identity is reflected in the question of the purpose of his work. While earlier scholars argued that the often openly obscene text was a satiric attack on the lax morality of contemporary clergy, more recently the ambiguity of the text has been celebrated as a sign of the openness of the medieval manuscript and of parody in general.

In any case, *The Book of Good Love* is a fascinating and often-shocking account of medieval Castile. The main story line, recounted in *cuaderna vía*, a verse form traditionally used for religious narrative, follows the archpriest as he searches for a likely mate, be she nun, Moor, well born, bakerwoman, or prostitute. The main narrative is frequently interrupted with fables, songs, and praises of the Virgin, often put in the mouths of various characters. The carnivalesque aspect of this work is most clearly shown in the battle between Lady Lent and Sir Flesh (*coplas* 1067–1314), which ends with the triumphant return on Easter

Sunday of Sir Flesh and Sir Love, whose parodic procession is joyously welcomed by troops of nuns and monks, celebrating not Christ's victory over death but the return of springtime and self-indulgence. Direct criticism of clerical lasciviousness and apparently sincere prayers contrast with sexually explicit wordplay, resulting in a heterogenous, ever-shifting text that reflected both the official and popular culture of medieval Castile.

Bibliography: F. J. Hernández, "The Venerable Juan Ruiz, Archpriest of Hita," *Corónica* 13 (1985): 10–22.

Denise K. Filios

Rupert III, King of Germany (b. 1352, r. 1400–1410), also called Rupert Klem or Clem, was born on 5 May 1352 as a member of the Wittelsbach dynasty and was the son of the elector Rupert II and Beatrice, who was in turn daughter of Peter II, king of Sicily. Rupert succeeded his father as elector in 1398 and was elected king by the German ecclesiastical electors in August 1400 as successor of *Wenceslas, who had been deposed the day before by the German princes. He was crowned at Cologne on 6 January 1401 and traveled to Italy to be crowned by Pope Boniface IX. To win over papal support for his claim to the throne, Rupert allied himself with Florence and attacked the duke of Milan, *Giangaleazzo Visconti, who had given financial support to Wenceslas in the 1390s. Rupert's forces were defeated outside Brescia on 14 October 1401, and he then returned to Germany.

Rupert was finally recognized as king of the Germans by Pope Boniface IX in 1403. The pope expected Rupert to assist the papacy against the Avignon popes; however, Rupert devoted his resources to combating the supporters of Wenceslas in Germany. Rupert was not able to rebuild the weakened German monarchy, but he had little to fear from Wenceslas, who was occupied in defending his Bohemian throne from his brother *Sigismund.

Rupert's fatal mistake came in 1408 when he supported Pope Gregory XII against the cardinals who wished to hold a council to heal the Great Schism. The archbishops of Mainz and Cologne and most of the powerful German clergy supported the position of the cardinals against Gregory. Wenceslas took advantage of the opportunity by pledging his support to the cardinals and in return was promised that the future general council would recognize his claim to the throne over that of Rupert. Civil war was imminent between the supporters of Rupert's claim to the throne and those factions who supported Wenceslas's claim, but Rupert died on 18 May 1410 before tensions could escalate. He is buried at Heidelberg.

Bibliography: F.R.H. DuBoulay, *Germany in the Later Middle Ages*, 1983.

John D. Grosskopf

Ruy González de Clavijo. *See* González de Clavijo, Ruy.

Ruysbroek, Jan (1293–1381). One in a rich tradition of Flemish mystics, Jan Ruysbroek stands with such giants of fourteenth-century Christian mysticism as *Meister Eckhart and *Juliana of Norwich. Ruysbroek was active as both an author and a spiritual counselor for most of his long life, and his writings, most notably *the Spiritual Espousals*, represent the apex of Trinitarian mysticism in the West. While Ruysbroek elaborated a mystical theology culminating in a "union without intermediary" with God, he vigorously opposed quietistic and autotheistic heresies, insisting on the dynamic relationship between the peace of contemplation and the virtuous works of the Christian life.

Jan Ruysbroek (or Jan van Ruusbroec) was born in 1293 in the village of Ruysbroek, near Brussels. At the age of eleven he went to Brussels to study, staying with his uncle, Jan Hinckaert, canon of the collegiate church of St. Gudula. In 1317, at the age of twenty-four he was ordained into the priesthood and spent the next twenty-six years as chaplain of St. Gudula. Much of his writing during this period stems from a concern to refute heretical mystical teachings, specifically the so-called Free Spirit heresy. *The Kingdom of Lovers* (1330s), *The Sparkling Stone*, and *The Spiritual Espousals* were all composed during this period.

In 1343 Ruysbroek and two confreres formed a small religious community at Groenendaal, also near Brussels, where Ruysbroek lived out the remainder of his life. Following some sort of misunderstanding, the group became canons regular of St. Augustine in 1349, with Ruysbroek appointed prior. In his free time Ruysbroek retreated alone into the forest to write on wax tablets, which he brought back to be transcribed by others. In later years he brought a brother with him and dictated his work. *A Mirror of Eternal Blessedness* and *The Little Book of Clarification* both derive from this period of his life. Ruysbroek regularly engaged his younger confreres in extended conversations and was often visited by spiritual seekers, including *Gerhard Groote, the founder of the *devotio moderna* movement. On 2 December 1381 Jan Ruysbroek died in the infirmary at Groenendaal at the age of eighty-eight. Ruysbroek was beatified in 1909, and his feast day was set on the anniversary of his death.

Central to Ruysbroek's mysticism was the inner life of the Trinity, a dynamic characterized by the Father's eternal flowing forth into the Son and the Son's return to the Father through the Holy Spirit (the love binding them together). The height of the Christian life, which Ruysbroek called "the common life" (*dat ghemeyne leven*), was participation in this rhythm of the Trinity—returning to God through love and going out into the world in love, a true balance between the active and contemplative lives.

Ruysbroek's Trinitarian view of the Christian life was expressed most comprehensively in the influential *Spiritual Espousals*. The *Espousals*, divided into one book each on the active life, the interior life, and the contemplative life, was a spiritual meditation on a line from the Gospel of Matthew that harks back to the Song of Songs: "See. The bridegroom is coming. Go out to meet him" (Mt 25:6). In book 2, Ruysbroek noted that the bridegroom comes into the heart of the mystic in three ways, unifying first the lower, sensuous powers of the soul (in desire for God), and then the higher powers of the soul (Augustine's memory, intellect, and will). Finally, in its most intense, most sublime form, the bridegroom comes as a "touch" or "inner stirring" (*gherinen*), which Ruysbroek compared to a spring or fountain welling up from within the depths of the soul itself.

Book 3 described the soul's being lifted into a pure unity with God, both in its essence and its activity (*weselijk and werkelijk*). For Ruysbroek, there were three types of union with God: a "union with intermediary," represented by the active life in which our virtues unite us to God; a natural "union without intermediary," meaning the life that all creatures live in God as a result of having been created by him; and third, a supernatural "union without intermediary," experienced by the contemplative alone after having entered "that dark stillness in which all lovers lose their way." But this supreme union was not the end point of the spiritual life, for "the mystic who has been sent down by God from these heights into the world . . . will therefore always flow forth to all who need him."

Ruysbroek was attacked vehemently on autotheistic grounds by *Jean Gerson, and this postponed or limited somewhat his immediate impact in France despite the defense mounted on his behalf by John of Schoonhoven. Among those influenced by Ruysbroek, who himself owed his greatest debts to Augustine, Pseudo-Dionysius the Areopagite, and Hadewijch of Antwerp, were Denis the Carthusian, who described Ruysbroek as a "second Dionysius the Areopagite," and Gerhard Groote, who translated two of Ruysbroek's works into Latin.

Bibliography: Louis Dupre, *The Common Life: The Origins of Trinitarian Mysticism and Its Development by Jan Ruusbroec*, 1984; Jan Ruysbroek, *John Ruusbroec: The Spiritual Espousals and Other Works*, trans. James A. Wiseman, 1985.

Jeffrey Fisher

S

Sacchetti, Franco (1334?–1400), was a Florentine writer and statesman who is best known for his collection of stories, the *Trecentonovelle*. Sacchetti's major themes were the harshness of fortune, political injustice, religious decadence, and the importance of moderation. The exact date and location of Sacchetti's birth are uncertain. Most likely he was born in Ragusa, in Dalmatia, where his father, the Florentine Benci di Uguccione Sacchetti, was a merchant. In 1352 Sacchetti moved to Florence, where in 1354 he married Felice di Niccolò Strozzi. He traveled extensively on business, returning to Florence in 1362 to begin his career in public service. Political life left Sacchetti cynical about his time, a trait that would find its way into his writing.

Domestic troubles and tragedies plagued Sacchetti throughout his life. In 1377 his wife died, and two years later his brother Giannozzo was executed for his role in the Ciompi revolt of 1378. Sacchetti traveled to northern Italy on diplomatic missions in 1381 and 1382, returning in 1383 to Florence, where he married Ghita di Piero Gherardini. The following years saw Sacchetti's political fortunes rise in Florence with his appointment as prior (1384) and as one of the Consigli del Comune (1388–92), and in Tuscany and Romagna when he became *podestà* (a ruling judge, usually invited from another city to ensure fairness). In 1396 Sacchetti's second wife died, and he returned from Faenza to Florence, where he married Giovanna di Francesco di ser Santi Bruni. In 1397 his property in Marignolle was destroyed by mercenary troops. Despite his financial and political losses, the Florentines continued to send him on assignments, first to Romagna in 1398 and then to San Miniato, where he died of the plague in 1400.

Sacchetti's literary career began in 1352 with his first work, *La battaglia delle vecchie con le giovani*, a poem describing a battle pitting the young and beautiful women of Florence against the old and ugly, ending with the victory of the former. Around 1363 Sacchetti began to write the verses that would later be gathered in the *Libro delle rime*, the definitive version of which was published only in 1936. These 309 poems of various kinds were largely composed of musical lyrics. In 1381, deeply affected by the untimely deaths of his wife and brother as well as the political troubles in Florence, Sacchetti wrote the *Sposizioni di Vangeli*, a treatise on Lent. There also exist sixteen letters written by Sacchetti, which hailed from about the same time period as the *Trecentonovelle*, as well as a collection known as the *Zibaldone*.

Although a precise date for the commencement of Sacchetti's most famous prose work, the *Trecentonovelle*, is unknown, it was probably written between 1392 and 1397. It was not published until 1724, however, and today there exist only 223 *novelles*, several of them incomplete. In the preface Sacchetti offered the collection as a diverting pastime and praised *Giovanni Boccaccio as his example. Whereas a unifying narrative frame characterized the *Decameron*, the *Trecentonovelle* was fractured. The narrator's voice was set not in the frame but within the stories themselves, providing commentary and explanation. The *Trecentonovelle* revealed a critical outlook on contemporary morality while reflecting Sacchetti's common sense and temperance. The simple language of the *Trecentonovelle* came close to everyday speech, and the variety of people and places depicted suggested the influence of Sacchetti's many travels.

Like other humanists of the period, Sacchetti's political life dovetailed with his literary life, at times contributing a distinctly pessimistic tone to his writing. His *Trecentonovelle*, while depicting individuals who managed their way out of dire circumstances with a clever word or trick, also presented the fickle ways of fortune. Yet Sacchetti nevertheless maintained a lighthearted quality in his writing, while emphasizing the importance of literature as diversion.

Bibliography: David Quint, *Origin and Originality in Renaissance Literature*, 1983; Richard Waswo, *Language and Meaning in the Renaissance*, 1987.

Anne M. Schuchman

Saint-Pourçain, Durand of. *See* Durand of Saint-Pourçain.

Sale, Antoine de La. *See* La Sale, Antoine de.

Salutati, Coluccio (1331–1406), was chancellor of the Florentine Republic and a celebrated humanist. Salutati is best known for his efforts to establish humanism within the mainstream of Florentine culture by demonstrating its practical applications in politics and society. Not only concerned with the study of classical literature, Salutati produced an enormous amount of writing, of which his public letters best reveal his talents in rhetoric and diplomacy. With the broad circulation of his letters, Salutati's reputation as a leading humanist scholar eventually spread throughout Europe.

The son of Piero Salutati, Coluccio was born in the Valdinievole in 1331. Due to the elder Salutati's involvement in the local Guelf party, the family was exiled after a Ghibelline victory in Turin when Coluccio was quite young. Between the ages of five and nineteen Coluccio lived in Bologna, where he received a formal education under the tutelage of Pietro da Moglio. In Bologna, the young Salutati encountered rhetoric and demonstrated an early literary talent. With the encouragement of his father, Salutati then continued his studies in law at the local university. From 1348 to 1350 he was enrolled in a notarial course instructed by Conte Francesco di Giordano Benintensi. Upon completion of his studies at the university, Salutati returned to the Valdinievole with his family. In the Valdinievole, he spent his time working as a government employee and private notary and participating in local politics. Although his formal education had ended, Salutati continued to educate himself by reading and mending manuscripts. He began building a library that would later contain over eight hundred manuscripts, including works by Virgil, Ovid, and Horace. He also wrote extensively on topics like fortune and the relationship between virtue and glory. Until 1374 he moved from one post to another throughout the Republic of Florence, but frequently returned to his primary residence in Stignano.

In 1356 Salutati was employed as the communal secretary of Uzzano. In 1366 he married Caterina di Tomeo Balducci, who gave birth to one son but later died while she was pregnant with the couple's second child. After Caterina's death, Salutati eventually remarried and had several more children. Eager to leave Stignano, Salutati joined the Florentine Guild of Judges and Notaries because the guild offered him more lucrative employment in larger cities. Shortly thereafter, he accepted a post in Todi that he later regretted. Eager to experience a more cosmopolitan setting, Salutati set off for Rome. He later accepted a post in the papal Curia in 1369. During his two years in Rome Salutati forged a valuable friendship with *Francesco Petrarch, with whom he corresponded for a brief period of time. After leaving Rome, Salutati spent some time working in Lucca but left shortly after Caterina's death in 1371.

Salutati's career continued to flourish in 1375 when he replaced Niccolò Monachi as the Florentine chancellor. As chancellor of the republic, Salutati's primary responsibility involved supervising the official correspondence of Florence. In particular, Salutati was charged with writing public letters, or missives. The letters were directed to Florentine officials and foreign administrators. The extensive letter-writing demands of the post required eloquence and diplomacy. Salutati's literary talents and legal background thus proved to be indispensable. During his thirty-one years as chancellor, the public letters provided Salutati with an opportunity to fight for the justice of the Florentine Republic and demonstrate his humanist leanings. Within a few years of his acceptance of the post, Salutati became renowned throughout Europe for his contributions to humanist scholarship. Salutati also used the letters as a means of reforming the sloppy writing style of his medieval predecessors and replacing it with the eloquent Latin of humanism.

Salutati's contributions to humanism, however, were more than mere stylistic adjustments. In his letters, Salutati related classical themes to contemporary moral and political problems as a means of demonstrating the usefulness of humanism. Not simply an idle intellectual pursuit, it instead provided valuable cultural, political, and diplomatic tools. Salutati also went to great lengths to revive knowledge of ancient Greek sources. For Salutati, the study of Greek was an essential component of the humanist education. In 1396 he convinced the Florentine government to commission *Manuel Chrysoloras, a leading classical Greek scholar, to teach at the local university (Witt, *Hercules*, 304). Despite his emphasis on classical literature, Christianity occupied a central position in Salutati's humanism. His own writing fused the Christian traditions of the church fathers with aspects of pagan culture drawn from the tradition of classical writers like Ovid and Cicero. During his lifetime Salutati composed a number of treatises that dealt with issues like ethics, the human will, and political legitimacy. Some of his works, like *De fato et fortuna* (1396), dealt with abstract issues surrounding the concept of fortune, while others, like *De nobilitate legum et medicinae* (1399), dealt with the contemplation of the primacy of law over medicine. Coluccio Salutati remained a prolific and eloquent writer until his death in 1406. An articulate and diplomatic chancellor, Salutati brought the benefits of the humanist curriculum out of academic isolation and into the forefront of public life in the Florentine Republic.

Bibliography: Berthold L. Ullman, *The Humanism of Coluccio Salutati*, 1963; Ronald G. Witt, *Coluccio Salutati and His Public Letters*, 1976; Ronald G. Witt, *Hercules at the Crossroads: The Life, Works, and Thought of Coluccio Salutati*, 1983.

Celeste Chamberland

Sánchez de Arévalo, Rodrigo (1404–70). Although Rodrigo Sánchez de Arévalo was a Spaniard by birth, he enjoyed an illustrious international career as a vociferous advocate of the papacy. Rodrigo Sánchez de Arévalo was born in Santa Maria de Nieva (near Segovia) in 1404. In his lifetime he held the bishoprics of Oviedo, Zamora, Calahorra, and Palencia. He never resided in any of his sees, however, since his ecclesiastical career in the service of *Juan II and *Enrique IV of Castile required his frequent presence in Rome and the courts of Europe. He is best known for his adamant stance against the conciliarists of the fifteenth century and their call for a general church council to supersede papal authority. He penned several treatises in defense of the papacy in response to the opinions of the conciliarists. He received an early basic education from the Dominicans and ultimately attended one of Castile's most prominent universities, the University of Salamanca. His initial plan was to study law, but his attention was apparently turned to theology, as indicated by his designation as a bachelor of theology in 1440.

He attended the Council of Basel with the Castilian delegation. In the wake of the disruptions of this council, Juan II urged Europe to support *Eugenius IV as the true pope and made Sánchez his spokesperson for this effort. Appearing before Emperor *Frederick III in Vienna, Sánchez suggested that a policy of neutrality in this dispute was heretical since it implied a lack of obedience to the papacy. From this point onward he became increasingly intolerant of a general church council, arguing that such councils could not achieve the work of reform. Around 1460–61 there was renewed conciliar agitation in France and Germany. This disruption was directed primarily against *Pius II's attempt to levy a tax on clergy and laity alike to pay for a crusade against the Turks. Sánchez wrote a treatise against these agitators, saying that a council could be used to mend a schism, but that none existed in this instance.

Although Sánchez was rarely in Castile during the heyday of his ecclesiastical career, he nevertheless retained some influence there. The reign of Juan II's successor, Enrique IV, was strife ridden, due primarily to the opinions of his critics, who portrayed him as a debauched ruler who had thrown Castile into disorder. Sánchez remained cautiously loyal to the king, despite the opinions of his detractors. Sánchez dedicated a mirror for princes, *El vergel de los príncipes*, to Enrique. In this work, he indicated which amusements were best suited to the virtue of princes, including arms, music, and the chase and hunt. Sánchez believed that each of these benefited a prince mentally and physically. Some scholars have suggested that the work also implicitly advised Enrique to follow a course of moderation and virtue. The king's immorality and impropriety were a constant source of discussion for his critics. Sánchez was also a staunch supporter of Enrique's heir, *Juana of Castile, "la Beltraneja," who was rumored to be the illegitimate offspring of Enrique's wife and one of his advisors. He loyally announced the daughter's birth in Rome and did not address the fights over succession that her disputed parentage brought about in Castile.

Sánchez wrote several other significant works, including *Suma de la política* (begun around 1455), which was a treatise on political theory that displayed his familiarity with Aristotle, Cicero, St. Augustine, and Thomas Aquinas. At the behest of Pius II, he wrote *Libellus de situ et descriptione Hispaniae* (1462), a biographical and historical account of Spain. His *De paupertate Christi et apostolorum* (1466) disputed the claims of the heretical Fraticelli, and he defended the pope's right to depose a secular ruler in *De monarchia orbis* (1466–67). He died in 1470 in Rome.

Bibliography: William D. Phillips, Jr., *Enrique IV and the Crisis of Fifteenth-Century Castile 1425–1480*, 1978; Richard H. Trame, *Rodrigo Sánchez de Arévalo, 1404–1470: Spanish Diplomat and Champion of the Papacy*, 1958.

Elizabeth Lehfeldt

Savonarola, Girolamo (1452–98), was a Dominican famous for his zeal for reform of his own order and the city of Florence. He was a powerful preacher, and after his permanent arrival in Florence in 1490, by means of his zealous appeal for repentance and spiritual renewal, he became the undisputed spiritual leader of the city and a major civil leader as well. He is noted for his apocalypticism and his millenarianism, both of which he applied to Florence and all of Italy. He predicted the invasion of Italy by a new Cyrus who would punish the earth and cleanse the church. Nearly all of Florence repented—he convinced the population to give alms, stop moral indifference, do penance, and live a nearly monastic way of life. When *Charles VIII of France invaded Italy in 1494, Savonarola was viewed as a prophet. He was able to negotiate a treaty with Charles to prevent the actual occupation of Florence, and he began to be viewed as the savior of the city. He declared Florence the "New Jerusalem," from which would spread the regeneration of Italy. His agreement with Charles stood directly contrary to Pope *Alexander VI's anti-French league, and so, with the pope as his enemy, Savonarola was eventually excommunicated, arrested, tried for heresy, and executed.

Savonarola began his career as a severe preacher of repentance and reform when he entered the Dominican Priory of San Domenico in Bologna in 1475. The priory was reputedly strict in observing the rule, a strictness that marked Italy and Savonarola for the rest of his life. He visited Florence in 1482, becoming a reader at the Convent of San Marco, which was later to become the headquarters of his religious revival. He left Florence in 1487, only to return at the request of *Lorenzo de Medici, and it was at this time that he began to preach. His sermons at first were typically apocalyptic, warning the faithful to prepare themselves for the judgment of God that soon would come upon the world. At the time of the French invasion, however, Savonarola, having been perceived as a true prophet, and with the Medici having been exiled from the city, increased in prestige and power and was able to effect religious and political reforms. He sought to bring about a spiritual regeneration in the city by preaching millenarian sermons, and he claimed that he would lead Florence out of the "abomination of desolation." Florence was the beloved city of Christ, and the promises of God would be fulfilled in her. Florence had in the past promoted the myth that she would be the new Jerusalem and the new Rome, that is, the spiritual and political leader of Italy. Eschatological preaching was widespread in Europe in the late Middle Ages, and Savonarola's message was the most successful of those proclaiming the judgments of God and the coming apocalypse of Christ. Savonarola was in the right place at the right time, and he was sincere as well in his desires for reform. His first actions upon the departure of the French army were to supply alms and employment to the needy. His preaching and status as a prophet were sufficient to bring about the "Burning of the Vanities" in 1497, when the population of Florence brought wigs, masks, pornographic artworks, jewelry, and other evil and worldly items and burned them publicly. The event marked the abolition of the Lenten carnival in Florence.

Savonarola's disfavor with the pope only increased, all of the reforms and spiritual renewal notwithstanding. Alexander VI resented Savonarola's independent treaty with Charles VIII, which put Florence under the protection of the French monarchy. Also, the pope was related by marriage to the exiled Medici. He dealt with Savonarola and his own jealousies by excommunicating Savonarola in 1497. The preacher rejected the excommunication on the charge that

Alexander's election had been a result of simony. He suggested a general council of bishops to certify that Alexander was not a legitimate pope and to elect a new one. However, Florence, too, turned against its prophet upon the pope's threat of an interdict against the city. Consequently, Savonarola was tried for heresy, tortured, and condemned at the order of Alexander. He was hanged and then burned at the stake on 23 May 1498.

Bibliography: Rachel Erlanger, *The Unarmed Prophet: Savonarola in Florence*, 1988; Ronald M. Steinberg, *Fra Girolamo Savonarola, Florentine Art, and Renaissance Historiography*, 1977.

Paul Sheneman

Schiltberger, Hans (1380–1440?), or Johann, was the author of a popular travelbook that included some of the earliest autobiographical accounts in German. Almost all biographical information about Hans Schiltberger is found in his travelbook, compiled at the beginning of the fifteenth century. The travelbook consists of three major parts: Schiltberger's life story, which forms the narrative frame; a chronicle of Muslim and Mongol rulers; and the actual account of his travels that led him from Greece to western Siberia.

Born around 1380 in Munich, Schiltberger left his native city at the age of sixteen to follow King *Sigismund of Hungary's call to crusade against the Turks. The travelbook's biographical frame, echoing other literary models, such as *The Book of John Mandeville*, began the prologue in the form of a first-person narrative, establishing the writer's identity and vouching for the veracity of the traveler's account: "I, Johanns Schiltberger, left my home at the time King Sigmund of Hungary left for the land of the Infidels. All that I saw in the land of the Infidels . . . you will find described hereafter." The first section (chapters 1–3, 6, 30, 67) contained his description of the Battle of Nicopolis (25 September 1394), his escape from the massacre due to his young age, his captivity among the Turks and later among the Mongols, and his eventual escape and return to Bavaria. There, in 1427, he entered the service of Duke Albrecht III of Bavaria as chamberlain and remained in his service until his death in old age. In a chroniclelike second part (chapters 4–29), Schiltberger changed his narrative perspective and primarily related the political events during the reigns of Sultan Bayzid I and the Mongol leader Timur in the years 1396–1405. The third part (chapters 31–66) followed the convention of guides for pilgrims and other travelbooks, describing the countries and cities, religions, languages, and customs of the peoples, as well as various marvels of the world that Schiltberger claimed to have observed. A good deal of the accounts, however, can also be found in other travelbooks, most notably in *The Book of John Mandeville*. Thus, in the typical fashion of the late medieval travelbook, the frame narrative of Schiltberger's captivity and escape facilitated the dissemination of a largely encyclopedic book knowledge about different peoples and their cultures. However, details about Schiltberger's life in Turkish captivity and in particular his eye-witness account of the Battle of Nicopolis have been used as sociological and historical sources.

Bibliography: Johann Schiltberger, *The Bondage and Travels of Johann Schiltberger, A Native of Bavaria, in Europe, Asia, and Africa, 1396–1427*, trans. J. Buchan Telfer, 1879.

Martin Blum

Schöffer, Peter (c. 1425–1502/3). One of the first successful printers, Peter Schöffer is famed for his editions of impressive liturgical volumes (the Psalter and a missal), the first easy-to-read Bible, and the first herbals and legal books, along with the numerous innovations he made in the printing process. He was active from 1455 until his death, operating initially in partnership with *Johann Fust and then on his own. His most famous work is the *Psalterium* of 1457, which has the distinction of being the first volume to include the date, the name of the publisher, and the origin.

Peter Schöffer was born sometime between 1420 and 1430 into a family of small landowners in Gernsheim, Germany. He attended school in Mainz before studying at the Sorbonne in Paris. By 1455 he was in Mainz working with *Johann Gutenberg. Fust foreclosed on a loan to Gutenberg and acquired his printing press in lieu of payment in 1455. Schöffer then went to work with Fust, and their partnership flourished until 1466, when the last imprint (Cicero's *De officiis*) appeared. When Fust died in 1466, Schöffer took over the business. By 3 June 1469 he married his wife Christina, and they had four sons. He wanted to produce more numerous less expensive volumes than those available in man-uscript and so developed his print type, the new *fere humanistica*, from manu-script hands. The *Psalterium* of 1457 incorporated skillful copies of manuscript ornaments in red, blue, and purple and a series of splendid initial letters in Gothic round or "Lombardic" design. Once he had developed the means of printing the *Psalterium*, he followed this model for producing liturgical volumes with little variation. The next book to which he turned his hand, the *Rationale divinorum officiorum* of Durandus, posed a different problem: how to produce a volume with a large amount of text. The difficulty was solved through the use of double columns with a new small typeface called "Durandus." The *Constitutiones* of Pope *Clement V, the first church law book, followed nine months after this on 25 June 1462. The text was printed in two columns using a new, smaller, clearer Bible type with a commentary in the smaller "Durandus" type surrounding the text in the margins. In 1465 he produced Cicero's *De officiis*, the first book to incorporate Greek letters, and from 1463 a regular printed title page was employed by both Schöffer and Fust. Two decades later, in 1484, Schöffer created the first printed herbal in Latin, the *Herbarius*, with 150 wood-cuts of plants. This was followed a year later by one in German, *Hortus sanitatis*, in a new typeface that proved popular with German printers. These herbals were an unusual departure for Schöffer, who was not especially interested in illustration.

Altogether, both with Fust and by himself, Schöffer produced 188 items of fixed date and 65 of uncertain date, half of which were books, including 76 on liturgy and canon law, 11 on Roman law, and 10 on philology and grammar. Most were in Latin, with 18 in German mostly dating from the period after 1480. Apart from printing books, he produced pamphlets and broadsides of topical interest, the precursors of newspapers. He also ran off papal bulls, briefs, letters of indulgence, governmental decrees, political documents, almanacs, calendars, and publishers' circulars. As one can see from this list, he was patronized by the church and the state. He was the first European printer to set up a successful business that involved the selling of books both from his own press and from others, the use of traveling representatives, and attendance at the fair at Frankfurt (he became a citizen in 1479). His success is evident in the fact that by 1496 he owned three houses in Mainz and one in Frankfurt and was part of a consortium of nine investors mining metals in Nassau.

Peter Schöffer led the way in the early years of printing, providing models for other printers to follow. Although he was a conservative man who took great care to imitate manuscripts closely, he was at the same time incredibly innovative in taking up the challenges that the new medium of printing offered. These innovations are his lasting legacy.

Bibliography: Hellmut Lehmann-Haupt, *Peter Schöffer of Gernsheim and Mainz*, 1950; John Glyde Oswald, *A History of Printing: Its Development through Five Hundred Years*, 1928.

Bonnie Millar

Schongauer, Martin (c. 1450–90),

was a painter and printmaker from Colmar. He came from a family of goldsmiths; his father and two brothers were of that profession, while Martin and another brother became painters. It is thought that he served his painting apprenticeship with Caspar Isenmann.

Scholars have seen in his style a close affinity with *Rogier van der Weyden. Because he came from an area that was close to the crossroads of trade among the regions of Germany, France, and the Low Countries, it is hardly surprising that Schongauer's style reflected popular artists of other locations. As was the case with so many artists of the time, Schongauer's paintings were not signed, causing scholars to attribute them to the painter by virtue of style. Two attributed to him are the *Madonna in a Rose Arbor* and the *Holy Family*. This last work is very close in composition and style to his engraving of the same subject. Although today he is best known for his prints, in his own time Martin Schongauer was noted for his paintings. It is likely that Schongauer's first teacher for engraving was his father. Even in his early prints, Schongauer illustrated a mastery of line and form, using subtle gradations of gray and black to create texture, space, and depth in his compositions. The date of his first work was around 1470–75, indicating that he likely pursued both painting and printmaking from the period of his apprenticeship. Influences of figure style and composition from van der Weyden and *Dirc Bouts occurred in Schongauer's first engravings, as may be seen in the *Madonna and Child with Parrot* and *Nativity*, both from around 1470–75. In his *Rest on the Flight into Egypt* (c. 1475), he anticipated the lush foliage and complex use of crosshatching employed by Albrecht Dürer.

One of the engraver's most influential prints was his *Temptation of Saint Anthony*, in which the saint was literally being pulled and tortured by demons of uncommon violence. This composition influenced Dürer and Michelangelo, who both owned his prints, and perhaps also Grünewald and *Hieronymus Bosch, whose later versions of this subject bore remarkably close kinship to the elements of composition and figure style found in Schongauer's work. In his *Crucifixion*, Schongauer introduced a wealth of drapery folds and textures that mirrored the work of the Flemish painters. In his ambitious *Carrying of the Cross to Calvary*, he illustrated more than fifty figures surrounding the figure of Christ, who had fallen beneath the weight of the cross. He set the scene in a darkening, atmospheric landscape. His graphic work was certainly the equal of that of the painters of his period and helped to establish engraving as a major medium for artistic expression in the fifteenth century. Schongauer's subjects ranged from the religious, as just discussed, to the secular, to ornamental. Most of his prints have the mark M (cross) S at the lower edge.

Bibliography: C. Minott, *Martin Schongauer*, 1971.

Marian Hollinger

Sebonde, Ramon de. *See* Sibiuda, Ramon de.

Sellyng, William (c. 1430–94). One of England's protohumanists, William Sellyng is best remembered for promoting humanist studies, namely, the study of Latin eloquence and the Greek language, and for his patronage of Thomas Linacre. During his career as prior of Christ Church in Canterbury, Sellyng served as envoy to Rome and as a peace negotiator with *Charles VIII of France.

William Sellyng was born sometime around 1430 in Kent, England. Early in life he entered the Benedictine order, and by 1448 he completed his studies at the monastery school in Canterbury. He was sent to Canterbury College, Oxford, to continue his education. At Oxford, Sellyng studied the classical authors, attended courses on Latin rhetoric that the Italian scholar Stefano Surigone was offering, and composed Latin orations. His interest in humanist subjects can be traced to these student years at Oxford. In 1454 he was ordained a priest and continued his theological studies at Oxford, earning his degree of bachelor of divinity on 7 February 1458. Sellyng obtained leave from Oxford in 1464 to continue his education abroad. Probably at the urging of Surigone, Sellyng departed for Italy. He studied at the Universities of Padua and Bologna, where on

22 March 1466 he was awarded his doctor of divinity. In Bologna Sellyng acquired his knowledge of Greek from the Byzantine scholar Andronicus Callistus. Sellyng returned to Canterbury in early 1469.

In October 1469 Christ Church Abbey in Canterbury sent Sellyng and a companion, a monk named Reginald Goldstone, to Rome to supplicate Pope Paul II for indulgences for the upcoming Jubilee of St. Thomas Becket. Sellyng was chosen for this mission because of his previous experience in Italy and his skill in Latin oratory. During their stay in Rome they were befriended by Pietro Mellini, an ecclesiastical lawyer well known in English monastic circles, and by the bishop of Urbino, whose assistance secured the sought-after privileges. This sojourn to Rome was short, and in 1470 Sellyng, back in Canterbury, was appointed chancellor of his monastery. At this time he began teaching Greek in the monastery school, and two years later he was elected prior of Christ Church. During his priorship he established the systematic teaching of Greek at his school, which became a center for the spread of Greek teaching to other parts of England. His most celebrated pupil was Thomas Linacre, England's most famous early humanist, who received his early instruction at Sellyng's monastery school and learned Greek from Sellyng himself. Sellyng took a personal interest in Linacre and sent him to study at Oxford in 1480.

Sellyng's reputation as a scholar, orator, and diplomat continued to grow, and in 1486 he was appointed one of King *Henry VII's ambassadors to the pope. In 1487 he was sent, along with the bishops of Durham and Hereford, on a mission to Rome. Sellyng invited his former pupil Linacre to accompany him to Italy so that Linacre could further his education; in Padua he introduced Linacre to *Angelo Poliziano. In Rome, Sellyng himself appeared before Pope *Innocent VIII to deliver the king's message. Sellyng's diplomatic activities continued in 1490 when he was sent to France as one of the envoys to negotiate for peace with Charles VIII of France.

In 1494, at the height of his political and scholarly career, Sellyng died. Sellyng's place in the history of classical scholarship and humanist studies is considerable. He contributed to improving the standards of Latin eloquence both at Christ Church and in the government more broadly. As a Greek scholar, he translated at least one work into Latin, collected an extensive library of Greek manuscripts, established the teaching of Greek at his monastery school, and encouraged its teaching throughout England.

Bibliography: Anthony Goodman and Angus MacKay, eds., *The Impact of Humanism on Western Europe*, 1990; Roberto Weiss, *Humanism in England during the Fifteenth Century*, 3rd ed., 1967.

Darin Hayton

Sforza, Caterina (1462?–1509). Born the illegitimate daughter of the second Sforza duke of Milan, Caterina Sforza became one of the most influential women in Renaissance Italian politics as a ruler and as a military strategist.

Though Caterina was illegitimate, she was still a Sforza and thus was valuable as a marriage pawn. Her 1477 marriage cemented an alliance between Milan and Rome. Her husband, Girolamo Riario, nephew of Pope, *Sixtus IV, was installed as vicar and virtual ruler of the city of Imola and served as a spokesman for the pope. Caterina now found herself thrust into the center of Renaissance political intrigue. The marriage was generally happy, and Caterina produced children quickly.

Girolamo's position at the papal court ensured Caterina's social standing, and she even had the semblance of her own court in Rome. With Sixtus IV's death in 1484, Girolamo and Caterina hoped to influence the next papal election. Riots broke out in Rome, and the pope's residence, the Castel Sant' Angelo, was besieged. A heavily pregnant Caterina swung into action, riding to the fortress and holding it against the rioters until the new pope could take over. Girolamo reached an agreement with the cardinals without Caterina's approval, and she was forced, reluctantly, to hand over the fortress, but her reputation as a military leader was made.

Caterina and Girolamo moved to the city of Forlì in Romagna and established a tenuous rule there; financially strapped, they attempted to tax their subjects. Girolamo fell ill, and Caterina became the real ruler of Forlì and Imola; Girolamo's illness resulted in fits of temper, which in turn angered his subjects. A conspiracy developed, and Girolamo was assassinated in 1488. At risk, Caterina barricaded herself and her children in the city's fortress, but it was quickly overrun. Through negotiation, however, she won her freedom once more and restored her rule with the help of Milan.

She avenged her husband's murder (quite brutally) and rather quickly embarked on a romantic affair with Giacomo Feo. They had a son together, and she continued to consolidate her rule in Forlì, but ignored complaints about the arrogance of Giacomo. Italy was plunged into war when France invaded in 1494, but Caterina remained neutral. Tensions in Forlì against Giacomo continued to rise and resulted in his assassination in 1495. The revenge Caterina wreaked in the aftermath of this murder was truly vicious, and her subjects respected and feared her as a result.

Caterina then looked to increase her dominions, but was prevented from doing so by Venice. She embarked on yet another love affair, this time with Giovanni de Medici, which seemed to bring her closer to an alliance with Florence. She secretly married Giovanni and had a son by him in 1498, though Giovanni died of illness a short time afterwards.

Pope *Alexander VI's son, Cesare Borgia, married into the French royal family and sided with France against Milan, forming a league between the pope, France, and Venice. Caterina was thus further alienated from Milan, and she became determined to hold on to Forlì and Imola. France conquered Milan and now seemed poised to take over Italy. Cesare saw the opportunity to consolidate the Papal States and moved to conquer Forlì and Imola. This time there was no one to help Caterina, and she eventually retreated to her fortress, which she defended to the last man. She was finally forced to surrender the fortress, and savage retribution followed; Caterina was turned over to Cesare, who raped her as his prize of war.

Caterina had sent her children away, and the French claimed her under rights of protection. Cesare, having taken Forlì and Imola, still wanted Caterina as his prisoner, but was forced to yield her to the French. The French imprisoned her until she signed over her rights to Forlì and Imola, which she finally did in 1501, after her sons had aligned with the Borgias. Released from prison, she still had hopes of regaining her position, but by the summer of 1504 she knew that her hopes were groundless, and she went into retirement. Instead, she concentrated her ambition on her children, particularly Giovanni, her Medici son. Her health began to fail, and she died in May 1509, leaving a legendary image behind—a man in a woman's body. Though Caterina was a woman, she embodied all the values and ideals of the Renaissance prince.

Bibliography: A. Braschi, *Caterina Sforza*, 1965; Ernst Breisach, *Caterina Sforza*, 1967.

Connie Evans

Sforza, Francesco (1401–66), was a mercenary soldier best known for his great resolve in battle and for his strength. He became a soldier in his father's army at the age of twelve and fought in his first battle at fifteen. Throughout his life Francesco battled for and against the duke of Milan, ultimately becoming the duke of Milan himself in 1450. Francesco devoted his last years to making peace in Italy.

Francesco Sforza was born on 23 July 1401 at San Miniato, an illegitimate son of Muzio Attendolo, founder of the Sforza dynasty and one of the most successful condottiere of his time. In January 1424 Muzio drowned in the Pescara River, and Francesco took command of his father's troops. Only twenty-three years old, he had already won twenty-two battles and held the confidence of his father's soldiers. Francesco and his army, like most soldiers at that time in Italy, were mercenaries, fighting for anyone who hired them.

Francesco Sforza served the duke of Milan, *Filippo Maria Visconti, faithfully for many years, but the relationship between the two men vacillated throughout their lives. In 1428 the duke, becoming suspicious of Francesco, imprisoned him for two years. However, the duke needed Francesco's great skill as a soldier to defend against the Florentines, so he hired him again to lead the campaign. In addition, the duke arranged a marriage between Francesco and Bianca Maria, the duke's daughter, in order to stabilize the relationship between himself and Francesco. At the time of this arrangement, Bianca was eight years old, and Sforza was thirty-one. The pair actually married ten years later.

After defeating the Florentines in Tuscany for the duke, Francesco went on to conquer the March of Ancona, a district along the Adriatic Sea, for himself. He captured the province in twenty-three days, and the pope made Francesco marquis of March in 1433, a title he held during the next fourteen years. Francesco continued to fight both for and against the duke of Milan during this time and in 1439 joined other armies in a war against Milan.

In the summer of 1441 Francesco married Bianca; she was then seventeen, and he was forty-one. Their marriage was against the wishes of the duke of Milan, who wished to postpone the wedding in light of recent hostilities. Despite these strains, their marriage was a happy one, producing eight children (Francesco already had one child by his first wife, who had died, and he had eleven illegitimate children throughout his life also).

The following year the duke of Milan formed an alliance with Pope *Eugenius IV and with two powerful rulers, the lord of Rimini and *Alfonso the Magnanimous. He wished to drive Francesco out of the March of Ancona. Thus began a five-year war, with Francesco losing badly toward the end. However, before it ended, Filippo Visconti realized that he needed his son-in-law's help with another war the duke was losing to Venice, and so he asked Francesco for aid. Refusing at first, Francesco changed his mind and demanded 240,000 gold florins and the right to rule the Duchy of Milan in the duke's name as his commander-in-chief; the duke had no choice but to agree.

On his way to Milan, Francesco received the news that Duke Filippo Visconti had died. Francesco now began to fight for possession of Milan, proclaiming himself the rightful duke because of his marriage to Bianca. Now, instead of defending Milan against the Venetians, he led the Venetians against Milan. The people of Milan felt that Francesco had betrayed them—they were starving and suffering because of the long war—and a proclamation went out that anyone who spoke favorably about Francesco would be executed. The political winds soon shifted once again as Venice sided with Milan against Francesco. Although each city had an army much greater than his, Francesco tightened his grip on Milan while the Venetians were slow to arrive on the scene. In March 1450 Milan surrendered to Francesco, and, taking possession of the city as its new duke, he was cautiously welcomed by citizens who were happy that the war was finally over.

As the duke of Milan, Francesco ruled one of the most important states in Italy, second only to Venice in financial and military power. He became a popular and beloved leader and accomplished many things in his last twelve years. He built a great hospital, and he continued the construction of the Cathedral of St. Ambrose in Milan and the Certosa of Pavia. Moreover, he created a new order of knighthood and initiated 150 of his officers and supporters into it. In 1459 Francesco met Pope *Pius II, who greatly admired him. All told, Francesco was a great statesmen, general, and diplomat. Francesco Sforza died on 7 March 1466 in Milan, of dropsy, at the age of sixty-four. His eldest son, Galeazzo, was his heir.

Bibliography: Denys Hay and John Law, *Italy in the Age of the Renaissance, 1380–1530*, 1989; Michael Mallett, *Mercenaries and Their Masters*, 1974; Lauro Martines, *Power and Imagination: City-States in Renaissance Italy*, 1988.

Sigrid Kelsey

Sforza, Ludovico, "il Moro" (1451–1508), is probably best known today for his love of Renaissance culture. Under Ludovico's direction, the Milanese court became a center for intellectual exchange and artistic initiative. In a period renowned as the "Golden Age of Milan," figures as exceptional as *Leonardo da Vinci and *Donato Bramante were drawn to his court and his generosity. The Milanese people affectionately referred to him as il Moro, a derivative of his baptismal name, Maurus, which can be translated simultaneously as both "Moor" and "mulberry." Ludovico adopted both meanings as his symbols, the Moors because he admired their culture and resourcefulness, and the mulberry because it was popularly assumed to be the wisest of all trees. These emblems are suggestive of the values he appreciated and cultivated.

Ludovico was born in 1451 at Vigevano, Italy, youngest son of the condottiere duke *Francesco Sforza and Bianca Maria Visconti. His parents' marriage marked the union of two of the most influential families in Milanese history. The Sforzas had a long history as fierce and shrewd condottieri, manifest in the name Sforza itself (meaning "the powerful"), a nickname given to Ludovico's grandfather, Muzio Attendolo, in recognition of his valor. The Visconti family had been dukes of Milan since 1395, when *Giangaleazzo Visconti bought the title from Emperor *Wenceslas for 100,000 florins. However, upon the death of his youngest son, *Filippo Maria, the duchy was left without a direct male heir. Francesco's claim through marriage to Filippo Maria's illegitimate daughter and his reputation as a great military leader were sufficient to win him the lordship. Ludovico was born the following year.

When Francesco Sforza died in 1466, he was succeeded by his eldest son, Galeazzo Maria. During his time in power, Galeazzo Maria proved to be both tyrannical and cruel. His harsh policies led to his assassination in 1476 by three young idealists, leaving his seven-year-old son and heir, Giangaleazzo Maria (named for his Visconti predecessor), with his wife, Bona of Savoy, as regent. Her regency was fleeting, however, as Ludovico forced her to resign in 1480; this left him, as male guardian, in complete control of the duchy. Even after he reached his majority, Giangaleazzo remained merely a figurehead in Milanese politics, and Ludovico's recognized primacy is evidenced by petitions from the Milanese provinces. Rather than appealing to the legitimate duke, these requests were habitually addressed to Ludovico il Moro. His position as usurper, essentially, went unchallenged by the Milanese owing to the weak character of the rightful duke. Giangaleazzo has been described as "sickly," "frivolous," and an "incompetent nonentity." He was easily manipulated by his uncle; and yet, ironically, it was Ludovico's capacity to manipulate that eventually led to his undoing.

In 1488 Ludovico arranged a marriage between Giangaleazzo and Isabella of Aragon, daughter of King Alfonso II of Naples. Three years later Ludovico himself married Isabella's cousin, *Beatrice d'Este. A great rivalry promptly sprang up between the two cousins. Isabella, disappointed with her impotent title and jealous of her cousin's authority, assailed her father with complaints and grievances. These protests against Ludovico's expropriation of ducal power multiplied after 1493 with the birth of Ercole (later called Massimiliano), Ludovico's first son and heir. Soon after this event Giangaleazzo unexpectedly fell ill and died, and contemporaries universally believed that he had been poisoned by his uncle. Following his death, the dukedom should have rightfully fallen to Francesco, Giangaleazzo's minor son, with Isabella as regent, but Ludovico intervened once again. He seized the dukedom for himself with the full support of the Milanese councilors, who deemed the political climate too tempestuous for the rule of a minor. With this act he not only dispossessed the duchess of Milan, but also made the Neapolitan king a permanent enemy.

In order to protect himself from the wrath of his Neapolitan in-laws, Ludovico took it upon himself to encourage *Charles VIII of France in his territorial ambitions. Charles wished to assert his claim to the Crown of Naples, rightfully his by descent from the Angevin rulers. Ludovico's support motivated Charles to pursue his pretensions. The French invasion of 1494 was a massive success, halted only by the onslaught of southern diseases. Charles died soon after and was succeeded by his cousin, Louis XII, who ardently resumed Charles's conquest with an added incentive, a dormant claim to the dukedom of Milan through the Visconti line. Ludovico Sforza fled Milan without a single blow in his defense. In 1500 he was captured by Louis and was imprisoned in France, where he died in a dungeon eight years later.

Ludovico Sforza was an enlightened and capable ruler. His extravagant tastes and aggressive foreign policy, however, greatly impaired his finances, leaving him without the necessary funds to hire and pay troops to fight against the French. During his time in power Milan experienced a period of political stability and artistic creativity. Nonetheless, at the time of his death Milan was thrust into an era of political chaos and cultural regression, suggesting that Ludovico's achievements were, in the end, shallow and evanescent.

Bibliography: David Abulafia, ed., *The French Descent into Renaissance Italy, 1494–95: Antecedents and Effects*, 1995; D. M. Bueno de Mesquita, "Ludovico Sforza and His Vassals," in *Italian Renaissance Studies: A Tribute to the Late Cecilia M. Ady*, ed. E. F. Jacob, 1960; Lauro Martines, *Power and Imagination: City-States in Renaissance Italy*, 1988.

Sara Butler

Sibiuda, Ramon (d. 1436), or Raymonde de Sebonde, has been described as the most significant philosopher in France in the early fifteenth century. His preeminent work, *Liber creaturarum*, has been available in print from the time of its completion in 1436 until the present. In the *Liber creaturarum*, Sibiuda provided an instrument by which humans could access the truths of God and of Christian living. Sibiuda conveyed his message through a combination of appeals to faith and reason.

Few facts surrounding Sibiuda's life can be confirmed. His date of birth is unknown, and his birthplace has been listed as both France and Spain. According to one account, Sibiuda left papers shortly before his death with the University of Tolosa in France, where he was both a professor and the university's rector, stating that he was born in Spain but naming no particular city. Even the spelling of Sibiuda's name is indeterminate; at least fourteen different spellings appear in the manuscripts and studies of his works, including Sabiendel, Sebundus, and Sebonde. Discrepancies in spelling appear even into the present, with Spanish scholars favoring Sibiuda, while French scholars prefer Sebond. Even the title of his great work, *Liber creaturarum*, has variants; thus in the second printing, his work was entitled *Theologia naturalis*. Although the former title, *Liber creaturarum*, is generally preferred, all nineteenth- and twentieth-century editions list both titles.

Sibiuda served the University of Tolosa until his death there in 1436. Living in the early fifteenth century, Sibiuda experienced the transitions in thought and philosophy characteristic of the shift from the Middle Ages to the Renaissance. His intellectual, theological, and philosophical environment was shaped by significant events in religious history, such as the church's active persecution of popular "heretics" like *John Wyclif of England, and in literary history, such as the invention and widespread use of *Johann Gutenberg's printing press. Philosophical thought was shifting from a more abstract and theologically based Scholasticism to one more informed by empirical methods, valuing the observance of nature and a focus on human beings and their relationship to nature. It is difficult to categorize Sibiuda's work, arising from this pivotal moment in history, as characteristic of any particular tradition. The *Liber creaturarum* reflects elements of major philosophical schools of thought, such as that of the Augustinians and of the adherents of *Ramon Llull; however, while most scholars recognize elements of these and other traditions in his texts, they do not argue for his work as representative of one particular approach.

According to several sources, the *Liber creaturarum* was begun in 1434 and completed in 1436. It was written in imperfect, late medieval Latin. While it was virtually unknown in Spain, it was widely disseminated in France and Germany, thanks in part to Gutenberg's press. The text can be described as an attempt to use philosophical ideas, such as those related to Llullism, to prove the truths of Christian faith. The text is divided into six parts that have been categorized as follows: (1) the human and God; (2) the kindness of nature and the comparison of humans with natural things; (3) the two loves, conversion and perversion, in the two cities; (4) love toward God and his honor; (5) fallen man and sin; and (6) justification of man, the Christian man, and the sacraments. Largely due to the contents of the Prologue, the text was placed on several indexes of prohibited books from 1559 to 1583. Such indexes listed works labeled by church leaders as heretical. The Prologue argued that the experience of humans and their faith in God can be proven. As a result of this ban, many of the earliest printed copies of the *Liber creaturarum* were published without the Prologue.

Sibiuda's work influenced many thinkers into the next century and beyond, largely as a result of Michel de Montaigne. Montaigne was so moved by the beauty of Sibiuda's text and by Sibiuda's piety that he translated the text into French and published it in 1569 under the title *Theologie naturelle*. Completed at the request of his father, Montaigne's translation has been judged to be very exact. Montaigne also composed an essay entitled *Apologie de Raymond Sebond* that he included in his *Essais*. Montaigne's interest in and praise of Sibiuda's work served to make Sibiuda and his work visible and accessible into the present.

Bibliography: J. N. Hillgarth, *Ramon Lull and Lullism in Fourteenth-Century France*, 1971; Friedrich Stegmülier, introduction to *Theologia naturalis seu Liber creaturarum*, by Raimundus Sabundus, 1852/1966.

Colleen A. Reilly

Siena, Bernardino da. *See* Bernardino of Siena.

Siena, Saint Catherine of. *See* Catherine of Siena, Saint.

Sigismund, Holy Roman Emperor (b. 1368, r. 1411–37). During his life Sigismund, the last emperor of the house of Luxembourg, a man who described himself as a second Charlemagne, received the titles holy Roman emperor, king of Hungary, king of Bohemia, king of the Germans, and king of Lombardy and was instrumental in healing the Papal Schism that divided the church. Sigismund was born on 15 February 1368, the younger son of Holy Roman Emperor Charles IV. Upon his father's death in 1378, he was sent to the Hungarian court to be near his betrothed, Mary, the daughter of King *Louis I of Hungary and Poland. Sigismund raised an army to persuade Louis to honor the arrangement made by Charles IV, and he was eventually married to Mary. Mary became queen of Hungary upon her father's death in 1382, and Sigismund was crowned king consort in 1387.

Sigismund's expansionist policies led him to intervene in the struggles between his half brother *Wenceslas, king of Germany and Bohemia, and the Bohemian nobility. After changing sides many times, Sigismund finally sided with Wenceslas in 1396 at the Battle of Nicopolis and was appointed vicar general of Germany as a reward for his support. In September 1396 Sigismund led a European army against the Turks who had moved into Serbia and Bulgaria. His army was defeated, and Sigismund himself barely escaped capture. This terrible defeat persuaded Sigismund that only a united Christian world could end the Islamic threat to Europe, and he spent much of his life pursuing that goal.

King Wenceslas was deposed in 1400, and Sigismund took advantage of the ensuing political confusion by trying to take Bohemia and imprisoning Wenceslas in 1402. An invasion of Hungary in 1403 forced Sigismund to return to defend his holdings, and so he released Wenceslas.

After the death of King *Rupert III of Germany in 1410, Sigismund and another contender for the throne, Jobst, were both elected king by opposing factions. Jobst's death in 1411 removed all competition, and Sigismund was named king of Germany, but the next few years were full of conflict. Sigismund campaigned in Italy against the Venetians and persuaded one of the three rival popes, John XXIII, to call the Council of Constance to settle the Great Schism. His coronation as king of Germany took place in Aachen in November 1414, and after his coronation he traveled to Constance to participate in the council.

At the Council of Constance, the Czech reformer *Jan Hus was burned as a heretic. Sigismund had personally invited him to defend his views at the council and had guaranteed his safe-conduct, but it is not known whether or not Sigismund had planned to have Hus arrested and tried after all. The outcome of the council was a reunited Western church.

Wenceslas died in 1419, and so Sigismund inherited the Bohemian crown, but a series of unsuccessful wars against the Hussites in the 1420s delayed his coronation. Since Sigismund was frequently absent from Germany during these years, the German princes formed the Union of Bingen. This union was supposed to allow the nobles to wage war against the Hussites more effectively while Sigismund was absent, but it also allowed them some autonomy from imperial control as well.

In 1431 Sigismund received the Lombard crown, was crowned emperor in 1433, and was finally received in Prague as king of Bohemia in 1436. As emperor and king of Hungary, he was aware of the importance of the bourgeois economy. In Hungary, he limited the control of feudal lords over market towns and strengthened these trade centers by giving them independent legal jurisdiction. He tried to achieve economic unity in Hungary with tactics like uniform export prohibitions. He also tried to block the import of Venetian merchandise into Europe.

As a crusader, Sigismund was always concerned with the presence of the Turks and with heretical teachings. He was an avid persecutor of heretical teachings and even organized an anti-Hussite crusade against his own subjects. Peace finally came in 1436 when Sigismund accepted the Compact of Basel, which permitted free preaching of the Hussite doctrine in Bohemia. He died on 9 December of the following year.

Bibliography: F.R.H. DuBoulay, *Germany in the Later Middle Ages*, 1983; Joachim Leuschner, *Germany in the Late Middle Ages*, 1980; Gerald Strauss, *Pre-Reformation Germany*, 1972.

John D. Grosskopf

Sixtus IV, Pope (b. 1414, r. 1471–84), formerly Francesco della Rovere (or Francesco da Savona). Born into a humble family engaged in commerce and civic affairs, Francesco was largely a self-made prelate who rose rapidly in the

Franciscan order due to his exceptional abilities as a theologian and an organizer. He was born on 21 July 1414 into the della Rovere family in or near the small town of Celle in Liguria, but he always regarded Savona, the nearest city, as his place of origin. Until he became cardinal, he went by the name Francesco da Savona, and as pope he was very generous to Savona and the Savonese. He received his education from the Franciscans before studying at the University of Padua, where he earned his doctorate in 1444. For the next several years Francesco pursued a university career. His lectures in logic and philosophy attracted enthusiastic listeners in Padua, Perugia, Bologna, Siena, and Florence. His growing reputation in academic circles was matched by growing respect and responsibilities within the Franciscan order. *John Bessarion, cardinal of Nicaea, admired Francesco's scholarship and made him his personal confessor sometime before 1459. On 16 May 1464 the assembled representatives of Francesco's order elected him minister general of the three Minorite orders. Largely on the suggestion of Bessarion, Paul II elevated Francesco to cardinal on 18 September 1467. Upon the unexpected death of Paul II in 1471, a conclave of cardinals took only three days to elect Francesco as the new pope, Sixtus IV.

The accession of Sixtus to the Holy See was typical of a period in papal history in which the familial and political concerns of the popes took precedence over their spiritual concerns. Within months of his election, Sixtus made a concerted effort to win the favor of the princes of Italy and Europe by lavishing gifts of benefices and spiritual concessions on them. His largess also extended conspicuously toward his own family; in addition to making six nephews cardinals (one of whom later became Pope Julius II), Sixtus usually did not hesitate to grant benefices to the many Ligurians who could claim to be related to him by blood or marriage. The nepotism for which historians remember Sixtus was not driven by mere generosity but helped him to fill high church offices with persons he could trust to carry out his policies. Nepotism as a policy of government led Sixtus into the Pazzi conspiracy of 1478 in which Girolamo Riarlo, Sixtus's nephew and preferred political advisor, instigated a feud between the Medici and the Pazzi families over monetary and commercial interests. Girolamo, with Sixtus's knowledge, attempted to oust the Medici from power in Florence by planning the murder of *Lorenzo and *Giuliano de Medici. Lorenzo escaped wounded, but Giuliano was killed, and Sixtus found himself at war with Florence from 1478 to 1480. Sixtus's nepotism and political activity threw papal finances into disorder, and in 1482, in response to complaints about the abuses of the papal court, Archbishop Andrea Zamometič attempted unsuccessfully to convene a council at Basel at which Sixtus would have had to justify his conduct.

Sixtus had mixed success in matters more directly related to church affairs. He worked for the reunion of the Russian church with Rome, but to no avail. In 1478 he established the Spanish Inquisition, and in 1482–83 he attempted to curb its abuses. He enthusiastically supported a crusade against the Turks, but failed to win the support of other European rulers, and his only notable success was in recapturing the Italian town of Otranto from the Turks in 1482. In that same year he canonized the Franciscan theologian Bonaventure.

Sixtus's greatest achievements came in his role as patron of the arts. He transformed Rome from a medieval to a Renaissance city. Under his direction, streets were opened, widened, and paved. The Ponte Sisto over the Tiber was built, and the new Hospital of Santo Spirito was founded. In addition to the churches of Santa Maria della Pace and Santa Maria del Popolo, he erected the Sistine Chapel and had it decorated by the Umbrian masters. He patronized many writers, musicians, painters, and sculptors, founded the Sistine choir, established the Vatican archives, and was the second founder of the Vatican Library. He was also the author of theological treatises on issues dividing the Franciscans and Dominicans, including *De sanguine Christi* and *De futuris contingentibus*. Sixtus died in Rome on 12 August 1484; his bronze tomb, created by Antonio del Pollaluolo and located in the grotto of Saint Peter's Basilica, is regarded as a masterpiece of Renaissance art.

Bibliography: Egmont Lee, *Sixtus IV and Men of Letters*, 1978; J.A.F. Thomson, *Popes and Princes, 1417–1517*, 1980.

Susan Arvay

Sprenger, Jakob (c. 1436–95), was a German Dominican, inquisitor general of the Rhineland, and a theologian and professor at the University of Cologne. Known for his zeal in the Inquisition, he was particularly interested in the prosecution of sorcery and was coauthor of the *Malleus maleficarum* with *Heinrich Krämer (Henricus Institoris). He also founded the first German Brotherhood of the Rosary.

Jakob Sprenger was born around 1436–38 in Rheinfelden, close to Basel. Admitted into the order of Friars Preachers in Basel on 25 November 1452, he took his vows in 1453 and remained in the Basel convent until 1467. Transferred to Cologne, he enrolled in the Faculty of Theology at the University of Cologne on 6 April 1467, and by 1468 he was already teaching at the university in preparation for the master's of theology. He acquired a preaching license in 1471 and his doctorate in 1474 or 1475. Meanwhile, he was appointed prior of the cloister of Cologne in 1472, a post that he held until 1488. Cologne at the time was the most important cloister in Germany, and Sprenger simultaneously held the position of grand vicar for the reformed convents of Brabantia. It was in 1475 that he founded the Fraternitas de Rosario. On 19 December 1478 he was named professor of theology at Cologne, and on 30 June 1480 he was elected dean of the faculty.

Sprenger's career in the Inquisition began in 1481 when Pope *Sixtus IV appointed him, along with Gerhard von Elten, to the post of inquisitor general of the dioceses of Mainz, Cologne, and Trier. He specialized in cases of witchcraft, with which the people of the Rhine valley in Germany were very nearly obsessed at the time. *Innocent VIII began his papacy in 1484 by issuing the bull *Summis desiderantes affectibus*, which treated sorcery as a relatively new threat and granted Sprenger authority to conduct an inquisition against witchcraft in the Archdiocese of Salzburg. The pope also called upon Sprenger's Dominican colleague Heinrich Krämer to prosecute this heresy. The two friars wrote the *Malleus maleficarum* (Hammer of sorceresses), which expanded upon the ideas of Innocent's bull and detailed the ways in which witchcraft was to be discovered and eradicated.

The *Malleus* was largely the work of Krämer, though editors and commentators later considered it mostly or solely the work of Sprenger. As the title suggests, its target was sorceresses, since the female gender was thought to have a predilection for this particular heresy. Women, according to the authors, were of inherently weak character, easily corrupted by carnal passions. It was felt that their depravity might lead them to consecrate themselves to demons, engaging in diabolical pacts, carnal acts with succubi and incubi, child sacrifice, and of course, total renunciation of the Christian faith. Marginal, maladjusted, and taciturn persons were particularly suspected of witchcraft. Most witches were supposed to be found among midwives, since they had the greatest opportunities to affect pregnancies, cause abortions, cast impotency spells upon men, and obtain children for devouring or sacrifice. The authors cited biblical injunctions, canon law, patristic writings, and examples culled from Alpine folklore on demonology.

First published in 1486, the *Malleus* was enormously successful and appeared in twenty-eight editions thereafter. More than 30,000 copies were printed between 1486 and 1669. Two important editions are those of Cologne, 1511, with an apology defending the work against its detractors, and of Frankfurt, 1582, with a second tome containing various other treatises on sorcery. It paved the way for the witch-hunts that ravaged Christendom in the next few centuries.

On 8 May 1488 Sprenger was elected provincial vicar of Pforzheim and was confirmed on 18 June. In the next few years he led the reforms of many cloisters, but accusations arose that he provoked discord in the convents of his province, and that he had a proud and haughty demeanor. On 23 April 1495 Pope *Alexander VI thus demanded that the Dominicans relieve him of his duties. The following 20 November, however, Alexander rescinded his order since the charges proved to be baseless, but Sprenger probably never received this news. He died unexpectedly on 6 December 1495 in the cloister of St. Nicolaus in Undis at Strassburg, where he was buried in the nave.

Bibliography: Heinrich Krämer and Jacob Sprenger, *Malleus Maleficarum of Heinrich Krämer and Jacob Sprenger*, trans. Montague Summers, 1971; Brian Levack, *The Witch-Hunt in Early Modern Europe*, 2nd ed., 1995.

Michael Lindsey

Suso, Heinrich (c. 1295–1366), or Seuse, whose original name was Heinrich von Berg, was also known as Blessed Henry Suso and by the pseudonym Amandus, adopted for his writings. One of the most famous German mystics of the late Middle Ages, Suso was a leader of the Gottesfreunde movement (Friends of God), a company of devout ascetic Rhinelanders, both men and women, who shunned the world and advocated an intimate association with God. In explicating the unitive spiritual relationship, Suso's works described the interior life as an intensely personal experience. Suso is widely regarded as the first important male mystic to incorporate autobiographical accounts of mystical experiences on such a large scale into his writings. His works, largely composed in the vernacular, were some of the most popular of the Middle Ages, and he was renowned in his lifetime as a preacher.

Suso was born at Constance in Switzerland on 21 March of a year around 1295. Of noble parentage, Suso entered the Dominican order at Constance at age thirteen, where he undertook his preparatory, philosophical, and theological studies. His family was probably the von Bergs who were originally ministerials to the archbishop of Constance but who, in Henry's time, had moved from the countryside into the town of Constance. While retaining their nobility, they had been forced by changing circumstances to take some sort of trade not considered demeaning. Henry's mother's name was Sus or Süs, and she came from the town of Überlingen, which, like Constance, was situated on the shore of Lake Constance. Later, supposedly out of respect for her, Henry assumed her family name.

Between 1322 and 1325 Henry studied theology in the Dominican *studium generale* (seminary) at Cologne under the tutelage of *Johan Eckhart, "the Master," and probably in the company of *Johann Tauler, both celebrated contemporary mystics. Around 1326 Suso returned to teach at Constance, where he composed his first work, the *Büchlein der Wahrheit* (Little book of truth) in defense of Eckhart, whose works had been denounced as heterodox in 1327. His masterpiece, *Das Büchlein der ewigen Weisheit* (Little book of eternal wisdom), was published in 1328. The practical nature of this work, written in plain language, appealed to the simple unperfected soul, and it became one of the most popular religious treatises of the Middle Ages. The work is often compared to the *Homilies* of St. Bernard and *The Imitation of Christ* of *Thomas à Kempis. Suso was also widely renowned as a composer of *Minnesang* and in modern scholarship has been called "the last of the *Minnesinger*." He was also one of the few lyric poets among the mystics of his time.

Suso's defence of Eckhart led to suspicion of his own works, but they were found to be entirely orthodox. However, sometime between 1327 and 1330 Suso was removed from the office of lector, probably because of his defense of Eckhart, who had been condemned by the pope in 1329. At this time he translated *Das Büchlein der ewigen Weisheit* into Latin, adding considerably to its contents and renaming it *Horologium sapientiae*. This extensively reworked edition, described by James M. Clark as "even more elevating than the original, finished in language, rich in figure, rhythmic in movement," became a favorite book in the cloisters at the close of the Middle Ages, not only in Germany, but also in the Netherlands, France, Italy, and England.

Toward the end of his life Suso edited his vernacular works as he wished them to survive in composite form into a volume that he called *The Exemplar*. This work contained his *Life*, the *Little Book of Eternal Wisdom*, the *Little Book of Truth* and the *Little Book of Letters*. Suso's focus on the interior life and the simplicity and accessibility of the language of his writings gave him mass appeal, hence his extreme popularity in later ages. His death date is recorded as 25 January 1366, and he was declared blessed by Pope Gregory XVI in 1831, who assigned his feast in the Dominican order to March 2.

Bibliography: James M. Clark, *The Great German Mystics: Eckhart, Tauler, and Suso*, 1949; Henry Suso, *Henry Suso: The Exemplar with Two German Sermons*, ed. and trans. Frank Tobin, 1989.

Claire McIlroy

Sweden, Saint Bridget of. *See* Bridget of Sweden, Saint.

Swineshead, Richard (fl. c. 1340–55). Also known as Suicet, Suisseth, and the "Calculator," Richard Swineshead was an Oxford theoretician of science and author of the *Liber calculationum*. Three contemporaries shared the name "Swineshead" at Merton College in the mid-fourteenth century, causing some confusion about identity. John, a Merton fellow from 1340 to 1347, was a bachelor of civil and canon law who died in 1372. Roger (d. 1365) was a doctor of theology who wrote *De motibus naturalibus*, an innovative work meant to serve as a bridge between earlier Aristotelian thought concerning the causes and types of natural motion and the more theoretically founded writing of William Heytesbury, John of Dumbleton, and Richard Swineshead, the Mertonian "calculators."

Richard was among the Merton scholars who revolutionized scientific thought, applying mathematical logic and structure to reasoning about physical phenomena. Three thinkers of the 1320s founded the Oxford movement: Richard Kilvington's *Sophismata* applied logical and semantic analysis to mathematical and scientific reasoning; *Thomas Bradwardine's *De proportionibus* provided the means to combine mathematical physics with logical *proofs*; and Walter Burley's *De intensione et remissione formarum* provided a theory by which alteration in the succession of forms could be mathematically analyzed.

Richard's *Liber calculationum* was the ideal expression of the Mertonian infusion of mathematics into physical science. It is the antithesis of modern practical physical science, for Richard's concern was to engage in a priori synthetic reasoning about the principles of the alteration of qualities in objects, referring to empirical situations only for illustrating his reasoning. Earlier philosophers like Burley and Roger Swineshead had assumed that one could not calculate variations of qualities like heat or wetness in individual subjects, but Richard devised a method of reasoning about the measurement of intensity and remission that allowed him to quantify the intensity of a quality more easily.

The first ten chapters of the *Liber calculationum* focused on the calculation of accurate measurement of alteration not only of quality within a subject but also of a subject's motion. Richard used his more basic arguments concerning analysis of intensity and remission, of density and rarity of a compound subject, as the foundation for reasoning about the mathematical measurement of power and resistance, and also the difficulties associated with measuring motion in media and over time. In later chapters he discussed light and the distribution of its illumination in differing media.

While this work did not augment technological innovation or experimental reasoning, fifteenth-century Italian humanists like Pietro Pomponazzi viewed the *Liber calculationum* as an important expression of the miscalculation of the relation of formal mathematics to scientific reasoning. In the seventeenth century Gottfried Leibniz saw Swineshead as a forerunner in introducing mathematics to philosophical reasoning, and his admiration ensured Swineshead a place in histories of philosophy and science for the next two centuries.

Bibliography: Edith Sylla, "The Oxford Calculators," in *The Cambridge History of Later Medieval Philosophy*, 1982: 540–63; James A. Weisheipi, "Roger Swyneshed, O.S.B., Logician, Natural Philosopher, and Theologian," in *Oxford Studies Presented to Daniel Callus*, 1964: 231–52.

Stephen E. Lahey

T

Tauler, Johann (c. 1300–1361), was one of the great fourteenth-century German mystics, along with *Meister Eckhart and *Heinrich Suso, all Dominicans. Born in Strassburg, Tauler is known as a disciple of Eckhart. His mysticism differed from that of Eckhart, however, in that Tauler insisted that the soul is distinct from God, and divine grace is essential to knowledge of God. He thus escaped the taint of pantheism with which Eckhart is sometimes charged. Tauler also was influenced by the mystical Friends of God during his time in Basel from 1339 to around 1346. Upon his return from Basel, he distinguished himself by his sermons advocating communion with God and by his faithful pastoral service. His charity influenced Martin Luther, as did his belief in human depravity.

Tauler entered a Dominican convent in 1315, and he also studied in Paris and Cologne. His duties included the instruction of Dominican nuns through sermons and writings intended to preserve them from heresy. At the same time he often instructed Beguines, spiritual communities of laywomen who lived near convents but who had not taken holy vows. Many of them were noted for their religious mysticism but were at times suspected of heretical beliefs. Eckhart and Tauler followed the thread of Neoplatonic thinking that appeared in the works of Thomas Aquinas back to Pseudo-Dionysius the Anerpagite. While Bernard of Clairvaux and Bonaventure had both emphasized a communion of human and divine wills, Eckhart and Tauler's mysticism was more ecstatic, a union of essence. Theirs was representative of the late medieval mysticism that influenced much of Europe and is considered the last great popular religious movement of the age. It called for an immediate experience of God and direct spiritual access without the need for an intermediary. Eckhart and Tauler interpreted the first chapter of John ("In him was life," 1:4) to mean that preexistent man was essentially one with God. He participated in the mind and will of God and was one with him, perhaps as a thought is one with its thinker—in God but not part of God's being. Tauler believed that only the very soul of God himself could satisfy the longing of the human soul, but the longing was a separate mystical substance from the will. Self-realization did not follow rational and willful pathways, for the soul turned in upon itself, where it experienced God. The dwelling of God was like an immeasurable abyss; it was more than heaven and more than the human soul. One who desired to enter this abyss would find God there and be joined to the eternal. Tauler offered Mary as an example of one being joined to the eternal, and that in a sense other than her conception of the Son of God. Mary lived as mother of the child Jesus, but she found her rest in the divine abyss, an experience available to all Christians. Nevertheless, Tauler held a dim view of the age in which he lived, even to the point of hyperbole. He declared that the love of one's neighbor was truly extinct in all the countries of the world, and he pictured God as pursuing people in the way a hunter pursues his prey. He tracks them down, in this case by means of punishments and temptations, but always for the good of the hunted souls. Tauler stated that God desires to "eat" what the hunt has yielded, the "eating" being a mystical experience that the hunted have with God as a result of the tests and trials he brings upon them.

When Tauler returned to Strassburg from Basel, he resumed his pastoral ministry, preaching sermons on the reality of a mystical union of the believer with God. He maintained his care for the faithful, serving them during the devastation of the plague in 1348, thus practicing in the face of death his belief that union with God results in love of one's neighbor and self-sacrifice. He preached to fully crowded assemblies of believers until his death in 1361.

Bibliography: James M. Clark, *The Great German Mystics: Eckhart, Tauler, and Suso*, 1949; Patrick Grant, *Literature of Mysticism in Western Tradition*, 1983.

Paul Sheneman

Thomas à Kempis (1379/80–1471)

Thomas à Kempis (1379/80–1471) was a renowned monk and religious writer. Thomas à Kempis was once reported to have said, "I sought for rest but never found it, save in a little corner with a little book." Although Thomas himself sought little more than to embrace a quiet life of spiritual contemplation, he has nevertheless come to have a profound impact on the history of Christian thought and practice. He emerged by the end of his life as one of the most influential religious authors of the late Middle Ages, and his eminent devotional treatise *The Imitation of Christ* remains even today an oft-read classic in Christian literature.

Thomas à Kempis was born in either 1379 or 1380 in the small village of Kempen (near Düsseldorf) within the Diocese of Cologne in the German Rhineland. His parents John and Gertrude Haemerken came from a peasant background, with his father serving as the village blacksmith and his mother teaching at the local school. However, despite his low socioeconomic status, young Thomas did enjoy the benefits of a formal education. As a small boy, Thomas no doubt studied at the village school under the tutelage of his mother. In 1393 Thomas moved to the Dutch town of Deventer and attended a school sponsored by a religious society known as the Brethren of the Common Life, where he concentrated on the discipline of Latin composition and the craft of document transcription. In 1399 Thomas decided upon a religious vocation and entered the nearby Monastery of Mount St. Agnes in the city of Zwolle in the Netherlands. In 1406 Thomas took his vows and officially became a novice in the order of the Canons Regular of St. Augustine.

After finally receiving ordination in 1413, Thomas occupied a number of posts at Mount St. Agnes. In 1425 and 1448 Thomas was appointed subprior of the monastery and at other times held such responsibilities as treasurer and master of novices. However, his most important contribution was his vast body of religious writings, which ultimately included biographies of *Gerard Groote and Florens Radewijns, founders of the Brethren of the Common Life, along with a history of the Mount St. Agnes Monastery itself. Most important, however, Thomas authored a number of purely devotional works, the most prominent of which is *The Imitation of Christ*, which he completed about the year 1427. For more than forty years thereafter, Thomas carried on with his monastic duties, until on 8 August 1471 he died at Mount St. Agnes, ending his life inside the walls of the small religious community to which he had devoted his best years.

Thomas's *Imitation of Christ* lies at the heart of a medieval religious movement known as *devotio moderna*. First developed by Gerard Groote in the late fourteenth century, *devotio moderna* was largely a reaction to the arid Scholasticism and moral laxity prevalent within the church during the late Middle Ages. Eschewing the deep metaphysical mysticism proposed by some reformers, the followers of *devotio moderna* instead urged believers on to a practical piety that recognized the expressions of God's love and grace present in everyday life. Following the lead of Groote, who had reportedly believed himself unworthy to enter the priesthood, disciples of *devotio moderna* initially avoided organizing their own religious orders and instead grouped themselves into informal societies that sought to encourage Christlike behavior within their membership. Indeed, to Groote and his followers, including Thomas, simplicity, charity, and a deep heartfelt devotion to God were the keys that unlocked the power of the divine hidden within the lives of average Christians.

Such was the major theme in *The Imitation of Christ*. In the *Imitation*, Thomas offered a set of practical guidelines for believers seeking the type of authentic spiritual experience advocated by the disciples of *devotio moderna*. Consequently, the *Imitation* tended to view the theological Scholasticism that dominated fifteenth-century Catholicism with great suspicion. "Deeply inquisitive reasoning does not make a man holy or righteous," warned Thomas, "but a good life makes him beloved by God. I would rather feel compunction of heart for my sins than merely know the definition of compunction." Instead, Thomas recommended a piety that first sprang from the heart, rather than the intellect. Ultimately, humanity's encounter with God was a mystical journey that could take place only within the spirit of each individual. However, Thomas's mysticism was not one of spiritual rapture so intense that it severed the believer's connection to the created order. Rather, it was a mysticism built upward from the most fundamental experiences of daily living. Thus those who would imitate Christ must first come to terms with the implications of that faith as it pertained to the struggles and temptations prevalent in the world around them.

The first step in Thomas's scheme to imitate Christ was the renunciation of the evils commonly encountered in life. "Who wages a stronger battle than he who labors to overcome himself?" asked Thomas in the *Imitation*. Thomas suggested that as the believer began to overcome the power of sin in his or her own life, rather than succumb to pride, his or her behavior would be increasingly characterized by the Christlike virtues of humility and love. Thomas cautioned believers against judging others, stating that "if you cannot make yourself as you would, how may you then look to have another regulated in all things to suit your will?"

Once the believer achieved a more Christlike demeanor in such external matters, it was time to concentrate on transforming the individual's inner nature. Although the seeds of the kingdom of God existed in the hearts of all people, the sinful nature of fallen humanity had rendered them dormant. In order to draw closer to Christ, the believer must learn to embrace God's earthly means of grace, especially as seen in the miracle of the Eucharist. Only then might one begin to overcome humanity's inherent sinfulness with the spirit of Christ. "The more nature is suppressed and overcome, the more grace is given, and . . . the soul is daily shaped anew, and formed more and more to the image of God."

Some twentieth-century scholars have challenged Thomas's authorship of *The Imitation of Christ*. Over the course of the years some twenty-five different writers have been credited with its composition, with many literary critics ascribing it instead to such figures as Groote or the French priest and University of Paris chancellor *Jean Gerson. However, no conclusive evidence exists to overthrow the authorship of Thomas, and most historians and literary scholars remain convinced that it was his work.

Bibliography: Albert Hyma, *The Christian Renaissance: A History of the "Devotio Moderna*, 2nd ed. 1965; J.E.G. De Montmorency, *Thomas à Kempis: His Age and Book*, 1970, Thomas à Kempis, *The Imitation of Christ*, edited with an introduction by Harold C. Gardiner, 1955.

Timothy L. Wood

Tomás de Torquemada. *See* Torquemada, Tomás de.

Tornabuoni, Lucrezia (1427–82). Lucrezia Tornabuoni de Medici was the wife of *Piero de Medici, "the Gouty," and the mother of *Lorenzo de Medici, "the Magnificent." She was also a writer of religious poetry and sacred stories, a patron and supporter of Italian vernacular poets, a charitable benefactor well known for her religious devotion to the Virgin Mary and St. John the Baptist, an astute businesswoman, and, above all, a shrewd political operator. A portrait of her attributed to *Domenico Ghirlandaio, painted sometime in the 1470s, hangs in the National Gallery of Art in Washington, D. C. Lucrezia is also supposedly represented in a fresco cycle in the Tornabuoni Chapel in the Church of Santa Maria Novella in Florence, appropriately in a scene depicting the birth of St. John the Baptist. A bust of Lucrezia that is known to have existed, probably as a companion piece to the one of Piero now in Florence's Museum of the Bargello, has yet to be positively identified.

Lucrezia was born in June 1427 (until very recently it was thought that she had been born about 1425) to Francesco di Simone Tornabuoni and Francesca Guicciardini, both from old, prestigious Florentine families. Francesco was a staunch supporter of *Cosimo de Medici. Lucrezia married Piero in June 1444 and had four surviving children: Bianca, Lucrezia (called Nannina), Lorenzo, and *Giuliano, the last of whom was murdered in the Florentine cathedral as a result of the Pazzi conspiracy of April 1478. Lucrezia also raised Piero's natural daughter Maria. Lucrezia's brother Giovanni became manager of the Medici bank in Rome.

Lucrezia's relationship with Piero was unusual for the time, a true partnership. They traveled to the Jubilee in Rome in 1450 and together had an audience with the pope, who granted them the right to have Mass said in the private chapel in the Medici Palace. Lucrezia may also have suggested the themes for several paintings Piero commissioned from *Filippo Lippi in the 1460s that were inspired by a favorite subject of Lucrezia's, the life of St. John the Baptist as a young child. Lucrezia had great influence with her husband and was appealed to by Medici clients because they wished her to intercede with him on their behalf.

After Piero's death on 2 December 1469, Lucrezia's influence and activities greatly increased. Lucrezia was not only a conduit for clients and supporters wishing to request something from young Lorenzo, but was also someone upon whom he relied heavily, as he later acknowledged upon her death. Lucrezia was also extremely influential in her own right, with a particular clientele among the poor and among women. She helped women as important as the exiled queen of Bosnia as well as poor girls in need of dowries or nuns requesting aid. Lucrezia often mediated disputes, and sometimes her mere request that a conflict be resolved was enough to ensure a successful outcome. Lucrezia's influence cast an even wider net, enabling her to obtain jobs for people, assist those in exile, and influence the outcome of clerical and legal contests. Her charitable and pious reputation resulted in many appealing to Lucrezia as a "mother," and she was even referred to as a saint after her death.

Lucrezia was an astute businesswoman. Piero had willed her the income of the Medici farm at Fiesole for the purpose of dispensing charity, but she also owned shops and farmland in Pisa and Florence. Lucrezia purchased the dilapidated thermal baths at Bagno a Morba in the late 1470s and turned them into a thriving business concern that included an inn for guests. Her decision to do so is not surprising; Lucrezia, like many of the other Medici, suffered severely from gout.

Lucrezia was also a well-known cultural patron of those who wrote religious vernacular poetry. Consequently, she supported religious writers such as Feo Belcari and vernacular poets such as Michele di Giorgante, Bernardo Bellincioni, and Luigi Pulci, from whom she commissioned the chivalric epic poem *Morgante*. One of her great friends was the humanist poet *Angelo Poliziano. Lucrezia herself wrote religious poems called *laude* as well as longer poems on the lives of St. John the Baptist, Susanna and the Elders, Judith and Holofernes, Tobias, and Queen Esther. Lucrezia probably wrote these works in the 1470s for the spiritual edification of her granddaughters.

Lucrezia died on 25 March 1482. Her son Lorenzo notified many important Florentines and other Italian dignitaries such as the duke and duchess of Ferrara. He in turn received many letters of consolation, reminding him of his mother's significant achievements and the importance of the tremendous assistance she had given him. Lucrezia's importance as a significant historical figure in her own right is undoubted.

Bibliography: F. W. Kent, "Sainted Mother, Magnificent Son: Lucrezia Tornabuoni and Lorenzo de Medici," *Italian History and Culture* 3 (1997); R. Russell, ed., *Italian Women Writers: A Bio-bibliographical Sourcebook*, 1994.

Natalie Tomas

Torquemada, Juan de (c. 1388–1468), was the outstanding papal apologist of the fifteenth century and a self-conscious "defender of the faith." Born in Castile, he joined the Order of Preachers at an early age. Trained at the convent in Valladolid, Torquemada later attended the Council of Constance (1414–18). Thereafter he studied theology at the University of Paris and then held administrative appointments in Castile. When the Council of Basel (1431–49) began, Torquemada was chosen both by his order and by the king of Castile to represent them in that assembly. In retrospect, it is possible that he was also sent to Basel by *Eugenius IV to defend papal interests there.

Torquemada was incorporated into the council in 1432, and he was assigned to the Reform Deputation. The friar was active in the council, intervening in a series of theological issues. Among these were the ongoing negotiations with the Hussites, censure of the doctrines of Agostino Favaroni, and suppression of resistance to the doctrine of the Immaculate Conception. Torquemada also defended the orthodoxy of the *Revelations* of *Bridget of Sweden. At the same time, wary of certain proposed reforms and their potential to harm the apostolate of the friars, which depended on papal privileges, Torquemada took up the cause of Eugenius IV, who was locked in a struggle with the council over its continuation in Basel. When Eugenius, who had been driven from Rome, granted the assembly grudging approval, he dispatched presidents to act in his place. The assembly, over Torquemada's protests, imposed on the pope's representatives the oath of incorporation (acknowledgement of authority of council), with its implicit promise of obedience. During this period, in 1434, Eugenius made the friar master of the sacred palace. Thereafter Torquemada found himself ever more opposed to the will of the conciliar majority in its attempted reform of the Curia and its refusal to meet the emperor of Constantinople and the Eastern prelates in Italy.

In 1437 Eugenius, buoyed by favorable events in Italy and by promising negotiations with the Greeks, announced that he was transferring the council from Basel to Ferrara. The majority of the fathers refused to move, but a minority left to work for reunion with the Eastern churches, and Torquemada was among them. For the next several years he alternated between residence in the Curia and diplomatic missions on Eugenius's behalf. The friar was in Florence, the new seat of the council of union, when an agreement was reached between East and West on the key theological issues dividing them. Torquemada was one of those chosen to draft the decree of union. The Basel assembly, meanwhile, deposed Eugenius, electing in his place Amadeus VIII of Savoy to reign as Felix V. Eugenius replied by condemning Basel's theory of conciliar supremacy. Torquemada then defended papal monarchy in a public debate with Giullano Cesarini, a former president of the Council of Basel.

When Eugenius returned to Rome, Torquemada, recently made a cardinal, took up residence at Santa Maria sopra Minerva. The cardinal participated in Curia business, upheld the interests of his order, and worked for monastic reform. He favored the Observant wing of the Dominican order, and he renewed religious life at his commendatory abbey in Subiaco. Moreover, Torquemada remained an active polemicist, backing papal plans for a crusade against the Turks with a refutation of the "errors" of Islam. He also wrote a condemnation of the heresy proceedings against converts from Judaism to Christianity that were then being held in Toledo (1449), following an uprising against royal taxes that a *converso* was charged with collecting. The question of the cardinal's own possible Jewish origin arose in this context.

Most notably, Torquemada undertook a refutation of the idea of conciliar supremacy. He began work on a commentary on Gratian's *Decretum*, the legal collection from which Basel's partisans had drawn many supporting texts. This project, which continued for many years, was interrupted for the composition of the cardinal's most famous work, his *Summa de ecclesia* (1453). This compendious work offered a coherent defense of the ecclesiastical institution against all threats to its saving work. Most important, it contained the most cogent and balanced polemic against conciliar thought written in that century.

Although Torquemada was a Thomist, he was not indifferent to the new cultural currents of the Renaissance. *Lorenzo Valla regarded the cardinal as a potential protector against his curial foes. The first German printers to reach central Italy did their initial print runs at his abbey in Subiaco. Although Torquemada may not have invited these printers to move southward, he certainly became interested in the printer's art. His *Meditationes* (1467) was the first illustrated book printed in Italy. Moreover, the illustrations reproduced paintings commissioned by Torquemada for the new cloister that he had built at the Minerva. The artist who decorated the cloister may have been *Fra Angelico, who already had painted a portrait of the cardinal kneeling at the foot of the cross.

Torquemada lived through the reigns of Popes Eugenius IV, *Nicholas V, Calixtus III, and *Pius II, helping elect their successors. These pontiffs, in turn, honored him and often supported his endeavors. Pius, when he held a congress of European powers in Mantua to organize a crusade in 1459, noted that only Torquemada and *John Bessarion, a Spaniard and a Greek, were firm supporters of that enterprise. The cardinal was old and ailing when he took part in the election of Paul II in 1464. Nonetheless, he continued writing, producing devotional and polemical works. Among the problems that attracted his attention were controversies over apostolic poverty, the theology of the Precious Blood, and the legitimacy of the Western Roman Empire. When the cardinal died in Rome in 1468, the library that he had assembled in support of his work was dispersed. Torquemada was buried in the Chapel of the Annunciation in Rome, the seat of a confraternity that he had founded to dower poor girls of good birth. His portrait by Antoniazzo Romano, presenting girls dowered by the confraternity to the Virgin Annunciate, can be seen in the chapel behind the altar.

Bibliography: Thomas M. Izbicki, *Protector of the Faith: Cardinal Johannes de Turrecremata and the Defense of the Institutional Church*, 1981; Juan de Torquemada, *A Disputation on the Authority of Pope and Council*, trans. Thomas M. Izbicki, 1988.

Thomas M. Izbicki

Torquemada, Tomás de (1420–98). The guiding force behind the Spanish Inquisition in its first two decades, Tomás de Torquemada has been memorialized as the archetype of religious fanaticism and is still the subject of intense historical controversy today. Ironically, little is known about Torquemada's early life. His uncle, *Juan de Torquemada, was a respected theologian and papal servant. One contemporary chronicler claimed that Tomás de Torquemada's paternal grandmother was a converted Jew, but later Catholic historians have hotly denied this charge. Tomás de Torquemada was born in or near Valladolid in 1420. At age fourteen he entered the Dominican Convent of St. Paul of Valladolid, where he studied for his doctorate in theology. In 1452 he was elected prior of the Monastery of Santa Cruz in Segovia, a position he held for twenty-two years.

It was in Segovia that he became confessor to the then infanta *Isabel. The story that Torquemada required her to promise that she would rid Castile of heresy if she were made queen is generally rejected as apocryphal. When Isabel did take the throne of Castile in 1474, however, Torquemada served as a trusted royal advisor and a confessor to several other high-ranking courtiers. Torquemada was probably among the Dominicans who prompted Isabel to request papal permission to establish the Inquisition in Castile in September 1478. Her request was granted two months later. In September 1480 *Ferdinand and Isabel delegated their authority to appoint inquisitors to Torquemada and Cardinal *Pedro González de Mendoza.

In February 1482, with inquisitors already operating in Seville, Pope *Sixtus IV issued a brief naming eight Dominicans, including Torquemada, to run the Holy Office of the Inquisition in Castile (and, briefly, Aragon) while reaffirming the route of appeal to Rome. Meanwhile, Torquemada's influence in Spain continued to rise as he became confessor to both King Ferdinand and Cardinal Mendoza. Isabel renewed her efforts to establish a Castilian Inquisition free from papal interference, and after considerable pressure from representatives of the Spanish Crowns, Sixtus finally named Torquemada inquisitor general for Castile on 2 October 1483. His authority was extended to Aragon two weeks later. That same year the six-member Supreme Council of the Inquisition, with Torquemada at its head, was established in Castile and Aragon by their respective monarchs.

After a conference of inquisitors in 1484, Torquemada issued the first of five sets of "Instructions for the Governance of the Holy Office." This consisted of twenty-eight articles establishing the procedure for opening an Inquisition tribunal in a given town, directing any confiscated property of heretics or apostates to the royal treasury, defining the Inquisition's jurisdiction over dead and absent suspects, and mandating the use of torture in cases where evidence was not decisive. Subsequent "Instructions" in late 1484, 1485, and 1488 extended Torquemada's personal power even further when they authorized inquisitors to ignore papal instructions and required all completed case dossiers to be sent to the Supreme Council for examination. Conservative estimates place the number of people killed by the Holy Office under Torquemada at perhaps two thousand. The apogee of Torquemada's influence came when he played a pivotal role in persuading the Catholic monarchs to expel all Jews from the kingdoms of Spain in 1492.

Torquemada spent his last years at the Monastery of St. Thomas in Ávila, from where he fought the unsympathetic Pope *Alexander VI to retain control over the Inquisition. In June 1494 the pope appointed four "assistants" with power equal to Torquemada's, citing the inquisitor general's advanced age. The role of supreme judge of appeal was transferred to one of these assistants five months later. Torquemada's influence with the Catholic monarchs continued unabated, however; they visited him in Ávila and buried their son at St. Thomas. In the spring of 1498 Torquemada convened the Supreme Council for the last time and issued a final set of "Instructions" to remedy various abuses that had appeared in the inquisitorial system.

There is considerable disagreement about Torquemada's way of life; one set of chroniclers claimed that he was distinguished for personal asceticism, while others reported that the inquisitor general traveled only with a 250-man guard and tested all his meals with either a unicorn's horn or a scorpion's tongue. Despite his appetite for power, he supposedly turned down the archbishoprics of Seville and Toledo. Given the intense polarization of opinion surrounding Torquemada, it is necessary to proceed with great caution in affirming or denying these anecdotes.

Torquemada died in bed on 16 September 1498 and was buried at St. Thomas. The administrative machinery of the Holy Office, however, long outlasted its creator, and the Spanish Inquisition was finally suppressed in 1834. Two years later, Liberal forces exhumed and burned Torquemada's remains in the same square where he had once presided over public confessions and burnings.

Bibliography: Henry Kamen, *Inquisition and Society in Spain in the Sixteenth and Seventeenth Centuries*, 1985; John Longhurst, *The Age of Torquemada*, 1962; Ben Zion Netanyahu, *The Origins of the Inquisition in Fifteenth Century Spain*, 1995.

Wendy Love Anderson

Tostado, Alfonso (1400?–1455), also known as Alonso Tostado and Alfonso Fernández de Madrigal, was a prominent fifteenth-century Spanish theologian and writer. Tostado created almost seventy Spanish and Latin exegetical treatises that helped shape Christian doctrine about salvation and papal fallibility.

Alfonso Tostado was born around 1400 into a family of manual laborers in Madrigal, near the province of Ávila in Spain. Quickly showing an active intelligence, Tostado was first educated in grammar by Franciscans in Arevalo before entering the University of Salamanca. After studying philosophy, law, science, and language for several years, Tostado received a theological degree from Salamanca in 1422. He then became a rector at St. Bartholomew's while remaining employed as a teacher of theology, law, and philosophy at Salamanca. Here his encyclopedic knowledge of classical and Judeo-Christian scholarship became manifest in his own exegetical writings. His commentaries followed a simple but persuasive method in which he raised multifaceted questions taken from particular biblical passages, which he then systematically answered. In each exposition, he preferred to examine several verses at once, rather than singly, thus keeping the entire passage in context. Displaying a keen understanding of the Judeo-Christian heritage, he offered biblical commentary on a wide range of subjects, including public and family morality, witchcraft, slavery, murder, and the potential and limitations of government.

Tostado's commentaries did not go unnoticed by church authorities. He soon developed an adversarial relationship with *Juan de Torquemada (the Dominican uncle of the grand inquisitor *Tomás de Torquemada), whom he addressed in 1433 at the Council of Basel. Their primary dispute centered on the question of whether the pope was more powerful, and thus superior to, a council of learned Christians. Although his early views regarding the papal plenitude of power had coincided with those of Torquemada, at Basel Tostado favored the superiority of the council. There he affirmed his stance on the limits of papal supremacy over the general council and, influenced by Platonic ideas, rejected the idea of papal infallibility. Tostado and Torquemada also opposed one another on several other theological disputes, including the date of Christ's birth (with Tostado arguing for the now-accepted date of 25 December) and the nature of salvation.

Tostado's teaching provoked further controversy in 1443 when Pope *Eugenius IV condemned him for heretical understanding of the nature of sin, absolution, and forgiveness. His fortunes changed, however, a year later when King *Juan II of Castile, an early advocate of humanism, summoned him to his council at court and named him royal chancellor. Here, in the midst of a Renaissance court, Tostado wrote his famous *Las Historias de Eusebius*, a testament to Greek scholarship. Five years later, his earlier disputes with the papacy seemingly forgotten, Tostado was approved as bishop of Ávila by the humanist Pope *Nicholas V. He stayed in this position until he died in Bonilla de la Sierra, outside of Ávila, in 1455.

His major works include *Las catorze questiones, Las historias de Eusebius, El tratado del amor y del amicitia*, and several biblical commentaries on such Old Testament books as Exodus, Genesis, Leviticus, and Numbers.

Bibliography: Solomon Gaon. *The Influence of the Catholic Theologian Alfonso Tostado on the Pentateuch Commentary of Isaac Abravanel*, 1993.

Susanna Calkins

Tyler, Wat (d. 1381), of Maidstone, England, alternatively Tegheler, Tylere, Helyer, or Helier, rose from the murky obscurity of common origin to a position of leadership in the Peasants' Revolt in June 1381. Little is known about this figure except from contemporary chroniclers who, not surprisingly, were less than keen on Tyler's character and goals. According to some sources, this man worked as a roof tiler in Kent and Essex, although one chronicler thought that Tyler had performed service in France in the employ of a rich merchant who, perhaps significantly, was killed by the Kentish rebels. In some of the chronicles, most notably that of *Henry Knighton, Tyler was misidentified as Jack Straw or Rakestraw, a mistake followed by some later commentators. From our meager resources, Tyler apparently was an intelligent and cunning yet also arrogant man.

For a variety of reasons, ranging from a fundamental dislike of servile status and the more immediate financial burdens the commoners of England had suffered as a result of the Hundred Years' War, including the infamous poll tax, peasants throughout England rose in revolt in 1381. Although hints of social revolution stirred the air, the rebels generally proclaimed their loyalty to their king *Richard II and insisted that they merely assaulted the young king's evil advisors. By far the largest and most dangerous rising occurred in Kent and Essex in June 1381, in the formative stages of which Wat Tyler assumed his brief career of prominence. On or about 7 June Tyler rose to a position of leadership among the rebels at Maidstone after he had attacked a poll-tax collector who had insulted his daughter, and by 10 June his band and others conjoined to capture Canterbury. About this time Tyler met John Ball, a priest, and

Jack Straw, a fellow leader of similarly obscure origins. With Tyler at its head, the rebel army marched from Canterbury to London in two days in a demonstration of incredible optimism and surprising discipline. Through the machinations of a fifth column within the city, the Kent-Essex bands infiltrated London on 13 June and proceeded to demolish the Savoy, *John of Gaunt's extravagant metropolitan palace. The sack of London witnessed the slaughter of foreign merchants, especially the hated Flemings, the capture of the Tower of London, and the murder of the archbishop of Canterbury, in addition to the customary pillage of a captured city.

At this time Tyler's power and prestige approached their zenith, for rebel groups throughout southern and eastern England invoked his name to mobilize and reinforce their own risings. John Wraw, the priest who mobilized rebels in East Anglia, claimed to possess Tyler's support, though it is unlikely that the two ever met. The peasants of St. Albans also sought Tyler's moral and military support in their attempts to sack the wealthy abbey. According to contemporary chroniclers, about this time Tyler and others gave some consideration to a strange plan to realign the political structure of the entire kingdom, envisioning not only bond men made free but also a radical decentralization of the realm, with mutually autonomous kings in every county led by a figurehead monarch. Unfortunately we possess not the slightest indication whether the rebels actually considered such a plan or whether it sprang from the overheated fancies of distant chronicles.

On 15 June Tyler and Richard II met at Smithfield. Although the series of events remains somewhat confused, after a brief parlay Tyler supposedly made some threatening gestures toward the king or one of his supporters, whereupon Richard ordered Tyler's arrest. In the struggle that followed, Tyler was murdered by the mayor of London, a convenience some analysts have attributed to royal machination. Tyler's death proved fatal for the rebellion. Deprived of their disciplined leadership, the sine qua non of any military organization, the bands in London disappeared like thieves in the night, while the sundry provincial risings either lacked sufficient strength to continue or else lost heart entirely. The sudden rise and equally abrupt collapse of the Peasants' Revolt of 1381 should be seen as an outgrowth of the leadership skills of this mysterious artisan who briefly ruled over England's capital.

Bibliography: R. B. Dobson, *The Peasants' Revolt of 1381*, 1970; R. H. Hilton and T. H. Aston, eds. *The English Rising of 1381*, 1984.

James C. Owens

U

Ubertino da Casale (c. 1259–c. 1329) was a prominent leader of the Franciscan Spirituals and author of the *Arbor vitae crucifixae Jesu*. Born near Genoa, Ubertino joined the Franciscan order in 1273. He studied in Paris for nearly a decade before returning to Italy in 1284. While Ubertino was teaching in Florence, he became ever more distressed at what he viewed as the corruption of the Franciscan order. Like a number of his fellow Franciscans, who became known as the Spirituals, Ubertino criticized the growing worldliness of the order and its failure to adhere to the ideal of strict poverty exemplified by the life of St. Francis and set forth in Francis's *Rule* and *Testament*. During 1302–4 Ubertino preached widely in Tuscany, urging the reform of the order and a return to true Christian discipleship. He attracted a significant following in this way, as well as the suspicion of church authorities.

In 1304 Ubertino went into retreat at La Verna, the mountain near Assisi where St. Francis had received the stigmata. There he wrote his *Arbor vitae crucifixae Jesu*, a lengthy work consisting primarily of meditations on the life of Christ but including many passages of speculative theology, autobiography, commentary on the apocalypse, and strident criticism of the Franciscan order and of the church. In the Prologue to this text, Ubertino spoke with great admiration of the Franciscan tertiary and mystic Angela of Foligno, whom he credited with exerting a major influence on his spiritual ideals and meditative practices.

During 1309–12 the Franciscan order, under the supervision of the pope, engaged in a series of debates about its future and about the issue of poverty in particular. In these debates Ubertino was a key spokesman for the Spirituals against the dominant Franciscan faction, the Conventuals. A number of tracts Ubertino wrote at the time of this controversy, including the *Rotulus* and *De paupertate Christi*, are among the most impassioned defenses of the ideal of strict poverty surviving from the medieval period. The debates did not resolve the tensions within the order; many of the Spirituals were persecuted during the ensuing decade, and Pope *John XXII put a decisive end to the resistance movement in 1322. In 1325 Ubertino was tried for heresy in Avignon, but he fled and lived thereafter as a fugitive. He is known to have preached against the pope in Como in 1329, but after this the historical record is silent.

Bibliography: John R. H. Moorman, *A History of the Franciscan Order from Its Origins to the Year 1517*, 1968; Ubertino da Casale, *Arbor vitae crucifixae Jesu*, intro. by C. T. Davis, 1961.

Sarah McNamer

Uccello, Paolo (1397–1475), whose adopted surname "uccello," means "bird," was a Florentine painter, frescoist, mosaicist, and designer of stained glass. One of the fifteenth century's most devoted students of the use of linear perspective as pioneered by *Filippo Brunelleschi and *Leon Battista Alberti, Uccello was described by Giorgio Vasari as "the most original and inventive genius in the art of painting since Giotto's day." Linear perspective became the nearly obsessive hallmark of his artistic style, dominating the compositional structure of every piece Uccello executed during his long career.

Paolo Uccello, whose original name was Paolo di Dono, was born in 1397 near Florence, Italy. His true birth date is not known, but can be surmised through Florentine tax documents. He married Tommasa di Benedetto Malefici late in life and had two children, a son, Donato (b. 1453), and a daughter, Antonia (b. 1456).

Early in his career he worked with the famous sculptor *Lorenzo Ghiberti during the years 1412–16. It was at this time that he began perfecting his signature linear style, a three-dimensional effect presented on a flat two-dimensional surface. He also worked in these early days on the bronze doors with Ghiberti for the Florentine baptistery, which were destined later to be known as the famed "Gates of Paradise."

We know nothing of Uccello's training as a painter, but it is recorded that he joined the Compagnia di S. Luca in 1414, and in 1419 he became a member of the Arte de Medici e Speziali, the guild of artists in Florence. Upon the death of *Cosimo de Medici, he was encouraged and patronized by Cosimo's son and successor, *Piero "the Gouty." Piero de Medici loved animals and was aware of Uccello's admiration for animals also. Because of their mutual interest, Piero commissioned Uccello to paint *The Battle of San Romano*, comprising three panels celebrating the victory of Florentine forces fighting in Siena in June 1432, but instead of highlighting soldiers, Uccello emphasized the horses of the combatants. Today each panel of the battle scene hangs in various art galleries in London, Paris, and Florence; they are collectively recognized as a masterpiece of perspective with their criss-crossed pattern of lances and prancing equestrian figures.

Uccello was employed as a mosaicist from 1425 to 1431 in Venice, but unfortunately his work there has not survived. There is one extant fresco that well represents his work in the 1430s, the equestrian portrait of Sir *John Hawkwood in the Florentine Cathedral of Santa Maria della Fiore. Uccello executed it twice since the cathedral fathers were not pleased with his original fresco. In 1447 Uccello painted the biblical scene *The Flood* in the Green Cloister of Santa Maria Novella in Florence, combining the linear perspective style of the High Renaissance with the older decorative style of the Middle Ages.

Uccello's most important and best-known painting remains *The Battle of San Romano*. This painting was later placed in the bedroom of *Lorenzo de Medici to remind the young ruler of the glorious past feats of Florentine arms. In his mature years Uccello created the panel *St. George and the Dragon*; he also painted the *Profanation of the Host* for the altarpiece of the Institution of the Eucharist and *The Hunt*, which well exemplified Uccello's use of simple dual structure and classic linear depth in support of dramatic realism.

Paolo Uccello, who worked until his death, passed away on 10 December 1475. He was buried in the Church of Santo Spirito in Florence in his father's grave. Today there has been a resurgence of interest in the paintings and frescoes of Paolo Uccello, primarily because it is thought that his works anticipated certain aesthetic trends in modern art. He has been described by Paul Hills as "both an imaginative decorative painter and a remarkable naturalist" and was certainly an important transitional figure between the medieval and Renaissance masters of the quattrocento period in Italy.

Bibliography: Jacob Burckhardt, *The Altarpiece in Renaissance Italy*, trans. and ed. Peter Humfrey, 1988; Paul Hills, *The Light of Early Italian Painting*, 1987.

Karen Holleran

Urban VI, Pope (b.c. 1318, r. 1378–89), formerly Bartolomeo Prignano.

Urban VI was elected as a compromise candidate by the first conclave to meet in Rome after the papacy's extended sojourn in Avignon (1309–77). His reign began with hopes for the reform and restoration of the papacy to Rome, but within a few months he had alienated a majority of the college of cardinals, who declared his election invalid and chose another pope. The resulting schism lasted until 1417.

Neapolitan by birth, Bartolomeo Prignano studied at the University of Naples, where he received a doctorate in canon law. By 1360 he had been appointed rector of the university, was a canon of the city cathedral, and was serving as the vicar general of the archbishop of Naples. In 1363 he was made archbishop of Acerenza and went to work in the papal chancery in Avignon. When Pope Gregory XI returned to Rome in 1376, he left Prignano behind in Avignon as regent of the chancery, and in 1377 he awarded Prignano the archbishopric of Bari. When Gregory died in March 1378, the college of cardinals met in Rome under heavy guard to elect a new pope. The Roman citizens, fearing that the predominantly French cardinals would elect a French pope and return the papacy to Avignon, rioted in the streets and at one point burst into the conclave itself, demanding a Roman, or at least Italian, pope. The cardinals eventually settled on Prignano, who was formally elected on 8 April 1378 and was enthroned as Pope Urban VI on 18 April. Although Prignano was not a cardinal, he was admired for his efficiency and morality, and his Neapolitan birth made him acceptable to the Roman people.

Soon after his election, Urban embarked on a series of reforms, ordering the cardinals drastically to reduce the size and splendor of their households and attempting to eliminate secular influence over the papacy. Unfortunately, Urban also began to exhibit a violent and unstable temper, treating the cardinals with contempt and abuse and deliberately humiliating secular rulers. He further alienated the French majority of the college of cardinals by adamantly refusing to return the papacy to Avignon. The French cardinals withdrew from Rome and gathered in Anagni, and in July 1378 they declared that Urban's election had been forced upon them by the Roman mob. On 2 August 1378 the majority of the cardinals, Italian as well as French, declared Urban's election invalid and invited him to abdicate. Urban refused, and on 9 August the cardinals declared him deposed. Urban responded by creating a new college of cardinals on 17 September. The original cardinals moved to Fondi, and on 20 September they elected a new pope, Cardinal Robert of Geneva, who took the name Clement VII. The two popes excommunicated each other, and each raised an army of mercenaries. In April 1379 Urban's army defeated Clement's at Marino, and for the remainder of his reign Urban retained control of most of Italy.

Ignoring Clement and the widening schism, Urban turned his attention to domestic matters. In 1380 he excommunicated and deposed Queen Joanna I of Naples, who had protected the rebellious cardinals and supported Clement. Joanna's cousin, Charles of Durazzo, seized the throne of Naples with Urban's help, but the two soon argued over the disposition of the kingdom. In 1384 Charles conspired with several of Urban's cardinals to place the papacy under a regency. While Urban was residing at Nocera, he discovered the plot and imprisoned six of his cardinals. Although Charles then laid siege to Nocera, Urban managed to escape to Genoa, where five of the imprisoned cardinals vanished. Throughout 1386–87 Urban attempted to recruit an army of mercenaries to invade Naples, but he was unable to raise enough money to pay for them. In 1388 Urban returned to Rome, where he died on 15 October 1389. According to some sources, he was poisoned.

Urban VI was a controversial figure in his own time and has remained so to this day. While some contemporaries regarded him as an austere and pious reformer, others, including the cardinals who elected Clement VII, denounced him as an apostate and tyrant. Among modern scholars, some have argued that Urban was, in fact, insane, while others have theorized that his disputes with the cardinals were the result of differences in social class and nationality. Whatever the cause of Urban's actions, his reign proved disastrous for the church and drastically reduced the influence and reputation of the papacy.

Bibliography: Yves Renouard, *The Avignon Papacy, 1305–1403*, 1970; Walter Ullmann, *The Origins of the Great Schism*, 1967.

Stephen A. Allen

V

Valdemar IV, King of Denmark (b. 1320, r. 1340–75), became ruler of a land completely dismembered by foreign powers, but his ambition, military prowess, and directness enabled him to reunite the kingdom of Denmark by 1361. His aggressive pursuits led to conflicts with Sweden, north German principalities, and the north German trading centers of the Hanseatic League. As the son of Christopher II, Valdemar lived after the age of eight at the court of Holy Roman Emperor *Louis IV. Raised at the courts of the emperor and of his brother-in-law, the margrave of Brandenburg, he was as ruthless and as unscrupulous as they and considerably more astute. In 1338 he left the royal court and began a diplomatic offensive to wrest Denmark from Gerhard and John the Mild, counts of Holstein. With the assassination of Gerhard in April 1340, Valdemar forced an agreement with John the Mild and was recognized as king of Denmark.

King Valdemar IV Atterdag (again day) ascended the throne in 1340 at the age of twenty when Denmark was perhaps at its lowest point. All but a single county in Jutland was under foreign rule, and at such a young age, Valdemar had to be content with the meager revenues of that small area. To gain necessary revenue, Valdemar confirmed an agreement made by his father to sell Skane and the province of Blekinge to King Magnus VII Ericson of Sweden, and he included the province of Halland in return for 50,000 silver marks.

Magnus's Swedish silver was of great use to Valdemar, and by 1349 he had driven the foreigners from a great part of Denmark, including Zealand and large areas of Funen and Jutland. In addition, in 1349 he interfered in north German politics, opposing the attempt of the German Charles IV (holy Roman emperor after 1355) to remove Valdemar's ally Louis of Brandenburg and to take Rugen and Rostock from Danish control. Valdemar liberated Louis's lands, reestablished Danish control of Rugen and Rostock, and reconciled Charles and Louis. On returning to Denmark in 1350, Valdemar faced the first of a series of uprisings against his rule, this time led by leading Jutland magnates. After all the revolts had been put down, a parliament met at Kalundborg in 1360 to consolidate the peace and to further define the rights and obligations of ruler and subjects.

In 1360 Valdemar completed the reunification of his father's kingdom when he invaded Skane, weakened by plague and political turmoil, with a large army and began negotiations with Magnus. Skane became and remained Danish for the next three hundred years, giving Valdemar and future monarchs access to its lucrative fishing industry. The following year Valdemar raided the treasures of the Hanse island of Gotland, giving him a strong foothold in the Baltic trade region and arousing the opposition of the Hanseatic League, Sweden, Mecklenburg, Holstein, and dissident Jutland nobles, which eventually led to war between Denmark and the Hanseatic League.

The Hanseatic fleet was defeated by Valdemar off Hälsingborg in Skane in 1362. The Hanse then allied itself with King Magnus of Sweden and his son Haakon (puppet king of Norway) to defeat Denmark. The alliance against Denmark was not entirely successful. Haakon rebelled against Magnus, and the church and the nobility, still smarting from overtaxation, followed suit; this was further exacerbated by Magnus's loss of Skane. The revolt recognized Haakon as king of Sweden. At this time Duke Albert of Mecklenburg, brother-in-law of King Magnus, claimed that his son, Albert, was the rightful king of Sweden. The Hanseatic League switched allegiance to Albert, and Magnus and Haakon (quickly reunited and in agreement) entered into alliance with Valdemar Atterdag of Denmark, the agreement being augmented by Haakon's marriage to Valdemar's daughter *Margaret, which united Denmark and Norway. Magnus and Haakon formed an army in Norway, but were decisively defeated in 1365, and Magnus was taken prisoner.

The 1365 defeat of Valdemar's allies did nothing to resolve his struggle with the Hanseatic League. A truce was agreed upon, which Valdemar repeatedly broke by interfering with Hanse trade. The Hanseatic towns, Mecklenburg, Sweden, and Holstein formed a coalition against Valdemar and began to prepare for war. The Hanseatic fleet attacked and defeated Valdemar's army in 1369 and took control of Skane. Via negotiations with the Danish Council, the Treaty of Stralsund was signed, giving the Hanse wide trade rights within Denmark, many additional privileges, and the right to approve all future candidates to the Danish throne. Valdemar Atterdag's humiliation was profound, and he died five years later.

Bibliography: Stewart Oakley, *A Short History of Denmark*, 1972.

Kristopher Bell

Valera, Diego de (1412–86). Diego de Valera enjoyed a career as a royal ambassador and chronicler in fifteenth-century Spain. Born in the city of Cuenca in 1412, he served in the household of the noble family of Zúñiga and eventually became a page in the court of King *Juan II. To complete his education and training, he was encouraged to travel abroad, and Juan II provided him with letters of presentation that facilitated this venture. As part of his travels, he spent time at the courts of both King Albert of Bohemia and *Charles VII of France. He returned to the court of Juan II, where he held the position of *maestresala*. During this time he also penned several didactic works, including *Defensa de virtuosas mujeres*, (Defense of virtuous women) and *Espejo de verdadera noble-za* (Mirror of true nobility). With the rise of *Enrique IV to the throne, he chose to withdraw from royal service and turned his attention instead to the study of philosophy and history.

He returned to royal service in 1474 when *Isabel acceded to the Castilian throne. He served as her *mayordomo* and the official chronicler of her husband, *Ferdinand. In these various capacities he also advised the royal couple, encouraging Ferdinand, for example, to pursue the reconquest of Granada. In 1481 he presented Isabel with the *Crónica abreviada de España*. The work was divided into four parts. The first was a description of Africa, Asia, and Europe, while the second was a description of Spain until the fall of the Roman Empire. The third addressed the Visigothic period, and the last traced Spain's history from the decline of Visigothic power until the death of *Alvaro de Luna. After this work he chronicled the reign of Enrique IV in *Memorial de diversas hazañas* (Memorial of various exploits), written during the 1480s. Despite the fact that some of Isabel and Ferdinand's chroniclers drafted accounts of Enrique's reign that portrayed him unfavorably, Valera attributed most of Enrique's failings as a monarch to trouble with the nobility. In the early twentieth century scholars determined that before his death Valera had also written an important chronicle of the reign of the Catholic kings, Isabel and Ferdinand. This work, *Crónica de los reyes católicos*, had previously been regarded as an anonymous chronicle.

Recently, scholars have critically analyzed the partisan nature of Valera's work. Although the earlier *Memorial* may have been somewhat even-handed, his *Crónica de los reyes católicos*, on the other hand, has been seen by some as a carefully crafted attempt to bolster the political legitimacy of Isabel, who came to the throne against the backdrop of a civil war against the partisans of Enrique's daughter, *Juana of Castile. In this work, for example, he did raise doubts about Enrique's ability to rule Castile with a firm and just hand. He died in 1486.

Bibliography: William D. Phillips, Jr., *Enrique IV and the Crisis of Fifteenth-Century Castile, 1425–1480*, 1978; Nancy Rubin, *Isabella of Castile: The First Renaissance Queen*, 1991.

Elizabeth Lehfeldt

Valla, Lorenzo (1406–57), was one of the most famous humanists of his time, an opponent of a secular papacy and secretary to *Alfonso V of Aragon. Lorenzo Valla (or della Valle) was born in Rome in 1406. Broadly educated in both Latin and Greek, Valla, after being rejected for an appointment as papal secretary because of his youth, received instead a post as professor of eloquence at the University of Pavia in 1429. Valla held this post until 1439, when he was forced to flee on account of his attacks on the juridical school of Bartolus of Sassoferato. By this time Valla had established a reputation as a Latinist and as a biblical scholar, noted for his then-modern, philological approach to ancient texts. Even before leaving his post at Pavia, Valla had come into contact in 1435 with Alfonso V of Aragon, then engaged in assembling one of the largest libraries in Italy and in bringing humanists to his court. Alfonso was also engaged in a protracted war against Joanna II of Naples and her French supporter, *René of Anjou, and so had need for literate propagandists as well.

Valla, who became Alfonso's secretary in 1437, a post he retained for eleven years, may or may not have written his famous *De falso credita et ementita Constantini donatione declamatio* (Treatise on the falsely believed and forged Donation of Constantine) at the behest of his royal patron. The work certainly suited Alfonso's interests since the pope was allied with Alfonso's enemies and Valla had, with the stroke of his pen, theoretically deprived the papacy of its secular base. According to the original Donation, Pope Sylvester I (314–35) and his successors had been given control over Rome and associated parts of the Western empire by the Emperor Constantine as a reward for curing Constantine's leprosy. Valla subjected the Donation to close philological analysis and in a highly technical discussion proved that it could not have been written when claimed but was in fact dated hundreds of years later and was thus a forgery. He then called upon the subjects of the papacy to rebel and deprive the pope of his secular territories and thereby restore peace to warring Italy, since Valla considered the worldly papacy a major cause of the disorder.

While the treatise on the Donation is Valla's best-known work, it was not perhaps his most immediately influential since the debate he initiated raged for many years before Valla's position was accepted by all. More important for Valla's contemporaries were his two great treatises on the Latin Language, the *Dialecticae disputationes* (Dialectical disputations) and *Elegantiarum linguae Latinae* (The elegance of the Latin language), completed in 1439 and probably in 1440, respectively. In the latter two works, Valla may be said to have invented Renaissance Latin by insisting on exact grammatical usage and by demolishing false assumptions about Latin that had stood for a thousand years. Another influential work by Valla was his *De professione religiosorum* (Concerning the faith of the religious). In it, he criticized the claims of the religious orders of the time that only by membership in them could believers live genuinely Christian lives, emphasizing the importance of faith and deeds. Valla also made contributions as a translator, producing Latin editions of Herodotus, Thucydides, Aesop, and parts of the *Iliad* and Xenophon's *Cyropaedia* (Education of Cyrus). As a historian Valla authored the *Gesta Ferdinandi regis Aragonum* (Deeds of King Ferdinand of Aragon), which he intended as a preface to a life of his patron Alfonso.

This latter work landed Valla in a great deal of trouble with the Spanish contingent of Alfonso's court, who were highly critical of Valla's use of evidence. His Italian enemies, and there were many since Valla had acquired a reputation for arrogance, used the occasion to launch a general attack on him, sometimes in the most insulting terms. Although Valla held his own in the acrimonious disputes that followed, in 1444 a more serious charge, that of heresy, was leveled against him. This allegation may have been a reflection, among other things, of changing politics in Italy now that Alfonso had finally secured his coveted throne of Naples. Since Valla still enjoyed Alfonso's favor and protection, he emerged from the trial little damaged, though he had to make a retraction of some unpopular views. Tired of continual disputes and struggles for influence at Alfonso's court, Valla reconciled with the papacy and moved to Rome with a high papal office under *Nicholas V in 1448. He died on 1 August 1457 in Rome, productive to the end.

Bibliography: Alan Ryder, *Alfonso the Magnanimous, King of Aragon, Naples, and Sicily, 1396–1458*, 1990; Lorenzo Valla, *The Treatise of Lorenzo Valla on the Donation of Constantine: Text and Translation into English*, ed. and trans. C. B. Coleman, 1922.

Paul D. Buell

Valois, Anne, Duchesse de Bourbon (1461–1522),

is also known to scholars as Anne de Beaujeau and "Madame la Grande." Anne Valois is best known for her role as unofficial regent of France for her brother, *Charles VIII, from 1483 to 1494, for strengthening France's central government and economy, and for facilitating the French annexation of Brittany.

Anne was born in 1461 in Genape in Burgundy to *Louis XI of France (then the dauphin) and Charlotte de Savoie. Anne spent her childhood in Amboise and in 1473 wed *Pierre II de Beaujeu, the future duc de Bourbon. The dauphin Charles, nine years Anne's junior, was sickly, and as Louis neared the end of his life, he became closer to Anne, whose keen intelligence matched his own. In 1483 he entrusted her to escort Charles's bride, the three-year-old Margaret of Austria, to Amboise. Louis died in 1483 after expressing the wish that Anne be Charles's guardian, but without naming a regent. Charles VIII had nearly reached his majority, but his ill health and incompetence made it clear that France's government would lie in other hands for some time to come.

Anne handled the duties of her unofficial regency with skill. Her most pressing task was to maintain the power of Charles's crown and to keep in check the power-hungry French peers, who had chafed under Louis XI's autocratic regime. In the meantime, she quietly continued to give order to the army and the ministers of state. She conciliated a number of the high nobility by giving them money and land, freeing political prisoners, and recalling exiles. She lowered taxes, dismissed foreign mercenaries, and punished the most hated ministers of Louis XI's government. She filled the Council and the Estates-General with persons loyal to her. She convened the Estates-General at Tours in 1484 that confirmed her as the king's guardian and thus the real, though unofficial, arbiter of power in France. Thenceforth Anne only nominally consulted the Estates while running the government. Anne combined the best of Louis's methods with a more generous treatment of servitors and allies. She gave money and troops to *Henry (VII) Tudor, facilitating his victory at Bosworth Field and securing his English alliance. In 1488 Anne became the duchess of Bourbon, strengthening her already-powerful position. That year also saw Anne quelling for good the insurrections against her. Louis d'Orléans, the heir presumptive, along with François of Brittany and other discontented nobles, continually tried to undermine Anne's power by leading a series of revolts—part military, part propaganda—known as the "Crazy War" against the government. Anne reacted swiftly and mercilessly to these assaults, which culminated in her victory at the Battle of St. Aubin de Cormier on 24 July 1488. Anne imprisoned Orléans and forced François of Brittany to sign a treaty that weakened the sovereignty of his duchy. This treaty was part of Anne's policy to bring Brittany under French control, a policy she continued with Anne of Brittany, François's heir. Anne Valois at first tried to buy Anne of Brittany's cooperation, sending her rich gifts; but the latter, attempting to evade French control, married *Maximilian of Austria by proxy instead in 1490. However, Charles invaded Brittany in 1491, and Maximilian could not send his wife any aid, due in part to Anne Valois's political machinations. Anne of Brittany was forced to sign a treaty with France, and on 13 December 1491 she married Charles VIII, Anne Valois having convinced Charles to repudiate Margaret of Austria.

Following Charles's marriage, Anne gradually withdrew from her role in the government. Charles was in his twenties and chafing under Anne's tutelage, and Anne had a daughter, Suzanne, in 1491, who commanded her attention, along with her estates in Bourbon. After overseeing the treaties of Barcelona and Senlis in 1493, Anne retired to Moulins in Bourbon, although she still advised Charles and other members of the government, particularly during Charles's fruitless invasion of Italy. She directed a number of modifications to Moulins, built a library of over three hundred volumes, and wrote the *Enseignements* for her daughter. She made a truce of sorts with Louis d'Orléans after his ascension to the throne, and Louis paid tribute to her abilities by asking her in 1514 to teach his new bride, Mary of England, French manners and customs. But Anne's fortunes and power steadily failed after the ascension of François I; her daughter Suzanne died in 1521, and the king and his powerful mother, Louise de Savoie, tried to take control of her property and brought legal proceedings against her. Anne retreated to Chantalle and died on 14 November 1522.

Anne Valois's political skill and effective fiscal policies allowed France to recover from the remaining ravages of the Hundred Years' War to achieve a strong government and a flourishing economy. She brought about many of these achievements through ruthlessness, austerity, and deception. But she showed a warmer, more private side as well in her letters expressing her joy at little Suzanne's happiness and her love of music, literature, and finery. Her most lasting contribution was a unified France, invigorated and ready at last to set foot upon the intellectual and artistic stage of the Renaissance.

Bibliography: P. S. Lewis, ed., *The Recovery of France in the Fifteenth Century*, 1972; Pierre Pradel, *Anne de France, 1461–1522*, 1986.

Miriam Rheingold Fuller

Valois, Jean, Duc de Berry (1360–1416). One of the greatest patrons of the arts in the history of the art world, Jean Valois made possible the creation of two of the most famous illuminated manuscripts known today, *Les Belles Heures* and *Les Tres Riches Heures*. Along with his brothers, the dukes Louis of Anjou and *Philip of Burgundy, Duc Jean de Berry was a power broker and trendsetter in the royal court of France.

Jean, duc de Berry, the third son of Jean II, "le Bon," the king of France from 1350 to 1364, was born on 30 November 1360 in the Château de Vincennes. By the mere accident of his birth, he was consequently the son, brother, and eventual uncle of the future and current kings of France. His proximity to the royal throne made him a potent political force, and this was enhanced by his vast landholdings. In 1360 he inherited the duchies of Berry and Auvergne, and he later added Poitou, a gift in 1369 from his brother, then King Charles V. At the age of twenty Jean married Jeanne d'Armagnac, a marriage contracted in part because of political considerations. He later married another Jeanne, Jeanne de Boulogne, in 1389, after the death of his first wife.

Jean Valois's involvement in politics centered on three aims: finding a conclusion to the Great Schism that had divided Christianity, reestablishing peace between France and England, and ending the rivalry between the houses of Burgundy and Orléans. He was forced to choose one of these houses in 1407 after the murder of his nephew, Duc Louis d'Orléans. The duc de Berry was reputed to be the head of an anti-Burgundian faction known as the "Armagnacs," an organization deeply hated by the Parisian people. In retaliation, his Parisian home, the Hôtel de Nesle, was ransacked, and his home on the outskirts of Paris, the Château de Bicétre, was destroyed. By 1413 sentiment against him forced the duke to take refuge in the Cathedral of Notre Dame. The political turmoil between France and England increased until the two kingdoms became once more involved in a war that resulted in the French defeat at Agincourt. This national tragedy weakened the already-fragile state of health of the duc de Berry, and he died on 15 June 1416.

Despite the political problems that eventually led to his death, Jean Valois was a connoisseur of beautiful art and amassed quite a collection. The entire royal family spent large amounts of money on lavish gifts. The lifestyle led by Jean Valois was indicative of this lavish spending; he owned at least seventeen residences, and he often moved his entire entourage from home to home. In order to maintain such a lifestyle, the duke cultivated the relationship between patron and artist. For example, his master architect, Guy de Dammartin, personally executed the renovations of both the royal palace and the chapels of Sainte-Chapelle in Bourges and Riom. The duke also requested the completion of the facade of the cathedral at Bourges. In so doing, he not only restored these buildings to satisfy his aesthetic tastes, but helped assure their survival for years to come.

As a collector, the duke's tastes covered a wide range of items. He owned exotic animals such as ostriches, camels, and bears, as represented in *Les Tres Riches Heures*; the bears sometimes went with the duke on his travels. Jean Valois was also the consummate showman; he collected all things exotic not only for his own pleasure, but also as exhibition pieces. In addition, he had a passion for collecting exquisite jewels, and he was known to possess a ruby weighing 240 carats.

His diverse tastes spanned the literary world as well as the artistic world. His library contained forty-one histories, thirty-eight chivalric romances, and several books on geography and nature such as Marco Polo's *Book of Travels* and Aristotle's *De caelo*. His collection of religious works included fourteen Bibles, sixteen psalters, and fifteen books of hours. The latter works were the most popular books of devotion in the later Middle Ages. Not only did they contain collections of prayer texts for each liturgical hour of the day, they also contained abstracts from the Gospels themselves. The books created by the Limbourg brothers are perhaps the best known, and they reveal the duke's desire to surpass the books of other connoisseurs in style, size, and beauty. Included in *Les Tres Riches Heures* were representations of months accompanied by the corresponding calendar. For example, the illustrations for the month of January depicted the duke sitting at his table surrounded by family and friends engaged in the exchange of gifts. These representations of the months revealed noble lifestyles in the France of Jean Valois, and this book of hours was in itself a representation of the custom of patronage. For the first time, the importance of the patron was depicted in artwork, as demonstrated in the image for the month of January. The rest of the months not only revealed the changing seasons in nature, but also the changing cycles of the Valois household as the duke moved his entire entourage from one dwelling to another in response to the changes in the seasons. In addition to the importance of cyclical changes, these books of hours also demonstrated the importance of the landscape, as farmers were depicted in the process of threshing wheat or preparing the fields for planting. These landscapes commissioned by Jean Valois were some of the first natural scenes, and they were full of light, a characteristic of the work of the Limbourg brothers.

Although works such as *Les Tres Riches Heures* were somewhat idealized, they did depict court life in medieval France. The fame of works such as this would have delighted Jean Valois, duc de Berry. He reveled in ostentatious display, and this opulent manuscript that so described his luxurious lifestyle well fit the man who commissioned it.

Bibliography: C.A.J. Armstrong, *England, France, and Burgundy in the Fifteenth Century*, 1983; William R. Tyler, *Dijon and the Valois Dukes of Burgundy*, 1971.

Jennifer L. Harrison

van Artevelde, Jacob. *See* Artevelde, Jacob van.

van der Goes, Hugo. *See* Goes, Hugo van der.

van der Weyden, Rogier. *See* Weyden, Rogier van der.

van Eyck, Hubert. *See* Eyck, Hubert van.

van Eyck, Jan. *See* Eyck, Jan van.

Vannucci, Pietro. *See* Perugino, Pietro.

van Ruysbroek, Jan. *See* Ruysbroek, Jan van.

Vasco da Gama. *See* Gama, Vasco da.

Veneziano, Domenico. *See* Domenico Veneziano.

Vergerio, Pietro Paolo, the Elder (c. 1370–1445). Pietro Paolo Vergerio was an early humanist educator, best known for his writings on and definition of liberal education. Vergerio's treatise on education had a profound impact on education in Italy during the Renaissance. Some other works of his include *On Restoring Unity in the Church* and a *Life of *Petrarch*. Also a Catholic, probably belonging to a minor order, Vergerio worked under two popes.

Vergerio was born in Capodistria, Istria (also Trieste, now Koper, Slovenia). As a young man, he studied rhetoric at the University of Padua. In addition, he studied canon law at Florence (1387–89) and Bologna (1389–90), most likely earning degrees in the arts and medicine at these universities. By 1390, at the age of twenty, he was teaching logic at Padua, and he remained at that university as a professor until 1406. At Padua, Vergerio wrote his most puissant treatise, *De ingenuis moribus ac liberalibus studiis* or (On the manners of a gentleman and liberal studies), which was the most influential educational treatise written at that time. It emphasized the importance of a broad liberal education including Latin, Greek, physical fitness, and a variety of subjects such as history, moral philosophy, rhetoric, literature, eloquence, poetry and the poetic arts, arithmetic, geometry, astronomy, and the study of nature. During this time Vergerio also served as a tutor to the sons of the lord of Padua, Francesco Carrara, and so his treatise was dedicated to Ubertino (also Albertinus), one of Vergerio's pupils.

In 1406 Vergerio left Padua for Rome and became secretary to Popes Innocent VII and Gregory XII, taking part in the Council of Constance in 1414 as part of Emperor *Sigismund's suite. The Council of Constance was an ecumenical council devoted to reforming the church; its participants included many European sovereigns and princes in addition to ambassadors of the kings of Denmark, England, France, Scotland, Poland, Naples, and the Spanish regions. In 1415 Emperor Sigismund endeavored to procure *Benedict XIII's renouncement of his claims to the papal throne, and Vergerio was one of a delegation to help effect this. After 1417 Vergerio became Emperor Sigismund's secretary and translated Arrian's *Anabasis* into Latin for the imperial library. Vergerio was one of the primary orators for the Catholic party at the Hussite synod in Prague in 1420, which Sigismund, now king, convened against the Hussites, on the charge that they were heretics.

Among Vergerio's works are several theological treatises, though he never advanced beyond the minor orders. He was never married. Vergerio died in Budapest, Hungary, on 8 July 1444.

Bibliography: William Harrison Woodward, *Vittorino da Feltre and Other Humanist Educators: Essays and Versions*, 1921.

Sigrid Kelsey

Verona, Guarino da. *See* Guarino da Verona.

Verrocchio, Andrea del (1436–1488), was the foremost sculptor of his day. He was also a respected painter and *Leonardo da Vinci's teacher, which cost him much reputation due to slighting comparisons, particularly by Giorgio Vasari. The son of a tile maker, Francesco Cioni, Verrocchio took his name from an early employer, Guiliano de Verrocchio, who taught him goldsmithing. He later became a painter and sculptor. His painted terra-cotta bust of *Lorenzo de Medici, "the Magnificent" (1480), is a remarkable portrait of the ideal Machiavellian prince. His most popular work in Florence still is the *Putto with Dolphin*, designed as the center of a fountain in a Medici villa. The dolphin spouts a jet of water as if it were being squeezed out by the putto. The putto, an angelic nude little boy, balances himself on one leg, as if doing a pirouette. Verrocchio's crowning achievement was the statue of the condottiere Bartolomeo Colleoni in SS. Giovanni Paolo square, Venice. It is his best-known work and arguably the high-water mark in equestrian statuary, rivaled only by *Donatello's equestrian statue of Gattamelata in the Piazza del Santo, Padua. Vigorous in its pose, as if Colleoni were poised at the head of an army, sword in hand, it is a contrast to the calm repose of Donatello's Gattamelata. Other important works are his *Young David* and the *Incredulity of Saint Thomas*, both in Florence.

Bibliography: G. Passavant, *Verrocchio: Sculptures, Paintings, and Drawings*, 1969; Giorgio Vasari, *Lives of the Most Eminent Painters, Sculptors, and Architects*, 1568/ 1972.

C. Thomas Ault

Vespasiano da Bisticci (1421–98) was a prosperous Florentine dealer of books and manuscripts. Among his patrons were kings, dukes, popes, and statesmen. His bookshop also provided a gathering place for prominent humanist scholars and writers. After retiring as a bookseller, Vespasiano began a second career as a writer. His most famous work was *Lives of Illustrious Men of the Fifteenth Century*, a collection of 105 biographies of Vespasiano's contemporaries. It included the lives of kings, popes, ecclesiastics, statesmen, and writers; some had been his patrons, while others had frequented his shop. His *Lives* provides not only portraits of these men, but also cross-sections of fifteenth-century life.

Vespasiano was born in 1421 in Florence, but his family was originally from Bisticci, a small village near Florence. Little is known about his early life. He began his career as the owner of a bookshop in Florence, and soon his reputation as a dealer of books and manuscripts spread beyond his native Italy. Vespasiano was able to locate Greek, Latin, and Hebrew manuscripts for purchase by his patrons, or he had manuscripts copied, illuminated, and bound for the private collections of Italian nobles. One of his prominent patrons was *Cosimo de Medici; Vespasiano hired forty-five scribes who worked for twenty-two months on producing manuscripts for Cosimo's library. Vespasiano's scribes also worked on manuscripts for the library of *Federigo da Montefeltro, duke of Urbino. Among his other patrons were Pope *Eugenius IV and Pope *Nicholas V, as well as *Alfonso the Magnanimous, king of Naples, and *Matthias Corvinus, king of Hungary.

Vespasiano's shop was a meeting place for humanist scholars and writers. At his shop, men gathered to discuss and debate the latest scholarly topics and political issues of the day. There they also had an opportunity to examine Vespasiano's large stock of books and manuscripts. Thus his shop became an influential part of Florentine intellectual and cultural life. In 1480 Vespasiano relinquished ownership of his bookstore to Andrea de Lorenzo. Printed books had by then become more accessible, while the demand and market for copied manuscripts had decreased. Rather than sell printed books, Vespasiano chose to retire to the village of Antella and pursue a second career as a writer.

From 1480 until his death in 1498, Vespasiano wrote several treatises, but his most famous work was *Lives of Illustrious Men of the Fifteenth Century*, which he wrote in vernacular Italian. The men portrayed in his *Lives* were his contemporaries, ranging from monarchs and nobles, popes, cardinals, and archbishops to statesmen, scholars, and writers. In addition to their deeds and accomplishments, Vespasiano related anecdotes from the everyday lives of these men, anecdotes that revealed their moral and human qualities. Vespasiano included three English men: John Tiptoft, earl of Worcester; William Gray, bishop of Ely; and Andre Hollis, a scholar and cleric. One woman was also included in the *Lives*: Alessandra de Bardi. Vespasiano praised her piety and womanly virtues and proclaimed her a model for other women to follow.

Only a few of the *Lives* had been published before 1839, but in that year

Cardinal Angelo Mai published 103 lives from a Vatican manuscript ascribed to Vespasiano. In 1859 Adolfo Bartoli published 2 additional lives, bringing the total to 105. Vespasiano was concerned in the *Lives* about religion and morality, and at times he sounds more like a preacher than a biographer. What he lacked in style, Vespasiano made up for in his vivid descriptions of people and events, which provide a fascinating picture of the complex political, economic, and social world of the fifteenth century.

Bibliography: Margery A. Ganz, "A Florentine Friendship: Donato Acciaiuoli and Vespasiano da Bisticci," *Renaissance Quarterly* 43, no. 2 (1990): 372–83; *Renaissance Princes, Popes, and Prelates: The Vespasiano Memoirs: Lives of Illustrious Men of the XVth Century*, trans., William George and Emily Waters, 1963.

Patricia Worrall

Vespucci, Amerigo (1454–1512), whose name adorns the continents of the Western Hemisphere, has a reputation as a swindler who stole the glory due to *Christopher Columbus. Although Columbus found new lands, which he thought were islands near Asia, Vespucci was the first to suggest that they constituted a new world wholly unknown to Europe. He also identified the stars of the Southern Cross, which still provides invaluable aid for stellar navigation.

Born on 9 March 1454, Vespucci began life amid the cultural and political ferment of Renaissance Florence. His family had strong ties to the Medici family, and he grew up surrounded by artists and scholars of all types. Educated by his uncle, a Dominican friar with a gift for the new learning, Vespucci absorbed a broad range of subjects, including Latin, astronomy, and geography. He began his public career in 1478 as a secretary for the Florentine ambassador to France. In 1484 he found employment in the service of the Popolanos, a Florentine banking family in Seville. His ability and discretion were such that by 1492 they trusted him as their bank manager.

Except for theoretical knowledge of astronomy and geography, Vespucci had no nautical training or connections to the sea. It is thus strange that he attained great fame for his ocean voyages. Acting on the desire to acquire knowledge and perhaps wealth, he joined Portuguese and Spanish expeditions to the territories discovered by Columbus. Between 1497 and 1504, in three or four trips, he may have sailed as far north as the eastern shore of Virginia, and he certainly saw the bleak land of Patagonia to the south. On these voyages Vespucci served as an observer and reporter.

Lacking his official reports, historians must rely on the published letters he sent to the rulers of Florence, *Piero de Medici, "the Unfortunate," and Piero Soderini. These letters revealed a keen interest in native peoples, who appeared as golden-age innocents one moment and bestial cannibals with unsavory sexual practices the next. His letters also showed a preoccupation with navigational matters. In recording the latitude of his travels, Vespucci came to the startling conclusion that the southern landmass was a continent completely unknown to classical geography and biblical tradition. In 1503 anonymous printers published a Latin translation of a letter that they entitled *Mundus novus*, giving Vespucci credit for the discovery of the New World. Shortly thereafter another letter describing his four voyages was published. The combination of vicarious titillation and astonishing geographical theory found in these letters guaranteed their widespread success and Vespucci's fame. The Spanish Crown, which needed able navigators and pilots to expand and exploit its newfound possessions, gave Vespucci citizenship in 1505. Three years later he received the post of pilot major, which entailed the training of new pilots and the continual revising of cartographic information. He died on 22 February 1512, and his body rests in the Church of San Miguel in Seville.

Though he never sought it, Vespucci achieved international fame during his lifetime. In 1507 a small group of scholars and printers at Saint-Die, France, published his letter as part of Martin Waldseemüller's *Cosmographiae introductio*. It included a map of the southern continent, which bore the name "America." The name caught on immediately, and even though later editions of Waldseemüller's work retracted it, America soon came to represent all of the new lands. Bartolomé de Las Casas, Columbus's biographer and champion, was the first of many suspected of foul play in this unlikely turn of events. Recent scholarship has shown that the naming of the western continents had more to do with the popularity of Vespucci's vivid letters and a printer's exuberance than with any ambition on his part. Despite his posthumous reputation as a thief, Vespucci seems to have been trusted and respected by all who knew him. Columbus's letters show that he thought of him as an ally and friend. Although most agree that America is misnamed, Amerigo Vespucci deserves distinction as the first man to understand the true nature of Columbus's achievements.

Bibliography: Germán Arciniegas, *Amerigo and the New World: The Life and Times of Amerigo Vespucci*, 1955; Edmundo O'Gorman, *The Invention of America*, 1961.

Brian G. Hudgins

Villani, Giovanni (c. 1276–1348),

was a Florentine merchant and historian. Villani was a prominent merchant and citizen, but he is best remembered for his *Chronicle of Florence*. His history of the city combined the myths and legends of the origins of Florence with his own detailed observations of mid-fourteenth-century life. His interest in the economic and social aspects of Florence and his use of detailed statistics made him a "modern" medieval historian.

Giovanni Villani was born about 1276 in Florence. His father was Villano di Stoldo, a prosperous merchant. Villani was probably educated at one of the city's grammar schools, and later he took an active role in his father's business affairs, even traveling to Flanders and France on family business. He was also associated with the famous banking families of Peruzzi and Buonaccorsi, but

all did not go well for Villani. He was caught up in the financial crisis of 1345–
46 and was briefly imprisoned following charges brought against him by one of
his creditors.

As a responsible citizen, Villani became involved in Florentine politics. In
1316, 1317, and 1321 he held the office of prior, the highest public office in
the city. He served as an official at the mint with the responsibility for the
records and for registering the new coins. During the severe famine of 1328 he
was also one of the city officials appointed to monitor food distribution. His
civic duty also extended to his involvement in some of the city's building projects. The most ambitious of these projects was the completion of the third wall
around the city.

Villani, however, is best known for his *Chronicle of Florence*. In the *Chronicle*, he related how he came to write his city's history. He had attended the
jubilee of 1300 in Rome, and while he was there, he realized that Rome was
decreasing in power and importance, while Florence was a city on the rise.
Villani felt that his beloved city deserved a comprehensive history that would
record Florentine greatness from its origins to his own time. His *Chronicle*
consisted of twelve books, beginning with the Tower of Babel and moving
through the history of Rome and Italy. It was not until the seventh book that
Villani began his discussion of Florence. For the earlier history, Villani depended upon available authorities, whose works were in turn based mainly on
myth and legend.

Of particular interest today are the sections of the *Chronicle* that deal with
the history of Florence beginning with the mid-thirteenth century. For these
sections, Villani relied on his own knowledge and observations and on primary-
source witnesses. Thus his account provides an invaluable source of information
not only about Florence, but also about diplomacy and foreign affairs. Villani,
unlike other medieval historians, was interested in facts and statistics. He provided a record of general information on aspects of life such as commerce,
institutions, population, weather conditions, calamities, and taxes. For instance,
based on the consumption of grain, he calculated that the population in 1338
was 90,000. He noted that there were 110 churches, 5 abbeys, and 24 monasteries, which indicated the importance of the church and religion in daily life.
He also recorded that in 1338 there were 80 banks and 2,000 wool shops,
suggesting that the economy of Florence and the wool industry were thriving.

As part of the *Chronicle*, Villani included descriptions of certain calamities
that had struck Florence. He described the devastating fire of 1304 and its consequences. The three hundred deaths caused by the flood of 1333 were noted,
as was the property that was carried away. He also provided a firsthand account
of the effects of plague in 1340 and in 1348; his description of the terrible
plague of 1348 rivaled *Giovanni Boccaccio's famous description in the introduction to the *Decameron*. It was in fact the plague of 1348 that ended Villani's

life. In the *Chronicle* he wrote that "the plague lasted until," leaving the date blank because his death intervened.

Villani spent almost fifty years gathering material and writing his history. After his death, Matteo Villani, his younger brother, continued the *Chronicle* up to the year 1363, the year that Matteo himself died of plague. He added eleven books, but he did not have his brother's keen sense of observation and interest in detail. After Matteo's death, his son Filippo contributed to the *Chronicle* through 1410. Thus, through their combined effort, the *Chronicle* recorded the mythical and legendary origins of Florence, but more important, it provided a detailed source of information about fourteenth-century life in Florence.

Bibliography: Gene Brucker, *The Civic World of Early Renaissance Florence*, 1977; Giovanni Villani, *Selections from the First Nine Books of the Croniche Fiorentine of Giovanni Villani*, ed. Philip H. Wicksteed, and trans. Rose E. Selfe, 1896.

Patricia Worrall

Villena, Isabel de (1430–90), was born Elionor Manuel de Villena. An erudite nun and mitred abbess, Isabel was the most celebrated female writer during the medieval golden age of letters in Valencia, Spain. Her principal extant work, *Vita Christi* (1497), is notable for its realistic and eloquent narrative and its motif of the dignity of women.

Elionor Manuel de Villena was born in 1430 in Valencia, the illegitimate daughter of the renowned Castilian humanist, writer, and translator Enrique de Villena. Nothing is known of Villena's birthplace nor of her mother. After her father's death in 1434, Villena was raised in the court of *Alfonso the Magnanimous under the tutelage of Queen Mary of Castile. There Villena received a remarkably complete education in Latin, Greek, and theology, among other disciplines. She entered the Franciscan Convent of the Holy Trinity in Valencia in 1445, was elected superior of the convent in 1463, and remained so until her death in 1490. The court of the Catholic kings and Valencian society at large coveted her company and wisdom.

With her *Vita Christi* (The life of Christ), Villena transformed a commonplace genre of her time into an intimate and largely biographical reflection on a series of biblical passages. Addressed to her fellow nuns for pedagogical purposes, the *Vita*, composed in Catalan, offered her insights on myriad themes, including the grace of everyday life, the drama of biblical scenes, and the richness of contemplative prayer. Its narrative tone was equally diverse, offering examples of popular language, courtly discourse, and eloquent theological rhetoric. This stylistic composite indicates influences from the thirteenth-century *Libre de contemplació en Deu* by the Catalan poet and theologian *Ramon Llull, the works of Francesch Eiximenis, and the *libros de caballería* in general. The *Vita* consists of 241 chapters and is based on the four Gospels as well as on apocryphal texts. References to classical literature and philosophy are interspersed throughout the exegesis, revealing Villena's syncretic interests. The *Vita* is, however, fully orthodox in its treatment of religious themes and does not reveal an interest in alchemy or sorcery, subjects that eventually cost her father Enrique favor with the court.

It is thought that the *Vita* is partially a response to Jaume Roig's satirical and misogynist poem *L'espill* (1460). A serious work pointedly dedicated to devout women, the *Vita* offers original and affirming images of mothers, wives, and religious women. The book's sincere tone appeared in marked contrast to Roig's mocking narrative. Whereas Roig emphasized the pernicious influence of Eve, Villena highlighted the new Eve, Mary, the Mother of God, while the Mysteries of the Virgin Mary, particularly that of the Assumption, were vivid in their representation. In addition, Villena created three striking allegorical female figures to represent Purity, Humility, and Contemplation. The *Vita*'s most original aspect is its representation of a woman capable of direct spiritual contact with Jesus Christ and the Virgin Mary, a literary theme and, indeed, a theological principle generally unacknowledged in the Middle Ages. In the case of Roig, such a possibility was flatly denied. In 1497 Queen *Isabel of Castile, an enthusiastic Latinist in her own right, requested that Villena's successor at the Convent of the Holy Trinity edit the *Vita* and have it published for public consumption.

Villena was also a talented illuminator. She illustrated *Speculum animae* (Soul's mirror), a two-volume manuscript consisting of, first, a missal, and second, a work of Christian meditations similar to the fourteenth-century *Speculum humanae salvationis* (Way to human salvation). Villena completed seventy-five miniature illuminations for the *Speculum animae*, sixty-three of which were full-page size.

Villena was considerably influential at court and in polite society during her lifetime. Her intellectual and literary accomplishments can best be discerned in her *Vita Christi*. Composed in Catalan rather than Castilian, the *Vita* has consequently not received the critical attention it deserves. Villena's narrative appeared as a precursor to the Spanish mystic writers of a century later.

Bibliography: Carlos G. Noreña, *Studies in Spanish Renaissance Thought*, 1975; Isabel de Villena, *Libre anomenat Vita Christi, compost per Isabel de Villena*, ed. Miquel i Planas, 3 vols., 1916.

Margaret Harp

Villon, François (1431–1463),

otherwise known as François de Montcourbier or François des Loges, was perhaps one of the finest fifteenth-century French poets. Villon was a Renaissance man of letters responsible for a large body of works, but he was also a man constantly in trouble with the law. His masterpiece, *Le testament*, embodied the medieval conception of life with its emphasis on spirituality and the importance of death. However, the works of Villon were different from those of his predecessors, such as Marie de France or Chrétien de Troyes. In order to appreciate Villon's imagery, it is necessary to be familiar with his favorite haunts and habits. The Paris of Villon's day was not the metropolis of today, but was rather an urban island in the midst of France, completely surrounded by walls that isolated the inhabitants from the rest of the country.

Villon made his poetry come alive, a feat made possible by the fact that his poetry often mirrored his life. He was born in Paris in 1431, the year of the burning of *Joan of Arc. Whether one believes in the concept of coincidence or not, Villon's life was never to be mundane. His birth was clouded by questionable circumstances, and this cycle repeated itself throughout his short life. For example, in 1455 he was involved in an altercation with a priest by the name of Philippe Sermoise, who was mysteriously killed after the annual Fête-Dieu celebration in Paris in 1455. It was quite possible that Villon was the murderer, and that he was the first to throw a rock at Sermoise. However, as luck would have it, Villon received two royal pardons. Villon often seemed to have luck on his side when it came to the authorities, for he usually escaped with only a reprimand. The dust had hardly settled over the 1455 incident when Villon was charged in the burglary of the College of Navarre in December 1456. The crime was not discovered until early January 1457, but by this time Villon had managed to disappear into hiding, where he stayed for five years. On 5 January 1463 Villon received a pardon from the death sentence pronounced against him in 1456. On 8 January 1463 Villon vanished from France without leaving a trace, and so the man who had entered the world under murky circumstances left it in the same way.

In his poetry, Villon ignored the concept of social class, and all became his targets, whether rich or poor, male or female. The themes of death, love, and spirituality were evident in all of his works. His masterpiece, *Le testament*, liberally employed all three themes. Many of his characters were female, and with the exception of the references to both his mother and the Virgin Mary, Villon hardly wrote well of women. His attitude toward women was perhaps best represented in "La belle Heaulmière," a ballade found in *Le testament*. In this piece the term "Heaulmiére," a feminized form of the French word for warrior, was not exactly used in a positive way. Villon combined the sexual connotation with the classic story of the foibles of human nature. When the poem is seen in such a light, it is possible that "La belle Heaulmière" was a mask for Villon himself.

Throughout his poetry, Villon tried to communicate the autobiographical details of his life to the reader. He constantly referred to himself as "le pauvre Villon," and like many of his characters who died as martyrs, Villon wanted to be a martyr too. He wrote, "De quelconque condition . . . Mort saisit sans excepcion" (death knows all without exception . . . on any condition). This autobiographical tendency can also be found in his use of acrostics, the letters in a name that stand for an underlying meaning, to explain his thoughts on both death and life.

In order to comprehend Villon's work, one must understand his tone and whether or not he was trying to fool the reader. By beginning several of his pieces with a date, he gave a certain validity to his work. He was also bluntly honest: "Je suis pécheur; je le sais bien" (I am a sinner; I know it well). He lamented his lost youth in the lines "Bien scay, si j'eusse estudie / ou temps de ma jeunesse folle" (If only I had studied during my wild youth). In addition, Villon employed the technique of closure, as in the example of the conclusion to *Le testament*, "Icy se clost le testament / Et finist du povre Villon" (Here ends the Testament, and here finishes Villon). It would be a few years before Villon disappeared from Paris, but perhaps this was an indication of what was to come. Such foreshadowing encapsulated the life and message of Villon; he entered the world on uncertain terms, but he left it on his own terms by defining his own poetic character.

Bibliography: David Fein, *A Reading of Villon's Testament*, 1984; Evelyn Birge Vitz, *The Crossroad of Intentions: A Study of Symbolic Expression in the Poetry of François Villon*, 1974.

Jennifer L. Harrison

Vincent Ferrer, Saint (1350–1419),

was a renowned Dominican friar who preached and worked miracles throughout Europe in the late Middle Ages. Choosing the side of the Avignonese obedience during the Great Papal Schism (1378–1417), Vincent eagerly defended his Spanish compatriot, Pedro de Luna (the antipope *Benedict XIII). Refusing the honors conferred on him, he chose instead the life of an itinerant missionary, converting, according to his hagiographers, heretics, Muslims, and Jews in Spain, Italy, and France. He died in Vannes, Brittany, on 5 April 1419 and was canonized by Pope Calixtus III on 3 June 1455. His feast day is on April 5.

Vincent Ferrer was born in Valencia, Spain, on 23 January 1350. He was the second son of a notary of some standing, William Ferrer. His younger brother, Boniface, is also of historical importance. He practiced law until the death of his wife when, on Vincent's advice, he entered the Carthusian order, eventually becoming their general. Taking cause with the antipope Benedict XIII during the schism, he eventually led several diplomatic missions in Spain for the latter.

Vincent's education took place in Valencia, where he studied grammar, rhetoric, the humanities, and dialectic. He joined the Dominican order in February 1367. In 1368 he was sent to Barcelona to further his studies, and by 1370 he was teaching philosophy at Lérida. Three years later he returned to Barcelona and there worked one of his most famous miracles: in the midst of a famine, he foretold the coming of a cargo of wheat. He continued his education in Toulouse in southern France in 1377.

In 1379 Pedro de Luna, legate in Aragon for the Avignonese pope Clement VII, retained him in his entourage. After this mission he went back to teaching theology in Valencia between 1385 and 1390. Shortly thereafter, Queen Yolanda of Aragon made him her confessor, and he resided in Salamanca between 1391 and 1395. He escaped the Inquisition for preaching that "Judas had done penance" when Pedro de Luna, now as Pope Benedict XIII, received the case before his tribunal and dismissed it. Pope Benedict favored him further when he made Ferrer papal confessor and apostolic penitentiary in Avignon. It was during this Avignonese period that he refused the cardinalate offered to him.

During the French subtraction of obedience and the ensuing siege of the pope's palace by French troops, Vincent became seriously ill, but a miraculous cure sent him again on his missionary path. In November 1399 Benedict XIII granted him the full power of a legate *a latere Christ*, a diplomatic representative of the pope. He preached penance and repentance for the next twenty years. Walking away from Avignon, he made his fame converting Cathars and Waldensian heretics in the Franco-Italian Alps. Heard by large crowds, he maintained in good order a large group of followers, male and female disciples. From southern Europe he moved north to Flanders and into France.

By 1408 he was back in Genoa, Italy, hoping that a meeting between the two rival popes, Gregory XII and Benedict XIII, would take place and end the schism. It never happened. Disappointed, he returned to Spain, and between 1408 and 1416 he preached and converted (according to his hagiographers) thousands of Muslims and Jews throughout the Iberian Peninsula. At the death of the Aragonese king, he was one of the judges appointed to establish a succession to the Crown. He participated in the Compromise of Caspe and helped the election of Ferdinand of Castile as king of Aragon.

His preaching and miracle working did much to maintain the legitimacy of the Avignonese pope, but by 1416 Benedict XIII's stubbornness forced Vincent to withdraw his obedience, even though he profoundly respected Benedict. Vincent skipped the Council of Constance (1414–1418) and its solution to the schism for his evangelic mission. He spent the last two years of his life preaching in Brittany, where he died in 1419.

Vincent was called "the Messenger of Penance," preaching repentance of sins and preparation for Judgment Day. He was extremely successful and was renowned in his own time for his sermons, miracles, and conversions. He led an austere life, fasting, sleeping very little and on bare floors, praying much, and traveling on foot in humble attire. He wrote many sermons and various tracts, including the *Treatise of the Spiritual Life* and a defense of the Avignonese papacy.

Bibliography: Francis Oakley, *The Western Church in the Later Middle Ages*, 1979; Laura A. Smoller, "Miracle, Memory, and Meaning in the Canonization of Vincent Ferrer, 1453–1454," *Speculum* 73 (1998): 429–454.

Joelle Rollo-Koster

Vinci, Leonardo da. *See* Leonardo da Vinci.

Visconti, Filippo Maria, Duke of Milan (1392–1447),

was born at the family home in Milan, the Castello di Porta Giova, to *Giangaleazzo Visconti and Caterina di Bernabò. Giangaleazzo became the first duke of Milan after purchasing his title from the Emperor *Wenceslas in 1394 for 100,000 florins. During his time in power he extended his lordship to encompass Verona, Padua, Pisa, and Siena. He regarded this expansive territorial agglomeration as a family property rather than a political state, and consequently, on his death in 1402, he divided his domains between his sons according to Italian tradition. The eldest son, Giovanni Maria, was made duke of Milan, while Filippo Maria was to rule under him at Pavia. Giangaleazzo had maintained his rule successfully through the employment of condottieri, great mercenary captains who led their own armies in support of Giangaleazzo's ambitions. At his death, however, his condottieri rebelled against the new duke, and anarchy ensued for the next decade. Giangaleazzo's chief captain, Facino Cane, led the most successful insurrection. He attempted to found an independent tyranny in Milan, though his efforts were cut short by his natural death on 16 May 1412, the same day that Giovanni Maria was murdered in the Church of S. Gottardo, thus propelling Filippo Maria into the position of duke of Milan.

His first decisive step as duke was to secure peace with Facino's armies by marrying his widow, Beatrice da Tenda. This marriage was short-lived, however; within three years of their wedding, two of Beatrice's maids accused her of infidelity with one of her pages. Visconti imprisoned both Beatrice and the page, had them tortured until they confessed, and then executed them in September 1415. Both the allegation and the extracted confessions remain dubious, though, as Visconti also had the two witnesses executed and all of the records of the process destroyed. Nevertheless, despite suspicions of foul play, Beatrice's execution went unchallenged politically. Her absence permitted Visconti to resume his affair with Agnese del Maino, the mother of his only child, Bianca Maria, and his lifelong companion.

Visconti was a master of manipulation. He spent most of his career playing his captains off one against the other. In order to recover the full extent of his father's estate, Visconti employed Francesco Bussone, known as Carmagnola, to be captain of his armies. Carmagnola labored for ten hard years and finally managed to regain this lost territory. Despite Carmagnola's devotion and his connection through marriage to the Visconti, Filippo Maria began to fear that Carmagnola had accumulated too much power and would eventually turn on him. Thus the duke preempted such actions by retaining *Francesco Sforza as his captain instead. Sforza came from a long line of condottieri and had already gained for himself a reputation as a brutal, yet brilliant military leader. Enraged by Visconti's betrayal, Carmagnola turned to Venice for assistance. After two years of warfare and political wrangling—during which Visconti took his second wife, Maria of Savoy, a strategy designed to eliminate Venice's most powerful ally—both sides finally reached a peaceful agreement. During this time Francesco Sforza proved himself to be not only a worthy captain, but also a leader in his own right.

Over the next twenty years Visconti wavered in his loyalties, imprisoning

Sforza at least once, while on two other occasions he promised him the hand of his only daughter. He deployed the famed condottiere Piccinino against Sforza, yet he was compelled to follow through with the marriage of Sforza and Bianca Maria once Piccinino's power grew beyond his control. Soon after Visconti's death in 1447, Sforza was recognized by the Milanese as his ducal successor.

Had he been less suspicious of his captains, Filippo Maria might have had a more auspicious career as duke of Milan. This extreme cynicism was only one of the idiosyncrasies that marred his character. His biographers wrote that in his later life, Filippo Maria became so sensitive about his obesity and homely countenance that he never appeared in public and rarely left the family home. Moreover, his fear of thunder led him to commission the building of a room with double walls in which he could take refuge during stormy weather. Nonetheless, Visconti did achieve a measure of success. When he first came to power, Milan was greatly reduced in size and was reaching the end of a decade of political chaos. At his death, however, Milan was once again a wealthy and powerful state. This profound transformation speaks not only to his shrewdness in creating beneficial alliances through his own marriages and those of Visconti women, but also his ability to procure military leaders of superior quality.

Bibliography: Jacob Burckhardt, *The Civilization of the Renaissance in Italy*, 1860/1990; Lauro Martines, *Power and Imagination: City-States in Renaissance Italy*, 1988; Dorothy Muir, *A History of Milan under the Visconti*, 1924.

Sara Butler

Visconti, Giangaleazzo, Duke of Milan (1351–1402).

Under Giangaleazzo Visconti's rule, Milan became a powerful state comprising much of northern Italy, and his military power was strong enough to defeat invading French forces. He was politically astute, using not only military strategies to gain power, but also intrigue and diplomacy. During his lifetime he was a generous patron of the arts, and his library at Pavia was one of the greatest libraries of the fourteenth century.

Giangaleazzo Visconti was born in Milan in 1351, the son of Galeazzo II and Bianca of Savoy. In 1360, at the age of nine, Giangaleazzo married Isabella of Valois, and four years later Giangaleazzo and Isabella set up their own household. Valentina, their first child, was born in 1366. They also had three sons; Giangaleazzo, who died in infancy, and Azzone and Carlos, neither of whom survived childhood. After Isabella's death in 1372, Giangaleazzo married his first cousin Caterina, the daughter of his uncle Bernabò. In 1388 Giangaleazzo and Catherina had a son, Giovanni, who would become the second duke of Milan, and in 1392 another son, *Filippo Maria.

Giangaleazzo was a tall, handsome man and a competent horseman. He was also well educated and knew French, German, and Latin; his interest in learning is apparent from his library at Pavia. The library contained almost a thousand manuscripts, which made it one of the largest fourteenth-century manuscript collections in Europe. Among the manuscripts were the works of *Dante, Plato, and Virgil, as well as St. Augustine and St. Ambrose. Giangaleazzo's interests also extended to contemporary authors, and both *Francesco Petrarch and *Christine de Pizan were invited to Pavia. Giangaleazzo was also a patron and collector of art. His interest in architecture led to his involvement in the rebuilding of the Cathedral of Milan. During his rule the University of Pavia prospered, the University of Piacenza was restored, and the Academy of Architecture and Painting was established.

Giangaleazzo is best known, however, for his political achievements, both domestic and foreign. When Galeazzo, his father, died in 1378, Bernabò, Giangaleazzo's uncle, took over the government of Milan, but in May 1385 Giangaleazzo captured and imprisoned Bernabò. After his coup against Bernabò, the citizens of Milan recognized Giangaleazzo as their ruler. He was thirty-four years old. Once he had firmly established his power in the city, Giangaleazzo then turned his attention to foreign affairs. He was concerned about French interference in Italian matters, and during his life he strove to weaken that influence. Three times Giangaleazzo had to confront invading armies backed by France. One such aggressor was John of Armagnac, a great French noble who wanted to avenge Bernabò and put Bernabò's son in control of Milan. In July 1391 Giangaleazzo soundly defeated the French force, and Armagnac was killed. The battle was a great victory not only for Giangaleazzo, but for Milan. In 1395, in an effort to enhance his international standing and prestige, Giangaleazzo bribed and coerced Emperor *Wenceslas into bestowing upon him the dignity of duke of Milan, a hereditary title to be passed down to Giangaleazzo's male descendants.

While he was establishing an international reputation, Giangaleazzo was also expanding his own empire though intrigue and conquest. His first significant acquisition was Verona in 1387. The city was taken with the help of a traitor. After hearing the news of Verona's surrender, Vicenza also submitted, and Padua fell soon thereafter. In 1389 Giangaleazzo began what turned out to be a long-drawn-out conflict with Bologna and Florence. It was not until 1401 that Giangaleazzo's forces attacked and finally captured Bologna. Florence was to be next, and it appeared that Giangaleazzo would have little trouble defeating the Florentines and thus would gain control of northern Italy. Florence, however, was saved from conquest when Giangaleazzo was suddenly taken ill on 10 August 1402 and died from fever on September 3 at age fifty-one. His death saved Florence, but it was devastating for Milan. He left two young sons, but the regents for fourteen-year-old Giovanni, the second duke of Milan, were unable to maintain control over Giangaleazzo's vast acquisitions. After his death, Giovanni ruled over a state that was greatly diminished in size.

Over a period of seventeen years Giangaleazzo Visconti was able to defend against foreign invasions and, at the same time, consolidated and extended his power. At his death he controlled a large portion of northern Italy. He was, however, not only a conqueror but also a generous patron of literature and art.

Bibliography: E. R. Chamberlin, *The Count of Virtue: Giangaleazzo Visconti,* 1965; Edith W. Kirsch, ed., *Five Illuminated Manuscripts of Giangaleazzo Visconti,* 1991.

Patricia Worrall

Vitry, Philippe de (1291–1361), was a French poet, composer, and music theorist, royal secretary to three French kings, and bishop of Meaux from 1351 to 1361. He was a leading representative of the *ars nova* movement. Notwithstanding his reputation as an exceptional polymath, it appears that most of what he wrote has been lost. His extant work comprises three poems in French, remnants of Vitriacan theory on musical notation (the so-called *Ars nova* treatise) and a handful of motets.

Philippe de Vitry was born, probably in the province of Champagne, on 31 October 1291. He began his career in government as a notary cleric under King Charles IV and subsequently served as a royal secretary and *maître des requêtes* under Philip VI and Jean II. He fulfilled several diplomatic missions, notably to Avignon in 1327 and 1350, and took part in a military siege at Aiguillon in 1346. A cleric in holy orders, he accumulated prebends at Soissons, Cambrai, Clermont-en-Beauvaisis, Verdun, and elsewhere prior to his nomination as bishop of Meaux. In 1357 he served as one of several reformers general selected by the Estates-General to investigate financial irregularities within the upper echelons of the royal government.

Contemporaries held Vitry in high esteem as a poet, as an authority on music, and as a scholar, yet surprisingly few of his works have survived the ravages of time. His three extant poems, including *Dict de Franc Gautier, Chapel des trois fleurs de lis,* and *De terre o grec Gaulle appellée,* provide only a glimpse of his poetic inclinations. In *Dict de Franc Gautier,* he extolled the virtues of rural life free from the constraints of court. The pastoral scene he described became a literary commonplace, one that *François Villon evoked a century later in his derisive *Contredits de Franc Gautier.* The *Chapel des fleurs de lis,* a significantly longer poem, revealed the author's devout sense of patriotism and was written in support of Philippe de Valois's call for a crusade (1332–34). The three lilies invoked in the title represent cardinal virtues of the French nation: Faith, Science, and Chivalry. In *De terre o grec Gaulle appellée,* a ballade, Vitry rebuked a contemporary poet, Jehan de La Mote, for his use of obscure classical allusions and for his preference for the English court over that of France—criticism he appears to reiterate in the motet *O creator deus.*

As a composer and a theorist, Vitry contributed much to the development of Western music. Whether he actually wrote a treatise titled *Ars nova,* merely "compiled" one, or just served as an authority and a reference to other *ars nova* theorists is a matter of current scholarly debate. Fragments of Vitriacan notational theory nonetheless survive in five manuscripts, three of which contain passages derived from a common textual source. Of the twelve to sixteen motets that modern historians typically ascribe to him, five are recognized on the authority of reliable contemporary citations. These include *Garison selon nature*, a French-language motet based on the traditional theme of courtly love; *Gratissima virginis species*, a devotional piece; *Hugo, Hugo*, a remonstrance against hypocrisy; and *Petre clemens*, a tribute to Pope *Clement VI. The music for *O creator deus*, originally written for four voices, is now lost; only the texts have survived. Several of Vitry's motets appear as anonymous musical interpolations in the *Roman de Fauvel*; however, scholars do not always agree on their number. In music and theory, Vitry belonged to the avant-garde of his generation. He promoted imperfect mensuration, use of the minim, and isorhythmic structure. He very likely also introduced the use of coloration (red ink) as a notational device. He died at Meaux on 9 June 1361.

Bibliography: John Douglas Gray, "The Ars nova Treatises Attributed to Philippe de Vitry: Translations and Commentary," Ph.D. diss., University of Colorado at Boulder, 1996; Daniel Leech-Wilkinson, "The Emergence of *ars nova*," *Journal of Musicology* 13 (1995): 285–317.

Jan Pendergrass

W

Walsingham, Thomas (c. 1345–1422), was a Latin writer who is often described as the last of the great medieval chroniclers, yet his major historical works were both a revival of an earlier tradition at the Abbey of St. Albans and an extension of that tradition that influenced other contemporaries like John Capgrave (1393–1464), the Augustan friar of Lynn. Little is known of Walsingham's early life, although it is generally accepted that he came from Walsingham in the county of Norfolk, entered St. Albans in 1364, and probably attended Oxford. At that time the abbey was the most prestigious Benedictine center in Britain, and its abbot, Thomas de la Mare, was a vigorous leader who imposed intellectual rigor and religious devotion, who supervised the building of a new scriptorium, and who probably encouraged Walsingham to revitalize a number of declining activities at St. Albans. Whatever his motivation, Walsingham applied himself conscientiously and produced a body of works whose breadth, scope, and quantity were unmatched by any of his contemporaries. His work-included traditional commentaries, chronicles, and rules for a musical-notation system, the *Regulae de musica mensurabili.*

Walsingham spent much of his career under de la Mare's supervision and did not become precentor (music educator) and *scripturarius* (head scribe) at St. Albans until the mid-1380s. A dozen years later he was appointed prior of the Benedictine house at Wymondham in Norfolk, but he retired after two years, preferring to pursue his studies and writing. He returned to St. Albans freed from all of his responsibilities for the scriptorium and other administrative duties. In the remaining quarter century of his life he continued his historical commentaries but devoted most of his effort to classical and clerical studies, producing several works on the gods of the ancients, a commentary on Ovid's *Metamorphoses*, an account of the Trojan War, and a biography of Alexander the Great.

Influenced by earlier chroniclers of St. Albans, Walsingham produced his

Chronica majora (Great chronicle), a continuation of Matthew of Paris's narrative history, which is notable for its comprehensive coverage of political events between 1372 and 1420. Walsingham wrote a *Short English Chronicle*, also called *Historia Anglicana brevis*, which was essentially an abridgement of the larger account with a narrower focus. He is also well known for his *Ypodigma Neustriae* (Account of events in Normandy), which continued early accounts of the duchy's history. It also justified England's invasion of France and focused heavily on contemporary English politics. *Ypodigma Neustriae* was intended to provide instruction and was dedicated to Henry V, and it may have earned its author the title of royal historian or *regis historicus*.

Walsingham also wrote a continuation of *Ranulf Higden's universal history, entitled *Polychronicon*, which used the same name, included the works of other authors, and extended the account into the 1380s. He produced a hagiographical *Book of Benefactors* and a similar account of *The Deeds of the Abbots of St. Albans*, or *Gesta abbatum*, using a variety of older sources and extending it through the abbacy of Thomas de la Mare.

Walsingham's works were unique because of their abundance of detail, the diversity of their sources, the strength of their opinions, and their expression of contemporary viewpoints. They remain a major source for all accounts of the reigns of *Richard II, *Henry IV, and Henry V and include discussions of *Wat Tyler's insurrection and the activities of *John Wyclif and the Lollards. Walsingham strongly condemned peasant revolts and was intolerant of moral frailties; thus he criticized *John of Gaunt and portrayed Wyclif as the Antichrist, while he increasingly defended the Lancastrians' patriotism and chivalry. While his work was highly derivative and redundant and lacked originality, Walsingham's writings were informative, detailed, and interpretive and marked the culmination of the tradition at St. Albans of compiling Latin chronicles.

Bibliography: Antonia Gransden, *Historical Writing in England*, vol. 2, 1996; John Taylor, *English Historical Literature in the Fourteenth Century*, 1987.

Sheldon Hanft

Wenceslas IV, King of Bohemia (b. 1360, r. 1378–1419), was also the

uncrowned German emperor. Wenceslas's incompetence as a ruler led to the Hussite revolt that split Bohemia from the Catholic church. Wenceslas was the son of Holy Roman Emperor Charles IV. It was during Charles's reign that an element of nationalism was introduced into the religious struggle to reform the corruption of the Bohemian church.

This struggle intensified when Wenceslas came to the throne in 1378. Much given to leisure pursuits, Wenceslas was the polar opposite of his father, and only his father's able councilors, whom Wenceslas retained, made the first ten years of his reign relatively peaceful. Wenceslas's capacity for drink and his ungovernable temper gave him an extremely unsavory reputation, though he did follow his father's example as a patron of the arts and learning. He also refrained from the unnecessary imposition of taxes and so enjoyed a dubious popularity, but he had no substance of character to withstand any serious challenge to his authority.

Anti-Jewish pogroms in 1389 revealed the king's inability to take resolute action, and the replacement of his father's ministers with men from the lower nobility and the burgher class created resentment among the older Czech magnates, who, in concert with Wenceslas's brothers and cousins, joined in a conspiracy against him in 1394. Wenceslas was imprisoned, but was later released through the intervention of his brother, *Sigismund, king of Hungary, after promising to honor the ancient rights of the nobility, which he did half-heartedly after 1398. Desiring to be crowned emperor, Wenceslas subsequently left Sigismund as regent for Bohemia, only to have Sigismund seize the opportunity to imprison Wenceslas and seize power himself. The rejection of Sigismund by the nobles, however, allowed Wenceslas to escape and regain power, though dealings between him and the nobility remained very tenuous.

Two national institutions, the Catholic church and the University of Prague, were also brought into the conflict. Wenceslas's quarrel with the archbishop of Prague led to the king's alliance with the pope, a move that alienated Bohemian clerics who now openly opposed both monarch and pontiff. The alliance led to a financial exploitation of the Czech church, and corruption grew rife. Calls for reform came from university professors, who generally supported nationalism; they were joined in these efforts by reformist preachers such as *Jan Hus, who aligned on the side of the nobility against the king and the pope. The reform views expressed in Bohemia were translated from the influences of the English reformer *John Wyclif, whose criticism of the church hierarchy mirrored the Czech situation.

In 1402 Hus was appointed rector of the University of Prague and launched a campaign of criticism of the abuses of the church. The church began a countercampaign against the reforming clerics, and tensions built until Wenceslas convinced Hus to retire to the country. The Council of Pisa, which had failed to resolve the Great Schism in 1409, exacerbated the divisions in Bohemia by recognizing a third pope. Hus traveled the country spreading the spirit of reform, and so the church moved to silence him. Hus was summoned to the Council of Constance in 1415 and was there burned at the stake for heresy, thus becoming a martyr and hero to Czechs who pledged to defend his heterodox teachings in defiance of king and pope.

Wenceslas was prevailed upon by the pope to suppress this reform and protest movement by issuing a series of decrees, but they proved ineffective; meanwhile, the council closed the university, and Hussite priests were refused consecration by the archbishop of Prague. In this atmosphere, the administrative functions of both the king and the church failed, and lawlessness and disorder followed. In 1419 the king was ordered by the new pope, Martin V (the Great Schism having ended), to enforce peace, and his attempts led to riots and chaos in Prague, where mob violence took over. The king's anti-Hussite councilors were lynched, and anarchy reigned. Wenceslas was terrified, completely withdrew from the disorder, and died of a heart attack a few days later, leaving his kingdom in total disarray and torn by religious strife.

Bibliography: J.F.N. Bradley, *Czechoslovakia: A Short History*, 1971; F.R.H. DuBoulay, *Germany in the Later Middle Ages*, 1983.

Connie Evans

Weyden, Rogier van der (c. 1399–1464), a Flemish artist of international

repute, was praised in early Italian sources for the "technical perfection" and "expressive strength" of his work. It was his inventive combination of geometric harmony and emotive intensity that has ensured van der Weyden his place, alongside *Jan van Eyck (whose work he undoubtedly knew), as the most influential Flemish painter of the fifteenth century.

Born in Tournai around 1399, the son of cutler Henri de la Pasture, van der Weyden was in 1427 apprenticed to the Tournai painter *Robert Campin, and in 1432 he became a master of the Tournai guild. He was also a pupil or follower of the Master of Flemalle, a figure who is often identified with Robert Campin and whose influence can be seen best in van der Weyden's early works. Before or in 1427 he married Elisabeth Goffaert (their children included the painter Pieter van der Weyden), and by 1435 he had settled in Brussels, where he was the town painter from 1436 until his death. Prosperous and well connected, he was a generous donor to charitable foundations and by 1462 was a member of the elite Confraternity of the Holy Cross. Evidence shows that he ran a large and prestigious workshop (including at least one visiting Italian painter), but no study has yet revealed the names or number of his assistants or their role in the shop's collaborative projects, though *Hans Memling is sometimes numbered among his pupils. In 1450 van der Weyden traveled to Rome. There he was influenced by Italian compositional, but not stylistic, models and seems to have especially admired the work of *Fra Angelico, in particular the Dominican's reduced color scheme and use of limited and stylized space. There is evidence of continued contact with Italy (in part via the Italians resident in Burgundy), and although he was not salaried, he worked on a number of occasions for Duke Philip the Good. Van der Weyden also kept up his ties with Tournai and its guild of painters, and although he was buried in Brussels, a funeral service in his honor was held in Tournai in 1464.

Sparse evidence and an imperfect understanding of van der Weyden's workshop practice make inevitably speculative any attempt to arrange the painter's oeuvre chronologically. Three surviving works can, however, be confidently authenticated and dated with reasonable accuracy. These include the *Miraflores Triptych*, representing scenes from the life of the Virgin (c. 1435; Berlin, Gemaldegalerie); *Descent from the Cross* (c. 1442; Madrid, Prado); and the Escorial *Crucifixion* (c. 1455–56; Madrid, Escorial). The quality of these three works sets the standard by which other attributions are authenticated.

Given in 1445 to the Charterhouse of Miraflores, near Burgos, by *Juan II of Castile (from whence it derives its name), the *Miraflores Triptych* (comprised of three immobile panels representing the Nativity, the Pietà, and the resurrected Christ appearing to the Virgin) exemplifies the distinctive quality of van der Weyden's work while still recalling his debt to the Master of Flemalle. Despite the elaborate architectural frames, each exhibiting "sculpted" figures of immense iconographic complexity, the overall effect of the painting is to draw attention to the stylized figure of the Virgin and her relationship with Christ, carefully distinguished by the interplay of color (white, red, and blue), line (particularly the dramatically diagonal Christ at the center), and emotion. Also commonly dated to this early period is the fragment *Magdalene Reading* (London, National Gallery) as well as *St. Luke Painting the Virgin* (Boston, Museum of Fine Arts), a work that marks the beginning of a new genre. No longer inspired by a vision, St. Luke paints the Virgin from life; the painter directly confronts his sacred subject, and the pair soon became a vehicle through which the artist could illustrate his own conception of painting. Van der Weyden is also credited with introducing the Italian model of the Pietà into the Netherlandish tradition.

Descent from the Cross, probably first painted for the Great Archers' Guild at Louvain, signaled van der Weyden's decisive break from the Master of Flemalle. The painting exhibits extraordinary compositional coherence, a harmony of design that is inseparable from the heightened emotional content while showing scant consideration for the illusion of realistic space. The figures, cramped together yet neatly balanced (the Virgin, figured as coredemptor, parallels Christ's movement while the attendants literally bracket and then fuse with the central event), give the impression of static, changeless grief. They are all, however, precariously posed, and a closer look reveals the agitated emotion that finds its echo in Christ's precisely delineated wounds and the tears of his mother and the bystanders. Van der Weyden's indirect, even abstract, control of emotion is the work's most enduring quality. The Beaune *Last Judgment* (Beaune, Hôtel-Dieu) is also regularly assigned to the painter's middle period. A nine-panel polyptych painted for Nicholas Rolin, chancellor of Burgundy, it offers evidence of extensive workshop collaboration. The terror of the piece, conveyed by the now-familiar intensity of emotion, is all the more remarkable for the total absence of devils in its hell scenes.

Painted as a gift for the Charterhouse of Scheut (Brussels), the *Crucifixion* (given to the Escorial by Philip II of Spain in 1574) is notable for its simplicity and restraint, the more so because, as the donor himself, van der Weyden was completely free of the demands of a patron. The painting is provided with a red background, a hanging neatly folded, or demarcated, into squares. This explicitly geometric pattern dominates the composition. The central, elongated Christ is flanked by his mother (left), whose broken diagonals offer an eloquent contrast to the unbroken verticals of the resolute St. John the Evangelist (right).

Curiously, van der Weyden was also renowned as a portrait painter. Fourteen (excluding donor portraits) are extant, and almost all were conceived according to a similar pattern. Half-length, the sitter is contrasted with a dark, neutral background; the hands are usually shown, joined, while the eyes move away from the spectator. The impression of the whole is one of serenity; see, for instance, *Portrait of a Young Woman* (c. 1460, Washington, D.C., National Gallery). In his portraits, van der Weyden strove not to individualize the sitter but to fix him or her according to an imagined ideal, even if this required distortion. Indeed, it was this impulse to distort, to subordinate realism to the dictates of an individual vision, that most fully characterized van der Weyden's accomplishment.

Bibliography: Lorne Campbell, *Van der Weyden*, 1979; Martin Davies, *Rogier van der Weyden*, 1972.

Nicola McDonald

William of Ockham. *See* Ockham, William of.

William of Wykeham. *See* Wykeham, William of.

Wyclif, John (c. 1330–84), was an Oxford theologian and philosopher known as "Doctor Evangelicus," the founder of the Lollard movement, and an influential advocate of ecclesiastical reform and the creation of a vernacular Bible. Likely born in Yorkshire, Wyclif went to Oxford, graduating as a bachelor of arts in 1356. He became master of Balliol College in 1360, began theological studies in 1363, and remained in Oxford until 1381. As was common for ordained scholars, Wyclif held benefices in Lincolnshire, Gloucestershire, and Buckinghamshire while he was in Oxford, and he retired to Lutterworth, Leicestershire, where he died in 1384. Before 1371 Wyclif was known as Oxford's foremost metaphysician and logician. He entered royal service at the invitation of either *John of Gaunt or *Edward the Black Prince, representing the king at a negotiation with papal nuncios in Bruges in 1374. Later he supported John's actions against the Good Parliament of 1376 and defended John in the Hauley-Shakyll incident in 1378.

During his royal service Wyclif wrote voluminously on the need for ecclesiastical reform, pointedly condemning clerical corruption and arguing in favor of secular control of the church's possessions. In 1377 Bishop William Courtenay attempted a formal confrontation with Wyclif that was foiled by popular unrest. Shortly thereafter Gregory XI called for Wyclif's arrest and examination, and again in 1382 Courtenay summoned Wyclif to a council at Blackfriars, where twenty-four propositions connected to his writings were condemned as heresy. Wyclif enjoyed John of Gaunt's protection throughout his life, but after he died, the Council of Constance declared him a heresiarch, and his remains were exhumed, burned, and thrown into the river Swift in 1428.

Wyclif was his generation's preeminent philosopher at Oxford, known for his strong advocacy of Augustinian themes in the face of the influence of *William of Ockham. Wyclif did not disagree with several important aspects of Ockham's approach, including sensitivity to logical and semantical nuance in philosophical reasoning, and impatience with Thomistic and Scotistic "moderate realist" theories of the relation of individuals to universals. His opposition was in response to Ockham's rejection of universals; Wyclif believed that God knows all creatures primarily through universals, and only secondarily as individual creatures. These universals exist primarily in the divine nature as second intentional concepts, and secondarily in individually created essences as first intentional concepts. This arrangement, Wyclif explained in *Tractatus de universalibus*, allowed one to accept Ockhamist innovation without compromising theological truth. Wyclif's realism was less an evocation of earlier Augustinians like Robert Grosseteste than it was a development of the contemporary Augustinianism of Walter Burley and Gregory of Rimini.

Attendant upon Wyclif's realism was a particularly deterministic theology. If God knows humanity primarily through the universal "humanity" entity, then God knows eternally who will be saved (the predestinate) and who will be damned (the foreknown). Here Wyclif's metaphysics articulated Archbishop *Thomas Bradwardine's earlier anti-Pelagian theology, which grounded his doctrine of the nature of the church as developed in *De ecclesia*. The true church, he argued, is the totality of the grace-favored predestined, and so "Christians" devoted to avarice evince an absence of grace indicating their true, foreknown status.

The fullest articulation of Wyclif's diagnosis of the church's ills and prescription for its cure appeared in his *De civili dominio* and *De officio regis*. Here he argued that God's perfect lordship is a universal in which instances of true created lordship participate. All people were created with natural, communal lordship, which was lost with the Fall. Christ's institution of the church allowed the return of this natural *dominium* for the grace-favored, who regained communal harmony by enjoying apostolic poverty. The present state of the church, Wyclif charged, was marred by clerical corruption and greed and must be returned to the ideal state of purity from without by a grace-favored civil lord or king. The king was charged with radical disendowment of all church property, rigorously enforcing clerical discipline while providing for the church's material well-being. In brief, Wyclif envisioned a host of national churches, each directed by a grace-favored king serving as God's steward by protecting the Christian natural lords within the kingdom.

Another aspect of Wyclif's ecclesiology was his indictment of the clergy. Because no one can truly know whether he or she is grace favored, no one can claim spiritual superiority; thus the duty of a "spiritual lord" involved not temporal authority but service of the soul's needs. There was no real need for clerical offices beyond bishops, whose responsibility was to serve God and king by rooting out incipient clerical corruption. Indeed, Wyclif argued that all grace-favored Christians were equally priests, stopping just short of a "universal priesthood of believers." His scorn for fraternal orders grew as increasing numbers of friars opposed him, leading him to accuse Franciscans and Dominicans of being more devoted to their founders than to Christ.

While Wyclif's *dominium* philosophy and deterministic ecclesiology attracted swift papal condemnation, his eucharistic theology and his writings on the Bible ensured his lasting reputation. In *De eucharistia* he argued that since accidents cannot remain without a substance after consecration, and since matter cannot be destroyed, Christ cannot take the physical place of the element's substance, making transubstantiation impossible. Wyclif also outlined a revision of traditional Catholic approaches to Scripture, holding that the Bible was the sole source for Christian truth, and that each Christian ought to develop his or her own understanding of it by reading it himself or herself. Consequently, Wyclif advocated the Bible's translation into the vernacular, and his students produced the late fourteenth century's Wycliffite Bible.

Wyclif did not restrict himself to academic audiences. His public sermons were filled with these teachings, and his disciples in Oxford and London formed the nucleus of what was to be the Lollard movement, a scripturally oriented revolutionary phenomenon that swept England over the next 150 years with demands for social and ecclesiastical reform. While leaders of the Peasants' Revolt of 1381 falsely claimed Wyclif's authority, the revolt of Sir *John Oldcastle in 1414–15 had Wycliffite roots. Although Wyclif's thought sparked Lollardy, his legacy is not restricted to England. The Bohemian *Jan Hus was strongly influenced by Wyclif's ecclesiology, and the Hussite rebellion, while not truly Wycliffite, has its foundation in his theology.

Bibliography: Anne Hudson, *The Premature Reformation*, 1988; Anthony Kenny, ed., *Wyclif in His Times*, 1986; K. B. McFarlane, *John Wycliffe and the Beginnings of English Non-Conformity*, 1952.

Stephen E. Lahey

Wykeham, William of, Bishop of Winchester (1324–1404), served two

kings, *Edward III and *Richard II, as lord chancellor of England during 1367–71 and again in 1389–91. He was denounced by *John of Gaunt, duke of Lancaster, and was convicted of government corruption and mismanagement in the wake of the Good Parliament of 1376, but was soon pardoned by Richard II in 1377. Wykeham was a noted pluralist who amassed great wealth during his tenure as bishop of England's richest see (1367–1404), but he was liberal in using that wealth to found two of England's most prestigious educational establishments, Winchester College and New College at Oxford. He is also remembered today for his reconstruction of Winchester Cathedral in the fourteenth-century perpendicular Gothic style.

William of Wykeham was born in the summer of 1324 to poor farming parents of "free condition" in the Hampshire village of Wickham. He was apparently bright, for an unnamed patron helped young William to his only formal education at the grammar school in Winchester, after which he first became secretary to the constable of Winchester Castle, Robert of Popham, and then entered the service of King Edward III in 1347 through the good offices of Lord Treasurer William Edington, bishop of Winchester. Wykeham seems to have been adept at acquiring lucrative government offices early in his life, for he was soon serving the king as master of the works (refurbishing) of the manors of Henley and Easthampstead and of the royal castle at Windsor, where he supervised the construction of meeting rooms for members of the new Order of the Garter. By 1366 he had also served as warden of the royal castles at Leeds, Dover, and Hadleigh, was joint warden of royal forests south of the river Trent, and had even been keeper of the royal dogs for a time. Although he did not even enter into holy orders until 1361, Wykeham was appointed the king's chaplain in 1349 and went on to hold a wide variety of rich secular livings, deaneries, prebendaries, and archdeaconries before he was finally ordained a priest in June 1362. Oxford theologian and religious dissident *John Wyclif later poked fun at this wealthy prelate who was less religiously spiritual than he was "wise in building castles." By 1365 a pluralities return showed Wykeham's annual income from these church benefices to be around 873 pounds sterling, a sum that made him one of the wealthier pluralists in the realm by the time he was "elected" bishop of Winchester in October of the following year. The pope at Avignon, Urban V, balked at confirming Wykeham in that most lucrative of sees, perhaps because the papal court at Avignon had been snubbed by King Edward during the war with France, perhaps because the French pontiff had another candidate in mind for Winchester. Papal provision was, however, finally secured in July 1367, and so Wykeham was duly consecrated, invested with his episcopal livings, and enthroned in his new diocese by the following summer.

As his ecclesiastical star was in the ascent, so too did William of Wykeham rise quickly to the highest levels of Crown service. Keeper of the privy seal by 1364, the bishop-elect of Winchester was appointed lord chancellor of England for the first time in September 1367. Although we know little of Wykeham's impact on royal policies, the French chronicler *Jean Froissart said of Edward III's chief minister that "all things were done by him, and without him nothing was done." His first term as chancellor coincided with several military reverses in the Hundred Years' War, and, blamed for these and for unpopular Crown extravagance, Wykeham resigned as lord chancellor in spring 1371 and prepared to devote himself to educational patronage and to needed reforms of his cathedral chapter of St. Swithun and the Hospital of St. Cross in Winchester.

Such a life was not yet to be, however, for Wykeham was soon recalled by the commons of the Good Parliament in 1376 to help curb the influence of William Lord Latimer and John of Gaunt, duke of Lancaster, in the government of the ailing King Edward. The bishop of Winchester played his role as asked, but when the Good Parliament was dissolved and his friend and protector *Edward, the Black Prince, died in June 1376, Wykeham was left exposed to the counterattack now launched by the angry duke of Lancaster against him. Wykeham was impeached by Lancaster's new royal council on charges of financial graft and misconduct of the French war and, having been fined the outrageous sum of nearly one million marks for his alleged misdeeds, was stripped of his episcopal temporalities and sent packing to his diocese. He was saved, however, when old King Edward III died in June 1377 and his successor, the son of the Black Prince, King Richard II, pardoned Wykeham and returned his episcopal temporalities. The wary bishop of Winchester now managed to avoid politics until, in the wake of the Merciless Parliament of 1388, when King Richard once more needed councilors he could trust, William of Wykeham again served uneventfully as lord chancellor in the years 1389–91. He was an old man by the time Henry of Bolingbroke, duke of Lancaster, overthrew King Richard in 1399, and although he was duly appointed to *Henry IV's council and even attended a few of its meetings, the bishop of Winchester's attention and energies had long since turned to other concerns.

William of Wykeham's enduring legacy will always be his endowment of two of England's great educational institutions and his rebuilding of much of Winchester Cathedral. Ever mindful of his own humble origins, Wykeham began buying land for "St. Mary's College of Winchester" in Oxford in 1369. A charter was issued in 1379, the first stones were laid for the new buildings—designed in the perpendicular Gothic style by architect William Wynford—and the warden and seventy "pore" scholars were formally installed in what came to be called "New" College on 14 April 1386. Meanwhile, in 1373 Wykeham had begun planning for "St. Mary's College of Winchester" to train eventual New College students in grammar in his cathedral city itself. Again intending an establishment for scholars "suffering from want of money and poverty," Wykeham founded his grammar school in 1382, began construction in 1387, and installed a warden and 104 scholars and clerics in what has been known since as Winchester College on 28 March 1394. In that year the bishop of Winchester also began remodeling the nave, apse, and triforium galleries of his cathedral in the perpendicular Gothic style, again under the watchful eye of architect and stonemason William Wynford. Following his death on 27 September 1404, William of Wykeham, bishop of Winchester, was buried in a white marble tomb topped with his effigy in a small chantry chapel on the south side of what is probably the longest (550 feet) and certainly one of the most beautiful cathedral naves in Europe.

Bibliography: William Hayter, *William of Wykeham: Patron of the Arts*, 1970; Peter Partner, "William of Wykeham and the Historians," in *Winchester College: Sixth-Centenary Essays*, ed. Roger Custance, 1982.

Clayton J. Drees

Wyntoun, Andrew of (1350?–1420/25?),

is best known for his vernacular verse chronicle of Scotland. He did much to develop that language known today as "Scots" and also contributed to Scottish national consciousness in a land of diverse peoples, languages, and customs. Beyond what he himself tells in his chronicle, little is known of his life. He claimed that he was born one Andrew of Wyntoun, perhaps as a younger son of one of the Wyntoun families prominent in fourteenth-century Scotland, though he himself made no such claim. Elected prior of the important Abbey of St. Serf's inch in Lochleven in 1395, after first serving as a canon regular of St. Andrews, he resided there until his death sometime between 1420 and 1425. This part, at least, of his story remains undoubted due to several entries of his name in the register of St. Andrews between 1395 and 1411. At the request of his patron, Sir John of Wemyss, Wyntoun wrote his chronicle in his declining years, most likely in 1406, though with additions to 1420 or perhaps 1425.

Like most medieval chronicles, Wyntoun drew upon or lifted much of his work from other sources. These included an unidentified Latin verse chronicle, a Scots verse chronicle now lost, some three hundred lines of John Barbour's poem *The Bruce*, and a number of other sources no longer extant. He included several entertaining tales and stories found in neither *John of Fordun's *Chronica* or Walter Bower's *Scotichronicon*, including the original tale of the meeting of Macbeth with the weird sisters. Many of these stories not merely informed later Scottish views of the country's past, but also found their way into English views of its neighbor, as seen most notably in William Shakespeare's *Macbeth*.

Wyntoun modeled his work on the popular history of the day, *Ranulf Higden's *Polychronicon*. The *Cronykil* thus began with the Creation and moved down through the years, chronicling not merely the history of that land called Scotland, but also its claim to superior antiquity and thus its claim to independence from its southern neighbor, England. Written in octosyllabic couplets, Wyntoun's *Cronykil* is known not for its poetry, but for its accurate depiction of events, especially from the time of the Bruce onwards. There exists, however, a certain unfamiliarity with, perhaps even a disdain for, the honors, gallantries, and rules of late medieval chivalry, and this may reflect Wyntoun's life as both canon and prior. Though it is highly concerned with dates, the work as a whole, considered as a literary production, is of little merit. It is, however, one of the earliest extant works in the vernacular of lowland Scotland, that offshoot of English (indeed, Wyntoun called it "Ynglis Sawe") now distinguished as "Scots." He did hold a definite, perhaps even virulent, anti-English bias, something he shared in common with his contemporary, John of Fordun. Together, as later embellished and elaborated, Wyntoun and Fordun forged a national history for a diverse land, one that not only gave it the backing of antiquity, but also one unsullied by foreign conquest and occupation. For the time, these constructions—though largely mythical, if not fictional—served as powerful ideological weapons against English claims to both superiority and rule over Scotland and thus profoundly and fundamentally shaped Scottish consciousness to the present day.

Bibliography: Alexander Grant, *Independence and Nationhood: Scotland, 1306–1469*, 1984.

Jerome S. Arkenburg

Z

Zabarella, Francesco (1360–1417), cardinal, was among the most highly regarded Italian ecclesiastical officials of his day. He was a legal scholar and an eloquent speaker, with wide-ranging interests such as poetry and history. As the Western church underwent the turmoil of schism and the theological challenges of *John Wyclif and *Jan Hus, Zabarella took a leading role in attempting to reform Catholicism.

Francesco Zabarella was born in Piove di Saco, near Padua, on 10 August 1360. He earned a doctorate in law in Florence and taught there from 1385 until 1390. Zabarella rose quickly in ecclesiastical circles and was soon appointed vicar general in Florence. In 1398 he was named archpriest in Padua and was entrusted to carry out diplomatic missions for that city. Zabarella supported the antipope John XXIII, and in turn, John appointed him bishop of Florence in 1410.

Zabarella was made a bishop during a time of considerable turmoil within the church; Gregory XII was the pope in Rome, but *Benedict XIII in Avignon also claimed the papal throne. Both Gregory and Benedict schemed to remove each other and were summoned to a council in Pisa in March 1409. They refused to appear and subsequently were found to be contumacious, were declared schismatics and heretics, and were excommunicated since schism was a heresy that offended the doctrine of *unam sanctam ecclesiam.* Peter Philgari was elected Pope Alexander V, but he died before even arriving in Rome. After Alexander's death, John XXIII was elected, and there were now three claimants to the title: Gregory XII, Benedict XIII, and John.

In order to terminate the schism, Holy Roman Emperor *Sigismund called another council. John XXIII hoped that the council would simply validate his claim to the papal throne and reaffirm the condemnations of Gregory and Benedict. He sent Zabarella with Cardinal Chalant of Savoy to discuss the matter with the emperor and to ask Sigismund to call a council in Genoa or Nice. To

John's disappointment, though, Sigismund called the conference for Constance in Switzerland instead.

The council opened with debate on conciliar theory, that is, the authority of a church council in defining doctrine over the authority of the pope. Given the historical context of the council—a time in which three claimed the papacy— the concept of the authority of a body of bishops commanded considerable support. While some observers asserted that Zabarella was influenced by *Marsiglio of Padua (d. 1342), who held that the papacy was not divinely instituted and that authority lies within the body of believers as a whole, Zabarella's thought was actually quite different. Zabarella defended the papacy as a spiritual institution and sought to reconcile the view of the papacy's godly characteristics with the belief that the community also held authority. He accepted the understanding that a civil leader (like Sigismund) could convene a council, but he defended the right of the bishops to act independently of the emperor.

The question of which claimant should be recognized as pope also posed a vexing difficulty. John offered to renounce his claim to the papacy, provided that Gregory and Benedict also renounced their titles. John exacerbated the situation by lashing out at his two rivals and then slipping out of town. Zabarella had tried to convince John that his resignation was inevitable and that it would be better for the church if he were to do so voluntarily rather than as the result of force. John sent messages to Zabarella and two other cardinals to ask them to represent him, but they refused. Gregory agreed to renounce his claim, but the council was forced to depose John and then to depose Benedict in absentia.

Zabarella also spoke in Rome in favor of the condemnation and burning of John Wyclif's works as heretical. He was less opposed to Jan Hus than some of his detractors. He participated in the questioning of Hus and did find him contumacious. He then tried to convince Hus to sign a statement by which he would have retracted some of his views and saved his life, but to no avail.

Zabarella attempted to balance the authority of popes and councils and of church and state. He strove to reform the church from within, but he was to an extent reacting to crises within the church rather than proactively promoting needed changes. He died in 1417, a century before Martin Luther posted his ninety-five theses on a church door, launching corrections of the church that surpassed those that Zabarella would have wanted.

Bibliography: Louise Ropes Loomis, trans., *The Council of Constance: The Unification of the Church*, 1961; Thomas Edward Morrissey, *Franciscus de Zabarellis (1360–1417) and the Conciliarist Traditions*, 1973.

John Donovan

Zacuto, Abraham (1452–1525), was a Jewish astronomer, mathematician, and historian. He is best known for his astronomical tables and for crafting the first metal astrolabe, which was more precise than the earlier wooden models.

Both his tables and his copper astrolabe were used by *Christopher Columbus and *Vasco da Gama. Thus Zacuto was a major contributor to the success of the Spanish and Portuguese voyages of discovery.

Abraham Zacuto was born in Salamanca, Spain, around 1452. Zacuto probably taught astronomy at the University of Salamanca, although the records are missing for 1481–1503. In 1492 Zacuto was forced to leave Spain because of the expulsion of the Jews. He sought refuge in Portugal and soon held a prominent position first at the court of King *João II and then in 1495 at the court of John's successor King *Manuel I.

In 1473–78, while Zacuto was still in Spain, he wrote his major astronomical work, which in 1496 was translated from Hebrew into Spanish and Latin by Joseph Vecinho. The work has come to be known by its Latin title, *Almanach perpetuum*. Zacuto's *Almanach* contained astronomical tables for determining the position of the sun, moon, and planets and also for calculating solar and lunar eclipses. Vecinho gave a copy to Columbus, who carried it with him on his voyages, and an annotated copy of the *Almanach* was found in his library. Columbus also consulted Zacuto when he was petitioning King *Ferdinand and Queen *Isabel to finance his expedition. In 1504 the *Almanach* was particularly beneficial to Columbus. In Jamaica, he and his crew were threatened by natives. Knowing from Zacuto's tables that a lunar eclipse was imminent, Columbus told the natives that he could control the sun and the moon. The eclipse happened as Zacuto's tables had indicated, and Columbus and his men escaped unharmed. Zacuto also contributed to the success of Vasco da Gama's voyage from Portugal to India. King Manuel consulted Zacuto about the voyage and asked Zacuto to aid in the planning. Da Gama personally consulted with Zacuto before the voyage and carried aboard ship Zacuto's tables and the metal astrolabe, which was used to determine the position of the sun.

Unfortunately, Zacuto did not learn the outcome of the expedition because in 1497 he was forced into exile by the expulsion of the Jews from Portugal. Accompanied by his son Samuel, Zacuto reached Tunis in 1500 after a difficult journey during which they were twice held as prisoners. In Tunis, Zacuto composed his *Book of Genealogies*, which chronicled Jewish history and events from the Creation to the year 1500. In 1510 the Spaniards captured Tunis, and once again Zacuto had to flee, this time to Turkey. Little is known about his last years. He was in Jerusalem in 1513 and in Damascus about 1515. Although certainty is impossible, the terminal date for his death is generally accepted as 1525.

Because of his religion, Zacuto spent much of his life fleeing from one country to another, yet he was still able to make major contributions to the study of astronomy and, in turn, the improvement of navigational methods. Through his contributions, Spain and Portugal, the very countries from which he was exiled, were able to accomplish amazing feats of discovery and establish their vast empires.

Bibliography: M. Kayserling, *Christopher Columbus and the Participation of the Jews in the Spanish and Portuguese Discoveries*, 1968; Janet Podell and Steven Anzovin, *Old Worlds to New: The Age of Exploration and Discovery*, 1993.

Patricia Worrall

Appendix I: Figures by Geographical Region

BOHEMIA

George of Podebrady, King of Bohemia

Hus, Jan

Jerome of Prague

Matthias of Janov

Milič, Jan

Wenceslas IV, King of Bohemia

BURGUNDY

Binchois, Gilles

Charles the Bold, Duke of Burgundy

La Marche, Olivier de

Margaret of York, Duchess of Burgundy

Philip the Bold, Duke of Burgundy

ENGLAND

Baconthorpe, John

Beauchamp, Richard

Beaufort, Henry

Beaufort, Margaret

Bourchier, Thomas

Bradwardine, Thomas

Cade, Jack

Caxton, William

Chaucer, Geoffrey

Chichele, Henry

Colet, John

Edward III, King of England

Edward IV, King of England

Edward of Woodstock, "the Black Prince"

Fortescue, Sir John

Free, John

Gascoigne, Thomas

Gower, John

Grocyn, William

Hawkwood, Sir John

Henry IV, King of England

Henry VI, King of England

Henry VII, King of England

Hereford, Nicholas

Higden, Ranulf

Hilton, Walter

Hoccleve, Thomas

Humphrey, Duke of Gloucester

John of Gaunt, Duke of Lancaster

Juliana of Norwich

Kempe, Margery
Knighton, Henry
Langland, William
Lydgate, John
Lyndwood, William
Malory, Sir Thomas
Morton, John
Netter, Thomas
Ockham, William of
Oldcastle, Sir John
Paston, John
Pecock, Reginald
Purvey, John
Repyngdon, Philip
Richard II, King of England
Richard III, King of England
Rolle, Richard
Sellyng, William
Swineshead, Richard
Tyler, Wat
Walsingham, Thomas
Wyclif, John
Wykeham, William of

FLANDERS AND HOLLAND

Agricola, Alexander
Artevelde, Jacob van
Bosch, Hieronymus
Bouts, Dirk
Broederlam, Melchior
Eyck, Hubert van
Eyck, Jan van
Goes, Hugo van der
Groote, Gerhard
Memling, Hans
Ruysbroek, Jan
Weyden, Rogier van der

FRANCE

Ailly, Pierre d'
Albarno, Montréal d'
Amboise, Georges d'
Aureoli, Peter
Beaujeau, Pierre de, Duc de Bourbon
Beauneveu, André
Bertrand, Pierre
Bondol, Jean de
Buridan, Jean
Campin, Robert
Cauchon, Pierre
Charles VI, King of France
Charles VII, King of France
Charles VIII, King of France
Chartier, Alain
Chastellain, Georges
Christine de Pizan
Commynes, Philippe de
Coeur, Jacques
Deschamps, Eustace
Durand of Saint-Pourçain
Fouquet, Jean
Froissart, Jean
Gaguin, Robert
Gaston III, Count de Foix
Gerson, Jean
Gersonides, Levi
Guesclin, Bertrand du
Joan of Arc
La Sale, Antoine de
LeRoy, Guillaume
Louis XI, King of France
Machaut, Guillaume de
Marcel, Étienne
Marigny, Enguerrand de
Molay, Jacques de
Oresme, Nicole

Perréal, Jean, Maître de Moulins

Philip IV, King of France

René, Duke of Anjou

Robert of Artois

Valois, Anne, Duchesse de Bourbon

Valois, Jean, Duc de Berry

Villon, François

Vitry, Philippe de

HOLY ROMAN EMPIRE

Agricola, Rudolf

Biel, Gabriel

Boner, Ulrich

Brant, Sebastian

Celtis, Conrad

Conrad of Geinhausen

Ebner, Margareta

Eckhart, Meister Johan

Frederick III, Holy Roman Emperor

Fust, Johann

Geiler von Kaysersberg, Johan

Gutenberg, Johann

Hegius, Alexander

Heinbuche, Henry, of Langenstein

John of Jandun

Kraft, Adam

Krämer, Heinrich

Langmann, Adelheid

Lochner, Stephan

Louis IV, "the Bavarian," Holy Roman
    Emperor

Luder, Peter

Maximilian I, Holy Roman Emperor

Nicholas of Cusa

Nicholas of Flüe, Saint

Pacher, Michael

Regiomontanus (Johann Müller)

Reuchlin, Johann

Rupert III, King of Germany

Schiltberger, Hans

Schöffer, Peter

Schongauer, Martin

Sigismund, Holy Roman Emperor

Sprenger, Jakob

Suso, Heinrich

Tauler, Johann

Thomas à Kempis

HUNGARY

Louis I, "the Great," King of Hungary
    and Poland

Matthias I Corvinus, King of Hungary

ITALY

Alberti, Leon Battista

Angelico, Fra

Bardi, Contessina

Bellini, Gentile

Bellini, Giovanni

Bernardino of Siena

Boccaccio, Giovanni

Botticelli, Sandro

Bracciolini, Gian Francesco Poggio

Bramante, Donato d'Agnolo Lazzari

Brunelleschi, Filippo

Bruni, Leonardo

Castagno, Andrea del

Catherine of Siena, Saint

Chrysoloras, Manuel

Dante Alighieri

Domenico Veneziano

Donatello

Este, Beatrice d', Duchess of Milan

Este, Ercole I d', Duke of Ferrara

Ficino, Marsiglio

Ghiberti, Lorenzo

Ghirlandaio, Domenico
Giotto di Bondone
Gonzaga, Ludovico
Guarino da Verona
John Capistrano, Saint
Landini, Francesco
Landino, Christoforo
Leonardo da Vinci
Lippi, Fra Filippo
Manetti, Giannozzo
Mantegna, Andrea
Manutius, Aldus
Marsiglio of Padua
Masaccio
Medici, Cosimo de
Medici, Giovanni de, "di Bicci"
Medici, Giuliano de
Medici, Lorenzo de, "il Magnifico"
Medici, Piero de, "the Gouty"
Medici, Piero de, "the Unfortunate"
Montefeltro, Federigo da
Montefeltro, Guidobaldo da
Nogarola, Isotta
Orsini, Clarice
Pacioli, Luca
Perugino, Pietro
Petrarch, Francesco
Pico della Mirandola, Giovanni
Piero della Francesca
Poliziano, Angelo
Pontano, Giovanni
Quercia, Jacopo della
Sacchetti, Franco
Salutati, Coluccio
Savonarola, Girolamo
Sforza, Caterina
Sforza, Francesco
Sforza, Ludovico

Tornabuoni, Lucrezia
Uccello, Paolo
Valla, Lorenzo
Vergerio, Pietro Paolo
Verrocchio, Andrea del
Vespasiano da Bisticci
Vespucci, Amerigo
Villani, Giovanni
Visconti, Filippo Maria, Duke of Milan
Visconti, Giangaleazzo, Duke of Milan
Zabarella, Francesco

PAPACY

Alexander VI, Pope
Benedict XII, Pope (Avignon)
Benedict XIII, Antipope
Bessarion, John
Clement V, Pope (Avignon)
Clement VI, Pope (Avignon)
Eugenius IV, Pope
Innocent VI, Pope (Avignon)
Innocent VIII, Pope
John XXII, Pope (Avignon)
John of Ragusa
Nicholas V, Pope
Pius II, Pope
Rienzo, Cola di
Sixtus IV, Pope
Ubertino da Casale
Urban VI, Pope

PORTUGAL

Abravanel, Isaac ben-Judah
Alfonso V, "the African," King of
   Portugal
Dias, Bartolomeo
Eannes, Gilberto
Escobar, Andrés de

Gama, Vasco da

Henry "the Navigator," Prince of Portugal

João II, King of Portugal

Lopes, Fernão

Manuel I, King of Portugal

SCANDINAVIA

Bridget of Sweden, Saint

Margaret I, Queen of Denmark, Norway, and Sweden

Valdemar IV, King of Denmark

SCOTLAND

Douglas, Sir James, "the Black Douglas"

Fordun, John of

Henryson, Robert

James I, King of Scotland

James III, King of Scotland

James IV, King of Scotland

Wyntoun, Andrew of

SPAIN

Alfonso V, "the Magnanimous," King of Aragon, Spain, and Sicily

Avignon, Juan de

Beltrán de la Cueva

Columbus, Christopher

Cresques, Abraham

Enrique IV, King of Castile

Eymeric, Nicholas

Ferdinand V, King of Aragon and Spain

Ferrante I, King of Naples

Galba, Joan Martí de

Gonzáles de Clavijo, Ruy

Gonzáles de Mendoza, Pedro

Halevi, Solomon

Huguet, Jaime

Hurtado de Mendoza, Diego

Inglés, Jorge

Isabel, Queen of Castile

Jaime II, "the Just," King-Count of Aragon and Catalonia

Jiménez de Cisneros, Francisco

Juan II, King of Castile

Juana of Castile

Llull, Ramon

López de Ayala, Pero

López de Córdoba, Leonor

López de Mendoza, Iñigo

Luna, Álvaro de

Manrique, Jorge

Manuel, Juan, Prince of Castile and Adelantado of Murcia

March, Ausias

Martin I, "the Humanist," King of Aragon

Martorell, Joanot

Mena, Juan de

Metge, Bernat

Nebrija, Antonio de

Palencia, Alfonso Fernández de

Pedro IV, "the Ceremonious," King of Aragon

Philip I, King of Spain

Ruiz, Juan

Sánchez de Arévalo, Rodrigo

Sibiuda, Ramon

Torquemada, Juan de

Torquemada, Tomás de

Tostado, Alfonso

Valera, Diego de

Villena, Isabel de

Vincent Ferrer, Saint

Zacuto, Abraham

Appendix II:
Figures by Occupation

BANKERS

Coeur, Jacques

Medici, Cosimo de

Medici, Giovanni de, "di Bicci"

CHURCH LEADERS

Amboise, Georges d'

Beauchamp, Richard

Beaufort, Henry

Bertrand, Pierre

Bessarion, John

Bourchier, Thomas

Bradwardine, Thomas

Bridget of Sweden, Saint

Catherine of Siena, Saint

Cauchon, Pierre

Chichele, Henry

Gonzáles de Mendoza, Pedro

Morton, John

Rienzo, Cola di

Wykeham, William of

EDUCATORS

Celtis, Conrad

Chrysoloras, Manuel

Gascoigne, Thomas

Groote, Gerhard

Guarino da Verona

Hegius, Alexander

Luder, Peter

Netter, Thomas

EMPERORS

Frederick III, Holy Roman Emperor

Louis IV, "the Bavarian," Holy Roman
Emperor

Maximilian I, Holy Roman Emperor

Sigismund, Holy Roman Emperor

EXPLORERS AND CARTOGRAPHERS

Columbus, Christopher

Cresques, Abraham

Dias, Bartolomeo

Eannes, Gilberto

Gama, Vasco da
Henry "the Navigator," Prince of Portugal
Vespucci, Amerigo
Zacuto, Abraham

GOVERNMENT MINISTERS

Amboise, Georges d'
Beaufort, Henry
Beaujeau, Pierre de, Duc de Bourbon
Beltrán de la Cueva
Bourchier, Thomas
Gonzáles de Clavijo, Ruy
Humphrey, Duke of Gloucester
Hurtado de Mendoza, Diego
John of Gaunt, Duke of Lancaster
Luna, Álvaro de
Marigny, Enguerrand de
Morton, John
Robert of Artois
Sacchetti, Franco
Wykeham, William of

HERETICS

Hereford, Nicholas
Hus, Jan
Jerome of Prague
Marsiglio of Padua
Molay, Jacques de
Ockham, William of
Oldcastle, Sir John
Pecock, Reginald
Purvey, John
Wyclif, John

HISTORIANS AND CHRONICLERS

Chastellain, Georges
Commynes, Phillippe de
Fordun, John of
Froissart, Jean
Higden, Ranulf
Knighton, Henry
La Marche, Olivier de
Lopes, Fernão
López de Ayala, Pero
Palencia, Alfonso Fernández de
Paston, John
Sánchez de Arévalo, Rodrigo
Schiltberger, Hans
Valera, Diego de
Villani, Giovanni
Walsingham, Thomas
Wyntoun, Andrew of

HUMANISTS

Agricola, Rudolf
Alberti, Leon Battista
Bessarion, John
Bracciolini, Gian Francisco Poggio
Bruni, Leonardo
Celtis, Conrad
Chrysoloras, Manuel
Free, John
Gaguin, Robert
Grocyn, William
Hegius, Alexander
Heinbuche, Henry, of Langenstein
Jiménez de Cisneros, Francisco
John of Ragusa
Landino, Christoforo
López de Mendoza, Iñigo

Luder, Peter

Manetti, Giannozzo

Metge, Bernat

Nebrija, Antonio de

Nogarola, Isotta

Petrarch, Francesco

Poliziano, Angelo

Pontano, Giovanni

Reuchlin, Johann

Salutati, Coluccio

Sellyng, William

Valla, Lorenzo

Vergerio, Pietro Paolo

Vespasiano da Bisticci

INQUISITORS

Eymeric, Nicholas

Krämer, Heinrich

Repyngdon, Philip

Sprenger, Jakob

Torquemada, Tomás de

KINGS

Alfonso V, "the African," King of Portugal

Alfonso V, "the Magnanimous," King of Aragon, Naples, and Sicily

Charles VI, King of France

Charles VII, King of France

Charles VIII, King of France

Edward III, King of England

Edward IV, King of England

Enrique IV, King of Castile

Ferdinand V, King of Aragon and Spain

Ferrante I, King of Naples

George of Podebrady, King of Bohamia

Henry IV, King of England

Henry VI, King of England

Henry VII, King of England

Jaime II, "the Just," King-Count of Aragon and Catalonia

James I, King of Scotland

James III, King of Scotland

James IV, King of Scotland

João II, King of Portugal

Juan II, King of Castile

Louis I, "the Great," King of Hungary and Poland

Louis XI, King of France

Manuel I, King of Portugal

Martin I, "the Humanist," King of Aragon

Matthias I Corvinus, King of Hungary

Pedro IV, "the Ceremonious," King of Aragon

Philip I, King of Spain

Philip IV, King of France

René, Duke of Anjou, King of Sicily

Richard II, King of England

Richard III, King of England

Rupert III, King of Germany

Valdemar IV, King of Denmark

Wenceslas IV, King of Bohemia

LITERARY FIGURES

Boccaccio, Giovanni

Brant, Sebastian

Chaucer, Geoffrey

Christine de Pizan

Dante Alighieri

Galba, Joan Martí de

Gower, John

Hoccleve, Thomas

Langland, William

La Sale, Antoine de

López de Córdoba, Leonor

Malory, Sir Thomas

Manuel, Juan, Prince of Castile and
    Adelantado of Murcia

Martorell, Joanot

Mena, Juan de

Sacchetti, Franco

Villena, Isabel de

MILITARY LEADERS

Albarno, Montréal d'

Douglas, Sir James, "the Black Douglas"

Edward of Woodstock, "the Black
    Prince"

Guesclin, Bertrand du

Hawkwood, Sir John

Hurtado de Mendoza, Diego

Joan of Arc

Sforza, Francesco

MUSICAL COMPOSERS

Agricola, Alexander

Binchois, Gilles

Landini, Francesco

Machaut, Guillaume de

Vitry, Philippe de

MYSTICS

Bridget of Sweden, Saint

Catherine of Siena, Saint

Ebner, Margareta

Eckhart, Meister Johan

Hilton, Walter

Kempe, Margery

Joan of Arc

Juliana of Norwich

Langmann, Adelheld

Rolle, Richard

Ruysbroek, Jan

Suso, Heinrich

Tauler, Johann

PAINTERS

Angelico, Fra

Bellini, Gentile

Bellini, Giovanni

Bondol, Jean de

Bosch, Hieronymus

Botticelli, Sandro

Bouts, Dirc

Bramante, Donato d'Agnolo Lazzerini

Broederlam, Melchior

Campin, Robert

Castagno, Andrea del

Domenico Veneziano

Eyck, Hubert van

Eyck, Jan van

Fouquet, Jean

Ghirlandaio, Domenico

Giotto di Bondone

Goes, Hugo van der

Huguet, Jaime

Inglés, Jorge

Leonardo da Vinci

Lippi, Fra Filippo

Lochner, Stephan

Mantegna, Andrea

Masaccio

Memling, Hans

Pacher, Michael

Perréal, Jean, Maître de Moulins

Perugino, Pietro

Piero della Francesca

Quercia, Jacopo della

Schongauer, Martin
Uccello, Paolo
Weyden, Rogier van der

PATRONS OF CULTURE

Alfonso V, "the Magnanimous," King of Aragon
Bardi, Contessina
Beaufort, Margaret
Charles the Bold, Duke of Burgundy
Este, Beatrice d', Duchess of Milan
Este, Ercole I d', Duke of Ferrara
Ferdinand V, King of Aragon and Spain
Ferrante I, King of Naples
Gaston III, Count de Foix
Gonzaga, Ludovico, Marquis of Mantua
Henry VI, King of England
Humphrey, Duke of Gloucester
Isabel, Queen of Castile and Spain
James IV, King of Scotland
Jiménez de Cisneros, Francisco
John of Gaunt, Duke of Lancaster
Margaret of York, Duchess of Burgundy
Martin I, "the Humanist," King of Aragon
Medici, Cosimo de
Medici, Giuliano de
Medici, Lorenzo de, "il Magnifico"
Medici, Piero de, "the Gouty"
Orsini, Clarice
Richard III, King of England
Rupert III, King of Germany
Sforza, Caterina
Sforza, Ludovico, "il Moro"
Tornabuoni, Lucrezia
Valois, Jean, Duc de Berry
Vespasiano da Bisticci
Wykeham, William of

PHILOSOPHERS

Abravanel, Isaac ben-Judah
Ficino, Marsiglio
Fortescue, Sir John
Gersonides, Levi
Halevi, Solomon
Llull, Ramon
Marsiglio of Padua
Pico della Mirandola, Giovanni
Sibiuda, Ramon

POETS

Boner, Ulrich
Chartier, Alain
Dante Alighieri
Deschamps, Eustace
Henryson, Robert
López de Mendoza, Iñigo
Lydgate, John
Machaut, Guillaume de
Manrique, Jorge
March, Ausias
Ruiz, Juan
Villon, François

POPES

Alexander VI
Benedict XII (Avignon)
Benedict XIII, Antipope
Clement V (Avignon)
Clement VI (Avignon)
Eugenius IV
Innocent VI (Avignon)
Innocent VIII
John XXII (Avignon)
Nicholas V

Pius II
Sixtus IV
Urban VI

PRINTERS

Caxton, William
Fust, Johann
Gutenberg, Johann
LeRoy, Guillaume
Manutius, Aldus
Schöffer, Peter

QUEENS AND CONSORTS

Bardi, Contessina
Beaufort, Margaret
Este, Beatrice d', Duchess of Milan
Isabel, Queen of Castile
Juana of Castile
Margaret I, Queen of Denmark, Norway, and Sweden
Margaret of York, Duchess of Burgundy
Orsini, Clarice
Sforza, Caterina
Tornabuoni, Lucrezia
Valois, Anne, Duchesse de Bourbon

REBELS

Cade, Jack
Marcel, Étienne
Tyler, Wat

RELIGIOUS REFORMERS

Ailly, Pierre d'
Bernardino of Siena
Bridget of Sweden, Saint
Colet, John
Gerson, Jean
Groote, Gerhard
John Capistrano, Saint
Marsiglio of Padua
Matthias of Janov
Milič, Jan
Nicholas of Cusa
Nicholas of Flüe, Saint
Pecock, Reginald
Savonarola, Girolamo
Thomas á Kempis
Tostados, Alfonso
Vincent Ferrer, Saint

RULERS OF PROVINCES AND CITY-STATES

Artevelde, Jacob van (Ghent)
Charles the Bold, Duke of Burgundy
Este, Ercole I d', Duke of Ferrara
Gonzaga, Ludovico, Marquis of Mantua
Medici, Cosimo de (Florence)
Medici, Lorenzo de, "il Magnifico" (Florence)
Medici, Piero de, "the Gouty" (Florence)
Medici, Piero de, "the Unfortunate" (Florence)
Montefeltro, Federigo da (Urbino)
Montefeltro, Guidobaldo da (Urbino)
Philip the Bold, Duke of Burgundy
René, Duke of Anjou, King of Sicily
Sforza, Francesco (Duke of Milan)
Sforza, Ludovico, "il Moro" (Duke of Milan)
Visconti, Filippo Maria, Duke of Milan
Visconti, Giangaleazzo, Duke of Milan

SCIENTISTS, MATHEMATICIANS, AND PHYSICIANS

Avignon, Juan de
Buridan, Jean
Free, John
Gersonides, Levi
Leonardo da Vinci
Oresme, Nicole
Nicholas of Cusa
Pacioli, Luca
Regiomontanus (Johann Müller)
Sibiuda, Ramon
Swineshead, Richard

SCULPTORS AND ARCHITECTS

Alberti, Leon Battista
Beauchamp, Richard
Beauneveu, André
Brunelleschi, Filippo
Donatello
Ghiberti, Lorenzo
Kraft, Adam
Verrocchio, Andrea del

THEOLOGIANS

Abravanel, Isaac ben-Judah
Ailly, Pierre d'
Aureoli, Peter
Baconthorpe, John
Bertrand, Pierre
Biel, Gabriel
Conrad of Geinhausen
Durand of Saint-Pourçain
Escobar, Andrés de
Geiler von Kaysersberg, Johan
Gerson, Jean
Halevi, Solomon
John of Jandun
Lyndwood, William
Netter, Thomas
Ockham, William of
Thomas à Kempis
Torquemada, Juan de
Tostado, Alfonso
Ubertino da Casale
Vincent Ferrer, Saint
Zabarella, Francesco

Selected Bibliography

GENERAL WORKS

Aston, Margaret, ed. *The Panorama of the Renaissance*. 1996.
Burke, Peter. *The European Renaissance: Centres and Peripheries*. 1998.
Curry, Anne. *The Hundred Years War*. 1993.
Hale, J. R. *The Civilization of Europe in the Renaissance*. 1994.
Herlihy, David. *The Black Death and the Transformation of the West*. 1997.
Holmes, George. *Renaissance*. 1996.
Horrox, Rosemary, ed. *The Black Death*. 1994.
Jensen, DeLamar. *Renaissance Europe*. 1992.
Mollat, Michel, and Wolff, Philippe. *The Popular Revolutions of the Late Middle Ages*. 1973.
Neillands, R. H. *The Hundred Years War*. 1990.
Rabb, Theodore K. *Renaissance Lives: Portraits of an Age*. 1993.
Sumption, Jonathan. *The Hundred Years War: Trial by Battle*. 1991.
Waley, D. P. *Later Medieval Europe*. 2nd ed. 1985.

CENTRAL, NORTHERN, AND EASTERN EUROPE

Banac, Ivo, and Sysyn, Frank, eds. *Concepts of Nationhood in Early Modern Eastern Europe*. 1986.
Berenger, J. *A History of the Habsburg Empire*. 2 vols. 1994–97.
Derry, T. K. *A History of Scandinavia*. 1979.
DuBoulay, F. R. H. *Germany in the Later Middle Ages*. 1983.
Hughes, Michael. *Early Modern Germany, 1477–1806*. 1992.
Kirby, David. *Northern Europe in the Early Modern Period*. 1990.
Leuschner, Joachim. *Germany in the Late Middle Ages*. 1980.
Macartney, C. A. *Hungary: A Short History*. 1962.
Maczak, Antoni, et al., eds. *East-Central Europe in Transition*. 1985.
Prevenier, Walter, and Blockmans, William. *The Burgundian Netherlands*. 1986.

Robisheaux, Thomas. *Rural Society and the Search for Order in Early Modern Germany*. 1989.
Sawyer, Birgit, and Sawyer, Peter. *Medieval Scandinavia*. 1993.

ENGLAND AND SCOTLAND

Aston, Margaret. *England's Iconoclasts*. 1988.
Brown, A. L. *The Governance of Late Medieval England, 1272–1461*. 1989.
Clayton, Dorothy J., et al., eds. *Trade, Devotion, and Governance*. 1994.
Cowan, Ian, and Shaw, Duncan, eds. *The Renaissance and Reformation in Scotland*. 1983.
Davies, R. G., and Denton, J. H., eds. *The English Parliament in the Middle Ages*. 1981.
Duffy, Eamon. *The Stripping of the Altars*. 1992.
Frame, R. *The Political Development of the British Isles, 1100–1400*. 1995.
Given-Wilson, Chris. *The English Nobility in the Late Middle Ages*. 1987.
Grant, Alexander. *Independence and Nationhood: Scotland, 1306–1469*. 1984.
Griffiths, R. A., and Thomas, R. S. *The Making of the Tudor Dynasty*. 1985.
Hudson, Anne. *The Premature Reformation: Wycliffite Texts and Lollard History*. 1988.
Jacob, E. F. *The Fifteenth Century, 1399–1485*. 1993.
King, Edmund. *Medieval England, 1066–1485*. 1988.
Lander, J. R. *Government and Community: England, 1450–1509*. 1980.
———. *The Limitations of English Monarchy in the Later Middle Ages*. 1989.
Pollard, A. J. *The Wars of the Roses*. 1988.
Storey, R. L. *The End of the House of Lancaster*. 1986.
Swanson, R. N. *Church and Society in Late Medieval England*. New ed. 1989.
Taylor, John, and Childs, Wendy, eds. *Politics and Crisis in Fourteenth Century England*. 1990.
Waugh, Scott. *England in the Reign of Edward III*. 1991.

FRANCE

Allmand, Christopher, ed. *Power, Culture, and Religion in France, c. 1360–1550*. 1989.
Armstrong, C. A. J. *England, France, and Burgundy in the Fifteenth Century*. 1983.
Braudel, Fernand. *The Identity of France*. 2 vols. 1988–90.
Briggs, Robin. *Communities of Belief: Cultural and Social Tension in Early Modern France*. 1989.
Davis, Natalie Zemon. *Society and Culture in Early Modern France*. 1975.
Febvre, Lucien. *Life in Renaissance France*. 1977.
Jackson, Richard. *Vive le Roi! A History of the French Coronation from Charles V to Charles X*. 1984.
Kaeuper, R. W. *War, Justice, and Public Order: England and France in the Later Middle Ages*. 1988.
Miskimin, Harry A. *Money and Power in Fifteenth-Century France*. 1984.
Potter, D. *A History of France, 1460–1560*. 1995.

IBERIAN PENINSULA

Boxer, Charles R. *The Portuguese Seaborne Empire, 1415–1825.* 1977.

Deyermond, Alan, and Macpherson, Ian, eds. *The Age of the Catholic Monarchs, 1474–1516.* 1989.

Hillgarth, Jocelyn N. *The Spanish Kingdoms, 1250–1516.* 2 vols. 1978.

Kamen, Henry. *Spain, 1469–1714: A Society of Conflict.* 1983.

Lewis, Bernard. *Cultures in Conflict: Christians, Muslims, and Jews in the Age of Discovery.* 1995.

Lomax, Derek. *The Reconquest of Spain.* 1978.

Lunenfeld, Marvin. *Keepers of the City: The Corregidores of Isabella I of Castille, 1474–1504.* 1987.

Nader, Helen. *The Mendoza Family in the Spanish Renaissance, 1350 to 1550.* 1979.

Netanyahu, Ben Zion. *The Origins of the Inquisition in Fifteenth Century Spain.* 1995.

Ruiz, Teofilo. *Crisis and Continuity: Land and Town in Late Medieval Castile.* 1994.

ITALY

Baron, Hans. *The Crisis of the Early Italian Renaissance.* Rev. ed. 1966.

Bentley, Jerry H. *Politics and Culture in Renaissance Naples.* 1987.

Bonfil, Robert. *Jewish Life in Renaissance Italy.* 1994.

Brown, Alison. *The Medici in Florence.* 1992.

Brucker, Gene. *Renaissance Florence.* 1983.

Burckhardt, Jacob. *The Civilization of the Renaissance in Italy.* 1860/1990.

Burke, Peter. *The Italian Renaissance.* 1987.

Dean, Trevor. *Land and Power in Late Medieval Ferrara.* 1988.

Grafton, Anthony, ed. *Rome Reborn: The Vatican Library and Renaissance Culture.* 1993.

Hay, Denys, and Law, John. *Italy in the Age of the Renaissance, 1380–1530.* 1989.

Lansing, Carol. *The Florentine Magnates.* 1991.

Lubkin, Gregory. *A Renaissance Court: Milan under Galeazzo Maria Sforza.* 1994.

Mallett, Michael. *Mercenaries and Their Masters: Warfare in Renaissance Italy.* 1974.

Martines, Lauro. *Power and Imagination: City-States in Renaissance Italy.* 1988.

Norwich, John. *A History of Venice.* 1989.

Queller, Donald. *The Venetian Patriciate: Reality versus Myth.* 1986.

Simon, Kate. *A Renaissance Tapestry: The Gonzaga of Mantua.* 1988.

Stephens, John. *The Italian Renaissance: The Origins of Intellectual and Artistic Change before the Reformation.* 1990.

Stinger, Charles. *The Renaissance in Rome.* 1985.

Trexler, Richard. *Public Life in Renaissance Florence.* 1980.

Waley, Daniel. *The Italian City Republics.* 3rd ed. 1988.

CULTURAL LIFE

Brown, Howard Mayer, and Stein, Louise K. *Music in the Renaissance.* 2nd ed. 1999.

Campbell, Lorne. *Renaissance Portraits: European Portrait-Painting in the 14th, 15th, and 16th Centuries.* 1990.

Chartier, Roger. *The Order of Books: Readers, Authors, and Libraries in Europe between the Fourteenth and Eighteenth Centuries.* 1994.

Cochrane, Eric. *Historians and Historiography in the Italian Renaissance.* 1981.

Cohen, H. Floris. *The Scientific Revolution: A Historiographical Inquiry.* 1994.

Copenhaver, Brian, and Schmitt, Charles. *Renaissance Philosophy.* 1992.

Debus, Allen. *Man and Nature in the Renaissance.* 1978.

Eisenstein, Elizabeth. *The Printing Press as an Agent of Change.* 1979.

Elliott, S. *Italian Renaissance Painting.* 2nd ed. 1993.

Goldthwaite, Richard. *Wealth and the Demand for Art in Italy, 1300–1600.* 1993.

Hartt, Frederick, and Wilkins, David. *History of Italian Renaissance Art.* 2nd ed., 1979.

Holmes, George, *Art and Politics in Renaissance Italy.* 1993.

Huizinga, Johan. *The Autumn of the Middle Ages.* 1996.

Humfrey, Peter. *Painting in Renaissance Venice.* 1995.

Kelley, Donald. *Renaissance Humanism.* 1991.

Kent, F. W., and Simon, P. eds. *Patronage, Art, and Society in Renaissance Italy.* 1987.

King, Margaret. *Venetian Humanism in an Age of Patrician Dominance.* 1986.

Kristeller, Paul Oskar. *Renaissance Thought and Its Sources.* 1979.

Leff, Gordon. *The Dissolution of the Medieval Outlook.* 1976.

Luscombe, David. *Medieval Thought.* 1997.

Nauert, C. G., Jr. *Humanism and the Culture of Renaissance Europe.* 1995.

Olson, Roberta. *Italian Renaissance Sculpture.* 1992.

Overfield, James. *Humanism and Scholasticism in Late Medieval Germany.* 1984.

Park, Katharine. *Doctors and Medicine in Early Renaissance Florence.* 1985.

Rabil, Albert, Jr., ed. *Renaissance Humanism.* 1988.

Seymour, Charles. *Sculpture in Italy, 1400–1500.* 1994.

Siraisi, Nancy. *Medieval and Early Renaissance Medicine.* 1990.

Smith, Christine. *Architecture in the Culture of Early Humanism.* 1992.

Strohm, Richard. *The Rise of European Music, 1380–1500.* 1993.

Thomson, David. *Renaissance Architecture.* 1993.

Trinkaus, Charles. *The Scope of Renaissance Humanism.* 1983.

Turner, R. *Renaissance Florence: The Invention of a New Art.* 1997.

Weiss, Roberto. *The Renaissance Discovery of Classical Antiquity.* 2nd ed. 1988.

White, John. *Art and Architecture in Italy, 1250–1400.* 3rd ed. 1993.

Wilson, Katharina, ed. *Women Writers of the Renaissance and Reformation.* 1987.

RELIGION

Baron, Salo. *A Social and Religious History of the Jews.* Vol. 14. 1969.

Bossy, John. *Christianity in the West. 1400–1700.* 1985.

Crowder, C. *Unity, Heresy, and Reform, 1378–1460.* 1977.

Haliczer, Stephen, ed. *Inquisition and Society in Early Modern Europe.* 1987.

Kieckhefer, Richard. *Unquiet Souls: Fourteenth-Century Saints and Their Religious Milieu.* 1984.

Ladurie, Emmanuel Le Roy. *Montaillou.* 1978.

Mollat, Guillaume. *The Popes at Avignon, 1305–1378.* 1965.

Oakley, Francis P. *The Western Church in the Later Middle Ages.* 1979.

Oberman, Heiko. *Forerunners of the Reformation: The Shape of Late Medieval Thought*. 1981.

Partner, Peter. *The Pope's Men: The Papal Civil Service in the Renaissance*. 1990.

Renouard, Yves. *The Avignon Papacy, 1305–1403*. 1970.

Stump, Phillip. *The Reforms of the Council of Constance, 1414–1418*. 1994.

Thomson, J. A. F. *Popes and Princes, 1417–1517*. 1980.

Weinstein, Donald, and Bell, Rudolf. *Saints and Society: The Two Worlds of Western Christendom, 1000–1700*. 1986.

WOMEN AND SOCIETY

Burke, Peter. *Popular Culture in Early Modern Europe*. 1978.

Davis, Natalie Zemon, and Farge, Arlette, eds. *A History of Women: Renaissance and Enlightenment Paradoxes*. Vol. 3, 1993.

Duby, Georges, ed. *A History of Private Life*. Vol. 2. 1988.

Herlihy, David. *Women, Family and Society in Medieval Europe: Historical Essays, 1938–1991*. 1995.

Jardine, Lisa. *Worldly Goods*. 1996.

King, Margaret L. *Women of the Renaissance*. 1991.

Klapisch-Zuber, Christiane, ed. *Silences of the Middle Ages*. Vol. 2 of *A History of Women in the West*. 1992.

Miskimin, Harry A. *The Economy of Early Renaissance Europe, 1300–1460*. 1975.

Mollat, Michel. *The Poor in the Middle Ages*. 1986.

Wiesner, Merry. *Women and Gender in Early Modern Europe*. 1993.

Index

Page numbers in **bold type** refer to main entries in the dictionary.

Contributors

Stephen A. Allen

Wendy Love Anderson

Jerome S. Arkenburg

S. Dorsey Armstrong

Karen Arthur

Susan Arvay

C. Thomas Ault

Kristopher Bell

Staci Bernard-Roth

Andrew Bethune

Martin Blum

Susanne Breckenridge

James Proctor Brown III

Paul D. Buell

Donna Bussell

Sara Butler

Susanna Calkins

Gregory E. Canada

Peter E. Carr

Celeste Chamberland

Susannah Chewning

Richard Copsey

Patricia Cossard

Christina Brunson Defendi

John Donovan

Clayton J. Drees

Deborah S. Ellis

Connie Evans

Michael Evans

Denise K. Filios

Jeffrey Fisher

Angela B. Fulk

Mark K. Fulk

Miriam Rheingold Fuller

Rebecca L. R. Garber

John D. Grosskopf

Sheldon Hanft

Jaimie B. Hanson

Margaret Harp

Jennifer L. Harrison

Darin Hayton

Kristin R. Hofer

Karen Holleran

Marian Hollinger

Wendy Marie Hoofnagle

Brian G. Hudgins

Thomas M. Izbicki

Kathryn Jacobs

Sigrid Kelsey

Kathryn Kiff

Clay Kinsner

Roger A. Ladd

Stephen E. Lahey

Elizabeth Lehfeldt

Frans A. van Liere

Michael Lindsey

Wentong Ma

Nicola McDonald

Timothy McGovern

Claire McIlroy

Sarah McNamer

Laura McRae

Bonnie Millar

Rowena Hernández Múzquiz

James C. Owens

Jan Pendergrass

Susan Perry

Kristine Lynn Rabberman

Lynn Ramey

Colleen A. Reilly

William B. Robison

Joelle Rollo-Koster

Dana L. Sample

Catherine Sanok

Michelle M. Sauer

Andrew Scheil

Anne M. Schuchman

Paul Sheneman

Tim Sullivan

Dominique Tieman

Natalie Tomas

E. Helene Tronc

Dan Wages

Alan S. Weber

Timothy L. Wood

Patricia Worrall

About the Editor

CLAYTON J. DREES is Associate Professor of History at Virginia Wesleyan College, where he has taught European and African history since 1992. He has been department chair since 1998. He is author of *Authority and Dissent in the English Church* (1997).